T3-BNJ-729

The Adams Papers

C. JAMES TAYLOR, EDITOR IN CHIEF

SERIES I

DIARIES

Diary and Autobiographical Writings of Louisa Catherine Adams

Diary and Autobiographical Writings of Louisa Catherine Adams

JUDITH S. GRAHAM, BETH LUEY,
MARGARET A. HOGAN, C. JAMES TAYLOR
EDITORS

Volume 1 • *1778–1815*

THE BELKNAP PRESS
OF HARVARD UNIVERSITY PRESS
CAMBRIDGE, MASSACHUSETTS
AND LONDON, ENGLAND
2013

Printed in the United States of America

Funds for editing *The Adams Papers* were originally furnished by Time, Inc., on behalf of *Life,* to the Massachusetts Historical Society, under whose supervision the editorial work is being done. Further funds were provided by a grant from the Ford Foundation to the National Archives Trust Fund Board in support of this and four other major documentary publications. In common with these and many other enterprises like them, *The Adams Papers* has continued to benefit from the guidance and cooperation of the National Historical Publications and Records Commission, chaired by the Archivist of the United States, which from 1975 to the present has provided this enterprise with major financial support. Important additional funds were supplied from 1980 to 1993 by The Andrew W. Mellon Foundation, The J. Howard Pew Freedom Trust, and The Charles E. Culpeper Foundation through the Founding Fathers Papers, Inc. Since 1993, *The Adams Papers* has received major support from the National Endowment for the Humanities, and matching support from The Packard Humanities Institute, through the Founding Fathers Papers, Inc., and from The Charles Francis Adams Charitable Trust, The Florence J. Gould Foundation, The Lyn and Norman Lear Fund, and anonymous donors. Any views, findings, conclusions, or recommendations expressed in this publication do not necessarily reflect those of the National Endowment for the Humanities.

∞ This volume meets all ANSI/NISO Z39.48–1992 standards for permanence.

Library of Congress Cataloging in Publication Data

Adams, Louisa Catherine, 1775–1852.
Diary and autobiographical writings of Louisa Catherine Adams / Judith S. Graham . . . [et al.], editors.
(The Adams papers: Series I, Diaries.)
Includes bibliographical references and index.
1. Adams, Louisa Catherine, 1775–1852—Diaries. 2. Presidents' spouses—United States—Diaries. 3. Adams, John Quincy, 1767–1848. 4. Presidents—United States—Biography. I. Graham, Judith S., 1945– . II. Title. III. Series: Adams papers: Series I, Diaries.

E377.2.A33 2013 973.5′5092—dc23 2011042297

ISBN 978-0-674-05868-2

This edition of *The Adams Papers*

is sponsored by the MASSACHUSETTS HISTORICAL SOCIETY

to which the ADAMS MANUSCRIPT TRUST

by a deed of gift dated 4 April 1956

gave ultimate custody of the personal and public papers

written, accumulated, and preserved over a span of three centuries

by the Adams family of Massachusetts

The Adams Papers

The acorn and oakleaf device on the preceding page is redrawn from a seal cut for John Quincy Adams after 1830. The motto is from Cæcilius Statius as quoted by Cicero in the First Tusculan Disputation: *Serit arbores quæ alteri seculo prosint* ("He plants trees for the benefit of later generations").

Contents

Descriptive List of Illustrations

In Record of a Life, Louisa writes that in the early 1790s "the family portraits were painted or rather began" (below). A set of miniatures of the girls of the Johnson family exists from around 1792, but the only full-size likeness of Louisa from the years before her marriage is this portrait by the American artist Edward Savage (1761–1817). He likely painted it and similar ones of Louisa's sisters Nancy, Carolina, and Harriet—along with portraits of their parents, for which see Descriptive List of Illustrations, Nos. 3 and 4, below—prior to his departure from England for the United States in 1793. This image captures Louisa around age eighteen in a billowing white dress with a sheer, patterned overlay and blue sash. She holds a wreath of pink roses in one hand and black bands encircle both her slender wrists (Grove *Dicy. of Art*; D/JQA/44, 28 Nov. 1844, APM Reel 47; Oliver, *Portraits of JQA and LCA*, p. 22–27, 45–48).

Courtesy of the National Park Service, Adams National Historical Park.

In 1796, while serving as minister resident in the Netherlands but temporarily posted to London, John Quincy sat for a three-quarter-length portrait by John Singleton Copley. Set against a crimson velvet curtain and a landscape of rolling hills and open fields, John Quincy exudes the confidence of a young man embarking on his diplomatic career. John Quincy recorded in his Diary several sittings from February to April, and he surprised his mother with a delivery of the portrait in Philadelphia in June. She considered it a "striking resemblance of my dear absent Son . . . as fine a portrait as ever was taken" and family members claimed that his features resembled either Abigail or his brother Thomas Boylston. Louisa Catherine Adams, however, may have considered John Quincy's portrait a bit too idealized. He wrote to Louisa to suggest that she might prefer a 1796 miniature by Thomas H. Hull to the Copley "because it is *not so much flattered*" (D/JQA/23, APM Reel 26; AA to JQA, 23 June 1797; JQA to LCA, 2 June 1796, both Adams Papers; Oliver, *Portraits of JQA and LCA*, p. 34).

Courtesy of the Museum of Fine Arts, Boston.

3, 4. CATHERINE NUTH JOHNSON AND JOSHUA JOHNSON, BY EDWARD SAVAGE, CA. 1793 48, 49

"O home! sweet home!" Louisa Catherine Adams wrote of the years of "domestic felicity" enjoyed at her parents' home on Great Tower Hill in London, where her father, Joshua Johnson, was a partner in an Annapolis mercantile firm and U.S. consul. Louisa described the home he established for his English wife, Catherine Nuth Johnson, and their children as "not sumptuous or extravagant, but such as the first Merchants in London at that day usually had." Maintained by a staff of eleven servants, it was "perfectly regulated though large." Reflecting on her time with her parents and siblings, Louisa commented, "I have never had a home since I left my fathers house, and it is a matter of perfect indifference if I never do" (Record of a Life, Adventures, both below; LCA to JQA, 18 July 1826, Adams Papers).

Edward Savage captured likenesses of Joshua and Catherine Johnson during this time of prosperity and family happiness, prior to the failure of Joshua's mercantile business and reversal of fortune and the family's departure for the United States in 1797. They were likely part of a series of family portraits, for which see Descriptive List of Illustrations, No. 1, above. "My Father was the handsomest man I ever beheld," Louisa wrote, and "My Mother . . . was at this time very lovely, her person very small, and exquisitely delicate, and very finely proportioned." Savage depicts Joshua at his writing desk with documents in hand; Catherine sits in an elegant velvet chair and wears an elaborate hairstyle interwoven with a gray silk scarf (Grove *Dicy. of Art*; Record of a Life, below).

Courtesy of the Massachusetts Historical Society.

5. PRINCESSES LOUISE AND FREDERICA OF PRUSSIA, BY JOHANN GOTTFRIED SCHADOW, 1797 102

In 1794 Frederick William II commissioned his court sculptor, Johann Gottfried Schadow (1764–1850), to create portrait busts of Princesses Louise and Frederica of Mecklenburg-Strelitz, the sisters who were to marry his sons Frederick William III and Louis Charles, respectively. Pleased with the results, Frederick William II then requested that Schadow produce first a life-sized plaster sculpture and later a marble version of the same, illustrated here, which was completed in 1797. After his father's death, Frederick William III had the sculpture crated and put in storage. When Queen Louise died in 1810 at age 34, the marble statue was redisplayed in the palace but in a distant corner. Over a century later, it was more prominently displayed in the palace and in 1949 was transferred to the National Gallery in Berlin (H. W. Janson, *19th-Century Sculpture*, N.Y., 1985, p. 66; Chandler Rathfon Post, *A His-*

tory of European and American Sculpture from the Early Christian Period to the Present Day, 2 vols., Cambridge, 1921, 2:100–102; Claude Keisch, *The Alte Nationalgalerie, Berlin*, London, 2005, p. 19).

Louisa Catherine Adams admired Queen Louise, whom she called "the Queen of Queens" because her "grace affability sweetness amiability and the most irrisistable beauty formed a combination of loveliness to which no language can do justice and which the painters art never could depict." The queen was an active partner to her husband in affairs of state and popular among her subjects. After her death, Prussia established the Order of Louise to honor women who contributed to the country's war efforts (Record of a Life, below; Christopher Clark, *Iron Kingdom: The Rise and Downfall of Prussia, 1600–1947*, Cambridge, 2006, p. 316–317, 376).

Courtesy of Bildarchiv Preussischer Kulturbesitz / Art Resource, N.Y.

John Quincy Adams met the German landscape painter Johann Christian Reinhart (1761–1847) in Hirschberg, Silesia, in August 1800 while he and Louisa Catherine Adams were touring there. Reinhart was by then a resident of Rome but returned to Germany each year to paint two landscapes for the Berlin Academy of Sciences. Some of these works were engraved by Daniel Berger (1744–1824) and colored by an unknown artist. During the visit, John Quincy purchased four engravings, three of which are exhibited at the Old House in Quincy (JQA to TBA, 7, 9 Aug. 1800, Lb/JQA/10, APM Reel 134; Fritz Novotny, *Painting and Sculpture in Europe 1780–1880*, New Haven, Conn., 1995, p. 75).

This engraving, despite its small size, illustrates the detail and realism for which Reinhart was known. The ability to paint foliage was especially prized at the time as a measure of how close an artist came to nature, and Reinhart excelled in forest scenes, the depiction of trees, and the accurate representation of leaves. The colors are deep and brilliant. The mountain range in the background—a common feature of the engravings purchased by John Quincy—is the Riesengebirge, or Giant Mountains. The conical peak, called the Giant's Head, was reached by steps carved into the mountainside (Hubert Schrade, *German Romantic Painting*, transl. Maria Pelikan, repr. edn., N.Y., 1977, p. 52; JQA to TBA, 7 Aug. 1800).

Louisa wrote almost nothing about the visit to Silesia in her Adventures memoir, but John Quincy described their tour in detail in a series of letters to his brother Thomas Boylston Adams, which were published in London in 1804 as *Letters on Silesia, Written During a Tour through that Country in the Years 1800, 1801.*

Courtesy of the National Park Service, Adams National Historical Park.

7. "WASHINGTON CITY," BY ANNE MARGUERITE HYDE DE NEUVILLE, 1821 208

When Louisa Catherine Adams first visited Washington, D.C., in 1801, she was "quite delighted with the situation of this place and I think should it ever be finished it will be one of the most beautiful spots in the world." By 1803, when the Adamses arrived in the city so that John Quincy could begin his term in the Senate, the buildings shown from left to right in Anne Marguerite Hyde de Neuville's watercolor—the State, War, and Navy Building; the White House; and the Treasury Building—had been completed. As Louisa then noted, however, much work remained to be done: "The City not being laid out; the Streets not graduated; the bridges consisting of mere loose planks; and huge stumps of Trees recently cut down intercepting every path; and the roads intersected by deep ravines continually enlarged by rain." Even in the 1820s, despite rebuilding after the British burning of the city in 1814, the city lacked basic amenities (LCA to JQA, 16 Sept. 1801, Adams Papers; Adventures, below; Green, *Washington, 1800–1878*, p. 3, 105–106).

In this watercolor, the buildings are seen from Decatur House, at the time the residence of the artist, Anne Marguerite Joséphine Henriette Rouillé de Marigny (d. 1849), and her husband, Jean Guillaume Hyde de Neuville, the French minister to the United States from 1816 to 1822. De Neuville painted a variety of scenes during her time in America, including sketches of Washington residents, scenes of rural New York, and drawings of members of the Iroquois nation. She and Louisa were friends, meeting for tea and exchanging visits, and the Adamses were frequent guests at Decatur House (Beale, *Decatur House*, p. 2, 13, 15; Margaret Bayard Smith, *The First Forty Years of Washington Society*, ed. Gaillard Hunt, N.Y., 1906, p. 140–141; Jadviga M. da Costa Nunes, *Baroness Hyde de Neuville: Sketches of America, 1807–1822*, New Brunswick, N.J., 1984, p. 4–14).

Courtesy of I. N. Phelps Stokes Collection, Miriam and Ira D. Wallach Division of Art, Prints and Photographs, The New York Public Library, Astor, Lenox and Tilden Foundations.

8. EMPEROR ALEXANDER I, BY FRANÇOIS GÉRARD, 1814 296

Alexander I succeeded to the throne of the Russian Empire after the palace coup of March 1801, in which his father, Paul I, was assassinated. Louisa Catherine Adams had a complicated relationship with him during her time in St. Petersburg, between 1809 and 1815. He was solicitous of Louisa's health, yet he thoughtlessly forced the Adamses to move from their lodgings during her pregnancy. He opened their private mail and questioned one of their servants—an incident that many years later led political opponents to claim that John Quincy Adams had procured prostitutes for the emperor. He also took undue interest in Louisa's sister Catherine Johnson, whose invitation to official occasions despite not having been formally presented at court led to malicious gossip (Adventures, below).

In 1814 Alexander spent time in Paris negotiating with his allies over the future of Napoleon, France, and much of Europe. While there he found time for several sittings with François Gérard (1770–1837). The artist had begun painting before the French Revolution but became well known in 1794 with his entry in a government-sponsored competition, *The French People Demanding the Overthrow of the Tyrant on 10 August 1792*. Although he continued to paint historical and mythological scenes, he was best known for his portraits of socially and politically prominent figures. His ability was recognized not only by Napoleon but also by Louis XVIII and other figures of the empire (Palmer, *Alexander I*, p. 282; Christopher John Murray, ed., *Encyclopedia of the Romantic Era, 1760–1850*, 2 vols., N.Y., 2004; La Comtesse de Choiseul-Gouffier, *Historical Memoirs of the Emperor Alexander I and the Court of Russia*, transl. Mary Berenice Patterson, 2d edn., Chicago, 1901, p. 83).

Courtesy of The State Hermitage Museum, St. Petersburg. Photograph © The State Hermitage Museum / Photograph by Vladimir Terebenin, Leonard Kheifets, and Yuri Molodkovets.

9. EMPRESS MARIA FEODOROVNA, CA. 1801

Louisa Catherine Adams was presented to Empress Elizabeth Alexeievna and the Empress Mother Maria Feodorovna, the widow of Paul I, on 12 November 1809. Thereafter, Maria often invited the Adamses and Louisa's sister Catherine Johnson to state functions. Despite her dowager status, Maria was a powerful force on Russia's social and political stage. She had married Paul in 1776, when she was seventeen years old, and over the next twenty years gave birth to nine children, two of whom became emperors. She participated in her husband's public activities and political development, and when he became emperor in 1796 upon the death of his mother, Catherine the Great, Maria advised him on domestic matters. She was devastated by his assassination in 1801, keeping the bloody linens on which he died and seeking revenge against the conspirators. She continued to wield considerable influence during Alexander's reign, taking precedence over the empress at court, advising her son on foreign affairs, and helping to marshal opposition to Alexander's reforms.

In this portrait, by an unknown artist, Maria Feodorovna is dressed in mourning for her husband and for her daughter Alexandra, who died during childbirth at the age of eighteen. Maria is wearing a medallion with a likeness of Paul and, on her shoulder, the Order of St. John of Jerusalem, the Knights of Malta, of which Paul had been Grand Master (Roderick E. McGrew, *Paul I of Russia, 1754–1801*, Oxford, Eng., p. 2, 95, 104, 107, 187, 202, 271; Palmer, *Alexander I*, p. 74–76, 148–149, 151, 157, 170, 185–187, 418–419; The Most Venerable Order of the Hospital of St. John of Jerusalem, "The St. John [Order] Regulations," n.p., 2003, p. 29–30, 34).

Courtesy of The State Hermitage Museum, St. Petersburg. Photograph © The State Hermitage Museum / Photograph by Vladimir Terebenin, Leonard Kheifets, and Yuri Molodkovets.

10. "VIEW OF THE PALACE SQUARE FROM NEVSKY PROSPEKT," BY GABRIEL LUDWIG LORY THE ELDER, 1804 329

This engraving shows three of the sites that Louisa Catherine Adams frequented in St. Petersburg: Nevsky Prospect, the Winter Palace, and the Hermitage. Nevsky Prospect, one of the city's grand boulevards, was part of the master plan drawn up for Peter the Great by the architect Jean Baptiste Alexandre Le Blond around 1716. Under Empress Elizabeth, trees were planted, and regulations required that all buildings along the street be made of stone. Here Louisa walked with her sister and her son, an activity encouraged by the emperor, who "would often stop and speak to us very politely." The street was lined with palaces and churches (Colin Amery and Brian Curran, *St. Petersburg*, London, 2006, p. 27–28, 31, 42–44; Adventures, 29 April 1810, below).

The large buildings visible in Palace Square are the Winter Palace, in which is also housed the Hermitage. The first Winter Palace was begun in the 1730s by the architect Bartolomeo Rastrelli. In 1754 Empress Elizabeth ordered it demolished so that Rastrelli could build a larger, grander palace with more than a thousand rooms. Catherine the Great oversaw the building of the first (Small) Hermitage within the palace. Designed by Jean Baptiste Michel Vallin de la Mothe, the Hermitage was both a retreat and a showplace for Catherine's art collection, and it was later a site for balls and official ceremonies. Louisa first saw the Hermitage at a ball on 13 January 1810. She returned on 5 April to see "its pictures its curiosities and all its splendors; with its sad associations of Vice talents and greatness" (Amery and Curran, *St. Petersburg*, p. 41, 43, 56, 60, 65; Adventures, 13 Jan., 5 April 1810, below).

Gabriel Ludwig Lory (1763–1840) was born in Bern and studied with Caspar Wolff in the studio of Swiss artist Jean Louis Aberli. In 1797 he was recruited to execute a project commissioned by Emperor Paul I, who wanted to promote Russian cities abroad by publishing a series of engravings made from paintings of St. Petersburg and Moscow. Delayed by the Swiss revolution, the work was not completed when the project ended in 1801 with Paul's assassination. Most of Lory's engravings were destroyed in the Moscow fire of 1812; the only surviving works were those owned by collectors or retained in Lory's own portfolio (Conrad de Mandach, *Deux Peintres Suisses: Gabriel Lory le Père (1763–1840) et Gabriel Lory le Fils (1784–1846)*, Geneva, 1978, p. 13, 14, 21, 27–31).

Courtesy of The State Hermitage Museum, St. Petersburg. Photograph © The State Hermitage Museum / Photograph by Vladimir Terebenin, Leonard Kheifets, and Yuri Molodkovets.

Before leaving St. Petersburg on 12 February 1815, Louisa Catherine Adams acquired three passports: a French one issued on 7 February, a Russian one issued on 28 January [9 *February* N.S.], and a Prussian one issued on 9 February. The French passport was signed by Antonin Claude Dominique, Comte Juste de Noailles, who had been appointed ambassador to Russia in 1814, after the return of Louis XVIII to France. Louisa used the Russian passport until she reached Riga. The Prussian passport, which she used throughout the German states, has stamps on the back indicating her stops from Riga to Kehl (Pères Anselme, Ange, et Simplicien, *Histoire généalogique et chronologique de la maison royale de France*, 9 vols., Paris, 1879, repr. edn. 1968, 9:243; LCA Prussian passport, 9 Feb. 1815, Adams Papers).

When she reached Berlin, Louisa acquired a second French passport, shown here, signed by Victor Louis Charles de Riquet, Duc de Caraman, whom she had known when she lived in that city during John Quincy Adams' diplomatic service there from 1797 to 1801. Unlike the Juste de Noailles passport, which simply gives her name, this one identifies Louisa as the wife of the U.S. minister to the Russian emperor. She presented the passport in Strasbourg, where it was stamped by a customs officer at the town hall on 19 March. On 23 March, when challenged by French soldiers loyal to the resurgent Napoleon, Louisa's ability to speak French and to identify herself as an American proved critical to her ability to proceed to Paris unharmed (Narrative of a Journey, below).

From the original in the Adams Family Papers. Courtesy of the Massachusetts Historical Society.

By the time Charles Bird King painted this portrait of Louisa Catherine Adams, he was well established in Washington, D.C., as a fashionable painter of prominent Washingtonians. The Adamses visited his studio and gallery frequently to see the paintings he had on display and, eventually, to sit for their portraits. Louisa had written in her Diary for 3 January 1821 that King "sent me a small painting for a present which will cost me a sitting for a portrait," but it was a few more years before she sat for him (Andrew J. Cosentino, *The Paintings of Charles Bird King (1785–1862)*, Washington, D.C., 1977, p. 37; CFA, *Diary*, 3:xvi–xviii; Diary, 3 Jan. 1821, below).

The decision to paint Louisa at the harp may have been hers. She had played the harp as a young woman and some of her acquaintances had been painted in similar poses. As Louisa noted in her Diary on 6 December 1820, it was "now the most fashionable instrument" (below). The turban Louisa chose was also the height of fashion, popular in France and England in the 1790s and adopted in the United States by Dolley Madison. Years later Louisa informed King that she was giving the portrait to her son John's children, and "as their Mother has always disapproved of *my taste* in the Costume, it was my wish to please her, by having it new dressed." She added, "At a former period of my life the *Portrait* might have possessed some intrinsic value even to you but now its possession can only be craved by the descendants of one who have learnt to pity and to love her for her misfortunes" (LCA to JQA, 20 Jan. 1797, Adams Papers; Herbert Norris and Oswald Curtis, *Nineteenth-Century Costume and Fashion*, repr. edn., Mineola, N.Y., 1998, p. 35; Allgor, *Perfect Union*, p. 238–239; LCA to Charles Bird King, 16 July 1836, PHi).

Courtesy of the Smithsonian American Art Museum.

13, 14. GEORGE WASHINGTON ADAMS AND JOHN ADAMS 2D, BY CHARLES BIRD KING, 1823

Charles Bird King painted these portraits of Louisa Catherine and John Quincy Adams' elder sons, George Washington and John, at his Washington studio in 1823. They are two of the paintings King did of various members of the Adams family between 1819 and 1827; for that of Louisa, see Descriptive List of Illustrations, No. 12, above. In fact, on at least one occasion, George and his father sat together for their respective portraits. George had been studying law with John Quincy since fall 1821, leaving for Boston in October 1823 to continue his training with Daniel Webster. John had moved to Washington earlier in 1823 after being expelled from Harvard; when John Quincy became president, John served as his private secretary (D/JQA/23, 31 May 1823, APM Reel 26; D/JQA/34, 7, 11 Oct., APM Reel 37; Bemis, *JQA*, 2:94–95).

For a lengthy discussion of the provenance of these two paintings, and the identification of their subjects, see CFA, *Diary*, 3:xv–xviii.

Courtesy of Mrs. Gilbert T. Vincent, Cooperstown, New York.

15. CHARLES FRANCIS ADAMS, BY ANSON DICKINSON, 1827

In the summer of 1825, Charles Francis Adams, having graduated from Harvard, moved to Washington, where he lived with his parents in the White House while studying law with his father. Two years later the young man returned to Boston to study with Daniel Webster and to continue his courtship of Abigail Brown Brooks, daughter of the wealthy merchant Peter Chardon Brooks and his wife, Ann Gorham Brooks. Charles and Abigail married on 3 September 1829. Charles acted as his father's agent in Quincy, and the two families visited in Boston and Quincy during the summers.

In March 1827, soon after his engagement, Charles arranged for Anson Dickinson to paint this miniature portrait as a gift for Abigail, who was in Washington visiting her sister Charlotte Gray Brooks Everett and Charlotte's husband, Edward, then a congressman from Massachusetts. Dickinson (1779–1852), a distinguished miniaturist, had a studio in New York but traveled to Boston and Washington to execute commissions. The portrait, in watercolor on ivory, was completed before Abigail left on 22 March to return to Boston. Charles does not note how well either he or Abigail liked the miniature, but John Quincy was "much taken" with it (CFA, *Diary*, 1:ix, xxxii–xxxiii; 2:31, 104–108, 110–113, 115–116, 423–424, 432–433; *Biog. Dir. Cong.*; Mona Leithiser Dearborn, *Anson Dickinson: The Celebrated Miniature Painter, 1779–1852*, Hartford, Conn., 1983, p. 14–16).

Courtesy of the Smithsonian American Art Museum.

16. "BALL GIVEN BY MRS. JOHN QUINCY ADAMS AT WASHINGTON, JANUARY 8, 1824," 1871 682

"A beautiful plan in my head which I shall endeavour to have executed," Louisa Catherine Adams wrote in her Diary on 22 December 1823 of her preparations for the most anticipated Washington ball of the new year (below). She expected the grand event—to be held on 8 January 1824, the anniversary of Andrew Jackson's victory at the Battle of New Orleans, with Jackson in attendance—would "attract not only all the Strangers but even the old residents of the City who never thought of coming to see me before." What was thereafter remembered as the Jackson Ball honored Jackson as a national hero and, by association, brought John Quincy into the spotlight of the presidential race (LCA to GWA, 1 Jan. 1824, Adams Papers; Allgor, *Parlor Politics*, p. 176–177).

Almost fifty years later, this photoengraving of the ball accompanied an 18 March 1871 article in *Harper's Bazar*. Jackson is positioned at the center of the scene, and John Quincy and Louisa appear at the far right. John Quincy's anachronistic portrait is probably based on an 1845 painting by George Peter Alexander Healy, and the likeness of Louisa suggests the Charles Bird King portrait from around 1824, for which see Descriptive List of Illustrations, No. 12, above. A newspaper description of the ball reported that she wore "a silk dress sparkly with ornament, with a sort of Spanish hat loaded with plumes." In one of the few mishaps of the evening, "while sitting in the dancing Room one of the lamps fell upon my head and ran all down my back and shoulders." Louisa's company good-naturedly joked that she was "already anointed with the sacred oil and that it was certainly ominous" (Oliver, *Portraits of JQA and LCA*, p. 104–106; New York *Commercial Advertiser*, 15 Jan. 1824; Diary, 8 Jan. 1824, below).

Courtesy of Widener Library, Harvard College Library.

17. GEORGEANNA FRANCES ADAMS, BY ASHER BROWN DURAND, 1835 695

Louisa Catherine Adams had a close relationship with Mary Catherine Hellen Adams, her niece and the wife of her son John, and with Mary's two daughters, Mary Louisa and Georgeanna Frances, called Fanny. The two families lived together in Washington, D.C., for much of the 1830s, and after John's death in 1834, John Quincy became the children's guardian. He wrote frequently in his Diary about reading with the girls and taking them to church and public events. Both grandparents escorted them to the May Ball, and Louisa wrote poems encouraging them to apply themselves and to be "vraie et bonne." When Fanny died in 1839 at the age of nine, Charles Francis Adams commented in his Diary, "The family were of course in much distress but my mother's grief touched me the most deeply. To her who has so few objects of pleasure around her it is grief indeed" (Diary, 7 May 1836, below; D/JQA/33, 4 May 1837, APM Reel 36; M/LCA/5, APM Reel 268, p. 54–55, 149–150; CFA, *Diary*, 8:330).

This portrait of Fanny was painted by Asher Brown Durand (1796–1886) in June and July 1835, at the same time that he was painting one of John Quincy, both at the request of his patron, the New York merchant Luman Reed. John Quincy had Durand paint Mary Louisa's portrait that summer as well, as a gift for her mother. After Fanny's death, Louisa wrote two poems in her memory: "To Fanny / In her Tomb / 20th Novbr 1840" and "To the Memory of / Georgiana Frances Adams" (CFA, *Diary*, 8:xi; Oliver, *Portraits of JQA and LCA*, p. 171–174; M/LCA/5, p. 242–244, 262, APM Reel 268).

Courtesy of the Smithsonian American Art Museum.

18. HEPPLEWHITE SECRETARY, BOSTON, CA. 1795–1810 730

Henry Adams recalled in his *Education* visits with his grandmother Louisa Catherine Adams in Quincy: She was "a little more remote than the President, but more decorative. She . . . seemed a fragile creature to a boy who sometimes brought her a note or a message. . . . He liked her refined figure; her gentle voice and manner; her vague effect of not belonging there, but to Washington or to Europe, like her furniture, and writing-desk with little glass doors above and little eighteenth-century volumes in old binding, labeled *Peregrine Pickle* or *Tom Jones* or *Hannah More*. Try as she might, the Madam could never be Bostonian, and it was her cross in life, but to the boy it was her charm."

Her secretary, however, was Bostonian. Its style suggests the desks of Thomas Seymour, a noted cabinetmaker active in Boston in the early 1800s, but it is unsigned, and the workmanship indicates that it was made in a different shop. John Quincy and Louisa purchased furniture in December 1801, soon after returning from Berlin, for their first home in Boston. In 1803, when they moved to Washington, D.C., they sold that house and stored the furniture in Quincy. It was brought out of storage in 1807 when the family again lived in Boston, and they bought additional pieces to fill out their home. The secretary might have been purchased on either of those occasions. It was likely sent to the Old House in Quincy when the Adamses left for Russia in 1809 and has remained there since (Wilhelmina S. Harris, *Furnishings Report of the Old House, The Adams National Historic Site, Quincy, Massachusetts*, 10 vols., Quincy, 1966–1974, 5:480; Robert D. Mussey Jr., *The Furniture Masterworks of John & Thomas Seymour*, Salem, 2007, p. 237; D/JQA/24, 7 Oct., 27 Nov., 17, 18, 21, 23, 24 Dec. 1801, APM Reel 27; D/JQA/27, 18 March, 4, 27 April 1807, APM Reel 30).

Courtesy of the National Park Service, Adams National Historical Park.

19. JOHN QUINCY ADAMS, CARTE DE VISITE, POST 1860 757

The daguerreotype, which was introduced into the United States in 1839, was a technological and commercial innovation, and American daguerreotypists were eager to include famous people among their subjects as a way to promote their studios. Several convinced John Quincy Adams to sit for them, including Philip Haas, Albert Sands Southworth, and John Plumbe. As the technology advanced, inexpensive reproductions of these images allowed further commercial exploitation. The example shown here is of a carte de visite, made from a process imported from France to the United States in 1860 that used a multilens camera to reproduce up to eight identical images per sheet. The carte de visite could be created as an original work or from an existing image. Whether famed photographer Mathew Brady created the original image shown here, which likely dates to the late 1840s, is uncertain, but the carte de visite bears the label of Brady's National Photographic Portrait Galleries on the back (Keith F. Davis, *The Origins of American Photography 1839–1885: From Daguerreotype to Dry-Plate*, New Haven, Conn., 2007, p. 15–16, 24, 40, 171).

In his Diary John Quincy provides an account of his experience in Plumbe's studio, where he was seated in a rooftop room resembling a greenhouse so that sunlight shone "obliquely on the side of my face." "There was a small telescope nearly in front of me pointed directly at me, and at a corresponding angle on the other side a mirror—a tin or metallic plate was fitted into the telescope, and on that metallic plate the photographic impression was made." For each exposure Adams was required to keep his head perfectly still, looking steadily at an object. "They kept me there an hour and a half, and took seven or eight impressions, all of them very bad for an exposition of sleep came over me. . . . How the impression is taken [or] came upon the plate is utterly inconceivable to me" (D/JQA/43, 27 Sept. 1842, APM Reel 46; Oliver, *Portraits of JQA and LCA*, p. 281–295).

Courtesy of the Massachusetts Historical Society.

20. LOUISA CATHERINE ADAMS DIARY, 14 MARCH 1847 764

Louisa Catherine Adams' concern for her husband's health had grown since John Quincy suffered his first cerebral hemorrhage on 20 November 1846 at the Boston home of their son, Charles Francis. Louisa had gone ahead to Washington, D.C., but on learning of John Quincy's condition, she quickly returned to Boston. On 8 February 1847, the Adamses traveled back to Washington, accompanied by a nurse.

In this Diary entry, dated 14 March 1847, Louisa prays to God to spare her husband: "With deep humiliation and a breaking heart, I implore thy help in this my great necessity; and O graciously hear my prayer for the restoration of thy Servant, my Dear Husband; imbue him with thy grace, and ease his heart of the heavy burthen which oppressessies his spirit. . . . And we petition thee merifully to support and sustain him by thy grace; that he patiently submit to thy will; and through the redeeming love of our Saviour, he may be enlightened in thy Gospel truths through his holy Spirit!— Amen!" She also recounts John Quincy's demand that she locate his will and other legal records, so that she would be prepared if he were to die (below).

On the same day John Quincy began what he called his "Posthumous Memoir," so called because from the moment of the hemorrhage "I date my decease, and consider myself for every useful purpose to myself or to my fellow creatures dead." He described his convalescence as "slow—scarcely perceptible, but without any painfull attack, and without any substantial restoration of health." He recovered from this illness eventually but lived less than a year, dying of a stroke on 23 February 1848 (D/JQA/46, APM Reel 48).

From the original in the Adams Family Papers. Courtesy of the Massachusetts Historical Society.

Introduction

Of her introduction to the home of her husband, John Quincy Adams, in late 1801, Louisa Catherine Adams famously wrote, "Quincy! What shall I say of my impressions of Quincy! Had I steped into Noah's Ark I do-not think I could have been more utterly astonished– . . . Even the Church, its forms, The snuffling through the nose, the Singers, the dressing and the dinner hour, were all novelties to me; and the ceremonious partys, the manners, and the hours of meeting 1/2 past four were equally astounding to me."[1]

Louisa sensed that her husband's family and friends judged her to be a "*fine* Lady," one who lacked the strength and skills "to *work* as they call it." Abigail Adams' attempts at household instruction deepened her feelings of ineptitude, but John Adams' kindness consoled her: "the old Gentleman took a fancy to *me*, and he was the only one."[2] Louisa set down these impressions of Quincy almost four decades later, in her memoir The Adventures of a Nobody. As her recollections suggest, she never did adjust to New England ways. Her family heritage, the circumstances of her marriage, and the demanding and unsettled life she shared with John Quincy shaped a strikingly individual member of the Adams family.

1. A COSMOPOLITAN LIFE

Born in London in 1775, the second of nine children–eight of them daughters–of the Maryland merchant Joshua Johnson and his English wife, Catherine Nuth, Louisa was raised and educated there and in Nantes, where the family spent the war years 1778 to

[1] Adventures, 1 Jan. 1802, below.
[2] Same.

1783. Joshua Johnson became the U.S. consul in London in 1790, and his home was a bustling social center for American officials and visitors. One young man who found his way there in November 1795 was the eldest son of the American vice president, then serving as the U.S. minister resident to the Netherlands. John Quincy Adams was enchanted by the pretty and musically talented Louisa, and the two became engaged in the spring of 1796. John Quincy was inclined to postpone their marriage until some indefinite time when he was settled in his career, but with some prodding by Louisa and her family, the wedding took place in July 1797 at the Church of All Hallows Barking, Great Tower Street, London. Just weeks later, the couple learned that Joshua Johnson's mercantile business was in ruins. In October Louisa accompanied John Quincy on the diplomatic posting ordered by his father, now the U.S. president, to the court at Berlin, and it was there that their first child, named for George Washington, was born in April 1801. After John Adams' defeat by Thomas Jefferson in the election of 1800, Adams requested that his son be recalled from Prussia. In July 1801 the young family sailed for America, where John Quincy took his place as a Massachusetts state senator (1802–1803), U.S. senator (1803–1808), and Boylston Professor of Rhetoric and Oratory at Harvard (1806–1809). Louisa gave birth to John 2d in July 1803 and Charles Francis in August 1807. In August 1809 she set out for what would be a long period abroad, as John Quincy served as U.S. minister in Russia—where their daughter, Louisa Catherine, was born in August 1811—and then, beginning in 1815, as minister in Great Britain. The Adamses returned to the United States in 1817 when John Quincy was appointed secretary of state, a position he would hold until he took office as president in 1825. After his defeat for reelection, the two returned to Quincy. In 1830 John Quincy was elected to the House of Representatives from the Plymouth district, an office to which he would be returned until his death in 1848.

In the years just preceding her first encounter with Quincy, Louisa had experienced her share of unusual customs as she mingled with the princesses, diplomats, and adventurers of the Prussian court. By 1840, when she began to write Adventures of a Nobody, Louisa had seen far more of the world. She had steered herself through the quaint manners of Quincy and Boston and then entered the more cosmopolitan society of the new federal city of Washington, D.C., where it was a matter of course to meet the Tunisian minister Sidi Soliman Melli Melli or for a party of Cherokees to pay a call.[3] In the era of the Napoleonic wars Louisa and John Quincy traversed the perilous sea route to Russia to reach the splendor and decadence of Alexander I's court. There, as virtually the only minister's wife resident in St. Petersburg, Louisa socialized with members of the imperial family, women accomplished in the arts and literature, and the mistresses of foreign diplomats. She would hazard an overland journey from St. Petersburg to Paris to meet her husband, who had gone ahead on diplomatic business, before departing with him for London to spend two years in the familiar environs of the Court of St. James. Back again in Washington, D.C., as the wife of the secretary of state, she regularly dealt with office seekers, rough frontier politicians, eccentrics, and men and women of great pretension. The "snuffling through the nose" of Quincy's townspeople may once have astounded her, but in her writings she is unperturbed by the odd and exotic inhabitants of imperial Europe and Washington City.

2. LOUISA CATHERINE ADAMS AS A DIARIST AND AUTOBIOGRAPHER

Louisa's writings would be of interest if only because she was a woman of great charm who lived for more than fifty years as the constant companion of one of the most distinguished statesmen of the era. But her writings command attention because of the ardor with which she applied herself to her task. To the prodigious record left by the Adams family, Louisa adds her highly personal works—most notably her Diary and memoirs, published here, and her letters. Her writings provide a fresh perspective on the family, and particularly on John Quincy, who emerges from her pages as a gallant and generous husband as often as he confirms his image as the ambitious and duty-bound Adams scion. Louisa's sharp observations of human foibles and her uninhibited expressions of emotion give color and authenticity to her record of the Adamses' comings and goings. She offers opinions on the great issues of the day, in so many of which her husband played a central role, but what makes her writings most arresting are the descriptions of life in the ballrooms and drawing rooms of Europe and America, the parlors of friends, and the family home, wherever that might be. The writings are notable too for the reflections she composed in the solitude of

[3] Same, 9 Dec. 1805; Diary, 9 Jan. 1823, both below.

her chamber. It was in her room with a garden view at the Old House, with its Dutch tiles and a "writing-desk with little glass doors above," that Henry Adams most vividly recalled the grandmother whose delicacy of figure, voice, and manner, and "vague effect of not belonging there, but to Washington or to Europe" he so admired.[4]

How Louisa composed her autobiographical writings, and why she did so, are closely connected questions, though both must be a matter of some conjecture because related journal books or notes are mostly lacking. In Record of a Life, begun in 1825, Louisa wrote from memory about her childhood and education, courtship and marriage, and the first months in Prussia. By the time she began The Adventures of a Nobody, a continuation of Record of a Life that covers events from late 1797 to 16 February 1812, she was familiar with her husband's Diaries, having "perused" them for her own interests, copied passages to assist him in legal proceedings, and written entries for him. She consulted those Diaries, sometimes quite closely, in constructing Adventures, and she wrote the memoir largely in diary form. Louisa states that she composed Record, and presumably Adventures, in the hope that one day her children would be "amused" and edified by it, and that "a review of past incidents may have a good effect upon myself." She had "no pretensions to be a writer and no desire to appear any thing more than a mere commonplace personage with a good memory and just observation enough to discover the difference between a man of sense and a Fool, and to know that the latter often do the least mischief of the two."[5] Beyond the function of edification, it is clear that these memoirs were to stand as testimony to the Johnson family's honor and patriotism, as a defense against the view she believed the Adams family and others held that Joshua Johnson had inveigled John Quincy into marrying her as the merchant saw his business failing and his fortune lost. Whether the self-effacing title "The Adventures of a Nobody" was intended to be taken literally or ironically, Louisa does not say, but in declaring herself a nonentity, she may have hoped to exempt herself a bit from the constraints of being an Adams writing for the ages.

In Narrative of a Journey from Russia to France, dated 27 June

[4] Henry Adams, *The Education of Henry Adams: A Centennial Version*, ed. Edward Chalfant and Conrad Edick Wright, Boston, 2007, p. 13. See also Descriptive List of Illustrations, No. 18, above.

[5] Record of a Life, below.

1836, Louisa described her trip of 12 February to 23 March 1815 from St. Petersburg to Paris entirely from her own memory, without John Quincy's Diary or a contemporaneous diary of her own to guide her. It was her lofty goal that the memoir would "at some future day serve to recal the memory of one, *who was*—and show that many undertakings which appear very difficult and arduous to my Sex, are by no means so trying as imagination forever depicts them— And that energy and discretion, follow the necessity of their exertion, to protect the fancied weakness of feminine imbecility."[6] The narrative is Louisa's tour de force, not the least because the strength and self-assurance with which she wrote it matches the boldness she demonstrated throughout the journey.[7]

Louisa is less explicit regarding the purpose of her Diaries except for the Russian Diary covering the period from 22 October 1812 to 15 February 1814. She kept that Diary strictly for herself, to assuage her grief at the recent death of the baby Louisa Catherine, for which she needlessly blamed herself: "I have procured this Book with a view to write my thoughts and if possible to avoid dwelling on the secret and bitter reproaches of my heart for my conduct as it regarded my lost adored Child whose death was surely occasion'd by procrastination."[8] The Russian Diary is the only contemporaneous record of Louisa's experiences in that country.

That Louisa enjoyed putting her own stamp on personal writing forms is evident not only in Adventures, the memoir constructed as a diary, but also in the Diary for 24 January 1819 to 8 January 1824, years when she assumed her responsibilities as the wife of the secretary of state and likely heir to the presidency. Louisa directed these Diary entries to particular people—her father-in-law, John Adams; her husband; her son George; and her brother, Thomas Baker Johnson. She then sent similar sentiments, still in diary entry form, as "journal letters" to the person addressed. This procedure accomplished two tasks efficiently and permitted her to polish the writing in the sent version. Louisa's purpose in this Diary extended beyond record keeping and self-scrutiny to include communication of a most spontaneous kind with distant family members, most prominently John Adams, eager for news of his son's political fortunes in Washington, D.C.

Louisa kept her late Diaries, those for 6 November 1835 to 28 May

[6] Narrative of a Journey, below.

[7] LCA's grandson BA published a version of this work; see same, note 1, below.

[8] Diary, 22 Oct. 1812, below.

1841 and 11 March 1844 to 18 March 1849—years when John Quincy served in Congress—only sporadically, writing entries here and there in her journal book, often in no particular order. After one period of light diary-keeping, Louisa explained her reticence, observing that diaries were "amusing while you are drawn into the focus of active society, where events follow each other in rapid succession. . . . But when time speeds his course in a monotonous circle of given things; a Diary becomes a memeto of puerilities."[9] The journal books that contain these Diaries also served as repositories for occasional writings, including poetry and religious and philosophical essays, that may have brought Louisa some solace as she took the measure of her life.

The writings presented here are somewhat uneven in quality, as works so varied and wide ranging are likely to be. But Louisa was a graceful and engaging writer, deft in her descriptive powers and skilled at summoning apt passages from scripture and such favorite authors as Shakespeare, Dryden, Sir Walter Scott, and Madame de Stael. She had a gift for capturing notable people at revealing moments, as when she tells of the Russian emperor Alexander I pursuing her pretty sister Catherine through the palaces and promenades of St. Petersburg, Aaron Burr diverting her "troublesome" children as they sailed aboard a packet, and Thomas Jefferson instructing her in the art of eating "Canvass back Ducks" at his White House table.[10]

Neither diaries nor autobiographical writings have been found that cover two highly significant periods of Louisa's life, the years when the family resided in England while John Quincy was U.S. minister to Great Britain, and the term of John Quincy's service as U.S. president, though it was at the beginning of the latter period that Louisa wrote Record of a Life. Narrative of a Journey and Adventures of a Nobody were written during the period when she composed the first of her two late Diaries.

The Diaries and autobiographical writings stand firmly on their own, but they are only part of the record that Louisa left behind—the remainder, of course, comprises her correspondence, as well as a considerable collection of poetic works, dramatic pieces, and prose sketches. The achievements of Louisa Catherine Adams as an individual, a wife and mother, and a member of the Adams family

[9] Diary, 17 June 1839, below.

[10] Adventures, [*19*] March 1805; 13 Nov. 1807; 29 April, 23 May, 29 Nov., 16 Dec. 1810, all below.

are most fully realized when her correspondence is joined to the writings presented here.

3. THE JOHNSON FAMILY

Louisa's upbringing provided little preparation for her life as an Adams. In Record of a Life and Adventures of a Nobody, she takes pains to describe Joshua Johnson's dedication to his native country and service to patriots abroad during the Revolutionary period. But despite the connection to America that her father could claim by his heritage and work, Louisa was formed mainly by European sensibilities. She writes of her indulgent parents, of sisterly rivalries and faithless suitors, as if she were composing a charming English novel. But she returns again and again to the dark events that unfolded at the time of her marriage: Joshua Johnson's business failure and his departure in the night for America with his wife and Louisa's sisters, leaving creditors behind. Louisa lays the blame for her father's ruin to dishonest business associates and the vicissitudes of credit and trade. The causes of Johnson's predicament are complex, but it is clear that he was slow and evasive in responding to John Quincy's letters to him in America requesting that he address the complaints of the creditors then knocking on the young couple's door.[11] Still wounded by these events as she looked back at them in her memoirs, she idealizes her parents, and particularly her father, contrasting the "roseate hours" she enjoyed in his home with the trials of her peripatetic existence in support of John Quincy's high public purpose.

John Adams assisted the Johnsons in America, securing a place for Joshua in the Stamp Office. When Louisa arrived in the United States from Prussia, she would have only a brief reunion with her father in Maryland. He soon fell gravely ill, and Louisa understood on her departure for Quincy that she would never see him again. Catherine Nuth Johnson was left destitute, dependent on her children and the connections her more fortunate daughters would make. Louisa maintained close ties with her siblings, and she and John Quincy offered support to them in times of trouble. Several of them figure prominently in these writings, most notably Catherine, who was a companion to Louisa during the years in Russia.

[11] See Record of a Life; Adventures, note 25, both below.

4. LOUISA'S LIFE WITH JOHN QUINCY

Throughout Record of a Life and Adventures of a Nobody, Louisa laments that she was unfairly judged to have been "palmed" off by her father on an unsuspecting John Quincy. She believed that her husband's confidence in her and her family had been irreparably damaged, though she makes it clear that John Quincy responded to her father's ruin with tact and forbearance. He evidently made no complaint about the £5,000 dowry lost with the Johnson fortune. Several years after Johnson's death, John Quincy examined his papers and, in the face of evidence that was at best inconclusive, assured Louisa that her father had been the most honorable of men.[12]

Louisa's youthful grace complemented John Quincy's austere demeanor, and she proved a great asset to him in his diplomatic errand to Prussia. She claimed ignorance of the affairs of state. John Quincy, she wrote, had taught her that women had no place in politics, "and as he was the glass from which my opinions were reflected, I was convinced of its truth, and sought no farther."[13] Nonetheless, in Berlin, Louisa's wit and fluency in French would enable her to represent the American republic, which she had not yet seen, as a cultured, fully fledged nation. Later, when a more experienced Louisa arrived at the St. Petersburg court, she would delight in upending European notions about American backwardness: Her familiarity with the great cities of Europe surprised the Russian empress dowager, who had expected to "quiz my ignorance. . . . The Savage had been expected!!"; she dressed her son Charles Francis as an Indian chief for a costume ball given by the French ambassador "to gratify the taste for Savages."[14]

John Quincy carefully and, in his way, affectionately taught Louisa what was required of her as the American minister's wife. When, against her husband's wishes, a wan Louisa applied rouge—as she had been urged to do by Queen Louise of Prussia—and attempted to leave for a party under cover of a darkened room, John Quincy "took a Towel and drew me on his knee, and all my beauty was clean washed away; and a kiss made the peace." That peace was breached some months later when Louisa made a bolder attempt to wear rouge to court, causing John Quincy to dash off in a waiting

[12] Adventures, note 25; Oct. 1803; note 209, all below.

[13] Same, 4 April 1799, below.

[14] Same, 12 Nov., 14 Dec. 1809, both below.

carriage, leaving her behind.[15] Although the admonition against rouge may have taken some repeating, John Quincy's example of republican simplicity and economy was not lost on Louisa. She understood that in comparison with others at the Prussian and Russian courts, her family's clothing and lodgings would be exceedingly modest, and their participation in mere frivolities would be circumscribed. Louisa tried to avoid the Prussian "harpies" who were intent on "fleecing" her at the card tables, and she saw the wisdom of barring Charles Francis from "a lottery of choice and expensive toys" at a St. Petersburg ball. She needed no convincing that the American public would be outraged if the Russian emperor were to stand as a sponsor at the christening of her daughter, Louisa Catherine.[16]

Louisa deferred to John Quincy on the matter of the children's religious training, and she herself followed his New England ways to provide an example for the family. But she had her own ideas about religion. The plain "forms" of the Quincy church had been unsettling to the newly arrived Louisa because her previous experience had been decidedly high church. Although Joshua Johnson's faith was Unitarian, he raised his family in the Church of England, convinced that for women there was "little danger in believing" but "*destruction* in doubt."[17] Louisa had attended a convent school during her family's residence in France, and she found her exposure to the Roman Catholic Church deeply affecting. She recalled "the heartfelt humility with which I knelt before the Image of the tortured Jesus and the horror I felt at the thought, of mixing with hereticks."[18] On tour during the Prussian posting, she had occasion to attend a service at the Dresden cathedral, and she wrote admiringly of the music, works of art, incense, and priestly paraphernalia, which "all sieze upon the senses, and steal insensibly upon the heart with rapt enthusiasm."[19]

By the time Louisa began to write Adventures, she had experienced a still broader array of religious observance. In Russia she became familiar not only with Orthodox ritual but also with that of the Greek and Lutheran churches. Her daughter was christened in St. Petersburg's English Factory Church and buried a year later in the

[15] Same, 1 Jan., 14 Oct. 1799; 1 Feb., [31] Dec. 1800, all below.

[16] Same, 24 Jan. 1798, 14 Dec. 1809, 9 Sept. 1811, all below.

[17] Record of a Life, below.

[18] Same.

[19] Adventures, 15 Sept. 1799, below.

so-called Lutheran Cemetery on Vasilevsky Island, the resting place for those not of the Russian Orthodox faith. By 1823, seasoned by her experiences at the English court and then in Washington, Louisa would describe the Catholic Church as an instrument of despotic or monarchical nations, and she would roundly condemn the Russian clergy as ignorant drunkards. She had found little to praise in the public worship services offered at the Capitol by visiting clergymen of different denominations, heaping particular scorn on one "miserable Rhapsodist." Louisa's critique of "Yankee Unitarians" as a "sect enveloped in a cloud of Mist" and her belief in the divinity of Christ intensified as she grew older and more burdened with losses and regrets.[20] While reflecting on religion in her late Diaries, Louisa seems to have given a nod to the Quincy church of her husband's forbears. She took a moment to pay tribute to the "old Puritan character," which, though unduly harsh, had adhered to a faith "calculated to raise the soul above the mere sublunary pleasures of this life; and to check the grovelling mind in its too ardent passion, for the distinctions, the wealth, and the paltry aggrandizement of mere worldly pursuits."[21] At Louisa's death in 1852, her preference for an Episcopal funeral service was respected.

In her years with John Quincy, Louisa was often ill or indisposed. She suffered numerous miscarriages, the first not long after her arrival in Prussia, and on several occasions she gave birth in difficult circumstances: George was delivered by a "Drunken Accoucheur" in Berlin; a son was stillborn in Washington during the summer of 1806, when the rest of her family was far away in Quincy; and her namesake was born in a rented house on the outskirts of St. Petersburg.[22] As a diplomatic and political wife she kept an exhausting schedule of social events, lasting late into the night in crowded ballrooms and stuffy drawing rooms, ideal situations for contracting illnesses. The Adamses' place in society, whether in the imperial courts or at home in Massachusetts and Washington, ensured the ready availability of eminent doctors, whose remedies—laudanum, blisters, bleedings—undoubtedly worsened Louisa's distress. As family separations and losses mounted, and as John Quincy's public achievements and disappointments exacted their price, Louisa often sank into depression, vivid descriptions of which can be found in

[20] Diary, 18 Feb., 4 March 1821; 12 July 1839, all below.

[21] Diary, 15 Sept., [*ante 29 Sept.*] 1839, both below.

[22] Adventures, 24 March 1801, and note 122; April, 29 June 1806; 8, 11 July, 11, 12 Aug. 1811, all below.

her Russian Diary and late Diaries.[23] She understood the nature of her suffering and evidently discussed her condition with her husband. In 1814, when Louisa was still grieving deeply for her daughter, John Quincy gave her a copy of *Medical Inquiries and Observations, upon Diseases of the Mind* by Dr. Benjamin Rush. She wrote in her Diary that the book provoked fears that she was insane, as she imagined herself "afflicted with every particular symtom described."[24]

Still, in 1815 this seemingly fragile woman undertook a journey that would require a high degree of physical endurance and nerve. John Quincy, in Paris after negotiating the Treaty of Ghent, instructed Louisa to quit St. Petersburg and join him as he awaited confirmation of his posting to London. Louisa set off in the Russian winter with seven-year-old Charles Francis and several unfamiliar servants, traveling in a carriage with detachable runners on a 40-day, 2,000-mile journey. Such preparations as John Quincy had directed for the trip proved wholly inadequate, but Louisa would demonstrate great resourcefulness as she encountered dangers—not the least of them Napoleon's resurgent forces—along the way.

Louisa served her husband by maintaining a warm bond with his aging, widowed father. The affection between Louisa and John Adams that was sparked when she first arrived in Quincy is evident throughout her writings. It is especially clear in the journal entries Louisa directed to him in the Diary for the period when John Quincy, as secretary of state, had little time to spare. John Adams surely enjoyed her candid reports of the follies and hypocrisies of Washington's political and social elite. Describing the congressional leadership's machinations over the Missouri question, Louisa wrote, "it is a pity that we have not a Homer to chant in the most elevated strains the glory of *such patriots*— At least we shall be allowed to . . . delight in the glory of *tricks atcheived* which would do honor to a gamester or a blacklegs."[25] She shared with her father-in-law her personal anguish and satisfactions, and she felt free to make little jokes about the punctilious John Quincy, even expressing relief that his monumental survey to further the cause of standardized measurements had been completed: "Thank God we hear no more of Weights and Measures."[26]

[23] For another such description, see also Diary, 7–13 Jan. 1821, below.
[24] Diary, 7 Feb. 1814, below.
[25] Diary, 3 March 1820, below.
[26] Diary, 6 Jan. 1821, below.

Because Louisa and John Quincy were abroad in Prussia, Russia, and London during many of the years preceding Abigail Adams' death in 1818, the works presented here afford the reader only a limited view of the relationship between the two women. Louisa writes that the misunderstandings that marred their early connection were set aside after her years in Russia, presumably because she had more than proved her mettle on the journey to Paris. Researchers who peruse their correspondence will find ample evidence of Abigail's kindness toward her daughter-in-law and the Johnson family. In 1836, while reading the letters of Abigail Adams that Charles Francis was preparing for publication, Louisa wrote of her: "we see her ever as the guiding Planet around which all revolved, performing their separate duties only by the impulse of her magnetic power, which diffused a mild and glowing radiance over all who moved within the sphere of her fascinating attraction." Here Louisa added, "from the hour that I entered into his family, The Ex-President John Adams never said an unkind word to me; but ever to the hour of his death, treated me with the utmost tenderness, and distinction the most flattering– I loved him living, and I venerate his Memory."[27]

Unlike Abigail, who had assisted John Adams mostly from afar, keeping home and family intact while, through letters, serving as his most valued advisor and friend, Louisa spent relatively little time apart from her husband. It was Louisa's presence, her personal charm and cultural acumen, pressed into the service of her increasingly canny political instincts, that helped to advance John Quincy's career. Once he became secretary of state, a stepping-stone to the presidency in the new republic, it became Louisa's responsibility to promote, by social means, her husband's goal of succeeding James Monroe. It was, she wrote, "a very painful thing to me to be dragged into public notice, and made an object of debate in every company– but these are the penalties I must pay for being the Wife of a man . . . who by his real and extraordinary merits throws those who are more ambitious than himself into the shade."[28]

In this social role Louisa was forced to enter the fray over the "ettiquette question," that is, the protocols for first visits, which had vexed all of Washington society, including President Monroe and his family. Giving John Adams an amusing report of his son "every morning preparing a set of cards with as much formality as if he was drawing up some very important article, to negotiate in a Commer-

[27] Diary, 1 Sept. 1836, below.
[28] Diary, 21 Dec. 1819, below.

cial Treaty," she went about the stultifying business of paying calls, or discharging her duty by merely leaving her calling card at the door.[29] She hosted parties, balls, and regular Tuesday "sociables" to gain the support of influential Washingtonians, and particularly the congressmen who would be instrumental in determining the presidential election of 1824. Her efforts so pleased John Quincy that after one ball, "he joined in a Reel with the boys and myself," she told her father-in-law, "and you would have laughed heartily to see the surprize of our people, and the musicians, who were the only witnesses of the sport."[30] Louisa came to embrace her social duties, carrying them out with a good measure of confidence. She took a wry view of the hazards of being in the public eye, commenting on the impossibility of ascertaining what republican virtue demanded of her: "my very dear five hundred friends begin to think my manners too generally *courtly* the fashionable expression and that I am not choice enough in the selection of my company."[31]

In January 1824 Louisa and John Quincy hosted a ball to honor Andrew Jackson, the hero of New Orleans, and, not coincidentally, to cast a spotlight on themselves as worthy aspirants to the White House. The response to their 500 invitations was so overwhelming that it was necessary to install pillars to support the upper stories of their F Street house. Louisa's elaborate plans were rewarded, as the rooms, decorated with chalked floors and festoons of laurel and roses, and piled high with refreshments, were the scene of the social event of the season.[32] As the election approached, Louisa wrote that should John Quincy lose, "the disgrace will not fall on him but heavily on that *very enlightened* Country and people who could not discriminate between sterling worth and base intrigue."[33]

Like other prominent women in Washington, Louisa attended the proceedings of the House and Senate, particularly when important issues were being discussed or a distinguished or flamboyant speaker was to take the floor. She kept track of censure proceedings against Andrew Jackson for his actions in Florida during the First Seminole War; took an interest in the wrangling over the Adams-Onís Treaty that her husband had so painstakingly negotiated; and followed the fiery debates on the Missouri Compromise. She also

[29] Diary, 22 Dec. 1819, below.

[30] Diary, 18 Jan. 1820, below.

[31] Diary, 5 March 1821, below.

[32] See Descriptive List of Illustrations, No. 16, above; Diary, 20 Dec. 1823, note 1, 27 Dec., both below.

[33] Diary, 30 Nov. 1823, below.

lent her hand to good works, serving on the board of the Washington Female Orphan Asylum.[34]

Although Louisa insisted that she did not involve herself in her husband's professional duties, her writings provide a view of the domestic context in which John Quincy worked. When, during his postpresidential career as a member of the House of Representatives, John Quincy argued long and vehemently against the "gag rule"—the southerners' effort to block the presentation of antislavery petitions to Congress—Louisa found herself in conflict with her relatives, some of whom were slaveholders: "Every friend is turned into an enemy; and now the prospect terminates with the fear of losing the love, the friendship and the society of my own nearest and dearest connections." Louisa wrote despondently on the slavery question, fearing the violence that would attend its resolution, and she prayed that her husband might be spared "from becoming the scourge through which this great event is to be atchieved."[35]

5. LOUISA AND HER CHILDREN

In the early years of their marriage, miscarriages gave Louisa and John Quincy good reason to despair of having children, but with George's birth and—notwithstanding further difficulties—the arrival of John 2d and Charles Francis, the Adamses formed a lively family. Louisa recalled with particular poignancy the childhood adventures of her firstborn. On a trip to Washington, two-and-a-half-year-old George announced that he had tossed his shoes and the keys to the family's trunks out of their boat's window. When he was three, an uncle saved him from jumping from a wharf into the Potomac River, "to see how *deep* it was!" At age six, George was "thrown out of a swing as high as the Poplars by the Otis boys," dislocating his shoulder. He delighted his mother by using the reward his grandfather had given him for bravery at the bonesetter's to buy gingerbread for his schoolmates.[36]

But only two years after this display of munificence, John Quincy's appointment to Russia separated Louisa from eight-year-old George and six-year-old John 2d. Without consulting her, John Quincy and his parents decided that the older boys would stay be-

[34] See, for example, Diary, 24 [*Jan.*], and note 2, 26 Jan., and note 2, 26 Feb., 7 Dec., and note 1, 13 Dec. 1819, and note 1; 20, 21 Jan. 1820, all below.

[35] Diary, 21 Dec., and note 1, 24 Dec. 1835; 10 March 1836, all below.

[36] Adventures, 9 Oct. 1803; May 1804; 7, 12 Aug. 1807, all below.

hind for the sake of their education. On a last visit to Quincy to see George and John 2d, she was not permitted "to speak with the old gentleman alone least I should excite his pity and he allow me to take my boys with me."[37] During what turned out to be the nearly six-year stay in Russia Louisa found some consolation in having Charles Francis along and in the birth of her only daughter. But Louisa Catherine's death in infancy was a blow that left her "only desirous of mingling my ashes with those of my lovely Babe."[38] Years later, after the family had been reunited for John Quincy's mission in Britain and then resettled in America, Louisa wrote that since her daughter's death she had found nothing to "fill the void made in my heart." Beloved as her sons were, "I have always considered them more as subjects born to gratify my pride or ambition than as beings calculated in any shape to meet my feelings of affection or sympathy."[39]

All three sons would enter Harvard—George in 1817, John 2d in 1819, and Charles Francis in 1821. Louisa eagerly anticipated her sons' visits during Harvard vacations, if on occasion she found the high-spirited boys insensitive to her indispositions and "gloom."[40] Louisa and John Quincy encouraged their sons to enjoy Washington's bright social life, but their all-too-ready infatuations were a matter of some concern. The older boys' college studies did not go smoothly. Both George and John 2d were disciplined by the Harvard authorities for their participation in student rebellions, and while George was reinstated and went on to receive his degree, John 2d committed a second infraction that earned him a permanent dismissal. "My Children seem to have some very intemperate blood in them, and are certainly not very easy to govern," Louisa wrote at the time of John's first misstep. "John is somewhat like his Mother a little hot headed, and want of timely reflection will I fear often lead him to error."[41]

Both George and John 2d fell into dissipation and ill health and met untimely deaths. George, summoned from Boston to Washington to escort his parents home in 1829 after John Quincy's defeat for reelection, either fell or jumped to his death from a steamboat in Long Island Sound. John 2d died in 1834, leaving behind his wife

[37] Same, 4 July 1809, below.
[38] Diary, 5 Dec. 1812, below.
[39] Diary, 7 Jan. 1821, below.
[40] Diary, 8, 9 Jan. 1821, below.
[41] Diary, 15 Nov. 1820, below.

(and cousin), Mary Catherine Hellen Adams, and two children, Mary Louisa (b. 1828) and Georgeanna Frances (b. 1830). Although the deaths of George and John 2d occurred in a period not covered in these writings, Louisa's despair and self-reproach are manifest in Adventures of a Nobody and in her late Diaries. She dwells on her failure to be a proper mother, removed as she was from the two in their boyhood; more broadly, she laments her sacrifice to her husband's—and the Adams family's—ambition. Her stillborn son, she wrote, was "the only one of my Children whom I never deserted."[42] Charles Francis, the child who was not left behind when his parents went to St. Petersburg, mirrored his father in being the one Adams son of his generation to lead a full and high-achieving life. At home in Boston and Quincy with his wife, Abigail Brown Brooks, and their seven children, Charles Francis seems a remote figure in his mother's late Diaries. John 2d's family, however, is very much in evidence. Beginning in late 1829 Louisa and John Quincy lived in John 2d's I Street home, and four years after John 2d's death, his widow and children would accompany the elder Adamses when they returned to their F Street residence. The grandparents aided Mary Catherine in providing a secure home for the fatherless children. Mary Louisa and Georgeanna would give purpose to Louisa's later years, though the family would suffer the further blow of the younger child's death at the age of nine.

Louisa, never one to let troubles, much less profound losses, go unnoticed in her writings, had every reason to look upon her later years in desolation. That this was the very period when she created the optimistic and self-affirming Narrative of a Journey and then turned to her most ambitious and complex memoir, Adventures of a Nobody, testifies to her compulsion to bring order to her life with the written word. Louisa produced memoirs and diaries that amplify and complement the records of the eminent American family into which she had married, and her writings are worthy of inclusion in the Adams Papers Diary series with the works of John Adams, John Quincy Adams, and Charles Francis Adams.

6. NOTES ON EDITORIAL METHOD

Materials Included and Their Arrangement

The Diaries and autobiographical writings of Louisa Catherine

[42] Diary, 18 Aug. 1839, below.

Adams are printed here in their entirety in keeping with the requirements of the Adams Manuscript Trust, which donated the papers to the Massachusetts Historical Society and created the Adams Papers project. Materials found in the journal books other than Diary entries and autobiographical writings—such as poetry, essays, lists, recipes, and household accounts—are not included, but poems that are clearly integral to a Diary entry or memoir have been retained. The two volumes, arranged to present Louisa's life as it unfolded, rather than in the order in which she wrote the material, contain the following documents in the Adams Family Papers manuscript collection at the Massachusetts Historical Society:

1. Record of a Life, an autobiographical work begun in 1825, in M/LCA/2, a journal book.
2. The Adventures of a Nobody, an autobiographical work begun in 1840, in M/LCA/6, made up of folded sheets of paper.
3. The Diary of Louisa Catherine Adams for 22 October 1812 to 15 February 1814, in M/LCA/1, a journal book.
4. Narrative of a Journey from Russia to France, dated 27 June 1836, in M/LCA/5, a journal book.
5. The Diary of Louisa Catherine Adams for 24 January to 25 March 1819, in M/LCA/1; 6 December 1819 to 28 March 1821, in M/LCA/2; 19 July to 19 August 1821, in M/LCA/3, a paper-covered booklet; 17 August to 27 September 1821, in M/LCA/4, a paper-covered booklet; and 3 December 1821 to 8 January 1824, in M/LCA/2.
6. The Diary of Louisa Catherine Adams for 6 Nov. 1835 to 28 May 1841, in M/LCA/5; and 11 March 1844 to 18 March 1849, in M/LCA/7, a journal book. These Diary entries, written only occasionally and scattered throughout their respective journal books, have been placed in chronological order by the editors.

Treatment of the Texts

This is the first volume of the Diary series to incorporate the substantially revised policy concerning the presentation of documents first used in volume 8 of the *Adams Family Correspondence*, and so it seems appropriate to offer an overview of the project's editorial method, especially as it pertains to the Diaries. Readers may wish to review the statements of editorial policy in previous volumes, particularly the *Diary and Autobiography of John Adams*, 1:lii–lxii, and the *Adams Family Correspondence*, 1:xli–xlviii, which document the original conception of the Adams Papers project, some aspects of which have now been superseded.

Under the revised textual policy, the texts are rendered as literally as possible, given the limitations of modern typography and the constraints inherent in translating handwritten manuscripts into printed documents. While the editorial policy in effect for earlier volumes allowed for substantial intervention to regularize the presentation of the texts, the revised policy of literal interpretation preserves more of the original document and allows the reader to determine the significance of the authors' spelling, grammar, capitalization, and other mechanical aspects of writing. In that spirit, the following is a summary of the specifics of the project's new policy.

Spelling is preserved as found in the manuscripts. Irregular spellings and spelling mistakes, even when they are obviously simple slips of the pen, are retained. The index will continue to offer corrected spellings of proper names and places, but no such corrections are made in the text itself. If a proper name is otherwise unidentifiable without some clarification, that explanation is generally provided in a text note.

Grammar and syntax are preserved as found in the manuscripts. Ambiguous statements resulting from grammatical errors may be explained in text notes. Inadvertent repetition of words, however, is silently corrected, and all new paragraphs receive a standardized indent, regardless of whether such paragraphs are indicated in the original manuscript by indents, extra space, hanging indents, extended dashes, or other conventions.

Capitalization is preserved as found in the manuscripts, even when it violates conventional standards, as in the use of lowercase letters for proper nouns or at the beginnings of sentences. When it is difficult to determine whether the writer intended a capital or a lowercase letter, the editors follow modern usage.

Punctuation is preserved as found in the manuscripts. Occasionally, punctuation marks are supplied by the editors for the sake of readability. In those instances, the punctuation is enclosed in brackets and rendered in italics to indicate that it has been editorially supplied. Louisa makes frequent use of dashes, requiring the editors to distinguish short dashes from distinct periods and to determine whether a dash is intended as terminal or internal punctuation. When hints that normally apply for making these determinations, such as the proximity of the dash to the word it follows or precedes, are not discerned, the editors rely on context and follow modern rules of punctuation. Finally, the punctuation for abbreviations and contractions has been standardized only to the extent that underlining below a superscript is rendered as a period following the superscript, and two periods or marks under a superscript are rendered as a colon following the superscript.

Abbreviations and contractions, in general, are preserved as found in the manuscript. Ampersands and superscripts are retained, except in diary datelines where superscripts are brought down to the line.

Missing and illegible matter is indicated by square brackets enclosing the editors' conjectural readings (with a question mark appended if the reading is uncertain) or by suspension points within brackets if no reading can be given. Three points are used to indicate a single missing word and four to indicate two missing words. When more than two words are missing, a footnote is provided indicating an estimate of the total amount of missing material.

Canceled matter in the manuscript (whether scored out or erased) is disregarded unless the editors deem it to be of some significance. In those instances, the text is included but crossed out typographically.

Variant readings (variations in text between two or more versions of the same material) are ordinarily indicated only when they are significant enough to warrant notice, and then always in notes keyed to the basic text that is printed in full. For the present volumes, this policy pertains to second versions of Adventures of a Nobody and Narrative of a Journey. The editors have not treated the journal letters as variant readings of the corresponding Diary entries; that is, differences between the two have not been noted, although on occasion particularly revealing information from the journal letters has been related in the notes.

Interlineations are silently included within the body of the text unless the editors deem the placement of the interlineated material worthy of mention, most commonly when it is written at the bottom or along the margin of a page and marked for insertion. Such explanations are provided by text notes.

Editorial insertions are now relatively rare and used largely to indicate errors in dating or to supply necessary punctuation. The vast majority of editorial comment can be found in the annotation, rather than in the text. Editorial insertions are still rendered in italicized text in brackets.

The *diary dateline* is always placed at the head of the entry, even if it appears elsewhere in the manuscript (for instance, at the end of an entry). Missing dateline elements are editorially supplied and erroneous elements are corrected using italicized text inside square brackets. The standards for punctuation outlined above are followed except that superscripts are brought down to the line. The editors have relied on John Quincy Adams' Diaries to resolve most of the dateline questions encountered in these volumes.

The Adventures manuscript has been treated somewhat differently because here, in what was intended as an autobiography, Louisa uses diary form with datelines provided erratically, not always accurately, and often to cover a narrative that continues for days or months beyond its starting point. The editors have not routinely supplied or corrected datelines in Adventures except in a small number of instances when a precise date has been deemed necessary, but accurate dating can often be found in the annotation or the text itself. The few out-of-order datelines in Adventures have not been moved, but explanatory notes are provided. John Quincy Adams' Diary should be consulted for regular, accurate dating of the events in Adventures.

Annotation and Index

While the most important function of these volumes is to provide accurate and authoritative texts, the editors also strive to offer additional information to help readers fully understand the nature of the documents and the historical context in which they were written.

A note at the beginning of each new Miscellany describes the physical nature of the document, its scope and contents, and its Adams Papers microfilm reel number. Here titles and epigrams are printed as Louisa wrote them, with multiline text run together and marked with virgules to indicate line breaks. Other features of the document, such as unusual watermarks or author's markings, may be noted. Also at this note, as needed, the editors have made an effort to fill long gaps in the Diary record by summarizing, chiefly from information in the Diary of John Quincy Adams and the Adams family correspondence, the principal events that occurred during these intervals.

All other matters annotated—textual, biographical, bibliographical, and so on—are dealt with in individually numbered notes for each Diary entry and in consecutively numbered notes at the bottom of the page for each of the autobiographical writings. Adventures, despite its diary form, is treated as an autobiographical work in the numbering and placement of notes. In general, the editors hope that the Diaries and autobiographical writings in large part annotate themselves, that together they provide an overarching sense of Louisa Catherine Adams and the events she experienced. Still, certain categories of material require some additional explanation, and the editors attempt to supply that through brief factual notes. Among the categories of information offered in the notes, the following are the most common:

1. *Persons and personal names.* The single largest category of notes are identifications of individuals, whether family members, friends, political and diplomatic colleagues, or acquaintances. While not everyone mentioned in the documents can be meaningfully identified, brief biographies are provided for many individuals who played a role in Louisa's life, at their first significant mention. When an identification is tentative, the caveats "possibly" or "probably" are used to indicate the editors' level of uncertainty. Text notes are also used to clarify spellings of names when the variations are substantial enough to make locating them in the index difficult (in most cases, names are "corrected" or regularized only in the index) and to provide cross-references to identifications available in other Adams Papers volumes.

2. *Books and other publications; poetry.* The editors attempt to supply full bibliographical information on the books and publications mentioned in Louisa's writings, especially those being read by members of the Adams family. Lines of poetry that Louisa integrated into her text are identified whenever possible. Louisa herself enjoyed writing poetry, and the reader can assume that she wrote at least some of the unidentified lines of verse in these volumes.

3. *Correspondence among family members.* Demonstrating the network of correspondence among the Adams family members and with their other correspondents has long been a matter of great interest to the editors of this project. Consequently, whenever possible the editors provide information on letters mentioned in these volumes; those for which no record exists are designated in the notes as "not found." When precise identification of letters is not possible—most commonly due to faulty dating or vague references—the editors may offer likely suggestions.

4. *Other subjects* are annotated according to the editors' judgment to provide historical context or explain topics that might be unfamiliar to modern readers.

A chronology is provided giving a brief overview of the activities of Louisa Catherine Adams and her family during the period covered in these volumes. The chronology appears at the end of volume 2, following an appendix, the Johnson Family Genealogy.

The index appears at the end of volume 2. Besides serving as a guide to locating people, places, and subjects in the volumes, it offers an abundance of additional information. Wherever possible, the index provides each person's full name, whether or not it was used in the text, and a brief description that may include the individual's profession, place of residence, connection to the Adams family, or relationship to other persons. Birth and death dates are supplied for all members of the Adams family, including more distant relatives. To facilitate index searches, lengthy main entries are divided into subentries, which appear in page number order.

7. RELATED DIGITAL RESOURCES

The Massachusetts Historical Society continues to support the work of making Adams family materials available online to scholars and the public at its website, www.masshist.org. Four digital resources in particular complement the *Diary and Autobiographical Writings of Louisa Catherine Adams*: The Diaries of John Quincy Adams: A Digital Collection; the Adams Papers Digital Edition; The Adams Family Papers: An Electronic Archive; and the Online Adams Catalog.

The Diaries of John Quincy Adams Digital Collection provides digital images of John Quincy Adams' entire 51-volume Diary, which he composed over nearly 70 years. The images can be searched by date or browsed by volume. See www.masshist.org/jqadiaries.

The Adams Papers Digital Edition, a project cosponsored by the National Endowment for the Humanities, Harvard University Press, and the Massachusetts Historical Society, provides searchable text files of the 38 Adams Papers volumes published prior to 2007 (excluding the Portraits volumes), supplemented by a cumulative index prepared by the Adams Papers editors. This digital edition is designed not to replace the letterpress edition but rather to complement it by providing greater access to a wealth of Adams material. See www.masshist.org/publications/apde/.

The Adams Family Papers Electronic Archive contains images and text files of all of the correspondence between John and Abigail Adams owned by the Massachusetts Historical Society as well as John Adams' Diaries and Autobiography. The files are text searchable and can be browsed by date. See www.masshist.org/digitaladams/aea.

The Online Adams Catalog represents a fully searchable electronic database of all known Adams documents at the Massachusetts Historical Society and other public and private repositories. This digital conversion of the Adams Papers control file was supported by the National Historical Publications and Records Commission and the Massachusetts Historical Society, and was initiated with Packard Humanities Institute funds in 2009. The Online Adams Catalog allows the public online access to a database of over 110,000 records of documents related to the Adams family. Cross-reference links are supplied for at least 30 percent of the records in the catalog to the online, printed, and microfilm editions, or to websites of the appropriate repository, including the Adams Papers Digital Editions, the Adams Electronic Archive, and 608 reels of Adams Papers microfilm. Each record contains information on the author, recipient, and date of the document, and the location of the original, if known. See www.masshist.org/adams/slipfile/catalog.php.

Readers can gain perspective on the documents in the *Diary and Autobiographical Writings of Louisa Catherine Adams* by consulting material from the same time period included in *Writings of John Quincy Adams*, ed. Worthington Chauncey Ford, 7 vols., New York, 1913–1917; and *Memoirs of John Quincy Adams, Comprising Portions of His Diary from 1795 to 1848*, ed. Charles Francis Adams, 12 vols., Philadelphia, 1874–1877. Other resources are the unpublished diary that Thomas Boylston Adams kept while in Europe, available on the Adams Papers microfilm; Thomas Boylston Adams, *Berlin and the Prussian Court in 1798: Journal of Thomas Boylston Adams, Secretary to the United States Legation at Berlin*, ed. Victor Hugo Paltsits, New York, 1916; and William Steuben Smith, Diary of Voyage to St. Petersburg, 16 July – 29 Oct. 1809, MHi:Adams Papers, Second Generation, on deposit.

Louisa Catherine Adams became closely associated with the Adams family late in 1795, when her courtship with John Quincy Adams began, and so by a happy coincidence her letters, now available on microfilm, will be represented in the forthcoming volume 11 of the *Adams Family Correspondence*, which covers July 1795 to February 1797, and thereafter her correspondence will regularly appear in the volumes of that series.

L. H. Butterfield, the editor in chief of the Adams Papers from 1954 to 1975, championed Louisa as a key figure in the Adams dynasty, whose story should long since have been told, from her own point of view. Louisa, he wrote, "was bound to have been crowded from view" by a husband who seemed "more a natural force, like Niagara Falls, than a mere human being."[43] The editors hope that the present volumes help to fulfill this charge by advancing the manuscript and microfilm versions of the Diaries and autobiographical writings to a documentary edition easily accessible to scholars and an interested public alike. We hope, too, that this edition will provide the raw material for many probing works of history and biography, even as it affords readers the opportunity to become acquainted with a remarkable woman.

Judith S. Graham
October 2011

[43] L. H. Butterfield, "Tending a Dragon-Killer: Notes for the Biographer of Mrs. John Quincy Adams," Amer. Philos. Soc., *Procs.*, 118:165 (April 1974).

Acknowledgments

These volumes are the work of many hands. To adequately represent the contributions of the Adams Papers staff to this project would require an unwieldy list of editors on the title page, and so we must be content to express our appreciation here. We deeply appreciate the work of Gregg L. Lint, Editor of the *Papers of John Adams*; Hobson Woodward, Production Editor; Sara Georgini, Sara Martin, and Neal Millikan, Assistant Editors; Sara Sikes, Assistant Editor for Digital Projects; Robert Karachuk, Associate Editor; Amanda A. Mathews, Research Associate; James T. Connolly, former Transcriber; and Mary T. Claffey, formerly the Digital Production Editor. All accomplished a range of tasks with extraordinary proficiency, dedication, and good humor.

We are grateful for the care with which Ann-Marie Imbornoni copyedited the manuscript and Jeremie Korta assisted in the translation of French language passages. Amanda A. Mathews and Sara Martin lent their fine skills to the preparation of the index.

For facilitating our research, we thank Edward B. Doctoroff, former Head of the Library Privileges and Billing Division at Harvard University's Widener Library, and the reference staffs at Harvard's Houghton, Lamont, Widener, and Fine Arts libraries; the Rare Books and Manuscripts Department and the Fine Arts Department at the Boston Public Library; and the New England Historic Genealogical Society. Our thanks, too, to the staffs of the Thomas P. O'Neill Jr. Library at Boston College and the Newton (Massachusetts) Free Library.

Kevin and Kenneth Krugh of Technologies 'N Typography in Merrimac, Massachusetts, brought the volumes through typesetting with efficiency and skill. At Harvard University Press, we thank John F. Walsh, former Associate Director for Design and Production, for his ongoing support of Adams projects. Abigail Mumford, Assistant Director of Production, and Kathleen McDermott, Executive Editor at Large for History, have ably assisted with the publication, marketing, and sales of this and other Adams Papers titles.

The editors are grateful to Michael O'Brien, Professor of American Intellectual History, Jesus College, University of Cambridge; Catherine Allgor, Professor of History, University of California at Riverside; and historians Margery M. Heffron, Joan R. Challinor, and Cokie Roberts, who shared with us their scholarship and abiding interest in Louisa Catherine Adams. Our thanks, too, to Victor N. Pleshkov, Director, St. Petersburg Institute of History of the Russian Academy of Sciences, who so graciously provided his expertise on matters related to Russian history and culture and helped us to identify the men and women attached to Alexander I's court.

Our work has benefited from the warm encouragement of the staff of the Adams National Historical Park, Quincy, Massachusetts. Particular thanks are due Caroline Keinath, Deputy Superintendent; Kelly Cobble, Curator; and Patty Smith, Museum Technician, for sharing their knowledge of the Adams family, the setting in which they lived, and the treasures preserved in the Old House. We appreciate the work of J. David Bohl, who photographed Louisa Catherine Adams' Hepplewhite secretary at the Old House; and Richard Walker, who photographed the restored Charles Bird King portraits of George Washington Adams and John Adams 2d in the collection of Mrs. Gilbert T. Vincent of Cooperstown, New York.

The Massachusetts Historical Society provided this project with the use of its unrivaled collections and the assistance of its learned staff. We are especially grateful to Dennis A. Fiori, President; Peter Drummey, Stephen T. Riley Librarian; Brenda M. Lawson, Director of Collections Services; Anne E. Bentley, Curator of Art; Ondine E. Le Blanc, Director of Publications; Nancy Heywood, Digital Projects Coordinator; Laura Wulf, Digital Projects Production Specialist; Susan Martin, Manuscript Processor and EAD Coordinator; Elaine Grublin, Head of Reader Services, and all of the members of the Library–Reader Services department. We heartily thank the Adams Papers Administrative Committee for contributing their guidance and wisdom to our work on these volumes.

This project was made possible by the generous gifts of Levin H. and Eleanor L. Campbell and L. Dennis and Susan R. Shapiro. We deeply appreciate their support. All who are drawn to the Adams family saga have reason to be grateful for their keen interest in having the *Diary and Autobiographical Writings of Louisa Catherine Adams* take its place alongside the Diaries of her father-in-law, husband, and son.

Guide to Editorial Apparatus

The first three sections (1–3) of this guide list, respectively, the arbitrary devices used for clarifying the text, the code names for prominent members of the Adams family, and the symbols that are employed throughout *The Adams Papers*, in all its series and parts, for various kinds of manuscript sources. The final three sections (4–6) list, respectively, the symbols for institutions holding original materials, the various abbreviations and conventional terms, and the short titles of books and other works that occur in the *Diary and Autobiographical Writings of Louisa Catherine Adams*.

1. TEXTUAL DEVICES

The following devices will be used throughout *The Adams Papers* to clarify the presentation of the text.

[. . .]	One word missing or illegible.
[. . . .]	Two words missing or illegible.
[. . . .][1]	More than two words missing or illegible; subjoined footnote estimates amount of missing matter.
[ ]	Number or part of a number missing or illegible. Amount of blank space inside brackets approximates the number of missing or illegible digits.
[roman]	Conjectural reading for missing or illegible matter. A question mark is inserted before the closing bracket if the conjectural reading is seriously doubtful.
~~roman~~	Canceled matter.
[*italic*]	Editorial insertion.
{roman}	Text editorially decoded or deciphered.

2. ADAMS FAMILY CODE NAMES

First Generation

JA	John Adams (1735–1826)
AA	Abigail Adams (1744–1818), *m.* JA 1764

Second Generation

AA2	Abigail Adams (1765–1813), daughter of JA and AA, *m.* WSS 1786
WSS	William Stephens Smith (1755–1816), brother of SSA
JQA	John Quincy Adams (1767–1848), son of JA and AA

LCA	Louisa Catherine Johnson (1775–1852), *m.* JQA 1797
CA	Charles Adams (1770–1800), son of JA and AA
SSA	Sarah Smith (1769–1828), sister of WSS, *m.* CA 1795
TBA	Thomas Boylston Adams (1772–1832), son of JA and AA
AHA	Ann Harrod (1774–1845), *m.* TBA 1805

Third Generation

GWA	George Washington Adams (1801–1829), son of JQA and LCA
JA2	John Adams (1803–1834), son of JQA and LCA
MCHA	Mary Catherine Hellen (1806–1870), *m.* JA2 1828
CFA	Charles Francis Adams (1807–1886), son of JQA and LCA
ABA	Abigail Brown Brooks (1808–1889), *m.* CFA 1829
ECA	Elizabeth Coombs Adams (1808–1903), daughter of TBA and AHA

Fourth Generation

LCA2	Louisa Catherine Adams (1831–1870), daughter of CFA and ABA, *m.* Charles Kuhn 1854
JQA2	John Quincy Adams (1833–1894), son of CFA and ABA
CFA2	Charles Francis Adams (1835–1915), son of CFA and ABA
HA	Henry Adams (1838–1918), son of CFA and ABA
MHA	Marian Hooper (1842–1885), *m.* HA 1872
MA	Mary Adams (1845–1928), daughter of CFA and ABA, *m.* Henry Parker Quincy 1877
BA	Brooks Adams (1848–1927), son of CFA and ABA

Fifth Generation

CFA3	Charles Francis Adams (1866–1954), son of JQA2
HA2	Henry Adams (1875–1951), son of CFA2
JA3	John Adams (1875–1964), son of CFA2

3. DESCRIPTIVE SYMBOLS

The following symbols are employed throughout *The Adams Papers* to describe or identify the various kinds of manuscript originals.

D	Diary (Used only to designate a diary written by a member of the Adams family and always in combination with the short form of the writer's name and a serial number, as follows: D/JA/23, i.e., the twenty-third fascicle or volume of John Adams' manuscript Diary.)
Dft	draft
Dupl	duplicate
FC	file copy (A copy of a letter retained by a correspondent other than an Adams, no matter the form of the retained copy; a copy of a letter retained by an Adams other than a Letterbook or letterpress copy.)
FC-Pr	a letterpress copy retained by an Adams as the file copy
IRC	intended recipient's copy (Generally the original version but received after a duplicate, triplicate, or other copy of a letter.)
Lb	Letterbook (Used only to designate an Adams Letterbook and

	always in combination with the short form of the writer's name and a serial number, as follows: Lb/JQA/29, i.e., the twenty-ninth volume of John Quincy Adams' Letterbooks.)
LbC	letterbook copy (Used only to designate an Adams Letterbook copy. Letterbook copies are normally unsigned, but any such copy is assumed to be in the hand of the person responsible for the text unless it is otherwise described.)
M	Miscellany (Used only to designate materials in the section of the Adams Papers known as the "Miscellanies" and always in combination with the short form of the writer's name and a serial number, as follows: M/CFA/32, i.e., the thirty-second volume of the Charles Francis Adams Miscellanies—a ledger volume mainly containing transcripts made by CFA in 1833 of selections from the family papers.)
MS, MSS	manuscript, manuscripts
RC	recipient's copy (A recipient's copy is assumed to be in the hand of the signer unless it is otherwise described.)
Tr	transcript (A copy, handwritten or typewritten, made substantially later than the original or later than other copies—such as duplicates, file copies, or Letterbook copies—that were made contemporaneously.)
Tripl	triplicate

4. LOCATION SYMBOLS

DLC	Library of Congress
DNA	National Archives and Records Administration
MHi	Massachusetts Historical Society
MQA	Adams National Historical Park
MWA	American Antiquarian Society
NN	New York Public Library
PHi	Historical Society of Pennsylvania

5. OTHER ABBREVIATIONS AND CONVENTIONAL TERMS

Adams Papers

Manuscripts and other materials, 1639–1889, in the Adams Manuscript Trust collection given to the Massachusetts Historical Society in 1956 and enlarged by a few additions of family papers since then. Citations in the present edition are simply by date of the original document if the original is in the main chronological series of the Papers and therefore readily found in the microfilm edition of the Adams Papers (see below).

The Adams Papers

The present edition in letterpress, published by The Belknap Press of Harvard University Press. References to earlier volumes of any given unit take this form: vol. 2:146. Since there is no overall volume numbering for the edition, references from one series, or unit of a series, to another are by writer, title, volume, and page, for example, JA, *D&A*, 4:205.

APM

Formerly, Adams Papers, Microfilms. The corpus of the Adams Papers, 1639–1889, as published on microfilm by the Massachusetts Historical Society, 1954–1959, in 608 reels. Cited in the present work, when necessary, by reel number. Available in research libraries throughout the United States and in a few libraries in Canada, Europe, and New Zealand.

6. SHORT TITLES OF WORKS FREQUENTLY CITED

AA2, *Jour. and Corr.*

Journal and Correspondence of Miss Adams, Daughter of John Adams, . . . Edited by Her Daughter [Caroline Amelia (Smith) de Windt], New York and London, 1841–[1849]; 3 vols.

Note: Vol. [1], unnumbered, has title and date: *Journal and Correspondence of Miss Adams*, 1841; vol. 2 has title, volume number, and date: *Correspondence of Miss Adams . . . Vol. II*, 1842; vol. [3] has title, volume number, and date: *Correspondence of Miss Adams . . . Vol. II*, 1842, i.e., same as vol. 2, but preface is signed "April 3d, 1849," and the volume contains as "Part II" a complete reprinting, from same type and with same pagination, of vol. 2, above, originally issued in 1842.

Adams, *Geneal. History of Henry Adams*

Andrew N. Adams, comp. and ed., *A Genealogical History of Henry Adams, of Braintree, Mass., and His Descendants*, Rutland, Vt., 1898; 2 vols.

AFC

Adams Family Correspondence, ed. L. H. Butterfield, Marc Friedlaender, Richard Alan Ryerson, Margaret A. Hogan, and others, Cambridge, 1963– .

AHR

American Historical Review.

Allgor, *Parlor Politics*

Catherine Allgor, *Parlor Politics: In Which the Ladies of Washington Help Build a City and a Government*, Charlottesville, Va., 2000.

Allgor, *Perfect Union*

Catherine Allgor, *A Perfect Union: Dolley Madison and the Creation of the American Nation*, New York, 2006.

Amer. Philos. Soc., *Memoirs, Procs., Trans.*

American Philosophical Society, *Memoirs, Proceedings*, and *Transactions.*

Ammon, *James Monroe*

Harry Ammon, *James Monroe: The Quest for National Identity*, New York, 1971.

Annals of Congress

The Debates and Proceedings in the Congress of the United States [1789–1824], Washington, D.C., 1834–1856; 42 vols.

Ann. Register

The Annual Register; or, A View of the History, Politics, and Literature for the Year, ed. Edmund Burke and others, London, 1758– .

Appletons' Cyclo. Amer. Biog.

James Grant Wilson and John Fiske, eds., *Appletons' Cyclopædia of American Biography*, New York, 1887–1889; 6 vols.

Beale, *Decatur House*
Marie Beale, *Decatur House and Its Inhabitants*, Washington, D.C., 1954.

Bemis, *JQA*
Samuel Flagg Bemis, *John Quincy Adams*, New York, 1949–1956; 2 vols. Vol. 1: *John Quincy Adams and the Foundations of American Foreign Policy*; Vol. 2: *John Quincy Adams and the Union*.

Biog. Dir. Cong.
Biographical Directory of the United States Congress, 1774–1989, Washington, D.C., 1989.

Bobbé, *Mr. and Mrs. JQA*
Dorothie Bobbé, *Mr. and Mrs. John Quincy Adams: An Adventure in Patriotism*, New York, 1930.

Bosher, *French Rev.*
J. F. Bosher, *The French Revolution*, New York, 1988.

Boston Directory, [year]
Boston Directory, issued annually with varying imprints.

Boston, [vol. no.] *Report*
City of Boston, Record Commissioners, *Reports*, Boston, 1876–1909; 39 vols.

Brands, *Andrew Jackson*
H. W. Brands, *Andrew Jackson: His Life and Times*, New York, 2005.

Bryan, *Hist. of the National Capital*
Wilhelmus Bogart Bryan, *A History of the National Capital from Its Foundation through the Period of the Adoption of the Organic Act*, New York, 1914–1916; 2 vols.

Burke, *Geneal. and Heraldic Hist.*, 1875
Bernard Burke, *A Genealogical and Heraldic History of the Landed Gentry of Great Britain and Ireland*, London, 1875; 2 vols.

Burke, *Geneal. and Heraldic Hist.*, 1914
Bernard Burke and Ashworth P. Burke, *A Genealogical and Heraldic History of the Peerage and Baronetage, the Privy Council, Knightage and Companionage*, New York, 1914.

Calhoun, *Papers*
The Papers of John C. Calhoun, ed. Robert L. Meriwether, W. Edwin Hemphill, Clyde N. Wilson, Shirley Bright Cook, and others, Columbia, S.C., 1959–2003; 28 vols.

Cambridge Modern Hist.
The Cambridge Modern History, Cambridge, Eng., 1902–1911; repr. New York, 1969; 13 vols.

CFA, *Diary*
Diary of Charles Francis Adams, ed. Aïda DiPace Donald, David Donald, Marc Friedlaender, L. H. Butterfield, and others, Cambridge, 1964– .

Clay, *Papers*
The Papers of Henry Clay, ed. James F. Hopkins, Mary W. M. Hargreaves, and others, Lexington, Ky., 1959–1992; 10 vols. plus suppl.

Colonial Collegians
Colonial Collegians: Biographies of Those Who Attended American Colleges before the War of Independence, CD-ROM, ed. Conrad Edick Wright, Robert J. Dunkle, and others, Boston, 2005.

Col. Soc. Mass., *Pubns.*
Colonial Society of Massachusetts, *Publications.*

Columbia Hist. Soc., *Records*
Records of the Columbia Historical Society, Washington, D.C.

Cross, *Banks of the Neva*
Anthony Cross, *"By the Banks of the Neva": Chapters from the Lives and Careers of the British in Eighteenth-Century Russia*, New York, 1997.

DAB
Allen Johnson, Dumas Malone, and others, eds., *Dictionary of American Biography*, New York, 1928–1936; repr. New York, 1955–1980; 10 vols. plus supplements.

Davis, *Mass. Judiciary*
William T. Davis, *History of the Judiciary of Massachusetts Including the Plymouth and Massachusetts Colonies, the Province of the Massachusetts Bay, and the Commonwealth*, Boston, 1900.

Delaplaine, *Life of Thomas Johnson*
Edward S. Delaplaine, *The Life of Thomas Johnson: Member of the Continental Congress, First Governor of the State of Maryland, and Associate Justice of the United States Supreme Court*, New York, 1927.

DNB
Leslie Stephen and Sidney Lee, eds., *The Dictionary of National Biography*, New York and London, 1885–1901; repr. Oxford, 1959–1960; 21 vols. plus supplements; rev. edn., www.oxforddnb.com.

Doc. Hist. Supreme Court
The Documentary History of the Supreme Court of the United States, 1789–1800, ed. Maeva Marcus, James R. Perry, and others, New York, 1985–2007; 8 vols.

Duberman, *CFA*
Martin B. Duberman, *Charles Francis Adams, 1807–1886*, Boston, 1961.

Green, *Washington, 1800–1878*
Constance McLaughlin Green, *Washington: Village and Capital, 1800–1878*, Princeton, N.J., 1962.

Greenleaf, *Greenleaf Family*
James Edward Greenleaf, comp., *Genealogy of the Greenleaf Family*, Boston, 1896.

Grove *Dicy. of Art*
Jane Turner, ed., *The Dictionary of Art*, New York, 1996; 34 vols.

Grove *Dicy. of Music*
Stanley Sadie, ed., *The New Grove Dictionary of Music and Musicians*, 2d edn., New York, 2001; 29 vols.

Hamilton, *Papers*
The Papers of Alexander Hamilton, ed. Harold C. Syrett, Jacob E. Cooke, and others, New York, 1961–1987; 27 vols.

Harvard Quinquennial Cat.
Harvard University, *Quinquennial Catalogue of the Officers and Graduates, 1636–1930*, Cambridge, 1930.

Hoefer, *Nouv. biog. générale*
Jean Chrétien Ferdinand Hoefer, ed., *Nouvelle biographie générale depuis les temps les plus reculés jusqu'à nos jours*, Paris, 1852–1866; 46 vols.

Howe, *What Hath God Wrought*
Daniel Walker Howe, *What Hath God Wrought: The Transformation of America, 1815–1848*, New York, 2007.

JA, *D&A*
Diary and Autobiography of John Adams, ed. L. H. Butterfield and others, Cambridge, 1961; 4 vols.

JA, *Earliest Diary*
The Earliest Diary of John Adams, ed. L. H. Butterfield and others, Cambridge, 1966.

JA, *Legal Papers*
Legal Papers of John Adams, ed. L. Kinvin Wroth and Hiller B. Zobel, Cambridge, 1965; 3 vols.

JA, *Papers*
Papers of John Adams, ed. Robert J. Taylor, Gregg L. Lint, and others, Cambridge, 1977– .

JA, *Works*
The Works of John Adams, Second President of the United States: with a Life of the Author, ed. Charles Francis Adams, Boston, 1850–1856; 10 vols.

Jackson, *Papers*
The Papers of Andrew Jackson, ed. Sam B. Smith, Harriet Chappell Owsley, Harold D. Moser, Daniel Feller, and others, Knoxville, Tenn., 1980– .

Jay, *Unpublished Papers*
John Jay: Unpublished Papers, ed. Richard B. Morris, New York, 1975–1980; 2 vols.

Jefferson, *Papers*
The Papers of Thomas Jefferson, ed. Julian P. Boyd, Charles T. Cullen, John Catanzariti, Barbara B. Oberg, and others, Princeton, N.J., 1950– .

Jefferson, *Papers, Retirement Series*
The Papers of Thomas Jefferson: Retirement Series, ed. J. Jefferson Looney and others, Princeton, N.J., 2004– .

Johnson, *Letterbook*
Joshua Johnson's Letterbook, 1771–1774: Letters from a Merchant in London to His Partners in Maryland, ed. Jacob M. Price, London, 1979.

JQA, *Diary*
Diary of John Quincy Adams, ed. David Grayson Allen, Robert J. Taylor, and others, Cambridge, 1981– .

JQA, *Writings*
Writings of John Quincy Adams, ed. Worthington Chauncey Ford, New York, 1913–1917; 7 vols.

Kirker, *Architecture of Bulfinch*
Harold Kirker, *The Architecture of Charles Bulfinch*, Cambridge, 1969.

Lanman, *Biographical Annals*
Charles Lanman, *Biographical Annals of the Civil Government of the United States, during the First Century*, Washington, D.C., 1876.

Lodge, *Peerage*, [year]
Edmund Lodge, *The Peerage and Baronetage of the British Empire*, London, various years.

London Past and Present
Henry B. Wheatley, *London Past and Present: Its History, Associations, and Traditions*, London, 1891; 3 vols.

Madison, *Papers, Congressional Series*
The Papers of James Madison: Congressional Series, ed. William T. Hutchinson, William M. E. Rachal, and Robert Allen Rutland, Chicago and Charlottesville, Va., 1962–1991; 17 vols.

MHS, *Colls., Procs.*
Massachusetts Historical Society, *Collections* and *Proceedings*.

Miller, *Treaties*
Treaties and Other International Acts of the United States of America, ed. Hunter Miller, Washington, D.C., 1931–1948; 8 vols.

Morison, *H. G. Otis*, 1969
Samuel Eliot Morison, *Harrison Gray Otis, 1765–1848: The Urbane Federalist*, rev. edn., Boston, 1969.

MVHR
Mississippi Valley Historical Review.

NEHGR
New England Historical and Genealogical Register.

NEHGS, *Memorial Biographies*
Memorial Biographies of the New England Historic Genealogical Society, Boston, 1880–1908; 9 vols.

NEQ
New England Quarterly.

New Amer. Cyclo.
George Ripley and Charles A. Dana, eds., *The New American Cyclopædia: A Popular Dictionary of General Knowledge*, 16 vols., New York, 1858–1863. Subsequent editions, beginning in 1873, were entitled *The American Cyclopædia* and are cited by date.

Niles' Register
Niles' Weekly Register [title varies], Baltimore, Md., 1811–1849.

Norman, *Hermitage*
Geraldine Norman, *The Hermitage: The Biography of a Great Museum*, New York, 1998.

North Amer. Rev.
North American Review, Boston, etc., 1815–1940.

Notable Amer. Women
Edward T. James and others, eds., *Notable American Women, 1607–1950: A Biographical Dictionary*, Cambridge, 1971; 3 vols.

O'Brien, *Mrs. Adams*
Michael O'Brien, *Mrs. Adams in Winter: A Journey in the Last Days of Napoleon*, New York, 2010.

OED
The Oxford English Dictionary, 2d edn., Oxford, 1989; 20 vols.

Oliver, *Portraits of JA and AA*
Andrew Oliver, *Portraits of John and Abigail Adams*, Cambridge, 1967.

Oliver, *Portraits of JQA and LCA*
Andrew Oliver, *Portraits of John Quincy Adams and His Wife*, Cambridge, 1970.

Palmer, *Alexander I*
Alan Palmer, *Alexander I: Tsar of War and Peace*, New York, 1974.

Papenfuse, *Pursuit of Profit*
Edward C. Papenfuse, *In Pursuit of Profit: The Annapolis Merchants in the Era of the American Revolution, 1763–1805*, Baltimore, 1975.

Pattee, *Old Braintree*
William S. Pattee, *A History of Old Braintree and Quincy, with a Sketch of Randolph and Holbrook*, Quincy, 1878.

PMHB
Pennsylvania Magazine of History and Biography.

Princess Louise, *Forty-five Years*
Princess Louise of Prussia (Princess Anton Radziwill), *Forty-five Years of My Life, 1770–1815*, transl. A. R. Allinson, London, 1912.

Register of Debates in Congress
Register of Debates in Congress, 1824–1837, Washington, D.C., 1825–1837; 14 vols.

Remini, *Henry Clay*
Robert V. Remini, *Henry Clay: Statesman for the Union*, New York, 1991.

Repertorium
Ludwig Bittner and others, eds., *Repertorium der diplomatischen Vertreter aller Länder seit dem Westfälischen Frieden (1648)*, Oldenburg, 1936–1965; 3 vols.

Rowen, *Princes of Orange*
Herbert H. Rowen, *The Princes of Orange: The Stadholders in the Dutch Republic*, Cambridge, Eng., 1988.

Rush, *Autobiography*
The Autobiography of Benjamin Rush: His "Travels through Life" Together with His Commonplace Book for 1789–1813, ed. George W. Corner, Princeton, N.J., 1948.

Saul, *Distant Friends*
Norman E. Saul, *Distant Friends: The United States and Russia, 1763–1867*, Lawrence, Kans., 1991.

Schom, *Napoleon Bonaparte*
Alan Schom, *Napoleon Bonaparte*, New York, 1997.

Sen. Exec. Jour.
Journal of the Executive Proceedings of the Senate of the United States of America from the Commencement of the First to the Termination of the Nineteenth Congress, Washington, D.C., 1828; 3 vols.

Shaw-Shoemaker
Ralph R. Shaw and Richard H. Shoemaker, *American Bibliography: A Preliminary Checklist for 1801–1819*, New York, 1958–1966; 22 vols.

Sibley's Harvard Graduates
John Langdon Sibley, Clifford K. Shipton, Conrad Edick Wright, Edward W. Hanson, and others, *Biographical Sketches of Graduates of Harvard University, in Cambridge, Massachusetts*, Cambridge and Boston, 1873– .

Small, *Hist. of Swan's Island*
H. W. Small, *A History of Swan's Island, Maine*, Ellsworth, Maine, 1898.

Smith, *Charles Carroll*
Ellen Hart Smith, *Charles Carroll of Carrollton*, Cambridge, 1942.

Sprague, *Braintree Families*
Waldo Chamberlain Sprague, comp., *Genealogies of the Families of Braintree, Mass., 1640–1850*, Boston, 1983; repr. CD-ROM, Boston, 2001.

TBA, *Journal, 1798*
Berlin and the Prussian Court in 1798: Journal of Thomas Boylston Adams, Secretary to the United States Legation at Berlin, ed. Victor Hugo Paltsits, New York, 1916.

Travellers in Germany
A Handbook for Travellers in Southern Germany, 3d edn., London, 1844.

U.S. and Russia
The United States and Russia: The Beginning of Relations, 1765–1815, ed. Nina N. Bashkina and others, Washington, D.C., 1980.

U.S. House, *Jour.*
Journal of the House of Representatives of the United States, Washington, D.C., 1789– .

U.S. Senate, *Jour.*
Journal of the Senate of the United States of America, Washington, D.C., 1789– .

U.S. Statutes at Large
The Public Statutes at Large of the United States of America, 1789– , Boston and Washington, D.C., 1845– .

Washington, *Diaries*
The Diaries of George Washington, ed. Donald Jackson and Dorothy Twohig, Charlottesville, Va., 1976–1979; 6 vols.

Washington, *Papers, Revolutionary War Series*
The Papers of George Washington: Revolutionary War Series, ed. Philander D. Chase, Frank E. Grizzard Jr., Edward G. Lengel, David R. Hoth, and others, Charlottesville, Va., 1985– .

Williams and McKinsey, *Hist. of Frederick County*
T. J. C. Williams and Folger McKinsey, *History of Frederick County, Maryland*, 2 vols., Frederick, Md., 1910; repr. Baltimore, Md., 1967.

Winsor, *Memorial History of Boston*
Justin Winsor, ed., *The Memorial History of Boston, Including Suffolk County, 1630–1880*, Boston, 1880–1881; 4 vols.

WMQ
William and Mary Quarterly.

VOLUME I

Diary 1778–1815

Record of a Life

JULY 23D 1825[1]

The unparalled heat of the weather is such it is scarcely possible to pursue any occupation whatever. and the effect upon the mind as well as the body is such as to destroy all that elasticity and vitality if I may so express myself which renders existence a pleasure and makes us forget the toils and drudgery of mere animal matter. Reading is wearisome, work is tiresome, and all the common employments are insipid, and the mind is sink into a state of supiness without a desire to manifest its superiority to mere corporeal substance— In this state of absolute inertness we are expecting the visit of general Lafayette and look forward with a sort of horror to what at any other season would give us great delight from the conviction that it must force us into exertion, and call for those petit soins, which at the best of times enforce restraint. The publick mind is still full of this really excellent man and the Nation has acquired a great degree credit for its perseverence and general expression and manifestation of sentiments worthy of a great people. and although the sentiment may have been somewhat exaggerated it is still praise worthy and calculated to produce good consequence in a future generation.

Most sincerely do I wish the good old Gentleman was safe returned to his Native Country and to his happy family Circle blessed and blessing all who surround him The trials he now endures are

[1] LCA wrote her 85-page autobiographical work "Record of a Life / ~~Memoir of your Mother~~ / or / My Story" (M/LCA/2, p. 271–355, APM Reel 265) in a leather-bound journal with marbled endpapers, 8" x 10 1/2". LCA described her childhood and education, courtship and marriage, and early days as the U.S. minister's wife at the Prussian court. Her account, like the biographical sketch she published anonymously two years later, emphasized her father's patriotism and her American heritage, perhaps in response to criticism from JQA's political rivals ("Mrs. J. Q. Adams," *Mrs. A. S. Colvin's Weekly Messenger*, 2 June 1827). The same journal also contains LCA's Diary for 6 Dec. 1819 – 28 March 1821 and 3 Dec. 1821 – 8 Jan. 1824, a reflection on the death of her son GWA, and instructions for compounding cosmetics.

almost too much for human nature and lead to fearful apprehensions that the fatigue may at last prove fatal in a Climate to which he is so entirely unused.[2]

As some day or other my Children may be amused with it I will endeavour to give a slight sketch of my life until this time confining myself to those events which are worth recording only. They may perhaps think on this principle, that I need not write at all but a review of past incidents may have a good effect upon myself. I shall only write when in the humour or to speak learnedly when the Cacoëthes Scribendi[3] has siezed me and my flights will probably be excursive as I have no pretensions to be a writer and no desire to appear any thing more than a mere commonplace personage with a good memory and just observation enough to discover the difference between a man of sense and a Fool, and to know that the latter often do the least mischief of the two.

My Father was the descendant of an English Gentlemen who emigrated to this Country in consequence of a marriage with a Miss Baker of Liverpool then an Heiress and a Ward in Chauncery— As she was not of age to avoid the pursuit of the Law they came out to the State of Maryland and established themselves in Colvert among the Colvert family— They were wealthy and respectable and left one Son who inheritted the property and who married a young Lady from the Eastward or connected with the Sedgwicks she bearing the same name— My Father was one of eleven children and early in life was placed in the Counting House of a very respectable Merchant from Scotland a M[r.] Graham the Father of Major Graham of one

[2] In Jan. 1824, at President James Monroe's request, Congress invited the Marquis de Lafayette to visit the United States in recognition of his services during the American Revolution. He arrived in New York City on 15 Aug. and visited JA in Quincy two weeks later. He reached Washington, D.C., on 12 Oct. and stayed in the capital or nearby, visiting Mount Vernon, Monticello, Montpelier, and cities in Virginia and Maryland. From March through mid-June 1825 he traveled to the rest of the 24 states. He again traveled to Washington, arriving on 1 Aug. and staying at the White House, with brief trips to Virginia, until his departure for France on 7 September. The Adamses gave several dinners in his honor, including one on 6 Sept., Lafayette's 68th birthday.

By "trials" LCA may mean either the rigors of his travels or his experiences in France during and after the French Revolution. He spent most of his career in opposition to the French government and never recovered financially; he had borrowed money to make the trip to the United States. Thomas Jefferson urged that the nation reward Lafayette for his services, and before he returned to France, Congress awarded him $200,000 and a grant of land in Florida (CFA, *Diary*, 1:304; D/JQA/23, 1, 6–8 Aug., 6–7 Sept., APM Reel 26; Stanley J. Idzerda, Anne C. Loveland, and Marc H. Miller, *Lafayette, Hero of Two Worlds: The Art and Pageantry of His Farewell Tour of America, 1824–1825*, Hanover, N.H., 1989).

[3] An insatiable desire to write.

the most distinguished families of Scotland—[4] He had not the advantage of a Classical education My Grandfather retaining many of the English prejudices in favour of the eldest Son on whom was lavished all the expence to make him an object of consequence in the Country—At the age of two or three and twenty my Father entered into partnership with two Scotch Gentlemen by name Wallace & Muir and in consequence removed to London as second partner in the Firm—[5] There he became acquainted with my Mother of whose family I knew very little as some misunderstanding had subsisted for some years indeed ever since the death of my Grandmother which had cut of all communication between my father and Grandfather whose character was I am sorry to say very indifferent— My Grandmother was a Miss Young extremely beautiful and I always her represented as possessing qualities and virtues of the highest order My father loved and respected her to the hour of his death and always spoke of her to *us*, as an example of exalted goodness. My Sister Hellen was born in the December of 1773 and I was born in February 75.[6] In 78 or 9 in consequence of the American Revolution my Father took his Family to France finding it no longer safe to live in England being in heart and Soul friendly to the Independence of the Country and my earliest recollections are French; for the little knowledge I had of my own Language was soon obliterated by the acquirement of a new one—[7] All the scenes of my infancy come with such faint recollections they float upon my fancy like visions which never could have had any reality yet like visions of delight in which all was joy and peace and love. I perfectly remember the elegance of the mansion in which we resided the school to which I was sent the strong impression made upon my imagination by the Roman Catholick Church the heartfelt humility with which I knelt before the

[4] Probably Charles Grahame, a merchant in Calvert County, Md. (Johnson, *Letterbook,* p. 170).

[5] Joshua Johnson moved to London as a partner in the firm of Wallace, Davidson & Johnson in 1771. Charles Wallace (1727–1812) was an Annapolis merchant, and John Davidson (1738–1794) was a deputy naval officer of the port of Annapolis. The firm was dissolved in 1777. In 1781 Johnson joined Wallace and John Muir (1741?–1810), commissary of stores for the army in Annapolis, in a new firm (Papenfuse, *Pursuit of Profit,* p. 53, 93, 108, 234; Johnson, *Letterbook,* p. 167, 180).

[6] Both sisters were born at 1 Swan Street, Minories, in London (Johnson, *Letterbook,* p. xxii).

[7] Although his firm began to close down its London operations in 1774, Johnson had been reluctant to leave London because tobacco prices, and his profits, were rising. By 1778 dwindling tobacco supplies and surveillance of his activities, coupled with growing opportunities in France, led him to move his business and family to Nantes (Papenfuse, *Pursuit of Profit,* p. 73–75).

Image of the tortured Jesus and the horror I felt at the thought, of mixing with hereticks. The veneration with which I entered the Convents the great affection I bore to one particular Nun who used to bring toys for sale to School all these shadows of early life have flitted before my minds eye but without the possibility of fixing names or even remembering a countenance which then was so familiar—[8] One of the events which I [recur?] to most distinctly was the marriage of my fathers Coachman to which we were permitted to go. The Bride was a dark complexioned rosy looking woman dressed in a large flowered Calico with a most enormous bouquet— They went to Church in my fathers Carriage and had the use of it for the day. My father gave them a handsome Supper and Ball and I still seem to see the Bride and Bridgroom opening the Ball with all the gaiety of french sprightliness— One of the events most strongly imprinted in my memory is a great inundation in Montz which obliged the people to sail in Boats through the Streets. oh! with what glee we children beheld it shrieking with pleasure when the servants would get into the boats from the basement windows without an idea that that which was productive of such fun to us was the cause of misery to thousands—Is not one of the great blessings of infancy its thoughtlessness its aptitude for every thing like enjoyment and its total unconsciousness of danger Yet what is idiotism in an adolscent is it any thing more than mere Childishness or rather a mind immatured? Can we must we believe that mind grows with our growth and decays with our wasted forms— Is not mind or what we call spirit an etherial spark an emanation of the Deity and can any thing so pure an essence so divine suffer decay or be liable to desease— How profound the mystery how wise the Creator— Are we not called upon, forced to have faith in this mighty wonder and dare we say vile worms as we are that ought with the Omnipotent is impossible? From whence is the word impossible with whom does it originate? in those only whose power is limitted who are taught by God himself "thus far shalt thou go and no farther." Will all the wisdom that philosophers teach will all the learning to which the mind of man can attain teach what is death? what sleep? what the soul? all all is dark and God Almighty God alone in his own time

[8] The Johnsons lived in an apartment in the Temple du Goût on the Isle Feydeau. The school was probably run by the Ursulines (LCA to ABA, 2 March 1834, Adams Papers; "L'Instruction primaire dans le Comté Nantais avant 1789," *Revue de Bretagne et de Vendée,* 5:372 [1874]).

can shed the light which can clear our understandings— But where will this theme lead me— I am bewildered and afraid and must still cling to that blessed being who in mercy stands between me and my God to pardon thoughts which I cannot controul.

The last year which we passed in France was full of pleasure and being more at home I was more familiarized with the acquaintance of my Mother which was very large. Among them I distinctly remember many of her friends with whom I have renewed acquaintance in other Countries. My Father was intimate with the celebrated Paul Jones but I have utterly forgotten him if I ever saw him[9]

In the Month of Feby 1783 I was attacked severely by a Pleurisy which left me in so weak a state of health as to cause great apprehensions in my Dear Parents for my life as they feared that Consumption would ensue— In April 83 we left Nantz on our way to England the family had much encreased as my Sister Boyd and My Brother were added to the Stock and our number was four when we left Mrs. Hellen myself Mrs. Fry and my Sister Mariane who died soon after my Mother settled in Nantz in consequence of the great fatigue which my Mother had undergone on the journey— Of our journey I do not remember any thing until we arrived in Paris. There we had elegant Apartments in one of the best hotels and a day or two after our arrival the Children at the request of Mr & Mrs. Jay were all sent to pay their respects Mr. Jay was then in Paris I believe as Minister. Mrs. Jay was a very Lady like looking woman and she had two daughters children like ourselves but dressed in the plain english fashion white Frocks and Pink Sashes which appeared to me much prettier than the fine silk dress and hoop which I was used to wear. Their establishment was handsome and their kindness unbounded and I have always looked back with pleasure to this visit which is the only thing that occurred during my stay in Paris which has stamped itself upon my mind—[10] The sufferings we all endured on our voyage from Calais to Dover the Bustle of our embarkation

[9] John Paul Jones probably met the Johnsons at Nantes in 1778 (Samuel Eliot Morison, *John Paul Jones: A Sailor's Biography*, Boston, 1959, p. 119).

[10] John Jay was in Paris as one of the American commissioners negotiating peace with Great Britain. He had been accompanied by his wife, Sarah Livingston Jay; his nephew, Peter Jay Munro; and, as his secretary, his brother-in-law, Henry Brockholst Livingston. The two little girls were Jay's daughters, Maria (b. 1782) and Ann (b. 1783). (Given the girls' ages, LCA may be confusing them with another family or remembering a later meeting.) The Jays and Johnsons had known each other for some time: Joshua Johnson and Catherine Nuth Johnson had supplied the Jays with French goods, and the two men had corresponded (*DAB*; Jay, *Unpublished Papers*, 2:110–111, 127–128, 177, 208, 585).

the Packet itself were all objects of wonderment and fixed themselves as objects of admiration and dread never to be forgotten—

Of our arrival in England and London nothing materiel remains— We were sent to School to a M^rs. Carter a Maiden Lady and one of the greatest Ladies in England more especially as She was in every respect one of the largest and fattest that England ever produced[11] We were recommeded to be placed under her care and tuition by M^r & Mrs Hewlett the latter of whom had been a very particular friend of my Parents having been the Wife and Widow of an American Gentleman of whom my father was very fond[12] M^rs. Hewlett was a very excentric Woman of strong mind and still stronger passions of course susceptible of equally strong attachments. In the confusion and general derangement incident to the removal of a large family from one Country to another it is natural to seek assistance from some person already established and they by this means frequently acquire a degree of influence which they could never have obtained under any other circumstances— My two Sisters and myself were immediately sent to Shacklewell where in consequence of our extraordinary dress and utter ignorance of English we became objects of ridicule to the whole School which consisted of forty Young Ladies from the ages of seven to twenty— To this cause I am convinced I owe the haughtiness and pride of character which it has been impossible for me to subdue; to the sufferings I then underwent living in a state of constant torment, and being perpetually punished or mortified for those very things which had always before been subjects of admiration— A child is to a certain degree a reasoning animal; it can observe and strongly mark the differences and changes in its situation; but it cannot seek the why or the wherefore from whence these difficulties spring. This was my case and I became serious melancholy and almost gloomy—which caused me to be called Miss Proud by my schoolfellows, and placed me in a

[11] Elizabeth Carter (1717–1806), whose education matches LCA's description, published translations, poetry, and essays, but she did not live in Shacklewell (*DNB*). A different Mrs. Carter may have been the schoolmistress, or LCA may have meant Elizabeth Hewlett, for whom see Record, note 12, below.

[12] John Hewlett (1762–1844), a biblical scholar and tutor, presided at the marriage of JQA and LCA. Elizabeth Hewlett (d. 1822), his wife, was a witness to the marriage of LCA's parents in 1785. Other mentions of Mrs. Hewlett may refer to Elizabeth or to Mary (d. 1815), John's mother (*DNB*; *Shelley and His Circle, 1773–1822*, 10 vols., ed. Kenneth Neill Cameron, Donald H. Reiman, and others, Cambridge, 1961–2002, 1:73; Joshua Johnson marriage certificate, Archives of the City of Westminster:St. Anne Soho Parish Records, communication from Margery Heffron, 10 June 2010; *The Monthly Magazine*, 54:36 [1822]; *The New Monthly Magazine and Universal Register*, 3:174 [Jan.–June 1815]).

more painful situation than ever— Among many of these unpleasant scenes those occasioned by my religious feelings were the most powerful— The first time I was forced to go to Church at Hackney I perfectly recollect my horror when my Governess obliged me to kneel down among what I had been taught in France to call the *hereticks*; which was so great that in the very act of Kneeling I fell as it were dead upon the floor and continued so ill although only eight years old that my father was obliged to take me home and to vary the scene I was sent to stay sometime with Mrs. Hewlett— After two Months I returned to School with strict orders from my parents that I should not be harried or urged too much upon the subject of going to Church; and that if it should again affect me in the same way, I was to be accustomed gradually to the prayers of the school, until my fears wore off.— In consequence of my again fainting at Church and being obliged to be taken out the judicious plan adopted by my beloved and ever amiable father was put into execution and I quietly conformed to the usages and forgot insensibly all the prejudes which I had so early and so strongly ~~acquired~~ imbibed— As I am writing for amusement and as we all love to dwell on that age of innocence and thougtlessness when all is fresh with hope, and even our sorrows are like rainbow clouds dispersed ere they are seen; you will probably find my prolixity very tedious; but it is easy to skip what we do not wish to read and view it only as a blank. Every Vacation we returned home to my fathers house; the very thoughts of which was so delightful that we no sooner arrived at school than a List of the Months and days was made, and our greatest pleasure consisted in tearing one off every morning with a view to shorten the lagging of time; and this occupation seemed to bring us nearer home— O home! sweet home! thou ever wert to me the joy of life, and the domestic felicity for many years almost uninterupted of my beloved Parents placed a picture constantly before my eyes truly enviable—and in no one instance during my life have I ever met such an example.[13] My Mother had been beautiful; she was at this time very lovely, her person was very small, and exquisitely delicate, and very finely proportioned. She was lively; her understanding highly cultivated, and her wit brilliant, sometimes almost too keen. My Father was the handsomest man I ever beheld.

[13] The Johnsons lived in Cooper's Row on Great Tower Hill, London, from 1783 until a few days before they left for America in 1797. LCA's father conducted diplomatic business and commercial affairs from their home (JA, *D&A,* 3:149, note 2).

His eye or the power of his eye was indescribable: its usual expression was sweetness and benevolence; but when roused to anger, or to suspicion; it had a dazzling fixed severity that was absolutely awe-ful; and which seemed by its vivid scrutiny to dive into the very depths of the human heart— his temper was admirable; his tastes simple; his word sacred; and his heart pure and affectionate as that of the most unsophisticated Child of Nature. the greatest fault he had was believing every one as good, as correct, as worthy as himself— his establishment was large, not sumptuous or extravagant, but such as the first Merchants in London at that day usually had: he kept a neat Carriage and one pair of Horses, and every thing was conducted in the family with the neatest order and regularity— His entertainments when he made any, which was not often, were handsome; but his usual way of receiving company was unceremoniously social, and almost limitted to his own Countrymen who resorted to England, for business or pleasure; these found a home and a Friend in him at all times— In Religion or creed he was a Unitarian; but as those opinions were at that time much decried; he took particular pains to educate his Children in the Episcopal form as in regard to women he always said there was little danger in believing; there was *destruction* in doubt. When I was about nine years old I was siezed with what was then called a one and twenty day fever which is very much like the Typhus, if it is not the same—[14] Well do I remember my sufferings! the almost exessive tenderness of my indulgent parents! who watched me night and day with unwearied patience, and cheerfulness: and fondly supported my weary head, and soothed my aching brain. All the acquaintance of my father appeared to vie with each other in showing kindness to *me*: and every hour brought forth presents in toys and fruit, to charm my drooping spirit. My Mother while the tears ran down her cheeks sat by my bed anxiously noting every change: seemingly busied in dressing my doll, and making its clothes to amuse me— In sickness I was always patient, quiet, and manageable; and in this long and severe illness I was so in all points but one— My Sister Harriet was not three years old and a most lovely child on whom I had always lavished my affection: but this time, while devoured by this deadly fever, the sight of her would almost throw me into convulsions, and if my Mother looked at or spoke to her it reduced me to deaths door. To the poor child this

[14] "Twenty-one day fever" was another name for typhoid fever (Ralph Gooding, *A Manual of Domestic Medicine*, London, 1867, p. 153).

was anguish; as my room furnished a most attractive spectacle, ~~to the poor little thing~~ being filled with playthings of every description that could fascinate a childs attention; and it caused great affliction and wonder to my parents; my disposition was so affectionate; I had always clung with such ardent fondness to my brother and my Sisters, that this antipathy could not be accounted for: I had always been liberal even to extravagance; it therefore could not be avarice! but no matter what it was it occasioned great affliction– I was particulary fond of the Gentleman who attended me–he used to come three times a day to see me; his manner was so mild, so quiet, so soothing, that I always saw him with joy– It was on this occasion that Dr. Letsom was called in; my case was deemed hopeless. He sat by my bedside–he was a tall thin man; his countenance was agreeable and his conversation lively. he asked me many questions which I was too weak to answer; but I remember perfectly that he drew a pigeon with a pen and Ink, and gave it to me; which pleased me very much, and made him a great favorite with me– A Blister was ordered and if it drew it would augur favorably; if it failed my fate was decreed: at twelve o clock at night the blister was to be removed but my poor Mother was overcome and unequal to the task; and Mrs. Hewlett was to perform the operation– I had been very low all day and have little recollection of any thing until I was roused, by seeing Mrs. Hewlett fall upon the floor, and feeling the smart of the cold air upon my back– The Blister had drawn favorably and the sudden joy had deprived her of sense, who never had fainted before. I cannot express the extasy with which I saw my dear Mother return to me; and from that hour I got well– As soon as I could bear the fatigue my good Dr Letsome who took a great fancy to me, invited me to go and see him at Camberwell where he had a very beautiful place to which I afterwards went with my Mother–[15] Again was I sent to Mrs. Hewlett for two Months Country air, and gentle exercise being recommended: and I shall never forget the kindness with which they treated me particularly Mr Hewlett who from that time I looked upon in the light of a father– The weakness and delicacy which ensued in consequence of this second illness; left me for several years very weakly, and I became a pet as is usual in such cases Both my Sisters who enjoyed fine health were very lively and had

[15] John Coakley Lettsom (1744–1815), a Quaker abolitionist, botanist, and physician, lived at Grove Hill, Camberwell, a house that included a museum, library, and botanical garden (*DNB*).

little of that sensitiveness for which has always I was distinguished and which has proved[16] so great an obstacle to my happiness— M$^{rs.}$ Carter was an uncommonly fine Woman; exact in her discipline and Lady like in her manners— At the present day she would not have been qualified for her situation the stile of education requiring a degree of acquirement which she certainly did not possess— Many of the modern studies not then being thought requisite in the education of Women and being thought to have a tendency to render them masculine— Your Father is a fine reader but M$^{rs.}$ Carter was his superior. I have never heard her equal— My Sister Nancy was a great favorite of hers she possessed a sort of intuitive genius; it was perfectly indifferent to her what sort of business she was required to learn she was equally successful in the atchievement of all the useful and elegant accomplishments which adorn a woman. My mind was of a different stamp every thing in the shape of work I abhorred. dancing and singing I was very fond of, but the mere mechanical drudgery of music was utterly beyond my powers as a proof of which I was one year learning to play one Song in the Opera of Rosina.[17] The only way I can account for this excessive stupidity is that I could read music with the greatest facility and my voice was so flexible that I could execute almost any thing at the first reading and before I could learn the song or accompaniment on the piano I became so disgusted with the perpetual jarring discords of my performance that I would drop my hands and sing over all the songs in the book during the half hour or hour which was allowed for practice and my Master in despair informed my Governess he could do nothing with me as I had no taste for instrumental music— This however was a mistake and perhaps it was owing to too pure a taste that the difficulty with me was unconquerable or my ear was too sensitive to endure the horrid sounds which young beginners produce without an absolute degree of torture. Such an assertion will probably be called affectation but even now I cannot bear what is termed practicing by learners without a sort of nervous shuddering which jars my whole frame—

Orders were given that I should only be taught to sing and I was made to scream psalms with sixteen young Ladies all trying with all their hearts which should make the most noise. In hymns or An-

[16] The preceding seven words were interlined.

[17] The English comic opera *Rosina,* text by Frances Brooke and music by William Shield, 1782.

themns I was always selected to sing the Solo's or the first part in duets and by degrees acquired a great reputation in the School as a vocalist–

My Sister at the same time became a first rate performer on the Piano and played with so much real feeling taste and ease that my delight was to sit at work in the same room and to sing accompaniments to the pieces while she played; and from this habit I acquired a facility of execution which no master could have taught; but it utterly spoilt me–for the habit of performing our different parts together, made us entirely dependent on each other; and never since our parting have I met with one being to whose accompaniment I could sing, in a way to do myself justice– There was a soul in her touch, and in every part of her performance so much truth, it was impossible to do otherwise than well. Our voices were also united in duets; and these trivial accomplishments, seemed to add a link to our consanguinity; as each excelled in her particular sphere, no jealousy was excited, but on the contrary each endeavoured to add lustre to the other. My natural timidity which was excessive, often proved almost insurmountable; but she would say something to me when sitting down to the Instrument which would pique me, when she was particularly desirous that I should shine; and then I would sing *at her* and by pointing the words of the songs I selected; give them an expression of which I was unconscious but which generally produced the happiest effects on my Auditors– But I am running on and speaking of a much later period of my life when buoyant with youth and happiness I dreamt of nought but joy and gladness– Many traits of character I could recite, few of them would do me much credit– Pride and haughteur were my predominant failings, but they had the good effect of keeping me out of bad company, for I too thoroughly despised the vicious to associate with them. D^r. Parkinson used to attend the School as Dentist, and one day he insisted upon taking out two of my double teeth–the idea of it was so horrible that I refused to undergo it– After much vain entreaty, my Governess called the man Servant and told him he must hold me in His arms– This succeeded; for rather than be thus *poluted* I submitted, exclaiming "do you think I will be held by a servant–" The good old Lady was so amazingly struck by the look and manner in which these words were said, that instead of using the rod, she always used to say she was sure I was intended to be a very great personage– At School I was universally *respected*, but I was never beloved. The girls feared me because I would not enter into their schemes and intrigues—and always dreaded me knowing my horror and dislike of their plots and plans, lest I should betray them— One only young Lady could I become attached to: she was as remarkable in her temper and manners as myself: we slept in the same room; we read together, and were almost inseparable: she was an East Indian very dark, with long black indian hair; not handsome, but looked up to by all the Teachers and scholars as a girl of uncommon talents— Miss Young was head teacher a most extraordinary woman. Her Uncle had her educated with boys for many years; and obliged her to wear boys clothes: and in this way she had in a great measure acquired something like a Classical education knowing some Greek and the rudiments of Latin. Miss Edwards and myself were her decided favorites and as we were both apt and quick in learning our different lessons, and very fond of reading; she took much pains to improve us and conversed freely with us upon the books we read, pointing out and selecting, the most beautiful and striking passages, and cultivating our taste by her judment— Her person was masculine and her manners were forbidding; so that unless she took a particular fancy to any one; fear and dislike kept the young Ladies aloof. Her heart was excellent, and her mind full of the highest qualities— When I was about twelve years old she left M^rs. Carters, and established a large and respectable school at Kensington— Five years had thus elapsed when M^rs. Carter removed to a superb house in Mitchum Surry about 12 miles from London, bearing the pompous title of Barron House. All I recollect of home was during the vacations; when our greated ambition was to play Ladies or in other words to dress in my Mothers Hoops and train gowns, and to assume the titles of the great; aping as far as we could their airs and manners— I never would be anything but a *Dutchess*, and never answered to any title but that of her grace— As we went to the theatre several times during the vacation, from thence we took our Models; and the elegant Miss Farren, now Lady Derby was our standard of perfection, as well as M^rs. Siddons—[18] In dancing and in musick we were put forward in all the exhibitions; and ballets were form'ed to show the *three Sisters* to advantage— M^rs. Hellen always bore the palm for the excessive timidity of my Sister Caroline and myself, almost always obscured the eclat of our performance— My Sister

[18] Elizabeth Farren (1759?–1829), an English actress, married Edward, 12th Earl of Derby, in 1797, six weeks after his first wife's death (*DNB*). For Sarah Kemble Siddons, see *AFC*, 6:xiv–xv.

Nancy's health at this time became so bad, that my father thought the exercices of the School, too severe; and placed her as parlour boarder, that she might have more indulgence. Nancy was very fat and growing almost unwieldy; but notwithstanding she became cadaverously pale and the Dôctors pronounced her complaints dropsical; and recommended my father to take her home—for a time! She went for six months—during which much fear was entertained for her life—after which though by no means recovered it was thought Country air and riding on horse back would be of service, and she returned to Mitchum again in quality of parlour border; she was nearly fourteen, and gave promise of great beauty, not exactly that symmetrical beauty of feature, which an Artist would delineate; but that expression of beauty which is illumined by a vivacious soul, whose every emotion beams in the speaking eye, and gives an undescribable charm to every variation of the countenance— My Sister Caroline was 20 Months younger then myself a lovely child with a flow of natural spirits almost amounting to wildness blended with the most overpowering timidity of character which ever prevented her from taking that rank and standing in the school, to which her merit talents entitled her— It was the custom for the young Ladies to celebrate the birthday of Mrs. Carter I had exhibited several times in different characters in masquerade, always being made to sing some complimentary lines on the occasion— This year we were to perform the Tragedy of Cato the parts were all assigned my Sister Nancy was to play Marcia, and Lucia fell to me;[19] After several rehearsals however the difficulty of procuring dresses and suitable scenery obliged us to abandon the plan: and it was given up for a Ball, and congratulatory Letters; mine was written in french— Among the most singular events of my life that of being *untaught* the language which I had acquired in its native elegance and purity, to be taught the execrable jargon then heard in the english schools, was the most extraordinery— But as they had a french teacher who knew nothing of the language; to save her place, she was obliged to condemn that which she could not imitate; and as our good Mrs. Carter was totally unacquainted with it, she naturally prefered the *knowledge* of her teacher—

In the course of the year I was removed to the parlour, and allowed many privileges. Among the number was that of walking in the Garden; but there was an express prohibition concerning the

[19] For Joseph Addison's *Cato*, see *AFC*, 5:28. Marcia and Lucia are the only female roles.

fruit which we were forbidden to touch— One Evening, like Eve I met with a tempter, who persuaded me that there was no harm in taking some Grapes, as there was such an abundance the old Lady could not use them— I hesitated a long time; but the example of my companion soon produced its effect, and I not only eat some but put a number of bunches in my pocket, to distribute among my friends— The bell rung for supper; and I was obliged to go immediately into the parlour, like a thief conscience stricken— I was restless and uneasy; but when my Governess began to read Young's Night thoughts of which was to prolong our stay above an hour; I felt in perfect torture— While she was reading one of the finest passages, my Sister Nancy screamed out, that there was a great Spider on my Gown, and I began to jump and beg, that they would take it off, as I had a natural antipathy to this species of Insect, which nothing could ever conquer— Again we all sat down to listen to the reading, when again the alarm was given, and in my agony to get rid of the Spider, I pulled the grapes out of my pocket, and threw them on the floor, vowing that no earthly thing should ever make me steal again, as these creatures must have been sent as a punishment for my fault— My feelings on this occasion were indescribable and I long thought nothing could wash out my disgrace. The reprimand I received was severe; but the spiders and the exposure they produced, proved a much more efficacious Lesson, which stamped it in never to be forgotten Letters on my mind— I hated the fault, but I hated much more the Girl who had induced me to commit it; unjustly attributing to her the act which had alone been caused by my own weakness— How frail is our Nature— How easily does the human heart throw off its own depravity, and cling to every straw in its deceit— Had I not a will of my own? did I not know I was doing wrong? committing sin? then what was this girls example to me! Was I not a creature endowed with reason, and did I not at the very time despise *her* for the Act? and yet I did it; and hated her *not* because I had committed the act, but because she had shown by this act of my own, that I did not possess the proud superiority over my companions, to which I had pretended; and that my resolutions were as weak and as unstable as those of my neighbours— This was a proof that good may sometimes be extracted from evil! I no longer held my head so high; and was much more lenient to those who I had hitherto considered far inferior to myself; I was no longer a standard in my own eyes; and from this hour the unbending harshness of my Nature, began to be subdued—and I to learn, that Charity for others, which I so much needed for myself– Rumours and whisperings were abroad not creditable to the School, and it began to decline very rapidly. In the Winter on the usual occasion we performed the Search after Happiness, and I made my first and last appearance on any Stage, in the part of Euphemia– How strange it is that people can judge so little of their own powers. M^rs. Siddons it is said always had an ardent desire to appear in Comedy in which she notoriously failed, and M^rs. Jordan I have heard prefered Tragedy–[20] Thus it was with my Sister, and myself– The parts assigned to us were quite different; I was to have played Pastorella as being the best singer; and she was to have had some other part as she was too gay to play Euphemia; but she declared if she had not the part of Pastorella she would not act at all. The matter was adjusted, and it was universally admitted that the haughty Euphemia was exactly suited to me– Much ingenuity was exerted in the formation of Scenery– I planned a house which was made of Sheets of White pasteboard sown together in the form of a Cottage; and twined it over with Shrubs The Stage was formed with the dining Tables and an old green Baiz Carpet was used as a Curtain. Green Houseplants of various sizes adorned the stage and produced a very pretty effect, and succeeded beyond our best hopes– Two hundred visitors were collected to view this mimic scene, and as the moment approached the throbs of my palpitating heart could almost be distinctly heard– I was to speak the Epilogue; claiming the indulgence of our awful publick, and congratulating our Governess. Trembling with confusion and overcome with apprehension, I entered on the Scene and was received with the kindest welcome– I spoke but with a voice so low, so tremulous, and indistinct; the most indulgent must have been disappointed: but ere the play was done I redeemed my reputation, and was saluted with loud applause– My Sister performed her part to admiration: but as she was not in the habit of singing single songs, that part was thought a failure; she spoke the prologue with infinite grace; and our Evening closed with a handsome Supper and many compliments from our assembled friends. and a handsome address from our Governess thanking us for the manner in which we had entertained her– In a short time after this my father

[20] Hannah More (1745–1833), a religious writer and educator, wrote *A Search after Happiness*, a pastoral drama for schoolchildren, in 1762; it was published in Bristol, London, and Dublin in 1773 (*DNB*).

Dorothea or Dorothy Bland Jordan (1762–1816), an Irish-born actress who had her first London season in 1785, achieved fame in comedies (same; *AFC*, 6:482, note 4).

removed us from School altogether— Three more daughters had been born to him, and the expenses of his family were heavy; but as our education was by no means complete, he engaged a private Governess to superintend our Masters, and to instruct the little ones. My Sister was in her fifteenth year I a year younger My fathers establishment was so perfectly regulated though large, that every thing in it moved like clock work; his household consisted of eleven Servants; three of whom had lived with him from the time of his marriage; and all of them were devotedly attached to him. He was a very indulgent Master although strict, and as every thing was methodical, every thing was easy— My Mother superintended the whole establishment though her health was so delicate she was often obliged to trust to a substitute in whom she was obliged to place unlimitted confidence— At this time our old and valued Butler removed to France with his Wife, and we lost two faithful Servants and solid friends, which produced an unpleasant change in the family routine— The loss of an old confidential Servant however we may pique ourselves upon our independence, makes itself felt for years if not for life; more especially when we have grown old together, and formed the same habits and acquired in a great degree the same tastes; and we insensibly rely on them for our comforts— This change produced other changes, and in some measure altered the face of things— I am thus minute because, I derived some benefit from the circumstance of the New Cook becoming so very fond of me, that she insisted upon teaching me all she knew; and she could do nothing in her Department, without consulting Miss Weser—[21] From this time my father insisted upon our taking turn each alternate week, in the superintendance of the House keeping, which was very beneficial to us all; and early initiated us in all the labours and troubles of family eoconomy— My Fathers house as I have already observed was open to all the young Americans, and among them we formed some very agreeable acquaintance: two of these Gentlemen being in my fathers Office (he was Consul General from the United States appointed by General Washington) ~~boarded~~ ate at my fathers house; and this naturally produced a great degree of intimacy, although they were nineteen and twenty, and we were so much younger— My attachment to Mr. David Sterrett was very great— His character his manners, his person were all excellent; and his disposition was such as to ensure the esteem and affection of all who

[21] A nickname for LCA.

knew him. He was equally fond of me, and always termed me his little Wife: and every body delighted to teaze me about him until a sentiment was forming in my heart, which no one doubted, least of all myself— Our time was all marked out for different studies; and in the Evening we joined my father and Mother in the parlour, and there were few which did not give rise to some frolick in which they joined, and all the family partook— Whenever we did better than usual as a reward the Carpet would be rolled up and they would join the dance; and lend their aid to add to the merriment of the Evening: and home was thus rendered so delightful we did not dream of any pleasure beyond it, unless it was an occasional visit to the theatre— On the New Years day after we left School my father presented us a guinea each with a desire that we should expend it in whatever was most agreeable to ourselves— With what delight we went to the Shop each calculating how much they would get for their money! and fancying it an inexhaustible mine of wealth, never having possessed more than a Shilling at a time before— But alas! what a disappointment! when I found that Milton's Paradise Lost and Regained, with Mason's Self Knowledge,[22] was all that my guinea produced. These however were treasures to which I had long aspired, and I was proud of reading, "that all our knowledge was ourselves to know." It was a curious selection for so young a child; but this book had been put into my hand by the teacher, and I had become very fond of its serious and contemplative subject. How often since that time have I thought it injured me; by teaching me to scrutinize too closely into motives, and looking too closely at the truth— Much, much depends upon the reading of our early life— Children appear to read carelessly, and to note little of the subjects which are placed before them. But the impressions which are made on them are durable, and though apparently lost for years; frequently stamp the taste and mark the character of the mind at a later period of their lives— Time flew on and my Sister Nancy hourly improved in manners and in beauty: at sixteen she was a perfect Hebe. Her complexion was fair, her hair dark auburn curl'd in natu[*ral*] Ringlets round her forehead; her eyes were hazle, but their expression it is impossible to describe, for their brilliant gaiety seemed to call on those she looked on to be as gay and as happy as herself; and her dimpled mouth disclosing a beautiful set of teeth; completed the power of

[22] John Mason, *Self-Knowledge: A Treatise, Shewing the Nature and Benefit of That Important Science, and the Way to Attain It*, London, 1745.

her fascination— Her person was good, rather inclined to au bon point, and too short to be decidedly fine, but of nice proportions her deportment was easy and graceful and there was an affability and sweetness in her address that won all beholders— She was calculated by nature and education to move in a highly polished sphere where her natural charms and her accomplishments would have been duly appreciated: about this time a young gentleman arrived from America to study at the temple who brought the strongest recommendations to my Father with a request that he would act as Guardian to him during his residence in England.[23] He was a small man very handsome possessing first rate talents and of most insinuating manners such a guest received on such a footing was not likely to be admitted to the intimacy of the family without producing the consequences which must naturally be expected and in a short time an appeal was made by the young Gentleman to my father to sanction his addresses after some hesitation my father did so making it a condition that the marriage should be retarded as they were both so young until he had persued his studies and returned to his Native Country to establish himself and procure the consent of his friends and on these terms he was allowed to consider himself engaged. During part of this time my father had a Country House at Highberry[24] my dear Mothers health was in a very low state and she could not remain in London. At this time my fathers Nephew Walter Hellen resided with us he was the second Son of Mrs: Hellen and was placed by my father in his Counting House— He was a very sickly though a very handsome young man possessing no shining qualities and very indolent— My Sisters attractions had touched his heart and he could not view his rivals success without sufferering— Dr Sheaf a man of talents who was studying medicine was the bosom friend of Mr. Jennings and was one of my champions on all occasions He presented me with the first verses I ever received. These Gentlemen both sailed for America and it was supposed that in two years my father would return to his native Country— During the Summer my life was nearly ended by a singular accident while playing battledore with Mr. Hellen I turned my neck and displaced the bones which produced such extreme agony as to endanger my life— It was followed by a violent fever which again reduced me to a

[23] That is, the Middle Temple, one of the four Inns of Court in London.

[24] Highbury, in Islington parish, was a suburb that included Highbury House, built in the early 1780s (*London Past and Present,* 2:214).

state of weakness bordering on ~~fragility~~ infancy— Here we only saw my father on the Saturday and he would return to town early on the Monday Morng. It is singular that in reviewing the days of our youth I have not the most faint or glimmering recollection of Your Grandfather or Grandmother Adams. My Mother used to talk of them frequently and often pointed out their residence in Grosvenor Square and describ'd Mrs. Adams eyes and Miss Adams's complexion but we were kept so much at School that we probably never saw them—[25]

It was during the following winter that we were introduced into what is called society— The difference in the ages of my Sister and myself was so little it was thought proper to introduce us together— I have described her already and have but a few words to say concerning myself I was timid to shyness reserved and cold— When pleased delighted to ecstacy and attached with ardour— my disposition inclined me to read the countenances of all who approached me with extreme care and my judgment of character was almost immediately stamped upon this investigation— Sense and talent I almost worshipped Mr. Hewlett during my frequent visits had done much to expand my understanding and by his serious conversation had led me early to think— There was an old Gentleman by the name of Edmund Jennings who was likewise constantly at our House who was a man of fine sense whose conversation I was very fond of—[26] Mr Granville Sharp David Hartly Tom Payne and many others whom I have forgotten—[27] Society at home was ever delightful to me upon the footing on which it was received in my fathers family and our little unceremonious suppers were the very essence of social festivity— My Mothers conversation was brilliant. She was fond of reading and her manners were polished and the tone she gave to his company was easy and what the french call spirituél—

[25] The Adams and Johnson families had known each other since 1779, when JA and JQA spent time in Nantes waiting for a ship to take them back to America. JA later, and improbably, traced the romance of JQA and LCA to these visits, but they were twelve and four at the time, respectively. JA visited the Johnsons in 1783, and JQA was at their home frequently enough to recommend in 1784 that letters be addressed to him there. When JA, AA, and AA2 moved to London in 1785, the Johnsons and Adamses socialized, but LCA was only thirteen when the Adamses returned to America in 1788 (JA, *D&A*, 2:358–359, 3:149; *AFC*, 5:328, 8:463).

[26] For Edmund Jenings, see JA, *Papers,* 12:x–xi. He had been acquainted with Joshua Johnson since the latter's arrival in London (Johnson, *Letterbook,* p. 3).

[27] Granville Sharp (1735–1813), a British abolitionist and scholar of religion and constitutional history, corresponded with JA (*DNB*).

David Hartley the younger (1732–1813), a British abolitionist who supported American independence, was a member of Parliament and a signer of the 1783 Treaty of Paris (*DNB*; JA, *Papers,* 15:x).

My father seemed to hang on every word she uttered and gazed on her with looks of love and admiration "as if encrease of appetite had grown by what it fed on" never did man love woman with a devotion so perfect—[28] His sparkling eye beamed on her with an excess of tenderness and his smile seemed to blend all those good and amiable feelings which spring spontaneous from a faithful and benevolent heart— She was his pride his joy his love and in her and his Children was concentratd all that made life desirable— In disposition I was not half so amiable as either of my Sisters but it was my fathers idea that I was more steady and this induced him to treat me as if I was the eldest and to put much trust in my discretion. To me this proved often a very painful distinction exciting much justifiable jealousy but it gave me a habit of measuring my own actions by a pretty severe rule as I soon learned that any lapse on my part would be met with great severity in all quarters. I had not the advantage of possessing the personal attractions which adorned my two Sisters— I was so entirely happy I never looked or dreamt of any thing beyond the hour, and thoroughly detested every thing like society beyond my own home unless it was an occasional visit to the Theatre. So decided was this trait in my character that I would shed tears for hours previous to going out to a party never open my lips while there and return to my home in such glee that my father used to think himself oblged to rebuke me by showing me the contrast between my downcast looks my trembling knees and my awkward gate which he used to say made me appear as if some crime was heavy on my conscience— These lessons encreased my aversion and destroyed even the wish to be seen out of my own doors— In writing thus of self I am betraying a degree of unpardonable egotism— It is true and I acknowledge the fact most humbly but in looking back to myself or to the happy period of my early days my memory is filled with reminiscenses so delightful it revels in scenes of such kind affectionate attentions such heart bestowed tenderness that I must be pardoned; for little in after life can compensate for such privations— Is a young woman thus situated a fit object to enter the world? Ever the first object of attention at home every fault pardoned, every virtue loved, a consequence given to every action with a constant desire rather to elevate than to depress her, with a system of reward and punishment calculated to perfect and expand every good feeling of her heart; can such an education fit a young artless creature for

[28] Shakespeare, *Hamlet*, Act I, scene ii, lines 144–145.

an entrance into a corrupt world? Will she not constantly seek the models which where hourly before her eyes? and will not every variation from such a standard occasion mortal wounds in a heart formed to love and venerate principles of action which appeared so perfectly pure and steady— My Parents appeared to be loved and respected by all who knew them— Their servants treated them with respect and devotion and in return met with that affectionate steady kindness in sickness and in health in joy or in sorrow which alone evinces a strong sentiment of mutual worth between the servant and his master— If in sickness or trouble they bestowed care and attention on his children those children were taught as the highest pleasure they could know to reward the service by a permission to make them some little gift such as would afford them real pleasure and at the same time confer a real benefit— If my Mothers health required more than common care each in turn would volunteer their service and her recovery was always celebrated by a little fete in the Servants hall for which my father furnished the means—

> Oh halcyon days of bliss long past ~~away~~
> Too good too happy long to last
> Blyth as Aurora decked in saffron gay
> With joys as pure as yields young blushing May
> Oh winged hours on lightest pinions flown
> Elapsed [aslas?] ere yet their joys were known
> In saddest gloom of Night thou didst decay
> ~~And~~ With blighted hopes to sorrow soon a prey
> Wrecked on a foreign ruthless shore
> They sunk subdued to rise no more

Do not my children read this as romance for every word is true— Our family consisted of seven daughters and one Son as children they were remarkable for beauty and as it was my Mothers delight to dress them all exactly alike on a Sunday when we walked in couples to Church we were objects of general curiosity and permit me to say admiration to the publick— It was a goodly show and well I remember it— Time rappidly flew our education was progressing and we had the best masters to teach us those accomplishments which properly used are an ornament to female loveliness— At this time my father received a singular Letter from Gov$^{r.}$ Johnson[29] who he

[29] Thomas Johnson (1732–1819), one of Joshua's older brothers, was born in Calvert County, Md. He was a member of the Continental Congress, the first brigadier general of the

looked on as a father telling him that he had heard much of his daughters and desiring him to be useful that they should "form connections with none but *men of note* and distinction in his own Country." This Letter produced a great effect on him and induced him to limit as much as possible our acquaintance among the English— Mr Thorp's family whom you knew in England were all boys and had been intimate in the family as children but they were the only young men of that Country with whom we had any intimacy—[30] Our Evenings I have already described; but alone or in company my father required me to sing and nothing but sickness could furnish an excuse for non complyance; he listened with delight to our performancs which seemed to soothe his soul to peace and harmony after the labours of the day— It was now that we continually heard annecdotes concerning the American Revolution the risks my father had run ere he was obliged to quit England. He would talk to us of Dr Franklin of Mr Lawrence whom he had visitted in the Tower of Col Trumbull who had been confined in Bridewell of Stephen Sair of Mr Jay of Paul Jones and of Gen Washington of whom he spoke with a degree of enthusiasm which fired our young hearts with the purest love and admiration.[31] My Sister Frye had been named after the states of Maryland Virginia and the Carolina's in compliment to their acquiecence with the declaration of Independence as she was born in the October of the year which fixed this great event as a proof of his strong attachment to his Country and his zeal in her cause. Many were the Americans that he saved from imprisonment

Maryland militia, and the first governor of that state. He served as an associate justice of the U.S. Supreme Court from 1792 to 1793. The other siblings who lived to adulthood were Benjamin (1727–1786), Mary (1729–1801), Rebecca (1730–1767), Dorcas (b. 1734), James (b. 1736), Elizabeth (b. 1739), John (b. 1745), Baker (1747–1811), and Roger (1749–1831) (*DAB*; Delaplaine, *Life of Thomas Johnson,* p. 13–15; George A. Hanson, *Old Kent: The Eastern Shore of Maryland,* Baltimore, 1876, p. 50).

[30] Samuel Thorp (1741?–1823) had two sons, Robert (d. 1861) and John Thomas (d. 1836); the latter was an alderman, member of Parliament, and lord mayor of London (*The Gentleman's Magazine and Historical Chronicle,* 93:183 [Jan.–June 1823]; *The Gentleman's Magazine and Historical Review,* 10:705 [Feb. 1861]).

[31] Henry Laurens (1724–1792), a South Carolina merchant, planter, and statesman, was en route to the Netherlands to negotiate treaties with the Dutch in 1780 when his ship was captured by the British. He was imprisoned in the Tower of London on suspicion of high treason from 6 Oct. 1780 to 31 Dec. 1781 (*DAB*; *AFC*, 3:x–xi, 4:18).

For John Trumbull, see *AFC*, 5:269. He was arrested on suspicion of treason and imprisoned in Tothill Fields, Bridewell (*DAB*).

Stephen Sayre (1736–1818), an American merchant and banker, lived in London from the 1760s until the Revolution. In 1775 he was briefly imprisoned in the Tower, accused of plotting to kidnap the king and overthrow the government. The charge was dismissed, and he sued successfully for assault and false imprisonment (same).

while residing in London at his own risk furnishing them with clothes money and passage on board vessels owned by him or his friends which convey'd them safe from danger either to their homes or to France— Among this number was General Sam Smith of Maryland who never acknowledged the kindness who never repaid the debt but who to use your fathers expression witnessd the suffering produced by the "most blasting calamities" yet never held out a saving hand; but help'd to crush by arrogance and disdain those to whom he owed his life his consequence his all.[32] Alas how is it that the wicked flourish when the good are brought thus low. At this time we became acquainted with Vance Murray he almost lived at our house and as is usual when a young man frequents a family on terms of great intimacy where there are young Ladies one of them must of course be selected as an object of preference and I was perpetually quized literally without knowing what it meant for my heart was as free as the roving birds who spreads in wanton sport his plumage to the garish Sun— Out of my home I knew no joy I cared for nothing I wished for nought—and I think I never was what is termed a susceptible young Lady or easily won to love. and at this time I was a very child. He was a Student in the Temple and my father was his guardian and Banker— He was most undoubtedly a man of Talents but at that time what would now be termed a dandy of the first order—[33] In the Summer we again returned to Highbury and Vessels began to arrive from America which were now impatiently looked for but they brought not the expected freights of Letters full of love but a gloomy silence and dull whispers began to spark the lovers want of faith and to bring the usual anguish caused to sincere and cruelly disappointed affection and the bright damask tint on the fair cheek of poor Nancy began gradually to fade and her

[32] Samuel Smith (1752–1839) was raised in Baltimore, the son of John Smith, a wealthy merchant active in Revolutionary politics. He probably met Johnson when he was traveling in Europe as a young man, between 1772 and 1774; the two men corresponded in the 1780s, and Smith shipped goods on Johnson's ships. His title came from his rank as brigadier general of the Maryland militia in 1794 and as major general defending Baltimore in the War of 1812. He served in the House of Representatives from 1792 to 1803 and 1816 to 1822, and in the Senate from 1803 to 1815 and 1822 to 1833 (*DAB*; Papenfuse, *Pursuit of Profit*, p. 122, 245; John S. Pancake, *Samuel Smith and the Politics of Business: 1752–1839*, University, Ala., 1972, p. 1–3).

[33] William Vans Murray (1760–1803) studied law at the Middle Temple from 1784 to 1787 and became friendly with the Johnson and Adams families. He was a close friend of JQA's, and they corresponded frequently between 1797 and 1801, when Murray succeeded JQA as minister at The Hague. Although both LCA and AA2 were viewed by others as possible objects of his affection, he married Charlotte Hughins, an Englishwoman (*DAB; AFC*, 5:344–345, 7:161).

beauty to wither and decay— Her spirits declined and she was soon the shaddow of herself— Vice had assumed her sway over his inconstant heart and he was lured to his destruction by the wiles of a married woman and yet lives to show of how little avail are the finest talents fortune and connection to save us from ruin when our passions are suffered to predominate over the best gift of God our reason— During this Summer nothing very material occurred excepting the return of our poor old Servant Cecilia in a starving state her husband had deserted her and she came to my father in her need to implore his succour; as this was never refused to any one in distress it was instantly yielded to her and she again became an inmate of our house— Her story was a common one her husband had robbed her of every thing she had been left in debt had made every effort to support herself and conceal her shame and affliction, and had parted with all she owned in the world until having nothing left she had passed three nights and days without tasting food ere she could controul her pride sufficiently to make her situation known and in this alarming state with the utmost difficulty, famished and exhausted, she reached our house— Never shall I forget the eagerness with which she devoured the food placed before her or the horror with which we contemplated her ghastly looks and her piteous craving, until it was found dangerous to indulge her and we were obliged to remove the eatables from her literally longing eyes, to prevent fatal consequences. She had been our Nurse had enterred my Mothers family on her marriage had lived 18 years with her at home and abroad and we all loved her as a Mother— She was an object of general care from this time to all the family and each vied with the other in tendering her the services which her very delicate state required— I became a great favorite with our D^{r} who was somewhat of a naturalist he delighted to show me his stuffed Birds his Butterflys his glowworms and all the beautiful varieties of the insect tribes and endeavoured to cultivate in me a taste for natural history but I fear I was not an apt scholar and I often wonder how I could have been selected as I was on most occasions as an object worthy of improvement— My passion was reading and I read every thing I could get hold of but this was not calculated to be of much real benefit it was all crude and undigested ill chosen and often of a nature to produce bad effects as it encouraged a sensibility already too keen. When I say sensibility I do not mean the lovesick sensibility of puling girls this I never possessed I read Novels and Romances it is true but it was only characters of lofty excellence which excited my ambition or produced emulation and my models were generally too great to be pleasing In fact I gloried in the heroic and General Washington was my idol—

Mr & Miss Carroll came to England under the care of a Negro Woman to be sent to Liege in Flanders for education— My father was to be their Guardian in Europe and the black woman was to be sent back immediately Kitty Carroll was then about 13 the wildest child I ever saw and utterly unruly— It was thought very singular in London that the rich Mr Carroll should have sent his children under such an escort— The Slave was a novelty to us and the treatment of that Slave by her young Mrs. was a thing we could not comprehend as we had always been severely punished for improper conduct to Servants this matter produced many unpleasant scenes while the woman staid between us young people— She was sent home in one of my fathers Vessels and the young people were sent to Flanders under a proper escort—[34] The Winter we returned to London which passed in the usual way introducing many young Americans to our acquaintance among others an excentric creature by the name of Carter who became much enamoured of my Sister Nancy— He was half if not quite crazy and his visits were not agreeable— He was a man of large property and piqued himself very much on his family in Virginia almost all of whom appear to have a crack in the brain even to this very hour— His conversation was excessively wild and although apparently good hearted he used to tell strange stories of a dismal character which produced nothing but laughter very contrary to his intention or expectation— Among these was the account of his Mothers death which ocurred while she was being dipped by an Annabaptist preacher and always made him shed an abundance of tears although his description of the scene was more ludicrous than melancholy— He was entirely harmless and an object of perpetual diversion to us young people although often very annoying— Being nearly related to the Marchioness of Salisbury and Lady Essex he was received in their families on a footing of great

[34] Charles Carroll IV (b. 1775 and later designated Charles Carroll of Homewood) and Catherine (Kitty) Carroll (b. 1778, later wife of Robert Goodloe Harper) were the youngest children of Charles Carroll of Carrollton (1737–1832) and Mary Darnall Carroll. Their father, who had for many years consigned tobacco to Johnson's firm and bought European goods from them, was a Maryland delegate to the Continental Congress and a senator in the first federal Congress. Carroll had been educated at the Jesuit College of St. Omer, and in 1785 he sent his son to Liège to study. In 1788 Kitty was sent to an English convent school at Liège. The children returned to Annapolis in 1794 (*DAB*; Smith, *Charles Carroll*, p. 130, 206, 220, 234, 247, 262, 264; Papenfuse, *Pursuit of Profit*, p. 71).

intimacy and according to his own account was a constant Butt for their pleasantry– It was about this time that we became acquainted with Mr. Higginson who was a very handsome young man but my father was not very fond of the Yanky's and they were not much encouraged to visit at our house– I think it was about this time that Col Smith and Mr J B. Cutting came to England–[35] Mr Murdoch was also established in London and became very intimate in the family– I cannot pretend to mention all the Gentlemen with whom we were acquainted I can only say that in consequence of my Uncle's silly Letter although we lived in the midst of the city of London we were kept almost entirely out of English society and visitted only one family in the street in which we lived– My Sister Caroline was just entering into society. Her form was light her complexion dazzling her manners arch and playfull and her disposition sweet– Timid to a fault it was only among our most intimate friends that she displayed her real character and all those became extravagantly fond of her– She was the most admirable mimic and afforded us constant amusement by this talent but my father tried his utmost to check it although he seldom could restrain his mirth at her performance– Col Smith almost lived with us and was the mediator with our parents in all our little troubles– At this time Mr Gibbs of Carolina proposed to my father for my Sister Caroline– he was very wealthy a great dasher and a great Beau. This latter quality operated so unpleasantly on the old Gentlemans feelings that he quietly rejected the advances and we saw Mr Gibbs no more–[36] My Brother was at School under the especial care of Mr. Hewlett with Mr Ben Ogle the father of the young man with whom you are acquainted who returned to America in the course of this Summer– He was received among us like our brother and I never was aware that the young Gentleman had any predilection for my worthy self until my residence in Washington–[37] Alas how unthinking and childish I must have been never to suspect the power of my charm's but so it was and I have heard of a number of ardent admirers that I had at that time since I have grown old the rumour of which never reached my ear in my youth– There was a Mr John Taylor a Gentleman from

[35] WSS arrived in London in 1785 as secretary to the U.S. legation in London. For Dr. John Brown Cutting, see *AFC*, 7:122.

[36] For Henry Gibbes, see same, 7:27–28.

[37] Benjamin Ogle II (1775–1844) married Anna Maria Cooke (b. 1777); their son, Benjamin III, was born in 1796 (Alice Norris Parran, *Register of Maryland's Heraldic Families*, 2d ser., 2 vols., Baltimore, 1935, 2:150–151).

Mass$^{tts.}$ whom I disliked more than I can express Who was the only one that I was at all conscious of having smitten but my feelings towards him were always those of disgust It was at this time that the family portraits were painted or rather began most of them were thought good likenesses but mine never gave satisfaction to my friends nor indeed any one that ever was painted in those days– The one George has was thought the best and that squints–[38] In the Summer we went to Lymington and in the course of our journey had a fine opportunity of seeing a number of beautiful seats and of visitting the Isle of Wight Six weeks passed most delightfully and we returned home in fine health and spirits from our tour in which we were accompanied by a Mr West of Baltimore one of the most really amiable men I ever knew Here again my life was endangered by a singular accident as well as my Mothers we were riding in a large four wheeled Chaise and M$^{r.}$ West was driving when we met two large Waggons laden with Hay– The drivers were walking at some distance behind and did not notice our situation and as the road was bordered by two high banks it was impossible to get out of the way– The consequence was that the Waggons advanced on us threw down our horse and was literally coming over us when M$^{r.}$ West at the risk of his life jump'd out and endeavoured to stop the Horses while my Mother scrambled over the Shafts of the Waggon and made her way safe out; the Horses still pressing on to me, and I too lifeless to move: fortunately the men came up and I was taken out of the carriage more dead than alive– I never shall forget the agony of the poor young man. He was in a deep decline and I think the shock he underwent at the idea of our horrid danger hastened his death which took place not long after– As neither he nor my Mother could see any thing of me after they had extricated themselves from the peril; and as I neither spoke nor move they both expected to find me crushed to atoms, and you may conceive their astonishment when I came forth coolly saying to the men pray take care of my Wig which appeared to be the only object of my concern my head having been shaved in consequence of a severe illness and my vanity not admitting of so cruel an exposure of my bald head– This was the only adventure of importance that occurred during our stay excepting our meeting a most elegant woman by the name of

[38] Joshua and Catherine Johnson and their seven daughters had individual miniature portraits painted in oil ca. 1792. LCA is probably referring to the Gilbert Stuart portrait, 1821–1825, in which her left eye appears smaller than the right (Oliver, *Portraits of JQA and LCA*, p. 24–26, 86).

Nesbit who took great pains to throw herself in our way; and who was really a fascinating creature possessing the most polished manners and the most cultivated mind:— On our return to Town we learnt that this acquaintance was far from a reputable one and that the Lady's situation and character was involved in mystery. I never heard her name since that time— She did not like me but was perfectly enchanted with my Mother and Sister. all the other branches of the family remaind at home— Major Jackson and M[r] Francis of Philadelphia now became constant visitors at our house They were both engaged to be married but poor Francis could not behold my Sister Carolines charms without danger and ere he was aware of it became devotedly attached to her— Every day every hour seemed to encrease his passion but though it was evident to every one he behaved with strict honour by constantly avowing his engagement to Miss Willing and speaking of his marriage as a thing of course—[39]

It was at this time that my father took a french family into his House that is a man and his Wife by the name of Gallement french Emgrants in great distress and professedly Nobles. He was to be Tutor to my Brother She Governess to us Females for although the three eldest were introduced into company we were still obliged to attend to all our school duties— The French Revolution was then blazing in all its fury and the Emigrants became objects of general pity in England— My father had lived so much in France and so happily that he felt a sympathy for these poor people and was liberal in the services he rendered them— He had known the King; he had been graciously received by the beautiful Queen; had rejoiced with the Nation in the birth of the Dauphin; and he could not however he admired the *cause of freedom* witness or hear of the enormous cruelties of the period, without execrating its authors— Until this time Lafayette had been an object of idolatry like Gen[l] Washington; but now we knew not what to think— was it weakness? was it want of judgment? or what caused the unfortunate seizure of the King and Queen which brought them to the block with such unheard suffering? Something mysterious has ever attended this circumstance which no time can reveal— He is good he is amiable he is

[39] Major William Jackson (1759–1828), who had been an aide to George Washington, went to Europe in 1793 to represent his future brother-in-law, William Bingham, in business dealings. He was engaged to Elizabeth Willing, and they married in 1795. Thomas Francis was engaged to Dolly Willing, Elizabeth's sister. They married in 1794 (*DAB*; Charles Willing Littell, "Major William Jackson," *PMHB*, 2:366 [1878]; *Philadelphia Gazette*, 27 Sept. 1794). See also *AFC*, 4:170–171.

ambitious and in this instance he was unfortunate for I will not believe that he was capable of adopting the Stateman's horrible doctrine that we may sometimes do evil that good may come of it— but I will endeavour to believe that as creatures of circumstance he was prevented from saving the wretched beings who clung to him for existence by unforeseen accidents beyond his power to controul—

Gen[l] Pinckney was Minister to England from the United States and our families became very intimate— M[rs.] Pinckney was a truly lovely Woman and I became very fond of her. My father contrary to his usual custom allowed me to stay at her House very frequently and I there became acquainted with a number of young Carolinians among whom was M[r.] Huger and their singular relation M[r.] Horie who however only made them flying visits as he was too much devoted to France to be able to stay in England—[40] On one of his flying visits he took the trouble to ride down from Cumberland place to show me Lavaters Angel; which he assured me was my exact likeness at which I was very much surprized as he was one of the objects whom I most unmercifully quizzed—[41] Col Smith was gone to France and our society had entirely changed—And we moved in a more fashionable world through the medium of M[r] Pinkney and M[r] John Barker Church's family then living in a very splindid style in London and at Chiswick.[42] Through them we became acquainted with three most beautiful American ladies M[rs.] Falconnet and the Miss Hunters of Rhode Island— One of them was blind; and they were in search of some Occulist in the hope that Miss Hunter might recover her sight— Col and M[rs.] Smith arrived in England and again our acquaintance was enlarged and I will say improved— The very familiar footing on which we lived made their society delightful

[40] Thomas Pinckney (1750–1828) of South Carolina was U.S. minister to Great Britain from 1792 until 1795, when he was made special commissioner and envoy extraordinary to Spain. He married Elizabeth Motte in 1779; she died in England in 1794. Francis Kinloch Huger (1773–1855) of South Carolina studied medicine at the University of Edinburgh before continuing his training in London. Daniel Horry (1769–1828) was educated in England but lived in France most of his life (*DAB*; N. Louise Bailey, Mary L. Morgan, and Carolyn R. Taylor, *Biographical Directory of the South Carolina Senate, 1776–1985*, 3 vols., Columbia, S.C., 1986; Eric Stockdale and Randy J. Holland, *Middle Temple Lawyers and the American Revolution*, Eagan, Minn., 2007, p. 200).

[41] Johann Caspar Lavater (1741–1801) was a Swiss physiognomist. Two illustrated English translations of his *Essays on Physiognomy* were published in London in 1789–1799; a portrait in one of them may have resembled LCA.

[42] For John Barker and Angelica Schuyler Church, see *AFC*, 6:10. They had four children: Philip, John Barker II, Catherine (Kitty), and Richard Stephen Hamilton (NN:Schuyler Family Papers, Additions, Alexander Hamilton Church's Family Tree).

For WSS's activities, see *AFC*, 9:416.

to us. Whenever the Col dined from home Mrs. S. would bring her Children early in the morning and pass the day with us and as this happened very frequently it brought us together continually— It was my delight to dress her and I was often employed in making up Articles of Millinery which I used to insist upon her wearing and in which she looked beautiful— She was one of the most placid quiet beings I ever saw; very cold in her general manners; but when she laughed or entered into the spirit of our gaiety which was very often, she seemed to be the life of the party— She would romp or dance and partake of all the jokes like one of us and she was perfectly adored by the family— The Col's manners you perfectly remember were irrisistable and we seldom sat down to our favorite Suppers without him—

Thus years rolled on and we were too happy to think of the lapse of time— In the Summer the Col and my father took a house between them at Brighton where we lived together six weeks but the air disagreed so much with my Mother we were obliged to leave it and we all returned to Town together—

Mrs. Smith was one of the most really amiable women I ever saw, and under the appearance of coldness and reserve was very affectionate in her disposition— She became very much attached to my Sister Frye during her residence in England, and I believe retained that attachment to her death— I loved her then and still better after I became her Sister— At that period we had little idea that such a circumstance could ever happen— We had changed our Governess in consequence of the encrease of the family of our french one; who however lived in our neighbourhood and was an object of constant interest as well as expense to the family— My Brother left England for America under the protection of Major Jackson and Mr Francis; my father fearful lest he should imbibe european Notions was anxious to give him an American education and thus fit him to live among republicans a thing very difficult to people who have lived in the European cities as I have found to my cost; for a Republick in theory and a Republick in practice are two essentially different things as many wiser people have found as well as myself—[43] It was in the autumn that Mr. Jay came over to make the Treaty. Poor Mrs. Pinkney returned from a visit to one of the Watering places very sick and sent for me to stay with her. I was shocked when I saw her she

[43] Thomas Baker Johnson went to America in 1795; he attended Harvard from 1796 to 1798 (CFA, *Diary*, 5:xvii).

was so much altered and appeared to be so dangerously ill— Dr Warren a gentleman of great celebrity attended her; but I have always thought he mistook her complaint and she told me she was six Months advanced in her pregnancy but she was determined to keep it secret, as she had always said she would not have any more children, and she was ashamed to declare her situation— I staid entirely with her and made every effort to amuse her: but my father fearful lest the fatigue might injure me insisted on my coming home; and promised if I was well that I should return to her the day but one after leaving her— Her Physician thought her so much better that he pronounced her out of danger although she had not been able to lie down or to sleep in any position but that of laying a pillow on a Table and resting her head on her arms to seek repose— On the Sunday Evening I returned it was about six o clock and she had thought herself so much better that she had descended to the drawing Room, to receive us; and was immediately siezed with a convulsion in which she expired— The distress of the family was dreadful and no language can express the shock I experienced on hearing the afflicting intelligence— She was one of the most unaffected lively agreeable women I ever knew and an excellent Wife and devoted Mother— Many happy hours did I spend in her house most kindly treated by her whole family; and even Mr. Deas was friendly and unreserved—[44] Mr Pinckneys family and Mr Church's had lived in habits of the most perfect intimacy and in that family alone he found consolation after his severe loss— Mrs. Church was one of the most polished elegant women I ever beheld—but there was something so very artificial in her manner that she always appeared to me to be acting; and some parts were too unatural to her real character not to betray that they were only assumed for the moment. Her understanding was fine her mind highly cultivated; but there was a deficiency some where which I cannot explain or she never could have fallen into so gross an error as excessive affectation; which is only pardonable in weak minds— It probably proceeded from a too earnest desire to be thought fashionable— There are two Ladies who have figured the last two years in Washington who forcibly remind me of what Mrs. Church and her daughter then were, excepting that Mrs. Livingston has more natural vivacity and more nature— Miss

[44] William Allen Deas (b. 1764) was the acting American chargé d'affaires in London in 1795; he signed the certificate at the exchange of ratifications of the Jay Treaty in JQA's place (N. Louise Bailey, Mary L. Morgan, and Carolyn R. Taylor, *Biographical Directory of the South Carolina Senate, 1776–1985*, 3 vols., Columbia, S.C., 1986; Bemis, *JQA*, 1:68–70).

Church was very much then what Miss Livingston is now the belle that drew all eyes but that frightened all hearts from the blaze of her style; which always reminded her admirers that it required attributes to support it—[45] At this time the Governess of Miss Church was the object of universal admiration She was an Emigrant of family reduced by the Revolution to the necessity of seeking subsistance in this way to maintain herself and her mother— She was a lovely creature one of your true Novel heroines; beautiful accomplished, modest, and correct: living in a family the Master of which was notorious for his dissipated life she was an object of envy, of desire, of admiration, and pursuit to half the libertines in London—but she escap'd the tongue of calumny, and her conduct was so judicious that she made an excellent marriage; and lives in an elegant style in Paris with her husband, who is a man of Rank and merit— Kitty Church was a sweet girl entirely engrossed with pleasure, and formed to give as well as to enjoy it— Her tastes were all french and she was only fitted for the Parisian hemisphere to which she has removed with her family to settle for the remainder of her life—

Major Pinckneys constant visits at Mrs. Church's and the late hours at which he returned home roused the observation of the censorious, and caused much scandal in our little world: fortunately he was sent on a Mission to Spain and was for a time forgotten— As I write without attention to dates many errors will be found in my relation of events as to the exact time of their occurrences: but until the eara of my marriage or rather my engagement; time flew on unheeded and as I never knew what trouble was I had no data to make a strong impression on my mind— This is the real blessing of happy youth, and alas it vanishes while we are insensible of its enjoyment—

Mr Jay as I have before said came to England and while he was there Mr Adams and his Brother Tom arrived in London on their way to Holland.[46] Col & Mrs. Smith had returned some time to America— Mr Jay and your father and Uncle were invited to dine with us the latter were to leave England immediately, and they were

[45] Edward Livingston (1764–1836) represented New York in the U.S. House of Representatives, 1795–1800, and Louisiana in the House and Senate, 1823–1832. In 1805 he married Louise Moreau de Lassy, born Davezac de Castera, a widow from Jamaica. Their daughter, Cora, was born the following year (*Biog. Dir. Cong.*; William B. Hatcher, *Edward Livingston*, University, La., 1940, p. 122–123, 299).

[46] JQA and TBA sailed for London on 17 Sept. 1794, arriving in Deal on 14 Oct. and London the next day. On 28 Oct. JQA met Joshua Johnson and then left London for the Netherlands, where he had been appointed resident minister. TBA was his secretary (*AFC*, 10:486, 487; D/JQA/21, 28 Oct., APM Reel 24).

asked on account of the former acquaintance of the two families when your Grandfather was Minister in England— Your father was engaged: but your Uncle dined with us and so far were we from dreaming of a future connection in the family that from some strange fancy my Sister Nancy nick named your Uncle Abel and of course the brother whom we had never seen was called Cain. I mention this merely to show how little idea or desire there was in the family to plot or plan a marriage between the families— I also had a nick name in consequence of my habit of warning my Sisters if any thing was likely to go wrong; they called me Cassandra because they seldom listened to me until the mischief was done— My Sisters both possessed great vivacity and much playful wit; and every person who visited in the family were either objects of admiration or severity— Col Trumbull was our constant visitor and as a man old or young who visits frequently in a family of young Ladies must be supposed to be in love; I was selected as the object of his partiality. He was old enough to be my father I was therefore very much at my ease with him, it never entering into my imagination that he could think of me but as a favorite child— This I knew he did for he took every opportunity to mark the distinction between myself and my Sisters— He gave me some instruction in painting but I was a poor pupil and did not profit as much as I should have done from so good a preceptor— Once in his life he said he wished he was a young man for *then* he should certainly pay his addresses to me; and this was the utmost that ever passed between us that could be tortured into love or what we fashionably term a belle Passion— In consequence of our being at Mrs. Churchs the first Evening that Mr. Jay and his Son and the Col was introduced he also bore another name among us Girls— The Servant a frenchman announcing them as Mr Pétéràjay and Col Terrible—[47] You may suppose this was too good a joke to lose and it attached itself to them as long as they remained in England—

If I ever had any admirers no woman I can assure you ever had fewer lovers than your Mother— In all this time not a shadow of an offer was made to either of us excepting Mrs. Frye, who refused Mr Buchanan the Gentleman who afterwards married—[48] My Sister Hel-

[47] John Jay's nephew Peter Jay Munro.

[48] Andrew Buchanan married Anne McKean, daughter of Pennsylvania jurist Thomas McKean, in 1797. After Anne's death in 1804 Buchanan married Caroline Johnson on 21 July 1807. Following his death Caroline married Nathaniel Frye Jr. on 3 July 1817 (Roberdeau Buchanan, *Genealogy of the McKean Family of Pennsylvania,* Lancaster, Penn., 1890, p. 132).

len had got over her penchant for Mr. Jennings as all the news we received concerning him proved him utterly unworthy of her affection; and the scandalous chronicle had so thouroughly affiched[49] his vices that it was impossible to regret his loss— That there was much truth in these reports I have since had reason to know for all his prospects were blighted by his conduct and his chief support has been the favour of the wealthy married Lady who seduced him. We were too entirely happy to make marriage a *want* and we only looked forward to it as an evidence that we were not devoid of those attractive qualities which generally are the operating causes of affection in such connections; more especially as my father had always told us that the fortunes he would be enabled to give would not be large enough to prove a motive for an offer— We were constantly taught to believe that we should have five thousand pound Sterling a piece; and so thoroughly was my father convinced of possessing this Sum, that even when all his calamities came so suddenly upon him; he still believed could he have found one single friend in his distress that his children would be amply provided for—

We formed an acquaintance with a family by the name of Court Mrs. Court a Widow had formerly been in habits of intimacy with my father and Mother. She was a very sensible woman but very eccentric Hasty in her judgments and not always just— She became strongly attached to my Sister Hellen to whom she had stood Godmother, and she took as great a dislike to me of which I was utterly unconscious— But being a frequent visitor at our house I soon discovered it and made a point to keep out of her way— She was a woman of property and her husband had left his three daughters under her guardianship one of whom had married against her consent and was but little noticed by her—These with a Cousin of theirs of the same name were the only english acquaintance of young Ladies that we had.[50] The Copley family were considered american as were a number of the Refugees who we became acquainted with thro' Mrs. Col Smith.[51] The Vassalls were the most singular family consisting of three or five females I dont recollect which; very tall, guant, masculine women, entirely independent and wealthy—their

[49] That is, *affiché*, publicized.

[50] Possibly the widow of Christopher Court, a London merchant with whom Joshua Johnson had business dealings (Johnson, *Letterbook,* p. xii).

[51] John Singleton Copley (1738–1815), the American artist, had left Boston for London in 1774. He was joined a year later by his wife, Susanna Clarke (1745–1836), and three of his children: Elizabeth Clarke (1770–1866); John Singleton Jr., later Lord Lyndhurst (1772–1863); and Mary (1773–1868) (*DAB*; *DNB*).

manners were like their persons coarse and unpleasant; They were old Maids and even their large fortunes could not lure a husband— Each of them had some peculiarity but Miss Margaret was the most conspicuous— She had fourteen Dogs who always slept in her chamber, a number of them in her bed, and whenever she went out to dine she carried a paper bag to take the gizzards of the fowls which she always made a point to ask for of the Lady of the House, and the conversation almost always turned upon little exploits of these charming puppies for the pleasure and edification of the company which she did the honour to join— The Sisters echoed the cry and we had the felicity of hearing the hounds without the possibility of flying the chase. Lady Holland was the Cousin of these Ladies, and has likewise given some strong evidence of *brutish tastes*—[52]

It was about this time that a Gentleman called on my father a small neat looking man in a very handsome chariot with livery Servants &ce. He walked into the Office entered into conversation very agreeably and then presented some papers to my father which concerned some American business to be done before the Consul— My father returned the papers for signature and stood to see the name when to his utter surprize he discovered that it was the Traitor Arnold, and he deliberately took up the *pen* with the Tongs and put it into the fire— The gentleman sneaked off endeavouring not to notice the act—[53] This trait will give you a real insight into your Grandfathers character— He was a perfect Gentleman in his manners and universally respected— The American Sailors adored him and his house was their refuge on all occasions— Noble in his sentiments; noble in his Acts; he was ever ready to befriend the unfortunate, and his temper was so open and confiding he soon became the victim of fraud and hypocrisy— Mr. Hellen was sent to America as his Agent, and his Commissions amounted to three thousand dollars a year; my father relied upon him to collect the moneys due to him and to settle all his concerns independent of the partnership with Wallace & Muir— This was not done to his advantage but to the as-

[52] William Vassall (1715–1800), a loyalist exile, and his wife, Margaret Hubbard (d. 1794), had three daughters—Margaret (1761–1819) and twins Anne and Charlotte (b. 1762)—and two sons. Elizabeth Vassall Fox (1770–1845) became Lady Holland when she married (*AFC*, 6:201; Joseph Jackson Howard and Frederick Arthur Crisp, eds., *Visitation of England and Wales: Notes*, 14 vols., London, 1896–1921, 13:36, 38).

[53] Benedict Arnold, who had defected in 1780, fled to England with his family in Dec. 1781. In the 1790s he pursued a variety of unsuccessful commercial ventures and sought money and appointments from the British government. He received neither a military post nor the rewards and praise he expected (*DAB*).

tonishment of many who knew that his Agent was dependent on him, Mr. H. came out as a Merchant with a handsome capital having Ships &ce without any visible cause for his prosperity.[54] At the same time the partnership was dissolved by mutual consent and terms entered into with all the Creditors for a settlement of their debt—[55] It was their wish that my father should have come over to this Country in person and left my Mother and some part of the family in England as hostages— Happy would it have been for him could he have done so The Ship was prepared for his departure and every thing was ready but my Mother could never be persuaded to consent to it— She had never been separated from him and the responsibility attached to the care of so large a family was too great for her nerves— To this however all my beloved fathers misfortunes must be attributed as all the Lawyers whom he had employed assured him that his presence was essential to prevent the utter destruction of his property in the hands of Mr. Muir, who was even then attempting to embezzle the profits of the concern— My poor Mother has been severely reproached for this act by those who ought to have treated her with Respect; but if we consider her situation, many allowances must be made for her. The charge of so many young women to whom any connection in England was positively forbidden; who were never permitted to be out of sight a moment was not easy; and had any misfortune happened she would have been too great a sufferer—

It would be quite impossible for me to name to you all the persons with whom we became acquainted— About this time my father became very much alarmed at the idea of your Aunt Carolines having made a conquest of Lord Andover a young nobleman whom she frequently met at Mrs. Church's who was very attentive to her and talked a great deal about her beauty—from this time she was not allowed to stay at Mrs. Church and only went there with the family—

The only time I ever recollect to have gone out without my father or Mother was to a Ball at Chiswick given by Mrs. Church under the

[54] Walter Hellen married Ann (Nancy) Johnson in 1798 and Adelaide Johnson in 1813.

[55] For the events related to the dissolution of the firm Wallace, Johnson & Muir, see Papenfuse, *Pursuit of Profit*, chs. 5, 6. By the financial settlement decided by arbitrators Uriah Forrest, James Carey, and James Mason in Feb. 1798, Johnson was to receive credit for £1,200 sterling for each year of the partnership as compensation for living expenses, and Wallace and Muir, who together had a half share in the business, an equal amount. The remaining assets were to be divided among the partners after the firm's London debts were deducted. Johnson was to receive £42,468 in specie and lands in Virginia and Georgia, and Wallace and Muir £37,330 in currency. Johnson disputed the settlement until his death (same, p. 108, 229–231).

protection of Col Trumble where we staid all night— It was on this occasion that I first saw M[rs.] Siddons and her two daughters— I formed an acquaintance with her daughter Maria one of the most beautiful girls I ever met with— She died about two years afterwards M[rs.] Siddons was a most dignified Woman— She looked the Queen every where but her manners were very good. It was here that I heard her say that Belvedera was the most difficult part she played and that her feelings became so excited during the performance she was generally carried home in convulsions— She talked much but she talked well and to the purpose—[56]

In the Autumn of this year M[r] Adams was introduced by Col Trumbull. The first Evening he supped with us he was in high spirits conversed most agreeably and after he retired all the family spoke well of him. His dress however produced some mirth as it was completely dutch and the Coat almost white— Col Trumbull was to leave town immediately after for France he being concerned in some speculation in which he was principal actor— He joked us and said M[r] Adams was a fine fellow and would make a good husband but his dress did not impress us agreeably as it made his person appear to very great disadvantage and Col Smith was the great model that we young Ladies most admired—[57]

After this introduction M[r] Adams came frequently to see us and as his devotions were supposed by every body to be paid to my Sister Nancy we all became very intimate and I rattled on quite unconcerned on the subject— He was a great favorite of my Mothers but I do not think my father admired him so much— He always had a prejudice towards the *Yankees* and insisted that they never made good husbands. When M[r] Adams passed the evening with us my Sister and myself were regularly called upon to play and sing to him which we did for two or three hours. My father never would retire to his chamber without requiring what he called the same indulgence and it in fact became a habit almost as regular as our meals— I never observed any thing in M[r] Adams's conduct towards me that

[56] The character of Belvidera in Thomas Otway, *Venice Preserv'd*, London, 1769, was one of Sarah Kemble Siddons' greatest roles. She had three daughters living in 1795: Maria (1779–1798), Sarah (1775–1803), and Cecilia (1794–1868) (*DNB;* Philip H. Highfill and others, *A Biographical Dictionary of Actors, Actresses, Musicians, Dancers, Managers & Other Stage Personnel in London, 1660–1800*, 16 vols., Carbondale, Ill., 1973–1993). JQA greatly admired Siddons, whom he had seen perform as early as 1783; see JA, *Papers*, 15:329, note 2.

[57] JQA returned from Holland to London on 10 Nov. 1795. The following day he wrote in his Diary, "Dined with M[r:] Trumbull, at M[r] Johnson's. . . . After Dinner M[r] Johnson's daughters entertained us with good music" (D/JQA/24, APM Reel 27).

1. LOUISA CATHERINE JOHNSON, BY EDWARD SAVAGE, CA. 1793
See page ix

2. JOHN QUINCY ADAMS, BY JOHN SINGLETON COPLEY, 1796

See page ix

indicated the smallest preference but used to be surprized some times at his dislike of some of the songs which I used to sing— All those which he knew to be favorites of Col Trumble were so disagreeable to him he would immediately take his hat and bid us good night when I began one of them. Hearing that he was a poet I told him that I expected he would write me a Song— This was a subject of perpetual banter between us and as I have before said being convinced by the observations of many Gentlemen that visited the family besides bets which were made on the subject that my Sister was the object of his preference and being likewise aware that she thought so I never dreamt of the possibility of drawing on myself his attention or regard— You will probably think this was a great degree of stupidity or simplicity whichever you may please to term it but it is the sacred truth and it proceeded from the habit of thinking myself less attractive than my Sisters owing in part to the consequence which my father always gave me and which I could only account for in a manner not flattering to my personal vanity however agreeable on the score of mind— In addition to this my Sisters had even assumed a tone of superiority towards me which had contributed to produce a constant doubt of my power to please— My Mother was always talking to me of my awkwardness my father of my bashfulness my Sisters made me the block on which all their fashions were tried and in this way I was constantly exposed to the ridicule of the whole— Indolence of disposition and a settled indifference made me careless of every thing and music and reading were the only things in life I thought worth living for excepting to laugh at all the oddities which fell in my way— As an evidence of my silliness one day when we were going to a Ball my Sisters sent for a very fashionable hair dresser and as usual there was some difficulty about who should be dressed first. My Sister Nancy whose influence was irrisistable pursuaded me to sit down— At all times this hair dressing was perfect torture to me and I generally fainted before it was done but this unlucky day I supported the torture with great philosophy entirely unconscious of what was going on— When the curl papers were taken out the hair dresser announced that he was going to dress me en téte de Mouton and you may conceive my horror when I found all my hair cut short and curl'd close to my head in imitation of a sheeps wool and powdered quite white and both my Sisters laughing as if they would kill themselves at the beautiful appearance I made. My mortification was extreme for I was very fond of being well dressed but there was no remedy for the evil and bon gré mal gré[58] I was obliged to submit to the evil. circumstances of this kind had however often happen'd I resolved no more to be the but. This matter occurred long before the period at which I am arrived but my eldest Sister always took delight in adorning Caroline and never even on my wedding day would in the smallest degree assist my toilet— But what where these troubles of an hour fleeting and evanescent as a morning dream leaving no trace behind— I think it was in the month of november that we first saw M^r. Adams Time flew on its lightest pinions and I looked not beyond the hour.—[59] I rattled and laugh'd then heedless of harm and never dreamt of change— matters went on thus for two or three months my father, my mother and all my friends being persuaded my Sister was the object of your fathers visits: when one evening at Supper he handed a paper across the table to me saying it was the song he had promised and I immediately opened it and began to read out; when Miss Henning the children's governess who sat next me whisper'd to me to stop and took it out of my hand— This as you may believe caused me to blush and behave like a fool; and as I have often since thought stamped a meaning on the verses which Mr A. never intended to give them, and which I never should have dreamt of had it not been for the act of that Lady, which for many days put the whole family into confusion— Long did I contend against the possibility of such an affection existing in the heart of your father—for but this woman argued so strongly that she had discovered it all the winter and that had foreseen how it would end that my vanity was enlisted and without a particle of affection at the time I suffer'd myself to be coaxed into an affection that lasted probably much longer than would have done love at first sight— The winter roll'd over we were engaged and on the 12 of Feby. as usual my father allowed me to give a Ball and at this ball Mr A. first made his attentions decidedly publick which brought much trouble on my head; as both my

58 For better or worse.

59 It is unclear when LCA and JQA became formally engaged. Her birthday ball was held on 27 Jan. 1796. JQA noted in his Diary, "Evening very agreeable. Danced with Miss Church, with Louisa &c." On 2 March he continued, "Ring from Louisa's finger. . . . Placed in a very difficult dilemma. Know not how I shall escape from it." On 30 March he wrote to AA that "I begin to think very seriously of the duty incumbent upon all good citizens to have a family," and on 5 May he told her that he was planning to marry, although not before leaving for The Hague. In his letters to AA, JQA never mentioned the name of his intended, but AA guessed, writing on 20 May that "if I remember right, She has classick Locks as Virgill Stiles them, Heavenly blew Eyes and plays musick delightfully." On 25 May she assured him that "whom you call yours Shall be mine also" (D/JQA/24, APM Reel 27; all Adams Papers).

Sister and Miss Church were my rivals, and they contrived to make me suffer so severely that even my first lesson's in the belle passion were pretty thickly strewed with thorns— love seemd to chill all the natural hilarity of my disposition, and those hours which had been spent in cheerful mirth were passed in gloom and anxiety in a sort of consciousness of some thing wrong without knowing to find the error— Shun'd by my Sisters, the unforgiving silence of Nancy made me wretched, and it required all the entreaties of Miss Henning to prevent my telling Mr Adams how I was situated— In the Spring we made a party to go to Ranelagh and M^r. Adams was to accompany us— I had jokingly told him that if he went with us he must dress himself handsomely and look as dashy as possible—not aware that on this subject he was very sore, and that some enemy of mine had made him believe I laugh'd at him. The night previous to the party he took leave very coldly and desired if we went that we should call for him at the Adelphi on our way, as he had engagements and could not see us sooner to which we readily agreed. Accordingly we took him up at the Adelphy and I obser'd immediately that he was very handsomely dressd in blue that he had a large Napoleon hat and altogether looked remarkbly well. as I had dressed myself very becomingly as I thought both my Sisters and myself being exactly alike we drove of in high spirits expecting a delightful evening.[60] On entering the Rotunda our party naturally separated and M^r A offered me his arm and while we were strolling round the room I complimented him upon his appearance at which he immediately took fire, and assured me that *his* wife must never take the liberty of interfering in those particulars, and assumed a tone so high and lofty and made so serious a grievance of the affair, that I felt offended and told him that I resign'd all pretensions to his hand, and left him as free as air to choose a Lady who would be more discreet. I then drop'd his arm and join'd my mother with whom I staid the

[60] The trip to Ranelagh, a fashionable public garden in Chelsea, took place on 11 May 1796. The Adelphi was a residential development built by the Adam brothers in 1768. JA and JQA stayed there briefly in Oct. 1783, as did AA and AA2 in July 1784, and JQA had lodgings there during his residence in London in 1796. After their marriage, JQA and LCA lived with the Johnsons until 2 Sept. 1797, when they returned to lodgings at the Adelphi. They were joined by the Johnsons on 4 Sept., prior to the Johnsons' departure for America on 9 September. On 7 Sept. JQA and LCA moved into a furnished house at No. 8, the Adelphi Buildings, which they rented at four guineas a week until leaving for Berlin (D/JQA/24, 11 May 1796, 1, 2, 7, 9 Sept. 1797, APM Reel 27; Mrs. Evelyn Cecil, *London Parks and Gardens*, London, 1907, p. 315–317; JA, *D&A*, 3:148–149; JA, *Papers*, 15:313, note 1; *AFC*, 6:173, note 4).

remainder of the evening— On our way home apologies were made and accepted but if lovers quarrels are a renewal of love they also leave a sting behind which however apparently healed reopens on every trivial occasion; and the smart frequently felt inspires the mind with a secret and unknown dread of something hidden beneath the rosy wreath of love from which we would in vain turn our thoughts; but which like the faint sunbeams through a dense fog only produce a momentary gleam of light to make the darkness which surrounds us still more impenetrable. Such is the obscurity which envelops a young mind under the influence of a first affection; the momentary flashes of reason which lead us to look to futurity are too evanescent to light us on our way, and only produce those weak and imperfect presentiments which inspire fear of some unknown and overhanging evil without guiding to the point by which the danger threatens— Thus it was with me there was a sense of unnecessary harshness and severity of character presented to my view which often led me to fear something I knew not what, and cast a damp upon my natural spirits which I never overcame— I loved with all the affection of a warm and untried heart, and the trials I underwent in the disatisfaction of a sister with whom I had always lived in love and harmony, taught me to reflect and to judge myself with sincerity and I often thought all had not been towards her as I could have wished— The time arrived for Mr. Adamss departure to Holland and he took leave of me stating that our engagement was for an indefinite term and he could name no period at which our marriage would probably take place: and desired that I would correspond with him. He recommended to me during his absence to attend to the improvement of my mind, and laid down a course of study for me until we met, which might be in one year or in seven— I urged him to give me a right to his name before he left me as I always had a horror of the banter and jests to which a young woman is exposed who is known to be engaged; and wish'd that he would have the marriage take place just before he left the house and leave me at my fathers, for I knew no happiness out of his house— You will smile my children and think this very romantic but I had the idea in my head that as the principal reason assign'd for our marriage not taking place was the then state of Holland, that as soon as things in that Country were sufficiently settled I could have join'd my husband without impropriety, and not have had the constant dread on my mind of being obliged to accompany my father to America, and thus add to the difficulty and lengthen the distance which was already between us.[61] I dwell on all these perticulars because however innocent my conduct and my thoughts; circumstances arose in the course of ~~two years~~ a few Months which gave a colour to every incident which blighted all my after happiness; and gave a cast to my mind and character which amounted almost at times to a derangement of understanding— I shall never forget the anxiety with which I awaited a letter from Mr. Adams and the terror which assailed me at the idea of answering it.— I felt my folly and my insignificance with a degree of inexpressible mortification and I vainly endeavoured to write. My officious governess however undertook to correct my letters and to give them such a tournure as she thought would be most elegant— It is true I was not young enough to need such assistance, but never having had a correspondent and at school having always undergone this process, I was too much afraid of trusting to my own performance to venture to write any thing without her approbation—[62] Our correspondence once begun was continued very steadily; but although I counted the hours that must elapse ere letters could arrive, when they came they oftener caused me the most undefined and uneasy sensations than pleasure, and I faded in health and appearance so rapidly that my father became alarmed and without my knowledge in the fullness of his affection and earnest anxiety for my happiness, sat down and wrote a letter to Mr. A. in which he represented my situation; and offered as he had business in holland which required his attention to go over himself with me and my Mother, that we might be married and I be restored to health and happiness— His intention was to have left England altogether to return to his own Country I never saw this

[61] JQA gave as the reason for the marriage's postponement the uncertainty of his employment and his inability to support a family. When JQA's appointment to Portugal was announced, he and LCA made plans to marry so that LCA could accompany him to Lisbon, provided that JQA could travel via London. JQA's departure was repeatedly postponed, and Johnson planned to move his family from London to America in March 1797. As 1796 drew to a close, the possibility faded of the marriage taking place before the Johnsons left (Joshua Johnson to JQA, 26 May 1797; JQA to Joshua Johnson, 9 Nov. 1796, 12 May 1797; LCA to JQA, 28 Aug. 1796; JQA to LCA, 2 June, 12 Oct., 12, 21 Nov., all Adams Papers). See also Margery M. Heffron, "'A Fine Romance': The Courtship Correspondence between Louisa Catherine Johnson and John Quincy Adams," *NEQ*, 83:200–218 (June 2010).

[62] Between 2 June 1796 and 6 June 1797, JQA and LCA exchanged 73 letters that survive. LCA's letters of 4, 24, and 25 July 1796 were brief, casual, and written in a childish hand. Her subsequent letters were longer, the penmanship more mature, and the language more mannered. Except for the angry letter of 17 Jan. 1797, for which see Record, note 63, below, they were affectionate. JQA's letters were lengthy. They gave few details of his official business but spoke lovingly of his hopes for their future. He occasionally offered advice but then apologized for doing so (all Adams Papers).

letter but I so well know my beloved fathers heart and principles that I am perfectly convinced it was written under the impulse of the most honourable feelings; and if he overstep'd the most rigid bounds of delicacy, it was only occasioned by those best of all human feelings the ardent hope of promoting the happiness of a child so dear to him— By return of Mail he received an answer so severe, so cold and so peremptory, that his feelings were bitterly wounded and all the pride of my nature was roused. I adored my father and I was proud— For the first time I gave way to my feelings and I wrote without assistance. I scorn'd the trammels I had borne with for I felt all and more than I could say—[63] so many many years have elapsed since that period that I have forgotten how the matter terminated but once more every thing went smooth— At the time these events took place I was utterly unsuspicious of evil, and every appearance as I have long since learnt was against me. My prospects in life appeared so fair I never dreamt of any thing that could arise to give a colour to improper motives, and I went on in the path I had adopted with all the guiless simplicity of unsuspecting and fearless youth— I had attain'd to the age of twenty but in knowledge of the world I was not fifteen— My husband was the first and only man with whom I was ever left alone or who ever dared to take a liberty with me and *he* never till after our engagement was sanction'd by my parents— If there is any thing to be proud of in such a boast I can swear before the living God that I came pure and virtuous to his arms, and that to this hour I have remained so; and that though the scorpion tongue of political slander assailed me ere I had been a wife a year; my Sons may look up with proud and unsullied honour to the mother who bore them who as far as chastity goes was pure as the azure of an unclouded sky. This is no boast as 'tis the boast of

[63] On 29 Nov. 1796 LCA wrote to JQA that she was going to ask her father to sail from London to America via Holland. On 20 Dec. JQA responded, "Although it is one of the warmest wishes of my heart to see you, yet I should in this case enjoy that satisfaction for so short a time, the bitterness of a new separation would be so severely renewed . . . that the pleasure of a short and transient meeting cannot even in a lover's calculation be put in a balance against the obstacles to your design." He also noted that a wedding in Holland was not feasible. In her response on 17 Jan. 1797, LCA denied having hoped for anything more than "the satisfaction of meeting once more, which satisfaction I fondly and foolishly imagined would have been mutual." Before their disagreement was resolved, JQA wrote on 31 Jan. that Joshua Johnson had written to him "and as plainly hinted to me, that it was with the view which I had inferred from your former letter." Although Johnson's letter to JQA of 16 Dec. 1796 mentions a possible family visit to The Hague, no letter with a more specific reference to the purpose of the visit has been found. By 20 Jan. 1797 LCA declared JQA once more "the tender and affectionate friend I had always found you" (all Adams Papers).

thousands of my sex— I had nothing to resist, I was without temptation— I lived during the time of my engagement or rather a part of it at Clapham Common in a very small house which my father rented expressly for me in a very retired way devoting myself to such studies as I hoped would lessen the immense distance which existed in point of mind and talents between myself and my future husband— and the only acquaintance I encouraged was that of M[rs] Falconet and her sister who lived about a quarter of a mile from my residence and whose society was delightful—[64] She had a large family of lovely children and lived very handsomely, at this time she was confined to her house in consequence of having been overturned in her carriage and seriously injured one of her limbs— Many evenings I passed in her bedroom in lively conversation more pleased and amused than if I had been in the most splendid ballroom— My friends from town used to visit me two or three times a week; and when ever my father and mother used to dine with me they would send provisions early in the morning that I might not be put to the trouble of seeking for them in the Country— Our servant Celia and a young girl were the only servants I had I was therefore often obliged to assist in preparing the lighter articles of our fare especially when I wish'd to exhibit my talents as a housekeeper to my delighted parents How often have I since thought that all this was kindly done with a view to prepare me for the change in my situation, and to familierize me with the cares and the expences of an establishment, that my awkwardness might not shock my husband after our marriage—but of what avail is care, precaution, or foresight against circumstances which break upon us with a force which nothing can controul; nothing can prevent— man is linked to man by a chain so mighty that he boasts in vain of his proud independence; alone he is nothing but a helpless animal, and in the world among his fellow creatures like a shuttlecock tossed to and fro not by his own volition, but by the impetus which is given to him by the multitude in which he happens to turn— A crafty and a subtle man will therefore make his way better than a good one; because he is ever on the watch to follow the current of prosperity while a good man using the best of

[64] Clapham Common was a parklike area of 220 acres in south London surrounded by the homes of prosperous city residents. On 5 July 1796 Joshua Johnson wrote to JQA that he had "taken Lodgeing at Clapham & the greater part of the Family is their, indeed I have only M[rs.] Johnson, Nancy & Caroline at home" (Adams Papers). LCA referred to her stay in Clapham, the family's summer residence, as her "retirement" (J. J. Sexby, *The Municipal Parks, Gardens, and Open Spaces of London,* London, 1905, p. 95–99; LCA to JQA, 28 Aug. 1796, Adams Papers).

his faculties for the benefit of his fellow creatures, is unconsciously drawn into the vortex of their vilainies, and becomes the dupe of his own benevolence and his own sincerity– After a painful summer I return'd to town with my youngest sisters and Miss Henning and there resumed my usual mode of living and my accustomed occupations– Mr Adams's election to the Presidency had been decided in the month of December but it was sometime before we hear'd the news of the event and much debating used to take place in our family concerning the event opinions and wishes were divided on the subject– Mr. Hall the late Sheriffe was staunch for the northern Candidate but the general leaning was towards Mr Jefferson–[65] My father was from Maryland then considered quite a southern state and his politicks and his prejudices were all of the same cast of character– It was during the Spring that Mr Adams wrote to announce his appointment to Lisbon and to request that I would be ready to receive him that our Nuptials must take place immediately after his arrival as he could only spare a few days to me and my family as he must proceed to his post without losing any time[66] Several letters came on the same subject and my Mother began to prepare my wedding finery which was all got ready for the expected occasion. weeks rolled on however without any further intelligence and considering it as a false alarm every thing was locked up and all the preparations concealed with as much care as if I had committed some crime in having made them. Time ran on until July when Mr A again wrote to beg my father to procure him a passage on board some vessel bound to Lisbon, and repeating his desire that he might not be detained in London–[67] My father and I understood him literally and he accordingly fitted up a small vessel of his own with every thing that could make us comfortable to take us to Portugal whenever it suited Mr. Adams's convenience. He arrived and owing to some trifling accident on his route could not come to see me until the day after when I met him with feelings of mortified affection more bitter than I could express; and with a dread at the idea of my

[65] Joseph Hall (1761–1848), Harvard 1781, of Boston was sheriff and judge of Suffolk County (James Spear Loring, *The Hundred Boston Orators*, 3d edn., Boston, 1854, p. 307).

[66] JQA received his commission as U.S. minister plenipotentiary to Portugal on 9 April 1797 (D/JQA/23, APM Reel 26).

[67] JQA wrote to Joshua Johnson on 13 Sept. 1796, "I must expect to take a Water passage from England.– In an English vessel I cannot go. I must therefore sollicit you to have the goodness to let me know whether there is any direct trade between England and Lisbon in American or any other neutral vessels, and whether it is probable I might find it practicable to embark in the course of the winter or spring ensuing in such a vessel" (Adams Papers).

3. CATHERINE NUTH JOHNSON, BY EDWARD SAVAGE, CA. 1793
See page x

4. JOSHUA JOHNSON, BY EDWARD SAVAGE, CA. 1793

See page x

immediate parting with my parents that almost broke my heart. Under all the impressions so strongly received by his Letters and wishing that some days after I became a wife might be passed with a mother from whom I had never been separated; when he asked me to fix a day for our marriage I named a very early one without hesitation; naturally supposing that it was what he most desired.[68] I dwell on the topic my Sons to show how the most simple acts may bear upon future events even when we cannot look into futurity, or in any way imagine the good or bad fortune which may be about to assail us— At this moment every thing seemed to combine to make my prospects brilliant— My father had entered into the most favorable arrangements with his creditors and was allowed to fit out a Vessel to convey his family home; he was to return in two years to England to wind up all the business of the house, and he expected to give each of his children a small fortune and to retire himself upon a handsome property without owing any man a shilling— We became acquainted with Mr T B. A— who accompanied his brother who soon won the hearts of all the family. On the Wednesday 26 of July 1797 I became a bride under as every body thought the happiest auspices— I must here observe that my mother expressed her surprize at my having fixed so early a day and rebuked me for not having consulted her; and I felt ashamed at the idea of being thought so indelicate the more so as it seemed to me upon reflection that Mr. A appeared surprized also—[69] Two days I think it was before I was married we went on board the Vessel to see our accomodations and I think soon after Mr. A. received Letters not to go but to wait for further orders and the Vessel sailed without us— Two happy weeks passed swiftly away, when suddenly I was overwhelm'd by a blow that prostrated my pride my pretensions I will say my happiness for ever— The man who had pretended to be my fathers best friend, in whom he had confided his trust for five and twenty years,

[68] JQA sailed from The Hague on 9 July 1797 and arrived in England on the 11th. He was detained because of wartime port regulations and did not reach London until the next day. He arrived at Osborne's Hotel at five o'clock in the afternoon of 12 July "and retired at an early hour." He went to the Johnsons' home the next morning. On 13 July he noted in his Diary, "Went down this morning to Mr Johnson's. . . . Found my friends there, and particularly my best friend, well" (D/JQA/24, APM Reel 27).

[69] On 21 July 1797 JQA told Joshua Johnson of "Arrangements relating to his Affairs and for my marriage." Three days later, JQA acquired a marriage license, and on 26 July, "I was married to Louisa Catherine Johnson, by John Hewlett at the Parish Church All Hallows." On 28 July JQA and LCA wrote to AA and JA to announce their marriage (D/JQA/23, APM Reel 26; Adams Papers).

brought the heaviest calamity on his head and stamp'd a wound upon that heart and that honour, which through life had been proverbial for rectitude— He was obliged to stop payment for the sum of *five hundred pounds* in consequence of the failure of a remittance, and the non arrival of a large East India ship, and to quit the Country with his family in a very different manner and under very different circumstances than he had ever expected—[70] Conceive my Dear Sons the shock I underwent, every appearance was against me; actions proceeding from the most innocent causes looked like deliberate plans to deceive; and I felt that all the honest pride of my soul was laid low for ever— I removed to your fathers lodging and too forcibly learnt that I had forfeited all that could give me consequence in my husbands esteem or in my own mind— No vindication could be offered on my part; appearances were too much against me; and all I could do was to mourn over that which could never be undone and which could only be aggravated by any effort to prove its falsity— In this I will say extremity of affliction; my mind seem'd rapidly to grow old and the bitter knowledge of real life was acquired in almost all its varied forms of agony and mortification— Never have I, never can I blame Mr. Adams for his feelings on this trying occasion, for I felt that thus situated my impressions would have been too strong to admit of either doubt or paliation; for he found himself exposed to a situation full of difficulties and as he thought disgrace and utter disappointment: from that hour all confidence was destroyed for ever in me and mine—[71] My marriage was not gay as acquaintance was very limitted; but the very exertions my poor father made to do us honour were afterwards set down to shameful extravagance— Mr. R King was then Minister in London but had left Town on a journey to Wales. I think he did not return until after my family had left England. He was so good so friendly had he been near perhaps this overwhelming ruin had been spared and I save from the pursuit of a phantom which has unceasingly followed me through every stage of life and which will follow me until the heart then so deeply wounded has ceased to throb—[72]

[70] The Johnsons sailed for America on 9 Sept. 1797 on the *Holland,* arriving at Georgetown, D.C., on 25 Nov. (*Alexandria Advertiser,* 27 Nov.; D/JQA/24, 9 Sept., APM Reel 27).

[71] In his Diary for 9 Oct. 1797 JQA noted, "Find the affairs of Mr: J. more & more adverse— This trial is a strong one—more so indeed than I expected—and I expected it would be strong.— I have done my duty—rigorous, inflexible duty, and no Event whatsoever shall convince me that by pursuing a more interested, and less faithful course, I should have been rewarded with better success" (D/JQA/24, APM Reel 27).

[72] Rufus King (1755–1827), who had represented Massachusetts in the Continental Con-

Never never as long as sense shall last shall I forget the worse than broken-hearted look of my adored father the last Eveng he passed with me in my own house: my poor Mother too I was not aware that they were to leave me so soon; but ere morning broke they had already left that Country in which all his children were born, and in which he had so long lived honoured and respected— When I arose and found them gone I was the most forlorn miserable wretch that the Sun ever smiled upon— I loved your father with the utmost sincerity but I learnt too quickly in spite of his utmost exertions, & how low I was sunk in his estimation without a hope of ever recovering the standing which was irreparably lost. It was strict and rigid justice and I had nothing to complain of— Such was my honey moon. I was found to be incompetent to the management of the family concerns: and they were put into the hands of Mr Whitcomb—[73] Every rap at the door made me tremble as every rap produced a dun to my father; and to me they appealed for payment believing that my father had left the means with me to settle them: and to crown my sufferings a Letter of the most barbarously insulting character was put in to my hands calling on my husband to save my fathers forfeited honour. In the midst of such really heavy afflictions I had no one to turn to but Mrs. Court an old friend of my family who by her unwearied kindness saved me from despair. Your Uncle Tom was kind and affectionate and to him I opened my heart and assured him of perfect innocence. As soon as Mr. King returned he came to see me and from him and his Lady I received all the consolation that could be offered under such circumstances— Until we quitted England my time was chiefly spent at Mrs. Courts when I could go out; but my Health was dreadfully impaired and I was in a situation in which there was little probability that it would mend— Two days after my fathers departure the fatal remittance arrived and the villain Maitland bribed the bookeeper in my fathers Counting house to give it to him which he did and thus took the sum which had been destined to settle all my fathers current debts; every one of which it would cover—[74] Thus things rolled on until our destination was changed and we were ordered to berlin—[75] Mr. Murdoch

gress and New York in the U.S. Senate, served as U.S. minister to Great Britain from 1796 to 1803 and again from 1825 to 1826. In 1786 he married Mary Alsop, the daughter of a wealthy New York merchant (*Biog. Dir. Cong.*; *DAB*).

[73] For Tilly Whitcomb, JQA's servant, see *AFC*, 10:210.

[74] Fludyer, Maitland & Company was one of the creditors of Wallace, Johnson & Muir (Papenfuse, *Pursuit of Profit*, p. 229).

[75] In June 1797 JA, now the U.S. president, commissioned JQA to go to Berlin, instead of

came often to see me but his visits only added to my grief— At my departure from London I was obliged to leave the old servant Celia whom I had taken into my service and she was so ungrateful that to add to all the pangs I endured she showered down every horrible imprecation upon my devoted head until I was seated in the Post chaise in which we drove away.— Owing to a long detention at the Duke of Portlands we did not reach Gravesend until after the Vessel had sailed and though late in the Evening we got into a boat and rowed some miles down the river to overtake her and I got on board just in Season to get to bed being very sick[76]—Here we began to breathe more freely— objects of novelty to me occupied my attention and the affectionate kindness of your father and Uncle once more cheered my drooping spirits and warm'd my sinking heart into something like hope. Amid all my distresses it was delightful to me to think I had incurred no new obligation for to my knowledge not a shilling was ever paid on mine or my father's account therefore the injury which Mr. A received by his marriage with me was the loss of the five thousand pound which my father had intended to give me and the having connected himself with a ruined house— When I first engaged myself to Mr. Adams I think my father had not lent his name to the speculation into which Mr. Maitland had plunged at any rate he had entered into no responsibility therefore their could have been no intention on his part of palming his daughter upon any one and his misfortunes were as unexpected as they were sudden— Never as long as I have being will I cease to defend your Grandfathers character from the foul aspersions of those who have accused him and no sense of after obligation can ever obliterate the pain I have endured when I have been forced to hear them—

We had embarked in a Danish Ship which fortunately for us was heavy enough to stand the tremendous storm which assailed and in which the Packet was nearly lost the Passengers being obliged to pump the Vessel during the whole of the voyage. Our Bark weathered the tempest and we crept on with a snails pace and after eight days hard sailling reach'd the port of Hamburg—[77] Our stores were excellent and we at least had the privilege of living well as far as

Lisbon, to negotiate a new commercial treaty with Prussia. JQA received notification of his new commission on 18 July (JA, *D&A,* 3:229; D/JQA/24, APM Reel 27).

[76] LCA was pregnant.

[77] JQA and LCA sailed on the *Frans,* Capt. Nommen Paulsen. The ship departed on 17 Oct.; JQA and LCA joined it at Gravesend on 18 Oct., arriving on 26 Oct. in Hamburg, where they stayed at the King of England Hotel (D/JQA/24, 30 Sept., 17, 18, 26 Oct., APM Reel 27).

good eating goes— Every Evening and morning the Crew were rung to prayers and it was in this vessel that I first saw in practice the dutch eoconomy in the use of Sugar. There was a piece of white sugar Candy tied to a string which was passed alternately to each who suked it and then sipped the tea. We took up our residence at Hamburg for a week or ten days having to prepare our Carriage for the journey and here I became acquainted with Sam Williams his brother Frank and Mr. Ross.— We received several visits I went once to the Theatre and I passed the day at Mr David Parish'es then English Consul and immensely wealthy— His Country house was very prettily situated on the banks of the Elbe and both he and his wife were kind and hospitable scotch people whose manners were such as to make you feel like old acquaintance after a visit of half an hour— Hamburg is a dreery looking City the Streets very narrow and the houses like described by travellers in Edingburg of many stories high— They are dirty and gloomy and the narrow canals which intersect some of the streets have a dirty gloomy and disagreeable appearance— One the peculiarities which struck the most unpleasantly was the spouts which lead from the tops of the houses to carry of the water as they nearly meet in the centre of the street the rain is conducted in distinct channels from the Roofs and produces a continuation of streams which falling from such an elevation cause a horrible sound of rushing waters which look at the same time like a threatening deluge— Our time passed agreeably enough and we left Hamburg in company with Mr S Williams Mr. Ross and the party who commenced the journey from England[78] What creatures of prejudice and circumstance we are and how seriously trifles sometimes affect us— You will laugh at me as much as I now laugh at myself but when my liveried footman was ordered to take a seat in my Carriage with me I felt as if the greatest insult had been offered to me and set it down as another consequence of the downfal of my family— An American can never understand the sensation of mortified pride which I endured but an Englishman would blaze at the idea and you must remember that even my father had never seen America since she had become a Republick Our journey was

[78] JQA and LCA were accompanied by Tilly Whitcomb and TBA (D/JQA/24, 18, 26 Oct. 1797, APM Reel 27). Samuel Williams (1760–1841) was the U.S. consul in Hamburg, 1797–1798, and became consul in London in 1798 (*Historical Index to the Pickering Papers*, MHS, *Colls.*, 6th ser., 8:555 [1896]). Charles Ross (1772–1817) was the only son of John Ross, a Philadelphia merchant, and Clementina Cruikshank ("Memoir of John Ross, Merchant, of Philadelphia," *PMHB*, 23:78, 84 [1899]; Jean Gordon Lee, *Philadelphians and the China Trade, 1784–1844*, Phila., 1984, p. 61).

dreadful the accomodations as bad as possible and the roads such as to make our Carriage a very dangerous conveyance and we were very thankful when we arrived at the beautiful City of Berlin as we had not met with one object of interest on the route– Berlin is a beautiful City and as we took up our residence at the most fashionable hotel in the Linden Strasse we had a constant opportunity of seeing the best part of this famed City–[79] The fatigue trouble anxiety of mind and sea sickness in the very delicate state in which I left London brought on a very serious illness and my life was despaired of for sometime It is almost impossible to imagine a situation more truly distressing for a woman of refinement and delicacy than the one into which I was thrown– Just arrived in a foreign land only three months married having suffered in that short space of time every calamity through others which can afflict the human heart excpting the pang inflicted by death thrown into the society and on the protection of young men without a female friend but a young servant girl of seventeen who was as wretched as myself and lying in the most helpless condition from sickness and disappointment with every sense of delicacy shocked by the disgusting and to me indecent manners of the people who attended me and in a noisy and publick Hotel. Never before having been parted from a father and Mother to whom I had been a darling child and sick unto death!!! An English Physician was sent for and this I believe saved my worthless life– As I lay gasping on my rude bed of agony after eleven days of dreadful anguish I heard M^r T B. A come into the room and ask if I was dead.– As it was reported in the house that I had expired– This was a new and a cruel scene for M^r. Adams and called forth all his kindness and most gratefully do I remember his tenderness and his affection during a trial so severe– I recovered my health very slowly and I think (as I write from memory without notes or help) it was three long Months that elapsed ere I was able to take that rank in society to which I was entitled– In that period no ~~one~~ female visited me and though I constantly heard of M^rs. Brown and her daughters as the most amiable good people still they never came near me.–[80] During this Interval the King had died

[79] They arrived in Berlin on 7 Nov. 1797 and stayed at "the Golden Sun, or Hôtel de Russie" (D/JQA/23, APM Reel 26).

[80] JQA reported that LCA became ill on 10 Nov. 1797. The next day he sent for Dr. Charles Brown, a British physician who had practiced in Russia and London before settling in Prussia. At Brown's request, Dr. Ribke, a professor, was also called in. LCA's ailments persisted, with occasional improvements, until December (D/JQA/23, APM Reel 26; Cross, *Banks of the Neva*, p. 155–156).

the present King ascended his throne his lovely Queen had been crown'd and Mr Adams and his brother had been presented at Court—[81] We removed from the Hotel to a small House at the Brandenburg Gate. Were I writing a book of travels I should certainly endeavour to describe this splendid object which may be termed the pride of Berlin but as it is I will only say that I had taste enough to admire it although I knew nothing of its architectural proportions— Immediately under my Windows was the Guard room and few days nay even hours passed without my ears being assailed and my eyes shocked by the screams and blows which were bestowed on the soldiers who inhabited them, and my weak nerves were not strengthen'd by the constant repetition of this scene of suffering.— My husband was now launched into the sea of dessippation which followed the coronation and it was only owing to the kindness of Mr. T. B. Adams that my lonely hours were cheered by the pleasure of society—[82] We kept no Carriage and as I have already said no female had yet paid me a visit— At last however I suppose from curiosity Miss Dorville afterwards the Wife of Mr. Jackson came to see me and she was immediately by the Countess Pauline Neale to whom I owe all the comfort and all the respect I ever enjoyed during my residence in that Country.[83] Expressing my astonishment to her at the difficulty I found in making acquaintance she told me it was because I

[81] Frederick William II (1744–1797), who had married his second wife, Frederica Louise of Hesse-Darmstadt (1751–1805), in 1769, died on 16 November. He was succeeded by his oldest son Frederick William III (1770–1840). JQA had presented his credentials on 9 Nov. but, because of the king's illness and subsequent death, was not presented to Frederick William III and the dowager queen until 5 Dec. (Princess Louise, *Forty-five Years,* p. 437–439; D/JQA/24, 9, 16 Nov., 5 Dec., APM Reel 27).

[82] On 29 Nov. JQA and LCA rented lodgings at Captain Stanckar's house at the Brandenburg Gate, moving in on 2 December. The house was adjacent to the palace, the guardhouse, and the Tiergarten, a park that extended from the gate to Charlottenburg. On 27 March 1798 they engaged an apartment from a Mr. Cohen at the corner of Friedrichstrasse and Behrenstrasse to which they would move in June. The Behrenstrasse was home to many of the capital's diplomats. JQA spent his time attending court functions, reading, and visiting the casino (D/JQA/24, APM Reel 27; Karl Baedeker, *Berlin and Its Environs,* 3d edn., Leipzig, 1908, p. 53, 55, 175).

[83] Miss Dorville was the daughter of Louis de Dorville, master of ceremonies to Queen Elisabeth Christine, the first wife of Frederick William II. In 1802 she married Francis James Jackson (1770–1814), the British minister plenipotentiary to Berlin, 1802–1806, and minister plenipotentiary to Washington, 1809–1811 (TBA, *Journal, 1798,* p. 12; *DNB*, entry on Jackson; *Ann. Register*, 1803, p. 479).

Pauline Néale (1779–ca. 1869) was maid of honor to Queen Louise of Prussia (1776–1810), the wife of Frederick William III. Her father, Ferdinand (1755–1828), had been chamberlain and grand cupbearer of the king of Prussia; her mother, born Josephine von Keller, was grand mistress of the household to Princess Ferdinand (*The Correspondence of Priscilla, Countess of Westmorland,* ed. Rose Weigall, N.Y., 1909, p. 104; *The Letters of Lady Burghersh,* ed. Rose Weigall, London, 1893, p. 49; Princess Louise, *Forty-five Years,* p. 430–431).

had not been presented and that the Queen had said unless I was presented soon that she should suppose I was not married— This was the first intimation I had had of the necessity Mr Adams never having suggested the propriety and I supposing in the then state of my feelings that it was owing to his mortification at his marriage that he did not wish to take me out— This however was a new and bitter stroke and I resolved to appear in publick— A party was made to the Theatre the first Even^g. that the Sovereigns went there and I, poor I, as timid as a hare became an object of general attention— Never shall I forget with what inexpressible admiration I saw the Queen of Queens—[84] In her every thing was combined that can shed loveliness on female beauty— Grace affability sweetness amiability and the most irrisistable beauty formed a combination of loveliness to which no language can do justice and which the painters art never could depict— Years have elapsed and I still see her in my minds eye moving in all the majesty of youthful royalty and followed by the admiring gaze of thousands who thought themselves blessed if they could catch a passing smile or have a glance of her beautiful form.— This may be enthusiasm but if it is it is the honest enthusiasm of grateful affection for kindness received at the hands of this angel which can never be obliterated from my recollection while the life blood animates my frame.— Much have I seen in the lapse of fifty years which have dragg'd over my weary head but never before or since has an object so unique met my sight— Arrangements were immediately made for my presentation and I waited on the Marquise Parella to request her to introduce me and to patronize me on my first entrance into society—[85] My acquaintance Miss Dorville was one of the court belles and at that time very celebrated as a beauty tho' not for discretion— I understood from M^rs. & the Miss Browns who now called on me that this young Lady had given a most curious account of my person and manners and represented me as having a face like a horse and being very ugly— This was however no disadvantage to me as people being prepared to see something very disagreeable were more inclined to be indulgent when they found me pretty much upon a par with my neighbours— Madame Parella according to appointment carried me to pay visits to all the Grande Gouvernates of the different Courts which then con-

[84] Queen Louise of Prussia.

[85] Marquise Parella was the wife of the Sardinian minister to Prussia, Marquis Provana de Parella di San Martino (*Repertorium*, 3:397; TBA, *Journal*, 1798, p. 10).

sisted of the Queens the Queen dowager Princess Henry's Princess Ferdinands Princess Louis Princess Radzivils and the Princess of Orange. Cards were left at all the great houses and among the Corps Diplomatique[86] My good little friend the Countess Neale gave me instructions concerning the dress and I was finally prepared for the eventful day— It was on a Sunday Eveng. that I was appointed to be at the Palace I think at about seven o'clock when I was usherred into the private apartments of her Majesty— My extreme debility and the terror incident to the novelty of my situation and the formidable appearance of Madame Voss in her great hoop and her tall upright person had such an effect upon me that I could not proceed as my knees seemed to refuse their Office and I trembled from head to foot—[87] The Queen perceiving my great embarrassment and pitying my situation waived all ettiquette and came forward to speak to me kindly telling me how much she had been interested for my situation which she had heard of very fully from my physician She asked me many questions in the most soothing tones and then observing my weakness and that I looked pale kindly dismissed me saying she hoped to see me again in the evening on which I curtsied and retired— I accompanied Madame Parella to the drawing room and was there presented to all the Corps diplomatique— I was delighted to return to Mr Adams and his brother from whom I had been separated as they were my world and I felt utterly lost when without them— When the Queen appeared and the circle was formed she again spoke most kindly to me and I was for-

[86] Princess Henry was Wilhelmina of Hesse-Cassel (1726–1808), the estranged wife of Prince Frederick Henry Louis (1726–1802) and great aunt of Frederick William III. Princess Ferdinand was Louise of Brandenburg-Schwedt (1738–1820), wife of Prince August Ferdinand (1730–1813) and also great aunt of the king. Princess Louis was Frederica Sophia Carolina of Mecklenburg-Strelitz (1778–1842), widow of Prince Louis Charles and sister of the queen. Princess Radziwill was Frederica Dorothea Louise Philippine (1770–1836), also known as Princess Louise, wife of Prince Anton Radziwill (1775–1833), a Polish-Lithuanian aristocrat; she was the daughter of Prince and Princess Ferdinand. The Princess of Orange was Frederika Sophia Wilhelmina (1751–1820), wife of William V, Prince of Orange (1748–1806), and aunt of Frederick William III (Princess Louise, *Forty-five Years*, p. 427, 432–433, 437, 438, 440, 441; O'Brien, *Mrs. Adams*, p. 148–151, 159). For portraits of the Prince and Princess of Orange, see JA, *Papers*, 12:442, 444.

LCA had a private audience with the queen on 21 Jan. and with the dowager queen two days later. She was presented to Princess Henry on 29 Jan. (D/JQA/24, APM Reel 27).

[87] The apartments were in the Stadtschloss, the royal palace. Sophie Marie, Countess von Voss (b. 1729), widow of John Ernest von Voss, had become the *grande gouvernante* or *Oberhofmeisterin*—mistress of the royal household—in 1793. She was responsible for supervising matters of etiquette (Sophie Marie, Countess von Voss, *Sixty-Nine Years at the Court of Prussia*, transl. Emily and Agnes Stephenson, 2 vols., London, 1876, 1:3, 179–180; O'Brien, *Mrs. Adams*, p. 146–147).

mally presented to all the Princesses of the Royal family and met with a most kind and friendly reception. To the kind offices of my good D[r] Brown and to my little friend the Countess I was indebted for my reception which was flattering beyond my most sanguine hopes.— The scene was so entirely new to me my senses were perfectly bewildered and when I was invited to stay supper and told that my husband could not stay I was distressed beyond measure. But the Marchioness Parella engaged to take me home and to sit next to me and in this way I was enabled to get through my difficulty— The Queen spoke to me several times during Supper with great sweetness and I was treated generally with the kindest attention— When I got home I had a great deal to tell as the novelty of the scene had exhilarated my spirits to a great degree and I thus afforded great diversion to both the gentlemen to whom these scenes had become quite familiar— From this time I was launch'd in the giddy round of fashionable life as successive invitations followed most of which were orders from the Courts as in strict ettiquette people are not allowed to refuse unless sickness prevents the acceptance At Court I was introduced to the Princess Louis Sister of the Queen but in no respect equal to her though a graceful fine looking woman. To the present Queen of Holland then Princess of Orange who was residing at the Prussian Court in a state of dependence and much beloved and respected. She was very amiable and so domestic it was painful to her to go much into publick She was very tall and so slender that she seem'd to stoop from weakness— Her manners were mild and rather retired. The Princess Louis on the contrary was showy dashing capricious and haughty and was generally more feared than loved— The Queen was excessively fond of her and she at this time possessed great influence with their Majesties— Her establishment was handsome and she held the high rank at Court of the Widow of Prince Louis. Princess Henry was the Aunt of the King and altogether of the old school— She was the wife of the famous Prince Henry but they had not lived together for some years— She was upwards of seventy remarkably stiff and stately in her manners and her suppers to which I was invited every Monday Evening the dullest and most tiresome I ever was at. The company played cards after which there was a Supper consisting of all sorts of meats in great joints and in great abundance very well calculated to produce indigestion— The first time I supped there I was seated opposite to the Princess and next to Lord Granville Levison Gore one of the handsomest men I ever saw and usually celebrated for his taciturnity but on this occasion he was so amused and made so many strange remarks a l'anglaise that I behaved myself quite childishly and with difficulty concealing my gigling from her royal highness who fortunately was to near sighted to observe me.—[88] I now became very intimate with M^rs. Browns family and much attach'd to her daughters Margaret was not handsome but she was a woman of very strong natural powers highly cultivated and improved by a constant intercourse with good society— Isabella was very pretty a dark brunette with less of mind but much more of that feminine softness which makes the charm of woman— Fanny was about twelve years old and as lovely a creature as poets fancy could create. William was the only Son very young very handsome and very wild. There was a friendly warm heart sociability about this family that can never be forgotten by those who had the privilege of visiting in their family and I should be worse than ungrateful if I did not speak of the constant kindness which they showed me during four years that I resided in Berlin. Many and many an hour of happy forgetfulness have I passed among them in the true and sincere enjoyment of their kind affection and never shall I forget a friendship so valuable and soothing to a young creature so new to the world and thrown thus helpless upon the kindness of strangers— My newness must have astonish'd them and I often think now I must have passed among them for a fool. In this family I was thrown entirely into English society and as it was the only society natural to me it was the only society I liked— I was invited to sup at Princess Ferdinands another Aunt of the King. She received me with extraordinary kindness which I attributed entirely to my good friend Countess Pauline Neale and there first met the Landgravine of Hesse Cassel Sister of the Princess she invited me to sit with her at her work Table and took great notice of me. The Princess was a very fine looking woman tho' not so handsome as her Sister and her manners were truly german sometimes so coarse that I used to blush with astonishment at what I then thought her want of delicacy— While I was seated by her she called up her Son in law the Prince Antoine Radsivil and introduced him to me and then turn'd to him speaking very loud and said she is very pretty look at her which surprized me so much I blushed scarlet when to add to my confusion she asked me

[88] Lord Granville Leveson Gower, 1st Earl Granville (1773–1846), a British diplomat, was in Berlin from early January to mid-March 1798 as special ambassador to congratulate the new king on his accession (*DNB*; *Lord Granville Leveson Gower, Private Correspondence 1781 to 1821*, ed. Castalia, Countess Granville, 2 vols., London, 1916, 1:144, 192).

what I blushed for and if I had never been told so before? Had I been accustomed to the freedom of a court this would have appeared as a matter of course but it occasioned to me a degree of embarrassment almost insupportable and I felt as if every eye in the room was fixed on me to see how I behaved— She made her card party after having asked me a number of curious questions such as if my husband loved me very much &c and I passed the remainder of the evening very pleasantly— The Princess Louisa was a woman of much finer manners and more cultivated mind than her Mother and very Lady like and agreeable. She was not handsome and was married to a very handsome man a Polish Prince who it was said was seven years younger than herself and not remarkable for his fidelity to his Wife—[89] These parties usually ended with a supper which was very gay I think it was at Belle Vue a pretty Country house belonging to the Prince situated in the Park about a mile from the City—[90] The Prince was old and very sickly and not at all a prominent character in his family— At this time I heard of Mr. Adams's attachment to Miss Frazer and I had another cause added to the misfortunes for regretting the marriage.[91] I had made as it appeared impossible for him to view me in any other light than as a person who had known all these impediments and who determined for the sake of what is called a settlement to marry him at the expence of honour truth and happiness—

[89] Philippine Auguste Amalie, a princess of Brandenburg-Schwedt (1745–1800), was the wife of Frederick II, Landgrave of Hesse-Cassel, and the sister of Louise, Princess Ferdinand (Princess Louise, *Forty-five Years,* p. 418).

[90] Bellevue was the home of Prince and Princess Ferdinand (same, p. 75).

[91] Mary Frazier, the daughter of Newburyport merchant Moses Frazier, had been courted by JQA, who years later recalled her in his Diary as "once to me the most beautiful and most beloved of her sex," explaining that he had hoped to marry her, but his father forbade "an unqualified engagement" (JA, *D&A,* 2:39; D/JQA/33, 18 Nov. 1838, APM Reel 36). See also *AFC,* 9:43–44, note 5.

The Adventures of a Nobody

WASHINGTON 1ST. JULY 1840[1]

I was pleased at the receipt of your last Letter my Dear Charles as from a recent one written by Abby I was led to believe that you could not spare time to write to me under the pressure of your business avocations The Letter itself was therefore an agreeable surprize and its tone altogether gratifying being indicative of repose and contentment two things utterly and entirely out of my reach—[2]

[1] This is the first entry of "The Adventures of a Nobody" (M/LCA/6, APM Reel 269), the narrative, mostly in diary form, that LCA began on 1 July 1840. The memoir covers the period from late 1797 through 16 Feb. 1812, during which time JQA served as minister to Prussia; Massachusetts and U.S. senator; Harvard professor of rhetoric and oratory; and minister to Russia. LCA gave birth to her children, saw the United States for the first time, and mourned her father's death.

The memoir comprises 70 loose and irregularly numbered sheets, most with gilded edges. A first set, numbered p. 1–56, consists of 14 sheets, 16" x 10", folded in half lengthwise and written on all four sides, though some sheets have split in half. The second set, numbered p. 57–264, consists of 56 sheets, 16" x 13", similarly folded; again, many of the sheets have split into separate pages. LCA also wrote a second version of Adventures, contained in M/LCA/6, that begins on 24 Jan. 1810 and extends to [*15 Sept.*] 1812. It is written on 6 sheets of paper, 14 3/4" x 9 3/8", watermarked 1842 and folded to 24 unnumbered pages. The editors have noted any additional or clarifying material from the shorter version.

Because LCA wrote Adventures as an autobiographical work, no matter that it is largely in diary form, notes appear at the bottom of the page, not at the end of particular entries. LCA uses datelines in the Adventures manuscript erratically, often to cover a narrative that continues for days or months beyond its starting point, and not always accurately. The editors have not routinely supplied or corrected datelines except in a small number of extraordinary cases, but more accurate and comprehensive dating can often be found in the annotation as well as in the text itself. For more complete and regular dating of the events covered in Adventures, see JQA's Diaries for this period, particularly D/JQA/23–28, APM Reels 26–31.

[2] CFA had written to JQA and LCA on 6 May and 24 June 1840 (both Adams Papers); ABA's letter has not been found. CFA was now LCA and JQA's only surviving child. Following their marriage on 3 Sept. 1829, CFA and ABA settled in a house provided by Peter Chardon Brooks at 3 Hancock Avenue, near the State House on Beacon Hill in Boston. From 1838 their family, which now included four children—LCA2, JQA2, CFA2, and HA—also spent time in a summer house on President's Lane in Quincy. CFA had built the house on land given to him by his father (CFA, *Diary*, 2:439; 3:x; 7:xxi; 8:vii–ix).

CFA's "business avocations" in this period included writing for newspapers and periodicals on political and historical subjects, and particularly on issues related to banking and currency.

My temper is so harrassed and I am I fear so imbued with strange and singular opinions, and surrounded by persons with whom it is decidedly impossible for me to agree, I feel that I am a torment to myself, and a still greater torment to your Father, who bears with me with the patience of Socrates; but who like Socrates glides smoothly on in the course which he has laid out for himself enjoying the turmoil, the very reflection of which is to me perfectly insupportable—[3] Conscious as I am of all his fine qualities, his easy temper, his quiet home habits, and his indefatigable powers of application; I am for ever ashamed of my-self for suffering my heart to crave for some social comforts; some soothing influence to fill up the lagging hours, which at my age in consequence of weakened faculties, and want of *essential* resources; hang with a tedious weight upon my time, and leave me to a too vivid and too painful contemplation of the past: where infancy and youth were fraught with bliss in the bosom of strong and unchanging Parental affection—

The faults of my character have never been corrected, owing to a happy, but alas a visionary education; which have made the disgusting realities of a heartless political life, a source of perpetual disappointment—

It has been asserted that I am inordinately ambitious! In what the evidence of this fact consists, it would puzzle any body to say, if by ambition is meant the thirst for place and mere worldly honours— Of such honours most assuredly as the Wife of your Father, I have had a large share— But such *honours* have never been sought by me; on the contrary they have been purchased at a most *bitter* expence of duty to my children, personal suffering to myself; loss of health and freedom of thought; and with all the cruel and stinging mortification of National pauperism, which most of the Foreign Mis-

He worked assiduously on the family papers, and in 1840 he completed an edition of his grandmother's letters. CFA's law practice was never large, but he was occupied with family business matters. After GWA's death in 1829, JQA transferred to his youngest son the task of managing his financial affairs in Boston, and in Feb. 1832 CFA assumed the additional responsibility of managing his father's Quincy property (Duberman, *CFA*, p. 33–34; CFA, *Diary*, 1:xxxiii; 2:393–394; 3:xxv; 4:249, 447–449; 6:413–415; 7:xvi; 8:279, 383–387).

[3] Among the contentious issues claiming JQA's attention at the time LCA began her memoir were the *Amistad* case, which he would shortly agree to argue before the U.S. Supreme Court on the Africans' behalf; the increasingly rigid imposition of the "gag rule" in the House of Representatives, which he took the lead in opposing; and the disposition by the U.S. Congress of the Smithson bequest, intended "for the increase and diffusion of knowledge among men," a goal JQA feared would be subverted by those who favored the ordinary instruction of youth over research and discovery (Bemis, *JQA*, 2:394–400, 420–422, 503–513).

sions present at the Courts to which they are sent—and the effects of which fall most heavily upon the Women; who dependent upon their Husbands, are obliged to make every sacrifice of pleasure, and often of comfort, that the paltry Salary may prove adequate to the necessities of her husband, to enable him to appear with due *decorum*; to accomplish the Mission on which he is sent!

When I married your Father mine was in prosperity— He was a Commission Merchant in England, and living as the first rate Merchants there live— He had resigned his Commission of Consul which he had received under General Washington, but I think his resignation had not been accepted—[4] I was two and twenty, accustomed to live in luxury without display, and too much beloved by my family for my *good*— Your Father and myself had been engaged for more than a year; and our marriage was made with the approbation of all my immediate friends, and as I believed those of Mr. Adams— He was appointed full Minister to Portugal: our House was taken; his baggage sent thither from Holland, and my Father had fitted up one of his own Ships, in the most comfortable manner for my accomodation, and we were married; but ordered to delay our departure by despatches from America— The consequence of these orders was a change of Station; a reduced Salary to half;[5] and one of those unforeseen misfortunes, which in these times have been so cruelly taught to our Mercantile Community, by the failure of a very small payment; which threw a shade over our brightest prospects, and

[4] While in Nantes, Joshua Johnson had learned that his public duties could be onerous, with reimbursement for expenses by no means certain. Still, in 1790, he agreed to serve as U.S. consul in London. In a 7 Aug. letter to Johnson announcing his nomination and setting out his duties, Secretary of State Thomas Jefferson gave assurance that his outlays for papers and postage would promptly be repaid and that, "as there will be little or no legal emolument annexed to the office of Consul, it is of course not expected that it shall render any expence incumbent on him." In Oct. 1792 an exasperated Johnson wrote to Jefferson asking to be relieved of his post. Johnson complained about the labor and time he had expended without compensation or "even a hint of Approbation," and he protested his lack of authority to collect the information required of him about shipping matters. At Jefferson's urging, Johnson remained at his post, mindful as he was of the hardships that the war in Europe was inflicting on American seamen and commerce (Papenfuse, *Pursuit of Profit*, p. 108; Jefferson, *Papers*, 17:119–120; 24:453–455; 25:415–417; 26:752–753).

[5] LCA is mistaken in her assertion that JQA's salary was reduced by one half. As minister resident to the Netherlands from 1794 to 1797, JQA had received a salary of $4,500. When President George Washington nominated JQA for Portugal, he elevated the diplomatic grade of that post from minister resident to minister plenipotentiary, which carried a salary of $9,000. In Prussia, the post to which JA reassigned him, JQA would also have the rank and receive the salary of minister plenipotentiary (Bemis, *JQA*, 1:50, 83, 87–90; *Repertorium*, 3:468–469).

gave a colour of imprudence to a marriage, formed under the brightest and most promising auspices—

My Father lost his voyage in consequence of the detention of the Vessel— A fortnight after I became a Wife amidst circumstances of the most painful kind I had to part with my parents, from whom I had never been separated, and who had distinguished me as a sort of paragon, in whom they could place every confidence:— I was left to mourn over events over which I had no controul; and under impressions powerful on my own mind, as to the harsh constructions generally adopted by an envious and ill judging world—

Anguish of mind and deep feeling of wounded sensibility, soon reduced me to a state of health which was attended by a total loss of sleep; which with other incidental causes almost unfited me for the exertion of travel; and during the remainder of my stay in London, I was content to abide my fate unknowing, and unknown; except by two old friends on whom I had never depended before—

In Nov$^{br.}$ we left London for Prussia our new Station, and arrived at Gravesend at nine o clock at night; the Vessel had dropped down and we were rowed down in an open Boat, and took possession of our Berths, to suffer the pangs of Sea sickness and all the discomforts of a Danish Merchant Ship; in which we continued eight days in a tremendous heavy *Gale*, in which the British Packet full of Passengers was nearly lost, the Passengers having been obliged to take turns at the Pumps to keep her from sinking—

We arrived safely at Hamburg, and through the constant and polite attention of M$^{r.}$ Williams, and some of his Hamburg Friends, we past a few days very pleasantly; the Peat turf however which they use as Fuel, being almost insupportable in my then situation— From thence we travelled in our own heavy English Carriage, through dreary and terrific roads, and the most miserable night accommodations, until we reached the Fashionable Hotel in Berlin, situated on the Linden Strasse—

Exhausted by fatigue, overcome by the constant danger of an overturn in consequence of the unfitness of our Carriage for the German high ways; with the flurry and agitation to which a Sranger is inevitably exposed in a Country where every object is a novelty, every usage new, and the language itself unfamilliar to the ear, and difficult to the tongue: the mind is disgusted by the singularity of the Scenes thus suddenly exhibited, and disgusted by its, at *first* unpleasant aspects meditates on and recur to the past, ere it has attained a knowledge even of the present, and pines for the loss of those comforts and those associations, which have heretofore formed the seat of happiness and contentment—

Here every thing was different in all its parts, from the english habits— The House was dirty, noisy, and uncomfortable— The Beds miserable; the Table execrable; the manners of the Mrs of the mansion coarse though kind, and between *us*, no means whatever existed of communication, which might have made my situation more agreeable— My voyage had introduced me to some odd Scenes, which had amused me during the Passage and I had there realized the Story of the Sugar Candy tied to a string, and practically passed from mouth to mouth by the Captain and his Men, every morning and Evening while I was on board.

With a mind prepared by reading and conversation with travelled men, I could not at all conceive that people could be so entirely different in their ways; and every moment added to my astonishment, and excited my curiosity beyond expression—

Mr. Adams was immediately engrossed by his public duties; and the three Gentlemen who had accompanied us were too busy in seeing sights, and perambulating the Streets, to be very companionable—[6] On the third day after my arrival, I was siezed with a very serious and dangerous illness; without a Female Friend, and for eleven days of acute suffering, exposed to every inconvenience excepting poverty, or rather *want*; which flesh is heir to.

My husbands time was entirely occupied by his publick avocations. My Nurse, and one of my Physicians did not speak a word that I could understand; but I was fortunate in having the attendance of Dr. Brown, an Englishman, and the then Queens Physician, who bestowed on me a fatherly care, and restored me to life—

During this period the King died— The late King ascended the throne, and my recovery was so slow that I was unable to see the funereal pomps or the Coronation, and its fêtes, which shed a lustre on the Nation in the beauty, loveliness, and accomplishments of the young Queen the popular idol of the day—

We kept no Carriage; and if memory does not fail me it was three month's ere we found a House suited to our Finances— In all this time, I had seen no Female face, but that of the Landlady, and I felt that I was an exile— We took possession of our House or rather apartments over the Guard House at the Brandenburgh Gate; most beautifully situated between that Gate and the Thiergarten or Park;

[6] Samuel Williams, Charles Ross, and TBA.

which to me issolated as I was, became a source of perpetual amusement; although it had its pains and its inconveniences for an invalid; as the drums beat whenever the numerous Members of the Royal Family passed for the Soldiers to present Arms, as well as for the Ambassadors or Officers of distinction— this of course was all day long and very annoying; and then I was exposed to see and hear all the bastinadoes which these poor fellows underwent for the slightest omission of duty— Mr T. B. Adams was the kindest brother and friend; and many a lonely hour has he beguiled, when I was too sickly to go out, and without a single solace to alleviate my situation— After a time Countess Neale, and Miss Dorville came to see me, having heard Dr Brown speak of me with some interest; and the former, with whom I was much pleased, kindly offered to do any thing for me, and expressed a wish to visit me again— A short time after this Mrs. Brown and her daughters accompanied by the young Countess, came to see me; and I was perfectly enchanted to see a family with whom I could speak english— a Second illness of the same nature had again reduced me very much and I was still very weak.

I was sitting at home one morning when Madlle. Dorville was announced. After some indifferent Chat "she asked me when I intended to be presented at Court:" that much surprize was expressed at the delay, and that it was *hinted* that if I was not soon introduced to the Queen, surmises not much to *my* advantage would take root, and make my residence in Berlin very unpleasant— The idea conveyed by this question was so disgusting, I immediately mentioned it to Mr. Adams—and measures were directly adopted, to put things en train for my presentation. As I had never been dressed by a Man Taylor, which my kind friend Countess Neale told me was the Fashion; and as they were enormously expensive, I borrowed a Dress of her and with the assistance of my Maid, I completed a plain but suitable dress for the occasion; and solicited the honour of a presentation of Madame the Marquise di Parella to the Queen, Princesses, and Nobility generally; according to the usage of the Court; it being the ettiquette to be presented by the Wife of a Foreign Minister, and Mr Adams having become very intimate with the Minister from ~~Naples~~ Sardinia— The Queen appointed an Audience half an before her Evening party on the 20 Janry —98— So weak that my knees knocked together as I stood, frightened almost out of my senses, at the idea of entering upon a stage so new; my husband not with me at this presentation, and the Lady who *was* with me a total

Stranger; I felt ready to sink into the floor: but the lovely Queen observing my trepidation, and probably knowing from Dr. Brown the real state of my health; came immediately almost to the door to meet me, and kindly expressed the desire she had had to become acquainted with me, and used the most encouraging expressions to set me at my ease and restore self confidence— She then invited me to her Court Circle, and graciously dismissed me— Madame Parella accompanied me to the Drawing Room, where emboldened by the presence of my husband the introduction to numerous Members of the Royal Family, ~~and to the King~~, which in consequence of the distinction with which your Father had been received; occasioned my reception to be made both flattering, and agreeable— Perhaps something was owed to the description of me, given by my *friend* Miss Dorville, a celebrated *Belle* herself at that time; and known here afterwards as the Wife of English Jackson of notorious memory; who had represented me as having a wretched complexion, a face as long as a *horse*, very lean, and without one good feature of face or person— It is true that there was but little of *beauty* to *boast*; but I was but little more than two and twenty, and so recently married; that this circumstance operated favorably, and in proportion as beauties lose by a system of injudicious puffing; so was a favorable re-action produced, because the *Monster* was not quite so frightful as she had been depicted— Ushered into the great world, we took handsome apartments in the Bearen Strasse; furnished two rooms merely genteelly; and made out in a very eoconomical manner with the family apartments according to our Straitened means; and bought a second hand Chariot with a pr. of Horses—

My house was within a few doors of Dr. Browns—and with them we formed a most intimate and friendly acquaintance— All the English Strangers of distinction or respectability assembled there every Eveng. when there were no great parties, to partake of their bread and Cheese Suppers; and the whole entertainment and establishment was conducted upon the simplest, and what in this Country might be termed, the most really democratic footing: and their guests always returned with delight from the Courtly scenes of the great world, with renewed zest, to the enjoyment of this unaffected, friendly, and charming society—

Dr. Brown was a very handsome courtly gentlemanly man; in his own person highly aristocratic, and almost constantly in attendance upon the different Members of the R. F.; with a very extensive practice among the Nobility and Gentry of the place— Showy in his manners, proud of his daughters, and fond of distinction; he was attentive and amiable to his patients; and generally esteemed and beloved— His Wife was a Welsh *lady*—accustomed to a Country life; I *think* but do not exactly recollect, the daughter of a Welsh Curate: her means of education had been very limited, and her superstition enlarged in proportion— She was the beau idéal of a good, honest, simple minded, kind hearted old Lady, of the old School; always decked in her close Cap, her dark Silk gown, her neat muslin neckkerchief, and her *apron*—always at home, busy with her housekeeping, or at her needle work; ready to hear the news, or to delight in the amusements of her girls; who she thought paragons, in their different lines of perfection— She would laugh continually at the impossibility of her ever acquiring the German language, and relate her mistakes with an irrisistible comic humour, that defied gravity, with all the simplicity of a Child—

One day having called in the morning, I found her with her Servant giving orders for her dinner; and she was repeating with earnestness, "that she wanted her to make a bitch and boy" to the great diversion of her daughters, who laughed till the tears rolled down their Cheeks: and at last translated pigeon pie into such German, as the Servant could understand— Many a time and oft have I laughed at my own equally comprehensive knowledge of the language; when necessity has compelled me to *affect* to know what I could not even understand; and wondered how I have been extricated from similar difficulties, in situations of actual necessity, at a later period of life— Margaret Brown was not handsome—though what is styled well looking— She was a very dark brunette, with sparkling black eyes and an expression too intellectual for feminine beauty: her education had been that of a youth, and her quick capacity, steady application, and retentive memory; had garnered large stores for future use more suited to a maturer age, than for the epoch at which we had become acquainted—; amiable but firm in her character, she was deficient in what is termed softness; though never course— Girls were afraid of her, and young men dreaded to converse with her, because they *felt* her superiority, and their own insignificance— She was her fathers special friend, and counsellor—her age 22.

Isabella was very handsome—also a brunette; but a perfect contrast to her Sister: the hair and the eyes were a shade lighter; her features more delicate, and the character of her countenance, and its general expression was less intellectual, but much more pleasing;

more especially as it corresponded with the gentle and unassuming tone of her manners, adding interest to her timid and unobtrusive attractions— She was my particular and devoted friend until her death; and while I write this little tribute of sincere and long felt affection to her memory; the tear glistens in my eye while I exclaim, "when shall I see her like again." Her Sister Fanny, but who could describe Fanny!! She realized the Poets dream of golden hair, a complexion of lilies and roses, fine features, eyes like the large and melting as the gazelle's; of the softest blue; a head placed with beautiful symetry on her Shoulders, and with the Hebe elasticity of joyous fifteen— The pet of the family, and the admired of all— She was very amiable; and being in the first blush of life, happy innocent and yet a child, was one of the loveliest girls I ever met with— one handsome boy made up this charming family, with whom I passed the happiest and most cheerful period during a sojourn of three years and a half in the City of Berlin.

In old age we look on the past days of our youth, with a degree of rapture, and howe're the sorrows of life may have assailed us: there is a cheering hope that buoys us up in youth in spite of ourselves; to hail a future change for the better— Forty two years and a half have elapsed since this period!—and with the garulity of age, I dwell upon the picture in all its freshness; and if it is tinted with *romance*; remember, that to me life was *new*; and with a mind so depressed by the fate of my family of whose safety I had not even *heard*; it was natural that the kind sympathy of such a family should have produced emotions in my heart of both affection and gratitude

My little friend Countess Pauline De Neale was not handsome, but full of animation and ésprit, and perfectly amiable, with all the bonhommie and sincerity of the German character— Well educated, and well read; a Maid of honour at the Court of Princess Louisa; full of anecdote, and gaining hourly experience in the busy world; she was to me a sort of Mentor ever ready to instruct me in the usages and customs of high life, and to assist me in the duties of its performance— Whenever we met she gave me an insight into the characters that passed before us; and this peep behind the Scenes, was always amusing, beneficial, and instructive— Ever the same, we lived in perfect harmony; and many of my pleasantest hours were passed in her society both at home and abroad. Her Father and Mother treated me with the same constant kindness during my stay at Berlin—

Miss Dorville was the Daughter of the Maitre des Ceremonie of the Queens establishment; and as I have already said was a *beauty*. She was tall not very fair, had a good deal of easy assurance; and being *un peu* passé betrayed rather too great an anxiety to obtain a Matrimonial settlement; the great object of her ambition, to which however the English Ambassador Lord Elgin, the main object of the day, turn'd a deaf ear, and while elegantly trifling with her hopes, allured only to disappoint Her features were prominent and of the roman Cast: but somewhat too masculine, and her air was altogether too *prononcée* to excite either love or respect— The Scandalous chronicle of the day was already busy with her fame, and many light jests were made at her expense; to which her after life unfortunately gave pretty strong credibility— Lord Elgin assured of his conquest, made a *bet* with some young Roué like himself, that he would invite a large party, and that *he* would present her with a pair of diamond Earings, on condition that she would allow him to kiss her in the presence of the whole company; to this she readily agreed, and went through the ceremony in the most gracious manner, and to the delight of his Lordship, and all the quizzers of Berlin—[7]

As it is necessary to give you a Carte du Pays ere we can complete our travels—I must introduce you to the Corps Diplomatique of that day, a Season prominent in history, as the close of the reign of William Frederick; and the beginning of a new era under the present King Frederick William—who so recently left this earthly Scene; and who if not the *greatest* King, was certainly one of the most suffering and the most worthy of the age in which he lived— I do not make this trifling eulogiem on selfish principles, although the distinction and kindness with which he treated me, during a residence of nearly four years calls forth my gratitude to his memory— Throughout the time of my residence there, his attention was unvarying and never failed to the hour of my departure in sickness and in health— I never saw him but on publick occasions— I owed all this to the effect produced by Mr. Adams who was universally liked—

Monsr Caillard was an old Gentleman formerly known to Mr. Adams in St. Petersburg; Minister from France— Baron Rozencrantz

[7] Thomas Bruce, 7th Earl of Elgin and 11th Earl of Kincardine (1766–1841), was an army officer and diplomat. In 1795 he was appointed the British minister plenipotentiary to Prussia. During Lord Elgin's later appointment to the embassy at Constantinople from 1799 to 1803, he undertook the removal to England of the Parthenon sculptures and other antiquities (*DNB*).

with a Wife who had for several years lost the use of her limbs— Minister from Denmark— The Marquis and Marquise Parella from Sardinia (not Naples) a little sprightly vulgur Italian, speaking but little french— Lord Elgin English; very handsome and equally presuming. Count and Countess Zinzendorf, Saxon, who had been residing there twenty two years; an excellent couple of the old School, stiff and formal as old Portraits; and with faces exhibiting about as much variety of expression— The Viscount Anadia of Portugal; fat, good humoured, and *half* agreeable— Baron Ompteda a man of doubtful reputation from Hanover Count Panin and Lady of Russia; since become famous as one of the conspirators in the reign of Paul— Baron Shultz von Ascheraden Sweedish Minister— The Marquis de Musquits Spanish; do Prince Reuss austrian—[8]

I have already mentioned my presentation at Court to the Queen, at a private audience, and the numerous presentations at the Circle to the different Princesses. Our means being small, my dress was of course simple— It consisted of a pale blue Satin Robe, a white Satin Skirt, and the body and Sleeves trimmed with blond—my hair dressed and a couple of Ostrich Feathers—white Satin Shoes, kid Gloves, and a Fan— I was not worth an ornament, and such things would have been injudicious— The only article of the dress bought for the occasion being the Robe; my Father having supplied me handsomely with clothes suited to the calls of fashionable society—

[8] The diplomats whom LCA lists here, with their dates of service in Prussia, are Antoine Bernard Caillard, from France, 1795–1798; Baron Niels von Rosenkrantz, from Denmark, 1796–1800; Marquis Provana de Parella di San Martino, from Sardinia (Savoy), 1789–1798; Lord Elgin, 1795–1798; Count Friedrich August von Zinzendorf und Pottendorf, from Saxony, 1777–1799; João Rodrigues de Sá e Melo, Viscount of Anadia, from Portugal, 1791–1801; Ludwig Konrad Georg von Ompteda, from Hanover, 1794–1800; Count Nikita Petrovich Panin, from Russia, 1797–1799; Baron Carl Gustav Shultz von Ascheraden, from Sweden, 1796–1798; Ignacio de Múzquiz, Marquis of Múzquiz, from Spain, 1797–1799; and Heinrich XIV, Prince of Reuss zu Plauen, from Austria, 1785–1799 (*Repertorium*, 3:51, 86, 131–132, 170, 189, 319, 362, 377, 397, 413, 439).

Panin (1770–1837) was Emperor Paul I's special emissary to Berlin in 1798 and 1799. Paul, who had succeeded his mother, Catherine the Great, at her death in 1796, was the scourge of the nobility and the officer class, and he was thought to be deranged. In 1800 as a member of Russia's council for foreign affairs, Panin prepared the ground for Paul's removal, though he was absent from St. Petersburg when the coup occurred, having been dismissed from the emperor's service and exiled to his estates. The conspirators' plan was to force Paul to abdicate or, failing that, to arrest and depose him in favor of his eldest son, Grand Duke Alexander. But when the coup was carried out in March 1801 the emperor resisted, and in the ensuing struggle he was strangled. The grand duke, who had given his assent to his father's removal but not to his assassination, took his place as Alexander I (*Cambridge Modern Hist.*, 9:34, 49; Roderick E. McGrew, *Paul I of Russia, 1754–1801*, Oxford, Eng., 1992, p. 323, 327–328, 331–335, 350–353).

When Supper was to be served, to my utter consternation, I was to remain, and Mr. Adams was informed that to avoid questions of etiquette, the Ministers never dined or Supped with the King— You can easily conceive my consternation when I found myself seated opposite to the King and Queen as a mark of honor shown to all Strangers of distinction; and obliged to converse, or rather to answer to the questions of their Majesties during the Meal This Presentation took place on the 20th of Jany 1798.

The next day paid visits to all the *great* and their *seconds* in command; and thus was launched into a world altogether new to me, and little to my taste; being totally unfitted by circumstances, disappointments, character and education to fill a sphere so novel, and so unsuited to the station to which I was born, and to the *then* fortunes of my family—

23 [*JANUARY 1798*]

The Marchesa di Parella sent me word early this morning that the Queen Dowager would recieve me between 1 and 2 o'clock; and that I must *wear mourning*— Countess Neale my Maid and myself literally *basted* up a Dress; and although it barely held together while I wore it; by the aid of a long black Veil I was ready when the Marchésa called for me, and went through the audience with more success than could possibly have been anticipated: thanks to the affability of her Majesty, who received me with the kindest distinction— Conceive my astonishment at the sight of this singular looking old Lady— She wore *Widows* mourning; a Bombazine Robe and Skirt, trimmed with white Cambrick up the sides like *weepers*; the Collar and Cuffs and body to match— Her hair was scratched out on each side in the manner of my old picture, only more á lá crazy Jane; with a long String of splendid diamonds fastened up in the front, then brought into a deep festoon on each side upon the hair; and over this a black Crape Veil, falling to her feet—being seated the effect was altogether extraordinary—and it was with the utmost difficulty that I kept my sérieux, with the dignity suited to the Wife of a foreign dignitary— When I got home the Judge laughed with all his heart at my recital of the Scene, and the gravity assumed by Mr A. who terribly dreaded some indiscretion on my part, could not controul our mirth— He was always kind as the most affectionate brother, and being less interested, was of course more indulgent to my follies or my griefs, than Mr. Adams; whose very anxiety for my success, rendered him uneasy, lest by some gaucherie I should fail–[9]

24

Went to sup at the Prince Ferdinands with Mr. Adams and his brother–reception of extraordinary kindness from the Princess; her daughter the Princess Radzivil, and the Landgravine of Hesse Cassel– The Princess Ferdinand was old, and her manners were rather abrupt– She invited me to sit by her, and began asking me how long I had been married? and how *old* I was? I told her, and she said she had not thought me *more* than sixteen– She then called across the room to the Prince Radzivil, a very handsome and gay young Spark; who had married her daughter a charming woman, but seven years older than her husband. "Prince Antoine venez ici!" He came up to her and I thought she was going to introduce him to me–but she fixed her eyes on my face and said to him, "regardè là, come elle et joliè?" He laughed; but I was so *raw* I blushed Scarlet, and then she cried out "Ah! voyez la? comme elle rougit.–" This capped the climax and I felt as if I should *cry* for very shame– The Landgravine saw my distress and kindly relieved me, by occupying the attention of both her Sister and the Prince; and from that hour took me under her peculiar protection, as long as I remained within the circle of her acquaintance– She was a superb looking woman, who had been very beautiful in her youth; and whose tastes appeared to be of a more simple and quiet order, than those of her Sister the Princess F—— The Party was small; no dancing, and the Supper was plain and unceremonious– My little friend Countess Neale, with her Father and Mother contributed by every kindness to remove the restraint naturally experienced on such occasions, to a novice like myself, altogether unlearned in the way of Courts, and naturally timid among Strangers–in addition to which that most corroding idea, that I had entered Mr. Adams's family under circumstances so inauspicious, and apparently so unfavorable to my own character, who alas, was one of the proudest women existing; acted upon my mind as a bar to all happiness; tho' I have no doubt that it produced an excellent effect, by checking the natural love of admiration existing

[9] TBA earned the title judge in 1811 when he was appointed chief justice of the Circuit Court of Common Pleas for the Southern Circuit of Massachusetts (Davis, *Mass. Judiciary*, p. 221).

in all women accustomed to the flattery of mankind; and to the doting love of warm hearted Parents; who had always gazed on me with delight as the ~~imagined~~ ideal perfection of beauty and loveliness— At my age when all the illusions of youth are over, and when the contrast between what *once* was, and what *is*, is so self evident; there can be no vanity in relating mere facts of the past age, from which I can derive no benefit— In my own eyes I never possessed beauty; and yet strange to say, I was so familiarized to the idea of possessing it; that when I was often mistaken as I rode or walked for one of the most celebrated women in London, Lady Elizabeth Lambert;[10] it never excited either surprize or vanity; as to my own eye there was no resemblance— Accustomed to consider both my Sisters superior to myself; surrounded by a beautiful growing family, and remarkably handsome Parents, it never appeared to me to possess intrinsic value; and though I ranked it high among the blessings which I had received from heaven, it seemed *too natural* to excite a puérile vanity in my mind— Haughty to excess my vanity was of a different character, and was not founded on so just a basis— The qualities of the heart and of the mind, excited a higher aim; and a romantic idea of excellence, the model of which seemed practically to exist before my eyes, in the hourly exhibition of every virtue in my almost idolized Father; had produced an almost mad ambition to be like him; and though fortune has blasted his fair fame; and evil report has assailed his reputation; still while I live I will do honour to his name, and speak of his merit with the honoured love and respect which it deserved— As long as he lived to protect them, his Children were virtuous and happy—amidst poverty and persecution; and it is only those who have lost such a Father, that can measure, or re-alize the destruction which such a loss brings upon his Orphans— If when I have thrown off this mortal coil, one single virtue; one amiable or deserving quality should ever have found favour in the eyes of my children let them see, feel, and understand, that amid all the trials of a suffering life; all the afflictions, calamities, and disap-

[10] Lady Elizabeth (1773?–1830) was the daughter of Richard Lambert (or Lambart), 6th Earl of Cavan. In 1792 Elizabeth was awarded damages of £4,000 in a suit brought against a London newspaper that had imputed to her an illicit relationship with her footman. Popular accounts of the case took note of her uncommon beauty. In 1793 Elizabeth married Capt. William Henry Ricketts (who later took the name Jervis), but he divorced her for adultery by an act of Parliament in 1799. She later married Rev. Richard Brickenden. George ("Beau") Brummell celebrated Lady Elizabeth's beauty, rating her high among the fashionable women of London (O'Brien, *Mrs. Adams*, p. 76–77; Lodge, *Peerage*, 1833, p. 378; "Trial of Richard Tattersall," *Walker's Hibernian Magazine*, Aug. 1792, p. 152–156).

pointments which have assailed me; that it was *his* watchful eye, and his protecting care that developped and strengthened that little, but abiding good; which has preserved me from the snares of evil; the meretricious fascinations of gorgeous Courts; and the more trying intrigues, insults, and gross contaminations of political struggles; in the cause of heartless and soul corrupting Ambition— Let this fact impress itself upon your hearts as it is not confined in its action to me, but to all the children who he lived to see grow up; on *whom* never was cast a reproach; one of whom lived and died in the performance of every virtue, as Daughter, Sister, Wife, and Mother; and another who in the exhibition of a long life in poverty, in affliction; in almost every trial of mind and body that can exercise the soul; has *proved* an example to her Sex in the practice of every virtue, that the purest christianity can exact.[11] It is forty three years since I became a Wife and yet the rankling sore is not healed which then broke upon my heart of hearts— it was the blight of every future prospect—and it has hung like an incubus upon my Spirit— It has been my reproach; but it has preserved me from temptation in this guilty world; and now at sixty five I can say to my Son; for my Children alone I valued reputation; and that through all my follies; all my inequalities of temper; that I have never commited in any sense an act, that should call a blush into their Cheeks for the conduct of their Mother, from the day of her birth to this hour— I had nothing but a fair reputation to bequeathe to them; and though in this Country such ideas are trivial, I have been differently schooled, and deem it a fair inheritance—

My next Sortie was to Princess Henry's; a very stiff old Lady who never went to Court, but always received at home— In consequence of a weakness of the Spine, she wore an iron collar, to support her chin and throat, which made her look like a stick—but her dress was so contrived with a quantity of Lace, as to conceal this appendage entirely— Hers were always Card parties, and immediately after my presentation I was siezed upon by two old Ladies and an old Officer to play Whist— Mr. Adams foreseeing the event, had furnished me with a Purse with some gold; timid, and a very indifferent player, the result was easily foreseen, and after fleecing me unmercifully; in despite of truth and justice, they made me pay for the lights and Cards; a perquisite as they said to the Maitre d'Hotel, and emptied

[11] LCA is probably referring, respectively, to her sisters Ann (Nancy) Johnson Hellen and Catherine Maria ("Kitty") Johnson Smith.

my fine purse of its contents— Just before Supper to which I was invited to stay without being able to say no; and without Mr Adams; I was introduced to Lord Levison Gower, one of the handsomest men in England about my own age, and Mr. Frere one of the most agreeable and the most talented men I ever knew—[12] His Lordship was sent as Ambassador to congratulate the King on his accession to the throne—Mr. Frere Secretary— As his Lordship and myself were the two Presentations of the Evening, we were honoured with the Seats of distinguished Strangers, and I fear that neither the Ambassador or myself behaved with the dignity or propriety exacted on such an occasion: and the scene was altogether so novel to us, and so contrary to English usage; that Lord Gower and myself being equally struck with the *novelty*; became quite intimate; and having the liberty to talk in (to the company an unknown tongue) amused ourselves without hesitation with the Scene displayed before us— The Supper was termed elegant— It consisted of all the delicacies of the Season in lavish quantities: but the style of the service produced in us almost irrepressible mirth— Conceive of four huge joints of Meat roasted, and adorning the four corners of the table!!! With every thing else in proportion, on a table laid for thirty Persons— Among the guest's there was an old Lady who seemed to fix the attention of my astonished neighbour; and he busied himself with counting the number of dishes of which she partook;[13] during which time he was obliged to watch the Princess, so as to answer any question which she might put to *him*; and then *I* was to remember the number, while he did the same for me in my turn— He got up to *nineteen*, when the thing became so irrisistably ridiculous, we were thankful to rise from table, lest we should commit some gross bévue which would have stamped our ill breeding, and shocked the whole company— Fortunately the Princess was nearly blind; therefore escaped the sight of our nonsense Mr. Adams was quite dismayed when I showed my purse; and we agreed that I should go as seldom as possible to Princess Henry's as I could not afford to lose, and could not avoid playing when there— The moment I appeared there the harpies would sieze on me; and whenever I was so unlucky as to stay, the same result was produced, and I was afraid to show the deficit in my purse made at an expence of all pleasure to me, and of real pain to my husband— Cramped as we were in our circum-

[12] Probably John Hookham Frere (1769–1846), a British diplomat and writer (*DNB*).

[13] Later in Adventures LCA identifies this woman as Madame Eichstadt.

stances, these were heavy taxes, but unavoidable to the Station which we filled—

The first private party at which I participated was one at General Kunheims at which there were assembled between four and five hundred persons, among whom I found myself almost a stranger— Judge Adams accompanied us; and as he was as much a Stranger as myself, we naturally remained together while Mr. Adams mixed in the throng of Nobles, with whom he had become intimately acquainted— The Ball began with english Country dances, and the Judge led me out to make my dèbut— The dance was long and fatiguing, but I was so extravagantly fond of the amusement, that the Strangers were forgotten and he danced so well and with so much spirit, I was quite delighted— Prince Radziville then invited me; and Prince Vitgenstein for the next dances; and I had a succession of partners until two o clock in the morning—when I returned home perfectly exhausted— It was thus that the Judge made me the fashion—and I became a *Belle*—

Unsuited to a life of almost constant dissipation, these incessant parties became very irksome to me; and I availed myself of every opportunity of excuse, where public duty permited me to remain at home, without giving offence— A most social and agreeable intercourse existed between us and the Families of Count Bruhl,[14] Dr. Brown, and Count Neale; and we met almost constantly without form or ceremony at tea, taking a Supper of the most simple kind, of cold provision, often of bread and Cheese (English) there deemed a great luxury— The House of Dr. Brown was the resort of all the English foreigners of distinction; and there we formed some of the most agreeable and distinguished acquaintances we have ever made, upon the easy terms of social familiarity; the only terms on which you can know the peculiar character of that Nation to advantage— The utter exemption from all the ettiquettes of idle pageantry; and the playful simplicity that pervaded the conversations, and amusements of the younger branches, were a source of continued enjoyment to the elders—and seemed to *youthify them*, while they

[14] In 1787 Count (and Gen.) Karl von Brühl (1742–1802), a member of a prominent Saxon family, was appointed military tutor to the prince royal of Prussia, later Frederick William III. Brühl's wife, Sophia Gomm, was the daughter of an English diplomat. LCA mentions their eldest child, Maria Sophia (Mary), and another daughter, Fanny. In 1810 Maria Sophia would marry Carl von Clausewitz, the Prussian general and military theorist (Roger Parkinson, *Clausewitz: A Biography*, London, 1970, p. 42, 128, 334; *The Correspondence of Edmund Burke*, ed. Thomas W. Copeland and others, 10 vols., Chicago, 1958–1978, 10:228).

participated in their innocent sports; and while I resided in Berlin; that house seemed the centre of attraction, as a relief from the formal monotony of the Courtly Assemblies; where

> Gewgaws shone with regal splendor
> and eyes of envy oped to wonder
> Not to approve fair beauty's smile
> But youthful innocence beguile—

the dazzling diamond seeming to posses a Circean charm, whose witchery could lure the passions of the young and lovely to their destruction—

We kept no Carriage as our stay was doubtful; but our Lodgings were so inconvenient in sickness; the Drums incessantly beating morning, noon, evening, and night whenever the Royal family or any Officer of Rank passed through the Gate; in addition to witnessing the corporeal punishment of the soldiers, without the possibility of avoidance; we sought and found a house a few doors from Dr. Browns in a fashionable and central quarter of the Town; but at a rent very unsuitable to our finances— Our Furniture was of course of the very plainest and cheapest description; and my good friend Mrs. Brown who was very plain spoken, taxed us with *meaness* sans cérémonie—

You will laugh at the minuteness with which I dwell on subjects apparently of little importance—but one of the objects of my writing this little history of past events, is to show you that *stations* that call forth the spleen, acrimony and jealousy of the multitude; are not the Bed of roses on which you may sleep, undisturbed by the scorpion care; but on the contrary they are *schools*, to teach forbearance, under the most bitter mortifications; and of perpetual and necessary privation in the midst of temptations, almost impossible to contend against— Few like your Father have resisted them, and persevered in a line of undeviating duty through life, with an unshaken purity and integrity beyond all praise; appreciated in every Country in which he has served, and from whom the highest tokens of respect and admiration have been loudly, unceasingly and honourably awarded— My love and respect for him was so unbounded; my keen regret at having become an added burthen to his cares so unpropitiously; my extravagant admiration of his superior talents, and his amiable character, had taught me to venerate his motives; though I often shrank from the severity of his opinions in passing judgment on others, less gifted than himself: and although the change in my life was *extreme*; taken from the midst of luxury, from a family who thought me almost,

> "The faultless monster that the world ne'er saw"[15]

and almost broken hearted, at the harshness of feeling elicited by their misfortunes, without the means of vindication, or the knowledge of the cause—the agony of believing myself suspected of connivance in knowing all the circumstance of my Fathers commercial difficulties; all bore upon my spirit; and bereft me of that greatest of all comforts; the talking of the absent, the joys of the past, and the fond affections which had blessed all the roseate hours of infancy— To condemn was impossible; and to destroy the gratitude and affection of years of unremited happiness, was equally impossible; and would have been unworthy: and nothing but the ardent affection I bore *him* made me think no privation too great, no mortification too severe, in mitigation of his disappointment— The mere loss of the very small property that I should have possessed I knew could not be the cause of so much bitterness— It must therefore have been the unfortunate *period* of my Fathers difficulties, owing to a protested bill; a misfortune to which every Merchant is liable in peculiarly hard times; that made the stroke so bitter; as his Station was sufficiently prominent to produce publick attention, and to shock his pride; and I am perfectly conscious that to a mind like *his* the wound could never he healed— ~~This idea has pursued me through life and will pursue me unto death— If it is wrong God forgive me— It may exist only in my own imagination, but it has been exemplified in the admiration of my Children to whom my connections have been objects of scorn—~~

In M^r. Adamss Library we had a List Carpet;[16] pine wood bookshelves; a mahogany writing desk, a second hand Sopha; and a few Chairs— My bed chamber had *no Carpet*; a Bedstead with white Cotton Curtains of the coarsest quality, bordered with a strip of Calico cut from a striped print; and made by myself, with window Curtains to match; a very common pine wood Toilet Table, with a muslin Cover; and an equally plain Toilet glass— No fire in the Winter; and half a dozen Chairs— The two drawing rooms I have already

[15] John Sheffield, "An Essay on Poetry," line 233. LCA used this literary reference again in her Diary at 30 June 1839, below.

[16] A carpet made of strips of woolen selvage, edging material discarded during the production of cloth goods (*OED*).

described one of these served for a dining room. They were very pretty–

Remember I was the *Wife* of a Foreign Minister, and daughter in law to the President of the United States–always addressed as your *Excellency*, and sometimes called *Princess Royal*–A capital epitomé of the Bathos in *dignity*– A charming family lived under the same roof with us with whom we became intimately acquainted; and I had a standing invitation to join a party at their house once every week during my stay at Berlin–[17] On my return to Berlin fourteen years after, *alone, and without rank*; a mere voyageuse; I met with the same welcome from Countess Golofkin; and received a kind Letter from her daughter since I have been in this Country; brought by Mrs. Rumpf, with a most cordial and friendly invitation to *Paris*; for myself or my Children; giving her address in the name of her husband the Count de Bruges– I mention these facts only to show that though your Mother was *poor*, she was *respected*–

Countess Neale or the Miss Browns were almost always with me when at home; and we amused ourselves with the scandal of the town, or satirizing the vagaries of the Court belles, or the follies of the Court Dowdies, or the prank of the young Foreigners; and the hours passed merrily on– I was sick almost all through the Month of Feby and of course could not go out; this was in 98.[18]

In March my visits were again renewed and as the Society was always a succession of Balls or Card Parties; I shall only occasionally mention any particular incident worth relating, and any remarkable character worth Noting– At a morning Concert at Prince Radzivilles; I there saw and heard Prince Plato Zeuboff: a man distinguished in the history of Catherine 2d of Russia;[19] handsome and covered with Orders; distinctions not the most honourably obtained, and wearing the Portrait of his *Misstress* richly set in Diamonds tied round his neck with a fancy Ribbon– grimacier a faire peur;[20] A fancied Musician but a poor performer; quite a contrast to

[17] Count Gabriel Golovkin, the grandson of Gabriel Ivanovich Golovkin, chancellor to Peter the Great, had been an officer in the Dutch service. His wife was the daughter of a Dutch nobleman (W. R. Morfill, review of *Comte Fédor Golovkine, La cour et le règne de Paul Ier*, by S. Bonnet, *English Historical Review*, 21:389–391 [April 1906]).

[18] This indisposition was due to LCA's pregnancy; see Adventures, note 22, below.

[19] Prince Platon Alexandrovich Zubov (1767–1822) was last in the long line of favorites of Catherine the Great. From 1789 until her death in 1796, the empress bestowed on him influence, money, estates, titles, military honors, and government positions (John T. Alexander, *Catherine the Great: Life and Legend*, N.Y., 1989, p. 223, 294–295, 319, 321–322).

[20] One whose grimaces are frightening.

Prince Radziville, who sang well and is an accomplished Man—Lord Gower (the present Ambassador in France Lord Granville); returned to england having called to take leave The Queen had a Circle en habit de Cours (a hoop) to which fortunately I was too sick to go— The King and Queen having just recovered from the Measles, this was a great congratulatory State affair, and very crowded and Stiff— Mr Adams of course attended— Mr Adams went to a ball at Princess Louis—Widow of the eldest brother of the King— She is very handsome; not so beautiful as her Sister the Queen but very graceful; very coquettish and by no means possessing the lovely disposition or character of her Majesty— She has two children and is treated with almost as much distinction as the Queen—[21]

Miss Estoff first Maid of honor to the Princess of Orange came with Countess Neale to see me; and proved another kind and highly esteemed friend during my stay in that Country

Princess Radziville sent to borrow some of my dresses as she wished the patterns— I sent them immediately— She was a very large Woman; I a very *small* one, and in trying them on she tore a favorite dress that my Mother had worked for me so, that I could never wear it again!— I grieved but to no purpose—

On the 23^d^ of April I was at a Ball at the Queens, where I was presented formally to the King, as was Judge Adams— Danced with Prince Radziville, and Prince Witgenstein, who entered into an engagement with me, to dance with them at any of the Balls where we should meet— Was obliged to accept as ettiquette made it impossible to say *no* to a *prince* on such occasions— Saw Prince Repnin of Russia— Went with Mr Adams to the Theater to see Emilia Gallotti—and fell off the Seat in a deep fainting fit— Poor Mr. Adams raised me with difficulty; and the Ladies of the Princess of Orange by her direction came to me, and assisted by every possible means in my recovery— having walked to the theatre had no carriage; and the Duke of Nassau Wilbourg kindly offered me *his* and sent me home—Treated with every possible kindness but even my *miseries* seemed to bring me *én spectacle*—completely undressed in publick—[22] The next

[21] For Princess Louis (Frederica Sophia Carolina of Mecklenburg-Strelitz) and her children, see Adventures, 1 Jan. 1799, and note 41, below.

[22] LCA fainted during the first scene of *Emilia Galotti*, a tragedy by Gotthold Ephraim Lessing. JQA's Diary for this period is filled with notations on his wife's difficult pregnancy, culminating in a 17 July 1798 entry in which he laments, "The case appears in allmost every point similar to that of last November— Patience and Resignation is all that we can have—" The next day he wrote, "The anticipation of evils that we cannot prevent is itself a great mis-

day I was too ill to go out; but on the day following called on the Princess of Orange, and her Ladies; who laughed and said that they did not apprehend that my illness would prove *dangerous*.— This was the 26 May— Mr Adams learning German; I could not afford to take Lessons—too expensive— Among my troubles was one of a singular character: Madame de Castel, the daughter of Madame de Voss the Grande Gouvernante to the Queen; pretended to attach herself to me with the warmest zeal, and wherever I met her I could scarcely extricate myself from her embraces— She was without exception the most disgusting Woman I ever knew, and I soon learnt that her character was so indifferent, that it might injuriously affect mine if any intimacy should take place— Mr. Adams was somewhat puzzled by this information on account of her affinity to Madame de Voss, and her near connection with the Queen; but my ill health confined me so much at home, that her great friendship gradually cooled off; and we met without these earnest marks of her affection— She was very ugly and all her pretence to notice in society, was founded on her Mothers high Station near the Queens person—

Mr. Adams now purchased a plain Chariot, and a pair of Horses; and my household now consisted of Whitcomb, my Maid Epps, who afterwards became his Wife;[23] a footman, a housemaid, a Coachman, and a woman Cook—

My ill health was a perpetual tax upon Mr. Adams's feelings—but his kindness was unremited in promoting my comfort— The perpetual anxiety which he displayed however had a tendency to defeat his wishes, and to keep me in a state of disquietude beyond my strength— My nervous system became affected, and the slightest agitation produced the very consequences which he so constantly apprehended—

Happy indeed would it have been for Mr Adams if he had broken his engagement, and not harrassed himself with a Wife altogether so unsuited to his own peculiar character, and still more peculiar prospects.— When we were married every disappointment seemed to fall upon us at once— My health was already injured by the anxieties by no means trifling attending my engagement—and the change of

fortune. I have these 8 months been convinced, with scarcely the shadow of a doubt what this Event would be—Yet now that it happens I feel it with no less poignancy than if it had been unexpected. The prospects of futurity that it still holds out to me are horrible— I realize them as if present. I have no more doubt of them than of death— They poison every moment of existence, and when they come will be not less bitter for having been foretasted—" (D/JQA/24, 26 May, 17, 18 July 1798, and *passim*, APM Reel 27).

[23] For the marriage of Elizabeth Epps and Tilly Whitcomb, see Adventures, note 148, below.

destination was as unfavorable to my constitution as possible— The consequences of our detention were likewise much more injurious to *me* even than the Climate to which I was removed— For a long time M[r] Adams in his Letters had urged me to be ready to accompany him at the shortest notice after the reception of his appointment to Lisbon; and had even informed me that a residence was already procured for us in that City, and I had been so accustomed to the idea; and these directions were so peremptory, that my Father had a Vessel prepared to convey us, which had been kept in waiting one Month so as to accommodate our removal— My wedding clothes had been prepared a *year*, and not an article was added to them when the event took place—so that there was ample time for deliberation, and for a thorough investigation into the character of my family, and my connections, which should prevent the possibility of deception: and I had had more than one misgiving as to the *fitness* of my *temper* to cope with the difficulties which presented themselves to my imagination— Educated in england I had already discovered that our views of things were totally different in many essential points; and that there was a severity bordering on injustice in some of the opinions which I heard expressed; for want of a more enlarged acquaintance with the customs of my Country: and more especially with those peculiar to *my* Sex—and on some points alarming to a young and inexperienced girl, a sensitive fractiousness about the minor concerns of life, which might occasionally create serious uneasiness; and a rupture of our engagement had nearly taken place in which I had at least evinced sufficient spirit to prove, that my *affections* were not to be sacrificed to my pride, or to any desire of ambitious *exaltation*— Brought up a *republican* and living in a Monarchy; I had learnt to consider the boasted greatness of ephemeral dignity, from which most of the Ministers with Whom I had been acquainted, had either returned impoverished, or involved in debt; were not worth much: and my own father had suffered too much in the cause of his Country, to raise any very great expectation— An American Minister was to *me* a very small personage; and in my eyes *is* so still, in as far as place goes—and the only superiority he can ever claim in any Country of Europe; *is*, the possession of superior talent to ensure him a real standing or reputation in those Countries—

Mere place in our Country, can never give even artificial rank; while the Salaries are too mean to place you on a level with your Colleagues, and *too* narrow to admit of your surrounding yourself with those appendages which through a little gilding, cover many little flaws in the understanding, and deficiencies in the manners— Talent acquirement, information and learning, is the only passport which will ensure respect, and claim and maintain its station all over the world; and this was the sterling gold to which I bowed in the choice of my husband, and which in every position in which he has been placed in this world; has been *felt*, *understood*, and *granted* in the midst of trial, persecution, disappointment and affliction— Such greatness bears its *own* stamp, and is the reward of *years*. With the consciousness of such powers, we cannot wonder that his measure of others less gifted, has often been unduly severe; and in early life, when the suffering which *experience* brings, has not taught us leniency to the casualties, the changes, and the calamities which no care can prevent, no forethought assuage, we are too apt to inveigh against the *effects* of misfortune, without a just appreciacition of its causes, and all the concomitant circumstances attending it; and to censure without mercy those ills which have deserv'd compassion and sympathy— I am induced to make these observations from a perusal of Mr. Adams's Journal— In which I find many allusions to my fathers difficulties conveying an idea altogether injurious to *him*, for want of a freer explanation—[24] Mr. Adams was in England a long time without even an invitation from them my parents— It was therefore his own choice that led him to seek *us*; while it is evident that some kind friend had warned him of his danger, and had carefully opened his eyes to *any* thing that might follow— Besides *his* Father, *his* Mother, and *his* Sister, had known us for years; and our marriage was not so hurried as to prevent their timely interference to prevent the connection— Letters from America announcing the arrival of my Father and the family in America— The information contained in them and the expression of acute suffering so evident in their tone, which forced themselves upon my memory, though so many years have elapsed, and they are laid in the peaceful tomb; have induced this painful retrospection;[25] and as this re-

[24] For one such allusion in JQA's Diary, see Record, note 71, above.

[25] Letters specifically announcing the family's arrival in America have not been found. LCA was probably referring to correspondence between her father and JQA, and to a letter she received from Catherine Nuth Johnson, all concerning Joshua Johnson's business failure.

In a 12 Sept. 1797 letter to JQA, Johnson wrote that he believed his hasty departure to be "the most proper to enable me to do speedy Justice to every one" (Adams Papers). Soon after that, one of Johnson's creditors, the Bremen merchant Frederick Delius, wrote to JQA to express his indignation at Johnson's "low mean & impardonnable conduct." He asked JQA to provide an accounting of his father-in-law's financial affairs, and he threatened that the mer-

cital of the past is not intended for the eye of any but my Children, I write freely and under the dictation of Truth; visible in almost every line in the accounts detailed at the time, concisely; but reviving all the links which have laid dormant on the tablet of memory, to be renewed with the vividness of present reality—

There being no *Lady* of the English Minister; I was a sort of substitute; having to perform double duty in the capacity of entertainer; at home the english sought *me*, abroad they flattered *me*; and I naturally felt much pleased with their acquaintance At a Ball at Court Mr Adams introduced Lord Elgin— He immediately entered into conversation, and insisted on my dancing with him which I positively refused; he persisted in urging me and at last, I was obliged to point to the dress which I wore a Robe as one indicating a predetermination not to dance—and stated that I had already contrary to established *ettiquette*, declined to dance with two of the Princes— He laughed heartily, and began to teaze me again; when Madame de Féikenback a very beautiful woman with whom he had a *liason* not very honourable; came up and took his arm— He immediately turned off, as he would not of course introduce her, and I never saw him afterwards—[26] He was a remarkably handsome rouè,

chant houses with which he was associated would "take necessary steps to safe my honor," perhaps by publishing the details of Johnson's actions. JQA's reply to Delius was no less indignant: "When you threaten *me* with a publication against *him* you cannot expect that I should receive the threat otherwise than with defiance. I have never received from Mr: Johnson any property whatever. I never asked any of him, and therefore have no arrangements to make on his account, with any person whatever" (Frederick Delius to JQA, 29 Sept., Adams Papers; JQA to Frederick Delius, 9 Oct., Lb/JQA/6, APM Reel 130).

JQA wrote to his father-in-law, enclosing a copy of Delius' letter. "Appearances and allegations are advanced which bring in question something more than merely your credit," JQA wrote, "and unfortunately your friends have not the means of refuting them in their power" (11 Oct., Adams Papers).

Although Johnson had received JQA's letter with its enclosure in Feb. 1798, he did not reply until December of that year, explaining that he had delayed writing in the hope—as yet unfulfilled—that his affairs would be resolved. He expected that the arbitration with his former partners would be completed in early 1799. Once he was rid of Delius and his other creditors, he would be able to provide "what I have told you, there will be for my Children" (Joshua Johnson to JQA, 1 Dec. 1798, Adams Papers).

Months earlier, LCA's mother had written to her regarding JQA's communication. Delius' letter, Catherine Nuth Johnson wrote, "Woud have Stampt its own infamy." Were JQA more familiar with their situation in America, "he woud be taught to know, that neither Exalted Worth or Exalted Station, are Sufficient to protect any man from Slander & Calumniatons." LCA assured her sister Nancy that their mother had misunderstood JQA, much as she herself had failed to allow for his "manner of writing" in his courtship letters, which she was "now fully convinced never were intended to give me a moments pain" (Catherine Nuth Johnson to LCA, 26 April; LCA to Nancy Johnson Hellen, 11 Sept., both Adams Papers).

[26] Elgin's supposed liaison was with a Madame Ferchenbeck (Susan Nagel, *Mistress of the Elgin Marbles: A Biography of Mary Nisbet, Countess of Elgin*, N.Y., 2004, p. 26).

since famous for a divorce from his Wife; and as the importer of the famous Elgin Marbles ~~He~~ Soon left the Country—[27] Count & Countess Brulh were charming people— He had I think been Governor to the King; and was highly esteemed at Court— She was an English Lady of some distinguished family; they had two daughters, and in them I found steady friends during my stay in the Country.—

Made a first appearance at the Russian Ministers—Count Panin's— His Countess was a very handsome Woman à lá Russe fair and fat, being only 22 years of age having six Children, and the appearance and àplomb of a woman of forty— They lived very splendidly, and she was said to be the proudest woman in Russia— Count Panin as a historical character became very prominent some years after in the assasination of Paul—with Zeuboff—[28]

We took a very pleasant journey to Potsdam with Mr Childs an American; Messrs Kent and Jarrett; and Mr. Hamilton, since a distinguished man in English Diplomacy, and then on his way to study at Gottenburg; with Isabella and William Brown Judge Adams, and the two latter on Horseback.[29] Saw all the great sights till Belle and I were perfectly exhausted— Mr Kent was a very sensible and gentlemanly man who travelled with young Jarrett, a very rich and wild West Indian; full of tricks and pranks, but amiably disposed— We parted at Potsdam with these two gentlemen, and returned to Berlin after a very pleasant and gratifying little tour— Mr. Hamilton of whom we had seen a great deal; and with whom we were much pleased, called to take leave of us to visit Dresden, and we lost a very pleasant and agreable companion the day after— Went to a grand Review— The Field crowded with people— The foreign Ministers always follow the Queens Carriage and thus find an easy pas-

[27] Not long before his departure for Constantinople in 1799, Elgin married Mary, the daughter of William Hamilton Nisbet, a wealthy Scottish landowner. In 1808 Elgin divorced Mary for adultery, in proceedings that put before the public her incriminating love letters and the humiliating testimony of servants (*DNB*; Susan Nagel, *Mistress of the Elgin Marbles: A Biography of Mary Nisbet, Countess of Elgin*, N.Y., 2004, p. 215–225).

[28] LCA is probably referring to Platon Alexandrovich Zubov. His brothers Nicholas and Valerian also took part in the coup against Paul I (Roderick E. McGrew, *Paul I of Russia, 1754–1801*, Oxford, Eng., 1992, p. 323, 341).

[29] The party set out on their four-hour journey to Potsdam on 6 Aug. 1798, and they would return to Berlin on the 9th. Mr. Childs, an "inquisitive traveller" from New York, had recently arrived from Dresden with a letter of recommendation from William Vans Murray. Kent, Jarrett, and William Richard Hamilton (1777–1859) were Englishmen. Kent, a clergyman, was the traveling companion of Jarrett, the son of a wealthy planter in Jamaica (D/JQA/24, 26 July, 6, 9 Aug., APM Reel 27; TBA to AA, 26 July, Adams Papers; *DNB*, entry on Hamilton).

sage through the field– It is a splendid sight; and the delight of the King, who only appears *animated* on such occasions–

Met the Duke & Dutchess of Sudermania–Great characters in Sweden– The Swedish Court dress most singular for Ladies, and frightful– These are prominent characters but they do not appear to be much admired *here*– They are very stiff, but very courteous; but have neither added to the gaiety or Splendour of the Court– Count Finckenstein is an old and very precise gentleman, who was Minister to Frederick the 2d, to the late King, and continues Minister to the present, Frederick William– The Count is said to be immensely wealthy– He has a family of eleven Children– Count Haugwitz is at the head of the Foreign Department though second to the old Count, *apparently* in command. This man Haugwitz is one of your Arch political deceivers, fully exemplifying the Jesuit and Machevelian doctrines, that *truth* is not needful, when *falsehood* will suffice– The old Count is worthy of all respect– His little peculiarities being only *tedious*, but not vicious; and originating in the severe discipline of a superior mind, to which he was subjected under the iron rule of his first Master– Count d'Alvensleben is another Minister; of an apparently easy character, cautious and judicious, but possessing no striking traits on which to found an episode or to adorn a tale–Not married– Count Finckenstein paid *me*–a visit in person– at this time I went occasionally with the Judge to visit my friends the Browns who were at their Country House at Charlottenburg where we enjoyed ourselves very much– I used sometimes to be afraid that my friend Bell was too sensible of the attractions of my *companion*– Mr. Welsh arrived on the 28th. of Sepber. 98–and two days after I lost the Society of my kind brother; who had proved a solace in my moments of mental anguish, and had uniformly contributed to my comfort, and my pleasure, both in sickness and in health–He soothed me in my afflictions–corrected gently my utter want of self confidence; flattered me judiciously, and by his unerring judgment, often prevented me from commiting mistakes, natural to my inexperience; and to which the innocence of unguarded youth is exposed in the trying Scenes of a Court– I never saw so fine a temper, or so truly and invariably lovely a disposition A years intimate acquaintance will attest this fact– I have always believed that he both respected and loved me, and did me justice in *times* when I needed a powerful friend–[30]

[30] JQA's new secretary, Thomas Welsh Jr. (1779–1831), was the son of Dr. Thomas Welsh

Mr. Garlick the english Chargé D'affaires became very intimate; and fortunately for me, many young Ladies constantly visited me at my own home, in the most social and agreeable manner— Some amused me with the Superstions of the Country—

> Where Ghost's and Goblin's formed the tale

others the scandals and peccadillo's of their neighbours—some annecdotes of the late Kings reign; an era prolific of themes of

> Quere and strange romancing, yet too true—

many of the Hero's and heroines being then at Berlin; having been principal performers in the guilty scenes; such as Madame Rietz (I think that was her name) Monsr. de Bishoffswerder the leader of the Illuminiti; and many others who soon after made their last appearance on the Stage, to give place to better rulers— The Lady abovementioned was the favorite Mrs. of the late King, who was banished the Court; and much of her property unlawfully gained, was siezed and resumed by the young King— Among the Stories *told* to me, was, one, which I think I can repeat, and which was current— The late King before his death being very low, and on whom every species of deception was practiced; had for some time resisted the extortionate demands of this Woman, and his Minister Bishoffswerder: and a *vision* was planed so as to shake his nerves, and thus atchieve through the terrors of religious apprehension, the base purpose which they so nefariously prosecuted— At the dead of the night, a figure representing our Savior, as risen from the dead, appeared to him; and commanded him to grant the prayers of his most *deserving* Minister, and most affectionate *friend*; and a failure to perform this *duty*, was to be punished everlastingly in the world to come— This scene was of course dramatized to suit the occasion; and fainting under the fears of an excited imagination, and the operation of powerful opiates, the King promised; and swooned— In

and his second wife, Abigail Kent Welsh, AA's first cousin. For the Welsh family, see CFA, *Diary*, 3:63; *AFC*, 3:189.

TBA left Berlin on 30 Sept. 1798. In Hamburg he secured passage on the *Alexander Hamilton*, Capt. Clarke, and sailed for America on 15 Nov., arriving in New York on 12 Jan. 1799. JQA gave AA a favorable account of his brother's accomplishments during his four years in Europe. He also informed her that he had entrusted his business affairs in America to TBA, since the stewardship of Dr. Welsh and CA had left his property in disarray (TBA, *Journal*, 1798, p. 32, 37, 40; TBA to JA, 27 Oct. 1798; JA to AA, 13 Jan. 1799; JQA to AA, 8 Oct. 1798, all Adams Papers).

the mean time the mystic paraphernalia was removed, and when he recovered all was as usual— In the morning he related his vision to one of the high Officers of the Court, and remarked "that he did not know before that *Jesus* wore a Watch Chain"!!! This observation led to the discovery of the imposition and banishment was the consequence— A queer anecdote!!![31]

The death of the Sweedish Minister introduced a new one to the Court. the Baron d'Engerstroum, a man qui à joué un grand role depuis, at the Court of Sweden as prime Minister— His Wife was a Polish Lady without beauty, although in her own conceit *beautiful*; very excentric; wealthy and with principles made easy by practical exertion— With them I now became acquainted and was thus ushered into a new school of morals, and as it turned out afterwards of female political tactics—[32]

After a lapse of five months I again took my place among the great world of Berlin, and again went through the same tread-mill round of ceremonious heavy ettiquette— At the Princess Henry's my greeting was polite— Again the vultures preyed upon my devoted purse, and though chagrin and spleen beset me, I endured the sight at Supper of the ruthful cuts upon the departing joints; and inwardly mourned at the want of capacity in myself, to enjoy with the delicious gusto of a *fasting* taste, the eates so amply set before me. Madame Eichstadt a Lady of eighty, who had done such honour at a

[31] Wilhelmine Encke (1752–1820), a trumpeter's daughter, was a mistress of Frederick William II and the mother of five of his children. Such was her influence from the time that he was a young prince until his death in 1797 that she was called "the Prussian Pompadour." In 1782 she married Johann Friedrich Rietz, Frederick William's groom of the chamber and later his treasurer. In 1796 the king gave her the title Countess of Lichtenau. When Frederick William III succeeded his father to the throne, the duchess was arrested, but she regained her freedom by surrendering her considerable property and accepting a pension (Princess Louise, *Forty-five Years*, p. 71, 72, 75, 159–161, 424, 443; *The Two Duchesses: Georgiana Duchess of Devonshire, Elizabeth Duchess of Devonshire*, ed. Vere Foster, London, 1898, p. 473–474).

Johann Rudolf von Bischoffwerder (1741–1803), a Saxon military officer, was an advisor to Frederick William II. In 1781 Bischoffwerder persuaded the king to join the Rosicrucians, a reactionary offshoot of freemasonry. He manipulated Frederick William with medical quackery, staged séances, and demonstrations of the occult, sometimes acting in concert with Madame Rietz (Princess Louise, *Forty-five Years*, p. 406; James Van Horn Melton, *The Rise of the Public in Enlightenment Europe*, N.Y., 2001, p. 267–268; Gertrude Aretz, *Queen Louise of Prussia 1776–1810*, transl. Ruth Putnam, N.Y., 1929, p. 67, 74–75; Charles William Heckethorn, *The Secret Societies of All Ages and Countries*, 2 vols., London, 1897, 1:229–230).

[32] Baron Lars von Engeström (1751–1826) was appointed Sweden's envoy to Berlin in 1798. He would serve as Sweden's prime minister, with responsibility for foreign affairs, from 1810 to 1824. His wife, Rozalia, was a member of the Polish nobility (*Repertorium*, 3:413; R. L. Tafel, *Documents Concerning the Life and Character of Emanuel Swedenborg*, 2 vols., London, 1877, vol. 2, part 2, p. 1242).

former mentioned supper Lord Gower[33] appeared with a splinded suit of diamonds new set, of a most costly description, and did her duty on this happy occasion, with equal fervour and unsubduing zeal— The wicked girls who let me into the secrets of the lesser lights, that shed their little rays on such occasions, had informed me that on these publick days; *dinners* were omited; lest the acuteness of the appetite should be blunted, and its keen edge be destroyed for the performance of the honors due to the Royal Viands— It is true that the amiable Lady above quoted was found dead in her bed supposed of an *indigestion*, after a supper of this kind at the same palace— My next appearance was at Bellevue, the Country house of Prince Ferdinand (I never saw the remarkably famed Prince Henry) and there the Princess extended her arms to embrace me, and from hers I passed to those of the Landgravine of Hessé Cassel who greeted me with the affectionate warmth of a Parent. Here I felt at *home*, The Landgravine made me sit by her at her work Table, and those who prefered work to play, sat with her and plied their needles; while a few Gentlemen joined in the conversation which was always light and agreeable— The Prince never sat down to Supper and the Princess prefered her Whist— Princess Radziville did the honors. Easy, and graceful, affable in her manners, she possessed that greatest of all *arts*, the power of ensuring the respect due to herself, while she gave a tone of social independence to her guests— The Chanoness Mad$^{lle.}$ de Bork was an elderly Lady of a great reputation for sense, observation, and reading— She possessed a great talent for drawing, which had been very highly cultivated; with a peculiar tact for siezing the likeness or expression of any features that happened to strike her fancy— With a small Card and a Crayon She would hold it under the Table, and while apparently conversing very animatedly, would perfect her sketch: The object of her work being utterly unconscious of the Act, and without suspicion of the fact— When the Supper was concluded I saw a large Card presented to the Princesses which seemed to fix all eyes on *me*; and much to my discomfiture I found she had taken what was generally pronounced to be a fine likeness of me: but I was not permited to see it until it was completed, a process always performed in her own apartment— A book of these likenesses was shown me at Princess Radzivilles; and a group of herself, her hus-

[33] LCA interlined "supper" then marked the words "Lord Gower" for insertion at this point.

band, and their little Child of three years old placed between them; gazing up in their faces with its lovely ringlets, and cherub Cheeks, as fresh as rosy morn, was one of the prettiest things I ever saw—

After these parties when I returned home I missed the Judge beyond expression— If he accompanied us, he had always something amusing to relate; and we would compare notes

> And o'er, and o'er again the past enjoy—

but Mr *Welsh*!! the contrast was complete! In appearance a perfect Cub—Stout, athletic, short necked, coarse complexioned, *raw*!—his manners abrupt; his conversation brusque; his voice vulgar; and exquisitely self-sufficient, th'ough very good tempered: the change was too much for my philosophy; and I could not help regretting, and perhaps making him sensible, how much *less* I thought of or admired *him* than his "*illustrious predescessor*"— An invetterate Yankee; every Fish was a Pickerel—Every Duck was a Brant; and like Cymon he wanted some bright *imagination*, to rub his newness off—[34] Whitcomb was his choice companion! and he soon made acquaintances out of our line—and we saw but little of him— Mr Adams recommended to him to take a french Master and he studied so assiduously, that in three months he could talk it fluently, and enter into society; corrected in many points and fashioned to appear in company— Somehow or other he did not succeed in the Grand Monde, and though I grew to like him better, I never could learn to like him much.— He never attained the lustre of the diamond, or the polish of pure gold, but like french or birmingham gilding the brass would show through—

Mr. Livingston a fine old Gentleman, a bonnie Scot, attached to the suite of the Prince Augustus of England, called on us, and we were quite charmed with him; and a day or two after I met the Prince with Mr. Livingston and Mr Arbuthnot at Dr. Browns— In very bad health, and suffering dreadfully from the Asthma the Prince could only sleep in an Arm Chair, and was frequently unable to go out of his chamber— Good humoured and pleasant, he was a general favorite. He was sent to Berlin I believe by the King upon a

[34] In John Dryden's 1700 poetical work *Cymon and Iphigenia*, Cymon, though well born, was "of a heavy, dull, degenerate mind." With his "clownish mien" and "stupid eyes," he "look'd like nature's error." But Cymon's chance meeting with the beautiful maiden Iphigenia inspired him "with liberal arts to cultivate his mind." He learned the ways of a gentleman and ultimately won the lady (John Dryden, *Cymon and Iphigenia*, lines 53, 56–58, 213; Stuart Gillespie and David Hopkins, eds., *The Oxford History of Literary Translation in England*, 4 vols. to date, Oxford, 2005– , 3:396).

stated allowance, with a view to separate him from his Wife Lady Augusta Murray; a marriage contrary to a parliamentary Law, but legal by the eclesiastical law; as the *bans* had been three times published in a Church in London, in the presence of the Congregation; under their proper names; and each being of age— This is a curious fact as *Guelph*, is a name extraordinary in itself to english ears, but being the name of the Royal family *only*; it seems almost incredible that it should have passed unnoticed— The Princes establishment was small yet handsome; but the most striking thing about it was, a South Carolina black Valet; of whom he appeared to be very fond.— The Prince travels under the title of Count de Diepholts—[35] Count Caraman called to see us; a very pleasant Frenchman of distinction Dr. Brown on a visit to England; but the family go on in the same style, and live very pleasantly—

My health failing again I could not accompany Mr. Adams on his weekly visits at Bellevue— Prince Ferdinand was very ill—and unable to appear— Princess Louisa was there with her Children— Some political difficulty had occurred to her Husband Prince Radziville, and the family appeared to be in trouble— Met Prince Augustus, Mr Livingston, and Mr Arbuthnot, at Madame de Voss's the Grande Gouvernante of the Queen: a visit of ceremony— An old Lady; tall, thin, and very stately! dressed in a hoop, and rich brocaded silk train and petticoat, with what used to be called a fly Cap, placed on the back of her hair, which was frizzed in the fashion of Mrs. Washington's portrait in the middle chamber—[36] Short Sleeves, large double Ruffles; Gloves, jewels, and fan— Her gait was stiff and formal, and she

[35] Prince Augustus Frederick, Duke of Sussex (1773–1843), was the son of George III. He studied at Göttingen and spent much of his time on the Continent in the hope of alleviating his severe asthma. While in Rome in 1792 Augustus met Lady Augusta Murray, daughter of the 4th Earl of Dunmore, and the two were secretly married there in April 1793 by a clergyman of the Church of England. To secure the marriage in an English jurisdiction, a second ceremony was performed that December at St. George's Church, Hanover Square, London, uniting "Augusta Murray" and "Augustus Frederick," without titles. The king learned of the marriage after Lady Augusta gave birth to a son, Augustus Frederick (later D'Este), in Jan. 1794, and later that year he declared the marriage void, acting under the Royal Marriages Act of 1772, which required the monarch's consent for the marriage of any descendant of George II under the age of 25. Augustus ignored the order for a time, and in 1801 a daughter was born. But in 1809 he complied and sought custody of the children (*DNB*; E. A. Smith, *George IV*, New Haven, Conn., 1999, p. 18).

The Guelph princely dynasty was represented in Great Britain by the House of Hanover (*OED*). Diepholz is a district in Lower Saxony.

[36] For Edward Savage's portrait of Martha Washington, which JA commissioned around 1790 along with a portrait of George Washington, see *AFC*, 9:xi, 56, 57. LCA is referring to the middle chamber of the Old House, the Adams family home in Quincy, where both portraits have been on display ever since.

exacted much more respect and homage than the Queen— Went with M[r] Adams to Madame de Salderns, but left the party, and returned home. M[r] Livingstone brought M[r.] Adams home— You will observe that at almost all these visits, M[r] Adams was obliged to play at Cards—therefore I was obliged to make my way as I could—and if I staid supper at Court, he was always at *home*, almost before I went in to table— And in this manner he acquired the habit of leaving me to myself on almost all occasions, since; not dreaming that a woman could feel lonely in company—and as it was the especial business of some appointed person to make the introductions; he has always been negligent of this ceremonial, much to the annoyance often of his family; always of Strangers—

The succession of Even[g.] parties for the Winter had begun; and we went to the Queen's first Court Circle for the Season; which were to take place once a week; the one a mere Circle and Cards— the other a Ball; thus alternating through the Season. A rigid scrutiny was kept up as to the omision of this mark of respect to their Majesties— It was therefore essential that a *good* and substantial excuse should be offered to avoid the appearance of neglect— To me these *duties* were a torment; being sickly and generally being obliged to stay Supper *alone*; much to my discomfiture, although always treated with particular distinction I did not play at Cards— After the Circle in which the King and Queen went round and spoke to their Guest's; She took her Seat at the Card Table having selected her own party; and She would often invite one of the Foreign Ministers as a mark of peculiar *honour*, to sit near her, that she might converse with him while she played Casinò— Behind her Chair stood four Maids of honour in waiting, and the Ladies where all obliged to go up to the Table, and make a low Courtesy, before they could participate in the amusements. The King and some of the Princes walked about the suite of rooms; and as it is not proper to sit or turn your back in the presense of Royalty; the watchfulness it imposes, keeps you in a perpetual fever, lest you should commit some blunder; sharply corrected by the Officers of the Court— A Novel by M[r.] Fay called the Countess; in this respect, gives a pretty accurate account of the difficulties in which strangers are placed; in the performance of the rigid ettiquettes sometimes rudely enforced—[37] The fashionable summary on such occasion as when speaking of them was, "the Queen lovely; the King silent; the Princesses gracious;

[37] Theodore Sedgwick Fay, *The Countess Ida: A Tale of Berlin*, 2 vols., N.Y., 1840.

the Princes affable, and the entertainment splendid— The Corps Diplomatique brilliant, and the English Prince elegant;["] this was the general formula for the Court— The little escapades of the young persons, were reserved for private intercourse; and distinction or disgrace was strongly marked by particular condescension, or pointed coolness—

At an evening party at Counts Panins. While dancing the string of my petticoat broke, and I was so frightened I nearly fainted. Retired to the Countesses boudoir and adjusted my dress— This accident caused her some mirth, and myself much confusion; I had a constant succession of Partners; and danced till three o'clock in the Morning— Madame Panin a fine Woman! At a party at Countess Bruhl's made to sing; accompanied by the Count on his Violin, and Mary his daughter on the Piano

~~NOVEMBER~~ DECEMBER 1898 [*1798*].

Spent the day at Countess Neales who had just returned to Town with the Princess— The Prince has been in disgrace!— At a dinner at D[r] Browns met Prince Augustus and his suite with Lord Talbot—a charming young Man, then very amiable and unpretending, and of very pleasant manners— The Prince very affable; but talking of his poverty and dependence upon his Father; which prevented his residing at Naples; the only climate which suited his Constitution—

13

Prince Augustus and his Family; Lord Talbot, M[r] Garlick, Secretary of the English Legation; The Hanoverian Minister Baron Ompteda; His Cousin The Chevalie Ompteda; a very remarkable person, measuring seven feet in height; A very Gentlemanly man of high Rank in the Military Service; but so embarrassed at being *so tall*, that it made him quite unhappy. I had much trouble with my Household arrangements my Cook being so intoxicated that she could not Cook; and dinner being delayed and spoilt in consequence— The Browns and M[r.] Sloper an Englishman of fortune completed the company— The party was social and after dinner the Prince said he would stay to *Tea*, he found himself so *comfortable*; if I would order my Servant, to desire *his* Valet to bring his dress Clothes, that he might make his toilet at our house, previous to his visit at the Baron D'Alvenslebens, where we were all invited to Meet the King and Queen— Every thing was arranged to his fancy, and I did the honours of the Tea Table in the old fashioned style— As at this period much was said concerning the quarrel between George the 4th. and his *Queen*, the Prince was standing at the Table talking to me, when Mrs. Brown very abruptly, and in her off hand manner, asked him (much to my confusion) "if *he* thought the Queen so *bad* as she was represented—" He hesitated a Moment; and then said "my Dear Madam" my brother is a *Beast*!!!—[38] It was quite late in the Eveng when the party broke up, and then I had to dress for the Ball. When I went up to pay my respects to their Majesties, the King said to me "so Prince Augustus dined with you to day"? I mention the fact to show you how well they were informed of every thing that passed

19TH

Went to dine with the Queen Mother; I was alone! She was very kind to me. I forgot to mention a visit made to her on a former occasion, at what they termed a Court of *Condolence*. The Ladies all went in full dress of deep Mourning, but without Veils— The Gentlemen full suits of black, Swords, &ca of the same— The Queen was Seated on one side near the Centre of a long Hall, hung with black— Her attendants in a half Circle behind her; and every one in deep black: herself in the deepest Widows weeds, with a Crape Veil flowing round her, and reaching the Floor— The Ladies and gentlemen passed very gravely, stopping before her; making a low obeisance, and then passing onward to give place to others— Not a word was spoken; not a smile seen and this mummery lasted two or more hours! Although it was a well known fact that this poor Woman, had been a wretchedly neglected and miserable Wife,— Her husband having installed two favorite Misstresses in high rank; and fortune;

[38] George, Prince of Wales (1762–1830), would rule Britain as George IV from 1820 to 1830 after serving as regent from 1811 to 1820 during the debility of his father, George III. The young prince amassed prodigious debts as he filled his residences with fine furnishings and works of art. For his unsanctioned marriage to Maria Fitzherbert in 1785, see *AFC*, 7:xi–xii. Within a few years of this union, George resumed his dissipations. To avoid financial ruin, in 1795 he married his cousin Caroline (1768–1821), daughter of the Duke of Brunswick. After the birth of a daughter, the two separated. Prince George attempted in vain to accumulate evidence of his estranged wife's indiscretions sufficient for a divorce. When, at his father's death, George prepared for his coronation, Caroline returned to England from her travels abroad to claim her place as queen. She was barred from the ceremony at Westminster Abbey. A sudden illness ended in her death three weeks later (*DNB*; E. A. Smith, *George IV*, New Haven, Conn., 1999, p. 46–47, 70–73, 77–81, 118–120, 174–178, 187–189).

who lived more courted and admired than herself; because more able to obtain favours for the parasites who hang upon the smiles of Royalty–

At a ball at Baron Alvensleben's–left early being engaged at Princess Ferdinands– She received us as usual most graciouly but insisted as I was fond of dancing that we should return to the Baron's Ball– Danced with Lord Talbot, Mr. Brummel and Mr. Graves, two English Gentlemen who had joined the suite of Prince Augustus–Brummel was famed for his beauty; and the finished grace of his manners–Graves a *rattle* full of wit and levity– They asked me "if the Queen was so beautiful as was reported? and insisted that they did not believe a word of it– That they were sure if she was any thing but a Queen; nobody would say any thing about her–["] I insisted that it was impossible to exaggerate upon the subject, and offered to *bet*, that when they had seen her, they would he more enthusiastic than any one else– Brummel smiled doubtfully; but Graves was positive that he should win the bet, and come off with flying colours– There was a Court at the Queens; two days afterwards, (I did not go); but the Gentlemen came to see me, and were perfectly rhapsodical in their admiration of (this it was thought) too lovely woman; for prudence to *Mr.* Graves–

Formed another new acquaintance a very pleasing but a very suffering Woman, Madame de Rozencrantz– Madame d Engerstroum introduced me– This Lady, Wife of the Danish Minister; had lost the use of her limbs, and for several years had been a most interesting and uncomplaining Woman– We sat with her some time and were charmed with her conversation.

The news of the deaths of two of Mr. Adams's friends cast a momentary gloom over the time; but his diplomatic duties did not permit retirement; and he was obliged to mix constantly in society irksome and painful to him, under such circumstances–[39] Under an engagement to the Princess Ferdinands and he being exceedingly unwell; *obliged* me to go alone though most reluctantly to make his

[39] JQA's cousin Elizabeth (Betsy) Quincy Shaw had died of consumption on 4 Sept. 1798. Thomas Crafts (1767–1798), Harvard 1785, had been admitted to the Suffolk County Court of Common Pleas in 1793, and he later served as a diplomat. As young lawyers in Boston, Crafts and JQA belonged to the Crackbrain Club, an informal social group that included Nathan Frazier Jr. and Daniel Sargent Jr. Crafts had died in August (D/JQA/24, 16 Dec. 1798, APM Reel 27; AA2 to JQA, 28 Sept. 1798, Adams Papers; Davis, *Mass. Judiciary*, p. 219; James M. Crafts and William F. Crafts, *The Crafts Family: A Genealogical and Biographical History of the Descendants of Griffin and Alice Craft, of Roxbury, Mass., 1630–1890*, Northampton, Mass., 1893, p. 189; Bemis, *JQA*, 1:26).

excuses; anxious and naturally timid, the trial was almost more than I could well get through with propriety—

Lord Talbot entertained Prince Augustus at the Hotel de Russie the party was select and well chosen, and the Evening so pleasent that the company did not separate until two in the morning— Lord Talbot has since been Vice-Roy of Ireland and much distinguished— You will see from the account of our first years proceedings, the general course of our lives; monotonous to read, but to us varied by the scandals of the moment; the politics of the day in which I took no part; the threatnings of War; and the disgraceful proceedings in England, of the heir to the Crown, and his wife; and the State of France at that time in the full blaze of her criminal revolution under the directory and the first Consul— In the Evening we were rarely alone at home; being constantly visited by a select few upon the most social footing; and the attendance at the Court parties filled up the time— At Court the Queen and the Royal family dressed with regal splendor; and diamonds, and Pearls, and precious Stones gave brilliancy to these Scenes of gorgeous display— In the midst of this apparently gay life; suffering was my portion, and anxiety that of my husband, to whose affectionate care I owed every thing— His affection was all I craved, and all the Court gew gaws and vanities were as nothing to me; as they only added regret to the memory of the past, in the bitter conviction that he might have formed a connection more suitable to the Station that he filled; and with more adequate means to support its consequence.—

1 JANUARY 99.

Began the year with the usual routine of congratulatory visits; the Even^g at Prince Ferdinands—but we did not stay to supper—my friend the Landgravine always kind—Sat at *her* table where M^r. Graves was very amusing, and quite in *ecstacies* with the exceeding beauty of the Queen—bantered him; because he had positively declared that he *would not* think her handsome!!

Had a small party at our House; the same as at Lord Talbots— Count and Countess Panin, M^r & Madame Bacounin, Count and Countess Golowkin, and their Daughter; all the English, and several of the Prussian young friends, with whom I was intimate— Prince Augustus sent an excuse—he was *obliged* to go and play at Blindsmans buff with the King and Queen; a diversion that the King was particulary fond of; but only play'd with the R family or any foreign

Prince who might be at Berlin– Ettiquette he said made it impossible for him to accept any other invitation however agreeable– He had accepted our invitation conditionally, anticipating this *call* which was often repeated– Prince Radziville and M^r. Sartoris came to supper, Count and Countess Bruhl and their daughters were of the party, and we danced until four o clock in the morning– Next day M^r. & M^rs. Errington were introduced to me at my own house–[40] Lord Talbot introduced an elegant man to us Mr St George–quite a Sir Charles Grandison–

At a large party at Count Shulemburgs–heard strange whispers of Princess Louis– The King and Queen both sick– The Princess Louis has made a faux-pas, and the result is so apparent, that she has confessed a private marriage to the King; but the Clergyman cannot be found who performed the ceremony– Her *Husband* is the Prince de Solms, an Officer of an inferior grade, without fortune, but handsome– They are ordered off to Anspach a Garrison Town on the Frontier– It is said that she cannot reach the Station before her confinement– Something was suspected from the change in her dress– She had suddenly become very modest and precise– This Lady is the present Queen of Hanover– The Queen has had no Court– She is dreadfully distressed at the conduct of her Sister– The amusements at Court postponed– The Princess Louis was confined at a poor miserable inn on the road, on the first night of her Journe'y– Three nights before I had seen her dancing the whole Evening, Waltzes and Country dances until eleven o'clock; the only difference in her *appearance*, being the extreme simplicity of her dress–in which hitherto she had always vied with the Queen in her ornaments, and in the richness of her apparel–[41] Whispers running

[40] George Henry Errington (1777–1843) of Chadwell Hall and Ashbourn and his wife Elizabeth Sophia (d. 1835) (Burke, *Geneal. and Heraldic Hist.*, 1875, 1:399).

[41] The party at the home of the Prussian official Frederick William, Count of Schulenburg-Kehnert (1742–1815), took place on 9 Jan. 1799. Frederica Sophia Carolina of Mecklenburg-Strelitz had married Prince Louis Charles in 1793, shortly after her sister Louisa's marriage to his brother, the crown prince. Louis took little interest in his young wife, but the couple had two children, Frederick William Louis (b. 1794) and Frederica Wilhelmina Louisa (b. 1796), before Louis died of typhus. When Frederica's "faux-pas" and secret marriage to Frederick William, Prince of Solms-Braunfels (1770–1814), were discovered, the two were dispatched to Ansbach in Jan. 1799. Frederica forfeited her royal title and coat of arms and was forced to leave her son behind. By Queen Louisa's intercession, the child Frederica, just over two years old, was allowed to remain with her mother, but only until the time came for her to be returned to the court to be educated. After the death of Solms-Braunfels in 1814, Frederica married Ernest Augustus, Duke of Cumberland, a son of George III. In 1837 the duke became king of Hanover (D/JQA/24, 9, 13 Jan. 1799, APM Reel 27; Jane-Eliza Hasted, *Unsuccessful Ladies: An Intimate Account of the Aunts (Official and Unofficial) of the Late Queen Victoria,*

round at the same time concerning one of her Maids of Honor, a very beautiful Woman, with whom rumour said the King was much smitten— She had had Twins supposed to be his Majestys; and this Winter had been married off to an Officer in the Army near the Kings person; who was promoted suddenly on the occasion—

At Court a Ball! not intending to dance, I wore a train; and when my Princely Partners asked me I declined dancing; and was quietly seated by one of my friends, chatting very pleasantly; when I saw Madame de Voss the Grande Gouvernante of the Queen, coming across the Hall; and while every eye was on her She advanced and stood immediately before me; "and announced to me, that the King intended to dance the first Country-dance with me— That I must sit still until I saw his Majesty take his place; and that I must then walk up alone and take my stand opposite to him—["] Conceive my situation! Madame de Voss no longer was the object of attention; She sidled off with her hoop shaking under her mincing step, erect as a may Pole; and every eye was on me, who being under the necessity of looping my train, thus betrayed the message, even before I was to go through the most painful part of the ceremony— The dance formed; the King took his place, fortunately for me next couple to the Queen, and I marched up ready to faint, and took my place— The King walked up and spoke to me, and the Queen with her usual loveliness; took my hands in hers, and stood and talked some minutes until I recovered myself— She told me I looked so pale she must make me a present of a box of rouge; I answered that Mr. Adams would not let me wear it— She smiled at my simplicity, and observed that if *she* presented me the box he must not refuse it, and told me to tell him so. She then beckoned to the King, and told him to begin the dance in the middle of the line, at the same time that She began it at the top; and *we* began the dance at the same moment— Prince Augustus and his Gentlemen all encouraging me, and kindly complimenting me when I returned to my Seat, upon the marked distinction with which I had been treated— My accustomed *partners*, who had claimed the engagements entered into for the Winter complained that although I was engaged to them; I could dance with the King; I got so flurried that Mr. Adams took me home before Supper—

I told Mr. Adams what the Queen said; but he said I must refuse

London, 1950, p. 163, 166–173, 179–180, 189). See also Descriptive List of Illustrations, No. 5, above.

5. PRINCESSES LOUISE AND FREDERICA OF PRUSSIA,
BY JOHANN GOTTFRIED SCHADOW, 1797
See page x

the box, as he should never permit me to accept it– At this Ball I saw Madame D'Harlberg a Lady from Vienna, who had formed a liáson with Mr. Graves, and had quitted her *Husband*, to follow her chére Ami to Berlin.– Her conduct displeased the Queen; and though she was a Lady of very high rank, she was treated very coolly– My health being again very delicate I staid much at home–

Mr. Siéyes Minister from France a Man famous in the revolutionary history of France– He had the worst countenance I ever saw; and was apparently very much out of his element in the Court Circles.[42] Made the acquaintance of Mr & Mrs Errington a young English couple just married– My life was now passed in a constant round of company. When my health became so delicate that I could not go through the fatigue of attendance at Court; and the numerous parties which follow in such quick succession during the Carnaval which usually begins on the 6th. of January twelth day– This year 1799 postponed supposed on account of the affair of Princess Louis The King had taken her Children–

During the Carnaval Every Night in the Week is engaged for Courts, Parties, or dancing *Teas* as they are called, not in full dress, Opera's twice a week in full dress, Mondays and Fridays; a Ridotto or masked Ball on Thursday. A box is appropriated to the Foreign Ministers and Kings Ministers at the Kings expence. The King and Queen have a box in the Centre, where they hold a Court for the Foreign Ministers, and strangers of distinction; but the Ladies are exempted from the duty of attendence– Tuesdays and Saturdays Dance, and Supper, at one of the Ministers; Sunday Ball at Court– Wednesday Circle in full Court dress; Hoops &ca. at Queen Mothers and Thursday Ridotto generally from a party at the House of one of the great Ministers followed by a Supper– The King and Queen always attend; and although the Prince of Orange had just deceased; the mourning was postponed and the amusements went on as usual– Went to the Opera with Mr & Mrs Errington; Mr. Adams in the Royal Box; The Opera Atalanta– Music was very good– I was very fond of this amusement[43] Went to a party at Count Arnims, stayed supper; and then followed the King and Queen, and the Foreign Ministers to the Ridotto– On these occasions the Ladies wear a black dress décolté! A Venetian Cloak in the Spanish fashion,

[42] In 1798, during the Directory, Abbé Emmanuel Joseph Sieyès was sent to Prussia as minister plenipotentiary (Bosher, *French Rev.*, p. lviii; *Repertorium*, 3:132).

[43] George Frideric Handel composed the opera *Atalanta* in 1736 to celebrate the wedding of Frederick, Prince of Wales, the eldest son of George II (Grove *Dicy. of Music*).

short and hanging full across the Shoulders; short sleeves—Diamond Earings and Necklace; black Shoes; a black Spanish Hat looped up in front with diamonds, and feathers of the same hue drooping lightly over the front of the hat, and inclining over the left shoulder; Bracelets of Jewels, or gold, and a Pr. of EYES; a Wire covered with black, and trimmed round with *very* very narrow ribbon, like a pr. of Spectakles, without glasses, instead of a Mask—

This dress was remarkably becoming to the Ladies who wore rouge, but made those who were pale look cadaverous—particularly when not relieved by the brilliancy of diamonds I who was remarkably pale, of course looked a *fright* in the midst of the Splendor, and in addition these things were so dull I took no pleasure at them at all—

At Court I presented Mrs. Errington to the Queen— We were dressed nearly alike; My Dress White Satin with gold embroidered in light draperies, the Skirt trimmed with gold fringe; and hers the same only trimmed with Silver— We danced all the Evening; I with my accustomed partners, and with the English; and a Mr. Pérponcher who was: a young Dutchman in the Prussian Service, and very intimate at Countesse golowkins our friend and neighbour. The Ball was given in honor of Prince Augustus, whose Birthday it was;[44] The Queen Mother sat opposite to *us*, next the young Queen; the company seated all around the room—excepting the Gentlemen; who formed a half Circles on each side of their Majesties— The Queen Mother beckoned to *me* to come to her! I pretended to be busy talking to Mrs. Errington, to avoid seeing her—but she insisted; and a gentleman informed me that the Queen wished to speak to me, and I was obliged to walk across the Hall between this circle of Gentlemen; and when I got there; She only wanted to ask me "how old I was"? How to get back without turning *my back*, was the difficulty; but I did so with the assistance of Prince Augustus, who complemented me upon extricating myself so *well* from the delemma— I believe they played me all these pranks to quiz me—being very raw—

Mr. Arbuthnot was one of the most charming Men I ever knew, and he and Mr. Livingston visited us on the most friendly terms, indeed few days passed without our meeting them at home or abroad, and this intercourse was delightful— They were men of classical

[44] The queen's ball to mark the birthday of Prince Augustus took place on 27 Jan. 1799 (D/JQA/24, APM Reel 27).

taste, highly cultivated, and with that experience and knowledge of the world which gives the last polish to man; by curing him of the narrowness of local prejudices; and teaching him, *that* liberality of opinion, which is acquired by travel through different Countries, where we find the same mixture of good and evil; although through the medium of different customs and usages, as we do in our own; and we learn that as fallible mortals, we must be lenient to the faults, which a more moral and better system of education, makes us disapprove. I sometimes went to small private theatrical parties, at the Princess Louisa's; acted by Mon$^{r.}$ and Madame de Sartoris, their Children, and my little affectionate friend Countess Pauline de Neale, and Mad$^{lle.}$ Borch, and the Prince. The performances were so excellent that they were soon more extended; and Count Galatin a Cousin of Mr Galatin,[45] and Count *Colentzel*, who I think used to figure at Catherine the 2^{d}s performances; were really excellent actors— We associated pleasantly with the Foreign Ministers—intimately with Mr Garlick. but their establishments were on a scale so magnificent, we could not attempt to entertain them often—

Went to Court; M$^{r.}$ Adams, M^{r} & M$^{rs.}$ Errington and myself: We wore hoops and the old fashioned Court dress à *l'anglaise*; As every body played Cards on a Sunday, *we* who both had a great objection to it; but who could not decline it; it being contrary to established ettiquette; M$^{r.}$ Errington, his Wife, Lord Talbot and I sat, round the Table; the gentlemen shuffling and dealing the Cards, while we amused ourselves with taking them up for them to renew the deal. Lord Talbot said we must endeavour not to attract attention, by an affectation of singularity— At Supper we had to manage our Hoops, which was very difficult; and the Chairs were so near together, that half of the Hoop on each side, rested on the knees of Lord Talbot and Count S$^{t.}$ George, who sat with us— M$^{rs.}$ Errington was two and twenty; pretty, well educated and highly accomplished. better acquainted with the great world than myself; sprightly, but not graceful— To me she was a charming companion, and we were almost always together— We there at Court saw Madame Piper a Sweedish Lady of distinction, who had accompanied the Dutchess of Sudermania; and Madame Armfeldt—wife of a distinguished Sweedish General; some years after suspected of a conspiracy by the Emperor Alexander in Russia— At the Ridotto—Where we saw a Splendid

[45] Pierre, Comte de Gallatin, who served the King of Württemberg as a diplomat (Henry Adams, *The Life of Albert Gallatin*, Phila., 1879, p. 3, 563).

quadrille which was enacted by the Queen, Prince Augustus, and all the most distingué of the Court— It was the Marriage of Philipè and Mary— The Queen exhibiting as Mary of England, and the Prince in the character of Philip of Spain— It had been in rehearsal for six weeks; and one of the Queens Maids of honour had told me, that I had been selected to take a part in one of the quadrilles— Mr. Adams told me to excuse myself on the plea of ill health; but the real reason was, that the expence was enormous; and the constant rehearsals, would have thrown me into a constant association with the gay person's of the Court, not agreeable to him, and perhaps hazardous to me— The invitation was flattering nevertheless; as I was the only foreign Lady so distinguished— Every Jewel that could be found was put in requisition on this splendid occasion, Every painting and historical work was examined, to ascertain the Costumes and manners of the Age— The dresses were all in character and in the highest style of magnificence— The Queen was covered with Diamonds; wearing all the Crown Jewels superbly set; and her *own*, which were magnificent! On her head she wore the Royal Crown, and her rich Robes of State, with the broad ermine, were supported by Youths brilliantly dressed as Pages; with her eldest Son, and the eldest Son of the Princess of Orange walking a little behind her, holding the large tassels attached to her robes, as little pages: and looking as sweetly as Children of four or five years old excited by the animation of such a Scene always appear— Her Suite of Course, consisted of Peers and Nobles of the English Court, and was as splendid as it could be made— The Procession entered, preceded by Marshals &cc and all the usual pomps of such occasions. The Music was composed by the best Masters; and the Ballet Master of the Opera House had composed and taught the quadrilles, danced on the occasion— The Procession marched gracefully round the hall, and the Queen took her stand on one side of the Stage, the attendants placing themselves in regular order behind her— King Philip then appeared; the Procession marching in the same manner, banners and Music &cc all Spanish! He looked remarkably handsome in the Spanish dress, which was as rich as money could make it; and having completed the march, he took his stand opposite the Queen: the Knights, Cavaliers, and Gentlemen of his train, ranging themselves so as to leave a vacancy for the exhibition of the Quadrilles on the Stage; consisting of English, Spanish, Scots, Flemish, and Mexicans each performed with great skill, as the National dances of the different Countries— The handsomest young Men, and the prettiest

Women had been selected; and the effect was admirable– The Ladies had not followed the Costume so closely as to wear gowns high in the Neck; their dresses were therefore very becoming, and made more display of jewelry, than they would otherwise of permited–[46] The King, Prince Augustus and Queen then joined hands; and the Processions united, and took their departure to the Palace where they finished the Eveng. Mr. Adams and I went and supped at Dr Browns the next Evening where we talked over the last Evenings performance very pleasantly, with Count Bruhls family, Lord Talbot and Mr. Sloper– Frederick William was only a Spectator– Madame de Pritwitz while at Cards at the Princess Henry's; was siezed with apoplexy; and being too ill to be removed from the Palace was carried to a chamber, and died there, next morning– Two days after, Princess Henry appeared at a Ball given by the Queen to her, on her birth day– The old Lady was 73 or 4– We did not stay to supper. We were introduced to Mr Thomas Grenville, a new Mission from England; consisting of Mr G—— Mr. Winne and Mr. Fisher–[47]

Mr & Mrs. Shickler were always very polite to us, and we dined there frequently– He was Mr. Adams's Banker, and they lived in a very showy style, and entertained very handsomely– Mr & Mrs. Cohen; very rich Jews; were also very polite to us; and lived in a style of great elegance, entertaining the first and highest persons of rank in the City–[48]

[46] The quadrille, which represented the 1554 nuptials of Philip II of Spain and Queen Mary of England, was presented on 13 Feb. 1799. JQA described the costumes as only "partly conformable" to the original ones: "The Ladies could not adopt the dress of the period so far as to cover their bosoms" (D/JQA/24, APM Reel 27).

[47] Thomas Grenville (1755–1846), the son of George Grenville, prime minister of Great Britain, 1763–1765, was on a special mission to Berlin to propose an alliance against France. His brother William Wyndham Grenville (1759–1834) was Britain's secretary of state for foreign affairs, 1791–1801 (*DNB*; *Repertorium*, 3:170–171).

[48] LCA is referring to one of two brothers, David (1755–1818) or Johann Ernst (1762–1801), the sons of Johann Jakob Schickler. The elder Schickler had married the daughter of his employer, David Splitgerber, of the merchant and financial firm Splitgerber & Daum. After Splitgerber's death, Schickler assumed control of the business. In the 1790s David and Johann Ernst took over, and the firm, now called Schickler Brothers, became primarily a banking house (W. O. Henderson, *Studies in the Economic Policy of Frederick the Great*, London, 1963, p. 8, 15–16).

Pessel Zülz Cohen (b. 1776) was the daughter of a prosperous silk manufacturer and the wife of Ephraim Cohen of a wealthy Amsterdam banking family. Ephraim Cohen had brought English spinning machines to Berlin and, in partnership with the state, established a wool factory near his home that employed hundreds of workers. By 1800 the Cohens had converted from Judaism to Christianity and changed their names to Philippine and Ernst. Philippine hosted a literary salon that thrived until 1804, when her husband's mismanagement caused the failure of the business and the loss of her family's fortune (Deborah Hertz, *Jewish High Society in Old Regime Berlin*, Syracuse, N.Y., 2005, p. 103–104; Deborah Hertz, *How Jews Be-*

Every Friday when able I accompanied Mr. Adams to Prince Ferdinands, where I took my work, and usually sat by the Landgravine of Hesse Cassel— In the Winter at the Ferdinand Palace, in the Summer at Belle Vue—

My health failing again I did not go out through the Month of March, excepting to visit Mrs. Brown my next Neighbour—

4TH [*APRIL*]

Mr Grenville and Suite, Mr Arbuthnot, the Browns, Lord Talbot, and Mr Sloper dined with us— Mr Grenville was a brother of Lord Grenvilles, then Minister of Foreign Affairs in England. He was one of the mildest, most agreable and most amiable men, and distinguished as a diplomatist— I knew so little concerning politicks, I seldom heard, and never enquired what was going on— I only knew that it was a period of great events, which I did not understand; and in which I individually took no interest— Mr Adams had always accustomed me to believe, that Women had nothing to do with politics; and as he was the glass from which my opinions were reflected, I was convinced of its truth, and sought no farther—

When my health failed the House of Dr Brown was my refuge—

At Mr. Cohens we saw the Barbier de Seville, and the Somnambula; a private performance: the first tolerably well performed— The party very large and crowded—

Mr. Mrs & the Miss Sanfords were introduced to me—An english family of great respectability and wealth— The Husband a complete English Squire of the old School; a regular Tally ho!!! Mrs. Sanford a most beautiful Woman; Young and apparently very ill, mismatched, and very unhappy—[49] They requested me to present them at Court, and we arranged to call upon the Grande Maitresses of all the Courts, amounting to six; and to ask an introduction to the Queen and Princesses: This was a ceremony always performed in *person*, from which no one could be exempted; An arrangement was then made between us in regard to their dress &ce and that I would accompany them at the time appointed. The two young Ladies were very pretty, but quite eclipsed by the beauty of their Sister— Mrs. Sanford was one of those exquisitely sensitive, and lovely creatures;

came Germans: The History of Conversion and Assimilation in Berlin, New Haven, Conn., 2007, p. 60).

[49] The Misses Sanford were the English gentleman's sisters; they lodged at the Hotel de Russie (D/JQA/24, 9, 21 April 1799, APM Reel 27).

that appeared like the sensitive plant, to shrink at the gaze of man, and to tremble at the rough tones of her husband, and his boisterous ways— Delicate to fragility; apparently far advanced in consumption, with all the elegant polish of the highest refinement; It was impossible to be acquainted with her, without feeling admiration and love for her fine qualities, and her lovely disposition: and compassion for her *lot*, which evidently was not of her own seeking: and you could not see her without feeling a conviction that she had been sacrificed by some dire necessity, most likely to the shrine of Plutus the God to whom so much of the adoration of this life is paid— We all went to Court where the Ladies were well received, and Mr. Garlick presented the Ursa Major, that accompanied them; much to the diversion of the Court, to whom such a character was new— Madame D'Harlberg on this Eveng. was so indelicately dressed; that the Queen sent her Mrs. Mistress of the Ceremonies to request; that she would retire and make some change in her arrangements, *or go home*— This unblushing Woman who was very handsome, returned into the Hall—and danced the whole Eveng— The Queen herself Waltzed with Mr. Graves, wherever she met him—[50]

A night or two after they went to the Queen Mothers— The Queen told Madame D'Halberg in the morning, that she had invited Mr. Graves on purpose to meet her— She was glad to see them so well together and hoped it would last!!! This Speech she made at a breakfast which her Majesty gave in a Green House at about a mile from Berlin—[51] The Sanfords also there— The poor old Queen was about half crazy—

Count Zinzendorf who had been Minister at Berlin for 22 years, was recalled to be Minister of War at Dresden— we were invited to a Féte given to him, prior to his departure—

At Count Panins; a party on her recovery from an illness two french plays; la Gageure imprevu and le Sourd—[52] They live in a Palace in which there is a regular built theatre:—very handsomely fitted up— Count Caraman a great performer—and Count Galatin—

At Count Zinzendorfs party—He gave it himself upon taking

[50] For Madame d'Harlberg, evidently the bright constellation of the evening, see Adventures, 1 Jan. 1799, above.

[51] JQA described as "curiously selected" the company at the queen mother's 13 April 1799 breakfast gathering at the greenhouse (D/JQA/24, APM Reel 27).

[52] *La gageure imprévue*, 1768, a comedy by Michel Jean Sedaine (1719–1797); and *Le sourd, ou l'auberge pleine*, 1790, a comedy by Pierre Jean Baptiste Desforges (1746–1806).

leave— It was a Ball and Supper. The young Ladies crowned him with flowers— I thought it was given to *him* With the Sanfords I went to Prince Ferdinands; as usual I sat with the Landgravine, and we stayed Supper—a new *Rule* At the Princess Henry's, with the Sanfords having presented them—Mr. Adams was invited to Supper— The Sanfords and I played Cards together—

While standing at the Window in the library I saw a child run over by a Cart— He was taken up dreadfully injured, and I fainted and fell— The consequence was a sudden illness full of disappointment, and ruinous to my constitution— The wretchedness of Mr. Adams aggravated the evil and only made the suffering more distressingly excruciating; At such seasons women want every solace, for they endure both corporeal and mental anguish— He was kind and affectionate in his attention; but his feeling of disappointment could not be subdued—[53]

Mr Forbes came very unexpectedly to see us— He is on his way to Hamburg from thence to England—[54]

Every Sunday regularly and without interruption, Mr. Adams read the Church Service to me in its regular form while we remained in the Country—

I had frequently breakfasted with my friend Pauline Neale at her appartments in the Radziville Palace: generally alone; sometimes with Louisa de Berg, a lovely Girl; and sometimes with Emily Zeuinert another charming Girl, a Maid of honour, of the Queen with whom I was very intimate— At breakfast one morning about a week or two before, I met there a Miss Dunderfeldt, a very beautiful and strikingly elegant Girl, of about eighteen—

Pauline introduced her very particularly—told me she was an adopted daughter of the Landgravines; and that she wished we might become intimate— I was charmed with her manners, and e're we parted she had sung for me, and we were quite acquainted— Pauline treated her with an extraordinary degree of respect; and there appeared to be some mystery about this young Lady, that I could not understand— I afterwards learnt that she was an incognita in Berlin; being a person of distinguished rank—and engaged to be married to, *I think*, one of the Princes of Wirtemberg

[53] LCA was experiencing a miscarriage and continued to be very ill throughout the month. As JQA noted, "A time of great anxiety now begins with much to fear, and little to hope" (D/JQA/24, 20 April 1799, APM Reel 27).

[54] For John Murray Forbes, a Harvard classmate of JQA's who visited on 28 April, see CFA, *Diary*, 1:1; JQA, *Diary*, 2:186, 188 (D/JQA/24, APM Reel 27).

The current of true love did not run smooth—as usual; and she was under the protection of the Margravine, until things should take a favorable turn—

We became very intimate; and I had conceived a very high opinion of her before we parted, never to meet again— I think her Romance ended with the marriage, and she became much respected at the Court where she resided— Who she was, or the mystery of the moment while she staid in Berlin, I never fathomed—

My Eveng's—when not at the great parties; I have already said were passed at Dr Browns, or at home; generally with the same company— When Mrs. Brown was alone a thing that rarely happened; she used to amuse me with long stories of Welsh Superstitions, and traditions highly interesting— Many of these wonderful events, had occurred to herself, and she implicitly believed the tales which she rehearsed; thereby giving them a character of sober interest, powerfully operating upon the imagination— I have often remarked, that the traditions, and Superstitions which you hear related by the uneducated, and ignorant, produce a much stronger effect upon the mind, than the varnished tales, depicted by writers of eminence, and accomplished Poèts— The action, the look, the words, infused with the faith in the details; produce a marked effect, and altogether give a reality to the depicted scene, which can never appear in written words; painting striking incidents with cold deliberation; which may inspire awe; but never produce that electric surprize, and suppressed fear, which is almost always realized by the listener, to a "horror" well related, blending the wistful look, and the half shuddering gaze; and the oft repeated glance at the door; with sudden and abrupt pauses; while the listening ear and the tremulous voice, awaken feelings of which you are ashamed, but which influence the imagination in despite of reason and resolution—

Miss Bishoffswerder was a person of a different calibre altogether. A woman of the world; who had played a grand Role in Society; She was as full of Superstitious notions as the before mentioned Lady. But she produced an entirely different effect upon my mind— Her histories were elaborate; and there was an appearance of worldly craft in her arrangement of the incidents, and in her manner of reciting; which blighted the interest by its artificial colouring; as too strongly contrasted lights, and shadows; destroy the beauty of an otherwise well concieved, and well finished painting— It is good! but it is not life!!! One Evening I went to take Tea with her at the Palace, where she had apartments, as Lady of honour to the Queen Mother— She accompanied me down the Grand Stair Case to Show me the Window at which it was *said*, that the Wife of the great Frederic appeared; always prior to the death of one of the Royal family— If she held a fan (I think) it was to be a female; if a glove a Male—and as She (Miss B) was in familiar intercourse with Spirits, she often saw, and conversed with her—[55]

Pauline Neale highly educated; remarkably well read; enthusiastic in her religion; was full of german mysticism in its most exaggerated sense; and a sincere and true believer— Hours I have spent in her society, when my blood has thrilled with her Rhapsodies; and she has related annecdotes of Bohemia, and Poland where she had long resided; and where she had collected the legendary tales of all the great families—*each* under the influence of a good or an evil genius; regulating their future destiny; foreshewing events monstrous and unnatural; from which they could not flee; which yet they must abide e'en through the wide world— I have returned home in a fever of excitement that has almost made my hair stand on end— Sometimes I woud try to banter her; She would instantly turn pale; shudder, look round the room and say she had *seen too much* to doubt the reality of her assertions; and then drop the conversation— Living in a school like this; sickly and weak both in body and mind; can you wonder that my mind became tainted, and infected by a weakness, of which I have *tried* to be ashamed; but which still clings to me as if it was a part of my nature?

Went with Miss Brown to the Review; a splendid military Scene— Mr. Adams having already seen them did not attend. 10000 Men—[56] Next day to a party at Mrs. Sanfords, at the Hotel— There we met Mr. Harris, the eldest Son of Lord Malmsbury; and Col Stuart; both men of distinction; and Mr. Harris in reputation a perfect nonesuch— Lord Talbot had just returned from Dresden, *and* the Arch Dukes Army— Attended the Review again Mr. Adams would not accompany me, being tired of them— In the Evening at a Ball given by the King and Queen who did not stay to supper—

[55] Opinions vary as to the identity of the "White Lady of the Hohenzollerns," a spectral figure whose appearance was said to presage the death of a member of the royal family. See, for example, Countess Terese Zalinski, *Noted Prophecies, Predictions, Omens, and Legends Concerning the Great War,* Chicago, 1917, p. 106–109; "Will the White Ladies of the Hohenzollerns and Hapsburgs Walk Again?" *New York Times,* 18 Oct. 1914; "Ghost Traditions of Hohenzollerns," *New York Times,* 20 Dec. 1914.

[56] The king's annual inspection of the military was held this year on 21–23 May (D/JQA/24, APM Reel 27).

We dined with a large party at M[r] Shicklers, and there met a very vulgar and disagreeable Englishman, who asked to be introduced to us;—and the next day we accompanied M[rs.] Shickler to Charlottenburg with a party. I could not bear to go out alone, but M[r] Adams always insisted on it.— The monotonous course of our lives at this Season of the year, gives but few subjects to write on— M[r.] Terry an Englishman formed a little variety—he sung delightfully; otherwise in no way remarkable— I consider this tedious account of past times as containing a gallery of striking pictures not hit off with the satiric keeness of a Mirabeau, but more just in the likenesses—

Count and Countess Gowlofkin called to take leave of us ere their departure for Teplitz, to which place they urged us to go, as they thought the bath's would be of great service to me—

The illness which had threatened me so long again occurred and I was kept at home 4 or 5 weeks— My Nerves were so terribly shattered by this last illness, that Dr Brown recommended a journey; and on the 17th of July, I was lifted into the Carriage, and by the time we arrived at Dresden, I had gained sufficient strength to participate in the pleasures, which the journey presented—

Went immediately after dressing to see my friend M[rs.] Errington, who I found with a sweet little Girl, who she had named Dresdina—[57] Almost as roughly handled as myself, she had narrowly escaped with her life—but she was blessed with a fine Child, while I only lived to witness the pangs of disappointment, which so bitterly distressed my poor husband, and destroyed all the comfort of my life— The Letters from America weighed me down with sorrow, and mortification; for anguish will have vent, and the heart will breathe its sorrows to the loved ones who have participated in our blessings.[58] It is a trite saying "that it does no good" but it is not true; for even the momentary relief, assuages the heaviness of grief, and softens its asperity— We dined with M[rs.] Errington, and there met two young Englishmen, M[r] Thompson, and M[r.] Wright— I accompanied M[r.] Adams to the Picture Gallery— I will not discuss the Paintings; but will only say that some of them inspired me with delight almost

[57] Elizabeth Dresdena Errington would marry Rev. James Wortham Hitch of Pembroke Hall, Cambridge, England, in 1826 (Burke, *Geneal. and Heraldic Hist.*, 1875, 1:399; "State of the Dioceses in England and Wales," *The Quarterly Theological Review and Ecclesiastical Record*, 4:498 [Sept. 1826]).

[58] AA wrote to JQA on 10 Feb. 1799, enclosing a letter from LCA's mother, which has not been found. In a letter of 1 Feb. AA had said that Catherine Johnson was depressed and concerned about her husband's financial affairs (both Adams Papers).

adoration—[59] On returning home met Madame De Berg and the beautiful Louise her daughter—

24 [*JULY*]

At four o'clock in the morning we started for Töplitz— The Geyersberg is a mountain so steep, that we could not descend in the Carriage; I was placed in an arm Chair, supported by two poles, and carried down gently by two men— On the side of the Mountain about half way down, stand the ruins of a Castle, said to have been magnificent in its day, and owned by a feudal Baron of a desperately wicked character— This Man having commited every crime, like the far famed Don Juan we were informed; had sold his Soul to his Infernal Master, for the privilege of a lengthened career; which was granted on condition, that the catalogue of his crimes should be complete— The Bond was signed in form; but the penalty was exacted in the midst of his successful triumphs; and his Lordship was siezed, and dashed from one of the loopholes of the highest turret, which caused a frightful gap; at the deriding laugh of the unrelenting spirit; who with malignant joy delighted in the agonies which he occasioned— 'Twas in this ruin that we were assured, that his Satanic Majesty revisited the Scene of his former glory, at a periodical Season; and that during his *stay*, the Ruins were brilliantly illuminated with most unholy fires; and that he kept up his Orgies with the most horrid sounds, and diabolical language, till the Cock crew; when he and his Satellites disappeared to renew the clamour at the dark hour of midnight; when the awful Tragedy was again rehearsed; the body thrown out, the shrieks and curses; and the laugh reechoing its horrid sounds, for miles around—[60]

We arrived safely at Töplitz—having met Madame de Castel, who informed us that our Lodgings were all ready; and immediately on

[59] The collection of the Royal Picture Gallery in Dresden dates to 1560, but the gallery itself was established in 1722. By the time of this visit, the collection was extensive and included works by German, Flemish, Dutch, Italian, and French masters. The best-known paintings were acquired by the elector of Saxony, Frederick Augustus II (who, as king of Poland, was Augustus III), under the supervision of Count Heinrich von Brühl (Karl Woermann, *Catalogue of the Royal Picture Gallery in Dresden*, transl. B. S. Ward, 5th edn., Dresden, 1902, p. 1–8).

[60] LCA was told similar tales about this unidentified castle ruin on the Geyersberg slope, which she and JQA passed on their route from Peterswald to Töplitz (present day Petrovice and Teplice, Czech Republic), and the castle of Dobrawska Hora near Töplitz, which they visited later, for which see Adventures, note 68, below.

our arrival took possession and found ourselves quite comfortable. Töplitz is situated in a deep Valley, through which runs a Stream of Water of different temperature, from hot to cold; seemingly graduted by Nature in its different degrees, to suit the temperaments of different Invalids– The Baths are built very roughly, immediately over the Stream; at intervals; and the Physician of the place prescribes the degree of warmth proper for the complaint of the Patient– The debility under which I laboured was such, he would not permit me to attend the publick Bath's; and the Water was brought to the House and the bath's were prepared in my Chamber in Tubs, until I should be strong enough to bear the fatigue of the bath, and the exercise together–[61] Three times a week the bath, and every day a bottle of Pyrmont Water[62] taken while walking in the gardens of Prince Clary, always open for the benefit of the Publick–[63] Our Lodging was quite near them, and close to the Catholick Church; the Music from which we found a perfect treat, during our stay; as it was remarkably good, and well performed– In the Even$^{g.}$ we went to the Tea Party at the Salon in the Garden; a sort of reception Room, where all the fashionable company met, and the Tea is given by different persons every Evening– This Evening the party was given by Countess Kollowrat; to whom we were presented by our friend Countess Golowkin, who likewise presented us to the Grand Dutchess Constantine, and to her Father Mother, and Sisters; the Prince and Princesses of Sax Cobourg family:[64] and to Prince Reuss, the Father of the Austrian Minister our acquaintance at Berlin; besides meeting some of our Berlin friends– We made a short stay, and returned to our Lodgings– The Country round Töplitz is magnificent, and we walked about to look at the magnificent prospects from the heights– The Tea party on the next Evening was

[61] Töplitz was a fashionable watering place and a favorite of royalty and nobility. The hot springs provided water for private baths that could be rented as well as free public baths (*Travellers in Germany*, p. 381–382).

[62] Pyrmont Water, bottled at a spring in Westphalia, was highly carbonated and had "an agreeable though strongly acidulated taste." It reportedly eased digestive ailments and menstrual complaints (Robert Hooper, *Quincy's Lexicon-Medicum,* Phila., 1817, Shaw-Shoemaker, No. 41081).

[63] Karl Joseph, Prince of Clary and Aldringen (1777–1831), owned much of Töplitz and the surrounding area. His palace, set amid gardens and a park, had an attached theater and garden room for reading, dining, and dancing (*Travellers in Germany,* p. 380–381).

[64] Juliana Henrietta Ulrica of Saxe-Coburg and Saalfeld (1781–1860) was the daughter of Duke Francis Frederick Anthony and Augusta Carolina Sophia Reuss Ebersdorff, and had three sisters: Sophia, Antoinetta, and Victoria. She married Grand Duke Constantine of Russia in 1796, taking the name Anna Feodorovna (Lodge, *Peerage,* 1892, p. liii–lvi).

given by Madame de Malnitz a Saxon Lady, and afterwards we went to the Theatre a small building in the Gardens.

Found myself so much fatigued could not go out after the bath— As there were Lodgers in the House with whom I was acquainted, they came to sit with me, and of course related the scandalous annecdotes of the day— The Grand Dutchess Constantine had been so severely beaten by her brute of a husband, that she could not make her appearance, until the yellow marks of the bruises had worn of from her eye, and her neck, and Shoulders— She was a pretty creature, not more than eighteen, and said to possess a sweet disposition— Paul had put Constantine under arrest for his brutality—[65] Mr Adams found the Evening party very dull—*Too* many Grandee's to make it pleasant— Went to Mass, but could get no Seats— The Church was filled to overflowing— A few minutes at the party, it being given by our old friend Countess Golowkin; the gayest and most charming old Lady I ever knew, who literally *lived* to *enjoy* every moment of her life— She was a Dutch Woman, her husband an Officer of distinction who had filled some high and important Offices— Always cheerful; always ready to participate in every thing that was passing, they were universally loved and respected, by the Class of Society in which they moved; the most distinguished and respectable in the City of Berlin—

29

Attended the Tea Party given by the Grand Dutchess: dull as usual—

30

Instead of the Tea Party at the Hall, we all accompanied Prince Clary to Dopperlberg, a Park belonging to him, distant about three English Miles from Town— The ride was beautiful; the Country varied and picturesque, with the beautiful mélange of Mountains, hills, and Valleys; producing a variegated Scene of exquisite gratification to the eye, in the grandeur of its rich and mingled beauties— We took Tea in a farmer House à la Chinoise, from which we could look into the Park, and see the Deer gambol in frolick sport, as they

[65] The couple became estranged and divorced in 1820 ("Sketch of the Life of the Grand Duke Constantine of Russia," *The Spirit of the Times*, 1:265–266 [4 Feb. 1826]).

ranged along through the leafy covert in which they roamed— We returned home at eight in the Evening!— The party mostly adjourning to the Theatre— Next Evening not well enough to attend a Concert at the Hall—

AUGST. [5?]TH

Mr. Adams was taken ill with a severe and violent intermitting Fever, and was obliged to keep on the bed. He rose however to see Lord Talbot and Mr. Harris, who called to see us, being on their way to Vienna with Lord Minto; and to proceed early in the morning[66] He Was obliged to go to bed the moment after the Gentlemen left us; and the Dr. informed him that he feared his complaint would prove the Ague and fever— This he would *not believe*— The day following he was quite sick; but rose to see Count!!! Neale, who was returning from Carlsbad, having been called there on account of the death of his Sister the Countess Zeinert, The Dr came and advised Mr Adams to keep in bed; but *he* believed that his fever was gone, and got up and dressed; when he was siezed with faintness, and we were obliged to put him to bed again directly, as the Dr had foretold— The Fever continued ten days with great violence; but he was so judiciously treated by the Dr, that he soon found himself better than he had been for a year: On the 12th day resumed his walks in the Gardens—

We walked out every morning as a part of the *system*, for the recovery of health. Mr Adams being better, began again to be anxious on my account, and forgetting the anxiety that I had suffered on his account during his sickness, seemed determined to believe that the waters had done me more harm than good— We met Count Panin, in the Gardens. The face of an old acquaintance when seen far from home, always gives pleasure, and we greeted him with delight—

At the Tea party we met Countess Panin; They were on their way home, the intercourse between Prussia and Russia having ceased altogether—[67] Again met Mr. Wright who we saw at Dresden, and

[66] James Edward Harris, 2d Earl of Malmesbury (1778–1841), and Charles Chetwynd Talbot, 2d Earl Talbot of Hensol (1777–1849), paid JQA a visit on 1 Aug. (*DNB*; D/JQA/24, APM Reel 27).

[67] Early in 1799 Count Nikita Petrovich Panin was instructed to offer Russian troops to Prussia if it would join the alliance of Russia, England, and Austria against France. On 1 Sept. Prussia refused, and Paul I ordered the removal of the embassy staff and archives from Berlin and appointed Panin vice chancellor (K. Waliszewski, *Paul the First of Russia, the Son of Catherine the Great,* London, 1913, p. 255–258; D/JQA/24, 2 Sept. 1799, APM Reel 27).

Count Bruhl— Mr Adams took me to the foot the Schlossberg, a mountain of considerable height, on the top of which was the Ruins of one of the Ancient Castle, which had belonged to a Rich and Cruel Baron; who made continual War on the Nobles who surrounded him, for miles around the Country— His retainers were numerous, and they were paid by the rapine and plunder of his neighbours, and their Serfs— Countrary to all the rules of romance, when the darkling shadows of night, are always chosen to exibit dæmons, and Ghosts; this valiant hero, was said to walk round the battlements in a full suit of Mail, and with his helmet Cap on, every morning at six o'clock, to mourn for the loss of his delapitated Castle, and Lands, which had been torn from him in the struggle of his warfare, and left a Ruin as an example, to a rising generation, of his fate— One turret alone was left standing; and in that one was a gap said to have been made by his Infernal Majesty; who in those days seems to have ruled with almost unlimited sway; when he dashed one of the Ancestors of the walking proprietor from the turret, down the steep precipice of the rocky mountain; where his mangled corse lay a prey to the carrion birds; as no one was found bold enough to bury it— Many a time and oft had his Successors tried to repair the breach, and thus conceal the disgrace attendant on the tale; but as soon as they had completed the work, a hideous storm would arise, accompanied by shrieks and groans, and the destruction would in the morning be found complete— The legends are mostly of the same character—[68] This effort was too much for my strength; and I returned home over come and exhausted— From the Gardens to the Ruin was four miles and a half, so that my walk out and home was at least four—

Our residence was very agreeable while at this place— The Evenings at the Gardens dancing or walking; sometimes at the Theatre—Often meeting our Berlin friends, and forming new and agreeable acquaintance among the daily arrivals— Mr & Mrs. Hildprandt of Prague we became very intimate with— We accompanied this family to Kloster Osegg a Monastery about six miles from Töplitz— They being well acquainted with the Prior, he treated us very handsomely, and shewed us all his Apartments, gardens, &ce The Monks appeared to be very illiterate, having no library, and nothing worthy

[68] The castle of Dobrawska Hora on the Schlossberg west of Töplitz was owned by Count William Kinsky until he was murdered in 1634 during the Thirty Years' War (*Travellers in Germany*, p. 382; *Cambridge Modern Hist.*, 4:242).

of curiosity; excepting a small Island in the middle of a Pond, in which were a number of small black Turtles; and on the Island a small *Fort* called Turtles Fortress–A number of small huts with thatched roofs containing turkish Ottomans, and Sophas, and two sets of machines for different Sports, for gentle exercise– We took tea in a Summer house at the bottom of the Garden, from whence we enjoyed a superb prospect; with various kinds of fruits; and then examined the Church; large, and full of fine Paintings and we returned home much pleased with our little tour at eight o'clock in the evening–[69]

The next day we went to look at the famous ruin on the Geyersberg which we passed on the road from Dresden– This ruin was then very Ancient; and its Owner we were informed had been the mortal enemy of the Baron of the Schlosberg Fort[70]–though the latter must have been a family of much more modern origin– We returned home to dine, and at 4 o'clock in the afternoon we sat off again on an expedition to *Dux*, the seat of Count Wallenstein–[71] I went in a Chaise with Miss Hildprand; the rest in a Carrige peculiar to the Country– It is called a Linée and is open, without a top; and consists of one long bench on which the Gentlemen sit across; it is very low and runs on four wheels– Count Wallenstein to whom Mr Hildbrand introduced us, shewed us his Stables; containing a hundred Horses of which he is very proud– They form the great obect of his care, and of his amusement– We did not see the inside of the Castle but walked through the Gardens, which are not very inviting– The prospects in every direction lovely and magnificent–That next day Count Bruhl called to invite us to a Tea Party given by Baron Krudener, the Father of the Minister of that name, who has since been in this Country; but we were too much fatigued to go; it

[69] The Cistercian monastery, founded in the twelfth century, had acquired, among other works of art, paintings that illustrated the history of their order (J. G. Kohl, *Austria,* Phila., 1844, p. 13–14). For a detailed description of the site, see D/JQA/24, 27 Aug. 1799, APM Reel 27.

[70] For extended comments by LCA on the Geyersberg ruin and the castle of Dobrawska Hora on the Schlossberg, see Adventures, notes 60, 68, above.

[71] Albrecht Eusebius of Waldstein (1583–1634), known as Wallenstein, was a leader of the forces under Ferdinand II, king of Bohemia, during the Thirty Years' War, for which he was made Duke of Friedland in 1623. Suspected of treason, he was assassinated, and his extensive properties were dispersed. Dux, one of his castles, housed a large art collection and relics of the assassination, including the duke's skull (J. G. Kohl, *Austria,* Phila., 1844, p. 14; J. Mitchell, *The Life of Wallenstein, Duke of Friedland,* 2d edn., London, 1853, p. 45, 87, 358–359, 363, 369–370).

being at Dopperlberg— In the Evening saw the Opera of the Zauberflöte by Mozart— The Princesses of S. Cobourg handsome—

Baron Hildprand and family called to take leave of us. They return home, and gave us a warm and urgent invitation to visit them at Prague—

1ST [*SEPTEMBER*]

I was too sick to go out— Count Panin called, and in the Even$^{g.}$ M$^{r.}$ Adams went to the Tea party given by Princess Reuss.—

A visit to Count Panin's— Appointed Vice Chacellor of the Empire; and he is preparing to leave Töplitz, which is beginning to thin very fast; another englishman by the name of Garvey called Went to the Hall in the Even^{g} and saw a play performed by the company of Ladies, and Gentlemen— It was not worth, much; and we staid later than usual— The Piece Jerome Pointu—[72]

Walked with M$^{r.}$ Adams to the Schlosberg, and ascended the mountain, having derived much benefit from the Pyrmont Waters; disgusting to the smell and taste— Did not go out in the evening, but received a visit from M$^{r.}$ Garvey—

At the Schlosberg again, took new milk on the top of the mountain, and amused ourselves with reading the names of the visitors carved on the walls; some of which were written upwards of a Century ago. wrote our own to pass down like the rest— Saw Countess Panin ascending the mountain in her *Carriage*; a proof of what the wealthy and great of this world can accomplish— At home in the Even

Took our leave of the Schlossberg— Count Bruhl having kindly made arrangements for our journey, and procured a Boat to take us down the Elbe on our way to Dresden, to avoid the Geyersberg Mountain, and to vary our route— Madame de Huernabine takes our Lodgings—The Lady of the Twins—very beautiful—

The 9th of September having in a great measure recovered my health, and taken leave of most of my kind friends at Töplitz; particularly our kind Doctor; we had taken an early dinner and were ready to step into the Carriage; when Countess Panin came to introduce Countess Ozarowska a Polish Lady of distinction— We started in our own Carriage at two o'clock in the afternoon, and arrived—at Ausig, were we stopped for the night; while our Carriage

[72] Beaunoir (Alexandre Louis Bertrand Robineau), *Jérome Pointu*, Paris, 1781.

was shipped, so as to proceed early in the morning— Commenced our Water excursion at five o'clock—Mr. Adams, Epps, Whitcomb, and myself— Epps had proved a treasure during the whole time of her Service in my family; almost educated by my Mother, she had been so accustomed to my habits, and manners; and was so attached to me, I always found her faithful and affectionate; and she attended me with the most unremitting care and attention— She was housekeeper, Nurse, Seamstress, Mantua Maker, and Clearstarcher and; thus saved me from a heavy burthen of expence— She afterwards married Whitcomb, who treated her ill, and the unhappiness which she endured, changed her habits and her character, which soon destroyed her constitutuion; and she died leaving a family of five Children— As a foreigner she had no friends; her crafty husband was pitied and approved; while the censure of the *honest* should have been his portion— Mr. Whitney was the only person who declared this *truth*, and it did him honour in proving his discernment—

arrived at Dresden we proceeded to our lodgings procured for us by Mr. Errington at the Hotel which they occupied, and they received us in the most friendly manner— We went to the Fair it being about to close and made some purchaces of table linen famed for its beauty and cheapness in Saxony— Mr. Adams sent some to his Mother— The Eveng Mr & Mrs Errington spent with us we called at Count Golowkins at the Hotel de Baviere and there we met Madlle. Bishoffswerder and her Mother with a large party of our Töplitz friends—

Mr & Mrs Greathead, and their Son Bertie, called on us and asked us to Tea in the Evening He was a gentleman of family and distinction, to whom Mr. Errington had introduced us. As we went in we met Mr. Hugh Elliot, the English Minister at the Saxon Court; a remarkably handsome and elegant man whose history I had heard before I had left Berlin— He had married a very beautiful German Lady, who after living with him a year or two had eloped with a Noble Countryman of her own, and taken her only child, a daughter with her— A few months after, Mr Elliot contrived through the medium of secret Agents, to steal the Child in its Cradle, and immedeately set out for England with her, where she was educated by his family—[73]

[73] Hugh Elliot (1752–1830), British minister to Saxony, had married Charlotte Kraut around 1779 while stationed in Berlin; their daughter, Isabella, was born in 1781. The next

14

In the morning we walked in the Gardens of Count Bruhl, a Man well known to history as the enemy of Frederic during the seven years war:[74] and in the Evening we again strolled out after being at the Gallery of Pictures an hour or two— Another day was lost to me as I was too ill to go out— The Evening Mr & Mrs Errington called, but I could not see them—

At Mrs. Erringtons where I met Mr. Elliot— We called at the Countess Worthern's one of our Töplitz friends; but she was out

15

Mr. Adams was presented by Mr. Elliot to the Elector of Saxony, and his Dutchess, the Princess Mary-Ann, Prince Max his brother, and his Wife a Princess of Parma— In the Evening he went to a Ball at the Governors: I stayed at home—

The Evening passed with Mrs. Errington and met a Mr Artaud[75] Dined with Mrs. Errington; Mr. Greathead and family, Mr Prescott, Miss Elliot, the stolen Child now grown up, and very beautiful; accompanied by several young Gentlemen, came in to spend the Evening— She was engaged to be married to Mr. Payne the Son of a great Banker in London— The next morning a Mr Oliver of Baltimore, brought Letters to us We went to the Gallery and then remain quietly at home all the Evening— Mr & Mrs. Errington and Mr Oliver dined with us, and Miss Elliot joined us at Tea—

The next day we dined and spent the Evening at Mrs. Greatheads They are very agreeable— She an elderly Lady of very pleasant manners and conversation—

Accompanied Mrs. Errington to the Catholick Cathedral— there is a grandeur and awful sublimity in these buildings very striking to the imagination of young and ardent minds—and the Music, the Paintings, and ornamented Alters; with the Showy paraphernalia of

year he was appointed minister to Denmark, but his wife refused to leave Prussia. Returning to Berlin to resolve the situation, he fought a duel with a cousin of Charlotte's whom Elliot believed to be his rival for her affections and subsequently obtained a divorce. Isabella married George Payne in 1801 and died in 1826 (*DNB;* Countess of Minto, *A Memoir of the Right Honourable Hugh Elliot,* Edinburgh, 1868, p. 209, 260–267, 415).

[74] Count Heinrich von Brühl (1700–1763) was prime minister of Saxony from 1746. The gardens of his palace in Dresden included a grand staircase and a half-mile terrace that was a popular promenade (K. Baedeker, *Northern Germany*, 11th edn., Leipzig, 1893, p. 272).

[75] Alexis François Artaud de Montor (1772–1849), French diplomat and scholar (J. M. Quérard, *La littérature française contemporaine*, 6 vols., Paris, 1842–1857).

the Priests; and the frank Incence; all sieze upon the senses, and steal insensibly upon the heart with rapt enthusiasm– The Arts are all called into action; and you gaze in wonderment at the works of man; while if you are of a reflecting mind, are led to think; if man can atchieve so much, how surpassingly wonderful must the Creater be; who combines all that greatness, and all that we behold of the great Waters, of the deep, and the lustrous magnificence of the Celestial Heavens, and all created things so full of might and glory!– So dazzling with perfection in all their vast variety; the same for ever; yet forever new!!! In the Evening we were at Mr. Elliots–

His Wife was a remarkably beautiful Woman, and had six of the loveliest Children that the world could display– She, Mrs. Elliot was the Niece of a former Housekeeper, who had lived in his service; and Mrs. Ap Jones (I think) of hot welch blood, thought it necessary to enforce her authority; and the pretty Peggy was so earnestly pressed upon her Master, that she took the name of Elliot by the Scotish law, and was henceforth received as his Wife by the English, and Strangers; although when I was *there*, the Elector had declined to receive her at Court– He had polished her manners and taken great pains with her education, but his very lovely Children were the passports to all hearts– He had found his former Matrimonial *bonds* so loose I suppose; he thought the Scotch Law would at least be *equally* binding; and they certainly appear to have been chains worn with more pleasure, and more durability– the party was large; Countess Panin was there and we all stayed Supper–

Mr & Mrs. Greathead, Mr & Mrs. Errington, with Messrs. Parry, Wright, Musgrave, and Oliver took Tea with us; and the next Evening we took a social Tea with Mrs. Elliot– She had been told by some German Lady to put blisters on her Arms so to remove an appendage that she did not like; and she was suffering great inconvenience from the application, which she feared would not prove a remedy–

A large party of us went to look at an elegant Country Seat about three miles from Dresden– Mrs. & Miss Elliot, Mr. & Mrs. Gray, Mr & Mrs. Errington, were of the Party– Mr. Elliot and two other Gentlemen, Mr. Hunter, and Mr. Long, had gone out hunting near the same place– We all returned to a late dinner at Mr. Elliots, and passed the Evening there– Mrs. Errington and I were always together; She at my Rooms or I at hers; and almost always in company with some of the English then at Dresden–

In the morning of Sunday we heard a Superb Requiem at the

Catholick Cathedral A ceremony celebrating the anniversary of the Death of the King of Poland—[76] ~~In the Evening at Mr. Elliots~~ The Coffin richly covered with Armorial bearings, Crown &ce We went with Mr & Mrs. Errington and saw the public Library after which we returned home to dine with them: Mr & Mrs. Greathead with their Son; and in the Evening there was a large party—

OCTOBER 99.

Countess Worthern and her daughters paid us a visit— Mr & Mrs. Errington, Mrs. Tylztzdtz and Mr Artaud, took Tea with us— Mr. Artaud amused us with an account of his Travels and adventures in Italy—A delightful companion—

We supped at Mrs. Greatheads; next day at Mr. Erringtons; and passed the Evening with a large company; and the last evening of our Stay, Mr & Mrs. Errington having dined with us; went together with us and sat an hour at Mr Elliots: whose family we took leave of, intending to begin our journey homewards the next morning—

I have been thus particular to give you an idea of our routine while at Dresden; which was nearly akin, to that which I led in Berlin: the only difference; here; it was all social, and that in Berlin when I was well enough to visit the great world; it was all *State* and very laborious—

One of our Trips was to the Fortress of Königstein! A Fortress of great Strength, which had withstood all the attacks of Frederic the Second— We were shown The Place on the sill of one of the loop holes, about a foot wide, and about 2000 feet from the ground on which a page had Slept— He had, being drunk had crept into the hole, and fallen asleep; and was only saved by passing a band gently round him, by which he was drawn into the window— He lived to be 108 years old—having under gone many perils— Mr & Mrs. Errington accompanied us and we had a delightful day— The rock in which this Fortress is cut is of great height, and almost perpendicular— There is a Well in it 1800 feet deep, it was forty years from its commencent to its completion— It was cut through the Rock—Of its military efficiency I shall say nothing, not being competent to the subject— The Saxon Regalia which we likewise saw, was there de-

[76] Augustus III of Poland, who as Frederick Augustus II was elector of Saxony, died on 5 Oct. 1763 (*Cambridge Modern Hist.*, 6:200).

posited during the seven years War; while the whole electorate was in possession of Frederic 2d.[77]

On the 9th of Septer at 4 o'clock in the morning we started on our return home—[78]

At half past eleven o'clock at night on the 10th. we arrived at Potzdam very much fatigued— In the morning acompanied Mr. Adams to the Palace at Sans Souci, where we saw the fine Gallery of Paintings and all the fine things commonly Shown to Strangers, but I returned to the Inn so ill I was obliged to go to bed—[79]

12

Being much better; after breakfast we went to visit the Peacocks Island a Small Island in the Havel, on which the late King had built a small pleasure house; an elegant little place and very neatly furnished— A Farm house at the other end; the Island being but half a mile long in imitation of a gothick Church; it is four miles from Potzdam—a very pretty spot—[80] We dined and immediately after pursued our course to Berlin delighted at the thoughts of once more being quietly settled in our Comfortable home— Just before dark we reached home and at our door stood our kind friend Mr Richards ready to receive us and welcome our return—

The next morning our friends the Dr. and his family called and insisted on our passing the Evening with them which we did: on our way calling at Count and Countess Gowlofkin, who were again comfortably established in their house—

[77] At the start of the Seven Years' War in 1756, when Frederick the Great invaded Saxony, Augustus III and Count Brühl sought refuge in the fortress. In 1759 paintings from the Dresden Royal Picture Gallery were sent there for safekeeping (Charlton T. Lewis, *A History of Germany, from the Earliest Times,* N.Y., 1874, p. 511; Clare Ford-Wille, "The Art Collection of Dresden," in Anthony Clayton and Alan Russell, eds., *Dresden: A City Reborn*, Oxford, 1999, p. 155).

[78] Their return trip began on 9 Oct. (D/JQA/27, APM Reel 30).

[79] Visitors to this summer palace, built by Frederick the Great in 1745–1747, viewed the royal rooms and the apartment that Voltaire had once occupied, along with lavish gardens. The picture gallery, housed in a separate building, displayed paintings by Leonardo da Vinci, Titian, Correggio, Peter Paul Rubens, and others (John Carr, *A Northern Summer; or, Travels round the Baltic*, Phila., 1805, p. 298–301; Martin Shaw Briggs, *Baroque Architecture*, N.Y., 1914, p. 161).

[80] This park was created in 1795 by Frederick William II. In 1805 Frederick William III altered the landscape to accommodate a menagerie (Harro Strehlow, "Zoos and Aquariums of Berlin," in R. J. Hoage and William A. Deiss, eds., *New Worlds, New Animals: From Menagerie to Zoological Park in the Nineteenth Century,* Baltimore, 1996, p. 63).

14

Pauline Neale came to see me and Spent the Evening with me, having heard of our arrival in the morning– The Queen was sick and the next morning the birth of a daughter was announced, being the second since our residence in the Country– Mr. Artaud and Mr Thompson called on us having just arrived, and we all passed the Evening at Mrs. Browns where we met Mr. Garlick– They were to have met us at Potzdam–

Mr. Artaud, Mr. Thompson, and Mr. Garlick dined with us–and we talked over our adventures at Dresden, and of the agreable persons whom we had left behind– I know nothing that yields more pleasure when the acrimony of scandal does not enter into the theme– The Miss Browns joined us in the evening– Next Eveng at the German Theatre saw Hamlet– Mr. Arbuthnot in the Evening– Staid at home to read the Memiors of Clairon sent to us by Mr Garlick–[81]

We dined and passed the Evening at Dr Browns, after three days of quiet at home; passed very agreeably in an hour or two of chat with our friends Garlick and Arbuthnot–and in reading the Memoires of Madlle. Clairon–Quite amusing–

Two more very quiet days No visitors– Next Evening at Dr Browns where we met Baron D'Alvensleben and Mr Arbuthnot–

Went with the Miss Browns to a Concert by Steibelt–

Took so violent a Cold that I could not go to a Concert at Mr. Cohens, where Madame de Genlis played superbly on the Harp:[82] A Lady Madame Paravacini performed on the Violin–

Went to the Theatre to see the Piccolomini–

Again at the Play Wallensteins death![83]

Mr John Murray came to see us from N.Y. Letters of recommendation from Mr King–[84] In the Evening met Count Bruhl and his family at Dr. Browns–

[81] Hyppolite Clairon, *Mémoires d'Hyppolite Clairon, et réflexions sur l'art dramatique*, Paris, 1799.

[82] Stéphanie Félicité du Crest de Saint-Aubin, Comtesse de Genlis (1746–1830), was a noted writer, actress, musician, and educator (Bonnie Arden Robb, *Félicité de Genlis: Motherhood in the Margins*, Newark, Del., 2008, p. 13, 239).

[83] Friedrich Schiller wrote a trilogy of plays about the life of Wallenstein. The second and third parts, *The Piccolomini* and *Wallenstein's Death*, were performed on 1 and 2 November. JQA notes in his Diary that the first part, *Wallenstein's Camp*, was censored in Berlin "because it exhibits an army in mutiny," but he would later see it in Leipzig (D/JQA/24, 2 Nov. 1799, 2 Oct. 1800, APM Reel 27).

[84] In his letter of 7 Sept. 1799 Rufus King explained to JQA that the traveler John Murray was "the Son and Partner of one of our most respectable merchants" (Adams Papers).

My little friend Countess Pauline called to take leave of me– Going to England with her Father– She is a real loss to me– A great Ball at Madame de Salderns was too sick to go: but went to Dr Browns– Engaged to go to the theatre with the Browns the following day if better– Went and saw King Theodore at Venice, by Paësiello a charming Opera Buffa–[85]

Mr. Murry dined with us and the Bruhls passed the Eveng– Madame D'Engerstroom introduced Countess Bunow wife of the new Saxon Minister– The Browns dined with us–

At Dr Browns to dinner In the Evening introduced Mr. Murray– The Brulhs, D'Alvensleben, Mr Arbuthnot, and Mr Curtois secretary of the spanish Legation, all there– Mr Murray dined with us, and we all went to Prince Ferdinands, where I was greeted with the utmost kindness by the Princesses– The Prince had been dangerously ill but was recovering, tho' not able to appear– We did not stay to supper–

Sick and confined at home for several days–

Received a Visit from Madame Ursinus to return thanks for an accidental service which *she* said I had rendered to her– Her husband was a Physician– They had not been long married and had one Child, an Infant about eight Months old– The Child was siezed with convulsions, and they were dreadfully alarmed. They lived on the floor over us, and they sent in great haste to me, to know if I could do any thing for them– The day or two before; I had heard that Madame de Mussow's Child when apparently *dead*, had been restored by an application of Oil of Amber, gently rubbed up and down the spine, and held to the Nostrils to inhale– I informed them of this Case, and advised them to try it– It had proved successful, and she came to return the thanks of her Husband and herself; stating that he was quite ashamed of having so lost his presence of mind; as he well knew the efficacy of the remedy– I mention this fact as there may be instances in which the remedy might prove useful, where convulsions are not the consequence of prolonged desease– The Baby was sent down to me full dressed, in a pink silk slip with a Gauze frock over it, and numerous bows of Pink ribbon–

This reminds me of the astonishment that siezed upon me at the sight of my housemaid, the first Sunday after my return– She came up to me dressed in an elegant Satin Cloak of pale Blue, trimmed with Fur–A National Cap, the Crown embroidered in colours; flat

[85] Giovanni Paisiello, *Il Re Teodoro in Venezia*.

to the head; with a very broad lace border, put very much off the face, and something in the form of the front of a bonnet, only put on in large fluted quils, like the portraits of Mrs. Washington— She was as proud as a Peacock; and in perfect ecstacy at her finery— As she had been accustomed to go almost without necessary clothing, and I had had great difficulty to make her wear Shoes and Stockings; and she had been a very good Girl; I was frightened lest she should have done Something wrong, to enable her to make the purchace: and I hastened to Mrs. Brown to relieve the quandary into which I was thrown— She laughed, and told me, there was no cause of alarm: as it was the uttermost height of the ambition of these poor Girls, to own a fine Cloak, to sport at Church, and in the Deer Garthen on a Sunday; and they would deprive themselves of every internal garment, and even their Tea, to save their money to procure such finery—

Went to a great Ball given by Baron d'Engerstroom on the occasion of the birth of the Crown Prince of Sweeden—[86] The House splendidly illuminated, and the Entertaiment very magnificent— The Marchese de Luchesini there—A very showy Woman who furnished much conversation in the private Coterie's of Berlin—Young Dorville a young Man of 22 was said to be too much smitten with her charms; but he had many Rivals to contend with— She was about forty and quite acquainted with les usages du Monde— The Marquis was a shrewd and crafty Italian as well as herself, and they both knew well how to play a political game— He served Frederic 2d—[87]

The Spanish Ministers Lady called on me with a request that I would present her at Court—[88] She was a beautiful Woman as to *face*, but of a fat unwieldy person, only 32; yet had a Son grown up— I accordingly paid the visits with her, and accompanied her at the presentation, where we were most graciously received

Accompanied Madame Ofarrel to Madame de Heinitz; Cards and introduction—

Eveng and Supper at the Baron de Hagen's to introduce Madame Ofarrel—

[86] The baby was the future Oscar I, king of Sweden and Norway (1799–1859) (*Cambridge Modern Hist.*, 11:687).

[87] Carlotta was the wife of Girolamo, Marquis of Lucchesini (1751?–1825), who had come to Prussia in 1780 (TBA, *Journal, 1798*, p. 24; Alessandro Carraresi, *Lettere di Gino Capponi*, 6 vols., Florence, 1882–1890, 5:121). On Dorville see Adventures, notes 108 and 109, below.

[88] Don Gonzalo O'Farrill y Herrera (1754–1831), a Spanish general, was appointed ambassador to Prussia in 1799 (Didier Ozanam, *Les diplomates espagnols du XVIIIe siècle: Introduction et répertoire biographique, 1700–1808*, Madrid, 1998; *Repertorium*, 3:439).

At the Theatre with Mrs. Ofarrel—

Evening and Supper at Baron d'Engerstrooms— The Lady who presents, must accompany the Strangers to parties, until the round is completed—

Went to a very large Party at Count Arnims— The King and Queen both there— The Queen again insisted upon the rouge, and threatened me with the box— Prior to our visit at Count Arnims we made our compliments at Madame de Voss's; a great crowd— This visit always expected as soon as the King come to Town

Went with Mrs. Ofarrel to visit all the Courts; after which we went to a very large party given in honour of the marriage of the young Countess Shulembourg, with Prince Hadzfeldt—a Lady since so celebrated in the history of Napoleon; which was said to have given rise to the famous Piece, called Trajan, in compliment to the Emperor for his clemency— She was a charming woman; but I did not admire her husband Prince Hadzfeldt, and thought him a cold, supercilious, haughty, flashy personage.[89] What College youth's call "all sufficient" the qualifications necessary for the completion of the character existing *only* in their own conceit— Mrs. Ofarel was standing immediately before me, when one of the Grandee's asked me to present him to her— I tapped her gently on the shoulder, and in turning she fell as gently on the Carpeted floor, and exclaimed that she had broken her Leg— I sank on one knee immediately, and rested her head on the other; when she fell into a dead fainting— She had barely recovered, when she again said she had broken the limb; which being heard by a Gentleman, who said it was only a sprain he took hold of her foot, and turned it; upon which she screamed and fainted again— Her husband had gone for a Surgeon, who raised her gently on a Sopha, and she was carried into another apartment, to which the Doctor desired me to accompany her. He then examined the *hurt*, and declared the bone to be fractured in two different places; and ordered me to cut the Stocking off, the leg being very much swolen; He gave me a pair of very sharp Scissors, and though I trembled like a leaf, I succeeded; and on examining

[89] Franz Ludwig, Prince of Hatzfeldt (1756–1827), was a Prussian soldier and diplomat. His wife was the daughter of Frederick William, Count of Schulenburg-Kehnert. When Napoleon captured Berlin in 1806, he intercepted a letter Hatzfeldt had sent to the king with intelligence about the French Army, and he charged the prince with spying. The visibly pregnant princess pleaded for her husband's life, and Napoleon relented, giving her the incriminating letter to burn (Sabine Freitag and Peter Wende, *British Envoys to Germany: 1816–1829*, London, 2001; *An Aide-de-Camp of Napoleon: Memoirs of General Count de Ségur*, ed. Count Louis de Ségur, transl. H. A. Patchett-Martin, N.Y., 1895, p. 306–309).

the limb, he prefered to have her carried home as she lay, prior to the operation while he would prepare Splints and all the necessary apparatus— I tried to find Mr. Adams that I might get home; but ere I could succeed, I fell down in a deep fainting fit; and was carried home—being attended by three or four Ladies who were alarmed at the length of time which the total insensibility continued:[90] A succession of these fits continued nearly all night, and they kindly staid with me until I was thought out of danger: but my recovery was slow, and though I was able to go and sit with Mrs. Ofarell, and assist to nurse her; at the end of a few weeks I suffered all the ill consequences of the fright, and again had the misery to behold the anguish of my husbands blighted hopes[91] Why do we so bitterly repine at evils, if such they really are, which are so utterly beyond our controul; and which probably are sent to soften the asperity of our natures, and to teach the high unbending spirit of man, submission to a Will too mighty to contend against, and which exacts for our sakes, that we may abide in the right path; with implicit and patient obedience to its decrees—

On the 19th of Janry. 1800 I again was able to take a ride and move about among the living—

The Old Queen Mother held a Court to Perform a Play in which she acted herself— Mr Adams did not go; I too weak to go out even to my friend Mrs. Browns— Mr. Adams became quite sick from anxiety, and want of Rest—

An American by the name of Ellison introduced to us—For ever at our house—a very disagreeable man—

FEBY 1ST [*1800*]

Went to Dr. Browns to pass the Evening, and to get rid of my disagreeable companion who staid late in the Evening whether Mr. Adams was at home or not: the ~~latter~~ former event being very rare. He became perfectly insupportable to me, and I forced myself to go out, to get rid of him— Received the News of the death of General Wash-

[90] These events occurred on 4 Dec. (D/JQA/24, APM Reel 27).

[91] On 8 Jan. JQA wrote, "Mrs. Adams taken ill this morning, in the process of a fourth misfortune, like three others which she has gone through since we arrived at Berlin— She remaine'd all day in bed, suffering no pain; and still entertaining some hopes." The next day he hoped that "the worst of her misfortune" had passed: "I can only pray to God, that there may never again be the possibility of another like event— A better hope, it were folly to indulge; for in cases like this hope itself is but an aggravation of misery" (D/JQA/24, APM Reel 27).

ington— Mr Adams was much affected by it Col Swan of Boston came to See us; and Mr. Adams after remaining at home several days, took him and presented him to the King—

Went to the Opera—but was not so pleased as at Dresden where the Music and the Acting was exquisite— The Opera was Tigrane[92] On the 6 went to the Ridotto— Being more than usually pale I ventured to put on a little rouge, which I fancied relieved the black, and made me look quite beautiful— Wishing to evade Mr. Adams's observation I hurried through the room telling him to put the *lights* out, and follow me down; this excited his curiosity, and he started up and led me to the Table, and then declared that unless I allowed him to wash my face, he would not go— He took a Towel and drew me on his knee, and all my beauty was clean washed away; and a kiss made the peace, and we drove off to the party where I showed my pale face as usual—

Next night at a great Ball at Madame de Wangenheims—King, Queen, and all the family there— The Queen blazing with diamonds~~— The Queen in the Character of an Indian Lady—~~

There was a change for the better in the french Mission; Genl Bournonville a pleasant elderly man, and two very genteel young men attached to his Suite; instead of that arch rebel Sieyés, who had disgraced his Country, and his Church, during the atrocities of the french Revolution— A man of great abilities; Napoleon prefered to keep him at a distance for a time, and his Mission was now ended, and a much more showy one substituted, à là Militaire—[93]

Shrove Tuesday being the last day of the Carnaval I went to a Costume Ball at the Princess Radzivilles—Myself in a plain ball dress— She recieved her company in the character of a Roman Lady; a Superb Costume, with a bunch of Keys fastened by a Gold Chain to her belt— The Queen, and Prince William, the Kings brother about 18, as young Greeks— There were three Quadrilles— One of them Asiatic, Representing A Harem— Mustapha Bey led the Procession—Several Officers in full Costume; Turkish; Then the first Black Slave keeper of the Seraglio: his attendants, followed by six Ladies dressed splendidly and with Silver gauze Veils reaching to the feet— They all marched up and were ranged immediately before

[92] By Alessandro Scarlatti.

[93] On 16 May 1799 Abbé Emmanuel Joseph Sieyès was elected to the Directory. Pierre Riel, Marquis de Beurnonville (1752–1821), who had been the minister of war, replaced him as the French envoy extraordinary and minister plenipotentiary at Berlin in 1800 (*Repertorium*, 3:132; Hoefer, *Nouv. biog. générale*).

the Queen; where they made there Salam's—and the order was given by the Chief Eunuch, for the beauties to unveil— The envious Curtains were upraised, and discovered, the bearded faces; of Six of the stoutest, and coarsest young military heroes; in the female garb; with all its light and brilliant embellishments, to the utter astonishment of the company, who were convulsed with laughter— Prince Augustus as a Bachus on his ton—with his followers— A Quadrille of Cossacs; and one representing Comedy with all her accessories—after Supper—Prince Augustus came in as Dulcinéa; Count Rothenbourg as Don Quixotte, and Perponcher (ofterner called Papillon being very volage)[94] as Sancho-Panza— I was obliged to go home before Supper, but the Ball lasted till near morning— There were few or no masks—but a multitude of Costumes of every known Nation under the Sun— It was altogether very brilliant; but like most things of the kind, after the first impression very tedious—

Mr Adams took a bad Cold and we were confined to the House—

MARCH 4

A great Ball at Mr. Dorvilles to which Mr. Adams went all the Royal Family there— I spent the Eveng at Dr Browns to meet the pretty Miss Elliot now Mrs. Payne, who was on her way to England—Here we saw General Stamford the new Minister of the Prince of Orange—

Could not go to a large Ball at the Minister Shroeters— All the Royal family there, one of the largest parties of the Season— I sat with Mrs. Ofarell who was recovering fast—A very charming Woman—

There was a great Ball at Court. It was the Queens birth day[95] but it was so intensely cold I could not go— My health was so delicate a decline was apprehended— I was pestered to death with the company of Dr Ellison— I could not endure him

20

A splendid Ball was given by Prince Hadzfeldt—The first since his marriage

[94] Probably Hendrik George Perponcher-Sedlnitzky (1771–1856), who served in both the Dutch and the British military and was later Dutch ambassador to Prussia (Albert A. Nofi, *The Waterloo Campaign, June 1815*, Conshohocken, Penn., 1998, p. 98).

[95] Queen Louisa was born on 10 March 1776.

The Princess of Orange was confined a few days since and has a daughter— Her situation in this Country is both painful and unpleasant; being entirely dependent upon the King her half brother, and the politics of the Country necessarily very unpleasant to her, since their hasty departure from Holland had compell'd them to seek a home in Berlin, without the means of supporting their rank— She was not handsome but very amiable, and nobody could know her without sympathizing in her situation—[96]

Most of my Evenings were spent with Mrs. Brown & family— Margaret by her wit and conversational powers, was always entertaining; Bell drooped, and no one knew why, but was as gentle and lovely as ever; while Fanny now near sweet seventeen, improved in beauty every hour, and still retained the childish simplicity of manners, which made her so attractive— She had no Beaux though every one loved her— Here we again met Lord Talbot, just returned from Italy; and he displayed to us the beautiful Drawings, and prints which he had collected— He was on his return to England— Mr & Mrs. Payne staid but a short time—they dined with us once—

MARCH 27.

At the Spanish Ministers where we passed the Evening— Marquis Luchesini gave a great and splendid Ball to the Royal Family, at which we attended— They came late and the Queen was much depressed, her youngest Child being very ill— (Misplaced) a few days—[97]

30

The weather had become very mild and I was out again. My visit was at Prince Ferdinands who were invariably kind to me— The Kings youngest Child died in the ~~morning~~ Evening—

Visits from Mr. Parry, and Mr. Carlyon; A New Russian Minister, a stiff odd looking old man, very talkative and conceited— Mr. Arbutnot, Mr. Parry, Mr Carlyon, dined with us; and my little friend

[96] The Prince and Princess of Orange were living in exile in Prussia because of the French occupation. Their daughter Pauline was born on 1 March 1800 (Rowen, *Princes of Orange*, p. 229, 230; *Walter Rathenau, Industrialist, Banker, Intellectual, and Politician: Notes and Diaries, 1907–1922*, ed. Hartmut Pogge von Strandmann, transl. Caroline Pinder Cracraft, rev. edn., Oxford, Eng., 1985, p. 101).

[97] LCA wrote and then crossed out, "The Queens youngest Child died," after the first sentence in this entry. Frederica died on 30 March.

Pauline came to see me immediately after her return from England, and France; delighted with her tour, and perfectly rhapsodical about the Empress Josephine, who had treated her with great distinction— The Letters of my friend, had already produced quite a sensation, and she had risen prodigiously in public estimation: which was evinced in her reception— M[r] & M[rs.] Greathead called on us— We returned the visit next morning, and in the Evening they took Tea with us, and passed the Evening— We dined the next day at D[r.] Browns and met them there— After dinner I took M[rs.] Greathead and introduced her to Madame de Voss, and asked an introduction for her to the Queen—and then to all the other Ladies— These are always dress visits— Occupied all the next morning in visiting, and riding with M[rs.] Greathead—

15 [*17 APRIL*]

I accompanied M[rs.] Greathead by appointment, and presented her to the Queen, and to the Queen Mother— The Queen had come from Charlottenburg to stand Godmother to the Princess of Oranges new born Infant— She was elegantly dressed, and loaded with Diamonds; this being a state occasion, and had fixed one o'clock at noon to receive us— The tears rolled down her Cheeks; as she related to me, the suffering of her Child, saying that it was a great trial to her to make the exertion of attending the Christening—but that she must perform the duty to her friend, however painful—

It was a private Audience and M[rs.] Greathead was received with great kindness— They, the Greatheads were relatives of the Duke of Ancaster— The Queen Mother a perfect *oddity*, likewise received us very graciously—

18

Prince Augustus, M[r] & M[rs.] Greathead, their Son Bertie, D[r.] Browns family, Miss Bishoffwerder, M[r] Arbuthnot, and M[r.] Garlick dined with us—Quite sociable—

We dined at Gen[l] Ofarells, and in the Evening went to see a play at M[r.] Cohen's; Le marriage Secret, and Les Lutin de Quervoisie—[98]

[98] The plays were Jean Louis Brousse-Desfaucherets, *Le mariage secret*, 1786; and "Les Lutins de Kernosi," an unpublished one-act play that Comtesse de Genlis wrote for the Cohens, based on a novel by Henriette Julie de Castelnau Murat, *Les lutins du Château de*

Madame de Genlis performed delightfully, and played on the Harp, on which Instrument she is de prémiere force— Mrs Greathead and I, were obliged to go to the Queen Mothers to supper—

The next Even[g] accompanied them to Prince Radzivilles—

22

They all called to take leave of us next morning, and sat out on their journey to Potzdam immediately afterwards— In the Evening Miss Dunderfeldt, and Miss Estoff came to take Tea with me—

Went with M[r.] Adams to See an Opera, The female Stratagem—Music by Cimarosa—[99] The French Ambassador and his Suite in the Box with us— The Gen[l] quite a pleasant, half vulgar illiterate, parvenue man—A Hero of the new school—[100] Count & Countess Brulh their daughter, Mary; Gen[l] Ofarrel his Lady, and Son, the Viscomte Anadia, Count Banow, Mess[rs.] D'Aroyn, and D'Aguilar, D[r] Brown, Margaret, and Pauline Neale, dined with us—

Whitcomb had become quite au fait in these Matters, and the Prince of Oranges Cook always officiated for us—

Three young Gentlemen from America called on us; M[r] Oliver, M[r.] Ogden, and M[r.] Fulton—to stay only a day or two: Mr. Oliver we had met at Dresden— Tom Welsh was very ill— The three Gentlemen dined with us, and proceeded on their journey the day after—

Obliged to appear at a party given in honour of the marriage of Count Hardenberg, and Miss Lederitz— I only staid an hour and returned home— The Bride and Bridegroom sat down together, with two others, Prince Augustus Ferdinand, and a Lady at Cards— this is the usage with new married people Since Prime Minister M[r.] Arbuthnot leaves for England in a few days and we lose a delightful friend and acquaintance, who has passed much time at our house, his conversation and charming manners proving a constant source of pleasure— Some years after on his passage to fill an appointment of importance I think at Ceylon, The Vessel in which he sailed was lost, and he perished in her—[101]

My health was very delicate and M[rs.] Brown who was at her

Kernosy, Paris, 1710 (Comtesse de Genlis, *Mémoires inédits de madame la comtesse de Genlis,* 10 vols., Paris, 1825, 5:60–62).

[99] Domenico Cimarosa, *Le astuzie femminili,* 1794.

[100] The general was Beurnonville.

[101] Robert Arbuthnot (d. 1809) was chief secretary of government for Ceylon, 1800–1807. He returned safely to England but was later lost at sea (Sir Charles Lawson, *Memories of Madras,* London, 1905, p. 273–274).

Country House at Charlottenburg, insisted upon my spending a week with her, as change of air might be of service— She was a Mother to me, and I passed my time very agreeably with her— M[r.] Adams came out of town to sleep, and returned usually before breakfast—sometimes he dined there— We all went to a large party given by M[rs.] Cohen on the return of her Husband from Holland— Madame de Genlis had written a Piece in honour of the occasion— Galatée animèe depuis vingt-quatre heures—A sequel to Pygmalion— The Cloison a Scene in which she performed *alone*, was very good—[102] returned to M[rs.] Browns. M[r.] Tyrwhit Secretary to the Prince of Wales, and A Member of Parliament dined there— M[r.] Tyrwhit the very smallest *man*, not to be a dwarf ever seen here—[103] M[r] Ditmar called after dinner with Letters for Silesia sent to us by Count Haugwitz, and returned with us to Town—

The next day we began our journey to Silesia; an account of which much more interesting than any I can write, M[r] Adams sent in letters to his brother—[104]

On the 23[d] of October after five weeks of lingering sufferring at Leipsic—We set off for Berlin, impatient to be at home once more; M[r.] Adams being in very bad health, and I in a situation to create perpetual alarm, and anxiety. We hurried on as fast as prudence would permit, and on the 21st we found ourselves once more at our comfortable home. Whitcomb having preceded us to make all necessary arrangements— Again I was surrounded by my loving friends, and was soon as much spoilt as ever— I was sick almost unto the

[102] Comtesse de Genlis wrote the one-act comedy *Pygmalion et Galatée; ou, la statue animée depuis vingt-guatre heures* (Pygmalion and Galatea; or, The Statue Brought to Life for Twenty-four Hours), to be performed after Rousseau's *Pygmalion. La Cloison* (The Partition) is another of her one-act comedies; in three of the scenes, the leading female character appears alone (Madame de Genlis, *Nouveaux contes moraux, et nouvelles historiques*, 2d edn., 6 vols., Paris, 1804–1806, 6:254–432).

[103] Thomas Tyrwhitt (1762–1833) held several posts in the royal household, where he was known by a variety of nicknames reflecting his short stature (R. G. Thorne, ed., *The House of Commons, 1790–1820*, 5 vols., London, 1986, 1:422–423).

[104] LCA and JQA began their trip to Silesia on 17 July 1800 and returned to Berlin on 25 October. Both of them visited churches and galleries and attended the theater, and JQA toured a number of textile mills and other factories. LCA was pregnant during the journey and ill much of the time; on 29 Sept. JQA wrote in his Diary, "M[rs.] A's illness rapidly approaching.— She is already very unwell, and will continue so untill the severe and inevitable trial has had its usual end." His fears were not realized: GWA was born on 12 April 1801. For detailed accounts of the journey see D/JQA/24, APM Reel 27, and JQA's seventeen letters to TBA, 20 July – 24 Sept. 1800 (Lb/JQA/10, APM Reel 134). The letters were printed in the Philadelphia *Port Folio*, 3 Jan. – 21 Aug. 1801 and were later published in London, in 1804, and in German and French editions. LCA briefly described the trip in a letter to her father on 5 Sept. 1800 (Adams Papers). See also Descriptive List of Illustrations, No. 6, above.

6. "DIE STADT HIRSCHBERG IN SCHLESIEN,"
BY JOHANN CHRISTIAN REINHART, CA. 1800
See page xi

death, and sadly wearisome to every one; but they bore with me with the patience of Angels, and never by look or word, made me feel the pang of *mortification*, by the most trifling indication of ennui at my complaints: but expressing the tenderest sympathy, and the most persevering and delicate attention, to an unfortunate creature; who as Mr Adams remarks in his journal "never knew what it *was*, to be well a whole day"—[105]

I was obliged to make some visits of ceremony after my return, and I formed some new acquaintance, one of whom proved most valuable to me; Lady Carysfort, wife of the English Ambassador, and the Sister of Lord Grenville, and M$^{r.}$ William Grenville, who had recently been here on an extra Mission— She was one of the finest women I ever knew—of very superior mind and cultivation: having received a Classical education like her Brothers— She was very plain in her person; somewhat masculine in her manners; and an premier àbord made one feel timid and afraid— But she took a fancy to me, and was so uniformly kind, and affectionate at all times; her conversation so instructive, so entertaining, and at times so delightful; I clung to her as if she had been my own mother, and loved her with equal sincerity—[106] M$^{rs.}$ St George a gay and dashing widow with M$^{r.}$ Kinaird also pleasant—

1st. [*November*]

Obliged to renew my dissipation—took Tea with M$^{rs.}$ St George with the Browns, Lady Carysfort, and the Bruhl family, and M$^{r.}$ Kinaired (the present Lord Kinaired)

At a great Ball at Madame D'Engerstroom's—3 hundred there—Supper superb. Next Evening at M$^{r.}$ Ofarels— The night after at Tea at M$^{rs.}$ S$^{t.}$ Georges—at Supper at Prince Ferdinands— As soon as the Princess saw me she as usual caught me in her Arms; and then called one of her Chamberlains, to put a Chair near her; all the company excepting myself standing; I was scarlet with susrprize—but you can never resist Royalty— The cause of this mark of distinction was too evident— We excused ourselves from Supper, and I

[105] D/JQA/24, 9 Oct. 1800, APM Reel 27.

[106] John Joshua Proby (1751–1828), 1st Earl of Carysfort, and his second wife, Elizabeth Grenville (ca. 1756–1842), had three daughters: Charlotte (b. 1788), Frances (b. 1789), and Elizabeth (b. 1792). He had four surviving children from his first marriage: William Allen, John, Granville Leveson, and Gertrude (*DNB;* John Debrett, *The Peerage of the United Kingdom of Great Britain & Ireland*, 13th edn., 2 vols., London, 1820, 2:1017).

passed the Evening as usual at the Landgravines Table— Prince and Princess Radziville had returned from Poland that morning

Evening again at Dr Browns to meet the Carysforts, the Bruhls, M^rs.^ St. George, and Mr Kinaird—

6.

Lord & Lady Carysfort, Mr Garlick, Mr. Proby, Mr Kinaird, the Browns, Mrs St George, Mrs Orby Hunter, and Miss Jones, dined with us— Mrs. Hunter, a most eccentric Irish Widow—Very wealthy—

Mr. Adams being quite sick, we remained at home some days—our friends generally spending the Even^g^ with us—

Mr. Maclure from Philadelphia— Mr Adams sent me to take Tea at Mrs. Schicklers—

15

At Madame Heinitz—met there Louis Bonaparte, and two Officers attached to his Suite; Flahault, and Follin— They were introduced, all three elegant young men—Louis very modest—[107] Staid but a short time, and then went to Lady Carysforts, to spend the Evening— Count Bruhl, and family were there—

Went to a very large party at Count Shulembourgs— We did not stay Supper, which was unusually splendid—

Dined at Genl. Ofarels, and spent the Evening at M^rs^ St. Georges—a young, wealthy, coquettish Flirt—but very pleasing in her manners, and rather showy than handsome

Evening at Countess Bruhls—Next at Mrs. St Georges—

Very sick; but went and dined at Lady Carysforts— She has three daughters whom she educates herself— He has three Sons and a daughter, the latter supereminently beautiful, but crazy—and confined in Ireland— The Sons, Lady Carrysfort herself prepared for College, where they were received with distinction— She was first Cousin of William Pit— Proud to excess of her family, and equally so of her Husbands Classical attainments— He was said to be one of

[107] Louis Bonaparte (1778–1846), Napoleon's brother, was en route to St. Petersburg as ambassador when Paul I was assassinated, so he cut short his trip in Berlin. The first officer mentioned was Auguste Charles Joseph, Comte de Flahault de la Billarderie (1785–1870), who later became a general (Blanchard Jerrold, *The Life of Napoleon III*, 4 vols., London, 1874–1882, 1:17; Hubert N. B. Richardson, *A Dictionary of Napoleon and His Times,* London, 1920).

the first Greek Scholars in Europe mild, silent, and good tempered; with nothing showy about him— She did most of the diplomacy— To many she appeared stern; to me she was a tender anxious *friend*—

We closed the month with a dinner to the two Mr. Headlems and Mr. Maclure, and the Evening had Dr Brown's family, the Bruhls, the young Lady Probys, Mrs St George, Mrs Hunter and Miss Jones, Mr Proby, with Mr Ridly. Played and danced,

1ST [*DECEMBER*]

Began the month of December badly—health always much worse—Situation more and more critical—

4TH

Went to the Minister Alvenslebens, only stead an hour— The Royal family not there— continued quite ill for several days, some of my young friends with me always— On the thirteenth again resumed my duties; a ball at the Minister Schröetters, between four and five hundred there—left the party to sup at another, at Mr. Cohens—

15

At a little ball at Mrs. St Georges, very pleasant, where we met the usual social set— Came home very late— Again very ill, an interval of several days in which the suffering was intense— The Evening at Mrs. Browns, The Dr thought it best to keep me amused— The mind too anxious for the body—

23

A visit of ceremony to Madame de Voss— Spent the remainder of the Evening with Mrs. St. George—

25

At a dance at Lord Carysforts; *obliged* to go, she would take no denial; a large company, and did not get home until midnight—

27

At the first Court for the Season— The Queen and King kinder than ever— She congratulated me upon my *prospects*; and said she *sincerely* hoped I should do well— The heat was so great, and the company so large, I was excused from the Supper; and we returned at nine very much fatigued— The English Ladies were presented by Lady Carysfort; and I fortunately in my then situation, was relieved from the harrassing formalities of such occasions—

Quite ill but dined in company at Mrs Browns, and also passed the Evening—

Again I passed the Evening at Dr. Browns, with Miss Bishoff-swerder, and Mr. Kinaird, a very gentlemanly man, of very agreeable manners—

21 [31]

On the last day of the year the Sweedish Minister gave a splendid ball, to dance the old year out, and the New year in— My Clothes were all laid out on the bed for me to dress, and I felt much tempted to go, but hesitated on account of the deadly faintings to which I was constantly subject—and about half an hour before the time, concluded to pass the Evening either with Lady Carysfort, or Mrs. Brown— Supposing that the former would be at the Party, I went to my neighbours, where Mr. Adams set me down as He passed— Lady Carysfort came from the Party, and joined us and we were all sitting laughing, and chatting, when Mr. Adams suddenly returned, looking so white, and flurried; that the Ladies drew him off, lest I should be frightened: and he thus had time to compose himself, and relate the painful event of the Evening to Lady Carysfort; who observing that I looked anxious, began to talk again about the ball; and in her own quiet way, related the incident which had just occurred, making many judicious, and solemn reflections as she proceeded— Poor young Dorville, a remarkably handsome and elegant young man,[108] while dancing a Country dance with a beautiful girl just introduced into company, not more than 16, while in the very *Act* of turning his Partner, had fallen on the floor, and never breathed more— Medical Aid was called, and every effort made to recover him; but it all proved vain, and the Corpse was removed in the midst of the dance, the lights, the fantastic Scenery put up for

[108] Probably the son of Louis de Dorville and brother of Miss Dorville.

the occasion, while the distressing shrieks of Women in fits, and young girls fainting in every direction; formed a contrast so dreadful, that the stoutest man quailed under its effects— The wretched Parents were conveyed to their homes senseless; and Madame D'Engerstroom in a poroxysm of the most ungovernable delirium, was conveyed to the house of Gen[l] Ofarils, dressed in her husbands *clothes*; to the utter horror, and astonishment of the company; and playing such extravagant *antics*, as made the women blush; and frightened the young men out of "their just propriety," into a state of the most ludicrous amazement, if not *amusement*; in the very heart of this melancholy tragedy— The young Man was little more than three and twenty; and the Surgeons thought that *tight clothes*, particularly the *Cravat*; and drinking while heated, a glass of iced Lemonade, had cauced his sudden death—[109] You who know M[r.] Adams can judge of his appearance when he came in, and therefore I need not describe it— and thus we see how wonderfully true the deleneations of Shakespeare are to life; for it almost always happens, that the ludicrous is so blended with the most melancholy and painful catastrophes: that it is not within the scope of mans reason, or mans will to guard against its effects— Is not this a truth calculated to make proud man start, and ponder on the limited nature of his *means*, and the littleness of his boasted powers? A mere buffoon; a common jester like the Grave digger in Hamlet; can banter his most sacred griefs, and turn *himself* to scorn; while the educated, the learned, the wise, and the Sage is brought to feel his nothingness to himself, and to his posterity—

My health now confined me to an intercourse alone with the families in which I visited sociably; without the labour and fatigue of Dress, and I was never alone—

We added two more very agreable acquaintance to our set. M[r.] Landon a gentleman and I think a Clergyman; and M[r] Caulfield his pupil, a wild young Irishman of large fortune and full of frolic— He sung most delightfully as well as M[rs.] St George—

I have mentioned Baron Krudener, and described *him*— At the last Supper party at M[rs.] Schiclers—I mention it to make you laugh; this old fool expressed his great admiration for ME; and invited me to breakfast with *him*, téte à téte in a Pavillion in his Garden— M[r.]

[109] JQA described these events in his Diary on 31 Dec. 1800, and LCA wrote "Death in the Dance. a *reminiscence*," [*post 31 Dec.*], although she had not witnessed them (D/JQA/24, APM Reel 27; Adams Papers).

Adams roared with laughing, when I informed him of my conquest— His Lady was a very handsome, but somewhat notorious person, of latitudinarian principles; with which for her own special comfort, she had innoculated her charming Cara Sposo—and I believe that he made the same proposals to all the ladies that he sat near; assuring them "that his Lady was always engaged with her own affairs"—

At Prince Ferdinands Mr Adams met the famous (it wants another Syllable) Count Tilly, who married Miss Bingham, and then left her for a pension from her Father—[110]

Poor Old Count Golofkin died about three or four Months ago— His Wife and he were sitting together, when a Letter was put into her hand by the Servant, which she gave to her husband— He opened it, and she told him, she would go and dress while he read it— Her chamber adjoined the sitting room— When she returned she spoke to him, but he made no answer— He was sitting in the same attitude with the open Letter in his hand, but entirely dead, and stiff— It was supposed that he had never read the Letter, a mere common place one upon business. He had a splendid Funeral: dressed in full Uniform, and with all the Insignia of the different Offices, which he had filled; and was to have been laid in *state*: but the suddenness of his death, precluded the possibility of such an exhibition— Immediately after the Funeral, the Widow received visits of condolence: all her guests appearing in deep mourning, the Customary form on such occasions— Fourteen years afterwards I saw my old friend the Widow again, at the age of 82 Dressed in a yellow brocaded Silk Gown, covered with large pink roses, interwoven in the Silk—participating in all the pleasures of the Place; and surrounded by young gentlemen, who seemed to delight in her pleasant and gay society— Her Children were all settled at a distance from her, and she lived alone—

I have already mentioned that I had determined not to go out in public I have not told you the why and the wherefore— The truth was, that I had dressed to go to Court. The everlasting teazing about my pale *face*, induced me to make another trial of a little rouge; and contrary to my first proceeding, I walked boldly forward to meet Mr. Adams— As soon as he saw me, he requested me to wash it off,

[110] Comte Alexandre de Tilly (1764–1816) and Maria Matilda Bingham, the daughter of William and Anne Willing Bingham of Philadelphia, eloped in 1799. The Penn. General Assembly annulled the marriage on 17 Jan. 1800 (*Doc. Hist. Supreme Court,* 8:40; James T. Mitchell, Henry Flanders, and others, comps., *The Statutes at Large of Pennsylvania from 1682 to 1801*, 17 vols., Harrisburg, Penn., 1896–1915, 16:390–391).

which I with some temper refused; upon which he ran down and jumped into the Carriage, and left me plànté là! even to myself appearing like a *fool* crying with vexation— As Soon a I had composed myself, I very cooly took off my finery; *re*dressed myself suitably: and stepped into the Carriage to joined my friends the Browns; who never guessed that I had made myself so ridiculous— In those days Anger seldom lasted with me more than ten minutes, and once over all was forgotten— When M^r. Adams returned from Court, he came over to M^rs. Browns, and we returned home as good friends as ever— I never went to any of the Courts after that—

FEBY [*JANUARY*] 1801

6

We had a little party at home a dance and Supper. I was too much exhausted—two oclock in the morning before the company separated— Nevertheless I went the next evening to a party at Mrs St Georges, where M^r. Adams and myself taught them to play Rerversi—

The Carnaval set in most brilliantly— It opened with a Court in Hoops, and was particularly splendid— As the political feeling of the Country was all French, Lady Carysfort seldom took the trouble to attend— The manifestation of marked coldness, to any particular Diplomatist, always being sufficiently decided to make it not only unpleasant, but painful— Her Ladyship was alone, and received me in her Boudoir—a sort of Sanctum Sanctorum as she informed me, into which she never admited any body, but her husband, and Children—and that *I* must consider my reception *there*, as one great proof of her affection— Here she sometimes gave way to her private sorrows—and *here only* she could talk to me of her private history; of her afflictions; of her own peculiar opinions; both religious and literary— This was too flattering from a woman of sixty, to a young woman of little more than five and twenty—and I used to sieze these occasions almost at the expense of my life— They were so impressive, and so interesting She told me how intensely she had suffered at the loss of her only Son! How long she had been before, even her strong sense of religion, her duty as a Christian, had brought her mind to the proper degree of unrepining submission, to the Will of her Almighty Father; and how she repented, and prayed that the rebellion of her heart, might be forgiven, by that merciful Father, who knew best what was good for her— She kindly said that she did not know why she thus opened her heart to *me*; it was an indulgence of which she rarely availed herself, but she could not help it— and she hoped I should consider it as a proof of great attachment and respect— She then told me to apply to her on all occasions when I wanted Motherly advice, and that she would be with me in my hour of trial, if I wished it—and asked me to come and see her again, when ever we could find an opportunity for an agreeable Causerie—

The next Evening I passed at Mrs. Browns, and witnessed a most ridiculous Scéne, between Mr. Garlick, and Mrs. Orby Hunter— She was one of the oddest, and most eccentric women to be *Sane*; that I ever met with—As tall as Mary Roberdeau; not graceful, very bony, between fifty and sixty; wearing a great deal of Rouge badly put on, with piercing black eyes; and very fond of Dress of the most expensive kind, but in very bad taste; Restless, presuming, cross; and perfectly absurd in her great Milesian pretensions;[111] she was a sort of half torment to us all, and we were sure to have something unpleasant whenever she appeared— Her poor little Dame de Compagnie Miss Jones, was an object of pity to every one— She dared not to *dress*, lest she should offend; She was afraid to *talk*, lest she should displease; She trembled to look at a gentleman, lest that look should be misinterpreted; and yet she was obliged to accompany her Tyranic Mistress to all the private parties, which Mrs. Hunter attended— These disgusting restrictions, seemed to operate on *us* all— and the situation of the poor amiable *dowdie*, half vulgar girl, who no one would have thought of; became an object of general compassion to our set, more especially, as she seemed too modest to fawn upon her persecutor— She had entered upon her painful and barren service immediately before leaving England, and could not extricate herself from the difficulties of her situation, for *fear* of being dismissed in a Strange land, without the means of paying her expences home— Garlick a good hearted, but blunt Englishman; the Secretary of the British Embassy, had all the labor of attending to his travelling Countrymen; *Men* and *women*, who visited Berlin; the

[111] Elizabeth Orby Hunter (ca. 1753–1813) was of Irish descent. Although the claims were later discredited as myth, in the seventeenth and eighteenth centuries church leaders and scholars asserted that the Irish were descended from an ancient, pre-Christian civilization, the Milesians. Against the English charge of Gaelic barbarism, Ireland's defenders equated the high civilization of the Milesians with that of the ancient Greeks and Romans (Colin Kidd, "Gaelic Antiquity and National Identity in Enlightenment Ireland and Scotland," *The English Historical Review*, 109:1197–1204 [Nov. 1994]).

Ambassador, only entertaining them once, and making his own selection for acquaintance—lost all patience with this Lady, and bantered and worried her in every possible way; and among the rest, in his pretended attentions to this poor girl, for whom he did not care one straw— The Irish Choler could not stand this, and from one thing to an other, to the utter amazement of poor gentle M^rs. Brown, and her terrified daughters; they got into the most violent quarrel; using the most violent language, which ended in a long and procrastinated Hysteric fit, terminating in a frightful burst of tears, through which Garlick, sat with the utmost composure, determined to see her out; and then to apolize to M^rs. Brown, and me, for his rudeness, brutality would have been a better term—and he accompanied me home trembling with fear, and mortification for them both: in having thus exposed themselves; and both exhibited traits of character so unsuitable, to the rank and Station in life which the held— Garlick was a sikly splenetic old Bachelor— We were very intimate and he was fond of M^r. Adams—

The Queen this Winter was more lovely than ever— Like myself, she was in *delicate* health; but she always danced and Watzed until the last moment, and made no change in her dress, excepting fancy Scarfs falling in draperies, tastefully thrown over her— Josephine of France loaded her with superb presents, and she literally reigned over all hearts Her Sister the Dutchess of Hildeburghausen was on a visit to her very handsome, but not so beautiful as the Queen— Princess de Salms (late Louis), at a Garison Town on the Frontier— Her brute of a husband is said to receive all his Officers while in *bed* with her at five o'clock in the morning, Smoking a Meer-shaum: What a change produced by unbridled passions!!!

The King and Queen were both ill: so that the amusements were suspended

The Hereditary Princess of Mecklenburg Shwerin a daughter of the Emperor of Russia likewise on a visit to the Queen, to spend the Carnaval; very handsome and distinguée—

The Browns passed the Evening with me, and Miss Bishoffwerder; the latter told me that at one of the Ministers Evenings; the Minister Werder had introduced two of his daughters to their Majesties— These Girls had been *reared*, I wont say *educated*, in the Country; and had never seen any thing like a town life, or the refinements of a Court. They were coarse, rough, boisterous girls; romps, talking loud, without an idea of the requisite formalities which enforce propriety, in a Circle of Courtly society— The Young

Men very improperly, instead of giving the poor things Lemonade; had plied them with punch, until they were perfectly intoxicated; and one of them while turning the Queen in the dance, was so overpowered, that her Stomach suddenly rejected the *stirring* beverage, and to the utter consternation of the Court, the royal Robes were *sullied*, and the Queen was obliged to retire— The young Ladies were sent back to the Country, next morning; and the Poor unconscious Minister the Father, came very near being punished for this *gross* offence—

FEBY 1ST

Mr Adams at Court— Fanny Bruhl with me—

2

Mr. Adams to day received the painful information of his brother Charles's death at N.Y. He was Deeply grieved—[112]

3

News of the Election of Mr. Jefferson and that the President Adams was ill of a Fever—[113]

Put on mourning, but Lady Carysfort came and forced me out to ride with her— My Situation more and more *critical*—

Mrs. Hunter and Miss Jones called to take leave of me— She said "mine was the *only House* in which she was *not* received, with chilling frigidity"— She was to leave the City on her way to France next day— This Lady had bought a Carriage on purpose to carry her Parrot; and Miss Jones, and her Maid, were to ride in it by turns, to take care of it. When she *died*, she left a Legacy to this *Parrot*, of five hundred pounds a year—[114] Young Caulfield kept a first rate Valet de Chambre, and a Chariot, for the especial use of his *dogs*—

We went to the Opera—And I there saw the Grand Dutchess This has been the most splendid Winter since we have resided here—

[112] JQA learned of CA's death, which had occurred on 30 Nov. 1800, in a letter from William Vans Murray ([24–27 *Jan. 1801*], Adams Papers), who had seen it reported in New York newspapers.

[113] They learned of the election results and JA's illness from the *Hamburg Gazette* and English newspapers sent by Benjamin Garlike (D/JQA/24, 3 Feb. 1801, APM Reel 27).

[114] The will is reprinted in *Kirby's Wonderful and Eccentric Museum,* 5:27–29 (1820).

Dined at Lord Carysforts only the Viscount D'Anadia beside the family. We stayed also to supper—

Dined again at Lord Carysforts to meet the Turkish Chargé D'Affairs and his Interpreter—[115] They had their dinner all brought ready cooked, and would taste nothing on the Table excepting a small piece of Salmon, of which they took a mouthful out of compliment to the Host— After dinner he came and sat by me, and gave me his Snuff Box to look at on the lid of which was painted a very ugly Ladies face, which he informed me was his favorite Wife— He talked a great deal to *me*; and Lady Carysfort quizzed me after he was gone, about his distinguished preference of my Ladyship.

Before I had retired from the Court Circles; Madame D'Engerstroom had taken it into her head, to make a Claim at Court; of a higher distinction than was customary as to the Seats at Supper at the Kings Table— As the Ladies of Foreign Ministers had the most distinguished Seats at Table; I could not imagine what it meant— She had paid me a formal visit to request my support, and I had told her that I had always been so kindly treated by their Majesties; and as the Wife of the Representive of a Republick I had no especial claims to press; that I therefore declined altogether having any thing to do with the subject—That Lady Carrysfort was a more proper person to apply to— She left me somewhat piqued; but insisted that I should aid *her*, in introducing the fashion of *Pockets*, as she was determined to wear them— I told her that my situation was such, that I doubted if I was of consequence sufficient to introduce *any* fashion, although I might follow one when it was established— She took her leave very coolly

Lady Carysfort sent for me to sit with her in the evening; and I mentioned the circumstance of Madame D'Engerstroom's visit, and asked how I should have acted. She laughed and said, "that she had gone through a similar Scene; and that she had positively *declined* to interfere in the established arrangements of the Court, which were highly satisfactory to the Corps Diplomatique; and she did not believe they desired any alteration or amendment—["] She laughed heartily about the *Pockets* and turned the whole affair into complete ridicule. Madame D'Engerstroom was a very flighty, and extraordinarily weak Woman; and her whole aim was to *magnify* herself into

[115] The Turkish chargé d'affaires was Muhammed Es'ad Effendi, who served in Berlin from 1800 to 1804 (*Repertorium*, 3:459).

some *super-eminence*, for which she did not possess one satisfactory quality— Superior beauty, Superior attainments, or superior virtues, may sometimes elevate themselves to great prominence in the World: but always blended with respect or admiration— Superior wealth may *enforce* attention, but without other accessories in *Europe*, it does not yield positive respect— It is a concomitant, but not the prime requisite— To finish this silly affair which—I mention in detail; because it was a useful lesson to *me*, when Mr. Adams was S. of State, with a restless Diplomacy of Foreigners at Washington— In spite of every advice, all the other Ladies of the corps refusing to participate— The first Court Supper she attended after making this pretention; the *other* Ladies were escorted to the usual Seats, assigned to them by the King; Every Lady holding any place at Court, when *she* attempted to move up; politely, but positively told her, that her *rank* did not entitle her to a seat above them; and thus *alone*, without her *Husband*, she was thankful to get a place, through the intervention of the Master of the Ceremonies; at the very foot of the Table; being at the same time informed, "that a rule had been adopted by the Kings Ministers to prevent all disputes on the subject of Precedence, to assign to each Lady a *place* by *courtesy*, as distinguished Strangers—["] Her situation was mortifying in the extreme: for she had wilfully brought it on herself; and the opportunity gave universal pleasure— Lady Carysfort enjoyed and laughed heartily at Madame's complete discomfiture— The punishment ceased with this exhibition, I *suppose* by order of the King; and at the next Court supper she was received as usual— This Lady has since been pre-eminent in Sweden—

I return to my visits in the Boudoir! Lady Carysfort was in low spirits and sick— She had been almost distracted with the tooth ache which was partially relieved; but she was feverish, and exhausted— Her conversation turned upon death, and futurity; (*she* knew that the Physicians thought me in a deep Consumption, tho' I did not at that time;) and I was very much astonished, nay almost confounded; to find, that with a mind so naturally strong, and so very highly cultivated; that the spirit of Superstition had taken the deepest and firmest hold on that mind; and that in fact it was too deeply engrafted, ever to be eradicated— I will not relate to you the many perfectly *attested* Stories, of supernatural influences, which *She* or her *family* had actually witnessed; and of which she had not the smallest doubt; and she told me that she had many years been acquainted with and actually *seen* the Arm, or rather *wrist*, of the far famed Lady Tyrconnel—[116] And she gave the most unlimited credit to the wonderful miracle, which she had attested with her own eyes— These mysteries of Nature *may* be disputed—but like religious *faith*, they create implicit belief in *many*, however incomprehensible; as addressed to our *senses*; and our Natures; in the mysterious realiaties of our actual being rather than to the cold and artificial presumption of what we term reason, not always proved to be genuine wisdom— The subtleties of Reason are often on a par with the refined subtleties of common Supestition—the one extracting all its powers from the distortion of natural truths; the other its *weakness* from the averseness of corporeal Nature, to the investigation of subjects, operating too strongly upon the nervous irritability of constitutional organization: The dread of things unknown presented to our view as if through natural instinct; palsies the mind with fear, and defies the sterness of judgment at its utmost need; leaving the wisest to a fearful imagination uncontrouled; for everything convinces mans mind, that there are things in this World, and the Next,

Man never yet hath dreamed of—

The death of my kind friend the Landgravine grieved me much— It was very sudden— All Berlin rang with the follies of Count Tilly and Madame Krudener She was a woman of the most extraordinary character, noted for talents and accomplishments of a very high order, but her conduct very doubtful, and at this period supposed to be very guilty— At a later period of her life she became a fanatic, and roamed through Switzerland and Germany; where she became the leader or head of a considerable Sect of severe morality, and self-denying doctrines; which she preached to very large audiences in the fields, over whom she obtained prodigious Influence—[117] I have never known the exact tenets of her Religious faith: but there is no doubt that she exerted a powerful sway over the mind of the Emperor Alexander, which changed his character, and induced him to exile his favorite Misstress, Marie Antoinette Narischkin; to

[116] Sarah Hussey Carpenter, Countess of Tyrconnel (1764–1800), was said to have an indelible mark on her wrist left by a ghost (R. E. G. Cole, *History of the Manor and Township of Doddington*, Lincoln, Eng., 1897, p. 158, 181; E. C. Cork and Orrery, "Early Romances of the Century," *The Pall Mall Magazine*, 9:262–263 [May–Aug. 1896]).

[117] Barbe Julie de Wietinghoff (1764–1824) married a Russian diplomat, Baron Bourkhardt Alexis Constantine Krudener, in 1783. In 1800 he was appointed ambassador to Prussia, and his wife accompanied him to Berlin. After his death in 1802, she wrote a novel, *Valérie*, Paris, 1804, and took an ardent interest in spiritual matters (Clarence Ford, *The Life and Letters of Madame de Krudener*, London, 1893, p. 4, 10–11, 46, 76, 92–93).

whom he had for years sacrificed his Wifes peace of mind, and happiness and she was the Mother of 3 of his Children

I have already said that My Friend the Landgravine died suddenly, and I grieved for her loss— In a foreign Country far from home, without connections or friends, to whom we have been accustomed to look; to share our sympathies, participate in our pleasure, or for consolations in our grief; we feel particularly flattered and grateful for marks of affection or attentions, even when they are casually offered—but when they are long sustained and continue undiminished for years, they insensibly elevate us in our own opinion—and gratitude for perhaps an imaginary discovery of *our* worth, binds the affection which otherwise might prove of very short duration—

My time was passed between Mrs: Brown and Lady Carysfort, either at their houses or my own; and my health was so weak, that few expected that I should survive the trial which I had to sustain—March sat in, and Mr. Adams was obliged to attend the Queens Court, where he met Prince Adolphus of England, now Duke of Cambridge—[118]

5 [*MARCH*]

We supped at Lord Carysforts with a party of thirty, and there met Madame de Riedésel, the Lady of General Riedesel, who was taken with Burgoyne— She has since published Letters during her residence in this Country—[119]

9

I was very ill all the morning and unable to sit up. Lady Carysfort called, and *insisted* that I should go to her in the Evening, and would not be denied; every hour or two I received a Note, intimating that she would take no denial, and at eight o'clock in the eve-

[118] Adolphus Frederick, Duke of Cambridge (1774–1850), tenth child and seventh son of King George III (*DNB*).

[119] Frederika Charlotte Luise, Baroness Riedesel (1746–1808), accompanied her husband, Gen. Friedrich Adolf Riedesel, to America, where he commanded German troops serving with the British Army. The baroness witnessed the first Battle of Saratoga in Sept. 1777. She published her letters and journals in Berlin in 1800 (Lina Sinnickson, "Frederika Baroness Riedesel," *PMHB*, 30:385–386 [1906]; *Baroness von Riedesel and the American Revolution: Journal and Correspondence of a Tour of Duty, 1776–1783*, transl. Marvin L. Brown Jr., Chapel Hill, N.C., 1965, p. xxi, xxx).

ning, as I was apparently better, Mr. Adams thought I had better go; that we could keep the Carriage, and I could return the moment I felt fatigued— I was too weak even to dress, and being in mourning, I tied a black Handkerchief round my head, with some black jet beads, in a proper dont care style; and wore a black mourning dress; and being within a Month of my confinement a black Lace Cloak— She promised me that I should not be in the Ball or receiving Room, but that I should stay in a small sitting room adjoining her boudoir, where I should undergo no fatigue— When we got into the Drawing room, Lady Carysfort came to me immediately, and took my arm, and led me into the apartment provided; and there in spite of all my efforts, *laid* me on a Sopha, and left some of my young friends to amuse me— I felt very badly; but an hour or more elapsed, and no one intruded— I was lying quite at my ease, talking and laughing, when I heard a Gentleman's voice asking Lady Carysfort, "who *that* Lady was"— And she answered the Lady of the American Minister— I did not dare turn my head round, the situation was altogether so ridiculous, but she brought him up to the Sopha, from which I attempted to rise; but he gently laid his hand on my Arm, and insisted that I should not move. This was Prince Adolphus, and I blushed all colours at being caught in such a position— He stood talking some time, and then sat down to the Piano, and with Madame de Caraman which I thought very odd, sung God save the King— I staid Supper and sat next to the Duke of Darmstadt, a German Lump of obesity; whose conversation kept me, and a young Lady who sat near to me; to use Abby's expression which I like, *in "a perfect gale"*— There were five or six *Great German Princes* there; Sovereigns as they are called; and among them the Duke of Saxe Weimar— This was the greatest Féte given by Lord Carysfort during our stay in Berlin—

Too ill to go out, I staid at home for several days; when Lady Carysfort again forced me to go to a Supper at her House; a small party consisting of the usual set— Prince Adolphus there— It was said that he had fallen desperately in love with Mrs. Sanford, and that her husband in a jealous fit, had brought her from Hanover to Berlin— A rumour having been circulated that the Prince was about to follow her, he had carried her off to England as the Prince could not go *there*, without his Fathers permission— And this poor Lady was dying of Consumption— Such is the World: who can escape scandal?

20

Prince Adolphus, Lord and Lady Carysfort and daughters, Baron de Reden, M[r.] Gentz, M[r] Ridley, and the Gentlemen of the Princes Suite, dined with us— The Prince received news while at Table, giving an account of the dangerous and alarming illness of his Father George III— He left us early— He would not permit me to serve the Soup, and took the ladle out of my hand, "lest I should be *fatigued*"—

Here I must observe that I *never* Waltzed and never had an *ornament*—[120]

22

My lovely and beloved Friend Bell Brown was siezed with violent and sudden illness—

24

M[r] Richards wrote a Note to M[r.] Adams informing him of the death of poor Isabella Brown—After an illness of two days of congestion— Prejudice of an unconquerable character, and not to be overcome, caused her so sudden dissolution; How careful Mothers ought to be, in early youth to familiarize their children to changes of circumstane and custom in life—and to prevent that local tenacity of opinion, which only sanctions the customary usages which hourly surround us— She was lovely in her character and her mind only wanted *expansion*, to render her all that could be wished— She in her last moments rejected the tears, the entreaties, the experience of her agonized Father, and the loss of life was the fatal consequence— Her strong attachment to me was evinced in her last moments— After taking leave of her Parents and Sisters She left a kind assurance of her affection for me, and desired that a Cap which I had presented and made for her, should be given to her— She laid it by her with a solemn request, that she should be buried in it, as the last proof of her love— All I loved seemed to be deserting me— This

[120] The waltz, which had its origins in a German country dance, gained popularity in Vienna in the latter part of the eighteenth century. Elsewhere, polite society was slower to approve of the seemingly formless dance in which couples were joined in long embraces (Arthur Loesser, *Men, Women and Pianos: A Social History*, N.Y., 1954, p. 158–159).

was a severe stroke— After the Funeral Lady Carysfort called to see and console me— Once I called at M^rs. Browns to see her after the loss of her dear daughter, but my health totally failed after that sad event;[121] and on the 12th day of April, I was blessed with a *Son*—but under circumstances so distressing; and treatment so cruel on the part of the Drunken Accoucheur, that my life nearly became the forfeit; and I rose from my bed of agony, a *cripple*, with the loss of the use of my left leg—[122]

For five weeks my life was despaired of and in the hope of saving *me*, and to keep the fever from the Brain, I nursed my boy, and a little Girl of six months old—The daughter of a kind english woman, then resident at Berlin— She never would nurse at her Mothers breast afterwards— The sixth week in a state to excite pity I was lifted into the Carriage— M^r. Welsh and Whitcomb carried me down in a Chair, and M^r. Adams from within the Carriage lifted me in—[123] I went to Lady Carysforts, she and her husband having stood Sponsors for poor George, when I was too weak and ill to attend the *Christening Service* on the 4th inst., which was performed by M^r. Proby, the Chaplain of the English Embassy;[124] and when I got there, I was kindly lifted out and carried into the House by Major Casa Major— Here I attended the morning Services—went through the ceremony of Churching, and received the Sacrament, with feelings I sincerely trust of devotion, and gratitude for the blessings bestowed on me— I was a *Mother*—God had heard my prayer.

Through my miserable confinement, the King had the ends of the Street barred up, that no carriages might disturb me; and the Queen sent every day to enquire how I was— In the situation of my health when I left my chamber; I was altogether unable to take leave of them, and express my grateful thanks for the unusual kindness shewn to me; and only through D^r. Brown and Countess Pauline, was I enabled to offer them after I was gone— All this was complementary to America—Not personally to *me*—

[121] LCA wrote "April" in the left margin at this point.

[122] LCA was probably attended at the birth of GWA by Dr. Ribke, whom she subsequently refused to see. She walked for the first time a month later, "with help and great difficulty" (D/JQA/24, 15 April, 11 May, APM Reel 27).

[123] LCA wrote "*16*" in the left margin at this point; the month was probably May.

[124] GWA was baptized on 4 May, and JQA wrote that LCA went out for the first time on 13 May and "rode out" on 27 May (D/JQA/24, APM Reel 27).

1 JUNE

Preparations were making for my departure as Mr Adams would not stay after his recall—[125]

4

George was innoculated with the Vaccine Matter preparatory to our departure[126]

8

Went to Charlottenburg could not walk without assistance attended the Services by M^r. Proby

15

I went to Lady Carysforts not having been able to go the day before, being again very ill; and after dinner took my final leave of her with bitter tears— When it was thought on the 4th day of my confinement that I was dying; that a mortification had taken place— I had entreated her to *take* my Child, until M^r. Adams should leave the Country; and she had faithfully promised to perform every duty to him, as I would myself—and I have not the slightest doubt at this moment that She would have conscienciously fulfilled the promise—

16

We dined at D^r. Browns and on taking leave of me he entreated me to persevere in nursing my Child for six Months; at that period my *constitution* might change—but he considered me in a deep consumption, and only trusted to this crisis to save my life— I had been fully aware of my situation and was rather pleased to learn that I might live to see my Parents, and perhaps die in their Arms—

[125] JQA had received his formal recall from JA and permission to return to the United States, dated 31 Jan., on 26 April (D/JQA/24, APM Reel 27).

[126] Dr. Charles Brown administered the smallpox vaccine (D/JQA/24, 3 June, APM Reel 27).

17

I was again lifted in the Carriage with hartshorn and all sorts of remedies for the deadly and sudden faintings which continually siezed me; and the change of Air, the idea of being once more in my blessed *home*, surrounded by my family, become ten thousand times more beloved to me by absence, and long suffering; had such an effect upon my spirits, I grew every moment better, and by the time that we arrived in *Hamburg*;[127] I could just put my toes to the ground, and leaning heavily on Mr. Adams's arm drag myself from our Lodgings to Mrs. Pitcairns—

Having spoken of the Christening of my poor boy: I was one day sitting at Borden Town with Joseph Bonaparte at his house;[128] when he suddenly turned round, and asked me how my *Son* did "that the King and Queen of England had stood Sponsors for"— I asked him what he meant? He said that the French Ambassador at Berlin had written the whole account of the Christening, and that Lord and Lady Carysfort had been the Proxies on the occasion— So many years after, I was perfectly astonished at this gross misrepresentation; and positively assured him, that there was not a single word of truth in it—

Our time at Hamburg passed very agreeably with Mrs. Pitcairn; her Husband was disgusting to me— I had known him an agreeable and very handsome man— Now he was surly, ill-humoured, and sick— She was an indefatigable Nurse, but for whatever cause he treated her like a dog. She had a beautiful little daughter, Lady Mary Fitzgerald by her first husband; Lord Edward Fitzgerald—and had just burried a Son by Pitcairn, of two or three Months old— She afterwards bore him a daughter, and then ran away from him with (I have heard) Prince Metternich— She was the daughter of Louis Philippe's *Father* by Madame de Genlis—[129]

[127] LCA wrote "21" in the left margin at this point. The Adamses reached Hamburg on 21 June (D/JQA/24, APM Reel 27).

[128] For Joseph Bonaparte, Napoleon's elder brother, see CFA, *Diary*, 2:74.

[129] Anne Stéphanie Caroline Sims (1776–1831), known as Pamela after Samuel Richardson's heroine, was generally believed to be the natural daughter of Louis Philippe Joseph, Duc d'Orléans (Philippe Égalité), and Comtesse de Genlis. In 1792 Pamela married Lord Edward Fitzgerald, who died in 1798. In 1800 she married Joseph Pitcairn, the U.S. consul at Hamburg. They separated soon after the birth of their daughter in 1803, and she resumed using the Fitzgerald name (*DNB*, entry on Pamela Fitzgerald).

8 [JULY]

Went on board of the Vessel in the Evening; having left Hamburg in a Lighter, and settled ourselves as comfortably as we could— My poor Babys Arm was very bad, and I was quite frightened at the appearance of it—

Sixty long and wearisome days passed over us— My Babe had the Dissentery so badly I feared we should lose him— No advice; inexperienced, and so ill and feeble I could scarcely drag myself about; the first half of the voyage was dreadful— My boy got well, and the Sailors had him constantly in their arms; and he throve so rapidly that *at* Sea, and though only three months old when we sailed, I had to set to work, and short coat him, lest some accident shou'd happen through his long Frocks— Epps loved him as if he was her own, and she was an admirable Nurse—

On my voyage I heard for the first time of Miss *Frazer*; and all the history; and my curiosity was much excited to see her— I candidly confess however, that poor faded thing as I was; the elaborate but just account which I heard of her extreme beauty; her great attainments; the elegance of her Letters; altogether made me feel *little*; and though I was not *jealous*, I could not bear the idea of the comparison that must take place, between a single woman possessing all her loveliness, and a poor broken consumptive creature, almost at the last gasp from fatigue, suffering and anxiety— It is true I had every confidence in my husbands affection, yet it was an affair of vanity on my part; and my only consolation was, that at any rate I had a *Son*— This was all very foolish no doubt, but is it not human nature?

On the 4th of Septb. we landed in Philadelphia; the weather was intensely hot, but it was of service to my limb, not yet perfectly re-established— With pain my old friends recollected me; and Tom Adams was shocked and distressed when he saw me— Here I first saw Mrs. Quincy and Mrs. Tudor—[130] And I went out several times though scarcely able to crawl; to dinner, and to Tea, and this continued as long as I staid— Dr Rush attended me—and was very kind to me—

[130] For Eliza Susan Morton Quincy, see CFA, *Diary*, 1:298. Delia Jarvis Tudor was the wife of William, JA's former law clerk (*AFC*, 1:146).

12 [*SEPTEMBER*]

At eight o'clock in the morning, Mr. Adams put me into the Stage for Baltimore, with Epps, my Bably, and Whitcomb, to visit my poor Father and my family in Washington. We had never been parted before; and though this Country was to be my home, I was yet a forlorn stranger in the land of my Fathers; and I could not reconcile myself to returning thus sick and desolate, among those who had so loved me— Mr. Adams felt the same anxiety to see his Parents that I did; and I could not complain of the feeling which occupied my own heart; When I arrived after a tedious and dangerous journey, my Father was standing on the steps at the door of the house, expecting his Child, yet he did not *know me*— After he had recovered from the shock at first seeing me; he kept exclaiming that "he did not know his own Child," and it was sometime before he could calm his feelings, and talk with me— Whitcomb remained a day, and then returned to Boston— Unaccustomed to the American Stages, I was perfectly exhausted, and the next morning waked in a high fever. A Physician was sent for, and he decided without a moments hesitation that early in October, I must wean my boy or he would not answer for my life— The kind care and affectionate attention of my Mother and my Sisters restored me in a few days to my usual state, and on the 12th of October I weaned my boy by absolute compulsion, against my will, and with great bodily suffering— Two little months escaped rapidly before Mr. Adams came on, and I had the misery to see my father fearfully changed; and delighting only in his Grand children Johnson, and George, and shadowing visions of brightness for future times—[131] Mr. Adams arrived on the 21st of October and was warmly and cordially greeted by the family, with delight by myself— Thus we were all once more united—[132]

27 [*OCTOBER*]

My Mother, Mr. Adams, Epps, the Child and myself, went to visit Mrs Washington at Mount Vernon— My Father was unexpectedly

[131] Johnson Hellen (b. 1800).

[132] JQA left for Quincy on 12 Sept., traveling via Newark, where he saw AA2. He stayed in Quincy from 21 Sept. to 14 Oct., visiting family and tending to financial matters. He met LCA and her family in Washington, D.C., on 21 Oct., settled his accounts with the treasury, and looked over Joshua Johnson's legal and financial papers. LCA and JQA arrived in Frederick, Md., on 3 Nov. and stayed until the 11th, when they departed for Quincy, arriving there on 25 Nov. (D/JQA/24, APM Reel 27).

called to Anapolis— There I saw Mrs. Lewis the celebrated Nelly Custis a beautiful woman—

28

At ten o clock the next morning we took leave, and returned to dinner at 1/2 past three— Mrs. Hellen come to stay there while her Husband was absent— I was better than I had been for a long time—

Caught a violent Cold and could not travel on the 31st the day appointed by Mr. Adams—

We were out a great deal while we staid at Washington—Dined at Mr Jeffersons, Madisons, Smiths,[133] and many other places— Never at Mr. Galatins—

On the 3d of Nover. we started for Frederic; I with a dreadful Cough, at 1/2 past two in the morning, accompanied by my Father, Mother, and two youngest Sisters— Caroline was to accompany *me*— About half way my Father, was taken very ill; so ill that it was with the utmost difficulty that he could reach Frederic, where he was immediately put to bed and a Physician called in—[134] I staid with him a couple of days at the Hotel; and was then forced to go to my Uncle Governor Johnson's, at Rose Hill, about a Mile out of the Town— All my relations received us with the utmost kindness, and treated Mr. Adams with the most marked attention and respect— Their Horses, their Carriages, Their Houses, all were at our command, and we were *petted* in every possible way during our stay, which was in every way painful, in consequence of my dear Fathers dreadful illness— Mr. Adams sat up with *him*— His danger was great— Our dear Babe became very ill with the Summer complaint—

8 [*11 NOVEMBER*]

At four o'clock on this day I was obliged to leave Frederick and my dying Father—My Baby being very ill of the Bowel complaint; and I not permited to take leave of my suffering Parent, lest it should agitate him; and me *so* much as to incapacitate me for the journey; Mr. Adams being anxious to proceed to Boston, lest the Winter should set in— Caroline would not leave my father in such a

133 Robert Smith (1757–1842), then secretary of the navy, had married his distant cousin Margaret Smith in 1790 (*DAB*).

134 JQA described Joshua Johnson's illness as "the gravel," or kidney stones (D/JQA/24, 3 Nov. 1801, APM Reel 27).

state, and remained to nurse him faithfully, on that dreadfull Bed of sickness, from which he was removed to his brothers; Baker Johnson's to die, after a lingering sickness of Six Months of intense and unremited agony, away from his home, and from the most of his family— I never saw him more—[135] We travelled all day only stopping once; the Child constantly shrieking so that we could not pacify him; by the Lancaster road, and arrived at the Ferry at 7 o'clock, so dark, that we were in imminent danger of running on the rocks in a very small Boat, and lodged at Columbia on the Eastern Shore— I had no proper Clothing for such a journey; and I cannot describe my suffering of both mind and body— At two the next morning, we again started from Columbia, and for 12 Miles we were alone in the Stage, over a very rough Turnpike road— We then took eight Passengers, and travelled 76 miles without stopping, and arrived at Philadelphia at 5 o'clock in the Evening; I extremely overcome and very ill—and my darling George not much better— Next day I was apparently better, and was taken to the Theatre— I was so severely ill, after this that Mr. Adams sent for Dr. Rush— Could my spirits be otherwise than bad; my situation was doubtful, and my fathers state enough to cause every apprehension— Mr. Adams remarks "that my Spirits were more depressed than myself *really* ill"—

15

I was a little better but still very poorly and remained quietly at home

16

At two o'clock we again set forward and went as far as Trenton where we arrived at eight in the Evening— Here we were all obliged to lodge in the same chamber, and the Child was so restless and uneasy, we could get no sleep—and soon after 4 o'clock, we resumed this dreadful journey, breakfasting at Princeton, dining at Elizabeth Town, and arriving at Newark at 4 in the afternoon at Giffords Inn—[136] Then I was obliged to walk to see Col Smiths *Mother*, who

[135] Joshua Johnson died on 17 April 1802.

[136] Archer Gifford's tavern on Broad Street (F. J. Urquhart and others, *A History of the City of Newark, New Jersey*, 3 vols., N.Y., 1913, 1:423–424).

insisted upon our staying and passing the Night at her House— Abby Adams, afterwards M$^{rs.}$ Johnson then a Child was with her—[137] The *evening* was very stormy with heavy rain— M$^{rs.}$ Smith an immense woman entertained us with a dismal family history—

18

At nine in the morning we rode to Pawles Hook, the roads dreadful, in a pouring rain; and then crossed the Ferry in an open Boat called I think a perogue, the Storm of wind and rain being so severe, that only *one* man could be found, who would cross with us— without even an Umbrella, dressed in a pale blue Satin pelice trimmed with black lace, and without one particle of covering, under which we could Shelter our devoted heads— We waited in the doorway of a house drenched to the Skin, while M$^{r.}$ Adams got a hack; a thing difficult to procure at that time—and we drove to M$^{rs.}$ Smith's,[138] who was too much shocked when she thus saw me drenched to the Skin, so ill, and weak, without stopping to ask any questions, she led me into a bed room, tore off my things, and insisted upon nursing me up in the kindest and most affectionate manner— What I had been and what I was!! the contrast was too great and my temper, my character entirely changed— Dearly did I love her—

19

The next day I was better, that is able to get up and received some of my old friends— In the evening She had company and I sat up quite late I was a favorite of the Col's—

20

At four o clock in the afternoon we took passage in the packet Cordelia weather very Cold— Many passengers—

[137] Margaret Smith, AA2's mother-in-law, and Abigail Louisa Smith Adams, daughter of CA, who would marry Alexander Bryan Johnson in 1814.
[138] AA2.

22

We went ashore at Newport and Lodged at Mrs Brentons,[139] and

23

the next morning to Providence and continued our Route in the Stage to Boston, where we arrived wet and tired; and fortunately for me and my babe, too late for the Quincy Stage, in which I was to have proceeded immediately— These were my first impressions of America! No one can wonder that they were not agreeable— Suffering and sorrow, sickness and exhaustion, with anguish of mind, all combined to harrass me; and hitherto I had been the spoilt Child of indulgence; could I realize the change? Impossible! and under such circumstances could I appear amiable? M^rs. Smith the Wife of Mr W. Smith of Boston received us very kindly, and we passed the night at her house, and breakfasted there in the morning—[140] At ten o'clock we started for Quincy, and arrived there just at Noon— Both M^r & M^rs. Adams received me very kindly, and were much pleased with the Child: for whose sake I had been thus hurried on from the South to gratify their wish and the necessity of M^r As entering into business— In the Evening Miss Beale came to see me (late M^rs. Wales)—[141]

26

Was thanksgiving day— We appeared at Church or rather Meeting— M^rs. Smith, M^r T Welsh, and W Shaw dined with us— M^rs. Cranch called in the afternoon— Capt Beale and Mr Peter Adams in the Evening—[142] From this period my Cough and breast were in a most distressing state, and Mr Adams could get no rest— The Quincy visitations were almost insupportable, and I longed for my home, with an impatience that made me completely disagreeable— M^r. Adams bought some of his Old Uncle Quincy's Furniture for

[139] Benjamin Brenton and his wife, Rachel Cooke, operated a boardinghouse at the Lopez House on Thames Street (George Champlin Mason, *Annals of Trinity Church, Newport, R.I.*, 2 vols., Newport, R.I., 1890–1894, 1:211).

[140] For Hannah Carter Smith, the wife of AA's cousin William Smith, see *AFC*, 7:422, 423, 444.

[141] Ann Beale (b. 1783) married Thomas Beale Wales in 1806 (Sprague, *Braintree Families*).

[142] Capt. Benjamin Beale Jr. (1741–1825), father of Ann.

our house—And I went with him to see the House in Hanover Street which he had purchased—[143]

On the 21st. of December we took up our residence in Boston—in Hanover Street, Epps, and Lydia Pray with us—[144] Very ill— Mr Hall and Mr. Smith called on us—

22 [*DECEMBER*]

Dr Welsh came to see me and bled me— Thought I might live a month but very doubtful— William and John Smith came from Atkinson on their way to N.Y. and dined with me— The old Gentleman dined at a publick dinner and took them both with him to Quincy in the Evening—[145]

William and John Smith came in from Quincy and passed the Night with us and then left us on their way to N.Y. I continued very ill—

25

Christmas day a little better from bleeding and blistering— Mrs. Welsh and Charlotte and Mr & Mrs. Quincy called on us Jos Hall and Mr. Shaw dined with us. T Welsh in the Eveng. Thus I had began the labours of House keeping but with Whitcomb and Epps—as Managers—

28

Very very ill—

29

Worse and the 30th a little better but in danger—

143 JQA bought 39 Hanover Street in Oct. 1801 from William Smith. JQA had lived there from 1790 to 1794 when he boarded with the family of Dr. Thomas Welsh, from whom Smith had bought the property in 1798.

144 Probably Lydia Pray (b. ca. 1784), a servant, the daughter of Sarah Harmon and Benjamin Pray of Quincy (D/JQA/24, 21 Dec. 1801, APM Reel 27; Sprague, *Braintree Families*).

145 William Steuben Smith and John Adams Smith had arrived from the Atkinson, N.H., home of Elizabeth Smith Shaw Peabody. "The old Gentleman" was JA.

31

Was so much better went out and returned some visits—

JANY 1ST. [*1802*]

M[rs.] Doble, M[rs.] Wilson, M[rs] Payne M[rs.] Bartlet and M[r] Boylston called on us— In the Evening was obliged to go to a small Tea party at M[rs.] Smiths, met the Welsh's; the Storers &ce—M[rs] Storer a fine woman.[146] Went out to Quincy— Weather so severely Cold could not endure it, and was very ill all the time I staid— Quincy! What shall I say of my impressions of Quincy! Had I steped into Noah's Ark I do-not think I could have been more utterly astonished— D[r.] Tufts! Deacon French! M[r] Cranch! Old Uncle Peter! and Capt Beale!!! It was lucky for me that I was so much depressed, and so ill, or I should certainly have given mortal Offence— Even the Church, its forms, The snuffling through the nose, the Singers, the dressing and the dinner hour, were all novelties to me; and the ceremonious partys, the manners, and the hours of meeting 1/2 past four were equally astounding to me—

In England I had lived in the City of London— In Berlin at Court! But the ettiquettes of Court society were not half so burdensome— I had promised M[r] Adams at his particular request never to talk about Berlin, and I faithfully kept my word—but we could not silence Epps, and she would make ridiculous observations; and the consequence was unfavorable to me— This was forty three years ago and forty three years in America is equal to a Century any where else; and do what I would there was a conviction on the part of others that I could not *suit*, however well inclined— This I necessarily *felt*, and the more particular the attentions that they thought it necessary to show me, the less I felt at *home*, and the more difficult my position became— I had a separate dish set by me of which no one was to partake; and every delicate preserve was brought out to treat me with in the kindest manner—but it always made me feel as if I was an apàrté in the family; and though I felt very grateful, it appeared so strongly to stamp me with unfitness, that often I would not eat of my delicacy, and thus gave offence— M[rs.] Adams was too

[146] Dr. Thomas and Abigail Kent Welsh attended the tea party with the two daughters of his first marriage, Harriet and Charlotte (D/JQA/24, 1 Jan., APM Reel 27; *AFC*, 7:203). For Hannah Quincy Lincoln Storer, the wife of Deacon Ebenezer Storer, see Adventures, note 193, below.

kind and I could not reject any thing— Louisa Smith was jealous to excess, and the first day that I arrived, left the Table crying and sobbing, and could not be induced to eat any dinner— No wonder that I was anxious to have a house—

The old Gentleman took a fancy to *me*, and he was the only one— I was literally and without knowing it a *fine* Lady— No qualifications had hitherto been demanded of me— Mr. Adams had made Whitcomb his Steward and had no confidence in any body else—but I had nothing to do but to see that the orders given were executed; and Epps, was the Housekeeper, as she kept the Linen, the Plate, and our Clothes in order— I had no private expences; because I had no means, therefore I had no res[. . .]ponsibility! Could it therefore be surprizing that I was gazed at with *surprize*, if not with contempt— The qualifications necessary to form an accomplished Quincy Lady, were in direct opposition to the mode of life which I had led—and I soon felt, that even my husband would acknowledge my deficiency, and that I should lose most of my value in his eyes— My dreadful ignorance ~~sickness~~ excited no sympathy, and I saw, and knew that I was totally unfit for my duties, and that I ~~could no longer please~~ under such circumstances could not be useful—and this *idea* added so much to the difficulties of my situation, that I became cold and reserved, and seldom spoke at all—which was deemed pride— All this was perfectly just; and I could not complain of any body but myself— I tried by every means in my power to *work* as they call it; but my strength did not second the effort, and I only made matters worse— Mrs. Adams gave me instruction and advice, but I did not readily learn—and in fact on my part all went wrong, and the more I fretted the worse things grew— Our pecuniary means were small; and of course eoconomy was essential. My people soon saw through my ignorance and took advantage of it, and in short I was in every respect any thing but what I should have been—

Mr. Adams could not hear these things eternally, without seeing my faults; and questions of expenditure and mismanagement highly merited on my part; caused perpetual uneasiness of a character painful to both, yet impossible to avoid— I state this merely to show how imprudent it is for a woman to form a connection in a foreign Country— I was a burthen to my husband; I felt it, and I grieved because I loved him; for what I could not repair— You all see my deficiency at this moment of writing—

In Boston I met with the most decidedly flattering reception— Every body talked to me of Miss Frazer as if they were afraid that I did not know the tale; and Mrs. W Smith told me the whole history, until I was perfectly convinced of the truth of the french Song

"Qu'on revient toujours à ces premieres amours."[147]

and that it would be impossible for me in any way to compete with this Lady; and that it was a great misfortune that so sickly as I was, I should stand in their way—

Mr. Adams could not afford to keep Epps, and offered to pay her passage back to England— This was a bitter stroke but I knew it was unavoidable— She declined the passage and married Whitcomb, and they set up in business which proved successful—[148] I was sorry but I too well understood the necessity either to grieve or complain—

The Charge of my darling boy then devolved upon me and the sleepless nights of Mr. Adams soon taught him to regret the loss of his loving and faithful Nurse— He was the great blessing in my cup; and he made up the sum of my joy—

All the élite of Boston called on me, and entertained me most handsomely, and it never entered into my head to regret Europe—

The situation of my Father was dreadful, lingering amid the pangs of poverty and agonizing sickness, for six long Months; it is true receiving all kindness from his Brothers—but far from his home, when a crisis took place and hopes were entertained that he might overcome the desease—but the news arrived that Mr. Jefferson had taken his place from him, and he sunk rapidly into his Grave; knowing that, that *place* kindly and mercifully given to him by President Adams, contrary to the advice of all his nearest friends; was the only support that he had for his numerous and distressed family—[149] He

[147] We always return to our first loves.

[148] Tilly Whitcomb and Elizabeth Epps were married in March. In 1804 Whitcomb became the proprietor of the Concert Hall on the corner of Hanover and Court Streets in Boston. Along with its musical functions, the hall served as a tavern and ballroom, and as a meeting place for political, fraternal, and civic organizations (Boston, *30th Report*, p. 479; *AFC*, 10:210; Samuel Adams Drake, *Old Landmarks and Historic Personages of Boston*, Boston, 1876, p. 68, 70–71, 149).

[149] In May 1800 Republicans in the Senate, along with several Federalists, opposed JA's nomination of JQA's father-in-law to the new and sought-after position of superintendent of the stamp office in the Treasury Department, with its annual salary of $2,000. Vice president Thomas Jefferson cast the deciding vote in Joshua Johnson's favor, an action he would affirm in the face of criticism. In April 1802 Jefferson directed his secretary of the treasury, Albert Gallatin, to reorganize his department, eliminating the position of superintendent of the stamp office and effecting other reductions and consolidations. While Johnson's family evidently took this to be a personal affront, Jefferson's reforms were aimed more broadly at eradicating Hamiltonian "pomp, patronage and irresponsibility" (AA to AA2, 4, 11 May 1800; TBA to JQA, 11 May, all Adams Papers; Jefferson, *Papers*, 32:477, 535–536; 37:158).

died on the 14th of April, leaving a large property which has been totally lost to his family, in consequence of the want of Means to administrate upon the Estate of himself, and his Partners—Lands in Georgia to a large amount situated in the neighbourhood of Augusta, and at this moment recorded and registered in every Court House in the Counties; where the Lands lie—In addition to large Sums, which have furnished fortunes to the Children of the Lawyers, in whose hands the Moneys had been collected— I mention this *fact*, only as a proof, that my Fathers were just Claims; and to exonerate his memory from every charge calculated to injure his character—[150] Kindly and affectionately treated by Mr. Adams's family, could I have enjoyed health, and fitted myself to perform the duties required by my change of life, I should have been happy— But I hourly betrayed my incapacity; and to a woman like Mrs: Adams; equal to every occasion in life; I appeared like a maudlin hysterical fine Lady, not fit to be the Partner of a Man, who was evidently to play a great part on the Theatre of life— These ideas will be called romantic.— They were so when young; but they exist to this hour— The moment in which my Fathers misfortunes occurred, gave a colouring to my future days, which could never be eradicated— It overtook *me* in the *zenith* of my happiness; at that peculiar period of life which marks a future destiny; and that colouring appeared to stamp my character, with a base deception which my Soul utterly *scorned*, and no evidence could ever be brought forward in my favour afterwards, to *prove* the perfect innocence of my conduct—

The loss of Fortune so small as the best to which all knew I could have pretended to, was scarcely a consideration—but the apparent

[150] Joshua Johnson's will of 12 Dec. 1801 bequeathed to his wife the use for her lifetime of his household goods and $800 per year. The remainder of his real and personal estate was to be divided equally among his children. He named as executors Thomas Baker Johnson, JQA, and Walter Hellen. The amount of money that the estate actually provided to Joshua Johnson's beneficiaries is not clear, but his widow was dependent on her children and their families for the remainder of her life. For the disputed settlement of the financial affairs of Wallace, Johnson & Muir, see Record, note 55, above.

Correspondence of a later date, occasioned by an inquiry from Maryland senator Alexander Contee Hanson Jr. (1786–1819), makes reference to the Georgia lands in which his family also had an interest. It was LCA's understanding that Wallace, Johnson & Muir had originally owned 60,000 acres near Augusta. JQA informed Hanson that he had reason to believe that Johnson had "conveyed away" his share of the Georgia lands before his death (FC, Joshua Johnson's will, Adams Papers, Genealogical Material; *DAB*; D/JQA/30, 8 Feb. 1818, APM Reel 33; LCA to AA, 23 Jan., Adams Papers; JQA to Alexander Contee Hanson, 23 March, Lb/JQA/19, APM Reel 143).

dishonour of palming myself upon a family under such circumstances, was a baseness from which my spirit has revolted; and it has and still does make the wretchedness of my life— It has turned every sweet into gall—and I have never thought it *possible* however desirous, and willing; to make a reparation for the bitter misfortune of a connection with a family so uncongenial, and so unfortunate as mine has proved to Mr. Adams, both in his private and publick situation— ~~Oh [. . .] to my Children~~

This is a sentiveness carried to excess many will think, but to a man in a public career in this Country a woman should be like Cæsars Wife.

Mrs. Knox was the most remarkable person that I became acquainted with in Boston— She was remarkably large, ugly, and course in her person; and altogether masculine in her manners, and understanding— Her conversation was pleasant and amusing—[151] Mrs. Swan was a very handsome woman of her age; what the french call brusque in her manners, and not the most refined in her conversation—[152] Mrs. Howard was a very pretty pleasing Woman— Mrs. Winthrop a very elegant and stylish person, with fine manners— Mrs. Sam Perkins beautiful, mais diable— Mrs. Otis, Mrs. Apthorpe, lovely— Mrs. Rufus Amory very handsome and very fashionable— The Welles charming— Mrs. Callender pretty— The Amory's, the Codman's, the Russells, The Sheaffes, the Sergeants, the Cushing's, The Paynes, the Sullivans, the Babcocks, the Gores, the Hubbards, the Tudors, the Quincy's, the Hitchborns, the Higginson's, the Salisbury's, the Twings, the Mason's the Powells, the Warrens the Codmans Fosters and many more; which formed a very large circle of acquaintance, and made me as dissipated as I had been in Berlin—besides which public Balls, and Assemblies; which kept me out much *later* at night—as we seldom returned before 12 or 1 o'clock— These Suppers were very elegant and expensive and the entertainment in high style— Mrs. Wilson Mrs. Doble and Miss Gray were Sisters all handsome and charming Women, with whom I became very intimate, as well as with Mrs. George Blake, one of the most

[151] For Lucy Flucker Knox, wife of Maj. Gen. Henry Knox, see *AFC*, 8:xiii–xiv, 264.

[152] Hepzibah Clark Swan, daughter of the Boston merchant Barnaby Clark, was the wife of James Swan (1754–1830), a Scot who had immigrated to Boston. Hepzibah's wealth enabled James to invest in loyalist property and speculate in land, but he fell into debt and in 1787 sought to recover his losses in France, where he eventually became an agent of the French Republic. In 1808 he was sent to a French debtors' prison, where he remained until his death (*DAB*; Small, *Hist. of Swan's Island*, p. 47).

unaffected and agreeable women I ever was acquainted with– The Parkmans and the Rogers's were also my visitors– Mrs. Morton was very beautiful at this time, and very much famed for her literary acquirements– Mrs. Dexter was an eccentric being as she is still, and I became very intimate with her– She was an ardent friend and admirer of Mrs. Adams, and through this medium extended her friendship to me–[153] Mr Tom Perkins's family and the Codmans were Neighbours– Mrs: Gardner Green and I were *great* friends; there was a sort of sympathy between us; both having been educated in England, where I had been acquainted with her– She often took me to Trinity Church with her in her Carriage–[154] The Joy's were also visitors–Mrs B Joy a most amiable being– To Mrs. W Smith I was indebted for many of the kindest offices and instructions in my family arrangements, and she was a true and kind friend to me, as long as she lived–

On the 13th of March my darling George broke out with the Measles, and thank God had it very lightly–

Whitcomb and Epps were married by Dr. Gardner on the 23d of March–[155] She was a dreadful loss to me, which although I have had many kind and good Servants, never has been replaced–

Went to Quincy and saw Mr & Mrs. Whitney– Returned on the monday Morning– My health began to fail again, and the old deadly faintings to return– After the departure of Epps, I was necessarily more at home–during her stay my Babe was in better hands than my own; and Mr. Adams had thought it necessary for *me* to accept the manifold kind attentions, which had so strongly been evinced in our reception at Boston– Had my Father been well, and could I have retained the Services of Epps; I should have had but very few wishes ungratified–

[153] Catherine Gordon Dexter was the wife of Samuel Dexter, who served for brief periods in JA's cabinet as secretary of war and secretary of the treasury. CFA described her as "one of the humourists of the last age" (*DAB*; CFA, *Diary*, 7:211).

[154] For Elizabeth Clarke Copley Greene, see *AFC*, 8:420. The first Trinity Church in Boston, a wooden building at the corner of Summer and Hawley Streets, served its parishioners from its consecration in 1735 until 1828, when work began on a new Gothic structure. When fire destroyed that building in 1872, the parish proceeded with plans to build the French Romanesque church, designed by H. H. Richardson, that still stands as a landmark at Boylston and Clarendon Streets (Moses King, *King's Hand-Book of Boston*, Boston, 1878, p. 150–152).

[155] John Sylvester John Gardiner (1765–1830) had been assistant rector to Samuel Parker at Trinity Church, Boston, since 1792. At Parker's death in 1805, Gardiner took his place as rector (*DAB*).

27 [*APRIL*][156]

The news of my almost adored fathers death overwhelmed me— and I became alarmingly ill— My Constitution had been so racked during my residence in Berlin, that the least agitation was dangerous to me— I had left my father on his death bed, without the power to help him; under circumstances the most distressing; He who had from my Infancy gratified every wish of my heart: who had placed the most unlimited confidence in my character; and had doated on me for what he imagined *excellence*. *Who* had told me on that very bed of sickness, that he loved and blessed me for I had never given him a *moments* pain— To think that I had deserted that father under circumstances so melancholy, after four years of absence; and that circumstances beyond controul compelled me thus to do; was heart rending; and self reproach of the bitterest kind seemed to sear my very heart— I knew I was among a people that thought it sin to indulge such feelings; but nature will have vent— I could not be comforted or consoled; He had prayed to be allowed to live to embrace me *once* more, and how literally that prayer was granted— Mrs Whitcomb came to me— *She* knew him, and loved him, and she grieved almost as much as I did— Mr. Brooks's manners to his Children, have always recalled my father to my memory, and I never see him without thinking of my young days—[157]

12 [*APRIL*]

My darling boys birth day passed almost unnoticed— He was a fine Child, and *I* was *too vain* of him— But the name which we had given him was not liked, and perhaps we ought to have given him the name of his Grandfather—[158]

[156] The entry is out of order in the MS.

[157] Peter Chardon Brooks, the father of ABA.

[158] AA wrote to TBA that the naming of her grandson for George Washington was "ill judged," just as her own failure to continue the names of her children's maternal grandparents had been. "I am sure your Brother had not any intention of wounding the feelings of his Father, but I see he has done it— had he calld him Joshua, he would not have taken it amiss—" The day after the child's baptism, JQA had written to TBA that the name was chosen to honor Washington's "public character" and to show respect for one who was "next to my own father, the man upon earth to whom I was indebted for the greatest personal obligations." But JQA had his own misgivings: "I know not whether upon rigorous philosophic principles it be wise to give a great and venerable name to such a lottery-ticket as a new-born infant" (AA to TBA, 12 July 1801, Adams Papers; D/JQA/24, 4, 5 May, APM Reel 27; Bobbé, *Mr. and Mrs. JQA*, p. 113).

15 [*MAY*]

On this day I went out to Quincy, I had not seen any of the family; and George went with me— Here I remained till the 24$^{th.}$ and M$^{r.}$ Adams came out on the Saturday and remained till Monday—

28[159]

M^{r} & M$^{rs.}$ Adams came to Town and passed the night at our house; my health and spirits both wretched— My fate was sealed— and all hope of my Fathers affairs being settled gone for ever—[160]

26

M$^{r.}$ Adams was now in the Legislature, and of course with so much business, was not much at home. The old Gentleman was in Town; M$^{r.}$ Adams did not see him, and I was very ill—as I had been so frequently in Berlin— M$^{r.}$ Adams delivered an address before the Fire Society, I was too ill to attend it the Ex-President and M$^{rs.}$ Adams attended the performance, and came to our House to Sleep— It was very successful—[161]

M^{r} & M$^{rs.}$ Adams left us and Louisa Smith staid— She had already made me a long visit in the Winter—

2D JUNE

M$^{rs.}$ Adams came into Town and dined with us and in the Evening returned with Louisa Smith to Quincy— Went to walk with M$^{r.}$ Adams and looked over a House on Beacon Hill—

159 The entry is out of order in the MS.

160 On the previous day, JQA had "acknowledged the instrument" by which he declined to serve as executor of Joshua Johnson's will. Responding to JQA's decision, Thomas Baker Johnson regretted his own lack of the legal and mercantile qualifications required to effect a settlement of the "complicated & dispersed" claims against the estate, though, he wrote, he was intent on assisting his "destitute" family. JQA encouraged Johnson to accept the role of executor, and to rely on relatives and family friends to assist him with questions of law and trade, but eventually Walter Hellen assumed the sole responsibility for administering the estate (D/JQA/24, 27 May 1802, APM Reel 27; Thomas Baker Johnson to JQA, 20 May, with a copy of JQA's resignation enclosed; JQA to Johnson, 27 May; Johnson to JQA, 29 June, all Adams Papers). For Thomas Baker Johnson's character, see CFA, *Diary*, 5:xvi–xvii.

161 JQA was elected to the Mass. senate in April and sworn in on 26 May. In his 28 May address to the Massachusetts Charitable Fire Society, the new legislator urged the use of brick and stone, not wood, for the construction of buildings (D/JQA/24, 5 April, 26, 28 May, APM Reel 27; JQA, "Address to the Massachusetts Charitable Fire Society," 28 May, Adams Papers).

On the 25 of June Mr. Shaw came to live with us—[162] My life was very quiet and agreeable— The family from Quincy often dined with us, and I went out there to stay from Saturday to Monday, whenever I was well enough; sometimes to stay a week. Every care was taken of me, and every kindness shown to me; but I was changed; I had lost my spirits and my health equally; and under such circumstances how could I please any one?—

22

Charlotte Welsh who had been on a visit to me left me this day and my Mother and Sister Caroline arrived this Eveng— I was *too* happy—

26

Mrs Adams came to Town and took us all out to Quincy— We stayed over Sunday—and My Mother and I and my boy returned to Boston, leaving Caroline there who Mrs. Adams was very fond of— We lived almost constantly at home, occasionally walking in the Mall; and Mr. Adams read to us in the Evening— My Mother had a great many friends in Boston—Mr. David Sears, Sheriffe Allen, Col Bradford, Capt Scott, husband of Mrs. Hancock; Jos Hall, Fitch Hall, the Appleton's now dead; Stephen Higginson, and William Gray of Salem; besides many others that I have forgotten—

I forgot to mention that Mrs. Murray, Wife of Dr Murray with Miss Mary Frazer called on me, and I found the latter *all* that she had been described— She was engaged to marry Mr. Daniel Sargent— This visit took place much earlier than I have mentioned—[163]

The Month of July passed without any event of consequence and our lives were altogether Monotonous— I much prefered it to a roaming restless life, and the Society of my Mother and Caroline, left me little to wish for— The Nature of the illnesses to which I was so constantly exposed, required repose; a thing almost incompatible

[162] William Smith Shaw came to board with LCA and JQA on 21 June. Shaw, who had served as JA's private secretary during the latter two years of his presidency, was at this time studying law in Boston (D/JQA/24, 21 June, APM Reel 27; *DAB*; AA2 to JQA, 28 Sept. 1798, Adams Papers).

[163] Mary Frazier called on LCA with Rebecca Orrick Murray, the wife of Dr. Henry Murray and mother of JQA's friend William Vans Murray. Daniel Sargent Jr. (1764–1842) and Mary Frazier were married on 4 Dec. 1802 (*AFC*, 7:28, 9:43–44; John H. Sheppard, "Reminiscences of Lucius Manlius Sargent," *NEHGR*, 25:210 [July 1871]).

hitherto with our situation; and even now, not approved: but my mourning authorized it, and it was of essential benefit to my returning strength—

My kind Sister took upon herself the cares of Housekeeping and released me from a thrall heavy enough to break the spirit of a Tyrant— My Experience's in this *line* in consequence of ignorance had been peculiarly painful; and my blessed Sister saved me from unspeakable discomfort— How singularly things turn out in this wonderful world! I had been the only *one* in my family who had gone through a regular *Cooking* education, in consequence of having been a favorite of a very superior Cuisiniere in my fathers family; and who was always delighted to have Miss *Weeser* with her, to learn her mysteries; and for several years my two Sisters and myself had been *compelled* to keep house weekly, for a very large family, under the judicious instruction of M[rs.] Nowlan and my Mother— But English housekeeping did not qualify me, and such a tàlànt was worth nothing in my circumstances— My Father was a Merchant, and a Stipulation was entered into by the Partners of the House, that he was to *entertain* the Americans who visited London; and of course to *receive* an equivalent for the expense thus incurred— It was the settlement of this question, that involved him in difficulties with his Partners when he returned to his Country; and which so materially contributed to his ruin— His house was always open to his Countrymen from every part of the Union; and those who have most cruelly censured him; made no scruple of enjoying its welcome pleasures, and social greeting; as long as it suited their convenience; although I have known but few that would speak in his favour when misfortune overtook him— M[rs.] Smith the amiable and loved Sister of my husband constantly at his house during her residence in england; and was invariably the same; and never changed in her conduct to my family nor the Col— She always wished that my Sister Caroline had been the object of my husbands choice— She knew *him*, and I was so much with *her* that she knew *me* almost as well; and her judgment was probably formed upon some striking characteristic, of which we were not aware—but so it was—and she was right— I am what the french call "àltiére"—She *firm* and *mild*— Few have laboured harder to correct the defects of their character than I have, or have studied their faults so keenly but there is a constitutional irritability about me of late years, trying to my friends and painful to myself, which is I know so disagreeable to all who live with me; it induces me to live much alone, that I may not burthen those, whose happiness I most desire in this life, and for whom I would willingly make any sacrifices to promote their welfare— this is written with the sincere consciousness of the defect—

The mere matter of fact life which I led yielded little to descant upon— Shaw was our every day friend; and Jos Hall's prozy stories our evening relaxation,[164] unless Mr. Adams read to us: who in the fervour of a lately acquired Parental duty; our Son being eighteen Months old; studied all the works on education; From Lock to Miss Edgeworth, in which studies I participated orally—I fear without deriving the benefit which aught to have rewarded his unceasing and arduous exertions for my benefit—[165]

I scarcely know of an anecdote worth repeating during the Summer— Mrs. Knox was a Lady as I have already observed of a masculine mind, and of very liberal opinions, which she often expressed more freely than was exactly prudent: but she was a very pleasant companion—when the topic of Religion was avoided— Mrs. Swan was of a different cast—of equally high pretension; but by no-means of equal standing in education, mental power, or conversational qualifications— Equally latidudinarians on many points, they would strike into extremes; and astound one with their remarks— The leading Women of that day were showy and prominent; and their individual characteristics were strongly marked— Mrs. Knox had been very unfortunate in the loss of her children; seven of whom I think she had buried;[166] and she had been in a sphere of constant action through the changes of the Revolution, and the Government: and she was not sustained by that unerring faith in the support of a merciful Providence, which was a source of such consolation to Mrs. Adams through her trials— Mrs. Swan was an outrageous pretender to *rank*, and *fashion*; and was much laughed at for regretting, that she must *bear Children like the Vulgar*; which she thought highly *derogatory* to a woman of fortune— She lived in a very handome style, and entertained a great deal—Often an object of envy; sometimes of scandal; I dare say without the slightest founda-

[164] Years later CFA, too, would comment on Joseph Hall's tendency to be talkative (*Diary*, 5:18).

[165] John Locke, *Some Thoughts Concerning Education*, London, 1693; Maria Edgeworth, *Practical Education*, London, 1798.

[166] By 1802 Lucy and Henry Knox had lost nine of their twelve children. Two had died of throat distemper (diphtheria) on the same day in April 1796. The three who would survive to full adulthood were Lucy Flucker, Henry Jackson, and Caroline (North Callahan, *Henry Knox: General Washington's General*, N.Y., 1958, p. 360, 401).

tion—[167] And here I will observe that the most extraordinary thing in Mrs. Adams's career was, that I never heard a word lisped against her reputation—

We all went to Commencement by invitation— Mr Shaw accompanied us—Mr. Adams too busy—[168]

One of the very prominent characters of the day was Mrs. Sullivan the Wife of the Governor— She was altogether an extraordinary Woman, of masculine mind, and fine person, very much like Madame de Genlis— *His* Son's it was said had derved the greatest advantage from *her* care in their education— There is generally a want of feminine grace and sweetness, in these showy, strong minded Women; which produce fear in us lesser lights: and this has always been my first impression on becoming acquainted with them—yet they alway appear to me to be *what God intended woman to be*, before she was cowed by her Master *man*—[169]

I now became acquainted with a charming woman; timid as a Nun, full of accomplishments, and when known loved— Her flashy husband I never admired— Very much in the Scott, and Macomb line, made to adorn their Uniforms— Mrs. Winthrop with beauty, grace, elegance and propriety; formed a striking contrast to Madame de Genlis, and all her tribe— Mrs. Humphries was a foreigner; a thing of course to be *despised* by the majority; but admired by the few.— All who really and intimately knew her, admired her, if it was only for her modesty— The mass of what is termed society, seldom know how to distinguish between this real virtue, and pride—

Genl. Humphreys was a Militaire; a Poet; a half Spanish Grandee, having been Minister to Spain, and a favorite of Washington—[170] Who can wonder that he *was great*— There was sublimity in his size;

[167] The Swans had three daughters—Hepzibah Clark, Christiana Keadie ("Kitty"), and Sarah Webb—and one son, James Keadie, who in 1808 married Caroline Knox. Charles Bulfinch is credited with the design for a house in the style of a French pavilion that was built for the Swans in Dorchester around 1796. With its high-ceilinged, circular salon and great dining room, the house was well suited to entertaining (Small, *Hist. of Swan's Island*, p. 55–58; Kirker, *Architecture of Bulfinch*, p. 128–130).

[168] From 1802 through 1848, Harvard's commencement day was the last Wednesday in August, which was the 25th in 1802 (Albert Matthews, "Harvard Commencement Days, 1642–1916," Col. Soc. Mass., *Pubns.*, 28:366 [1917]).

[169] For the two previous marriages of Martha Langdon Sullivan, the wife of James Sullivan, Massachusetts governor from 1807 until his death the following year, see *AFC*, 7:384. She was stepmother to the children of James Sullivan's first marriage to Mehitable Odiorne (*DAB*).

[170] Anne Frances Bulkeley, the daughter of an English merchant, was the wife of David Humphreys (1752–1818), the soldier, diplomat, and prolific poet. Humphreys returned to America from a post in Spain in 1802 with his wife, whom he had married in Lisbon in 1797 (same; *AFC*, 5:329; 9:394, 395).

and when his Wife rode with him to whom it properly belonged; there was divinity in his Chariot and six— He was an Aid of Genl Washington's— My Uncle Johnson arrived suddenly at the Camp, and this Sir Piercy Shafton came out to receive him; and with a mincing gaite, and a foppish tone told him, very *supercilliously*, that the General was *busy*, and would not see any body— Upon which my Uncle reiterated his demand, but was not *attended* to— At last my Uncle vociferated in language not very well suited for a Lady's pen— Go *puppy* I think was the word, and tell him it is Tom Johnson of Frederick and be —— to you; when the young *hero* moved off to the tune of a quick step, and bowing and cringing returned to usher Governor Johnson into the presence of the Genl, who greeted him with a warm embrace— I never saw my Uncle but once— He was then a little old man with sharp bright gray eyes, very active; and of the most animated conversation— His family adored him; and all his Children lived with him[171]

He had ruined a fine Estate by experimental farming—and that Estate, one of the finest in Frederick County called Richlands, had just been sold to pay his debts—and they all lived together at Rose Hill, with Major Graham the husband of his eldest daughter—[172]

This is a fine specimen of the rough and the Smooth—

My Mother was kindly treated by all her old friends ~~at 4 o'clock in the morning of the 14th. she left me~~ whose entertainments occupied the whole Month— Mr A, a Candidate for the Senate[173] At the commencement of this Month; The Child, Caroline, and myself were all extremely ill—

This Month passed away almost entirely at home; My poor

[171] Having already likened David Humphreys to generals Winfield Scott and Alexander Macomb, LCA now compares him to Sir Piercie Shafton, the character in Sir Walter Scott's *The Monastery*, Edinburgh, 1820, who was notable for his ostentatiously elegant manner of expression (Paul Harvey, comp. and ed., *The Oxford Companion to English Literature*, rev. edn., Oxford, Eng., 1933).

Thomas Johnson, brigadier general of the Maryland militia, set out from Philadelphia in early Feb. 1777 to deliver his recruits to Washington's army, which was then encamped at Morristown, N.J. (Delaplaine, *Life of Thomas Johnson*, p. 228, 230; Washington, *Papers, Revolutionary War Series*, 8:451–452). For LCA's only meeting with her uncle Thomas, see Adventures, 28 Oct. 1801, above.

[172] After the death of his wife in Nov. 1794, Thomas Johnson moved from his estate at Richfield (not Richlands), just north of Frederick, Md., to nearby Rose Hill, the home of his daughter Ann Jennings Grahame and her husband Maj. John C. Grahame. Major Grahame built the Rose Hill mansion on a 225-acre tract of land that Johnson had given to his daughter as a wedding present in 1788 (Delaplaine, *Life of Thomas Johnson*, p. 347, 492–493).

[173] At this time JQA was, in fact, the Federalist candidate for the U.S. House of Representatives (Bemis, *JQA*, 1:113).

Mother was to leave me, and the trial under all its circumstances, was *very*, *very* severe— My eldest Sister had kindly invited her to live with her, and Mr. Hellen; and she had accepted their invitation being left destitute— Washington seemed to be her home, and she made the journey in company with Judge Cranch and his family—[174] Mr. & Mrs. Adams had paid her much attention—but she was excessively disliked by the Latter, who never could overcome the sentiment— Too earnest in her entreaties for the place which the old Gentleman had granted to my father, *against* the decided judgment of Mrs. Adams, and her Son Thomas;[175] He had indulged the kindly feelings of his heart contrary to the interests of his future prospects; and this generous but imprudent act, of kindness; laid the foundation for Mr. Adams *future course*, from the moment we returned to America— My own sense of the injury to himself, was as strong as that of Mrs. Adams~~ and though I [decidedly] suffered from its consequences,~~ I could never condemn a sentiment, in which my own soul had fully accorded— I would rather that he had kept a Hotel than have resorted to such a means for a subsistence— This was the first and last time My Mother ever was in a house of Mr. Adams's— Caroline staid with me— I was again in a very bad way—[176] We passed all our winters with her at Mr. Hellens in Washington but one from that time—

I have been forty three years married and I have been but once since our first visit to Frederick and Mr Adams has never been there from the day that we left my Father— My poor Mother was no favorite with her husbands relatives She had been the spoilt Child of excessive indulgence and her change of fortune came hard to her in her old age— Many and many a time when she was sick, have I seen my Father roll papers round the handles of the Knife and Fork, and lay them before the fire to take the chill off, before she was allowed to touch it; and no matter how busy he might be, he always sat by

[174] JA had appointed William Cranch a commissioner of public buildings in the District of Columbia. When the U.S. Circuit Court of the District of Columbia was established in Feb. 1801, Cranch was named junior assistant judge, and the following year he became a reporter of the U.S. Supreme Court. In 1805 Thomas Jefferson would elevate him to chief justice of the circuit court, a position he held for fifty years (*DAB*; D/JQA/24, 10, 14 Oct. 1802, APM Reel 27).

[175] LCA may be misjudging the views of AA and TBA on Joshua Johnson's appointment as superintendent of the Stamp Office. Their letters on the subject are gracious in tone. See, for example, AA to AA2, 4 May 1800, M/CFA/31, APM Reel 327; AA to AA2, 11 May, AA2, *Jour. and Corr.*, 2:176–178; TBA to JQA, 11 May, AA to Catherine Nuth Johnson, 18 May, both Adams Papers.

[176] LCA was in the early stage of a pregnancy. On 4 July 1803 she would give birth to JA2.

her to cut the food which was presented to her, and gave it to her with his own hand, with the kindest looks and words— Hamlets description of his Fathers love for his Mother, is the only one which I have ever seen, that could realize the picture ever before my eyes, presented by my Parents[177]—and I was twenty two ere I married: and he was as a Father what he hourly proved himself as a husband— Was it wonderful that she should pine at the change in her situation? when she saw herself forced to *cook* and do all the drudgery of the family? and when that family so reared and educated, actually wanted the very necessaries of life?— It was too severe a trial, and she who I had always known, the most domestic, quiet, unobtrusive Mother; always at home, always at work for her children, all of whose Clothes she made with her own hands? Who had taught those children to help themselves by the work of their own ingenuity, and even under the greatest difficulties to maintain the appearance suited to the station in and in a Slave Country! could she be happy or contented?

Mr. Adams was much employed with his business as one of the Bankrupt Commissioners[178]

3D [*NOVEMBER*]

Mr Adams was a Candidate for the S. U. S. The election came on and in consequence of a Shower of Rain his opponent Dr. Eustis was elected by a majority of 59 votes—[179]

5

Mr. Adams's friend Mr Frazier died in the Night having been sick since last February and most carefully attended by his beautiful Cousin Mary— Mr Adams attended the Funeral—[180]

177 "So loving to my mother / That he might not beteem the winds of heaven / Visit her face too roughly" (Shakespeare, *Hamlet*, Act I, scene ii, lines 140–142).

178 By the authority of federal district court judge John Davis, JQA received a temporary appointment as a bankruptcy commissioner in March 1802. But the Republican Congress provided for the permanent appointment of commissioners by the president, and Thomas Jefferson did not retain JQA (D/JQA/24, 4 March, APM Reel 27; Bemis, *JQA*, 1:112).

179 JQA was narrowly defeated in the 3 Nov. election for the U.S. House of Representatives by Dr. William Eustis. Although JQA carried Boston, his Republican opponent prevailed in several neighboring towns annexed to the district. JQA remarked that the Federalists blamed the rain for discouraging Federalist voters from going out to the polls in the "remotest" part of town, adding that "this is one of a thousand proofs, how large a portion of federalism is a mere fair-weather principle" (D/JQA/24, 3 Nov., APM Reel 27; Bemis, *JQA*, 1:113).

180 Nathan Frazier Jr. had died on 1 Nov. after a long illness (D/JQA/24, 5 Nov., APM Reel 27).

DECEMBER 1ST 1802

1ST

The Club was at our house[181]

2

We went to the Ball which was very crowded. Caroline danced did not return until midnight— These public Balls were very amusing—[182]

3

Dr Tufts Mrs. Adams and Mrs. Cranch dined with us and returned to Quincy in the Evening—

4TH.

Both the Girls left us who lived with us; because, I had ventured to say that I thought they used more Sugar than was right— They insisted that they only took three piled spoonfuls in every Cup of tea, and as they were not accustomed to have things measured out to them, they should return home by the Quincy Stage— It was then two o'clock and they left me at four; stupified with astonishment and crying bitterly— Mr. Adams went off to Quincy in the Eveng—

6

On Monday morning Betsey Newcomb returned—quite ashamed—[183]

[181] For the Wednesday Evening Club, see *AFC*, 6:355.

[182] LCA and JQA occasionally attended public balls during this period; see, for instance, D/JQA/24, 2, 30 Dec., APM Reel 27. They probably took place at Boston's Concert Hall (Morison, *H. G. Otis*, 1969, p. 42, 528).

[183] The servant Betsey Newcomb cooked for the Adamses and cared for GWA (LCA to AA, [*ante 8 March 1802*]; AA to LCA, 8 March, both Adams Papers).

8

We dined at Mr Gardener Greens; Mr Adams myself and Caroline and afterwards spent the Evening at M^rs. Quincys—Met Bishop Chevereux[184]

13TH

Was invited to a large party at M^rs: M^c.Leans but was not well enough to go— This Lady was since that period married to William Lee— Mr Adams and Caroline did not go—

14

I was siezed with violent illness and M^r. Adams was forced to call the family up, and send for Dr Welsh— Mr Adams alarmed—

15

Still ill but getting better towards night— Caroline and Mr Adams dined at Dr Danforth's— I staid at home with my boy—

16

The weather so severely cold could not any of us go to the Ball—Caroline and myself being indisposed—

17

Invited to a Ball at Mr Babcocks Caroline too ill to go— Myself still indisposed—Sent an excuse—A great disappointment—

18

Could not go to Quincy; Caroline quite sick and the weather bitter cold

[184] John Louis Ann Magdalen Lefebre de Cheverus (1768–1836) had fled from revolutionary France and in 1796 sailed to Boston. He was a founder of the Holy Cross Church in Boston, designed by Charles Bulfinch and consecrated in 1803, for which JA and other leading New Englanders were subscribers. In 1810 Cheverus was consecrated the first Catholic bishop of Boston with New England as his diocese (*DAB*; Kirker, *Architecture of Bulfinch*, p. 161–162).

21ST

Mr. Adams went from Quincy to Plymouth with a party to deliver an Oration and lodged at Judge Thomas's— Was much amused with his little journey—[185]

22

He went in Procession to the meeting House and spoke an hour and ten minutes and then went to dine at the Town Hall— He visited Genl Warren,[186] and then returned to Sup at Judge Thomas's— I am infringing upon his history, and must therefore stop—[187]

23

He returned home with a violent Cold; but much gratified at his success.

25

Invited company to dine. All engaged, even *Shaw*; could not dine at home— I again quite ill— Xmas Day always a holyday before—

26

Mr Adams went to Quincy to dine, and returned in the Evening

28

At a large party at Miss Grays—Mostly of young persons— Miss Gray eccentric but very agreeable— The Ladies very pleasant and the men gay—

[185] In JQA's 15 Oct. 1802 untitled draft of his address commemorating the English colonists' landing at Plymouth, he extolled the colony as the only European settlement for which the desire for religious liberty was the "sole and exclusive actuating cause." JQA affirmed the claims of the aboriginal people to their cultivated fields, dwellings, and "whatever they had annexed to themselves by personal labour," but he asserted the greater claims of civilization and progress, and he judged that "the pilgrims of Plymouth obtained their right of possession to the territory upon which they settled, by titles as fair and unequivocal as any human property can be held" (M/JQA/46, APM Reel 241).

[186] JQA called at the home of James and Mercy Otis Warren, who appeared to be "broken down with years and infirmities, altogether" (D/JQA/24, 22 Dec., APM Reel 27).

[187] For JQA's full account of his visit to Plymouth, see same, 21–23 December.

30

Took Caroline and her friend Miss Dexter to the Ball— Miss Dexter returned with us and passed the night with Caroline— She was much attached to *Caroline*, who felt a great friendship for her— Of a very strong mind, highly cultivated by her Father, she was a Girl of great abilities, and charming conversation— Of Shaw what shall I say— He was the strangest looking man!!! kind hearted; always busy, apparently about nothing; a great admirer of the Ladies; awkward and unwieldy; In politics timid as a Hare, yet fond of bustleling in every thing that was stirring; and fond of good cheer; he was the oddest compound that ever crossed my path; yet very pleasant to live with— He appeared much smitten with my Sister Caroline but poverty taught him prudence; and he sighed, and fortunately for *him* said nothing— The old saying that "a friend in need is a friend in deed," surely was not exemplified in his person; for while fortune deserted *us*, he was afraid to speak to us;— but on our return from Russia, when She appeared to heap her favours on us, he was enthusiastic in his admiration, and universal in his approbation—[188] And was this remarkable? Did not the many uphold him? let the every day world of expediency answer the question— Amid the overflowing smiles of Fortune or success; complaints are seldom made of us; as long as we have something to *give*—but the moment that the *means* cease to be proportionate to the *demands*, our very virtues are turned to crimes; and all the light of a good life and faithful service, is o'ershadowed by heavy and black clouds; which if they do not obliterate the *truth*; so completely obscure its radiancy, that nothing but the tempest of the whirwind can clear the chaotic darkness, and in after ages restore its bright effulgence—

The Winter passed away amid party's and Balls in which I occasionally participated—and we lived pleasantly and happily— My health only being painfully delicate and thus causing anxiety impossible for me to controul; and making *me* wretched to witness—

We went frequently to Quincy; and our lives were passed in an agreeable routine of social intercourse; and the regularity of domes-

[188] William Smith Shaw's close relatives commented on his peculiarities of person and manner, but they were quick to affirm his good heart. Although Shaw justified his mother's fears that he would become "a *confirmed Old-Batchelor*, in the most extensive sense of the word," he would distinguish himself as a founder and benefactor of the Boston Athenæum (Mary Smith Cranch to AA, 22 June 1798; Elizabeth Smith Shaw Peabody to AA, 10 Nov. 1810, both Adams Papers; AA to Mary Smith Cranch, 11 Dec. 1799, MWA:Abigail Adams Letters).

tic comfort— I was surrounded by kind friends and all the labours of my household were carefully provided for by Mr. Adams, and my Sister—and my darling boy was the cheering comfort of my present days and the darling of my ambitious hopes—

7 [*JANUARY 1803*]

Had the first Party I ever gave in Boston—between forty and fifty we danced until one in the morning— The House being small I opened all the Rooms; and sat small Tables prettily ornamented in every direction and two larger ones in the Centre of the Chambers up Stairs: all covered with refreshments— This broke the formality of a Supper and seemed to please generally—

11

We had a Tea party of our friends—always stiff and cold—

13

We went to the Ball and bought home Miss Morton— These Balls always lasted until morning, or rather between one and two o'clock— They were generally pleasant— Mr Charles Bradbury was a devoted Beau of Mrs. Frye's; but never popped the question—

23

We observed a great smoke in the Bed chamber of my Sister; and particularly in the China Closet; and were very much perplexed, no fire being ever made in the apartment but on occasions of sickness— A small fire had been made a week or two before and Caroline became so much alarmed on seeing the smoke issue from under the hearth, that she called Mr. Adams to look at it— On sending for the Mason it was found that a large beam under the hearth, was nearly burnt through; and that if we had not fortunately poured a quantity of water down through the Cracks, it would have blazed out, and probably destroyed the poor old Rat hole; for the benefit of a future Generation, but seriously to *our* loss—

28

At a very large and handsome party at M[rs.] Gardner Greens— M[r] Adams did not come there until late in the Evening— His avocations were so constant we saw but very little of him—

31

Caroline left me to spend some days with M[rs.] Dexter at Roxbury Louisa Smith had spent some time with us and enjoyed herself much—

FEBY 3

M[r.] Adams was elected to the Senate—[189] Here again was to be a change in our Situation tolerable in perspective but requiring great sacrifices of domestic comfort— My establishment was very comfortable and I longed for quiet. Every thing had been so new to me on my arrival I had had so much to learn so much to be *reconciled* to; Even my Religious opinions were adverse to those of all the friends of M[r.] Adams a thing altogether new to me as from the first moment of my acquaintance with him he had apparently known no creed but mine— The change was so inconceivably great, it required time, judgment, and patience to realize; things of which I had never dreamt; and which were altogether contrary to that *fixedness* of opinion, which has proved through life one of the strongest traits of my character— Gradually they became familiar and although I could not sacrifice the sentiment which had

> "Grown with my Growth, and strengthened with my strength";[190]

though until I became a *Mother*; perhaps not properly weighed and considered; one more of precept, habit, and example than of meditated reflection— Yet since that period I had become a Member of my Church by reason of preference, and conviction; and my faith was fixed and unalterable— Between my husband and myself there

[189] JQA was elected U.S. senator from Massachusetts in Feb. 1803, after defeating Timothy Pickering in the state's Federalist party caucus. Pickering, the ardent Federalist whom JA, as president, had dismissed from the office of secretary of state, would shortly be chosen by the Mass. General Court to fill a vacancy created by the resignation of the state's other senator, Dwight Foster (Bemis, *JQA*, 1:113–114).

[190] Alexander Pope, *An Essay on Man*, Epistle II, line 136.

never existed a moments difficulty— He ruled his Children and I quietly acquiesced to his right of controul, on a point so materïal; and I likewise joined in the Duties of his religious exercises as a tribute of respect to him, and as an example to my little ones—convinced that where the heart is true, and faithful in its worship, God will mercifully accept the adoration of a Sincere believer, through whatever form it may be offered with heartfelt humility and decorous devotion—

My health became more and more delicate every hour, and suffering appeared to be *my* lot, and cruel anxiety *that* of my husband; He was now necessarily a man of active business; and I could no longer expect to be the engrossing object of his care as I had been; and like a petted Child I pined at that, which ought to have gratified me— I knew nothing of Politics, and of course was without ambition: and domestic life seemed to be the only life for which nature had intended me— The prospect of the birth of another Child, made every idea of change unpleasant; and under all these circumstances his election to the Senate yielded me no satisfaction— But there was no help for it—and such feelings were warmly disapproved by the family—

I think it was sometime in the Spring of this year, that I went with Caroline and Mr. Adams to pay the Wedding visit to Mrs Daniel Sargent; but I am not sure— She looked beautiful, and I believe that this was the last time that I ever saw her— Her married life was very happy and very brief, and she left but one Child a daughter—[191]

APRIL

Mr. Adams received the News of the suspenstion of Payment of the House of Bird Savage and Bird— This was another severe stroke to him—and it confirmed his dislike to Commercial Houses— To prevent the possibility of loss to his Father he immediately began to

[191] Mary Frazier Sargent died of consumption in 1804 shortly after the birth of her only child, Maria Osborne Sargent (1804–1835). Maria would later marry Thomas B. Curtis. When JQA happened upon Maria's grave at Mount Auburn Cemetery in Nov. 1838, he was deeply affected by "a mingled emotion of tenderness, of melancholy, and yet of gratitude to Heaven." Had he married Mary Frazier, he mused, "in all probability I should have lost her in the prime of life, and lost perhaps a child like this, cut off like this in the blossom." After his years of "exquisite wretchedness" over lost love were cured by the ocean that separated him from Mary and by his absorption in "the politics of a revolutionary period," his adventures and wanderings had led him to "more propitious ties—by which I am yet happily bound" (John H. Sheppard, *Reminiscences of Lucius Manlius Sargent*, Boston, 1871, p. 31; D/JQA/33, 18 Nov., APM Reel 36).

dispose of his property so as to secure his Father from loss—[192] The energy and decision with which he acted on this occasion was highly honourable and meritorious

12

My Darling boy was two years old, precocious and full of promise— How many prophecies of his future greatness I heard!!! Bishop Chevereux used to dwell upon his features, and then exclaim that he was born to accomplish great deeds of intellectual brightness. Did not I defeat this promise by my desertion of my children, to suffer exile amid the pomps and vanities of a Court, at the expense of every feeling of my Soul, and of the sweetest affections of the heart? and O how bitter has been the punishment— When woman, poor feeble powerless Woman, is called upon to act; what can she, what ought she to do, between conflicting duties— Should she desert the helpless Creatures who God himself has placed in her keeping, to follow the fortunes of one, who is in his strength, and master of his Will?

Friends however near or however well disposed, cann'ot perform the duties of a Mother, unless the life of a Mother is extinct; In that case a Child has but one person to look up to, as its guardian; and its affections are fixed upon one object as they are when the Mother is living— No substitute on the face of this Earth can be found for the Mothers attachment, or the Mothers devotion if she is virtuous; and if the strong and powerful instincts of her Nature have not been perverted by some unholy and worldly master passion— When this is considered; when the average portion of harmony in connubial life is measured; when the loss of youth and health, the rapid decline of beauty, the satiety of habit, and the constant and alluring temptations of a captivating and dangerous intercourse with Society render a Mans home insipid, what can compensate to a Wife, but the companionship, the cares, the tender caresses, and the fond love of her Children? Nearly Four years of lingering hope, of repeated disappointment, had rendered this *great* blessing dearer to me than it is to most women; and my religious opinions had rendered these continued frustrations of a sanctified hope, still more painful.— You can

192 JQA had recommended to his parents that they temporarily entrust funds from matured U.S. bonds underwritten by Dutch bankers to Bird, Savage & Bird, the highly respected London banking house of the U.S. Treasury. When the firm failed in 1803, JQA took steps, including the sale of his Hanover Street residence, to assist his parents (Bemis, *JQA*, 1:114–115).

then easily conceive with what ardent love I regarded this my first born Child, and with what earnest anxiety I watched his growth; and with what delight I traced each little thought or expression, that indicated brightness or promise of mind— He was at this period the delight of his Father, whose great ambition to have a Son had thus been so fully gratified—

Our time was pleasantly spent, sometimes in Society but more frequently at home; where Mr. Adams used to read to us every spare hour that the Evenings admited, or with visits from the family at Quincy— Constant faintings and violent attacks of illness short in their duration, prevented my visits to Quincy; as Dr. Welsh's assistance was always necessary, these attacks being incident to my situation and always alarming as to their results— One of the most painful peculiarities attending me in these situations from the period of my marriage, was the loss of the use of my hands which generally caused such agony, that they were obliged to be often tied up in laudnum poultices—

Mrs. Storer was one of the Ladies with whom I was most intimate— She was very tall and had it was said been very handsome— She was a remarkably showy woman in conversation, and had the art of displaying her reading, by a ready and well applied quotation, and a lively and active memory, which never failed when occasion offered for display— Agreeable, ready witted, and gay, she was always a welcome guest and the variety of her conversation, and its apparent good nature, made you feel desirous to see her often— Many years after I heard her history from Mr. Marston and the old Gentleman; and felt much surprized that she had been the heroine of a little Drama, in which she had displayed a great degree of fortitude and independence, much approved by both the Gentlemen— Facts of Notoriety may I suppose be mentioned without impropriety— She had married a gentleman to whom she was much attached and had selected him from a number of admirers as the best and who *loved her best*— A Short time after the marriage with Mr Lincoln her Fathers affairs became much deranged and I believe he *failed* Her husbands conduct immediately changed towards her and he treated her with so much contempt, and harshness, that she returned to her family; obtained a separation; and never lived with him after— He died a few years after, and she married Deacon Storer—a very worthy Man—[193]

[193] In early 1759 an eligible JA courted the young Hannah Quincy, whom he called Orlinda.

I forgot to mention that Mr. Hellen came on to visit us and went to Portland— When he returned as we were, (in consequence of Mr Adams's election to the Senate) to pass the Winter in Washington; arrangements were made that we were to board with him, and his family; and it was settled that Caroline, myself, and George, should go on with him, and that I should be confined at my Sisters under the care of my Mother— Every preparation was made; our Trunks all sent round by Water with our Clothes; when the whole plan was changed, and Mr. Hellen went off without us— This was a very severe disappointment to me, but I believe it was best—[194]

JULY 4

Nothing very material happened until the last Evening—Charlotte and Hariet Welch took Tea with Caroline and myself— Mr Adams at Quincy. Mr. Shaw out; My Nurse not to be found My two girls out and only the little girl at home— I made all my at 1/2 past ten my Nurse came home. Shaw also had gone to bed— But he went for Dr. Welsh who came at twelve and at three o'clock in the morning just as the first Guns fired my Dear John entered upon this world of care— He was laid upon the Carpet and took a violent cold; the young women in our service not thinking it *delicate*, to afford assistance to a fellow creature in such circumstances; but Caroline jumped out of bed, and ran into the room almost undressed, to assist; and took the Child immediately— Charlotte and Hariet Welsh had run away from the Tea table—I mention this as an example of the *false* delicacy, which is too often practiced even at the expence of life—

I recovered very slowly but as soon as I could crawl came out to Quincy to see Mrs. Adams, who was so dangerously ill that she was not expected to live—[195] My Boy was named *John* after his Grandfa-

At about that time, Hannah was at least informally engaged to Dr. Bela Lincoln of Hingham. They married in May 1760. JA remarked that Lincoln "treated his Wife, as no drunken Cobler, or Clothier would have done, before Company." Four years after Lincoln's death in 1773, Hannah married widower Ebenezer Storer, a merchant and the treasurer of Harvard College, who was known by the title Deacon for his earlier service to the Brattle Square Church (JA, *Earliest Diary*, p. 12–13, 80–81; JA, *D&A*, 1:176–177).

[194] Walter Hellen visited from 19 Feb. 1803 to 10 March. On 18 Aug. JQA wrote to Hellen about the terms of their residence with him (letter not found; D/JQA/27, APM Reel 30). The Hellen house, sometimes called the Peter House, was at 2620 K Street. LCA and JQA lived there while in Washington until 1808.

[195] AA had fallen down a flight of stairs in early June. By the end of the month she had begun to recuperate, but in August JQA noted in his Diary that she was "in extreme pain from

ther as soon as he could be carried to Church; and Long before I was able to rise from my bed— He was beautiful, and I fear I was too proud of being the Mother of two fine Children—

We made our preparations for our removal to Washington and although I was going to my relations I knew that my home could never be what it had been; and that the situation in which I returned, would be productive of uneasiness every ways— But the course was to be pursued, and it was met without Question—

The extreme kindness with which I had been received in Boston made in painful to relinquish my establishment—again to become a wanderer; and I surely did not behave with either the fortitude or the patience, which might have been expected—

Ambition was not one of my Sins and as I have observed before I felt that my husband should have had a Wife fond of display, with a soaring mind and qualities, of a much higher grade than those of a woman, who was content to live at home and nurse her tender babes

I have said little or nothing of the Gentlemen with whom I became acquainted in Boston— H G Otis was at that time my most intimate friend— He had been Guardian to my brother and both Mrs. Otis and himself had left a sense of obligation on the minds of my family which neither time, nor change could eradicate— Their House at this period was the very centre of fashion and they were both so calculated to shine by the ease of their manners, their distinguished minds, and their liberal hospitality; it was impossible to know them without feeling their claim to admiration and acknowledging it—[196]

George Blake who then had a charming Wife was likewise very polite to us and rendered his house delightful—[197] It would fill a volume to particularise the families with whom we lived on terms of

a large and highly inflamed tumour, on the spot where sometime since she had applied a blister.—" The tumor was "laid open," but the doctors were not hopeful of a recovery. AA's condition improved in early September, and LCA, who had herself been ill from the effects of childbirth, brought the infant JA2 to Quincy for a visit on the 6th (AA to TBA, 20 June; JQA to TBA, 19 Aug., both Adams Papers; D/JQA/27, 6, 30 July; 14, 17, 18, 22 Aug.; 3, 6 Sept., APM Reel 30).

[196] At this time Harrison Gray and Sally Foster Otis were living at 85 Mount Vernon Street on Beacon Hill, in a house designed by Charles Bulfinch and completed in 1802. Otis was known for his hospitality, and the house was the site of frequent formal and informal entertainments (*DAB*; Kirker, *Architecture of Bulfinch*, p. 158–159). For Otis' relationships with JA and JQA, see CFA, *Diary*, 8:174.

[197] George Blake (1769–1841), U.S. district attorney for Massachusetts, was married to Sarah Olcott Murdock (*NEHGR*, 11:181–182 [1857]).

the most social familiarity in consequence of their friendship for M[r.] Adams: and it Surely was natural to grieve for the loss of an intercourse so calculated to make life agreeable— Fortunes had not grown so large or so fast as they have since; and though living even then was luxurious; wealth was not so essential a quality as it is now, to enable the merely independent to enjoy the most extensive and general acquaintance— You were treated handsomely but not extravagantly; and the pleasures of social intercourse were more an object, than the gew-gaw display of meretricious show— I always recal the periods of time which I enjoyed during my residence in Boston with pleasure; and note them as the happiest periods independent of *politics*, which I have passed in this Country—

To the friendly kindness of M[rs.] Quincy M[rs.] Smith M[rs.] Storer and M[rs.] Welsh, I am indebted for many attentions in sickness and in health, which have left an impression of the deepest gratitude—

My Father and Mother Adams treated me with *too* much distinction—and whenever I met my Sister M[rs.] W Stevens Smith, she treated me with the kindest partiality and affection She had known me in England and there I had learnt to love her— In America that love and admiration encreased to enthusiasm— For here I saw her under every change of fortune, from the height of affluence and Station, to the misery of poverty and obloquy; sustaining herself and her family with a degree of persevering fortitude; uncomplaining sweetness, and patient resignation, with the Christian devotion of a Saint— Col Smith was a very elegant Militaire; a Man of the World to whom money seemed as dross, and to be used only in the promotion of every taste, and every gratification that it could purchase Up in the Clouds when prosperity cast its Sun gleams oer his head; or in Prison bounds when wanton recklessness had

> Strewn his golden fleece & scatter'd it away—

He was always the gay deluded toy, that wanton'd with the wind and good fortune was to him but the ebb and flow of a changing tide— He was a delightful companion; one of those beings who are born to be the charm, and the plague of doating Woman,

> Who feels the ill yet fondly loves the aggressor;

What he possessed he shared too liberally with all that he loved and that liberality was dispensed with a courtesy a *heartiness* cordiality does not imply enough to describe the *manner*; that it won all hearts until repeated follies turned the scale, and left him nearly friendless– Mrs. Smith loved this Man with the purest devotion; under all circumstances; and all, and every trial that wayward fortune could inflict; and was the most untiring exemplary Wife, that I ever saw without any possible exception She possessed great strength of mind; Gentleness of disposition, unswerving fortitude and deliberate and reflective firmness of religious principle, which bore her triumphantly through Scenes of difficulty and perplexity, to which few are equal in this world of trouble; and she left a reputation as free from reproach and as highly cherished, as that of the Infant Cherub whose pure and unspoted innocence had fitted her for the heaven to which she was so recently called—but whose memory lives in the hearts of all who were susceptible of love and admiration for her, alas, too precocious loveliness[198]

Col Smith was a brilliant rather than a solid man; but still he possesed powers which ensured him a high Rank among publick men, and has left in this respect a fair and handsome reputation—

George Blake was of a different stamp—A Lady's Man!!! proverbial for his gallantries; of agreeable conversation and showy manners— but there was a laxity of moral principle about him very disagreeable to me, and something in the tone of his conversation that like the noted rattle of the Snake gave warning of danger—

John Welles was an open hearted kind creature that we were always glad to meet with; his amiable Wife also who appeared to be endowed with the same qualities as himself– John Callender was a bon vivant lively and amusing, somewhat coarse, and not altogether à mon gout– His Wife a pretty woman undistinguished of the many– The Quincy's kind and solicitous to bring *me* out Rufus Amory a rattle full of good points; not too strict a moralist but suited to occasion as it rose, without a thought of care– His Wife one of the finest and most stylish Ladies of the times handsome lively and agreeable– Col Apthorpe stiff cold and somewhat *pomptious*! his Lady sensible beautiful but a *little* harsh– Genl Arnold Welles and Lady extra fashionable– English Tom Amory half usé his Wife beautiful as houri, and lovely as beautiful– And many more that I could put into my ["]Catalogue" too numerous to mention— The Suppers were delightfully social, and music, dancing, and Song, were all called in to enliven and vary the amusements of

198 The estate WSS built in 1795 on the shore of New York's East River had to be sold a year later, and his other business ventures were unsuccessful. For more on his misadventures, see JA, *D&A*, 3:183–184.

the passing hours— Can you wonder that I disliked the thought of change?

Mrs. Adams continued dangerously ill— My baby bore his Grandfathers Name—but she grieved that he did not bear his likeness, and that was a grief to one so sensitive as myself—

Under the necessity of procuring a Nurse ~~for myself~~ to take care of my two little ones I had twenty young women apply for the situation—and alas! for this Land of good or bundling habits—every one had *had* a *Misfortune* and had a young lady or gentleman to provide for, and were thus obliged to condescend to take a Service, even far from home— This however did not suit me, as I felt afraid I might have to provide for more; and I selected a very staid looking *Lady*, sent to me by Mrs. Otis with a recommendation— I engaged her, and fixed the time for her entrance upon when I received another a second Note, stating that this person could not suit me; as She had a Child by a coloured Gentleman, and was altogether an improper character— I immediately declined to take her, and engaged Patty Milnor, who I was obliged to send back early in the Spring, as *she* was constantly in hysterics, *because* she could not see her *Sweetheart*—[199]

Our residence in Boston I have already said was very pleasant—and I grieved to give up my House: a fact I fear too strongly evidenced when I gave up my house, and signed the deed of Sale— I cordially approved of the Act; but I sadly regretted its necessity—

I had no right to feel so it is true; for it was not my property and the total beggary of my family took away all claim— But to a Woman, her home is a blessing under every circumstance; and it is the only element in which her happiness should be fixed—

OCTBR. 1ST.

At last we departed, leaving Mrs. Adams recovered— We rode to Milton and there took up Mr. Allyne Otis, and from thence went to Providence and lodged at Mr. Ammidons—Caroline Patty the two Children Mr. Otis Mr Adams and myself—[200]

[199] Patty Milnor and Patty Walin are probably the same person; see Adventures, note 230, below.

[200] Alpheus Ammidon was the proprietor of the Golden Ball Tavern ("Amidon's or Ammidon's Inn," *Book Notes*, 26:66–67 [1 May 1909]).

2

The Fever in New York made it difficult to procure a passage across as all intercourse was suspended and the Capt of a small Packet called the Cordelia agreed to take us and Land us at Powles Hook—[201] The wind not being fair we remained in Providence—

4

We sailed. A Singular being named James Brown forced himself upon our attention and soon convinced us that he was one of those Crack-brain reformers who fancy that they can change the whole system of the World and new create the Age— These characters are a sort of pest when you are closeted with them as in a Packet at Sea and until the weather became so bad that we were confined to our Cabins or elegantly termed State Rooms by that most inexorable of all sickness le mal de Mer we were bored beyond all patience— Mr Otis left us to go on by Land—

The Weather being bad and the Wind very heavy we landed at Newport and Lodged at Mrs. Brinton's— Mr. Hore a young Englishman went with us— Here we found a French family from St. Domingo—Dirty beyond conception

5

As my poor George was playing in the Garden he nearly trod on a Snake and narrowly escaped its sting— The weather still continuing bad we could not sail and contented ourselves with our very kind hostess who I still remember with pleasure—

6

Again we took possession of our Berth's I and my two Babies in one State Room. My Sister and Patty in the other both too sick to move— The Night and day were dreadful. My Baby only three Months old would not leave the breast one moment— My poor George sick almost to death; but "saying nerver mind Mama;" I shall soon be better; myself so weak I could scarcely crawl and al-

[201] The yellow fever epidemic in New York caused many residents to leave the city; it was particularly virulent near the wharves (Alexander Ramsay, "Observations on the Yellow-Fever of New York in 1803," *Edinburgh Medical and Surgical Journal*, 8:422, 424 [Oct. 1812]).

most as sick as the Children— Even the boy who waited on the Cabin Passengers was constantly wanted on Deck, found it impossible to attend to us, and "our sufferings *was* intolerable"— and at last we were obliged to put into the Port of New London—

8

Mr. Hoare took my George, washed and dressed him, and carried him on Shore; and offered me every assistance in his Power— He was a very elegant young man, only 24 and apparently quite unaccustomed to such services, but performed them admirably— We landed at eight o'clock in the morning and got a comfortable breakfast; and then laid down to rest our exhausted frames— In the afternoon My Sister myself and Mr. Hoare took a short walk to see the Town, and at nine o'clock we all undressed and went to bed, in the hope of getting strength to renew our voyage—

9TH

At eleven I was waked; and had to wake my Babes, and dress them to go on Board, out of their warm and comfortable Beds, and at twelve we again set Sail upon this tedious and really perillous voyage—for the Sailors told Mr Hoare while I was in my Berth with the door open to the Cabin, "that the Rigging was so rotten, it would not bear them to the Sails"— George was now much better and sat in the Berth with his playthings— I did not observe that the window was open just wide enough to put his hand through; but when about to land he told me he had thrown the Keys of all our Trunks and his Shoes out of the Window, and they of course had fallen into the Sea— Here was a new embarrassment added to which I was in a raging Fever, and during our ride to New Ark of ten miles over a log road, quite delirious— Arrived at Giffords I was put to bed; with all the Family in the same chamber; and every one shrinking from me in the apprehension of the Yellow Fever—

10

Continued dangerously ill— Dr. Johnson attended me; but he was afraid to come near me, and made me stretch my arm out as far as I could for him to feel my pulse, and would not look at my throat; such was the panic occasioned by that frightful desease— Mr. Adams and my Sister Nursed me; and every thing was done for me that was possible to promote my comfort under such circumstances— Mrs. Smith Senr. and Mrs. C Adams took George with them to pass the days, and brought him home in the Eveng.—[202] On the day that we started from Quincy we had heard of the death of Mrs. Hellens Child, and she lay in a very dangerous state not expected to live— This delay was therefore very painful and distressing—[203] Col Smith called

12

My Fever having subsided I was lifted out of Bed, and put into Mrs. Giffords Carriage; and we rode six miles to Elizabeth Town The exertion appeared to revive me and my medcines were all prepared and punctually administered— We remained at Elizabeth Town very much in the same way; and with the same alarm as at New Ark— At Princeton and at Frankfort we were received on the same conditions as heretofore dining and sleeping in the same chamber, children and all-together; lest *I* unfortunately should carry this plague out of my immediate family, who were to derive all the benefit of infection from the dreaded yellow Fever; without a possibility of escape, if they sought protection under the roof of *Christians*

> "Lord what is Man, that thou shouldst be mindful of him"—

when in the hour of tribulation he has so little feeling for his fellow creature.— We did not enter into Philadelphia; but travelled round the outskirts and arrived safely at Washington then a scene of utter desolation— The roads were almost impassable and Mr Hellens house lonely and dreary and at least two miles from the Capitol— Judge Adams came to us here—

On our arrival we found Mrs Hellen in a high delirium, and without hope of recovery—[204] The Physician relied somewhat upon my appearance to produce a change, and I went into her chamber with

[202] SSA, along with Margaret Smith, lived in Newark (JQA to AA2, 10 Oct. 1803, MHi: Photostat Coll.).

[203] Nancy Hellen's son Washington, born in April 1802, died on 19 Sept. 1803. LCA's entry for 12 Oct., below, suggests that another child was born between January and August, but no record has been found (JQA to Walter Hellen, 28 April 1802, Lb/JQA/11, APM Reel 135; D/JQA/27, 28 Sept. 1803, APM Reel 30).

[204] They arrived in Washington on 20 Oct. (D/JQA/27, APM Reel 30).

my bonnet and Cloak on, just as I had descended from the Stage, and beheld her in the most pitiable condition which almost overcame my feelings— The experiment succeeded, and she slept that night, and gradually recovered— Poor thing; the loss of her babe within a few Months of the birth of another, had produced the worst consequences, and reduced her to the extremity of danger into which she had fallen—

My Sisters had grown almost out of my knowledge, as I had left the four younger ones *children*, kept under the most rigid restraint according to english custom— They were now in manners young women; and with all the pretensions of Belles, fond of society, without means to keep up the appearance to which they had been accustomed; and without the protection of *Father* or *Guardian*—[205]

My Mothers situation was utterly dependent, and she had never been an authoritative Agent in the controul of her family, having always herself, entirely relied upon her husband in this point— Accustomed to every luxury for 30 or forty years, very delicate in her health and in her person; the change in her circumstances was frightful; and being a *foreigner* in a Country where the helplessness of woman greatly indulged is unknown; she was often rudely condemned, when she deserved the sympathy and admiration of her Sex— In all Countries poverty *is* an *evil*— In this it *is* a *crime*! There are so many ways the most *reputable* as they are called, in which Women may make a subsistence by her own exertions; but *She* had a large family of single daughters; few friends; and besides, to contend with all the prejudices of the old Country which had become part of herself; and without a possibility of acquiring the means of entering on any useful career, without involving herself in a heavy Debt, which she probably would never have been able to pay— My Fathers Estate was too deeply involved to hope for release— Mr: Hellen, and my brother had lost their places under Mr. Jefferson at the moment of my Fathers death—and Mr. Adams had suffered difficulties from the Failure of Bird, Savage and Bird, which had reduced his income so much, as to render it only equal to the support of his family—[206]

[205] None of LCA's sisters except Nancy Johnson Hellen had yet married, so they were probably all living in Washington with their mother.

[206] Walter Hellen was a tobacco merchant and, by 1808, a director of the office of discount and deposit at the Bank of the United States. Thomas Baker Johnson had worked for Nathan Goodale, clerk of the federal District Court of Massachusetts in Boston, and later at the College of Charleston. From 1810 to 1824 he was postmaster of New Orleans (Charles E. Howe, "The Financial Institutions of Washington City in Its Early Days," Columbia Hist. Soc., *Rec-*

I am thus particular in my account of the State of things that you may perfectly understand my feelings towards my husband which can admit of no possible misconstruction— The unhappy circumstance of my beloved Fathers misfortunes at a moment so inauspicious to my future peace of mind by apparently connecting my marriage with the crush of his fortunes gave me personally the appearance of deception towards M[r.] Adams and his family in having palmed myself upon his honor while others were sensible of the fate which was about to befal my family to utter ruin— Utterly unconscious of the Stroke which hung over me I gave my hand and heart to your Father under the impression that I was to receive a small fortune and that M[r.] Adams was fully assured of its validity— To a being so sensitively fastidious as you have ever known me to be the idea that I should have appeared to this censorious world to have played a part so base with evidence strong against *me* and without the possible power of refutation has preyed upon my life and mixed gall with all the sweets that have been granted to me in such large abundance: and the more kindly and tenderly my husband has treated me, the more bitterly I have felt the pang, that a connection formed under such circumstances was an injustice on my part not to be overcome, as it has been followed as a natural consequence, by almost every species of misfortune and mortification to him, on the side of my family— The very elevation to which he raised me has been used against him and the hissing stings of calumny have been used to sting him to the quick to blast his success and to give pain to the children of his love through the medium of his Wife, and her relations; whose follies have given too much colour and opportunity to his enemies— That M[r.] Adams should have reposed any confidence in me or retained either affection or respect for me is the wonder, for how few *men* would have endured with patience and forgiveness the wrongs which he has sustained and which he has nobly pardoned—

There is something revolting even to a corrupted heart in even the slightest appearance of treachery; and to such suspicions my conduct was necessarily exposed. M[r.] Adams knew that my Fathers affairs were embarrassed but he had been absent for a long time; and was not aware of the working of his enemies who envied his unsullied reputation as a Merchant, and his irreproachable private

ords, 8:31 [1905]; *Sibley's Harvard Graduates*, 14:429; LCA to AA, 19 Dec. 1804; to JQA, 25 May 1806, both Adams Papers; CFA, *Diary*, 5:xvii).

character, and whose whole study was to get his American business out of his hands for their own advantage—

Prior to my marriage, his Creditors had made a most satifactory and liberal arrangement to enable him to return to his own Country; there to wind up his affairs, by a fair settlement with his Partners: and these Creditors had done so with the most decided conviction of his honesty, probity, and justice— On the strength of this arrangement, he had *publickly* prepared his Vessel for the Passage; had sent off all his furniture in the eye of day; had laid in all his Stores, engaged all his Servants, and waited for my Marriage *alone* to enable him to depart; when unexpectedly, without a possibility of avoidance through the malice of his pretended friends, and the shameless treachery of his Book keeper; *he stopped payment for a small Note*, and was ruined by the base persecution of one, who he had loved and trusted like a brother— Under these circumstances he became the prey of Sharpers immediately on his return to his own Country; after an absence of twenty five years; in which he had been a faithful publick Servant under four different Commissions, during the Revolutionary War; and in the performance of which duties, he had sunk a large portion of his own hard earned property, to benefit his suffering Countrymen in Foreign lands, without a just and due remuneration— It was in the confidence of a fair adjustment of such Claims, and a favorable settlement of his affairs with his Partners, with a partition of large tracts of Land purchased with his own money; that he made a *Will* in which he bequeathed to me a small portion I *think* ten thousand dollars, and left Mr. Adams joint Executor and Guardian to his *Children*— A Copy of the Will is I think at this day filed in Doctors Commons, in London, where it was duly certified and executed in all *Legal forms*— Judge Adams and I believe Judge Hall were witnesses—and Mr Murdoch in whose hands my fathers affairs were left—and who left a fortune of 100.000£ sterling at *his death*!!!

I am very particular in detailing these *facts* because they all prove that there was no intentional deception on his or on my part; and to show as a moral *lesson*, that with the utmost purity of intention, the strictest principle of honour, we may be sunk to the lowest ebb of calamity without any efficient means to vindicate innocence, or to shake off the Mask of guilt; forced upon us with as little mercy and justice, as that which for so many years hid Louis 14 Brother under the Iron Mask— The new career of life into which we now entered was one of entire novelty to me— The ideas formed of a republick *abroad* are very different in the theory from the practical effects upon mankind in the intercourse and habits of society— A Republick of *Equality*, is a sort of *non descript* only to be realized in musty tomes generated in the unpractised and unsocial brains of needy Book-Worms— The inequality of every living thing in human or animal nature, testifies too strongly to the fact to admit of denial; and the testimony of Ages bears record to this great and fundamental truth in the proved and acknowledged shortness of the duration of all such experiments— In governments where every man woman and Child is an *incompetent Sovereign*, who makes or unmakes the *efficient* and *able rulers* of the Land, according to the wisdom of party factions; the spleen and avarice of demagogues; the hireling greediness of grasping avarice; or the unprincipled recklessness of vicious profligacy; In such governments the vices of the *many* must ever be called into action; and until the coming of the Millenium when man shall be almost purified from the baleful nature of his frailties; such a government and such Institutions, will ever pander to the passions of the bad, instead of supporting and sustaining through the medium of Just and efficient Laws; the fortunes, the interests, and the virtues of the best and most worthy Citizens of the Community—

With M^r^ & Mrs. Gallatin I was then not acquainted; and during the whole of Mr. Adams's term, *he* never visited the family— As I have since been intimate with him, I will now observe, that he is one of the most charming, talented, nay, gifted men that I ever knew in any Country— This was a mind of the *highest* order; blended with a brilliant wit, and keen observation; which with a Womans intuitive readiness seemed to sieze the characteristic traits of his fellow men with quick perception; and with judicous adaptation to their prominent points, his tactics were applied to promote *his views* for the furtherance of his peculiar objects, and there were few in lifes intercourse, from whose knowledge, or their weaknesses, he did not derieve some lesson of experience, or some gleanings of worldly wisdom— Shrewed, subtle, and penetrating, few could cope with him; and many of the prudent and sagacious in society thought it necessary to be on their *guard* when brought into contact with him—as subtlety is a dangerous characteristic—

Who for his own uses sought mankind—

His Lady was not popular and the world kindly whispered that the all-conquering *Treasury*, bowed with humility to the deity of his household Sovereign— I never was acquainted with the Lady— Excentric in her Dress, singular and unattractive in her personal appearance, there was nothing to lure to her society either in manner or appearance; although I have no doubt that she possessed many amiable and fine qualities which would have rendered her a valuable friend.[207] The ettiquette of the day was rigid; and as there is no standard laid down in this City as *a rule of Action*; I blundered from ignorance as well as many others, unconscious of my fault— Each of these families entertained constantly excepting that of Mr. Gallatin, who only did so occasionally— An English Chargé D'Affaires Mr Thornton I think and no Minister was at this period at Washington who was followed by Mr. Merry and family— I believe they were already at Washington and a question of ettiquette arose between them

Senators where they always originate concerning first visits; which after a time put an end to our intercourse, which for a time was constant and familliar Merry was a heavy thorough-going John Bull of kindly manners, but very inelegant deportment— His Wife was a very showy Woman of vulgar extraction, suddenly raised to wealth and station, and possessing no feminine refinement, or of that "usage du monde" which teaches the proprieties of social intercourse, or the courtesies of polished life— Her Husbands principal duty when she entertained, seemed to be to attend to the *Waiters* in their circuit round the rooms with the refreshments, and side by side with the Liveried *help*, to officiate in the disposal of the Cakes, or Cates always well received by the guests— *She* assumed the Plenipotienry *attitude*, and did the honours of the Station with the insulting tone of british arrogance, feminine impertinence, and ill-bred parvenue coarseness— The first Ball I attended at her house "She insisted upon my opening the dance with Mr. Foster the step Son of the Duke of Devonshire, *because* I was no tramontane and had seen Court life;" and this in the hearing of the whole company; that she always had a Boars head disguised at *Supper*, "because the Americans could not sit down without hog meat &ce" which I give you as specimens; and she never took her Seat at the Table, but had her Supper sent or carried up to her by some of our exalted Sena-

[207] Albert Gallatin, secretary of the treasury from 1801 to 1814, married his second wife, Hannah Nicholson (d. 1849), in 1793. Gallatin himself described his wife's person as "far less attractive than either her mind or her heart," but others praised her stylishness and wardrobe (*DAB*; Gallatin to Jean Badollet, 1 Feb. 1794, in Henry Adams, *The Life of Albert Gallatin*, Phila., 1879, p. 108).

tors, who were too happy to play Cavaliéré Servente's to such an accomplished Misstress—[208] The Lady of Genl Tureau was altogether indescribable and can only be presented en Silhouette, in which Shade altogether predominates externally, and leaves us to idealize the lights *within*—

The general society consisted of charming families who bred in the School of Washington and Adams, had not yet clothed themselves in the buffoonery of the modern democracy; but who professed some respect for the moral obligations of civilized man, and *acted* up to the Doctrine— Their theories were not at perpetual variance with their feelings and principles; and they were therefore Citizens who respected themselves, and the Laws really well intended by the good and great, who created them; just and judicious Institutions of their Country, adopted and promulgated for the good of the whole Nation—and already subverted to accomplish the narrow and corrupting purposes of mere *party Spirit*—and personal jealousies—

The Society at My Sisters house was delightful— Talent, Wit, Good humour, and an easy and general desire to please promoted freedom, without the familliarity of rudeness; and the young and the old, were recieved with equal respect and pleasure, with the security of the surest welcome— Music, dancing, Cards, or more frequently social and brilliant conversation, varied the Scene, and our visitors seldom shortened their visits from "ennui"—

M[r.] Adams applied himself to his Senatorial duties with his usual fervour, and went through a close examination of my poor Fathers papers with the same zeal; and came to the conclusion that a more honourable and better man never lived; and that *he had been* the prey of all he had served through the benevolence of his heart; and the baseness of the Scoundrels who had ruined him to enrich them-

[208] Anthony Merry (1756–1835), the British minister to the United States from 1803 to 1806, married Elizabeth Death Leathes (d. 1824), the widow of a prominent member of the English gentry, in 1803. They lived on K Street near the Hellens. Disagreements over etiquette arose because Merry was unaware of Thomas Jefferson's egalitarian approach to protocol and viewed informality as a personal and political affront. In 1804 Jefferson codified the new rules of official social behavior in the "Canons of Etiquette" (Malcolm Lester, *Anthony Merry* Redivivus: *A Reappraisal of the British Minister to the United States, 1803–6*, Charlottesville, Va., 1978, p. 4, 10, 12, 13, 29–30, 32, 122).

Augustus John Foster (1780–1848), the son of Lady Elizabeth Foster, for whom see Adventures, note 227, below, and stepson of William Cavendish, 5th Duke of Devonshire, was the secretary of the British legation in the United States. He became minister plenipotentiary in 1811 (same, p. 20–21; *DNB*).

selves—[209] And thus was his memory justified; and a stain removed from *my* character, which had destroyed all my happiness, and reduced me almost to the death— Tis true I had been and ever was foolishly sensitive to the mere appearance of wrong in this cruel misfortune; but my *own* judgment alone, was sufficient to condemn me on the principles usually adopted by the world; and I had a sufficient insight into his affairs and into the unfair way in which they were managed, to see and feel the shadow cast over his fair fame; while the very men who caused his ruin, were robbing him of his hard earned gains, and reducing him and his family to beggary— Here was the truth illustrated by his own Books and papers; ably kept until within four days of his death; and this testimony was undeniable, but for want of *means* to carry on a suit, his family were crushed for ever—

If *I* felt sorrow and all the anguish of mortified pride under such a deep affliction; one so untimely; Mr Adams must have been more than *man*, more than *Angel*, not to have felt the bitter blow most keenly: for the very *prominence* of his Station, added to its sting, and rendered it almost unbearable— A man must be more than mortal to bear with philosophy so severe a shock; and a feeling of deep injury was natural and justifiable on his part, when we rationally and candidly consider his position— To me he was kind, devoted, and affectionate; but common sense indicated too clearly the impossibility of his feeling towards those whom I so fondly loved and respected, as every Woman; every daughter would have her husband feel, towards the Parents whose long unweared and tender affection, had impressed upon her heart and her understanding a deep sense of fillial gratitude, love, and veneration—

Of the Gentlemen most distinguished at the time I shall only mention a few of the most prominent who frequented our house during our residence in the City— Of the Senate Mr. Tracy of Cont. was one of the most witty, delightful and charming companions I almost ever met—[210] His character stood very high, and his reputation in the Senate was that of superior talent, and ability— It was remarked of him that though a brilliant Wit out of doors, he never

[209] In an effort to assist the Johnson family with Joshua Johnson's estate, in Dec. 1804 JQA perused his father-in-law's books and papers. He remarked in his Diary that they related to transactions "so extensive and complicated, that the more I advance the more the difficulties increase" (D/JQA/27, 5, 7, 9, 12–14 Dec., APM Reel 30).

[210] Sen. Uriah Tracy of Connecticut, an ardent Federalist, opposed the Louisiana Purchase and was a leader of the New England secessionists (Claude G. Bowers, *Jefferson in Power: The Death Struggle of the Federalists,* Boston, 1936, p. 229–231).

on any occasion displayed it in the Senate– His Speeches were dignified illustrations of the subjects which he handled with peculiar force, and in a masterly manner– His arguments were strong; his reasoning perspicuous, and his deductions and conclusions clear, with an emphatic power of eloquence carrying conviction to his hearers– Bayard Phil. B. Key Col White, Giles, Pickering, Mitchell, Ellery, S. Smith, Hillhouse, Dayton, De Wit Clinton a short time– with a number of others whom I do not immediately recollect–Burr was Vice President, and there has never been such a P of Senate since his day– He presided with dignity, yet with that firm urbane politeness, which makes the rude recoil, and Seals authority with its best stamp– The force of *manner* in this *little Man* was strongly exemplified in the difficult situation which he held; for independent of his known gallantry to the Ladies; he kept *them* under the most perfect and judicious controul during the daily Sessions at which they attended–

Mr. Adams was now a Senator of the U. S. Thus a distinction was immediately created between my *station* and that of my own family with whom I boarded; and though this fact produced a difference *out* of doors in this equalizing republick by the distinction shown to a *man* as a *Senator* by all the Officers of the Government &c; still this very distinction pointed the fact of a difference, and often occasioned unpleasant feelings very painful to myself, and not a little galling to others– Having lived abroad, all this operation of mere circumstance was new to *me*; and it had a very depressing effect upon my spirits– In other Countries *Station* is so defined, and the rules of Society are so clearly understood; *feeling* is seldom unpleasantly shocked by changes which stand on the firm and fixed basis of common custom– But with us, jealousies are immediately awakened, and even your children and your nearest and dearest connections, are *fearful* of being *supposed* to play a minor part on the great theatre, and despise the idea of a *secondary* place, even to age combined with dignity and wisdom– This is not the puerile observation of six and twenty; but it springs from the long tried experience of six and sixty, after a varied life of good and evil; and from the mind of one who never valued what is termed greatness by a vulgar world; but who being accustomed through her connection with a family whose real *greatness* emanated from great minds, morals, and qualifications, has raised a standard from which almost all others shrink; by which alone her judgment can be satisfied– The Winter was severe; but we frequented the parties, the dinners, the Assemblies, and all the routine of a Metropolitan Season at a Congressional Session, almost at the risk of life, in consequence of the difficulties of intercourse— The City not being laid out; the Streets not graduated; the bridges consisting of mere loose planks; and huge stumps of Trees recently cut down intercepting every path; and the roads intersected by deep ravines continually enlarged by rain—[211]

Mr. Jefferson was the President of the day—the ruling Demagogue of the hour— Every thing about him was *aristorcatic except* his person which was ungainly ugly and common— His manner was awkward, and excessively ineligant; and until he fairly entered into conversation, there was a sort of peering restlessness about him, which betrayed a fear of being scanned more closely by his visitors, than was altogether *agreeable* to his self complacency— while conversing he was very agreeable, and possessed the art of drawing out *others* and at the same time attracting attention to himself— The entertainment was handsome—French Servants in Livery; a French Butler, a French Cuisine, and a buffet full of choice Wine and Plate: had he had a tolerable fire on one of the bitterest days I ever experienced, we might almost have fancied ourselves in Europe— Mr. Madison and his Lady were present; and the French Minister Tureau; and among others whom I have forgotten John Randolph, who gave us a specimen of his wonted rudeness, in an attack which he made on the wine— Mr. Madison was a *very* small man in his *person*, with a *very* large *head*—his manners were peculiarly unassuming; and his conversation lively, often playful, with a mixture of wit and seriousness so happily blended as to excite admiration and respect— I never saw a man with a mind so copious, so free from the pedantry and mere classical jargon of University Scholarship—but his language was chaste, well suited to occasion, and the simple expression of the passing thought, and in harmony with the taste of his hearers— Mrs. Madison was tall large and rather masciline in personal dimensions; her complexion was so fair and brilliant as to redeem this objection, in its perfectly feminine beauty— Dressed as a Quaker with all the nâive simplicity of the sect; there was a frank-

[211] Although the Executive Mansion, Capitol, and buildings for the Departments of Treasury, State, and War were by now completed, the streets were not. Congress refused to fund any street improvements until 1807, and the few local taxpayers could not afford the cost of paving the wide boulevards called for in Pierre Charles L'Enfant's plan. LCA seemed pleased with the city on the whole: "I am quite delighted with the situation of this place and I think should it ever be finished it will be one of the most beautiful spots in the world" (Green, *Washington, 1800–1878*, p. 27, 38–39; LCA to JQA, 16 Sept. 1801, Adams Papers).

ness and ease in her deportment, that won golden opinions from all, and she possessed an influence so decided with her

little Man

that She was the worshiped of all the Idol-mongers, who hang on tinsel greatness— Genl. Tureau was one of the Revolutionary Hero's of France in its worst era in La Vendéé; who still retained such a love of *fight*, that he and his fair Lady often gave to the public fine specimens of Battle, which necessitated an interference from *neighbours*, and even constabulary *force* to protect the frail conquered party—[212] Of John Randolph what shall I say? Among some of the theories broached by mankind the World is said to be haunted by *Dæmons*; and if this idea could be re-alized, surely John Randolph in person, face, manners and mind, might have been the prototype of this *imaginary* monster, created to torment and bewilder mankind—[213] The dinner was agreeable enough—but when we retired to the Drawing Room in the *french* fashion, Ladies and Gentlemen together; We found a Grate of small size in the vast Circular Room, the fire not rising above the second bar of this coal grate, and the coals what there were of them barely kindled; in fact in such a State, that one of the Guest's said "he could have amused himself '*by spitting out the fire*'["]; Shaking with cold the company reduced to a state of [morne] silence, we were under the necessity of keeping our teeth close shut, lest their chattering should proclaim that, "our sufferins was intolerable." while the gallant President drew his Chair close into the centre of the hearth, and seemed impatiently to await our exit; which was sadly delayed by the neglect of the hackney Coachman; although we were countenanced by the blustering french hero, who amused himself with a gallopade backwards and forwards in the apartment, until relieved from the same inconvenience as ourselves— After a long and dangerous ride, over the *glacier's* between the Presidents and the lone house by the river side occupied by Mr. Hellen, we had a hearty laugh at the events of the

[212] Louis Marie Turreau de Garambouville (1756–1816), the French minister to the United States from 1804 to 1811, was known to physically abuse his wife, Marie Angélique, and to insult her in front of their servants. For the rebellion in the Vendée, see *AFC*, 10:256, 257. In late 1793 the Committee of Public Safety charged Turreau with suppressing the rebellion in the Vendée. From Jan. to May 1794 Turreau and his twelve "*colonnes infernales*" swept through the region massacring rebels and destroying their property, often indiscriminately killing civilians, including women and children (*Repertorium*, 3:145; Allgor, *Perfect Union*, p. 61; Arno J. Mayer, *The Furies: Violence and Terror in the French and Russian Revolutions*, Princeton, N.J., 2000, p. 351–358, 361).

[213] John Randolph of Roanoke (1773–1833), representative from Virginia, was known as an orator. Always eccentric and odd in appearance, he later was said to be insane (*DAB*).

day—and a cheerful Cup of Tea, that most welcome of all restoratives round a pleasant family Table in social chat, measuring the present by the past, thus brought in contrast to my view—and I saw but little to choose between the vulgar aristocracy of German Courtiers, and the time serving democracy of the borrowed luxuries and the stately assumption, of the Parvenue triumph of a political *hypocrite*, denominated the Leader of a faction—

My next exhibition was at a Ball at Mr. Robert Smith's— Here there was an ensemble, a whole in such good keeping and taste, that I was carried back to the sphere in which I was brought up among the class of Merchants in England— Mr. Smith was in manners and appearance a gentleman; courteous, well bred and doing the honours of his house with easy hospitality, without that excess of familiarity, which sometimes makes a company more uncomfortable than haughty restraint— Mrs. Smith was a perfect Lady, handsome, polite, dignified and affable— In her personal appearance highly aristocratick, and a fine epitomé of the old School— She was not a general favorite—why? because she was always *correct*— therefore said to be cold— Genl Dearborn and his Wife were kind friendly excellent people. He "told of Wars and hair breadth-'scapes;" assured me that from his *own* experience when taken by the Indians in the dread affair of Genl Hull (I think) that it only required "a fortnight for men like *him* to return from *refinement* to the Savage state," and that after two Months "*he* was as much an Indian as any of them"— and his good and amiable Wife, a true specimen of yankee housewifery, always kind was for ever regretting her Milch Cows, and her Chickens at Kenebunck, from whence she had been driven, not to assume the *purple*, but to assist in the honours of the Drawing Rooms— Here was a real genuine pattern of unsophisticated democracy, far superior to the affected blandishments of Mr. Jeffersons assumed greatness, accompanied by all the social virtues of benevolence, sincerity, and natural goodness of heart—[214]

Mr Levi Lincoln was the ~~District~~ Attorney Genl—A plain man with no very striking marks about *him*, that now live in my memory— His reputation was fair and good and his person and manners not re-

[214] Henry Dearborn (1751–1829), secretary of war from 1801 to 1809, and his wife Dorcas Marble Dearborn. LCA is compressing time here, however. In 1812, as the senior major general in the U.S. Army, Dearborn was responsible for planning the disastrous campaign, led by Brig. Gen. William Hull (1753–1825), against British and Indian forces on the Michigan frontier (*DAB*).

markable in any way; but of the average stamp of the prominent Lawyers of the day, with a good deal of Country bonne-homie—

Without Notes it would be impossible to detail the incidents of such a life after so long a lapse of time. I shall therefore confine myself to such facts as were vulgarly familiar and prominent, and which are recollected by many now living—

Balls, Dinners, Parties and Dejeunées Dansants succeed each other constantly; and although the roads were impassible, and but at the risk of life; the rage for pleasure, and the routine adopted by the Leaders of fashionable life in this *then* desert City "of magnificent distances," made it necessary for the Wives of Public men to frequent them more than was either agreeable or convenient to myself.—

Mr Adams was entirely engrossed in his political affairs the Lousiana Treaty being then before the Senate—[215] We made many most agreeable acquaintance. M^r^ & M^rs:^ Hugee of S C and Mr Purviance from N. C a very pleasant but most eccentric man—

M^r^ A Burr an elegant man in point of manners who I did not know.

DEC 24

Dined at the Presidents— M^r^ R Smith and Lady; Mr. Wright a very odd person Senator from Maryland and his daughter; M^r^ & M^rs^ & Miss Conway and Mrs. Livingston were the guests; dinner rather stif and being indisposed we left the party early—

The House, the manners of the Hosts &ce were all in better style than any that I met with in Washington— Mrs. Smith would have been a Lady of high fashion *any where* and their democracy was quite imperial— M^rs.^ H Livingston was beautiful arch, witty and playful, without the retenù's or dignity of the above Lady—

25

M^r^ & Mrs. Pichon passed the evening with— He is a formal and rather heavy frenchman; Mrs. Pichon was every way interresting.

[215] JQA had arrived in Washington too late to vote on the treaties related to the Louisiana Purchase, which were ratified on 20 Oct. 1803 with no Federalist votes. He supported the acquisition but was vocal in the debates over enabling legislation, much of which he opposed on constitutional grounds (Bemis, *JQA*, 1:119–121).

7. "WASHINGTON CITY," BY ANNE MARGUERITE HYDE DE NEUVILLE, 1821

See page xii

Pretty, graceful accomplished with sweet manners, unaffected and without pretention— She sung her National Ballads with sentiment, and was altogether a most attractive creature— Mr Pishon was the Consul General from France lived and entertained genteely; and was popular in the City.

JAN. 1 [*1804*]

According to the fashion of the day Mr Adams paid his visit to the President— A day which draws out an unruly Crowd of indiscriminate persons from every Class; peculiarly annoying to the Corps Diplomatique, whose fine clothing, Carriages &ce, become the gaze of the curious vulgar, only to be satisfied by tangible means, exceedingly trying and unpleasant to aristocratic feelings and education— Tom Jefferson as the founder of democracy; was obliged patiently to submit, and to *permit* these indignities: and to have his wardrobe ransacked that the People might admire his *red breeches* &c &c and amuse themselves at his expense, and *not a little* annoyance—[216]

5

My little boy was very ill of a fever and my time and cares were too necessary to his recovery to admit of my leaving him— Among the acquaintance which we made none were more kind than Judge and Mrs. Cushing— They seemed to belong to a patriarchal age; strongly imbued with the puritan spirit softened by that benevolence which a free association with men generally produces through observation and experience, when we have passed the age of the passions; and ambition been gratified by established popularity— Their persons, dress, manners, and the manner of their lives; equipage; all spoke of a primeval age; exciting astonishment in the mature; and risibility in the young; who under the idea of their *freedom*, are apt to make a use of *liberty* not exactly accordant with the rules of good breeding—

Gayéty was the order of the day and the House was thronged with visitors— My Sisters were very pretty and attractive and their education and accomplishments rendered them objects of general ad-

[216] Martha Washington had opened the president's house for receptions on Fridays, and AA maintained the practice of weekly public receptions. Thomas Jefferson, however, limited formal receptions to New Year's Day and the Fourth of July (*AFC*, 9:8; Allgor, *Parlor Politics*, p. 19–23).

miration— My manners were frigid, cold, and repulsive; and being naturally timid, and educated under much restraint; much was attributed to pride which was caused by fear of giving offence, or clashing with some usage which I did not understand, or some omissions of ceremonial with which I was totally unacquainted— At the Courts of Princes you get written instruction's to teach you the forms and ettiquettes—you are therefore seldom liable to give offence by erring— In a democratic government where all are monarchs; although *one* yourself, there is a perpetual struggle for a *position*, which gives rise to constant feuds, and demands utterly impossible to satisfy; & which lay the foundation for absurd enmities that can never be reconciled— A man intent upon business walking to his department, passes by a Gentleman who *bows* to him— *He* does not see it; but the consequence resulting therefrom, is an exaggerated enmity so violent; that howerver gifted by talents, knowledge or experience for Office; a vote is for ever cast against the offender however fit for the Office in question—

Many pretend that the Government of Moses was a *Republic* But the people did *not* create and select *him*, and enforce obedience to him and to Aaron: ~~under the Almighty's immediate Law~~? It was the Almighty who ordered his course; and who sustained him in Power; and without this special and divine support Moses would have been no better than common *men*: excepting from the education which he had recieved miraculously to fit him for the purpose— How could that be a Republick which had the King of Kings for a Ruler?

8

This is not intended to be a diary but merely a sketch of the times long past, and of many who have long laid cold in their graves— Mr. Pickering was in the Senate of the United States a bitter opponent to my husband, and an enemy to his Father— He was not an agreeable man—there was a degree of ascerbity in his manners altogether repellant; and few who had known him *long* could get over the difficulty of the first abord— Mr & Mrs. Lownds were very charming persons— Easy, agreeable and unpretending they produced no great *effect*: but they were esteemed, beloved and respected— A man of superior talents, modest to a fault, but sound in morals as in *mind*—[217] Mr & Mrs Daniel Hugee were also of the old Carolina

[217] Thomas Lowndes (1766–1843), a representative from South Carolina from 1801 to 1805,

standard; and were very much liked— More showey in his manners and more assuming in his style. They moved about with more pretension of fortune and fashion—

Genl Tureau the French Minister was ugly illmannered and every disagreeable— He had been one of the leading Gen in the War of la Vendée and had been noted for his cruelty and brutality throughout its existence Not having exhausted his love of glory and delight in warlike triumphs; he amused the people in Washington (though in a civil capacity towards the United States) with matrimonial *battles* in which his poor vulgar Wife was always so *beaten*, that the aid of the Constabulary *force* was frequently called in to protect her in the fray. He was shrewed and decietful; possess'd a good portion of Diplomatic Cunning; and though *hated* was every where well recieved— I had no acquaintance with the *Lady* and never saw her but once— Quantum sufficit—

Major Marin and M[r] De Cabre were his Secretaries both very agreeable Men, and constant visitors at our House. M[r.] Adams myself and the family being thoroughly acquainted with the language— Indeed the House was generally attractive to visitors— M[r.] Adams being much courted; and my Mother and Sisters all being possessed of very popular manners with every social quality as well as my brother in Law M[r.] Hellen, to make the House delightful to the leading men and foreigners of that period—

The petit soupers often consisting of little more than Crackers Butter Cake and wine—which however gave a zest to music, dancing, and wit— No one ever went there *once* that did not want to come again— M[r.] Tracy and M[r.] Dana of Connecticut the first, the soul of wit and pun out of the Senate; but ever grave serious and decorous in his Seat—The other cutting, sarcastic and epigrammatic in the H R full of laughter and jokes every where—sources of constant mirth and acting on each other as whetstones to sharpen the good humoured points of their friendly jests— But how can I detail or depict the numerous acquaintance which graced the house! not so freely perhaps, but on the easiest and most familiar footing Philip B. Key and his family; H G Otis: the Quincy's the Harpers of Baltimore; the Catons; the Smiths; The Wrights; the Chaces, the Thompson's, the Ogles, the Goldsboroughs, and how many many

and his wife Sarah Bond I'On Lowndes (Walter B. Edgar and N. Louise Bailey, eds., *Biographical Directory of the South Carolina House of Representatives*, 5 vols. to date, Columbia, S.C., 1974–   , 4:357–358).

more! Col White of Delaware was one of the élégans of that day admired and courted by all— Many Ladies from the different States of the Union visited the City; but accomodations were indifferent, scarce, and the inconveniences many; and only the more wealthy could afford to purchase the discomforts of the place

[*FEBRUARY 1805*][218]

One of the great events of the day was the Impeachment of Judge Chase for which alone among his manyfold errors not to say Sins it was no wonder he should when almost expiring have written the word *Remorse*!!! Let us pray that *that* word may have obliterated his faults as a proof of sincere repentance—[219]

John Randolph was the lyon of the day— A man perhaps the most extraordinary of his day— Full of all the attributes of mind which *forms* great men, his temperament was irritable and sensitive almost to madness; and he was incessantly goaded on in his political career by a wild ambition, ill regulated passions; petty jealousies; and indomitable perseverance— Every act was a phrenzy though the purpose was often good, and there was a *sort* of method in his Speeches; yet like Hamlet 'tis difficult even to this day to prove that he was insane— Ever in extremes he was at times a delightful companion; or an insolent bully—in fact "everything by starts and nothing long" enough to learn to love him or respect him![220] Surrounded by admirers who loved the excitement produced by his waywardness and his brilliant rhapsodies; he appeared to be the great man of his day, for he ruled the timid and amused the weak, till his *Antics* produced the most serious consequences; in the shameless persecution of men infinitely superior to himself; and to whom the Nation owed a debt of gratitude for long and faithful services To sum up the whole he was to congress what Shakespeares *Fool's* were to a Court. He kept Congress awake with "his quips and cranks" and made the *Ladies* smile—[221] Peace to his manes.—

[218] LCA placed this paragraph and that at [*post 14 March 1805*], below, out of sequence. The supplied dates reflect the occurrence of the events she described.

[219] Samuel Chase, a Federalist appointed to the Supreme Court by George Washington in 1796, was impeached by the House in March 1804 in proceedings managed by John Randolph. The charges included malfeasance in office during sedition and treason trials and in an address to a Maryland grand jury. The Senate failed to achieve a two-thirds vote on any of the charges, and Chase was acquitted. He remained on the Supreme Court until his death (*Biog. Dir. Cong.*; *DAB*).

[220] John Dryden, *Absalom and Achitophel,* line 548.

[221] John Milton, "L'Allegro," line 27.

MARCH [*1804*]

The next great event was the marriage of Jerome Bonoparte to Miss Paterson of Baltimore— She was beautiful and she was followed as person's are who have attracted public attention by any extraordinary act— Balls suppers and parties of every kind were the consequence and we lived in a perpetual round of dissipation—[222] To my Sisters this was delightful to me it was painful to leave a nurseling who required all my care and Mr. Adams health was not good and his labour excessive—

5 [*POST 14 MARCH 1805*]

My Sister Boyd was married and Balls and parties succeeded—[223] Her Husband Col Boyd was a very fascinating handsome man and they went to reside with his Mother in Washington— He was descended from the House of Killmarnock in Scotland and the next Heir.[224]

[*MARCH 1804*]

The marriage of Jerome Bounapate and Miss Patterson was in turn the wonder of the day. Beautiful as a houri she burst upon society with a startling èclat and the flattering hope of future greatness as Sister in Law of Napoleon with a Crown in prospect plucked from the head of some conquered King produced a great *sensation*— All these *pretensions* gave grounds for high admiration for we *Republican's* though detesting Kings and Rank &c &c &c have a great respect for the pomps and externals of such Stations and are apt to worship the *Stars* which sometimes irradiate our Spheres although they may be *only* of the sixth magnitude— Thus even the follies and vagaries of Jerome and his young Bride however absurd; or ill suited to the manners of our day— Mrs. Jerome showed a ready tact and

[222] Jerome Bonaparte (1784–1860), the youngest brother of Napoleon, and Elizabeth Patterson (1785–1879), the daughter of a Baltimore merchant, were married on 24 Dec. 1803, but Napoleon refused to acknowledge the marriage. In 1807 Jerome married a German princess, and in 1813 Elizabeth obtained a divorce (Bill Marshall, ed., *France and the Americas: Culture, Politics, and History*, 3 vols., Santa Barbara, Calif., 2005, 1:162–163).

[223] Harriet Johnson and George Boyd were married on 14 March 1805 (D/JQA/27, APM Reel 30).

[224] At this paragraph, LCA wrote "Omit" three times, twice in the left margin, and once in the right.

her beauty was heightened by all the Arts of a Parisian Toilet which the world asserted were always under the immediate direction of her Husband—

Mr. Stuart was then in Washington and his Studio was open to the public where I saw a Painting of his exhibing three heads issuing from on neck representing Mrs. Bonaparte in full face three quarters and profile all beautiful and admiral as likenesses in the full bloom of almost childish loveliness—[225] Years have elapsed disappointments innumerable have occured to mar those evanescent hopes; and yet the Star still scintillates to show how beauty can outlive care even in the wane of life in a cold and ambitious temperament unsubdued by sentiment or strong feeling—

T'was but a shooting Star, that twinkled but to fall!—

Mr. Pishon was furious at the match; and seemed to live in terror lest Napoleon should wreck his wrath on him for what he could not help—[226]

Mr Foster was the Secretary of Legation to the Englsh Minister Merry— A wild untameable young Irishman full of intelligence the Son of Lady Elizabet Foster since Dutchess of Devonshire very noted in England and said to be very beautiful but very different from the famous Dutchess of the Fox party whose place Lady Elizabeth filled after her death—[227]

Mrs. Harper. was one of the most excentric women I ever knew; living in Style in Baltimore married to a man of talents and of fortune; but night and morning could not be more different in every possible particular— She was lively almost wild in her character and her tastes. He was ponderous and heavy an old Law Book; and seldom awake long enough when he was in company to remember where he was— In the Senate he was much esteemed and thought a

[225] LCA and JQA visited Gilbert Stuart's studio on 29 March 1804 (D/JQA/27, APM Reel 30). For the triple portrait of Elizabeth Patterson Bonaparte, 1804, privately owned, see Carrie Rebora Barratt and Ellen G. Miles, *Gilbert Stuart*, N.Y., 2004, p. 251–253.

[226] Louis André Pichon (1771–1850), as chargé d'affaires in Washington from 1801 to 1804, was responsible for reporting Jerome Bonaparte's actions to Napoleon and for conveying the emperor's orders to his brother (*Correspondance des directeurs de l'Académie de France à Rome*, ed. Jules Guiffrey, 17 vols., Paris, 1887–1908, 17:130).

[227] Georgiana Spencer Cavendish, Duchess of Devonshire (1757–1806), supported and campaigned for Charles James Fox, the prominent Whig statesman. In 1782 she became friendly with Elizabeth Foster (1757–1824), who had separated from her husband and come to live with the duke and duchesss. Elizabeth is said to have borne children to the duke and, in 1809, after Georgiana's death, she married him (*DNB*).

handsome Speaker and writer— The Senate was at that full of distinguished men from all parts of the Union— There was a bright Constellation of talent and learning such as is seldom concentrated in one body; and Burr the Vice President presided with a dignity which has never been approach since— Though a devoted Servant of the *Ladies* he never permited a moments infringement of the Rules. And the little hammer in his graceful little hand would startle them into silence at the instant application— Mr. Giles was often Boisterous and unruly; but he was active for his State and thought a great Speaker Col White of Delaware was a polished and elegant man; a favourite of the Ladies, and a finished Orator— Phillip Barton Key was very handsome; a model in manners and one if not the most graceful Orator of the day. I cannot mention them all but as a body there were but few exceptions.—

The trial of Judge Pickering called forth much interest and much intrigue;[228] Mr. Wright the Member from Maryland was a restless active busy man whose self esteem rendered him very troublesome to the more judicious— Ambitious and irritable he was hot in argument and irrascible in debate; so much that out of doors his *sanity* was often questiond in consequence of his want of judgement— His daughter was a sweet pretty Girl and one of the belles of the Season— Sam Smith the thunderer was also in the Senate— Ambitious to excess; ostentacious in the same degree aristocratic and overbearing he appeared to have with the assistance of the Mason Family of Virginia the whole controul of the President and his Administration and his Brother Robert was dictator—then Secretary of the Navy.

Of Mr. Jefferson I can only state the impression which he made on me when I saw him— My prejudices were all in his favour when I arrived in the Country as I had been accustomed to hear my Father praise him— The first abord did not please me: his countenance indicated strongly the hypocricy of his nature and all about him his smile and his actions indicated a sort of tricky cunning, the sure attendant of a sophisticated mind devoid of a strong basis of substantial principle— His manners were neither elegant nor refined; his conversation was agreeable, but he ever appeared to be a great

[228] John Pickering (ca. 1738–1805) of New Hampshire was appointed to the U.S. District Court in 1795. In 1801 he suffered a mental collapse that affected his conduct as judge. In Feb. 1803 Thomas Jefferson brought the matter to the House of Representatives, which voted articles of impeachment. The Senate voted for his removal on 12 March 1804 (*DAB*).

man by fortuitous circumstance; but too unsound by *reality* to claim so lofty a position—

It was the sneaking greatness of mere good fortune attained in a lucky hour; and by a concurrence of propitious events— Showy, prosperous and backed by a strong party in his political career; his character was exactly adapted to lead restless demagogues and turbulent politicians, who needed only *gifts* without aspiring to qualifications— Nervously timid and totally wanting in personal courage, he was a *jest* among brave men; and M^r. Tracy used to say of him "that he never would take the Leg of a Chicken, because he was afraid of the *drum stick*"—

In short he was the Iago of the political world—
His God rejecting; to his race untrue—

M^rs. Randolph was a very amiable woman who to know was to respect. To my Mother Adams the two daughters (both lovely women) they owed all the early care and advice which a Mother could have bestowed on their friendless situation, while in Paris; without the blessing of Maternal care—[229]

APRIL 2

The winter passed under much uneasiness and anxiety of a domestic character: and the time having arrived for Mr Adams's departure we prepared every thing and he left us taking my Nurse Patty Walin with him under the most disagreeable circumstances She, having been subject to fits all the Winter and obliging to vacate his writing room besides many other inconveniences.—[230] Mr Allen Otis accompanied him and I remained with my two little ones at M^r. Hellens a fearfully responsible situation on account of the Climate to which none of us had been used—

This was the first long separation I had ever been exposed to since my marriage and my health and spirits were sadly depressed

[229] Martha (Patsy) Washington Jefferson (1772–1836) was married to Thomas Mann Randolph, who served as a congressman and later as governor of Virginia. After the death of her mother, Martha Skelton Wayles Jefferson, in 1782, Patsy traveled with her father to Paris while her sister Mary (Polly) was cared for by relatives (*Notable Amer. Women*). For the period of just over two weeks in June 1787 that Polly spent with the Adamses in London on her way to Paris to join her father and sister, see *AFC*, 8:92–93.

[230] Patty Walin, called Patty Milnor earlier, was very ill beginning on 4 March and was sick on the trip back as well (D/JQA/27, 4 March, 6 April 1804, APM Reel 30).

MAY

I weaned my boy which he appeared to bear very well; but he soon sicken'd and I was kept in a state of deep and constant anxiety under the apprehension that I must lose him—

The unintermiting care and attention which he required Night and day prey'd, upon my health spirits: and the active and ever restless spirit of my eldest Son who was ever in danger in consequence of a careless Nurse rendered cares almost beyond my strength to endure and the responsibility heavier than I can express although every kindness was shown to me. One day when I had sent my George out to walk his Uncle coming home from his Office thought he saw a Child alone on the wharf. He approached very softly behind him; and when he had fast hold of him he asked him what he was doing? He was pulling his Shoes and Stockings off he replied "to get into the water (the Potomac) to see how *deep* it was!" At another time his curiosity was roused to go down into the Garden by the Porch leading out of the third Story instead of going down the Stairs— He was not five years old yet this thirst after knowledge seemed to pervade every thought and action and I knew no peace—

The health of my Children was the sole object of my life and I was continually moving from the City to Bladensberg or to Clarksville about half way to Frederick for the benefit of change of Air which through Gods great mercy succeeded in restoring him and he gained so rapidly in the[231] occasionally I saw M^rs. Madison M^rs. Merry and some of the Ladies of the District and attended at the Episcopal Church; but I had no Carriage and the distances were too great to walk—The Church being in the upper part of George Town—[232]

My Sister Hariet since M^rs. Boyd was a ministering Angel in my distress and never left me alone night or day.

NOV

In November when Mr Adams returned to Congress I had the happiness to present his children to him in high health beauty, after

231 The page ends here, with "the" positioned as a catchword. On the following page the manuscript continues with the next passage given here, beginning mid-sentence with "occasionally."

232 St. John's Church, at the corner of Second and Potomac Streets (Benjamin Perley Poore, comp., *Congressional Directory*, 2d edn., Washington, 1884, p. 183).

seven Months of absence to pass thro' another winter of dissippation and fatigue—

6

Rode out with Mr. Adams on Horseback— When we got to the high Street in George Town my Saddle turned and I fortunately slipped my foot out of the stirrup, and was dragged away by a Gentleman into a Store as the Horse plunged kicked at a furious rate which would certainly have killed me—

He was soon caught and saddled and though still a little restive we took a long ride and returned home safe.—

We paid visits of ceremony according to washington ettiquette at the opening of the Session; but our lives were calm and quiet seeing a few friends of an evening and when alone Mr Adams read out to us while we worked—

Mr. Bayard appeared as a Senator from Delaware and Dr Mitchel of N. Y.— Congress is famed for its dullness until after the hollidays and it is not until after the Members have been satiated with the luxury of Christimas that their wit expands into a genial flow when it bursts forth in a flood of Speeches which often dazzle the senses without satisfying the judgement or the understanding—

Mr H G Otis was one of the favorites of the day—

Mr. Bayard possessed an extended fame and was quite the rage Going one morning to the Senate I heard a debate in which Mr Hillhouse of Con Dr Mitchell took part—& Mr Ellery of R. I. in which in a burst of great fury Mr E—— called Dr Mitchell a *Mad Bull*!! I mention these things to show that the manners "of our grave and reverend" Sengniours required polishing as much as they have done this winter—

Mr. Pitkin and Mr Dagget were also visitors at the House both able men and of Note in that day—

DEC

It was not the fashion to begin parties early in the Season and the first of January was the time usually fixed for the fashionables to open their Houses and Congress also became attractive as the desire to shine in the mornings appeared always to follow the wish to please the Ladies at the Balls and Eveng. Parties—

1 JAN [1805]

At this period of time 1804 & 5—only the *elite* of Congress entered into what was termed the best Society.— and the consequence was that the Society was quite select:— It consisted chiefly of the heads of Department and those Families or Residents whose independent fortunes enabled them to live handsomely and sometimes to entertain their friends and acquaintance— Luxury was unknown except in the Houses of the Foreign Ministers and there were very few who aimed at great and ostentatious display— There were no Confectioners &c or French Cooks and the Ladies prepared there own entertainments at the expence of much labour and anxiety but generally with success—

As there was no Lady at the Presidents there were no Drawing Rooms so that dinners were the only mode of entertainment— The aspect of the House *below* Stairs was very handsome— Up *Stairs* there were strong indications of the want of female inspection— Mrs. Madison so well known and so much admired usually officiated on these occasions and was universally popular for the amenity of her manners and the suavity of her temper— She seemed to combine all the qualifications requisite to adorn the Station which she filled to the satisfaction of *all*: a most difficult performance.—

Col Tayloe's family were wealthy and their House with his kind and amiable Wife and daughters to grace it was one of the most elegant in the City— Mrs. Ogle of Annapolis was an elegant Woman and greatly admired when she visited at Mrs. Tayloes her Daughter—[233]

To follow the routine of the day would be monotonous— Miss Wheeler was a great belle Miss Murray Miss Lee the Misses Chace Mrs. Caton & her daughters the eldest engaged to Mr R. Patterson— Miss Spear Miss M Smith and a number of others with the Merediths Daltons &ce and Miss Dearborn formed a Centre of attraction which gave great eclat to the City and Georgetown in which was also a number of beautiful Girls. The Miss Worthingtons Mason's Jennifers Stodarts &cc too numerous to mention—

Col Boyd was paying his addresses to my Sister Hariet; and the french Secretaries of Legation were often at the House of an eve-

[233] John Tayloe III (1770–1828), a Virginia politician and landowner, married Ann Ogle (ca. 1775–1855), daughter of Governor Benjamin and Henrietta Margaret Hill Ogle, in 1792. He built the Octagon House in Washington (Stella Pickett Hardy, *Colonial Families of the Southern States of America*, N.Y., 1911, p. 502).

ning the family being musical and speaking French— M^r. Adams health was not so good as usual and his application to business was incessant— I was much occipied with my young Children and could not go out much with my Mother and Sisters—

M^r & M^rs. Gallatin I did not know— He was Secretary of the Treasury— Genl. Dearborn Secretary of War.— His Wife was one of the kindest hearted beings in the world and his daughter was a St Giles's beauty of the most Showy Class—[234] The poor old Lady was for ever pining for the Chickens and Cows that she had left in Maine: and mourned for the loss of her occupation of Cheese making almost with tears of sorrow— Yet she entered with real glee into the routine of parties of pleasure and rendered her very agreeable by the general bon homie of her receptions— He was a pompous Militaire of the Democratic School and was full of annecdotes of his own martial experience He one day was recounting to me his having been taken prisoner by the Indian's and been kept among them a long time—And he observed with great gravity—"It was really astonishing how soon we lost the habits of civilasation; in *two* months we became as savage as any of them."— I could not help smiling and thinking that in regard to polish there was not much to lose: for the Secretary's education had not been very finish'd— He spelt Congress with a K. always and when his Wife lay hopelessly ill he met the Physician who asked him "how she was?" he answered almost with a sob, "Oh dear Doctor she is *convalescent*!" He was a kind family man a little puffed up by the Station into which he had popped: or according to Shakespeare into which

"Fortune had thrust him."[235]

As I interested myself very little with the Congressional business I can write very little about it— Mr Adams was almost always immersed in the business and passed much of his time in his room writing— We saw M^rs. Merry frequently and I think that it was at a Ball at her house that she brought the Secretary of Legation M^r. Foster and asked me to open the Ball with him, because she "said *I* had seen something in Europe." This will serve as a specimen of her manners— She was a prodigious favorite of John Randolphs— She

[234] A contemporary once said of Julia Dearborn, "We are told that Venus rose out of the sea, but I once thought she came out of the waters of the Kennebec" (*Revolutionary War Journals of Henry Dearborn, 1775–1783*, ed. Lloyd A. Brown and Howard H. Peckham, repr. edn., Westminster, Md., 2007, p. 15).

[235] Shakespeare, *Twelfth Night*, Act II, scene v, lines 158–159.

never favored her company with her presence at her Supper Table; but used to make some of the members of Congress fetch and carry what she a service which they always appeared to perform with great gusto as Gentlemen in waiting—

The Trial of Judge Chace occupied the publick and every body seemed to take great interest in the proceedings. To me it was of great interest— He had ever been a friend of our Family and had decided as an Arbitrator in the case of my Father in his favor— This decision was reversed by the Chancellor of Maryland *Hanson He* being the Heir to the property in question of which he became possessed to the ruin of myself and family—[236]

Judge Chace was a Man of the old School warm impetuous full of life and vivacity and with a sound judgement but little discretion in his wit— His was just such a character as Democracy under Mr. Jefferson could sieze upon and demolish with the assistance of a strong shrewed party with the help of the tricks and vagaries of a Harlequin could please and tickle the vulgar who cared but for the show: which with the aid of abstruse wiles could Law itself confound and lay a Giant in the dust—

And did remorse blot out the injury?!! Let the Age blush that sanctioned such iniquity!!

1 [*MARCH*]

The Sentence was passed and after all this violent and unjust persecution Samuel Chace was acquitted and declared not guilty of any of the charges brought against him by the House of Representatives—

The House was crowded with Ladies and Spectators and the interest was intense—

Thus owing to the violence of two Men proverbially supposed to be more than half insane was this perhaps imprudent but faithful old Servant of the Revolution goaded and persecuted for many a day, under the taunts and persecution of a mere boy to gratify the spleen of a *party*; whose nefarious plots had brought them into mo-

[236] LCA may be confusing Samuel Chase, for whom see Adventures, note 219, above, with his second cousin Jeremiah Townley Chase (1748–1828), a judge of the Md. General Court from 1789 to 1805 and chief justice of the court of appeals from 1806 to 1826. Alexander Contee Hanson Sr. (1749–1806) was appointed chancellor of Maryland in 1789 and served until his death (Jon L. Wakelyn, *Birth of the Bill of Rights: Encyclopedia of the Antifederalists*, 2 vols., Westport, Conn., 2004, 1:42–43; *DAB*).

mentary power at the expense many many have since thought to the real detriment of the laws and morals of the Country—[237]

But why do I make such observations!! Because experience is a rude though a salutary teacher—

3

Congress sat this day it being the day for adjournment although it was Sunday.— Mr. Burr took his leave of the Senate in a most elegant and even pathetic address delivered in the most graceful and touching manner, and Mr Adams who had never liked him came home quite affected by his manner, appearance, and sentiment— O! how winning is refinement and polished decorum! I fear it will ever white wash many Sin's which morality must condemn. I hated this man for his duel; but I had no acquaintance with him; and never spoke to him. My trial was to come—[238] At half past nine in the Eveng. Congress adjourned—

6

Mr Adams having some leisure from his Congressional pursuits examined my Fathers Papers and found them all in the best order being regular until within 4 days prior to his leaving Washington in company with us on my journey towards Quincy. He would have Administrated on the Estate had not the Securities been to heavy and the Affairs too complicated— I never could blame him

14

My Sister Boyd was married on the evening of this day I having requested that the wedding should take place previous to our departure The families of the Bride and Bridegroom only being present.— Balls and parties ensued when she went to reside with his Mother—

We prepared to return to the north and my Sister Eliza was invited to accompany— My Children were both sick and I had no

[237] The impeachment was led by John Randolph and William Branch Giles (*DAB*).

[238] The Burr-Hamilton duel took place on 11 July 1804. On 2 March 1805, the day after the Chase trial concluded, Burr delivered his farewell speech to the Senate (*DAB*; D/JQA/27, 1 March, APM Reel 30).

nurse so that I started on the rout with great apprehension as to my strength to accomplish the charge of them on such a journey—

2 [19]

This day Mr. Adams my Sister Eliza myself and my two Children left Washington in the George Town Stage for Baltimore in which Seats had been secured for Col Burr and Com Preble— They however had concluded to go in a private Carriage and we went on without them— I at that time felt a sort of loathing for this Col Burr who had recently killed Genl Hamilton in a Duel and I felt quite relieved when we were informed that he would not go— Arrived at Baltimore without we got the best apartments could the Col having secured the best apartments at Evan's and here we met Judge and Mrs. Cushing kind as ever loading George and John with *goodies* and assisting me in all possible ways—[239]

The Children were both quite unwell and of course very troublesome It was the first time that I had the entire charge of them and my anxiety was proportioned to my want of health and strength—

My Sister was not at a time of life when Girls are willing to devote themselves such confinement when circumstances of pleasure and excitement are for ever calling forth expressions of admiration and flattering attentions— When we arrived on board the Packet we found Mr. Burr and Com Preble already there and I took possession of a State Room with my two Children— When I returned into the Cabin Mr. Burr the Vice President was already there and I was formally introduced to him— He was a small man quite handsome and his manners were strikingly prepossessing and in spite of myself I was pleased with him— He appeared to fascinate every one in the Boat down to the lowest Sailor and knew every bodies history by the time we left— He was politely attentive to me devoted to my Sister— At Table he assisted me to help the Children with so much ease and good nature that I was perfectly confounded— We had a very rough Passage and to the astonishment of Com Preble fell out of one of the high Births and rolled upon the floor— At about twelve at Night we landed and it was diverting to see Mr Burr with my youngest Child in his arms; a bundle in his hand and leaning on his other

[239] The Indian Queen Hotel, on the corner of Hanover and Baltimore Streets, was owned by William Evans from 1796 to 1807 (J. Thomas Scharf, *History of Baltimore City and County*, Phila., 1881, p. 514).

arm to walk from the Wharf while my Sister Mr Adams and George followed us to French Town—[240] Yet it was all done with so little parade and with such entire good breeding that it made you forget that he was doing any thing out of the way. He talked and laughed all the way and we were quite intimate by the time we got to Philadelphia where he called to see us, and this the first and last occasion on which I ever saw this celebrated man—

At Philadelphia we remained some days the Children as we found By Dr Rush having the Whooping Cough and Chicken Pox; so that I obliged to engage a girl to attend to them with me: more especially as he insisted on my accepting several Even^g.^ invitations from his friends there with he wished me to become acquainted— Old Mrs. Roberts the good Quaker with whom we boarded undertaking the charge of my little ones while I was absent— It was under these circumstances that I first became acquainted with M^r^ & M^rs:^ Hopkinson a charming family with whom we formed a lasting friendship which exists to this hour—with her; and which continued with him as long as he lived— He was a most delightful companion— Intellectual learned gay and witty it was impossible not to love and esteem him.[241] The anxiety of my mind rendered me a tedious guest but my Sister made friends wherever she was seen.

We were at a great Ball at Mrs. Tench Coxes in the highest style of elegance— Many beautiful girls shone brightly at this gay party where wealth and luxury reign'd triumphant— I was obliged to leave it early much to the regret of my Sister—

How many charming families I then knew The Willings Francis Jacksons Peters Meredith's Mc. Pherson's Bishop White and Daughters the Harrison's Powells and how many others as Cox's Bird Hare &c &c— And here I met Nancy Smith a connection of the Adams family—

And where are most of them now?— This Lady Mrs Masters the only one of that branch of the family left!![242]

We arrived at Quincy after a tedious and unpleasant journey and our House not being ready we remained a week or two with the Gentleman's family— Mr Thomas Adams was married and himself and Wife resided with them with a Niece of Mrs. Adams Miss Le

[240] Frenchtown, Delaware.

[241] Joseph Hopkinson (1770–1842), a Philadelphia lawyer and politician, and his wife, Emily, the daughter of Thomas Mifflin, the first governor of Pennsylvania (*DAB*).

[242] Ann Smith Masters, sister of WSS.

Smith and her Gland Daughter the Child of her Son Charles.— The Family being so large we removed as soon as possible and not being able to procure any Servant or more properly *help* I had to cook and perform all the duties of the house with the assistance of my Sister who was more successful in milking the Cows as I confess with all my labor for want of *knack* I could not get a drop of milk.—[243]

Never did we laugh more heartily than while thus occupied our perpetual blunders rendering the whole scene so ridiculous; but we were highly gratified when Mr Adams pronounced his Meals excellent— One of my Neigbours kindy relieved us of the milking department: and at the termination of three days we began our usual routine with the assistance of a boy and two females with my assistance occasionally and superintendence—

My brother came on from Washington and obtained a situation in the Office of Mr. Goodale & which he remained some time. Mr. Adams was much from home—And my Sister who was a general favorite was also much abroad. The one attending to law business: the other on visits to different friends in Boston so that keeping no Carriage I was often alone with my Children—

Some of our time was spent in the study of Botany and our rambles among the rocks and woods were sources of amusement under the direction and instruction of Mr Adams who entered heart and soul in the pursuit of plants and wild flowers while his unfruitful scholars profited very little from his lessons.

One morning while hearing Mr. Adams read a book of some interest to us, the children playing in the paddock close to us my eldest boy came running into the room and called his Aunt to come and see his little brother who had fallen into the water— at first she took little notice; but got up and went out to see what was the matter; when she found the Child had fallen head foremost into the Rain water Tub, and was in imminent danger of losing his life— She lifted him out had a fire made immediately; stripped and used warm frictions of hot Rum; and sent immediately for the Doctor— I wondering that she did not return, opened the door of the Room and beheld my beautiful boy as I thought in the agonies of death black in the face and struggling for breath— I could not faint: but my agony

[243] JQA and LCA arrived in Quincy on 5 April but did not move to JQA's birthplace until 18 April, after having some work done on the house. The other residents of the Old House at the time included CA's elder daughter, Susanna Boylston, and Louisa Catharine Smith. TBA would marry AHA on 16 May (D/JQA/27, 5, 8, 18 April, APM Reel 30).

at this sight could only be understood by *him* who has created his Creatures, and in whose hands is life and death—

The presence of mind of his Aunt produced the best effect; and in the evening the Child appeared to be out of all danger playing about the Room— In the morning he waked in a high fever and for two days he was entirely delirious in a raving fever: which the Doctor feared was an affection of the brain—but God in his mercy spared him to me and he entirely recovered— Mrs. Adams had gone on a journey but the kindness of the old Gentleman who came to us immediately full of the most affectionate anxiety; was stamped on my heart never to be forgotten. God Bless him for all his goodness to *me*.—

The House in which we lived was nearly tow miles from the Family and the neighbourhood was in many respects unpleasant there being two or three insane persons under no controul of whom we were very much afraid—

My health was wretched and the fear that I should have to leave my Children when I accompanied my Husband to Congress harassed my spirits and embittered my existence— Mrs. Smith came on to visit her Mother with her daughter Caroline and in her society I took delight—[244] Mrs. Adams was in every point of view a superior Woman: and I loved her and respected her sincerely— But I felt that there was too great a distance between her and myself on every point to admit of that tender and intimate intercourse which existed between myself and her during a two years residence which she made in England with her family where I had learnt to love her with the warmest affections— I had never seen her brothers and at that time there was no prospect whatever of my ever becoming acquainted with any one of the family—Accustomed both then and long afterwards to hear Mrs. Adams spoken of as something much above the common standard of her Sex when I became acquainted with her as her daughter I felt that even my husband must contrast wofully to my disadvantage and that idea humbled me so much in my own conciet every sense was paralysed and I felt only the consciousness of my own inferiority— Looked up to with love and admiration by my own family unaccustomed to the customs and usages of this Country sunk under the deepest depression of spirits at the loss of and the weight of his misfortunes, and the utter destitution of my family, I felt as an unwelcome intruder into that of my hus-

[244] Caroline Amelia Smith (1795–1852) married John Peter de Windt (1786–1870) in 1814.

band who could believe or understand that I was not aware of my Fathers difficulties before I married—and the idea that I was *suspected* of having "drawn him in" (as is vulgarly said) seemed an incubus that was pressing me to the earth and crushing every hope of happiness: and yet this very fancy perhaps produced the very effect which turned all my blessings into evil— Mrs. Smith was a lovely creature beautiful patient and long suffering she was a christian and bore every ill with that patient equanimity which proceeds from the heart and mind of a religious woman—practiced in all the virtues of severely tried humanity and although we never had even a conversation on the past or the present events of my life— There was something so considerate, so soothing, so encouraging in her conduct to me that she seemed whenever she was near me as a guardian Angel sent to console me in my errors, and to correct me in my mistakes.—

Naturally proud I was suspicious of every thing therefore always unreasonable: My Brother attributed my fathers misfortunes to the delay of marriage which had retarded his return to his at when his Affairs had been honorably arranged by his Creditors— For that time I had been engaged and Letter after Letter had arrived to persuade me to be ready at any time for Mr. Adams arrival as he would be obliged to leave England immediately and my wedding clothes had been a year when he came not an article being added thereto and these Letters were so pressing that as my father had fitted up a Vessel at great expense to take us to Lisbon which had waited a month I naturally supposed that I must fix an early day for the marriage so as that I might be with my Mother as a bride while I remained— But just a few days after the time fixed a change took place in Mr Adams's destination: and my husband was order'd to remain in London and wait for despatches: and a fortnight after my *marriage* my father stopped payment for the small sum of £500 after 26 years of high standing as a Merchant through the treachery of a *Friend* who had drawn him into ruin; himself being *protected* by a Seat in Parliament— My Father left England with his family and I was left behind to tremble at every knock at the door of the with Bills of my Father to be presented to a husband of two weeks old

E're yet the *honey* Moon her softest sweets had shed!

One female friend alone was left to me in England; and to her kindness I owed my life— Sorrow had blighted all my joy—and I was indeed condemned to be a mourning Bride— To Mr Rufus King I was ever grateful for much kindness, as long as he lived—

Such was my history! can any one wonder at the feelings which so beset me when I came to America! impossible! and the more kind my husband was: the more keen and bitter was the sense of injury that I unknowingly had inflicted on him—

The time came for our departure for Washington and true to my fears my Children were left behind.[245]

Mrs. Smith accompanied us to N.Y. The journey was dreadful I could not help grieving for my Children— It was my first Separation from them and my heart was almost broken but our finances were low and the Children were troublesome and I concieved that I had no *right* to refuse what Mr. Adams thought just— But however strong our sense of justice may be it bears very hard upon the feelings and affections when it is too strictly carried out— ~~Went to the Wharf in Phila but found the Packet gone with the bagage~~

We remained a couple of days with Mrs. Smith and then we pursued our dreary journey ~~home~~ to Washington to spend another Winter in the midst of political intrigue and party cabals in which I could not take the smallest interest— We found the family all well and ready to recieve us stayed five days in Philadelphia The Boat left us.

NOV. 29

Many changes had taken place in Congress both in the Senate and the House—Like marriage for better for worse, but not irrevocable—

DEC 2

Congress opened this day: Mr. Tracy Mr Israel Smith and Mr Chittenden came on with us from Baltimore Mr Tracy in very bad health— The Presidents Message was sent in and Mr Adams returned early from the Senate: and we went to dine with the Boyds.[246]

245 GWA spent the winter of 1805–1806 with Mary Smith Cranch; JA2 stayed with his grandparents (D/JQA/27, 8 Nov. 1805, APM Reel 30).

246 The new Congress met for the first time on 2 Dec., and the next day Thomas Jefferson's secretary delivered Jefferson's fifth annual message, which was read to those assembled (D/JQA/27, APM Reel 30).

7

General Miranda a very agreeable Gentlemanly man called on M^r. Adams with Letters from Col Smith– He was a Spaniard of some fame at the time–[247]

9

Capt Landais also visited M^r. Adams an old acquaintance of twenty years and more since they had met. Capt Ladais had been on board of the Frigate Alliance as Commander who was to have brought out M^r. Adams and my husband to America in the year 1779 and they had met at Nantz and Orleans and Brest– But so fresh was his memory that he recognized old Captain in one of the rooms in the Capitol and accosted by name–which much astonished the Captain as my husband was a mere boy at that period and had of course entirely out grown his knowledge or recollection– The change in the destination of the Vessel prevented their return in her– Capt Landais and Paul Jones had been bitter rivals in the revolutionary war Jones commanding the bon-Homme Richard–[248] They came home in the Frigate la Sensible– Mr Adams dined with the President where he first met the Tunisian Ambassador with his two Secretaries– After greeting the company he proposed to retire to smoke his Pipe but the President requested him to smoke it there– Many curious jokes were every day passing concerning this great personage which afforded much amusement to the Public– He was a geat admirer of handsome Women; and always insisted up holding them under his Cloak as it possessed many *virtues*–desireable to those without families.–[249] M^rs. Madison was his great favorite especially as she was the reigning Sultana at the Court of Mr Jeffer-

[247] For the participation of WSS and William Steuben Smith in Gen. Francisco de Miranda's 1806 expedition to liberate Venezuela from Spanish rule, see JA, *D&A*, 3:183.

[248] Pierre Landais (1734–1820). JQA noted that while he and JA were waiting to return to America in 1779, he "was then reading Don Quichotte de la Manche in the Cabin of the Frigate Alliance, or walking the Streets of Brest with Captain Landais." During the battle between John Paul Jones' *Bonhomme Richard* and the *Serapis,* Landais was in command of the *Alliance.* He failed to come to Jones' aid and in fact fired several broadsides into the *Bonhomme Richard.* In 1781 Landais was court-martialed and dismissed from the navy. In his later years he often visited Washington in the hope of obtaining prize money and restoration of his rank. On 14 March 1806 Congress voted to grant him $4,000 (JA, *Papers,* 8:17; *DAB*; D/JQA/27, 14 March, APM Reel 30).

[249] Sidi Soliman Melli Melli, the Tunisian minister, arrived in the United States in 1805 to resolve a dispute over restitution for ships seized by the United States. His exotic clothing caused a sensation, and his expectations of gifts and women, consternation (Joseph Wheelan, *Jefferson's War: America's First War on Terror, 1801–1805,* N.Y., 2003, p. 319–320).

son and he was lavish of his presents of Shawls Stuffs &ce to her and her friends–

11

The Assemblys began and I accompanied my Sisters– It was thin cold and comfortless it not being fashionable to attend the first. The only prominent object was the Ambassador.[250]

13

We passed the Even[g] at M[rs.] Harrisson's a very large party– M[rs] H was a lovely amiable woman liked by every body– Her husband was an old friend of my Fathers and first Comptroller. G W Campbell of Ten was there also one of the prominent men of the day more showy than agreeable–and M[r] Sheldon who bore an excellent character and was a great favorite in the family–

M[rs.] Simmonds was a beautiful French woman married to a most disagreeable man who seemed very jealous of her–but his own reputation for fidelity was un peu lashes and the world was not blind to his follies– I never heard of any misconduct on her part and she was a very interesting woman.–

19

M[r.] Verplanck and General Van Cortland frequently visited at the House the former had a high reputation for talents and was a fine writer. The latter was one of the kindest and most delightful old men that I have known: every way amiable he seemed to be every body's friend and was hailed with pleasure wherever he appeared–the girls all loved him; the Women all praised him and the men respected him–so that he met with a universal welcome–

25

Christmas day. Mess Tracy Dana and Lewis with M[r.] Sheldon dined with us– M[r.] Adams and my Sisters went with M[r] Verplanck

[250] Beginning in 1802 the Washington Dancing Assembly gave frequent dancing parties during the winter season (Gaillard Hunt, "American Society a Century Ago," *Harper's Monthly Magazine*, 129:847 [Nov. 1914]).

to visit the Vice President Clinton and Miss Clinton they were not at home and Mr Adams was so unwell he was obliged to retire early in the Even$^{g.}$ Mr Petry the Secretary of the French Legation was a fine old man and a great favorite—

A whole party of Cherokee Indians came in. No Gentlemen in the house we felt very disagreeably. They insisted on hearing the Piano which my Sister played for them. and we were obliged to give them beads and ribbands and Feathers before we could get rid of them— The house was so isolated that it was impossible to divest ourselves of fear: and we were truly thankful to see them depart.[251]

Went to the Capitol. The preaching wretched.— There is something so every way unsuitable to all Religious feeling of solemnity or propriety in the Hall *itself*; independent of its intriguing and wrangling associations that you cannot think of the purity of heaven in a place so altogether worldly: where corruption faces you in every corner and where all the bad passions betrayed in the week arise like Ghosts to haunt the imagination with the baseness of Vice or the exhibition of follies which ought to bear a harsher name—[252]

JAN 1ST. 1806

Went to the Presidents a great crowd drawn by curiosity to see the Tunisian Ambassador— There is something very singular in their Costume and appearance— It was not new to me as I had already known one at Berlin— But in our Country where the manners are so familiar there is nothing to restrain Strangers from taking liberties nor of that retenú which in Europe exacts certain attention to forms as a protection from licence or personal rudeness. The House of the President is considered as the House of the *People*—Much like a Tavern only that in the one your money buys respect and convenience— In fact in this Station you are considered a *debtor* and you are treated pretty much as a Bankrupt—for no payment that you can make is ever satisfactory—

[251] In December sixteen Cherokee chiefs arrived in Washington to discuss a land sale. They would conclude a treaty with the government on 8 Jan. 1806 (William Gerald McLoughlin, *The Cherokee Ghost Dance: Essays on the Southeastern Indians, 1789–1861*, Macon, Ga., 1984, p. 58–60).

[252] Public worship at the Capitol began in 1795 in a temporary structure. When the Capitol was completed, the chaplain of Congress or visiting ministers of different denominations presided from the Speaker's desk. In Feb. 1805 the Marine Band began playing in the gallery after services (Bryan, *Hist. of the National Capital,* 1:260, 606–607).

26

On this day M[rs.] & M Randolph had a Son— M[rs] Whitewood who came to see me had attended her professionally and gave me a most amusing account of her distresses— After the Baby was born she was desirous of giving her patient something like nourishment— It was night and she could not find a bit of bread to make a little panada or a scrap of meal to make a little gruel: nor a Servant in the house of whom she could get any thing— It was Bachelor Hall! and not a single convenience had been thought of for the Lady; and female domestics were scarce: as the President was too deeply imbued with french habits to practice the homespun domesticity of American— and out of the immediate company rooms the House neither exhibited cleanliness or comfort—[253]

M[rs] Randolph was only a *visitor* and did not interfere with its internal arrangements— M[r] Madison had a fall which injured his knee pan which we had not heard until to day— M[r] Adams had called on him and informed us he would soon be able to go out. M[r] Adams was laboriously engaged all this Month in Congress and spent a large portion of his time in his Chamber— My health was particularly delicate and my spirits worse—[254]

M[r] Bayard produced a great sensation in the Senate as an Orator—but I did not like him so well as M[r.] Otis, M[r] Tracy or M[r] Key— To me he was never an agreeable man—

Went to the Capitol heard M[r] Davis— As a place of worship it is odious to me— Spent the remainer of the day with My Sister Boyd.—

12 [*FEBRUARY*]

M[r] Pickering M[r] Tracy M[r] Dana and M[r] Harper with several other Gentlemen dined with us— It was the celebration of my birth day—

13

At a party at M[rs.] Madisons— She is the cynosure of all eyes—A really charming Woman—A Quaker in education possessing a perfect equanimity of temper and manners:—possessing great influence

[253] James Madison Randolph, the second son of Martha Jefferson and Thomas Mann Randolph, was born in the president's house (*Notable Amer. Women*).

[254] LCA was pregnant.

in Society and considerable interest in the political world which she was said to *use* with much discretion— The Foreign Ministers were at her feet: and the world seemed to bow before her— Dancing never was allowed there: but music and cards were the mode of entertainment—and the then seldom consisting of more than seventy or eighty persons were very unpretend social and agreeable

17

My Mother and Sisters went to a Ball at M^rs. Merry's— M^r & I were not invited and we passed the even^g at home— Politics ran very high and Mr Adams acted a very leading part during the Session[255] Mrs Merry was a very showy and vulgar woman who assumed great airs on her husbands Station— Her conversation was coarse and her manner frequently insulting— She told my Mother that she had ordered a great deal of *hog meat* for the supper as the americans must have it on all occasions: but she had made a stipulation with her Cook that he should disguise it in every possible form *it was so vulgar* Yet this fine *Lady* made her husband accompany the Butler with his tray to every individual in the Room while she flirted with the most prominent men or withdrew from the general company to play Chess with John Randolph who she told him she did not consider *a man*.[256] This LADY of high pretentions was said to have been a Bar Maid at a tavern in Norfolk who charmed a rich country Squire who married her died soon after; and left her a large fortune—after which she married Merry who was *poor* for the sake of his rank in the Corps Diplomatique— This was the history told at the time—perhaps scandal—

MARCH

Judge Marshall and were two of the most charming men I ever knew in any Country—[257] they possessed a suavity of manner so prepossing it was impossible to know them and not to love them— Poli-

[255] During the first session of the 9th Congress, which ran from 2 Dec. 1805 to 21 April 1806, JQA served on several committees, including those concerned with revising the articles of war, making appropriations for roads west to the Ohio River, revising the Senate rules, settling Georgia land claims, and establishing the Library of Congress (Bemis, *JQA*, 1:125).

[256] John Randolph was slightly built, had no beard, and spoke in a high-pitched voice (*DAB*).

[257] LCA failed to include the name of the other man.

ticks were grown more vexed every and the Spanish Minister Yrujo seemed to be very troublesome and partially sustained by the Diplomats who at almost every Court from a real Esprit de Corps support each other in questions of difficulty unless at War with the Offender—[258] They are generally a restless set ready to teaze the Governments to which they are sent on the most trivial occasions and often prove very vexatious friends in a Country where the rules and ettiquettes of Courts cannot be established— The French Minister was a brute who on the ground of Mr Jefferson's admiration of the French Revolution and its atrocities was obliged to submit without notice to all the scandalous scenes practiced by the man and tamely to bow to his gross effrontery lest la Belle France should show her indignation—

13

Gen Tureau passed the Eveng. and brought his Violin— He accompanied my Sister Hellen who was an elegant performer on the Piano and to our astonishment proved himself a Master of sweet sounds. Another Nero! I passed the Eveng with my Sister Boyd.

15

Went to the Methodist meeting at George Town. How is it possible that Religion can be so perverted: and yet how fascinating to the illiterate and ignorant is the rhapsodical vehemence of a noisy uneducated man in the earnestness of his jestures and the seeming heartiness of his prayers to excite their feelings and ensure attention!

MARCH 23

I was very alarmingly ill this day and confined to my Chamber The news of Mr Pitts death caused some sensation to day—[259]

[258] Carlos Martínez de Irujo, Marquis of Casa Irujo, served as Spanish minister from 1796 to 1808, when the United States and Spain were in an extended dispute over the legitimacy of the Louisiana Purchase and the borders of Florida (*Repertorium*, 3:445; Junius P. Rodriguez, ed., *The Louisiana Purchase: A Historical and Geographical Encyclopedia*, Santa Barbara, Calif., 2002).

[259] William Pitt the younger, prime minister of Great Britain, died on 23 Jan. 1806 (*DNB*).

26

M[r] & M[rs.] Boyd M[r] Tracy M[r] Pitkin and M[r] Stedman passed the Eveng with us such Evengs. were always delightful

30

Went to the Capitol: heard M[r] Hargrove Sweedenborgian.— I do not like this diversity of doctrine— Perhaps while they amuse they shake the principles by filling the mind with new and strange ideas—

APRIL

Nothing remarkable occurred this Month I was constantly sick and M[r.] Adams determined to leave me in Washington as it was deemed dangerous for me to travel in my situation— Thus I was doomed to a separation from husband and children for Months to avoid a risk which the anguish of my mind was just as likely to produce— But the fiat of my Physician was not to be disputed and I was compelled to stay—

26

M[r] Adams left Washington on his return to the north with M[r] Tracy M[r.] Dana, and M[r.] Gilman and Arrived at Baltimore that night—

My time passed heavily almost always indisposed and only able to mix with the family occasionally— Occasional company in the Eveng. and gentle exercise in a Carriage varied the Scene my Sister Hellens health being as delicate as my own: and my only comfort was Letters from Boston—[260]

JUNE 29

Thus past the months of May and June—until the 21st when my Sister sent me word that her Child was dying— Having no Carriage and the request being pressing I walked over to my Sister Boyds a long Mile to see her: and while I was there the poor Baby died after struggling to live for several Month's in a state of constant suffer-

[260] Nancy Johnson Hellen was also pregnant. She gave birth to MCHA in September.

ing—[261] I walked home at eight or nine o clock in the Evening and at 3 oclock in the afternoon of the next day under circumstances of the most imminnent danger gave birth to a dead Child with the Thermometer at a hundred and neither Father or Children near me to console me for my sufferings—[262]

My health returned rapidly the kind nursing of my Mother and Sisters did much to renovate me: but the hope of soon seeing was the real panacea I must fairly acknowledge that I was not patriotic enough to endure such heavy personal trials for the political welfare of the Nation whose honors was dearly bought at the expense of all domestic happiness— But alas! how little can we foresee the events that are to befal us in this world and if we do foresee them how seldom can or will we make any effort to guard against them

JULY 26

On the 26 of July I started with my Sister under the protection of Com Hull for Boston and passed night at Baltimore— We there went to the Methodist Church where I witnessed a scene that was perfectly undescribable—and I will not attemp to paint it— The House was the best I ever was in but I do not recollect the name of it— my wedding day.

Sometime before the birth of my Child Mrs Merry introduced at our house the celebrated Thomas Moore The Author of Anacreon and a number of very beautiful Songs The loves of the Angells L'alla-Rock &c &c and the Judge Family— I heard him sing many of his Songs and two or three Evengs. sang with him— He said that I sang delightfully but I wanted *Soul*— He appeared to be the of Love and his style was so full of sentiment it would not have been very becoming or suitable for Ladies generally to echo his tones or the expression of his words or his manner! Warmed by his devotion to music and to his worship of the Muse delicacy appeared cold and

[261] Harriet Johnson Boyd's infant son Archibald died on 11 July.

[262] In her letter to JQA of 23 June, not found, LCA reported the stillbirth of their child. In his response of 30 June, JQA wrote that he received the letter when he was not alone. "On perusing it, I was barely able to preserve that appearance of tranquillity which could conceal the immediate impression upon my heart; I hurried hither to the retirement of my own chamber, where I could indulge the weakness, which the bitterest of sorrows is forbidden to discover to the world. . . . If the tears of affliction are unbecoming a Man; Heaven will at least accept those of gratitude from me, for having preserved you to me." JQA also suggested that LCA spend the rest of the summer in Boston (Adams Papers).

propriety formal and he could find no pleasure in the modesty of judicious restraint— As a companion he was delightful and we regretted that his stay was so *short*—

27

At Baltimore we met M[r] William Duer who was lodging at Barney's and D[r.] Davis and there was one other Passenger all of whom joined our party and we travelled together to Philadelphia—[263] Overcome by fatigue and weakness I fell into a succession of faintings which made it neccessary for me to remain a day.—

Towards evening I was so much better that I insisted upon continuing our journey the next morning and decided to pass the night at Princeton—

29.

Arrived there very weak and exhausted and President and M[rs.] Smith and her daughters a delightful family came to see me at the tavern and insisted on my going to their house and would take no denial—[264] Every kind attention was shown to me by these excellent persons and I can never forget the attention and sympathy displayed towards me by M[r.] Duer throughout the journey to New York—

31

In the morning after a good Breakfast we took leave M[rs.] Smith and the young Ladies one of whom was engaged to be married to M[r] Duer and arrive at my Sister Smiths who immediate recieved us my Sister and myself and was as ever lavish in her attention and care of the poor weak invalid— We remained with M[rs] Smith four days. I very quiet but my Sister Caroline in the enjoyment of all the sights that New York produces—

[263] William Alexander Duer (1780–1858), a New York judge and educator, was president of Columbia College from 1829 to 1842 (*DAB*).

[264] Samuel Stanhope Smith (1751–1819), a clergyman and educator, was president of the College of New Jersey from 1795 to 1812. He and Ann Witherspoon, daughter of John Witherspoon, president of the college from 1768 to 1794, were married in 1775 and had nine children (*Colonial Collegians*).

5 [8 *AUGUST*]

We sailed in the Packet for Newport and had such a stormy and dangerous passage that Com Hull to the management of the Vessel out of the hands of the *Capt* who he threatened to put in rons for his bad behavior and we did reach Newport on account of the Storm until very late on the night of the 7th. and to remain there till the next the whole of which was passed in beating up to Providence— There we passed the Night under the care of Mr Jarvis and proceeded as far as Walpole

10

and the next day arrived in Boston and passed the night at Whitcombs at Concert Hall— Mr Adams was glad to meet us and I was in an agony to be restored to my Children—

11

We went out to Quincy and were kindly greeted but my Children recieved me as a stranger and I was almost forgoten After dinner we moved to our own house and arranged every thing as well as we could for our accommodation— little or nothing had been done even in the arrangement of the Furniture and we had only a small boy to do anything for us for two or three days— God gave us strength and we soon became comfortable— Mrs. Judge Adams who lived with the Old Gentleman had given birth to a daughter on the 29 of July and of course they could not accommodate *me*.[265]

John would go back to his Grandmothers and it was with great difficulty that I could keep him at home—

14TH

Three or four days of labour and I was able to accompany my husband to Cambridge when he attended his Class. It was very fatiguing but the success of an experiment which I had not approved and very much mistrusted was a sufficient reward—[266] On one of thes occasions I saw several of the Proffessors; and Mr Hedge spoke

[265] Abigail Smith Adams (1806–1845).

[266] JQA had been appointed the first Boylston Professor of Rhetoric and Oratory at Harvard in Aug. 1805.

very highly of my Brother as a Scholar; and expressed his regret that he had left the College; as he would certainly have left it with the highest honors had he completed his education— It was singular that M[r] Johnson had not called on the Proffessor: but he felt the sting of poverty too bitterly to expose himself

"To the prouds man's contumely"[267]

So often exhibited in that said Institution of Harvard: where assuredly the purse strings of the wealthy are closely watched: and where Scholars are only *made* through the worship of the Golden Calf—or for some political *magnanimity* towards an old established *power*. This union of politics and purse is very *weighty*— The Idol set up are of a very vaccilating character: but on the *main* point they are always true: and their significancy is felt and understood by the devotees—the Gold ever in Statu quo.

But enough! Such digressions are useless.

16

We were much alarmed at a fall that our dear boy John had out of bed; in which he bruised his head sadly, and cut his lip— He soon went to sleep afterwards and we hoped that he was not much hurt—

M[rs.] Adams was quite ill— And the colored man in returning from Boston was thrown from his Cart, and run over—Fortunately not much hurt— He was an old Servant of the family—formerly a Slave—[268] The time passed very quietly— Often at the Old President's where we met the Family and were much with the Judges Wife, who was a very fine woman— The had a pretty little girl of whom they were very proud— It was the first Child—

27

At six o clock accompanied M[r] Adams to Cambridge through Boston— Arrived at D[r] Waterhouses where we met the Judge and Caro-

[267] Levi Hedge, for whom see CFA, *Diary*, 1:122, had been a philosophy tutor at Harvard when Thomas Baker Johnson attended. The line from Shakespeare, *Hamlet,* Act III, scene i, line 71, suggests that Johnson left the school due to a lack of funds; however, his father told William Cranch that he felt training in an Annapolis lawyer's office would be of greater benefit than a Harvard education to a young man who planned to work in Maryland (Cranch to AA, 4 June 1798, Adams Papers).

[268] William Abdee, who had married Phoebe, the former slave of Rev. William Smith and the longtime servant and tenant of AA and JA (D/JQA/27, 16 Aug., APM Reel 30; *AFC*, 7:75).

line—[269] We went to the Chapel and took our Seats— The performances began at eleven and closed at three: literally to me on the stool of *repentance*— Then went to dine with Mrs. T K Jones; an elegant dinner; laid out under a large Canvass Pavillion in honor of her Son, who had graduated that day with destinction— There were about 300 Persons—[270] My Sister returned to Boston with Mrs Danforth her friend. We returned to Dr Waterhouses where we passed an agreeable Eveng.

28

Mr Adams took me to see the Library; Philosophy, chamber (I picked up nothing that ever served me) and to the museum— Aand at 12 o clock went to the Phi Beta and heard a Poem from Mr Whitwell and an Oration by T B Adams his manner always good but his voice not loud enough— When the exercises were finished we dined at Dr Waterhouses again— Never was a greater Original seen! He always put me in mind of the Mountebank Quack Dôctors that I had see so often in England; with a Clown playing tricks to amuse the people; while the Charlatan sold his wares and filled his pocket— He was a man possessed of great learning but full of Paradoxes—full of wit, satirical, mordant in his invective, he yet was kind hearted, charitable, and beneficent— And his name stands recorded next to Jenner as a Saviour in the distruction of the direful Pestilence Small Pox which was so destructive in various forms to mankind— His Lady was a superior Woman of sweet manners: but she had the anxious look that all women who have married men who stand out as marks of singularity before the Public: and who always have something about them *out of Place*.

SEPT

"For the rain it raineth every day with a High
ho![”][271]

[269] For the physician Benjamin Waterhouse's career and long friendship with the Adamses, see *AFC*, 4:32–34.

[270] Polly Morton Jones, the wife of Boston merchant Thomas Kilby Jones, hosted the commencement party for her son, Thomas Morton Jones (1787–1857) (Boston, *30th Report*, p. 88; "Records of the West Church, Boston," *NEHGR*, 92:119 [April 1938]; *Harvard Quinquennial Cat.*). Such elaborate commencement parties were a longstanding Harvard tradition; for one given by Mary Smith Cranch in 1787 to honor her son, William, and JQA, see *AFC*, 8:121, 132–133.

[271] Shakespeare, *Twelfth Night*, Act V, scene i, line 401.

Went into Boston with Mr Adams on business returned in the Evening took George with us— The weather dreadful—

8

Went in the Even to a dancing masters Ball— I went as *I* thought very *smart*: but my toilet did not please— It was much too simple for the occasion; as I found many elaborate Costumes very different from what I expected; and in a *taste* altogether new to me— The Dancing Master himself appeared as a Zéphir; and wore a suit of the lightest colored Nankin; with a broad Pink Persian Sash across his Shoulders, fastened at the side with a large bow, Silk Stockings, black Shoes with large Rosettes the color of the Sash!! A short time after my entrance, wearing a small white french lace Cap ornamented on one side with a delicate bunch of Morss Roses; with a simple white India Muslin dress; a pink belt to match the flowers in my Cap and bouquet; & pink Satin Shoes. A Lady of about sixty without a Cap and dressed in a Lace Veil worn as a Nuns; was handed in at arms length by the dancing Cupidon; and I felt quite abashed by the ecstacies of admiration thus excited, in contrast to my negative appearance— My Sister and I however hid our blushing heads (to laugh) and got through the dance as well as we could with the contemptuous glances cast at us.

For two or three days after I had some lectures, and apologized for not knowing better— The error was utter *ignorance* on my part— The time was dull: frequent stiff set parties; my youngest Child sick: and was very uneasy about him: but his complaint was worms and he got better though his health fluctuated.

M^r^ & Mrs. Harper, Mrs Caton, her two daughters, Mr Rogers, Mr. Shaw, and Mr Bowdoin & M^r^ R Sullivan—came to see me.

I was making and baking Cake, and was obliged to *dress* before I could appear— The rooms of my house were literally too small to hold my company.— These Ladies were the elite of Baltimore—[272] There was something truly ridiculous in my position— The shaking off of the kitchen drapery for the parlour finery; and the assumption of the fashionable manners of my Station: was such a transition: as

[272] Catherine Carroll had married Robert Goodloe Harper, a Baltimore lawyer and politician, in 1801. Her sister Mary had married Richard Caton, an Englishman, in Baltimore in 1786. Three of their daughters married English noblemen, and the fourth married the British consul at Baltimore (*DAB*; Rufus Wilmot Griswold, *The Republican Court; or, American Society in the Days of Washington*, rev. edn., N.Y., 1856, p. 208–210).

robes Cinderella as a Princess; and I could scarcely fancy that the smoke spots had left me *fair*; when I presented myself to the company— M$^{rs.}$ Harper had lived with my family in England and knew full well what I was used to— My boy was so beautiful he took all the shine off his Mother, and she felt no jealousy on the occasion— My Sister was much acquainted with them: and had often staid at Mr Carrolls at Carrolton—

I undertook to drive my Sister Caroline to Weymouth to pay some visits the two Children were with us. We were going very gently up a Lane when a man came by with a red Wheelbarrow.— In an instant the Horse started and flew right up the bank; when we all found ourselves lying in the Road— Fortunately the horse satisfied with his *noble daring*: stood still, and I flew to my Children to ascertain their state. George had recieved no damage; but John had a heavy blow on his head which made him cry fearfully. My Sister and myself recieved severe contusions on the arms, and I one on the side of my face— As the accident occurred near the house of Dr Tuffts, we went there and had our bruises examined; and poor John got some cake and ceased crying, although the hurt on his head was considerable— ~~D$^{r.}$ Tuffts drove us home and~~ the Man took George and my Sister so that they arrived at our house without farther trouble— M$^{r.}$ Adams ~~was from home and did not hear of it until we had quite recovered from the fright~~ and came to the Dôctors and took John and myself home—

28

Went to meeting and afterwards dined at the old House accompanied by my Sister, children and husband— We returned early in the evening M$^{r.}$ Adams is quite a Gardiner; and we are all learning to *bud* and *graft*—

30

The month ended with dreadful weather— It was varied by occasional Parties: one at our *own house*, and others in the town— They were always *full* dressed; plenty of Cake and fruit; a number of Ladies; few Gentlemen; and Mosquito's in abundance: and they usually broke up at nine o'clock— Mr Adams spent most of his Evenings at his Fathers—

OCT 1ST

Miss H Welsh came out to see us— She is a woman of strong mind; masculine manners; and one of those ever busy persons who in the earnest desire to assist every body; continually creates confusion and mars their undertakings—

4

M^r^ & Mrs. Adams and the family and M^r^ & Mrs. Cranch dined with us and we had company in the Evening—

7

A party to German Town— In the Evening went to Tea with the family at the old house—

8

Mr. Adams as usual went to Cambridge and in consequence of a change in the hours he was obliged to sleep at Dr Waterhouses—

The old Gentleman often called in the morning to see us and was always very kind and affectionate—

After Mr Adams left us my John was taken ill with a sore throat and fever from which I also was suffering but towards evening was much better and recovering when my Husband returned

Miss Èdes was a lively agreeable girl very amusing in conversation She came to take tea with us accompanied by Miss Welsh.

Mr Adams is constantly immersed in business and of course seldom at home— The cares of his family become very oppressive to him and again it is concluded that I am to stay behind and he is seeking some place in Boston where he can board us.

Mr Adams and my Sister went to a party at Mrs. Beales in the Even^g.^ I remained at my Fathers with my Sister whose dear little girl was dangerously ill—And returned with them—

Went to Boston with Mrs. Adams and returned— Called to see how my Sisters baby was; found it still very ill, but Mrs. Harrod her Mother came out and we returned to tea. My Son was still quite unwell and I was in a state of great anxiety— The illness of M^rs.^ T B Adam's's Infant kept in a state of great alarm; and my Sister and myself devoted all the time we could spare to assist her in her cares—

23

M^r. Adams returned from Boston and brought out the news of the death of M^rs W Smiths youngest Child John with the Croup— It has been sick for some days but never thought dangerously ill until this day— My Sister Caroline went into Boston to stay a week with Miss Welsh— Miss Edes came to spend some days with me during my Sisters absence Miss Edes and M^r. Adams went out to walk I was too unwell to go— When returning from his Fathers the Boy met him and he hurried home as I had fainted, but soon recovered—

31.

Mr Adams drove me to Boston with John— We travelled the whole ride with the Snow blowing in our faces— I was left at Concert Hall; and he proceeded to Cambridge— In the Evening I went to see my Sister, and took Tea at Doctor Welsh's: Mr Adams came there and we walked back together to Concert Hall where we passed the Night— We returned home in the Evening after M^r. Adams came from Cambridge and were fortunate in getting home safe—

NOV 7

Time wore on with the usual course of the family: constant interchanges of social visits as far as strength and weather would permit: My house was two miles from my fathers residence; and it was a dreary walk in the long Evenings: and we possessed nothing in the shape of a Carriage and I was very delicate in health and weak in mind.

Mr Adams went into Boston and Cambridge and procured lodgings for us in a Street which we none of us ever heard of and every thing as usual was fixed without a word of consultation with the Family— The House belonged to a Mr Gulliver— He was to board us and we were to furnish the apartments and to keep a Man and a Maid Servant— And there we were to remain while he passed the Winter in the Sunshine of Washington—[273]

On returning from Boston in a Chaise that Mr Adams drove my Sister lost a Basket containing all her best dresses jewels &ce— They did not miss it for some time: then retraced their steps and went

[273] Benjamin Gulliver, a purveyor of West Indian goods, lived on Poplar Street (D/JQA/27, 6 Nov., APM Reel 30; *Boston Directory*, 1807, Shaw-Shoemaker, No. 12180).

nearly back to Boston but all in vain as they have never been heard of— The loss was very heavy but she bore it with great equanimity and distinguished herself by her conduct in this instance as she has done through life— Every preparation made we took leave of the family

13

We went this day into Boston in the Stage and Mr Adams took me to see the lodgings that he had procured for us— The House was pretty and new, but the distance from all habitations and from every friend and acquaintance barred us out from all Society and at that Season it was gloomy beyond description— But the agreement was made and there was no retracting: and the time was fixed for us to enter on *Gullivers travels*—

We returned to Quincy that night to sleep and the next day we packed up for our speedy removal— The Children were sent away and all was confusion

15

Our Furniture went into Boston— We being in a most uncomfortable plight and fatigued to exhaustion as I had but one assistant—

16

It poured with rain and we continued our wearisome employment while M^r. Adams gave directions about the Farm &c to his brother who was to manage his property during his absence—

18

We left Quincy this morning after breakfast in the Stage: myself Caroline and the girl Sally Cleverly who lived with us— While we sat at breakfast we were annoyed by a strong smell of fire: and looking round in every direction we discovered, that a red hot coal from the wood fire was burning the floor under my Sisters Chair and that her woollen garment was much injured— We arrived safe in Boston and took possession of our apartments— George went with *us*; but John was left at his Grand Mothers— We worked very earnestly to get fixed—

19

At eight o clock Mr Adams left us in the Hartford Stage to return to Washington: and we were left to make the best of our strange possition— It was a trial but I could not leave my *Children*—

During our sejours in this *Street*: we had but little variety we saw but few person's Mr Shaw the only Gentleman who visited us— My boys were in a constant state of excitement at the burning of O Selfridge in Effigy; who Shot young Austin in the Street: and the boys collected at the Mill Pond in mobs to practice these hanging matters much to their delight and *my* trouble—[274] One Eveng. at the earnest invitation of Miss Grey my Sister and I went to take tea with her where we met a very small company— As we got out of the Carriage I percied that the Maid looked agitated and I immediately asked what was the matter? were the Children well? and entering the House I found that she had left a Candle burning on a toilet Table; the Muslin over which has caught fire spreading to the Window Curtains and even to the Childens Beds— Fortunately the Woman was in the Parlor giving them their Supper; and they thus escaped; mercifully escaped a dreadful calamity— Mr Gulliver and the man Servant soon quenched the flames by tearing down the Curtains and making a free use of Water and my Boys were soon sleeping sweetly by me as I kept them in a Bed close to my own—

Miss Hanah Adams the Authoress came to visit me several times She was one of the most remarkable Women of the Age— The World was to her a vacuum— She breathed in it and had her being— But Books were the only things that she appeared to delight in; and her learning was of a very abstruse sort which fitted her for a companion to My Father Adams and his Son: but which overwhelmed one so ill taught as myself— She was peculiar in her appearance, her manners her conversation—So absent that to find her way in Boston it was only when starting from a given point that she could find her way and she was always obliged to have some one to take her to that given point on her return or she would lose herself—

One Evening she came to Tea and after talking of several writers Rousseau was named— To my utter astonish Miss Hanah burst forth in the most enthusiastic strain on *his* Abellard and Eloise: and the

[274] Thomas O. Selfridge, a Boston lawyer, had been embroiled in a dispute with Benjamin Austin. After Austin's son Charles accosted Selfridge in the street and beat him with a stick, Selfridge shot and killed him. Selfridge was tried for murder and acquitted (*Trial of Thomas O. Selfridge . . . for Killing Charles Austin*, 2d edn., Boston, 1807, Shaw-Shoemaker, No. 11474).

whole Evening she continued in a Strain of poétic fervor almost startling to an imagination warm even as mine— The contrast between the Woman and this rapt effusion would have been ridiculous had not she displayed its beauty in its rapt elation— This was the only time I ever heard *her* converse in this strain in my life and I really felt proud to have had the power to draw out a mind of such strength and such purity—[275]

FEB 12 [*1807*]

Mrs. Adams sent for us to Quincy to go to an Assembly there— My Sister had recently lost a Child and I was not very willing to go;[276] but arranged a Dress of Grey Muslin trimmed with black velvet and bugle fringe with a black bugle tiara on my head— Alas! when I appeared my dress was utterly contemned and my good looks in my own eyes terribly depreciated— All the other Ladies were praised proportion to my default— But few traces of beauty were left in me and my Husband was away so that there was nothing to excite my vanity on the occasion My Sister Adams was suffering severely as a Nurse and the old Lady and Gentleman did not go to Balls

My Sister was charming and looked sweetly— We all went to the Ball and I danced down the first dance with the Judge who was in high spirits but was so faint when I got through the very long Country dance I was obliged to sit still the rest of the Evening The Supper was substantial and inviting and Mrs Judge Adams myself Miss Smith and my Sister got home at twelve very much exhausted—

16

Every body appeared in exuberant spirits and some of the family did not get home until three o clock in the morning— We remained at my Fathers until the following Monday and then returned to Town.—

Our good hostess presented her husband with a little girl and we were left to the tender mercies of the Servant; and though we did not meet with the Brobdignags; we assuredly became very familiar with the Lilliputian Meals; which became "so small and beautifully

[275] For Hannah Adams, see JA, *D&A*, 3:243; *AFC*, 9:240.

[276] Walter Hellen (b. 1804), the son of Nancy Johnson and Walter Hellen, had died on 19 December.

less," that we were obliged to procure provisions from Concert Hall for a supply.—

21

We walked out every day and occasionally the Miss Welsh's came and frequently the Dr. also and we generally stopped at Concert Hall to procure something for the Children or at the Confectioners Mrs Nichols on our way—[277] Thus passed the month of February with the exception of another visit to Quincy, and one or two short visits from the family to see us for a few hours

March as usual was very Cold, and as Mrs. Gulliver found it very inconvenient to keep us: we moved as soon as we could into a house at the corner of Nassaw Street and Frog Lane which looked into the Mall and took possession on the 16—[278] Nothing was arranged and our situation was thoroughly uncomfortable— At about eleven o'clock at Night we were roused by a cry of fire and Persons knocking at the door and were obliged to take Water upon the roof which is flat and have the hot Cinders swept off the door steps and in this way we all took violent and Coughs and became quite sick—

18 [*MARCH*]

And on this day when Mr. Adams arrived from Washington he met with a most uncomfortable reception and the return to his family under such circumstances was any thing but agreeable— He immediately however sent for his Sister and her daughter and we accomodated her as well as we could— In the morning they left for Quincy—[279]

A great part of our Furniture had to come from Quincy and we could make no final arrangement of our house until they arrived—

My situation was very delicate— Threatened with Consumption

[277] Possibly a member of the Nichols family who in 1816 would run a confectionery on Court Street (Chauncey M. Depew, ed., *One Hundred Years of American Commerce*, 2 vols., N.Y., 1895, 2:625).

[278] JQA bought the property at the corner of Nassau Street and Frog Lane (later Boylston Street) in June 1806. The Adamses lived there when in Boston from 16 March 1807 until 5 Aug. 1809 (JQA to LCA, 13 July 1806, Adams Papers; D/JQA/27, 18 March 1807, APM Reel 30; D/JQA/28, 5 Aug. 1809, APM Reel 31).

[279] JQA arrived in Boston at 9 P.M. with AA2 and her son John Adams Smith and daughter, Caroline Amelia Smith. Unaware that LCA had moved, he first went to the Concert Hall. When he arrived at Nassau Street, he found the house unsettled and JA2 quite ill (D/JQA/27, 15, 18 March 1807, APM Reel 30).

and with great and constant pain in the side and most violent Cough I was almost unfited for severe duty and the fatigue and exposure was very trying to my Constition—[280] Thus afflicted; with sick Children to take charge of I was almost entirely confined to the House until June, and it was two or three weeks before my husband could get any quiet— His attendance at Cambridge was constant and he with my Sister participated in the pleasures of society—and passed almost every week at Quincy going early Saturday afternoon and returning on Monday— My poor John was very sickly in consequence of an Emetic having been administered to him by Dr Welshs own hand which caused him to throw up blood.—

JUNE 1ST.

Mr Andrew Buchanan a Widower in Baltimore made an offer of marriage to my Sister which she accepted; and he was invited to come on and stay with us; where the marriage should take place when he should have made the necessary arrangements to recieve his Wife at home— My house was so small I could not invite the family and my situation made it impossible for me to make any show about it— The bans were published all the forms settled— My time passed in occasional visits to my friends: and from them as well as from the family who sometimes staid three or four days at a time—

JULY 16

Mr. Adams the Judge came to pass the day and night— As he was leading me down to dinner my foot slipped and I fell; but fortunately for me he caught me by the Arm and saved me from going to the bottom— The jar however proved very injurious he staid the Night with us and left us next morning— Mr Adams had a new occupation and his time was still more absorbed—[281]

[280] LCA was pregnant with CFA, who was born on 18 August.

[281] JQA was one of seven commissioners the selectmen of Boston charged with concluding an agreement with the Boston Mill Corporation for filling in the Mill Pond, located in the triangle between Craigie's Bridge and the Charles River Bridge. On 24 July the commissioners executed the deed to be submitted to the town for ratification. By the terms of the agreement, the pond was to be filled within twenty years with soil from Beacon Hill at the expense of the corporation, and the town would receive an eighth of the new land area (Walter Muir Whitehill, *Boston: A Topographical History*, 2d edn., Cambridge, 1968, p. 78–79; D/JQA/27, 24 July, APM Reel 30).

I became very ill in consequence of my fall, but recovered soon— My sister passed a week at Quincy with Mr Tom Greenleafs Family Kind and excellent persons for whom I have ever felt the since-respect and regard—[282] Mr & Mrs. Adams passed the day and night with us the Child is very sickly— They returned to Quincy in the morning— Mrs. Adams is a woman whose mind has been highly cultivated and is celebrated for beauty— Versed in all the duties of a *bon Menage* she forms a most striking contrast to poor me; who know but little of it— And it was certainly not in London or at the Court of Prussia that I could learn the management of a Quincy establishment— I did the best I could and God mercifully requires no more of us if we do it with faith and good will—

19

Mr Buchanan arrived from Baltimore— He passed the Evening with us and the next day all was arranged and the day fixed— He could not dine with us but promised to stay with us every day at meals until the event took place— He was a most amusing and good humoured being—but I feared that my Sister was taking cares upon herself which she would find too oppressive; he having four children by his first Wife the daughter of Gov Mc·Kein and Sister of Madame Yruco; and not being in good business—But he had offered himself to her when she was a beautiful girl of sixteen and she had rejected him—and it was natural that she should be flattered by an affection which so tacitly acknowledged her worth—

21

The Judge and his Wife with Mrs. Smith and her daughter were invited as well as Mrs Adams and the Ex President— Between eight and nine in the Evening Andrew Buchanan was married to my Sister Carolina Virginia Marylanda Johnson— Miss Welsh was bride-maid— Mr. Hall and Mr Shaw, ~~their attendants~~ Miss Smith, and Susan Adams; Mr Emmerson the Clergyman[283] with Dr Welsh and his Lady were the company present at the Ceremony; and John

[282] Thomas Greenleaf (1767–1854), moderator of the Quincy town meeting, and Mary Deming Price Greenleaf (1767–1856?) had four children (Greenleaf, *Greenleaf Family*, p. 95–96, 210; Sprague, *Braintree Families*).

[283] William Emerson (1769–1811), minister of the First Church of Boston (*DAB*).

Smith was the groomsman—and the house was full of Company during the Even[g]— All the Quincy friends staid the *Night* as well as the Bride and Bridegroom.— No presents were offered or recieved— Our supper was pretty but the accommodation *every* way small—

22

A company of young Ladies and Gentlemen this Even[g]— M[rs.] Adams M[rs.] Smith and my boy John returned to Quincy: and Judge and M[rs.] Adams came in the afternoon: and the party danced until midnight— John Smith came to the Wedding but returned to Quincy after supper and came back again in the morning to be at the dance— We had a bed on the floor in the Nursery; and were glad to get back to our Chamber—

23

Rose much exhausted being so near my confinement which was hourly expected Miss Smith Susan & Caroline left us this morning for Quincy—

24

M[r] Adams walk'd to Cambridge as usual— M[r] & M[rs] Buchanan Charlotte Welsh and John Smith went out in a Carriage to hear the Lecture, and to see the Colleges, Libraries &c— &c— and they dined at D[r] Welsh's—did not return until night— M[r] Adams as usual dined at Cambridge, and never returned until Evening. George went to School—

25

My Sister and I passed the day alone with the exception of morning visits— The Gentlemen having gone to Quincy to a great Agricultural dinner given by the Ex President who entertained very elegantly—[284]

[284] JA served as president of the Massachusetts Society for Promoting Agriculture from 1805 to 1812 (*Transactions of the Massachusetts Society for Promoting Agriculture*, Boston, 1858, p. 42, 52).

26

After Church M^r & M^rs. Buchanan and John Smith dined at Dr Welsh's—and the whole family spent the Even^g. with us. Married ten years this day—

27

The Gentlemen dined with Mr Emmerson. met there Col Bomford and M^r. Lee— Went to see Fanneiul Hall[285] The Bridal party took Tea at M^rs. W Smith's—an excellent friend of mine and the family.

29

We had a company to dine with us—Mr Boylston, Dr Welsh, Mr Emmerson, Mr Kendall, Mr Shaw, M^r J Hall, Dr Rogers, and M^r. Shaw and Dr Waterhouse— The Gentlemen were very social and did not leave the table until after dark— We ladies did not dine with them—

It was so essential for Ladies at that time to superintend *all* the arrangemants of a dinner both in the culinary and the fixing departments; that they were oftten obliged to keep behind the Scenes—and though they did not publickly wait on their Lords as the Indian *Ladies* do: they certainly labored as hard and as positively: with less paint to shield their faces from the Steams of Ovens and Stewpans— O the Cakes that have been spoiled and Pies burned!!

30

M^r & M^rs. Buchanan and Charlotte Welsh went to pass the day at Quincy: they returned home early and spent the Evening at Miss Greys— As usual very ill after so much exertion—

M^rs. Buchanan quite ill but became better towards Evening— Mr B. would not leave her and he did not go to the fishing party—

[285] In 1805 Faneuil Hall was found to be too small to accommodate public meetings, and the selectmen voted to enlarge it. Charles Bulfinch was chosen as architect. The building was doubled in width, and galleries were added at three sides. The work was completed in 1806 (Abram English Brown, *Faneuil Hall and Faneuil Hall Market*, Boston, 1901, p. 152–155).

31

All better and the evening brought Miss Grey and M[r.] Hall— The Bride &c passed the Even[g] at M[rs.] Otis's

AUGST I

The party accompanied by M[r] Adams went to Trinity Church and heard D[r] Gardner preach— Dined at home and passed the Evening with D[r] Welsh's family

2

M[r] & M[rs.] Buchanan went to Salem with Charlotte Welsh: they returned in the Evening and found M[r] De Grand at the House who staid Supper— The idea of losing my loved Sisters society who had ever been so especially dear to me at a moment when my situation required so much soothing care: and it was a cruel effort to suppress my feelings within reasonable bounds: I fear I behaved very badly.

5

M[r] & M[rs.] Buchanan passed the Evening at M[rs.] S: Dexters with whom I was very intimate for many years— She was a strong minded shrewed Scotch woman; very excentric and very worldly wise— Her Husband was one of the great men of the Country: of brilliant fame; and more so of talent— He was one of our Giant Lawyers and Politicians—

But elevated powers and strong minds are not the best sources of success in highly democratic governments— Your middlemen, to whom it costs nothing to *stoop*; with the knac of pettyfoggers are the *sort*. they forever gain because the world are not *aware* that they have any thing to lose: while the eyes of the Universe are fixed upon the superior race; and to them a light *stumble* is a downfall—

6

M[r] Buchanan and his Wife my beloved Sister left us for Baltimore, and what were *my* thoughts? It was but a little more than a year since I had escaped death under the same circumstances:

and all allowed that my situation was perilous: and what had I to hope?

M[r] Adams staid at home with me that evening and George: and we walked little while in the Mall—

7

As I was sitting alone in my Chamber towards Evening, my poor George came into my Chamber looking deadly pale: and said, "Mama! I have been thrown out of a swing as high as the Poplars by the Otis boys." And he had got up all *alone* and come to me—!!

I examined him but could only percieve a bruise on his hip to which I immediately attended: and then took him and made him lay his head on my lap; until the D[r] could come: to whom I instantly sent— The poor fellow moaned piteously every now and then, and I was much alarm'd M[r] Adams was dining out— The Doctor came and said the Shoulder was a little swoln, but he thought there was no material injury— The Child began to play and seemed almost to have recovered— His Father came home and I told him of the accident, and what the Doctor had said and then proposed to take the Child to the swimming bath: they went and returned in about an hour and as he appeared much exhausted I had him put to bed— He was very restless and uneasy, and cried and sobbed almost all night— His Father sat by him and tried to soothe him: but it was impossible, and in the morning early the D[r] was sent for again— The Shoulder was so much swoln that he said he could do nothing at that time but put the Arm in a Sling—but still thought it was a *jar* and nothing serious— He gave him something to compose him and he fell asleep and when he waked he was as lively as a bird— His arm did not appear to hang naturally and I felt very anxious: but my fears were laughed at, as I must not bring up *my* boys to be delicate—

12

M[r] & M[rs.] Adams came into Town to see us— As soon as they saw the Child they told his Father to take him to a famous bone setter to examine him; and the moment D[r.] Hewit saw him he said that the Shoulder was dislocated and the collar bone was broken: and he set the one and fixed the other; before my poor boy knew what he was about—[286] When he came home his Grandfather gave him a quarter of a dollar as a reward for his *bravery*; and as soon as he got it he ran on the common, and meeting one of his School "told him to run and spend it all in Gingerbread for the boys, and when *he* was *President he* would make *him* Secretary of State"— This was a most amusing joke to us when the boy came with the Cake and informed us of the promise—and my poor fellow distributed it with the utmost delight to all the Children standing round him; having only one hand and keeping but a small piece for himself— He was but little turned of six years old!!

18

Unable to do any thing time passed heavily— I walked in the Mall until ten o clock— At two in the morning I disturbed the family; My Nurse towards morning was so alarmed at my Situation, that she burst in to tears and was sent away: and for the first time with my *fourth* Child Mr Adams was with me at the birth to: see another *apparently dead Child*—in about half an hour the Child had recovered the play of his lungs, and my husband had witnessed sufferings that he had no idea of—

What a contrast to my last birth! 500 Miles away from my husband—Children; and a dead but beautiful Child only fourteen Months before!!

For two days we were in great fear for the Child who had not entirely recovered—but after that time appeared to thrive rapidly and all went on prosperously— Thanks be to God!!

30

I had felt unusually strong and well and foolishly took the Child off the Bed and walked across the Room with it in my arms— He was very heavy and I was siezed with severe and dangerous illness which nearly cost my life and two weeks did not repair the mischief— Mrs. Smith kindly supplied the place of my Sister, and assisted me in the concerns of the family and in the care of poor George—who seemed born early to taste the ills of life.— A french Gentleman when he was three years old attached to the french Le-

[286] The Boston bonesetter Shubael Hewes attended GWA (D/JQA/27, APM Reel 30; *Boston Directory*, 1807, Shaw-Shoemaker, No. 12180).

gation had playfully drawn the Childs horoscope without my knowledge and brought it to me— I declined taking it but he told me that he was threatened with a great *peril* at the age of *eight* and *twenty* but that if he escaped it he would be one of the most extraordinary Men in this Country— I would have nothing to do with it for I had no faith—

5 [*SEPTEMBER*]

George was siezed with a fever; and Mr Adams was almost worn out in a day or two the Child grew better but my own situation was very critical— Mrs. Smith came to us and all began to grow well. Mr and I was able soon to ride— My youngest Son was brought from Quincy to see his new Brother but he would not look at him and seemed to think the little stranger was a *usurper*— His Grandmother was obliged to take him home—

12

Was able to ride out for the second time and we made preparation to have the babe vaccinated on account of our coming journey to Washington—

13

Our Boy was baptized this day by the name of Charles Francis— after a Brother of my Husbands who died before I came to this Country, and Judge Dana with whom Mr. Adams went to Petersburg as Secretary at the age of fourteen—[287] The Baptism took place in the first Church Chauncy place by Rev Mr Emmerson— I was not able to get out of the Carriage: ~~but my Sister held the Child~~ and the Nurse brought it back so that I could immediately return home. Mr Buckminster the far famed and extraordinary Preacher returned from England

Alexander Everett entered Mr Adams's Office as a Student— A young man of great promise—[288]

[287] For Francis Dana, see *AFC*, 1:362, 7:160.

[288] Alexander Hill Everett (1790–1847) studied law in JQA's office after graduating from Harvard in 1806 (*DAB*).

15

George being violently in love with Miss Virginia Foster having seen his Aunt Caroline recieve letters from M[r] Buchanan took one of her Letters out of her toilet drawer and carried it over to her telling her that She must *keep* it until he should have learnt to write one to her himself—[289] Poor boy this act betrayed at least some idea of constancy in his affection—not yet seven years old—And the desire to be remembered— It was such a thought as would fill both the heart and mind of an innocent and artless Child— And there was sound sense in it, though the deduction in real life might be erronious His Father punished him severely— And the next day he did not return from School until night having strolled about the Town all day without food; and fainted as soon as he got into the House— I was not permited to see him for fear of indulgence undue—

D[r.] Waterhouse vaccinated our Boy— M[r.] Adams went out to Quincy with his Sister who had brought John to see us and took George with him.— He made arrangements while there to Board out my two Children in *different* places and thus again was the family scatered to the winds He found M[rs.] Adams very seriously ill; and confined to her bed, and she continued quite ill when he was obliged to return to Boston— George came back with him

OCT 1

We went to what we supposed a social visit at M[rs.] S A Otis's; and found a very large dress party— Hariet Otis played and sung very well and was a sweet unaffected Girl— The company was brilliant and crowded and we met all the *Fashion* of Boston—

4

The Carriage came into Town with a request that we would all go out; so that M[r.] Adams and myself, my three Children and Nurse all sat off together— We arrived to dine and immediately after dinner it began to storm, and the Baby and I took violent Colds.— We left our dear John to pass the Winter with M[rs] Cranch; and took George with us to Boston

[289] Virginia Foster was likely the granddaughter of the Adamses' neighbor William Foster, a Boston merchant (Frederick Clifton Pierce, *Foster Genealogy: Being the Record of the Posterity of Reginald Foster*, 2 vols., Chicago, 1899, 2:940, 954–956).

7

John Smith took leave of us to go to Albany

9.

My poor George was so sick he could not go to Haverhill; and M[r] T.B Adams who fortunately came into Town, took him out with him to Quincy to stay until he should be *able* to go—

10

At eight o clock in the morning we started in the Stage for Providence and passed the night at Ammidons— After breakfast next morning we embarked, and I then met M[r.] Euston a gentleman who had travelled with my Sister and myself from N. Y. last August twelve months—

11

Went on board of the Packet at Providence and lay at Anchor about a mile below the Town the *whole day* in a Calm— In the Even[g.] a M[r] & M[rs.] Gamage and a M[r] Prentiss came on board: and through the day we by some means drifted down to Newport where we laid too all Night— We remained in the Vessell— After we passed Point Judith we were baffled by a head wind, and were beating about all day and all Night: in the Sound we arrived off New London at Sun rise—

14

The Packet beat up for the long Island shore, but she pitched and rocked so that every body was sick on board.

15

The wind abated a little but the Sea was very heavy until we reached Landers Point the entrance of the East river; but the tide being against us we had to Anchor for the Night— The Passengers all but five or six we among them staid on board— At ten o clock in the morning we beat through Hell Gate with a head wind and reached New York at Noon. M[r] Adams Went into New York to procure Lodgings at M[rs.] Anthonys and then came with a Carriage to take us there—from the Wharf

On Landing in New York we were walking up towards the Street to meet the Carriage when a man smatched my Baby out of the maids' arms and ran up the Street with it; myself and my Nurse running and screaming after him— He turned into a house and we followed but saw no one; and I was just about to mount the Stairs when he brought my boy and put him into my Arms; excusing himself by saying that the Child was such a perfect beauty, he thought he must show him to his Wife— The apology was irristable to a Mothers and we turned back, and met M[r] Adams who was in great agitation looking for us. We staid the night—

18

This morning we started again for Philadelphia crossed the Ferry in a gale and pursued our journey in the Stage— The weather changed suddenly from unusually warm to very Cold— We stopped at New Brunswick to sleep—

19

We got off again between four and five on our way to Philadelphia and arrived there at about seven in the Even[g] myself exhausted We could not get lodgings at the Indian Queen and M[r] Richards got us one in South fourth Street at a M[rs] Claytons M[r] Adams went immediately to secure Seats in the Stage to proceed in the morning— but my poor baby was so ill from the fatigue and shaking of the incessant motion; that he was in convulsions and we were obliged to get M[rs.] Clayton to send for the nearest Physician; and when he came he said it was the general affect of the cold and the fatigue; and the sudden transition from the cold air into a very warm room— He used frictions with brandy and gave him a composing medecine— Every bone in the babe appeared to ache— Utterly worn out with Sea sickness, fatigue and anxiety; added to the exhaustion of Nursing; my strength gave out, and I was siezed with successive faintings to a late hour—

In the morning I was better as well as my babe; and we left Philadelphia in the Newcastle Packet at 1/2 past seven o clock—

20

At seven in the Evening we arrived at Newcastle; and immediately took the Stage and arrived at Cecil point at eleven o clock at *Night*— Took Passage in the Packett Pinckney Taylor and sailed for Baltimore— We had a tremendous Passage and a heavy sea struck the Vessell and nearly capsized her— The Gale was so high she could not carry sail; and we were obliged to anchor under a Lee shore for the night; but before his Anchor was dropped the wind changed and

21

we pursued our course some miles further to Pools Island; and lay there until day break: and though the wind was still against us, it gradually abated and we got into Baltimore at Noon.

22

We dined at Evans's Tavern— And after dinner we rode over to my Sister Buchanan's who lived four miles from Baltimore. we were greeted with the kindest affection; but my anticipations were fully re-alized; for I saw that even thus early her multifarious cares were beyond her strength; and that instead of diminishing they were to encrease in due time— She was beloved by every body round her, and the Children doated on her— The House was very small but very pretty; and under her auspices a pattern of neatness— We remained one Night with her; and my Dear Mother who was staying with her; agreed to return to Washington with us on the day but one after we left them; all of us being engaged to pass the day with Mr & Mrs. Johnston Mr Buchanans Sister a very beautiful Woman— Here I met my old Beau Lawson Alexander more than half crazy but still very good looking—

24 [23]

We were invited to dine at Mrs: Harpers who called while we were absent but were obliged to decline on account of our departure— We were engaged to dine with Mr Lloyd Buchanan at a place called Woodbine We there met her Mother and Brother Mrs. Stuart and her Son—Miss Blodget and a Mr. West— It was about two miles from Baltimore— Mr. Henry and Lawson Alexander formed the company—

We returned early in the Even[g] to Baltimore and there I parted with my loved Sister again—

24

At eight o clock this morning we took the Mail Stage and arrived at Washington at dusk—and we were set down at M[r] Hellens after all the Passengers had been landed: we were set down after a day of wearisome fatigue at eight or nine o-clock— They were delighted to see us and my Mother who they did not expect and perfectly charmed with my boy— I earnestly thanked the Almighty for having saved us from so many perils: and for having preserved my poor babe from vital sickness— He was under eight weeks old when we started from Boston— Congress should not gridge mileage nor the people when their Members thus peril life and comfort to get to their Post.

26

My Sister Boyd and her husband dined with us and the family were all united again but my Sister Buchanan— M[rs.] Hellen lovely as ever had a little daughter to introduce; and M[rs.] Boyd had a Son named after my husband—[290]

Visits began and I had the pleasure of again meeting my old acquaintance— M[rs] Mason was a charming Woman for whom I had the highest respect— Miss Murray was one of the great belles of the day as also Miss Lee since M[rs] Horsey Miss Holliday the Miss Worthington Miss Jeniffer The Miss Stoddarts and many more beautiful Girls who formed the charm of the Washington Society— My old Friend M[rs.] Duvall was one of the most capital Housekeepers! the kindest hearted being and the most incessant talker that I ever met with— Her house was as open as her heart and hand: and her knowledge was lavishly dispensed to all who would accept it— To young Housekeepers she taught the mysteries of curing Bacon, making Soap, pickles, Preserves, Pies, Puddings, &ce &ce with all other *matérial* so essential to family management; and at such Seasons; she *armed* with Floating Islands, Whipt Syllabubs, Cakes and every other nicety to please the eye and gratify Palate; and if M[rs.]

[290] John Quincy Adams Boyd (1806–1831) was born on 21 November.

Dearborn was famed for raising Chickins and milking Cows, Mrs. Duvall was her superior *far* in *raising* the rich Staples of the South and West; which Mrs. Merry was so zealous to procure to adorn her Table in Masquerade—

Having started once more into the focus of the great World, I shall generalize and quit the diary style as tedious and monotonous

Politics are ungenial and I know nothing about them but their miserable tràcàsseries:[291] and shall run on as wild as an unbroken colt; in my relation of men and things through this Winter— Mrs. Madison was as popular as ever— Mr Adams resumed his Seat in the Senate with all the usual routine: and the social intercourse of the family and the House was resumed on the accustomed agreeable footing— The races were gay and well attended the young Ladies making small bets—[292]

Loo Parties became quite fashionable and regular meetings took place at particular Houses every Evening for the especial purpose—

16 [26]

Congress Assembled and the Message went in— This of course was the topic of conversation for several days and the Message was reviewed and criticised according to party feelings and standards; and was lauded or decried accordingly. Poor old Mr Wheaton was put out and Mr Dunn was chosen— Wheaton was a *faithful old Servant*— The other *wanted* the *Place*— Thus closed the Month of October[293]

NOV 3

At length Mrs. Adams wrote and we heard that our children were both well—[294] Mr Quincy called—: Mr Gailliard &c Mr Smith took their Seats in the Senate and the deaths of our old friends Mr

[291] Worries, bothers.

[292] Horse racing had been popular in Georgetown since 1769. By 1803 races were held at the Washington Jockey Club, south of Columbia Road between 14th and 16th Streets. The racing season, which lasted for several days in November, included a ball (Bryan, *Hist. of the National Capital*, 1:304, 609–610).

[293] Joseph Wheaton of Rhode Island, the first sergeant at arms of the House of Representatives, had served since 1789. He was replaced by Thomas Dunn of Maryland, who served until his death in 1823 (Robert V. Remini, *The House: The History of the House of Representatives*, N.Y., 2006, p. 510).

[294] AA to LCA and JQA, 25 Oct. 1807, Adams Papers.

Baldwin and Mr. Tracy were announced— Tracy was a delightful man and we sadly missed his Society—[295]

~~7~~ 3

Mr. Adams dined at Mr Jeffersons— When he returned he said the dinner had been very agreeable; and the conversation lively—[296]

I became quite sick with the Ague in my head— Congress on the attack of the Chesapeake Frigate—[297] Ah take him all in all where shall we find his like again—[298]

6

A severe Snow Storm— Most of us got colds and remained quietly at home to Nurse— Mr. Adams walked all the way to the in the Snow Storm

13

Mr. Adams as usual went to the Senate— Afterwards dined at Mrs. Madison's with a large company— Mrs. Madison was not present having recently lost her Mother—[299]

We Passed the Eveng at Col Thompson's not a large party and there I met Mr & Mrs. Erskine, the British Minister and his Lady— We had exchanged visits but I had not become acquainted with her— She was a very pretty Woman; and being an American her manners accorded so well with ours she was quite popular: added to which her husband was a genteel unpretending man, agreeable and

[295] Abraham Baldwin died on 4 March; Uriah Tracy died on 19 July (*Biog. Dir. Cong.*).

[296] JQA provides a lengthy description of the dinner in his Diary (D/JQA/27, APM Reel 30).

[297] From October through December, Congress considered responses to the British attack on the *Chesapeake*. In June the British frigate *Leopard* had stopped the *Chesapeake* on its way from Virginia to the Mediterranean and demanded to search it for Royal Navy deserters. When the captain refused, the British fired on the *Chesapeake*, with casualties to the crew. The captain surrendered and permitted the search, and the ship was released. In his annual message to Congress, delivered on 27 Oct., Thomas Jefferson included an account of the affair and of measures he had taken in response to it. After extended debate, Congress passed measures to fortify ports and build gunboats (E. B. Potter, ed., *Sea Power: A Naval History*, 2d edn., Annapolis, Md., 1981, p. 95; *Annals of Congress*, 10th Cong., 1st sess., p. 15–16, 787, 1065–1171; *U.S. Statutes at Large*, 2:451, 453).

[298] The quote, from Shakespeare, *Hamlet*, Act I, scene ii, lines 187–188, probably refers to Uriah Tracy.

[299] Mary Coles Payne had died in October (Allgor, *Perfect Union*, p. 117).

modest; and his brother was odd, awkward and innoffensive— They were the Sons of Lord Erskine who was also admired in this Country, and altogether they seemed to suit the publick taste—[300] The party was pleasant but I prefered the company of my Nurseling; and was glad to get home—

My Mother my two Sisters and Mr Adams and myself dined at Mr. Jeffersons:— I sat on his left hand, Mrs. Erskine on his right— Being occupied with Mrs. Erskine he said but little to me; only instructing me how to eat Canvass back Ducks—A raw carcass being on his Plate which he assured me was the perfection of eating— He was a great epicure and his Table was served in very handsome style— There was nothing particularly agreeable in the dinner, and the President was very sparing of his Fuel— We returned home early—

My Brother left us to go to South Carolina for his health and this was the last event of interest that occurred in this Month of dreary November—

DEC

We lived very quietly as the fashionable Season had not commenced until to day, when we attended at a great Ball given by Mr Elias B Caldwell a company of more than 200 and very gay— We returned home between eleven and twelve at night— Mr Caldwell was of a great Revolutionary family, and had married Col Boyds Sister— She was a very pretty Woman and he was a very amiable Man— Politics were growing very hot and Mr. Adams was very busy and very anxious— The Whigs began to be jealous of him, and the old Federalists hated him: so that we were fast getting into hot water— Mr Jefferson took but little notice of *him* and of me none at all—[301] Christmas day we spent together and Genl Van Cortland dined with us— In the Evening a small party at Mr Erskines Music and Sup-

[300] David Montagu Erskine, 2d Baron Erskine (1776–1855), and Fanny Cadwallader of Philadelphia were married in 1799. Erskine served as minister plenipotentiary to the United States from 1806 to 1809. His brother, Henry David, was a clergyman (*DNB*; *Ann. Register*, 1877, part 2, p. 145; Burke, *Geneal. and Heraldic Hist.*, 1914, p. 735).

[301] On 22 Dec. Congress passed the Embargo Act of 1807, which prohibited American ships from traveling to foreign ports and required the posting of large bonds for ships traveling between American ports. Massachusetts politicians and the Federalists generally were strongly opposed to the embargo. JQA nevertheless voted for it. He wrote to JA on 27 Dec., "My views of present policy, and my sense of the course enjoined upon me by public duty, are so different from those of the federalists that I find myself in constant opposition to them— Yet I have no communication with the Administration, but that which my place in the Senate of course implies" (*U.S. Statutes at Large*, 2:451–454; Bemis, *JQA*, 1:142–144; Adams Papers).

per: but few guest's: Mr & Mrs Nat Cutting a very pretty French Woman— He was a Doctor and a Poet— John Randolph was very troublesome and the theme of general conversation—and there was a great fuss about John Smith of Ohio[302]—but troubled myself very little about them—

JAN 1 [*1808*]

Went with Mr Adams and my Sisters to pay the New Years visit at the President's— It was very crowded with men women and Children and it was difficult to find the President— Most persons disapprove of this sort of company: but with all my *supposed* arristocratic tastes I think it is a privilege due to the *People*; to permit them to see their President in his house *once* a year, that they may evince their respect for *him* and their homage to the Nation that they love and cherish— And this cold brow beating Scorn sits but poorly on the uppermost Class of Society in this Country where a man can never feel sure of his Station for a year; and is up to day and down tomorrow— Order should be observed and decorum required and then the privilege would be esteemed— A Lady mentioned to me that at one of my Drawing rooms; a Coachaman with a whip in his hand stood close to her and that she feared he would spoil her dress— I had remarked this personage myself, and enquired how he got in— The answer that *he* made was that he was the Coachman of a gentleman from New York who was there with his family and of great wealth— *He* had been a driver; the man *said* and he thought therefore he had a right to be there also—

5

We dined at Mr Erskines— Tolerably pleasant— England and America not on a very agreeable footing— We heard of nothing but the Embargo.

Mr & Mrs. Erskine too Tea with us— She is pretty and innofensive— He is gentlemanly and agreeable *et tout dit*—

12

A large Ball at Mr. Erskines I could not leave my Babe so often Mr. Adams and the family went—it was brilliant

[302] For John Smith, see Adventures, note 306, below.

13

A Ball at the Mayors: M[r] Brent— All went but myself I staid with my babe who was quite sick— M[r] Rose the New Envoy from England was there; and the party was large— My boy was quite ill all night— The North Chamber was so cold we were obliged to take my husbands chamber. A terrible change to *him*— He went with the family to a large party at M[rs.] Duvalls— All three of us sick; M[r] Adams a bad Cold: I an ague in the face—and the Child very ill— My Mothers old friend Col Jno Williams spent the Evening with us: My Baby better—

The family all went to a party at M[r] Erskines and M[r] Adams made me go with him— We staid a short time and then went to M[r] Riggs's a house warming: but I was too unwell to stay; and we left the family at the Ball and returned home

My baby was much better and I was better of course— M[r] Adams had also got well and I took my boy and passed the day with my Sister Boyd; and staid as late as I dared—

A large Ball at D[r] Worthingtons it rained so heavily no one could go—

Again at M[r] Erskines M[r] Rose was a mild elegant man; who I had heard much spoken of in Berlin where he was a favorite— His manners were charming and his conversation interesting though not brilliant— The M[r] Casamajors were the delight of the Girls; and were very pleasant men. They were quite an acquisition to our Society— Thus closed the Month of Jan[y] 1808.

FEB 1

A large party at D[r] Thorntons— All the Corps diplomatique there; Politics ran very high— Miss Wheeler the belle of belles—

6

M[r] Randolph is the subject of conversation. Has had a bad fall and is very ill at M[r.] Keys— M[r] Dana came frequently to see us and then we missed M[r.] Tracy still more— We had many visitors M[r.] Verplanck Gen[l] Van Cortland M[r] Steadman and many more too numerous to mention by name— Nothing heard of but his conversations— About a year ago he was engaged to marry a beautiful Girl of a high Maryland Family— The day was fixed all the arrangements were made but at the moment of its completion it was all broken up for ever— The mystery was never explained—

11

Mr & Mrs. Erskine and a number of Gentlemen dined with Mr Hellen— The Casamajors passed the Eveng here—

16

We passed the Eveng. at Mrs. Erskines—Cards &c no dancing I never played— Mr. Duer and my Sister came from Col Boyds and Mr. Marin Mr de Cabee— Music all the Evenings They Sang and Marin accompanied my Sister on the Clarionet— The Family went to a great Ball at the Navy Yard last night and returned quite charmed with the party—

21

Col Boy and his Wife with my Sister Catherine and stayed the Evenning as did also the younger Lewis Casamajor and Mr Duer to supper—

22

A great Ball at Stelles to celebrate the birth day[303] My Sisters went I remained at home— I spent the great proportion of my time with my Sister Boyd— On returning home in the very dark Night we were nearly upset in the Carriage—as my Infant was with me we were much frightened having lost our way in the old fields—

23

A Party at Mrs. Erskines we did not go— The Family all there—dined at Mrs. Duvalls— At a Ball at Col Thompsons in the Evening I heard frequently from my Children—

[303] George Washington's birthday was celebrated at Stelle's Hotel, opened in 1800 by Pontius Delare Stelle on the site where the Library of Congress now stands (Cliff Sloan and David McKean, *The Great Decision: Jefferson, Adams, Marshall, and the Battle for the Supreme Court*, N.Y., 2009, p. 143).

27

Mr Story and Mr Bacon passed the Evening with us—with Mr Ellis a young man from N Y.

29

A large party at home— The Rose the Erskine and the Caton families and most of the Fashionables passed the Evening and supped at Mr H's and thus closed the Month— Mrs. Hellen was lovely and beloved—

MARCH 1

At a Ball at Mrs. Erskines: all the world there—very gay—

2

Mr G W Campbell and Gardenier went out and fought— G—— badly wounded! fears for his life— Campbell came back and took his Seat in the House— G was an elegant man handsome in Person with excellent manners— A shining light in these respects among our hoard of half Savages in the H R.[304]

25 [5]

A large party at Genl Masons in George Town—

7

A quiet day— Louis Casamajor in the Evening— Mr. Hellen a hot Federalist—

8

The last party for the Season took place— My Mother and Sisters all went I attended neither Mr Adams nor I—

304 Barent Gardenier (d. 1822), a representative from New York, accused those supporting the embargo of being influenced by the French. George Washington Campbell (1769–1848), a representative from Tennessee, accused him of slander. They met at Bladensburg, Md., and Gardenier was shot but survived (Joyce Appleby, *Inheriting the Revolution: The First Generation of Americans*, Cambridge, 2000, p. 42).

12

Supped at my Sister Boyds—

13

Col & M$^{rs.}$ Boyd dined with us Louis Casamajor in the Evening

17

Mr Buchanan came from Baltimore to see us. left my Sister there— At a small party at Gen S Smiths— Molly a very fine girl is said to be engaged to Mr Mansfield of Eng—[305]

30

We all dined at M$^{r.}$ Boyds met there Mr Caldwell— It was a family party— After Tea hastened home to avoid a heavy thunder gust—

31

Col & Mrs Boyd dined with us and came to take leave of my Mother and Adelaide who were to go to Baltimore with Mr Buchanan— M^{r} H Erskine spent the Even with us— He was a Strange young man in his manners—agreeable when you knew him: but not pleasant at first sight—

In this way in constant interchanges of visits with my Sister the time passed rapidly— Mr Adams was so deeply engrossed with business he had scarcely time to speak to the family—and we had but little conversation on any subject— With politics I never interfered for I never could endure them

APRIL 5

M^{r} & Mrs Erskine Mr Verplanck and Gen Van Cortland passed the Evening with us partly but did not stay supper—

[305] Mary Buchanan Smith married John Mansfield in 1809 (Lodge, *Peerage*, 1890, p. 543).

9

Mr Smith of Ohios case decided–[306]

11

Mr Smith resumed his Seat in the Senate– Parties nearly even

12

Georges Birith day 7 years old and for ever separated– 4 years ere the Lord in his goodness granted me one; and now never with my little ones–

15

Mr Crowninshield of Mass died this day.

16

The remains were taken to Baltimore to be buried at Salem– Procession &c as usual

25

Congress adjourned and we made preparation to adjourn

27

Took leave of my Sisters and Catherine, myself, Mr Adams, and the Child and Nurse got into the Stage for Baltimore– Arrived there we found that Evan's was full and that lodgings had been taken for us in a house opposite kept by a West Indian and not very comfortable– My Mother Eliza and Adelaide were at Mrs. Harpers and came immediately to see us– They were going to the Theatre and Catherine went with them– Mr Adams went to the Wharf to secure a passage–

[306] John Smith (1735–1824), a senator from Ohio, had been charged with treason in Aug. 1807 for having taken part in the Burr conspiracy. JQA chaired a Senate investigative committee that recommended his expulsion. On 9 April 1808 the Senate voted not to expel Smith, but he resigned on 25 April (D/JQA/27, 27 Nov. 1807, APM Reel 30; *Annals of Congress*, 10th Cong., 1st sess., p. 55–56, 324).

29

My Mother and Sister took leave of us and we sailed at nine o clock and arrived at French Town at nine in the Evening; and there took the Stage for New-Castle—

We arrived at Philadelpha at eight in the morning and found some difficulty in getting— A Passenger by the name of White was very friendly and we at last were accommodated at a Mrs. Decharms— Being much fatigued I staid quietly at our lodgings where Mr Adams immediately went and Mrs. Hopkinson confined to her Chamber with four Children sick of the Measles and one had been buried the day before— Mrs Nicholas and Mrs Marloe called on us and Mrs. Dames and Mrs McEwing walked out with us. and took Tea with— Mr. Adams took Seats for monday Morng.— The Stage was upset coming from Baltimore and Mr Gilman was badly hurt—

MAY 1

Mr Adams was out all day: dined at Mr Hopkinsons and came home quite late in the Evening— My Babe was very ill and we had to send for Dr. Rush who sent his Son who remained with the until past ten in the morning—[307]

The dear baby was so ill we could not travel In the Even—the Child was better and we took a short walk and returned to Tea—

3

At eight oclock we started again on our weary pilgrimage and we arrived at Brunswick at eight in the Evening— Our companions in the Stage were very disagreeable; and we stop'd at Mr Guests and then proceeded to a tavern Between four and five we started again and our very troublesome Passenger left us very much to our comfort— We had a very short Passage cross the Ferry and we tried to get lodgings at Mrs. Anthony's but she had removed— We then went to Mrs. Bradishes; where we found a couple of chambers in the Garret

We were prevented from sailing by a very violent Storm Mr John Smith and Mr Rufus King came to see us

[307] Benjamin Rush's son James (1786–1869) was his father's medical apprentice. He would graduate from the University of Pennsylvania medical school in 1809 (Rush, *Autobiography*, p. 371).

6

We went on board the Packet At about 5 oclock next morning we had a very heavy wind and tremendous swell all were sick on board and we suffered severely— We landed some Passengers at Newport after a passage of twentynine hours—

7

We pursued our rout to Providence and were overtaken by a violent Squall of wind and rain: it was five in the afternoon when we landed at Providence— We remained for the night.

8

In the morning we left Providence in the Stage where we rode to Walpole and dined and then took a Carriage to our own House in Nassau Street— We found the House all ready for our reception— I was to have gone to Quincy with Mr. Adams but he was unwell—

10

Went to Quincy with Mr Adams and Charles Mr. Adams went to Mrs. Cranch's and brought my John again to my heart and arms we dined and passed the afternoon there; and returned to Boston in the Evening

Mr Adams could not go out to Cambridge being quite sick and obliged to see a Physician Mr Hall and Mr Dexter called— Mr Adams awoke quite ill but as usual in despite of all entreaty went to Cambridge accompanied by Dr Welsh— He delvered his Lecture performed all the usual business: and returned home stopping on the way to leave an excuse at Mr Austins not for not dining with him on the plea of indisposition and returned home so sick he was confined to his Chamber the rest of the day—was much better in the Evening—

14

This Evening Mr. Adams though still quite unwell went to Quincy to see his Father and Mother with his brother who had come to town with Miss Welsh— Nothing about was settled and home was any thing but agreeable—

16

May visits from my Lady friends— all sick— The Judge and Mrs Adams and Child came to see us.

Dr Welsh and family came and spent the Even^g^ and Mr Degrand—

18

At a large party at M^rs^ S Dexters— The company agreeable but people shy—

19

Mr Emmerson was suddenly seized with a heamorrhage of the Lungs— It is thought that he can never recover—[308] Mr Shaw promises to go to bring home my poor George— My Children are quite estranged already.

20

Went to a large party at Mrs. Allen Otis's

24

Mr. Riply called and the old Gentleman came into Town to a Meeting of the Accademy[309]

25

Our dear George reached home just before dinner Mr Shaw brought him— They were detained by an accident which befel their

[308] Rev. William Emerson recovered sufficiently to resume preaching in July (D/JQA/27, 21, 31 July 1808, APM Reel 30).

[309] For Samuel Ripley, see Adventures, note 327, below. For JA's role in founding the American Academy of Arts and Sciences and his long service as its president, see *AFC*, 2:75–76; 9:390–391.

Chaise and from which they fortunately escaped uninjured His health was miserable— once again we were a family—[310]

Mr. Adams took the George out to Quincy to see his Grandparents and brought them back on Monday when he took them to John would not there either Morning or Evening—

JUNE 1

The time passed in this way occasional parties; visits to Quincy— A large party at Dr Danforths which was gay and pleasant. On the eigthth of the Month Mr. Adams sent in his Resignation to the Legislature as his policy was not approved and it was accepted and Mr James Lloyd was chosen in his Place on the 9th of the Month.[311] Thus ended my travels for a time and began a system of persecution painful to our Family but disgraceful to the State of Massachusetts whose Citizens are ever Slaves to a handfull of Men who right or wrong submit to their dictation— They utterly incapable of an enlarged and noble policy: but with all their boasted independence hang on the Skirts of Great Britain, as Child Clings to its Nurse— And with the true slavish spirit The more they are scorned the deeper the worship—

The old Gentleman came into Boston to dine with the Agricultural Society; and took Mr Adams out with him and George left him there and brought in John—

At a party at Mr S A Otis's His Son was not there Mrs Otis and daughters were there— Otis as was is and ever has been his custom was playing a double game talking one way and acting another— He is so proverbial for his insincerity that he bears the palm for political treachery above all competitors—[312]

[310] GWA had been living with the Peabodys in Atkinson, N.H., since Oct. 1807 (D/JQA/27, 8 Oct., APM Reel 30).

[311] JQA had attracted the enmity of Massachusetts Federalists not only by voting for the embargo but by attending the Republican caucus that nominated James Madison for president. Meeting in late May, the Massachusetts legislature elected James Lloyd Jr., a merchant and member of the state senate, to succeed JQA in the U.S. Senate and instructed the state's senators to urge a repeal of the embargo. JQA saw this action, taken when his term still had six months remaining, as a rebuke. In response, he resigned on 8 June (Bemis, *JQA*, 1:144–149; *Biog. Dir. Cong.*).

[312] Harrison Gray Otis opposed JQA's stand on the embargo and favored closer relations with Britain. Samuel A. Otis, however, declared himself "mortified" at the state senate's rejection of JQA and claimed that his son shared this feeling. Like LCA, JQA noted the younger Otis' absence from social events at his father's home during this period (Bemis, *JQA*, 1:144, 147; D/JQA/27, 7, 9 June, APM Reel 30).

My Son George returned from Atkinson with a very troublesome sickness and I was obliged to shut myself up alone with him and not mix with the family until it was removed— How cautious Schools be in their care of Children and not thus by neglect lay the foundation for desease in the blood which may never be eradicated— He soon got well and grew quite fat— Catherine returned home much to Mr Adams's satisfaction as we were *very* dull—

The Old Gentleman went to dine at Water Town at Mr Prebles and Mrs. Adams dined with us: and Mr Adams returned with her and took John with us— One of the belts broke and it was obliged to be repaired before they could proceed— It was late when they arrived at Quincy—

30

Catherine went with Mr Riply to pass the day at Concord He had entered into an engagement with my Sister Eliza altogether ill assorted in every way and I seriously opposed it— He was an excellent young man not yet settled in the Church; She a gay dashing beauty accustomed to Washington Society of a different Creed and not a sixpence between them— Was I wrong? God knows: but I thought her trial would be too severe—

JULY 4

Catherine went out to Quincy to pass the day—my Johns birthday— Mr Adams attended the public ceremonies and dined at the Governors a party of thirty most of them Officers and the old Gentleman who lodged with that night[313]

Kitty and I and the Children returned home John very ill— My poor George who followed Dr Waterhouse and his Father to the St Door was *knocked* off the Stone steps on to the Pavement and brought in fainting—then very sick at his Stomach— The Dr came and found a large hurt on the back of his head— Applica of Cloths steeped in Vinegar seemed to relieve him and our agony of alarm was partially relieved—

[313] JQA attended ceremonies at the State House, Brattle Square Church, and the South Church, followed by a dinner given by Gov. James Sullivan (D/JQA/27, APM Reel 30).

25

The monotoney of our lives produced little or no incident worth relating— On this Evening we had a party of about forty Ladies and gentlemen at Tea—

We walked every fine Even in the mall and freqently had

5 [3 *AUGUST*]

Mr. Adams and Mr. Degrand went out Bathing Degrand got out of his depth and had some difficulty to save himself they had George with them

Thus passed the time only varied by visits from our relatives— My Father came in from Quincy and Mrs. H G Otis seeing at the Window stoped her Carriage and came in to visit *him* as also Mr J Rutlege

11

We all went out to dine with Mr. Ward Nichalas Boylston at Jamaica Plains—A very excentric man who was always telling he would leave his fortune first to one and then another of the family because the old Gentlemans Mother was a Boylston—[314] met the family and Judge Parsons—[315] Returned home early—

We remained in Town and Mr Adams though very unwell went to Quincy and took George

18

My boy a year old large healthy and beautiful— My Sister and I passed the Evening at Miss Danforths— Mr Adams did not go.

23

We went to Cambridge with Mr. Adams to the Exhibition—heard from Quincy that Mrs. Adams was sick— Mr Adams attended con-

[314] Ward Nicholas Boylston, who died in Jan. 1828, bequeathed to JQA 400 acres of farmland in Weston. When JQA visited the property, he declared that it was "a Bill of Expence of Mr Boylston, and may very easily become one to me—" (JA, *D&A*, 1:295; Bemis, *JQA*, 2:100; D/JQA/36, 28 July 1829, APM Reel 39).

[315] For Theophilus Parsons, see JQA, *Diary*, 2:xiii; JA, *Legal Papers*, 1:cvi.

stantly to his business at Cambridge and as constantly to his Club which he never missed

Mr Verplanck Jun of N. Y. came to see us and stayed the Evening with us. He is a very sensible man: singular; and not always very agreeable— Lady Temple and Mr & Mrs. Bowdoin met with an accident to their Carriage and we invited them in— It was soon repaired and they left us in a short time—A vist from Mr H Erskine—

Catherine went to a Ball at Mrs. Dexters with Mrs. Foster and Mr Verplanck Mr. Riggs called—going to George Town next morning; and we saw Mr John Coles— Catherine went to spend the Evening at Mrs. H G. Otis. I called at Mrs. W Smiths with Mr. Adams but was not well and obliged to return home— Mr King called—[316]

19 [*SEPTEMBER*]

Mr. Erskine and Mr Sterling passed the Evening as also Mr King a heavy thunder-gust and my Sister and myself both sick— Mrs. Charles Adams and Susan came in Mr. Adams dined at Mr H G Otis's with a small party of Gentleman— Mr. Erskine and Mr. Sterling were of the company— Mrs. Adams with Mrs. Charles and Abigail staid the Night and left us for Quincy next morning Abby is very pretty—

Went to Mrs P. Fosters to pass the Even.[317] Her Sister Mrs T B Adams on a visit of a week Catherine at a Ball at Mrs H G. Otiss and the month ended and we entered upon October very quietly—

I was very ill in consequence of weaning my baby, but he took it very well— Mr Cutts and his family and Mr Cook and his Lady called on us— They were on their way to Washington: At a Ball at Mrs. Fosters returned home at ten oclock with Mr. Adams—

OCT 19

Went to Cambridge to the exhibition and dined with Mr & Mrs Parkman—[318] Returned tired to death immediately after dinner— The mere commonplace routine of every day life suits me very well— Mr Adams and George went to Quincy

[316] The events in the two preceding paragraphs occurred between 8 and 19 Sept. (D/JQA/27, APM Reel 30).

[317] Frances Harrod Foster, the wife of Boston merchant Phineas Foster and sister of AHA.

[318] The oratorical exhibition at Harvard took place on 18 Oct. (D/JQA/27, APM Reel 30).

Mr Adams M^rs.^ T B. A Louisa Smith and George came into Town to a Ball which I was to give in the Even^g.^ It was prettily got up in the next House to ours which was empty and there was a handsome Supper— At eight occlock the company assembled mostly old friends and connections of the family with a few young men—Notes of excuse being sent by all the political clique who thus dissmissed us. They danced until one o clock and H G. Otis came in to see what sort of a thing it was after we had sat down to supper—and did not quit until the last—

26

Mrs. Adams and Louisa Smith returned to Quincy—And Mr. Quincy took leave to go to Washington—

29 [*NOVEMBER*]

Went out to Quincy and staid until Monday. John lived almost entirely with his Grand Mother

The whole month passed over without one circumstance of peculiar interest— Catherine went to a Ball at Mrs Apthorps which we declined— The Children all sick with the Chicken pox

DEC

The Children all sick and myself not much better. The month glided on quietly— We passed Thanksgiving at Quincy where the Children had been five days for change of air alternately they visited their Grandfather but neither of them enjoyed any health— George was kept to close a Student— His brain was overcharged with all sorts of things and his imagination kindled into a Flame— At one time he fitted up the Cellar in the ~~old~~ next house to perform Hamlet in with his School boys and at others the Circus seemed to take all his attention and there was nothing curious in the Town of any kind that escaped his attention— Thus he was always in trouble and in punishment— A total want of system caused all and not apportioning his studies to his age

My three Children were all dangeroulsy ill of fevers and the dreadful restless anxiety of my husband almost made me crazy— It was too distressing to see him at such times for he could not controul his feelings— And it was such a mixture of odd sensations that even in the midst of alarm, we could scarcely help smiling The Season was extraordinarily severe and we all suffered accordingly

JAN 1 [*1809*]

John returned home better Charles continued quite ill and George still Coughed badly— Catherine went out as usual—

26

Mr. Adams again left us for Washington And we were left with all the political World frowning us down with but few friends to protect us. Catherine went out very frequently and I staid at home with my Children— We often heard from Mr Adams and I had the satisfaction to learn that the Senate had rejected Mr. Adams's Nomination to Russia a thing perfectly abhorrent to me and which I hoped was done with forever—[319] O how unfit I always have been for the Wife of a *great Man* and a Politician— Content to glide on in the plain routine of domestic duty I seldom took any part in what was going on unless it was to loathe intrigue and persecution— How different had Mr. Adams married one of his own Country women—

FEB 15

Went over to pay a visit to my Neighbour Foster— The Ice was thick on the Pavement and being exceedingly timid and having no one to help me—I slipped and fell with my back against the Curb Stone and an hour after I got home was taken very ill and being in a delicate situation and the consequence was inevitable and a sickness somewhat dangerous ensued from which I did not recover for three weeks— My Sister then had a Pleurisy and Charles had an ugly eruption both painful and troublesome—

Time wore on until the 26 March and on that day Mr. Adams returned and again we had a prospect of tolerable quiet

[319] For the course of events that would, after all, result in JQA's appointment as minister plenipotentiary to Russia, see Adventures, note 330, below.

I MARCH

we went out to Quincy and I immediately went to see George who was placed there to attend to Mr Whitneys school—[320] Was laid until Monday morning and returned to Boston with the Children

Nothing occurred to vary our lives— The Fosters Mr & Mrs. W. and Daughter came frequently to see us. Mrs F was a french Woman and spoke but little English and they resided with the old People who spoke no french so that our house was quite congenial to them—

Visits to and from Quincy were frequently exchanged and these were the regular course of our lives— Mr Adams attending his Cambridge duties with great regularity—[321]

APRIL 16

We went to the Theatre and took our Children for the first time. Hamlet was performed by Master Payne— We were more diverted by the questions of the boys than by the performance although young Payne greatly excelled the most favorable anticipations— He promises well—[322]

22

George went to the dancing School— His Father scorns the idea of instilling the graces.[323] Why should not a man move well? is it preferable to be like Clown? Surely not when we have the means of improvement— Dr Johnson *mind* might have been softened and less brutal had he been mellowed by the polish of gentle and easy motion— Dancing may not be a necessary part of instruction: but in its association as we cannot dance alone: it has the effect of subduing rude egotism and teaches the art of abstaining from that roughness which is an almost inevitable consequence of ill breeding—and by teaching persons how to associate with Familiarity and ease under judicious and proper restraint—

[320] John Whitney taught at the Quincy schoolhouse, built in 1793, from 1808 to 1811 (Pattee, *Old Braintree*, p. 329).

[321] JQA returned to Boston from Washington on 26 March 1809 (D/JQA/27, APM Reel 30).

[322] John Howard Payne (1791–1852) had made his acting debut in New York in February (*DAB*).

[323] Despite JQA's fears that GWA's regular schoolwork would suffer, the boy attended George Labottiere's dancing school on Thursday and Saturday afternoons (D/JQA/27, 22 April, APM Reel 30; *Boston Directory*, 1809, Shaw-Shoemaker, No. 17067).

MAY 4

Went with my Sister and Mr. Adams to hear Mr Ogilvie's Lecture and was much pleased— It was against duelling—[324] The boys had got a new idea and instead of playing Minister and preaching all the afternoon they played and buried Ophelia my Dressing Case being the Coffin and und the Bed the Grave— And the Duel between Hamlet and Laerties always finished the performance—

6

Dined at George Blakes and staid until late in the Evening: His dinners were very pleasant The company was quite large— The Judge went with us and staid the night at our house—

At a party at Dr Danforths

18

Went again with Mr Adams and Kitty to hear Mr Ogilvie Mr De Cabre a young french man went with us— We all returned together but he did not stay Supper

19

Mr De Cabre spent the Evening with us—Playing and singing kept us up until near 1 oclock.

20

Walked on the Mall met Mr De Cabre and Mr Degrand who came in and supped with us—Again staid until midnight[325]

22

Mr De Cabre in the morning— Mrs. W Foster in the Evening—

[324] James Ogilvie (1760–1820), a Scottish-born educator, began a career as a traveling lecturer in 1809 (*DAB*; *DNB*).

[325] Peter Paul Francis Degrand (1787–1855), a French émigré who became a Boston stockbroker, served in the Massachusetts legislature and was later a strong supporter of JQA for the presidency (CFA, *Diary*, 1:155–156; 3:33).

24

Mrs Knox and her daughter took Tea with us also Mr De Cabre— Staid singing and playing until a late hour— Mr Adams liked the Music but not the hours.

The Club at our house Mr. Adams invited Mr De Cabre to come and he accepted the Invitation— Mr Ogilvie also came by invitation— As we Ladies had nothing to do with the Club Frenchman like Mr De Cabre seeing us walking in the Mall prefered to join us and Mr. Adams was not pleased— We went to here Mr Ogilvie's invitation on the progress of Society— Mr Caseau and Mr De Cabre joined and came home with us. Staid an hour and departed— Going to Washington.

27

Mr De Cabre came and took leave going tomorrow morning.

JUNE

Began with the same routine which was becoming very tedious— Catherine was becoming weary and Mrs: William Gray was in a fidget— Her Son William appeared to seek my Sisters society more than she approved as she had already chosen a Wife and things were not altogether pleasant as she did not admire my Sister at all—[326] I had to announce to poor Ripley that the engagement was broken off between him and my Sister Eliza and it seemed as if every concured to produce disagreeables[327]

[326] William Gray (1750–1825), a merchant of Salem and later Boston, and Elizabeth Chipman Gray were the parents of William Rufus Gray (1783–1831), who married Mary Clay in October (M. D. Raymond, *Gray Genealogy*, Tarrytown, N.Y., 1887, p. 271–272).

[327] Samuel Ripley (1783–1847), Harvard 1804, the son of Rev. Ezra Ripley of Concord, Mass., had been a tutor to the children of Col. John Tayloe of Mount Airy, Va., and Washington, D.C. He returned to Cambridge in 1807 to study for the ministry while preaching in area churches and would be ordained in Waltham in Nov. 1809. Eliza Johnson's family apparently objected to Ripley's modest financial prospects as a clergyman. He married Sarah Alden Bradford in 1818 (Joan W. Goodwin, *The Remarkable Mrs. Ripley: The Life of Sarah Alden Bradford Ripley*, Boston, 1998, p. 67–71; AA to Catherine Nuth Johnson, 15 Oct. 1809, Adams Papers).

3 JULY[328]

Charles was very bad with the Measles very badly and my anxiety is dreadful— He grew better in the Evening but the eruption was very thick and hot.

2

Ripley returned from Washington all was settled but not to his satisfaction— He was deeply attached to my Sister and the stroke was terrible to him— My Brother was to have come on with him but changed his mind— We dined at Quincy with the Agricultural Society— A fire broke out not far from us: and enquiries were made of Mr Adams concerning a black man who we had just and who had entered on his service this day—Being a West Indian suspicion had fallen on I believe without cause[329]

4

This day the news arrived of Mr Adams's appointment to Russia and I do not know which was the most stuned with the shock my Father or myself— I had been so grosly deceived every apprehension lulled—and now to come on me with such a shock!—[330] O it was too hard! not a soul entered into my feelings and all laughed to scorn my suffering at crying out that it was affectation— Every preparation was made without the slightest consultation with me and even the

[328] The entry is out of order in the MS.

[329] JQA's new servant, Nelson, a Trinidadian, was suspected of setting a fire at the home of his previous employer. Because JQA had secured his house and been "wide awake" all through the night of the fire, he was able to assure investigators that Nelson was with him and could not have caused the fire (D/JQA/27, 1, 2, 4 July, APM Reel 30).

[330] In March, while in Washington, D.C., arguing a case before the Supreme Court, JQA had readily accepted President James Madison's offer of the post of minister plenipotentiary to Russia. Thomas Jefferson had nominated William Short to be the first U.S. minister to Russia in 1808, but the Senate refused to confirm him, judging a legation to be an unjustifiable expense. Initially JQA's nomination was also rejected, but Madison's persistence and events in Napoleonic Europe finally led to JQA's confirmation on 27 June 1809, and he received his commission on 4 July (D/JQA/27, 6 March, 3, 4 July, APM Reel 30; Bemis, *JQA*, 1:151, 159; Saul, *Distant Friends*, p. 49–50). For JQA's account of the considerations he weighed before accepting the position, including "the age of my Parents, and the infancy of my children," see D/JQA/27, 5 July, APM Reel 30.

St. Petersburg would be a familiar place to JQA. In 1781 fourteen-year-old JQA, who had accompanied his father to Europe two years earlier, joined Francis Dana on a diplomatic mission to St. Petersburg, serving for fourteen months as a translator and secretary.

disposal of my Children and my Sister was fixed without my knowledge until it was too late to Change—

Judge Adams was commissioned to inform me of all this as it admited of no change and on the 4 of August we sailed for Boston I having been taken to Quincy to see my two boys and not being permited to speak with the old gentleman alone least I should excite his pity and he allow me to take my boys with me—[331]

Oh this agony of agonies! can ambition repay such sacrifices? never!!— And from that hour to the end of time life to me will be a susession of miseries only to cease with existence—

Adieu to America—

5 [*AUGUST*]

We went to see on the 5 of the month to undertake this long voyage to me painful in every possible shape for many more reason's than I can mention— Mr. W. S. Smith was Secretary Messrs. Gray and Everett as attachès—[332] I had urged every thing against my Sisters going— She was entirely dependent with out one sixpence in the world not even clothed properly when she started and I *knew* that *I* could never supply her— But it would not do against my Mothers and my pleadings: the temptations on the other side were too powerful to be resisted and fate was settled by the privation of my Children— Before we had been a fortnight at Sea with three young men—Squabbles and jealousies commenced and the future was laid bare to my eyes as clearly as if it had passed—[333] Broken

[331] On 23 July JQA visited Mary and Richard Cranch in Quincy to arrange for GWA and JA2 to board with them. JQA met with TBA in Boston on the 25th to discuss matters related to the departure for Russia. TBA returned to Quincy that day, and on the 26th, LCA and the children "went out to Quincy, to my father's." It may have been during LCA's visit that TBA informed her of the plans for her two older sons. JQA went to Quincy on the 29th and said farewell to his two sons there before returning home on the 31st. JQA reported that on 3 Aug., LCA, who had returned to Boston, went back to Quincy, accompanied by her sister Catherine, "to take leave of my Parents and children— I could not go" (D/JQA/27, APM Reel 30).

[332] LCA, JQA, and two-year-old CFA, with Catherine Johnson, departed on the ship *Horace*, Capt. Bickford. Accompanying them were JQA's nephew William Steuben Smith, his private secretary and later officially the secretary of the legation, and Alexander Hill Everett and Francis Calley Gray, whom JQA had agreed to attach to the legation on the condition that they pay their own expenses. Gray (1790–1856), Harvard 1809, was the son of William Gray, the merchant and owner of the *Horace*. JQA's manservant Nelson and LCA's chambermaid Martha Godfrey were also in the party (D/JQA/28, 5 Aug., APM Reel 31; Bemis, *JQA*, 1:153–154; Edward Gray, *William Gray of Salem, Merchant: A Biographical Sketch*, Boston, 1914, p. 19; *Harvard Quinquennial Cat.*).

[333] LCA refers here to events that unfolded in St. Petersburg after the period covered in this memoir, as it became evident that the relationship between Catherine Johnson and Wil-

hearted miserable, *alone* in every feeling: my boy was my only comfort— I had passed the age when Courts are alluring— I had no vanity to gratify and experience had taught me years before the meaness of an American Ministers position at a European Court— Nothing but mortification presented itself to my imagination with the loss of all domestic comforts to give me fortitude to support the change—

If it was to do again nothing on Earth could induce me to make such a sacrifice and my conviction is that if domestic separation is absolutely necessary cling as a Mother to those innocent and helpless creatures whom God himself has given to your charge— A man can take care of *himself*:—And if he abandons one part of his family he soon learns that he might as well leave them all— I do not mean to suggest the smallest reproach— It was thought right and judicious by wiser heads than mine but I alone suffered the penalty— They are known only to God—

Our voyage was very tedious— All but Mr Adams and Mr Smith very sick and as usual I having the whole care of the Child who suffered as much as any of us.—

SEPT 17[334]

We had not seen a Vessel since we passed Fair Isle in the North Sea—[335] We had had a heavy gale all day and night and the Swell was frightful— The Swell continued terrific— At about five o clock in the Afternoon a British Brig was discovered she fired a Gun to the Leaward, upon which our Colors were run up: within an hours time she came up with in Speaking distance and hailed us:—[336] Where

liam Steuben Smith had become intimate. In Jan. 1813 JQA "had a long and very serious conversation with Mr Smith, who finally avowed a disposition to do right." William sent Catherine a proposal, which she accepted, but his commitment was not "definitive" until JQA intervened again. Catherine and William were married on 17 Feb. 1813. On 19 March 1814 they had a daughter, Caroline Amelia (D/JQA/28, 18, 19, 20, 23 Jan., 17 Feb 1813, APM Reel 31; D/JQA/29, 19 March, 14 April 1814, APM Reel 32).

[334] For her description of the voyage to St. Petersburg, LCA drew freely from JQA's Diary. Beginning at this point, she paraphrased, summarized, and excerpted her husband's entries, sometimes adding information about her own experiences.

For a clearer and more comprehensive account of the voyage, see JQA's Diary. Also useful is William Steuben Smith, Diary of Voyage to St. Petersburg, 16 July – 29 Oct. 1809 (MHi: Adams Papers, Second Generation, on deposit).

[335] Fair Isle is about midway between the Orkney and Shetland Islands, off the northern coast of Scotland.

[336] In 1807 Britain had acted to prevent neutral and strategically located Denmark from complying with Napoleon's demand that it help to enforce his Continental System intended

from?— From Boston! Whither bound? To Russia! Let down your Boat and come on Board: After some minutes the order was repeated— The Boat was very small and the Capt thought it could not live in the Swell— The order was repeated and a Musket with ball fired ranging along the side of the Ship— It was dusk the wind blowing in Squalls like a Gale with a very heavy sea— The Mate went into the Boat with three men in her but cried out that she could not live and the Brig Shot a head and was out of sight in a few minutes— All this time the Boat and people were in the most imminent danger but got on board at last in safety

18

Another dreadful night— The Sea mountains high and the Vessel rolling and pitching as if she would upset— In the morning we made the Land on the Coast of Norway and at Noon were abreast of the Naze— The water became smoother and we got into the Sleeve so called between the Coasts of Norway and Jutland—and we had a quiet night—[337]

19

We were awakened this morning with the news that an English Cruizer was near us— She came along side of us and sent an Officer on board without speaking us and four Men— She was in pursuit of a Danish man of War for two days— He said it was fortunate that he had not seen us last night as he should have fired into us supposing it was her— At about 7 in the Evening we saw another Brig under Danish Colours. She fired a Gun to bring us too and lay close beside us. She hoisted English Colours after she had ascertained the

to block trade between Britain and Europe. When the Danes refused an alliance, the British bombarded Copenhagen and seized the Danish fleet. Denmark declared war on Britain and joined the Continental System. The British ships that the *Horace* encountered were patrolling the seas to prevent merchant vessels from reaching hostile Baltic ports (*Cambridge Modern Hist.*, 9:235–236; Charles Esdaile, *Napoleon's Wars: An International History, 1803–1815*, N.Y., 2007, p. 311–313; O'Brien, *Mrs. Adams*, p. 11).

For a summary of the major events of the Napoleonic wars up to the time of the Adamses' arrival in St. Petersburg, see Bemis, *JQA*, 1:156–158.

[337] The Naze, also known as Lindesnes, is a cape at the southern tip of Norway projecting into the North Sea. This "sleeve," or channel, was the Skagerrak Strait between Norway and the southwest coast of Sweden, and Denmark's Jutland Peninsula. The Skagerrak connects the North Sea with the Kattegat Sea area, which leads to the Baltic Sea.

usual questions and sent an Officer on board of us with four Men— The Officer did not know as they the English were it with Denmark whether we might proceed or not— The Boat soon returned with an answer that we might proceed without interruption having a Minister on Board—

We sent for a Pilot and while considering which place to put in a small Craft with two with about 15 or 20 Men armed and a Swivel came under Danish colours fired a gun and ordered us to bring too. A Danish Lieut of the Marine by the name of Kauff and told the Capt he must go into Christiansand— The Capt became alarmed and declared he would not put any where and turned his Ship about to stand out to Sea— The Lieut immediately made a Signal and about fifteen men came from the Boat heavily armed and climbing up the rigging and took possession of the Ship walking the quarter deck while others from the boat were preparing to board us— The Lieut however made a signal to them to withdraw— He and the Pilot were afraid that the Capt would carry them out to sea— The Capt concluded to go into the harbour of Flecknore[338] about four miles distant from Christian Sands.

I was perfectly indignant at being taken by this boat and was clear for, maintain our position as we had six Guns—

Mr Isaacson an Agent for American Seamen a very Gentlemanly Man; the next day and we all had a charming dinner in this little nook in Norway Mr Thorndike came on board the Ship and passed the night— Met Lawson Alexander and a number of Americans taken by the Danes—[339]

We were detained on Shore by a heavy Storm and Mr Isaackson to his great inconvenience accomodated us all with lodgings where we were compelled to stay until the next Even^g.^ when the Gov's Boat was sent and Mr Adams obliged us to return to the Ship in a heavy Gale and that night we sailed for the Catigat— We saw four or five Vessels ashore

[338] Flekkeröy Island, Norway.

[339] Danish privateers harassed American shipping in these waters, forcing merchant vessels with their valuable cargoes into harbor for violations of the Continental System. After being tried in local courts, the American seamen were further detained by lengthy appeals to higher courts. JQA found 36 captured American ships at Kristiansand, Norway, and took up their cause within the constraints of his authority and time. But it was left primarily to Peter Isaacson, a Danish citizen who served as the U.S. consul at Kristiansand, to attend to the Americans (Bemis, *JQA*, 1:170; Alfred W. Crosby Jr., *America, Russia, Hemp, and Napoleon: American Trade with Russia and the Baltic, 1783–1812*, Columbus, Ohio, 1965, p. 133–134; D/JQA/28, 19 Sept. 1809, APM Reel 31).

25

At Sun rise this morning we came abreast of Koll Point but the wind veered and came a head, and in the midst of the Passage of the Sound we saw a Ship of War at Anchor—[340] And a Sloop with several other Vessels anchored near them— We made up directly to the Man of War; and a Lieut from her soon came on board—who on examining the Papers of the Crew was very troublesome and threatened to take one of them off— The Officer not understanding Mr. Adams Commission told him he had better go on board the Admirals Ship and see him himself— He went accompanied by the Capt and the young gentlemen and we were left under the protection of the Officer We were nearing the Port of Elsineur when at about eleven o clock at night the Vessel was drifting up against the Man of War— The wind was fair for our progress. The wind was at the same time blowing fresh, and we put down another small anchor which however did not arrest the drift— At about five in the afternoon she began to drift again and we droped our third and last Anchor a very heavy one— We had drifted within the Ships length of a large Brig whose bowsprit was threatening our Cabin windows and we were within a mile of the Shore At the approach of Night I was anxious to send the Ladies and Child ashore for which purpose a signal was made at the Masthead—but none came out— Shortly before Sun set a boat from the British Man of War came out to us and gave some advice to the Capt— He told him that one good anchor, would be better than three and recommended to him in case the wind should change to cut his Cable and go out to Sea— He returned on board his Ship: the night came on.— the night came on with foul weather about midnight which hove in Channel off till about midnight— The wind then changed and continued freshening till morning

25 [27]

All the morning was employed in weighing the Anchors; two of them were successfully got on board— At this work all the hands were engaged and most of the Passengers part of the time with the rest— An American Vessel came in but was sent back by the Admiral

[340] Koll Point, Sweden, is at the entrance to the Sound (Øresund). The Øresund Strait connects the Kattegat to the Baltic Sea.

The wind came continually more a-head and the Vessel would not wear round and the Capt ordered the Cable to be cut away and we stretched out so that we hoped to get to Elsineur that Night— At the third attempt the Capt lashed down the helm put the Vessel under close reefed Mainsail Topsails Maine and fore stay sails but the fore Yard Arm had broken right in two in the middle and they were obliged to take it down— We were between the shores in a narrow see and expecting every instant to be dashed on Khol Point a fearful spot in the history of Wrecks Fortunately it was not very dark and not cold and no Sea so— The next night the Storm continued The light in the Binnacle went out and there was not a light to be had in the Ship— Mr. Adams got his tinder Box

To go through the horrors of this most terrible and tedious voyage is beyond my streng—A

28

on this day we landed at Elsineur and got lodgings— two of the Gentlemen went off to Copenhagen with the Capt— Mr. Adams accompanied us to see the sights with Mr & Mrs. Ellah who was Consul at the place from the United States— There is not much to see and Hamlets Gardens as they were still called ornamented with heavy leaden Statues were the great object of curiosity—[341]

When the Capt returned with the Gentlemen Mr Gray and Mr Everett—Mr. Adams was prevailed upon to go to Copenhagen by the Americas to make some effort in their cause and we continued on Shore until their return.[342] Any thing was better than Sea as we could at least sleep without alarm—

[341] Beginning in the late eighteenth century, Helsingör (Elsinore), the setting for Shakespeare's *Hamlet*, attracted European tourists, who found there the disappointingly restored Kronborg Castle. To enhance the visitors' experience, an allegorical garden was created, with such features as the Kingdom of Heaven, the Hermit's Hut, and a broken column to mark an imaginary grave. By 1805 the garden had come to be known as "Hamlet's Garden," and the "grave" as "Hamlet's Grave" (James Harpur and Jennifer Westwood, *The Atlas of Legendary Places*, N.Y., 1989, p. 186, 188).

[342] Capt. Bickford, Alexander Everett, and Francis Gray made a preliminary visit to Copenhagen on behalf of the American seamen detained there by the heavy costs assessed in the adjudication of their cases. JQA and William Steuben Smith then made the trip and sought assistance for the Americans from Hans Rudolph Saabye, the U.S. consul in Copenhagen (D/JQA/28, 28, 30 Sept., 1 Oct. 1809, APM Reel 31; JQA to Hans Rudolph Saabye, 30 Sept., Lb/JQA/12, APM Reel 136).

OCT 2

We all embarked again on our dismal course with a tolerable wind: but in half an hour it was a-head again—then a Calm in the Eveng head wind and there we had to stay with the Shore on both sides of us

14

Thus we continued with every variety of bad weather and at last provisions began to give out and Mr Adams began to think that we could Land somewhere and go the rest of the way by land but the Capt would not agree for fear of the British—

We lay off the Island of Bornholm—And a boat came off with a polite message from and from the ridiculous there is but one step it is asserted; so we found it verified in the midst of sickness distress of mind, weariness of body constant alarm & not daring to put our last Anchor for fear we should lose it— wer recieved an invitation to a Ball at the Governors on the Island of "Burnt Hollum" as our Capt named it for eight o clock in the Evening while the Vessel was rocking rolling and pitching as if she would go to pieces— We were obliged to decline the honor—

16

We started to go back—and with an intention to put into some Port— But I had no hope— I knew that Mr Adams would never give up and we were obliged to make the best of our miserable condition— They were no imaginary dangers that assailed us, and our sufferings were pitiable— Dangers accumulated every moment as the Season and now we had cold added to our burthens—

Thus we went on day after day—beating about and worn down with fatigue and anxiety

20

Our pilots anxiety at missing sight of both Gotland and Dago was so excessive that he was almost distracted We met a Vessel within speaking distance and found that we were near some known light and our Pilot became a little more easy.— We gained gradually and passed several Lights well known as far as Revel[343] in the Gulph of Finland

22

At last we reached our destination though some distance from the and an Officer coming up the Admirals Boat we dressed ourselves and accompanying him left every thing in the Vessel so as not to detain and landed perfect beggars though supposing that our Trunks would follow us immediately—

My Sister and myself wore hats which had been chosen at Copenhagen that we might appear fashionable—and we could scarcely look at one another for laughing: immense Brown Beaver of the most vulgar imaginable as much too large as our American Bonnets were too small— Thus accoutred fancy us immediately from the Ship usherd into an immense Saloon at the Admirals House full of elegantly dressed Ladies and Gentlemen staring aghast at the figures just introduced and with extreme difficulty restraining their risibility Maid and Child and all taking their place in the Farce and our Black Servant following— It was exquisite beyond all description and too ridiculous in the first moments to be mortifying as we naturally supposed it would only be momentary— Not a place could be be found to put our *heads* in (Bonnets not excepted) the Admiral politely urging us to stay at his as well as his Lady but which we could not accept being such a number and so situated— And at last the Vice Consul gave us apartments and a very nice supper and we went comfortably to rest—

23

At Breakfast Mr. Sparrow informed us that a heavy had sprung up; the Vessel been blown many miles down (leagues) I mean and the she probably would not get back for ten days— Here was a position agreeably defined— Myself a *white Cambric* Wrapper; my Sister the same; A Child of little more than two years old with only the suit on his back, and the Minister with the Shirt he had on; solus!!

343 Gotland is an island in the Baltic Sea off the southeast coast of Sweden. Dagö is the Swedish name, and Khiuma the Russian one, for Hiiumaa, an island off the west coast of Estonia. The Russian seaport of Revel, on the Gulf of Finland opposite Helsinki, is today Tallinn, the capital of Estonia.

We did appear quite in the Garb of the Aberiginals of our Land but as near as possible to do it honor—

We embarked again in the Admirals all the Females the Child M[r] Adams M[r.] Everett and M[r] Gray en suite and Nelson—at twelve at noon we started: and were two hours before to warp out of the Mole[344]—and we were four hours more before we arrived at the Wharf at Petersburgh and had to wait until a Carriage could be procured to take us to and the water had already affected the Child very much so that it required to be more than a philosophic Squaw to bear up against our varied trials M[r] Martin an American Gentleman whom we met at Cronstadt accompanied us and kindly had a dinner served up and every as comfortable as possible in the horrid Hotel that could possibly be got—[345]

Immediately after dinner M[r.] Harris the Consul came[346] and all the Shop keepers were set in motion to procure the requisites for ready use— And we had an outside garment and the Minister was dressed from top to toe much to his discomfiture in a superb style Wig and all to be presented to the Chancellor of the empire[347] when he should be ready to receive him—

25

The Chancellor appointed seven o clock in the Even— M[r.] Harris dined with us gave M[r] Adams much instruction as to how many bows he must make— Amost what to say; and told him to be careful not to dwell upon business but to be careful to introduce something light and pleasant into the conversation as the Russians must be

[344] The waters enclosed by a stone breakwater (*OED*). Everett explained the travelers' situation and the maneuver: "Preferring a voyage by water from Cronstadt to Petersburgh on account of the difficulty of procuring land-conveyances we came up in the packet on the morning of Monday the 24th and reached Petersburgh in three hours after leaving the Mole. The operation of warping out of the Mole employed as much as one hour. It is done by fastening ropes to piers erected at considerable distances from each other in the Mole and hauling up to them by windlasses" (Alexander Hill Everett Diary, 1809–1811, MHi:Everett-Noble Papers).

[345] The Hotel de Londres, at the corner of Nevsky Prospect opposite the Admiralty, accommodated the Adamses, Catherine Johnson, Alexander Everett, and Francis Gray with "an Apartment of five indifferent chambers" (A. B. Granville, *St. Petersburgh: A Journal of Travels to and from that Capital*, 2d edn., 2 vols., London, 1829, 1:448; D/JQA/28, 23 Oct. 1809, 12 June 1810, APM Reel 31).

[346] Levett Harris of Philadelphia had been U.S. consul in St. Petersburg since 1803 (Alfred W. Crosby Jr., *America, Russia, Hemp, and Napoleon: American Trade with Russia and the Baltic, 1783–1812*, Columbus, Ohio, 1965, p. 94).

[347] Count Nikolai Petrovich Rumiantsev (1754–1826), Alexander I's foreign minister and chancellor (Palmer, *Alexander I*, p. 172–173).

amused; and that he must immediately get a Carriage for the fact was that in S[t] Petersburgh "Ill faut rouler."

At seven o clock in the Evening they departed—M[r] Adams looking very handsome all but the Wig. O horrid! which entirely disfigured his countenance and not to his advantage— They soon returned as the visit was short but the reception courteous— M[r] Harris passed the Evening with us.

26

M[r] Smith arrived with only a small part of the baggage and that was carried to the Custom— An invitation from the Chancellor for M[r.] Adams to dine with him on Saturday M[rs.] Khremer the Lady of the Court Banker called on me and was kindly polite—[348] She entered fully into our situation and appeared to take great interest in the Child who was sitting on my knee when she came in— About an hour after her visit every requisite for our toilet was sent with a Note express a wish that we would make a free use of the Articles as long as they could be convenient—with a large supply for the Child she having one of the same age— The whole business was so elegantly performed that I felt very grateful and readily used the favour for the Child—

27

We this day recieved our Clothes and baggage from the Custom House every article plumbed— We my Sister and myself went to visit M[rs] Krehmer and accompanied her to some Millinere & Mantuamakers and Furniture— M[r.] Adams looked over a suite of appartments very suitable but just engaged—

I was quite ill! The Water was dreadful in its effects and both the Child and myself suffered every thing— The Chamber I lodged in was a stone hole entered by Stone passages and so full of rats that they would drag the braid from the table by my bed side which I kept for the Child and fight all night long—and my nerves became perfectly shattered with the constant fright least they should attack the Child— We were all more or less sick

[348] Anna Dorothea (Annette) Smith Krehmer, the daughter of an Anglo-Russian merchant and the wife of the banker Sebastian Krehmer, a Baltic German from Narva (O'Brien, *Mrs. Adams*, p. 32).

Mr Crame and Mr Smelt paid visits— Mr Krehmer invited us to dine Mr Adams and myself were too ill to go— The young Gentlemen went The Emperor sick can not recieve—

The dinner at the Chacellors at which Mr Adams attended was in the highest style of magnificence

NOV 1

The style of expense is so terrible here it seems as if it would be impossible for us to stay here— We are in pursuit of lodgings but can procure none— The Emperor signified through Count Romanzoff Chancellor of the Empire that he would recieve Mr. Adams as Minister U S A an hour after the ~~Te Deum~~ Mass and afterwards to the Empress.—

The Commandeur de Maisonneuve sent a gentleman to enquire when Mr Adams could see him that he might make arrangements for his presentation to the Emperor— M^r^ A sent word at eight o clock in the Evening— He came and we found in him an old acquaintance who had done the same service for us at Berlin—A most delightful old man[349]

Mr Adams was presented the Emperor in his Cabinet steping forward to meet him at the door when he addressed him in french "Sir I am happy to see you here"[350]

8

This morning Mons de Maisonneuve called and informed me that I must write a Note to the Chancellor requesting to be presented to the Empress Mother and to the Reigning Empress and that Mrs. Adams must also be presented and the time fixed was after the Mass and Te Deum on Sunday[351]

[349] Commandeur Joseph de Maisonneuve (d. 1812) had represented the Maltese Order of the Knights of St. John of Jerusalem (Knights of Malta) in the Prussian court in 1797, when JQA was minister there. Maisonneuve, who had come to St. Petersburg in the time of Paul I, was made master of ceremonies under Alexander I (D/JQA/28, 30 Dec. 1812, APM Reel 31; *Repertorium*, 3:214).

[350] Alexander I (1777–1825) was married to Elizabeth Alexeievna (Louise of Baden, 1779–1826). Their only children, two daughters, had died before the age of two, the second in May 1808. Alexander's mother was Maria Feodorovna (Sophia Dorothea of Württemberg, 1759–1828), the widow of Paul I (Palmer, *Alexander I*, p. 16, 39, 154, 418). See also Descriptive List of Illustrations, Nos. 8 and 9, above.

[351] LCA copied this paragraph, making minor modifications, from JQA's Diary, which accounts for the reference to "Mrs. Adams." See D/JQA/28, 9 Nov. 1809, APM Reel 31.

That it would be proper for me to call on the Countess Litta on Saturday Evening as Mrs. Adams would then be able to recieve such directions as would put her au fait of the ceremonial— In the Evening we went by appointment to the Bavarian Ministers Baron de Bray— We saw Madame de Bray Madame de Bray was young and very pretty and the only Lady of the Corps Diplomatic besides myself— Several of the foreign Ministers were there and also the Mother and Sister of Madame de Bray who reside with her— Her account of the forms of presentation differed very much from those we had heard before[352]

11

We entered our new lodgings to day—somewhat better but very bad at the Hotel de Londre—[353] Mr & Madame de Bray returned our visit just after we had got in— Just before seven o' clock according to appointment by Mr. De Maisonneuve we went to Countess Littas The Count & Countess recieved us very politely— The Countess told me that I was to be presented the next day directly after Mass to the Empress Mother— But she did not know if I was to be presented to the Empress Elizabeth or Mr: Adams— He was to be presented before Mass— The forms of my presentation had been correctly given by Mr De Maisonneuve and were altogether different from those given by Madame de Bray—

12

Mr Harris took Mr Adams to the Palace at eleven o clock and just as he was starting he recieved a Note from Mr de Maisonneuve with

[352] Ekaterina Vassilievna, Countess Litta, the grand mistress of the court, was a niece, heir, and erstwhile mistress of Prince Grigori Alexandrovich Potemkin. Now nearly fifty years old, she had survived her first husband, a Livonian count, and in 1798 married Count Giulio Renato de Litta. Originally from Milan, Litta had been an officer in the Russian Navy and was serving as the Knights of Malta's envoy in St. Petersburg (O'Brien, *Mrs. Adams*, p. 12–13).

Chevalier François Gabriel de Bray had served France as a diplomat until the fall of the monarchy. He then traveled through Europe and went on missions to St. Petersburg and London for the Knights of Malta, having entered the order as a young man. He met his wife, the daughter of a Livonian count, while serving as the Bavarian ambassador in Berlin. In 1809 he assumed the same position in St. Petersburg (Joseph de Maistre, *St. Petersburg Dialogues; or, Conversations on the Temporal Government of Providence*, transl. Richard A. Lebrun, Montreal, 1993, p. xvii).

[353] Unable to find a house or furnished apartment, the Adams household, including Catherine Johnson, Alexander Everett, and Francis Gray, moved on 11 Nov. from the Hotel de Londres to the Ville de Bordeaux, another public house (D/JQA/28, APM Reel 31).

8. EMPEROR ALEXANDER I, BY FRANÇOIS GÉRARD, 1814
See page xii

the words tres press's on it stating that my presentation was put off until 1/2 past two— Of this Mr Adams informed me and I was left alone to go through all the fears and frights of the Presentation perfectly alone at the most magnificent Court in Europe— Three or four messages arrived from the Palace changing the time for my presentation and I was obliged to hurry as the last ordered me to be at the Palace at 1/2 past one—

Off I went with a fluttered Pulse quite alone in this foreign among people whom I had never seen dressed in a Hoop with a Silver tissue skirt with a train a heavy crimson Velvet Robe with a very long train lined with White body and sleeves trimed with a quantity of Blond; my hair simply arranged and ornamented with a small diamond Arrow—White Satin Shoes gloves Fan &ce and over all this *luggage* my Fur Cloak— I was attended by two footmen—and thus accoutred I appeared before the Gentlemen of our party who could not refrain from laughter at my appearance—

Arrived at the Palace after ascending with great difficulty in the adjustment of my trappings I was recieved by a Gentleman and shown in a long and large Hall in which I found Countess Litta superbly dressed and covered with diamonds— She was the Niece of Potemkin and inherited all his wealth—Very handsome and very fat— She recieved me very kindly—Told me that I was to be presented to the reigning Empress first and then defined my position for the presentation— She placed me in the centre of the Hall fromting a large folding door and informed me that the Empress would enter by that door and that I must stand unmoved until her Imperial Majesty walked up to me—that when she came up I must affect to kiss her hand which her Majesty would not *permit* and that I must take my Glove off so as to be ready and take care in raising my head not to touch her Majesty— She then retired to the embrasure of a window and left me thus drilled to act my cue— Naturally timid I felt as if I was losing all my composure and with difficulty could command the tremour

Two Negroes dressed a la Turque with Splendid Uniforms were stationed at the doors with drawn Sabres with gold handles— At the opening of the doors I saw a suite of long rooms at each door of which stood two Negroes in the same style[354] and the Grand Mar-

[354] It was Peter the Great who first took an interest in acquiring Africans, whom the Russians referred to as blackamoors, Ethiopians, or Negroes, to adorn the imperial court. The Africans, who generally arrived as slaves by way of Constantinople, Tripoli, or Amsterdam, were granted their personal freedom in exchange for a lifetime commitment to service in the

shall in a splendid Costume preceded the Emper and Empress who came up together with a long train of Ladies and Gentlemen following and as their imperial Majesties passed the door the Grand Marshall fell back and the door were nearly closed and they approached me— The Emperor was in Uniform and the Empress like myself in a rich court dress—

I went through the forms which the Empress made easy by her extreme affability and the Emperor assumed the conversation the Empress only joining in with a word or two— I think the audience was of about fifteen minutes ending with some complimentary words and they with drew as they came and I remained in the same position until the doors were re-closed— And thus ended act the first— Countess Litta who had never approached during the ceremony came up and congratulated me on the success of introduction and said the rest of it would be more simple—

We then went to the Apartments of the Empress Mother every thing superb but not so elaborate and there knowing my Lesson I was more at my ease— She recieved me very graciously and evidently expected to quiz my ignorance putting many questions to me as to the effect on me of the wonders that struck my eyes every where in Petersburgh— I expressed in strong language my admiration of every thing and mentioned that I had seen London Paris Berlin and Dresden—&ce but that I had certainly no City that equaled S[t] Petersburg in beauty— Ah mon dieu vous avez tout vue!! and she appeared to regret it very much— The Savage had been expected!! She was wonderfully gracious and after an audience of twenty Minutes I was dismissed with a hope that she should soon see me again— It was beneath the dignity of Madame Field Marshall Litta to present me to the Grand Dutchess so I was transfered to Madame Lieven a fine old Lady and by introduced to the Grand Dutchess a girl of 14 of an elegant presence and most distinguished manner but not very handsome—[355] The Audience was very short— At last I returned home with an additional budget of new ideas almost as oppressive and unsuitable as my Robes— I was very much

court (Allison Blakely, *Russia and the Negro: Blacks in Russian History and Thought*, Washington, D.C., 1986, p. 13–16). For Nelson's entry into this service, see Adventures, 3 June 1810, and note 400, below.

[355] Grand Duchess Anna Pavlovna (1795–1865), sister of Alexander I, was at this time an object of Napoleon's interest as a replacement for the Empress Josephine, who had not provided him with an heir. Alexander delayed his response to Napoleon's inquiries out of concern for his sister's youth and on account of Maria Feodorovna's objections to a Bonaparte-Romanov connection (Palmer, *Alexander I*, p. 162–163, 185–188, 418–419).

fatigued with all this variety of agitation but Madame Litta gratified me by intimating that I had got through very well–

13

Mr. Adams Catherine and I went pay the visit of Courtesy after the presentation to Countess Litta: and from thence went to Mad de Brays where we were introduced to a Madame d Buzow and her daughter and Madlle Lesseps daughter of the French Consul a very agreeable girl– returned home early–

14

Between 8 and 9 in the Evening we went Mr Adams and myself to a great Ball at Count Romanzoffs given to the Empress Mother and attended by the Emperor and Empress– It was very splendid– It was very splendid like those at the Court of Berlin The dresses very magnificent and every body covered with diamonds I was dressed in a Silver Tissue which was all fixed on me by a French dress Maker and when I appeared before our young party it was approved and I started in tolerable spirits–

Count Romanzoff recieved us with distinction and the Emperor and Empresses spoke very kindly to us– I did not know a creature in the Room but I only saw Miss Lesseps who I had met at Madame De Brays a few nights before– She invited me to walk into another with some Ladies and we went there– The Emperor followed us and politely offered us wine and entered into conversation with me– Returning to the Ball Room the Grand Duke Constantine bowed to me but I was not presented–[356]

Mr. Harris at last arrived– He had been upset and was obliged to return home and dress– He asked me to dance a Polonaise I was much afraid I should blunder but I soon fell into the step and made out without mortifying my fastidious partner–

There were fifteen supper Tables–That of the Emperor ornamented and served on solid gold. That of the Corps Diplomatique with Silver–and all the others were legant though in a less degree– The party broke up at 1 in the morning and no one was alowed to depart before the Emperor; I was introduced to the whole Corps

356 Grand Duke Constantine (1778–1831), who in 1822 would renounce his right to succeed his brother Alexander I to the imperial throne (Palmer, *Alexander I*, p. 386, 418).

diplomatique The Chancellor was said to have 300 Servants of different grades 150 at least wearing magnificent Liveries according to their grades— The wines and every thing on the same scale— I was glad to get home— All this was too much like a fairy tale—

17

I was siezed with violent illness and a D[r] Galloway was sent for—[357] who ordered that I should be confined to my bed until he came again voyage: the excitement: and the uneasiness of Mr Adams at the expence entailed upon us bore me down and again I sadly regreted that I had not stayed at home—

19

Invitations to a dinner at Madame De Brays sans cérémonie arrived—tomorrow— I was obliged to decline Another to a Ball at the French Ambassadors on the 20— This invitation was accepted— An invitation to Madame de Brays to a dancing party en petite Committée on Thursday Evening—

I was much better—

20

In the Evening we all excepting Mr Smith went to a Ball at The French Ambassadors— The early part of the Evening 8 o clock was for a Childrens Ball— It was a beautiful sight— The Children retired between nine and ten and then the company consisting of about forty persons danced and stayed to an elegant Supper— Made several acquaintance Madame de Vlodeck a reigning belle very handsome and a favorite of the Ambassador—[358] We were struck with the

[357] Dr. Galloway, a Scot, was among the British physicians who prominently served the Russian imperial court in this period (D/JQA/28, 17 Nov. 1809, APM Reel 31; Cross, *Banks of the Neva*, p. 158).

[358] Armand Augustine Louis de Caulaincourt, Duc de Vicence (1773–1827), was the French ambassador to Russia from 1807 to 1811. Caulaincourt had been with the French entourage in July 1807, when Napoleon and Alexander I concluded the Treaty of Tilsit, which formed an uneasy alliance between the two empires. With a generous allowance from Napoleon, the ambassador enjoyed a place of precedence in the diplomatic corps, and he entertained lavishly at his palace near the Hermitage, country house on the road to Peterhof, and villa on Kamenny Ostrov (Stone Island), on St. Petersburg's Neva delta. His mistress, Madame de Vlodek, was the wife of a military officer (Palmer, *Alexander I*, p. 135–136, 151, 177–178; *Repertorium*, 3:133; R. R. Madden, *The Literary Life and Correspondence of the Countess of Blessington*, 2d edn., 3 vols., London, 1855, 2:491; D/JQA/28, 24 Oct., 10 Nov. 1810, APM Reel 31).

9. EMPRESS MARIA FEODOROVNA, CA. 1801

See page xiii

Splendor of the Embassadorial residence which is quite Regal— The Duke is a very elegant man his Secretaries are pleasant but nothing remarkable and his Palace is one of the Imperial residences.— Among the company was a Prince at about one we sat down to Table— The Ambassador told me *I* was too serious for a pretty woman; and that when "we were at Rome we must do as Rome"— I told if I should go to Rome perhaps I might— We got home at two—

26

The Duke de Mondragoni called on a visit—[359] He is an elegant man: but of a dark and melancholy turn of mind in consequence of some great family misfortune and the situation of his Country. Madame Bacounin and Madame Sablonkoff came to see me— She was one of my old english acquaintance the daughter of John Julius Angerstein a rich Merchant in London— Madame Bacounin was I believe a Sister of her husband—[360] They were both very agreeable women— I went with my Sister and *Charles* to Madame de Brays and passed the Evening—

I forgot to mention that the last night I went to the French play and sat in the Duc de Mondragoni's Box.

27

This morning Mr Harris sent us a present my Sister and myself of an elegant Turkish Shawl— We wore them that Evening at the French— Mr Harris had suffered agonies at the idea that american Ladies should appear without such indispensables and Mr Adams allowed *me* to accept it— We went at 4 oclock to dine with the Ambassador and found every body there but the Duke of Mondragoni— My Sister was quite enchanted with all these parties but the want of variety of toilets was a dreadful drawback— What would have

[359] The Duke of Mondragone of Naples, minister to Russia since 1808 (*Repertorium*, 3:259).

[360] John Julius Angerstein (ca. 1732–1823) was a man of obscure Russian origins. At the age of fifteen he immigrated to England, where he was successful in the marine insurance business and notable as a philanthropist. His fortune enabled him to buy the great works of art that would form the core of the collection now at the National Gallery in London. His daughter Juliana married the Russian Army officer Nikolai Alexandrovich Sablukov (*DNB*; D/JQA/28, 25 Nov. 1809, APM Reel 31; Algernon Graves and William Vine Cronin, *A History of the Works of Sir Joshua Reynolds, P.R.A.*, 4 vols., London, 1899–1901, 1:25).

dressed one modestly was by no means competint for two more especially for a younger Lady and we had much to endure from the rigid parsimony of the Salary. our expenses were very heavy and our difficulties encreased every hour at a Court so showy and every way extravagant—[361]

The party was small divested of all cérémony— But I was not fitted for the sphere and "could not do as Rome does." The liason of the Ambassador was notorious and I could neither admire nor respect the Lady: and this circle of almost unrestricted gallantry did not suit my ideas of les convenances.

Princess Viazemski Madame de Vlodeck and the Countess Tolstoy & her Sisters and two or three other persons of Rank with all the Corps Diplomatique attached to the french party were there— We were about two hours at Table and we returned to the Saloon we found Mademoiselle Bourgoin a french Actress there who declamed parts from different plays Phedre—Zaire—l'Ecole des Maris and le Florentin—[362] M de Rayneval read the alternate parts— This was very amusing— A band of musick was then introduced struck up a Polonaise which we walked round the and then we passed through a Suite of apartments to a Theatre where another Actor performed a number of tricks of slight of hand. We then returned again to the Hall and a dance began which lasted until Supper and we got home at 2 o clock—

14 [*DECEMBER*]

Thus we went on occasionally making visits and going to the theatre until this time when we all went to a fancy Ball for Children at the Duke de Vicenza's We took Charles who I had dressed as an Indian Chief to gratify the taste for Savages and there was a general burt of applause when he marched in at which he was much surprized— There were forty Children admirably costumed from two to twelve years old some beautiful fancy dances performed by the elder and Charles led out Miss Vlodeck supposed to be the daughter of the Ambassader and they with the assistance of their Mamas opened the Ball— He was three years and a half old no quite—[363] Af-

[361] JQA's salary as minister was $9,000 with another $9,000 provided for travel and household expenses (Bemis, *JQA*, 1:164).

[362] Racine's *Phèdre*, 1677; Voltaire's *Zaïre*, 1732; Molière's *L'école des maris*, 1661; and La Fontaine's *Le florentin*, 1685.

[363] CFA was two years and three months old.

ter the dance there was an elegant supper oceans of Champaign for the little people and the Mothers all stood full dressed behind their Chairs— When supper was finished there was a lottery of choice and expensive toys—but M[r] Adams hurried us away when the Child left the table and would not permit him to take a chance— We all returned home together

8 [17]

Invited to dine with Madame Severin— We went and after dinner found that there was a Ball to which Madame Severin insisted on our staying— We remained until two in the morning when we sat down to supper and it was between 3 and 4. when we got home— I was quite knocked up—

23

Recieved a Notification for M[r] Adams and myself to attend at the celebration tomorrow Evening of the Emperors's birth day by the Empress Mother—to a Ball—

Having but one dress in which I had already appeared several times I declined on the plea of ill health and went to take Tea with Colombi Wife of the Spanish Consul and a lovely Woman who we visited most sociably—[364] We passed a delightful Evening and I had gone to rest long before Mr Adams came from the Ball—

30

Went with M[r.] Adams to a small party at Mrs Krehmers but was so sick I was obliged to return home— My Sister had been quite sick for a week— I left him and the Gentlemen there—

[364] Countess María de Bodé y Kinnersley de Colombi (1782–1872) had married the Spanish consul general in Russia, Count Antonio Colombi y Payet (1749–1811), two years earlier. She was the daughter of Mary Kinnersley, an Englishwoman, and Baron Charles Auguste Louis Frederick de Bodé. At the time of the French Revolution, the Bodé family had fled from their estate in Alsace. In 1795 Catherine the Great responded to Baroness de Bodé's appeal for lands in Russia, granting the family a domain on the Dnieper River. The following year Paul I agreed to a second request, providing them with a more suitable estate near Narva. Although the baron died before settling there, his wife saw to the children's education and entry into Russian society (O'Brien, *Mrs. Adams*, p. 33–34; Didier Ozanam and Denise Ozanam, *Les diplomates espagnols du XVIIe siècle*, Madrid and Bordeaux, 1998, p. 232–234).

JAN 1ST [*1810*]

On this day I went with Madame de Bray and paid my visits– I was informed that her Majesty the Empress Mother having heard of my being out at Tea with a friend the Evening of the Ball to which I had been invited intimated that it must not occur again or I should be *omited* on future occasions– This was charming pour l'économie!! more especially as I had heard her tell a Lady who had worn the same gown several times that she "wished that *She* (the Lady) would get another for that She was tired of seeing the same colour so often."– Charles went with Mrs. Krehmer to pass the day with her Children–

3

A Ball at Madame de Brays met all the Corps diplomatique–Baron Blome the Danish Minister was in his person manners and Establishment the very pink of elegance–Refined to effeminacy; yet he was entirely devoid of affectation and very free from mental weakness– He was a Bachelor had a great reputation for gallantry but never shocked in society the sense of propriety of other people–To *me* he was not an agreeable man but he was what in Society *a gentleman*– The Ball was very brilliant and in the course of the Evening the F. Ambassador invited to a Ball at his house for Monday.

The Chevallier de Bray was a German full of Bonhommie displayed altogether in the German style– All gène was excluded in his House and everybody felt at home and at ease there– Without pretence to great fortune he lived handsomely nothing extravagant, nother outrée and a total banishment of all pretention– It was the house of rè-union of the whole Coprs who in Petersburg live much together–

6

Passed the Evening at Mrs. Krehmers–a small party of about fifty Count St Julien the new Austrian Ambassador was there and his Secretary Baron Marreschall both charming and quite an acquisition to the Corps– Count Einsiedel the Saxon minister was the Wit of the Corps and in his company it was difficult to keep the sèrieux suited to the dignity of our *body*– Mons D'Alopéus was also there–

9

At the Ball at Caulincours given in honor of Princess Viasemskey's birth day.— There were about 130 persons there— Supper was served at two in the morning and we left at four after dancing all night—

Heard of the Empress Josephines divorce—Rumour says to marry the Princess of Saxony—[365] Introduced to Count Cshernischoff the favorite of Alexander— He was one of the handsomest men I ever saw—age five and twenty five—

10

Dined supped and *passed the night* at M^rs^ B Cramers—four o clock when we got home Reeceod Tickets for the Ball and Supper at the Pallace Had a company of our Countrymen to dine with us— This was a Masquerade Ball and ten Tickets were sent besides the three for Mr Adams Mr. Harris and myself— The French Am—— called to pay us a visit enquired if we were to be at a fète given by Mr Narischkin— We were not invited. He said it was a great party always given to close the old and begin the N.Y.

11

Being according to Russian custom New Years day we sent Cards round to all the world according to the fashion of distinction and recieved ditto in return.[366] There were illuminations a Ball and a Spectacle— There were no invitations given but he was going for the fourth time—

[365] Determined to secure the Bonaparte dynasty on the French throne, Napoleon arranged for the annulment of his civil bond and religious vows to Empress Josephine, and on 15 Dec. 1809 the two signed the document that dissolved their marriage. Napoleon considered three prospective brides: Grand Duchess Anna of Russia, the daughter of the king of Saxony, and the daughter of Emperor Francis I (formerly Francis II) of Austria. In early Feb. 1810 he settled on eighteen-year-old Marie Louise, Archduchess of Austria and Princess Royal of Hungary and Bohemia (Schom, *Napoleon Bonaparte*, p. 545–548; Palmer, *Alexander I*, p. 162, 181).

[366] The Old Style (O.S.) or Julian calendar, at the time twelve days behind the Gregorian calendar, was used in Russia until 1918. It was on 13 (not 11) Jan. 1810 O.S., New Year's Day, that the Adamses sent visiting cards "to all our acquaintance, and to all the persons of distinction who are entitled to be visited" and received the same in return (D/JQA/28, 13 Jan., APM Reel 31).

13

Mr Adams Mr Smith and Mr A Everett went to Court and heard Mass after which a Circle at which the Foreign Ministers were recieved—Ladies never attended— At nine in the Evening we went to the Ball at the Hermitage with Mr. Adams— It is impossible to describe the Splendor of the Scene— All the Palace that is the two united the Imperial and the Hermitage with all its magnificent embellishments are laid open to the Public— The nobility all appear in full Court Dress The Gentlemen wearing black Venetion hats with large Plumes of Feathers and Cloaks and the Ladies rich dresses of the most splendid style— The illuminations exceed all description and the Pictures vases and rich ornaments of every description produce an effect perfectly dazzling to the eyes and the imagination—[367]

The brain bewilder'd floats in gay delight
The sight enchanted swims in rays of light—
Mellifluous sounds invade the list'ning ear
While Horns resound iviting to the Cheer—
While Tables groaning pall the varied taste
Luxurious splendours of profusion waste—

I was walking with Madame de Bettancourt an English Lady the Wife of Genl Bettancourt Chief of the Polytecnic School and was gazing at the Pictures when I observed the Empress Mother make a sign to me to come to her—[368] I immediately walked up to her and she told me that she wanted to introduce her Sons to *me* and then presented the Grand Duke Nicholas then about 16 and the Grand Duke Michaal a year or two younger—[369] Nicholas was the most

[367] The imperial family's Winter Palace, commissioned by Empress Elizabeth Petrovna in 1754, was completed in time for Catherine the Great to make it her residence in 1763. Catherine ordered the construction of the adjoining Small Hermitage, where she entertained guests and displayed works of art. As her art collection expanded, she commissioned the adjacent Great or Old Hermitage, completed in 1787, to which she added a loggia for her copies of Raphael's Vatican frescoes. Catherine also commissioned the Hermitage Theater, constructed between 1783 and 1787. A truly public museum would not be realized until Nicholas I ordered the construction, near the Winter Palace, of the New Hermitage, which opened in 1852 (Norman, *Hermitage*, p. 1, 3–4, 19–20, 37–38, 67, 73).

[368] Political turmoil in Spain had caused the military engineer Augustin de Betancourt y Molina to seek refuge in St. Petersburg in 1808. There he oversaw civic planning and construction, and in 1809 he established the Institute of Engineers of Communication Routes (O'Brien, *Mrs. Adams*, p. 35; Marco Ceccarelli, ed., *Distinguished Figures in Mechanism and Machine Science: Their Contributions and Legacies*, 2 vols. to date, Dordrecht, 2007– , 1:34–35).

[369] Grand Duke Nicholas (1796–1855), who would succeed his brother Alexander as emperor in 1825, and Grand Duke Michael (1798–1849) (Palmer, *Alexander I*, p. 386, 410–412, 419).

beautiful boy I ever looked on— His manner was elegant and he addressed me in a style of the most polished breeding— Michaal would have been very handsome had he not been near his brother and was also ready and perfectly well bred— I believe that my *astonished* admiration gratified the Empress more than any words could have done— At the Supper in the Theatre Transparencies beautifully designed shut in the Boxes and the Horns so celebrated for their exquisite melody played occasionally sending forth sounds like the music of the Spheres so perfect was the harmony—

The Emperor walked round the Table of the Foreign Ministers and addressed a few obliging words to every one— To me he was very courtious and seemed pleased at my expressions of admiration of the Scene— It was contrary to ettiquette to rise—

14

Madame de Bettancourt and her daughters and spent part of the Even. with us. We then went to visit Princess Viasemski and from thence to the Duke of Serra Capriola his Wife being the daughter of the Princess— The Prince Duke was upwards of 80 and the most handsome and delightful old Gentleman that I ever saw: and after these visits we went to a Ball at Mr P. Severin— Returned home at one before Supper—

16

At three o clock we went to the Ice Hill party at Kamini Ostroff to Caulincourt's Country House— The Cold was severe— The Ambassadors Hills not being in order The company rode half a mile to the Emperors and near the Palace— We did not go—and the company returned at 4: o'clock— The company was as usual—The Diplomats and The family of Madame de Vlodcek— A few young men were added— Prince Kourakin a Son of the Minster of the Interior— The Evening dancing and the Gentlemen exchanged clothes with some of the ladies, and danced a Cotillion— We returned home at 10 o clock— I retired from the dressing Room having no toilet to make: and Mr. Six the dutch Minister remarked the Act in a manner to make it unpleasant to the other Ladies: my situation was very ~~unpleasant~~ disagreeable—but the old man owed a grudge to Caulincourt, and kindly payed it through me— I acknowledge I felt very much out of my element—But I had no right to censure other people—[370]

18

The blessing of the waters took place this Morning It is a grand Ceremony of the Church which takes place on the Neva right opposite to the Palace in the Presence of the Imperial family—the troops in the City and all the Foreigners and strangers of distinction— We obtained a seat in a window of a house in the Square and saw the Procession of Priests with the Archbishop at their head performing the Ceremony— Magnificent Furs covered the Balcony and The Emperor and all the Imp family attended by the Grandee's with all the Foreign Corps in superb costumes accompanied them— After they retired the Emperor and Caulincourt the Troops all in full uniform and on most splendid Horses drawn up in a hollow square and not deviating the breadth of a hair from the Line— This is the most splendid sight that can be imagined G D Constantine was in Command— Went to a Ball at M^rs S Cramers and at Supper the 12th. Cake was cut and M^r. Adams was made King; but declined the honor being a Republican— The Bean was transfered to Count Einsiedel and he chose M^rs. Krehmer for his Queen—[371] We danced, and it was past five o clock when we got home— The Haute Commerce as it is termed live in a style of great expence and entertain continually once or twice a week beginning with dinners ending with Balls which do not break up until four in the mornings Cards form a constant part of the amusement— The Foreign Ministers frequent them very much— Mr Krehmer was the Court Banker—

[370] The -6° F temperature probably dissuaded LCA from joining those guests at Armand de Caulaincourt's villa who went sleigh-riding on the hills of the emperor's nearby palace. In the evening JQA "played at whist" while some of the young men danced in "female attire." The Dutch minister, Willem Six van Oterleeck, evidently remarked with favor on LCA's decision not to participate in the exchange of clothing, to the chagrin of the women who had joined in (D/JQA/28, 16 Jan. 1810, APM Reel 31; Palmer, *Alexander I*, p. 185–186).

[371] The procession gathered in a pavilion erected on the Neva River over an opening in the ice. The archbishop plunged the cross into the water, to the sound of trumpets and cannon fire. Had JQA accepted the bean from the Twelfth Night, or king's, cake of the Feast of the Epiphany, he would have offended republican virtue, and he would also have been required to provide "a treat to the Company in the course of the Winter" (J. H. Schnitzler, *Secret History of the Court and Government of Russia under the Emperors Alexander and Nicholas*, 2 vols., London, 1847, 2:391–393; D/JQA/28, 18 Jan., APM Reel 31).

24[372]

A Ball at the Empress Mothers Her Birth— As usual enquired of Mr Adams why I was not there— He informed that I was quite ill and unable to attend being confined to my bed—

FEBY

Mrs. Krehmer sent for Charles and She kept him until after ten at night— This Lady is particularly kind and we are under great obligations to her— He is a Swede she is a German and a great favorite of the Emperors.— Gen Pardoe the Spanish minister is quite charmed with the Society of Mr. Adams and comes frequently to see and converse with him— He is a Greek Scholar an Author and very learned and full of Court annecdotes of this and the last reign—[373]

3

My illness encreased very rapidly and again I was afflicted by suffering and disappointment— This mode of life is dreadful to me and the trial is beyond my strength—

21

Just getting about when Mr Adams was siezed with a violent Cold and was quite ill— Sent for Dr Galloway who ordered him to bed and to keep very quiet—[374] I have omited to mention that Count Romanzoff came in State to visit *me*— He was in his State Coach with six Horses out Riders 3 footmen with Flambeau's all in full dress— Not being aware of the intended honor and our apartments very mean I did not recieve which was as great an oversight as that of politeness as could have been commited—

3 FEBY. [*MARCH*]

Princess Amalia the Sister of the reigning Empress came to take Tea and spend the Evening with me. and the same blunder occurred

[372] LCA's 2d version of Adventures begins at this date. For a description of that manuscript, see Adventures, 1 July 1840, note 1, above.

[373] The diplomat Benito Pardo de Figueroa served King Joseph Bonaparte of Spain from 1808 to 1812 (*Repertorium*, 3:428, 440).

[374] The 2d version adds here, "Just getting up myself."

neither my husband or myself ever having expected such distinctions— My presentation Madame de Bray informed us had been quite of the usual line: and I presume these honors were offered as compliments to the Country this being the first regular Mission from America—

Recieved a notification through Mrs. Krehmer to send my Boy to the Princess Amalias room in the Palace To see the Emperor and Empress who would be there on monday Morning at twelve o clock— Thus I was obliged to make him a suitable dress— It consisted of a white[375] Satin Frock over which was worn a sprigged Muslin dress white Satin Pantelets—The Shoulders and bosom bare and the Sleeves tied up with Satin Ribbon with a white Satin Sash to fasten the waiste of the Frock and white Satin Slippers— He was about two years and a half old— Martha Godfrey attended him— They were all anxious to see her in consequence of an impertinent Letter which had been intercepted and carried to the Emperor in which he was very disrespectly mentioned—[376]

7

Mr Adams who was confined by a violent Erysipelas in one of his Legs: insisted that I should go to a Ball given by the English Club to the Emperor and Empresses— I had had Blisters behind my ears which were not healed and I could not dress properly— But no excuse could be offered and I went with my Sister and the Gentlemen of the Legation and we could not return home until two in the morning— The Imperial Family recieved me with the usual distinction and exprest their regret at Mr Adams's indisposition— It was an elegant Ball—

8

Obliged to go to a Ball at the French Ambassadors escorted by the Gentlemen of the Legation—[377] We went at nine o clock the party

[375] At this point LCA wrote "Feb. 5." in the margin, though the month should be March.

[376] JQA noted that Martha Godfrey, in a letter to her sister, "spoke of this Country severely." LCA later wrote that her maid's letter to her friends "related many anecdotes which she had picked up concerning the Imperial family" (D/JQA/28, 5 Dec., APM Reel 31; LCA to CFA, GWA, and JA2, 1 May 1828, Adams Papers). For LCA's further remarks on this incident, see Adventures, 5 Dec. 1810, below.

[377] The 2d version replaces the previous seven words with "without my Husband—"

brilliant as usual— Mad[lle.] Gourief the Daughter of the Minister I think of the interior was dancing a Quadrille with Count Saxbourg— In waltsing round in the Chene des Dames She slipped and both fell on the Floor she being a very large coarse Woman: Her position was not an agreeable one as she found some difficulty in rising while her Partner stood and said Eh bien! Levez vous et ne faites pas des grimaces!!! This was too bad her Mother and I who was close by her led her to a seat and she soon after quitted the— Count Nesselrode was then a young man addressing but it was not then supposed he would be permited to marry her by her Family— He was a young man of great promise but then not much known to the world—[378] Supper as usual and dancing— Nothing amused me so much as the instructions of our Consul Levet Harris— It was some time after we arrived before M[r] Adams's Carriage was ready for us and M[r.] Harris used to give me a Seat in his; while my Sister went with M[r.] Adams: and during these rides he would favor me with Instructions as to my conduct and deportment &c— In the first place although I might take his arm on the Stair way where nobody could see it; *he* must drop it before he enterred the room and I must walk up to the Lady or Gentleman of the house alone—least our acquaintance should seem too familiar— It was not ettiquette for a Lady to stand by a gentleman after the reception: as it would be thought very improper— That a Lady must not go to the Theatre with a Gentleman but only under the protection of her footmen: and last of all that he hoped M[r.] Adams would soon have his Carriage lest it should that *we* had an improper *Liaison*!! This was quite too much for my gravity and I laughed in his face assuring him that whatever fears he might have for *his* reputation I had none whatever for my own and this entretien put an end to such discourse and to all future rides with Levet Harris— He was a petit Maitre, with Quaker habits of exceeding neatness and in his household, his furniture, his Equipage and his person there was a refined elegance amounting to effeminacy in the best possible taste— He had many amiable traits of character and I always regreted that association

[378] Count Karl Robert von Nesselrode (1780–1862), a Russian statesman and diplomat, was descended from German nobility. He married Marya Dmitrievna Gurieff, the daughter of Alexander I's finance minister and the maid of honor to the Empress Mother. Count Nesselrode would serve as Alexander's state secretary for foreign affairs at the Congress of Vienna, and in 1844 he would become chancellor of Russia (Palmer, *Alexander I*, p. 190, 304; Serena Vitale, *Pushkin's Button*, transl. Ann Goldstein and Jon Rothschild, N.Y., 1999, p. 133–134; *New Amer. Cyclo.*).

with Men of corrupt habits had led him into practices which the strict principles of my Husband could not approve—[379]

9

Mr Adams was able to ride out[380] but the severity of the attack was only subdued and he became much worse after riding out—
This is the height of the Russian Carnival—

12

M^r. Adams continues ill: very feverish:[381] and although Gentlemen kindly visit him he is unused to confinement and time hangs sadly on his hands— He never permits me to nurse him— My Sister reads to him and we make out as well as we can—

20

Mr Adams rode out in company with me returned much fatigued but the general health better— Leg still sore: but the humour having fallen there has saved his precious eyes—

21

M^r. Adams sat up the whole day without injury—[382]

[379] Levett Harris enriched himself by facilitating the clearance of questionable ships and cargoes past Russian neutrality commissioners. William David Lewis, an American merchant in Russia, publicly accused Harris of corrupting his office. Harris, in turn, sued Lewis for libel. In proceedings that began in 1820, Harris conceded that he had reaped a fortune but argued that in these transactions he was acting as a merchant, not as the U.S. consul. After seven years of litigation in Philadelphia, Harris prevailed but was awarded only nominal damages (Saul, *Distant Friends*, p. 58–59, 83–86; Bemis, *JQA*, 1:169). See also Diary, 17 Dec. 1819, and note 1, below.

[380] In the 2d version the remainder of the paragraph is replaced by "and we stayed a couple of hours."

[381] JQA noted that, as a treatment for his erysipelas, a disease much later understood to be caused by a streptococcus bacterium, Dr. Galloway advised that he apply "a continual fomentation of lead-water mixed with Brandy upon my leg" (D/JQA/28, 11 March 1810, APM Reel 31).

[382] The 2d version replaces the previous two words with "his Leg being better and rode out:—"

22

Thank God my husband was able to resume his place in the Drawing Room— Mr. Six came and sat with him— He has recieved great attention from the whole Corps Diplomatique—

APRIL 1

Mr Adams went to visit Count Romanzoff and the duties of his Office were all renewed very actively— His health was still weak and mine was wretched— I had taken a violent Cold[383] in consequence of sitting with my back to an open "was is das" and an attack of Erysepelas the desease of the Country of a very inflamatory character which settled in the back of my head and neck and subjected me to an occasional deafness altogether painful; and very inconvenient when associated with royalty— Mr John Spear Smith arrived— Another Attaché—[384]

Some Gentlemen generally passed the Evening with us and we were seldom alone[385]

5

Went to see the Hermitage—Its Pictures its curiosities and all its splendors; with its sad associations of Vice talents and greatness—[386] The Empress Catherine seemed to rise on memory in all the Majesty of Power abused; Intellectual strength and abilities misused; Morals debased and the worst corruption encouraged and protected— And yet in defiance of all this: every where tokens of taste, of cultivation; of Respect for the Arts; and deference for Science pervade the Place and while it created the most agreeable sensations of pleasure—we silently regreted that under all circumstances our impressions were more painful than pleasurable— What a contrast between that day and the present Reign!!!

Mr Labenski did the honors of the Hermitage— Came hope per-

383 The 2d version indicates this occurred "at the F A's masquerade."

384 Like Alexander Everett and Francis Gray, John Spear Smith, the son of Gen. Samuel Smith of Baltimore and the nephew of Secretary of State Robert Smith, served at his own expense (D/JQA/28, 30 March, APM Reel 31; Bemis, *JQA*, 1:154).

385 The 2d version adds the following paragraph: "Of my Children I thought for ever and all these honors were worth less compared with the blessing God had granted me and of which I was entirely deprived—"

386 The 2d version adds here, "Alas! Alas! what is man?"

fectly exhausted— Invited to a Ball at M[rs.] Krehmers. M[r] Adams my Sister and myself declined— The Gentlemen went—

9

M[r.] Adams and my Sister (rather a breach) of rules went to the Ice Hill Party at the French Ambassadors Caperoonage[387] being deemed essential— It is a very difficult thing for Americans to conceive of the restraints exacted by European Society, and what are termed delicate proprieties— But I have found that we cannot reason upon mere forms with those who cannot or will not understand them when long established; and if we break thro' them we must submit to evil construction without asking the why or the wherefore— Custom is the Law—

14

My health declines so much I could not go to Madame de Brays dancing party.— Besides which the expence of dress is too heavy for our apportioned Salary— I have tried every experiment even that of dressing in Mourning but it would not answer, and our motive was suspected— What mortifications attend an American Mission!!!

M[r.] Adams dined with the Dutch Minister M[r.] Six—A real plain spoken Dutchman shrewed keen and very castic—An enthusiastic admirer of Napolean—Proud of his Station while he lives in perpetual fear of losing it— He took a great fancy to *me*. but his injudicious praises did me more harm than good—[388]

29

Easter Sunday is a great day at S[t] Petersburg and we recieved Presents from some of our friends of painted and Cut glass Eggs without paying the Fee generally asked for the complement—as a religious ceremony and were obliged to accept them.[389] They are very handsome and sometimes very costly—[390] Every one even of the

[387] That is, a chaperone.

[388] The 2d version adds, "He was a man of sense and very shrewed. Through Lent we were quiet."

[389] JQA noted that on Easter Sunday "the muzhik's present real eggs, hard-boiled and died red with log-wood; for which they receive roubles" (D/JQA/28, 29 April, APM Reel 31).

[390] The 2d version adds, "My health was so wretched I remained much at home thankful even at that expense for the privilege—"

People have a right to kiss the Emperors hand on this sacred day. It is a privilege however mostly claimed by the Court which sometimes keeps him up until a very late hour of the Night— Ladies are not admited or he would have no hand left— The Gentlemen all went to Court where there were grand doings—

My Sister and myself were accustomed to walk out occasionally when the weather was not too cold on the Newssky Perspective; and the Emperor would often stop and speak to us very politely— As my Sister was a great Belle among our young Gentlemen this circumstance though customary with the Emperor towards many Ladies whom he met gave umbrage to Beaux and occasioned so much teazing and questions that we left off our promenades for some time— But the weather being now very fine we resumed our walks[391] and again met his Imperial Majesty who again stoped us and enquired "why we had left off walking out" and without waiting for an answer; turned to me and said "that it was good for my health and that he should expect to meet *us* every day looking at my Sister." that the weather was fine— This was a real Imperial command in its tone and manner; and he gracefully touched his hat and walked on— When we met at Table the usual question and sour looks greeted us from the young gentlemen and my Sister answered yes! repeating the order that we had recieved to vex them: they were all in a blaze and I related the conversation of the Emperor without exaggeration and precisely in the manner it had taken place

"Adding nought in malice as my Sister did"[392]

The Minister looked very *grave* but said nothing— The young Gentlemen disapproved and hoped that we should not do it.

That however diplomatic usage did not permit and we continued our walks occasionally taking Charles with us who always had a kind greeting from his Majesty and a shake of the hand but the Emperor complained that he could not make him sociable—

MAY 10

The Ice in the Newa broke up A handsome sight but perfectly delightful to us poor poor exotics—

[391] The 2d version adds, "the Carriage always following."

[392] "Nothing extenuate, / Nor set down aught in malice" (Shakespeare, *Othello*, Act V, scene ii, lines 342–343).

12

The Ice though broken takes time to float the Masses to the Gulph of Finland and still longer for it to come down from the Lake Ladoga— But it is a matter of great rejoicing to the—[393] The Gov of the City waited on the Emperor with a glass of the Water—and when all the Ice is gone the chain Bridge of Boats is put across the River and the Country is free to the Petersburg Public—[394]

13

It is customary to celebrate May day in Russia and the French Ambassador[395] to his Country House to see the Fete— All the Nobility Gentry and Citizens who can go out in Procession in their Summer dresses and Carriages Drozkis &ce &c of the finest kind of Horses which they cannot use in the Winter as they cannot bear the exposure to the Climate and drive to a Palace called Caterérimenhoff about two miles from the City at nine o clock in the Evening— Caulincourt had borrowed[396] of a Merchant for the occasion— We did not go—the Gentlemen all went—

15

Invited to dine with Mons & Madame de Laval de Montmorency of which family it was said he was a Scion— A Frenchman who had married a Russian Lady whose beauty had certainly not kindled the flame of love in his heart. Cupids arrow would certainly have been shivered in an attack on such charms— A Gentleman asking Count Eensiedel what the attraction could have been He coolly answered "Elle à une mine de Fér"— The équivoke was delightful—

23

Went to a Ball at the French Ambassadors in honor of the Marriage of Napoleon with Maria Louise of Austria— Obliged to go as

[393] The 2d version completes the sentence with "People—"

[394] JQA noted that the breaking of the ice in the Neva River, which occurred later in 1810 than it had since records were first kept in 1719, was a joyful event and the object of "innumerable wagers." It marked the beginning of the summer season, a time when the nobility and wealthy merchants left for their country estates, the double windows were taken down, and boat travel resumed (D/JQA/28, 10, 12 May 1810, APM Reel 31).

[395] The 2d version adds, "invited us."

[396] The 2d version adds, "a House."

the Imperial Family were to be there—[397] The Palace (a Palace belonging to the Emperor in which he resided rent Free the Russian Ambassador in Paris having the same honor) was superbly illuminated; as were the Houses also of the Spanish Ambassador Pardoe and Count de Bushe Heinfeldt of whom I have said very little and Count St Julians the Austrian Ambassador but they made comparatively but little show—

The Emperor was remarkably gracious— He enquired of Mr. Harris where I sat and immediately came to me and tapped me on the Shoulder as I was talking to a Lady next to me and that *I* must walk or dance the next Polonaise with him— I was very much confused as I did not know what to do when a Lady of the Court came and informed me that as soon as I saw the Emperor take his place in the dance I must walk up *alone* and take my place by him— Naturally timid this idea almost overcame me but I got through ackwardly enough— He immediately took my hand and we started off— Fortunately for me the Polonaise was very short and I bowed when the music stoped intending to return to my Seat when he said "that the dance had been so short he wished to converse with me"! Imagine my confusion every Lady in the Hall was seated but myself. He did not hear well and I what with the flurry caused by the prominence of my position and the unfortunate loss of hearing which the Climate had could only betray my stupidity without being able to understand a word— Thus we stood for about five minutes when he bowed low and retired leaving plantè là until some one whispered to me to go and take a

The Music soon struck whe his Imperial Majesty again cane up and asked me "where my Sister was"? I told him I did not know but would go immediately and seek he. "He said no I must not as he would go and do that himself"— He sought Her and took her out himself to dance and she not knowing the ettiquettes began laughing and talking to him as she would have done to an American partner herself beginning the conversation contrary to all usages du Monde—and he was so charmed with the novelty that he detained Caulincourts Supper twenty five minutes to prolong the Polonaise— She had never been presented at Court so that this extraordinary

[397] Having been married by proxy to Napoleon in a religious ceremony at Vienna on 11 March, Archduchess Marie Louise of Austria was formally married to him in a civil ceremony at St. Cloud, near Paris, on 1 April. She would give birth to a son in March 1811 (Schom, *Napoleon Bonaparte*, p. 542, 548–549, 553, 588).

distinction produced a Buz of astonishment and poor Madame de Bray being the only Lady beside myself of the Diplomatic ~~were in such a state of astonishment they could scarcely refrain from excepting~~ my ~~self~~ was so distressed at not being noticed that the Emperor through the medium of Caulincourt took the Lady out and thus appeased the jealousies— The truth was the Emperor wished to become acquainted with my Sister and the honor confered on me was only a passport to the act— The Emperor Supper Table was magnificent and the wonder of the night was a gorgeously ornamented Bast of wrought gold containing Seven large Pears which strange to say had been cultivated in one of the Emperors Hot Houses and which his Imperial Majesty had treasured and guarded for the Fete of his Mother which would soon take place— Tho a little suspicious instituted enquiries on the next day and found that his pears were gone and that Caulincourt had paid one hundred Rubles apiece for them— We got home at two o clock in the morning and it was broad day light—[398]

JUNE 3

At last there is a prospect of our getting out this horrid Hotel where I cannot sing at my work or be accompanied on the Piano by my Sister when we think ourselves alone without hearing loud clapping of hands and brava's from the neigbouring apartments on one side and on the other the directions of a Gentleman for the finishing touches of the toilet which always terminates with Rouge— The looking Glass must hand near the partition door— The Emperor wants to have Nelson for his own Servant.[399] He has fourteen Blacks who on entering the Service take an Oath never to leave him— They wait upon the Imperial Family alone wear Turkish dresses very rich and expensive and take their turns of Service— They have a handsome Table a Carriage and four at their service and as perquisites the remains of the Desserts of the Imperial Table—White Coachman Postillion's and Footmen quite in style— But he had tasted of freedom and the golden Pill of this new Slavery ~~the bondage became so bitter~~ he sunk and died under its operation.[400]

[398] The 2d version adds, "It was a most tedious Ball—"

[399] The 2d version adds, "I am sorry to lose him."

[400] After entering the emperor's service in Sept. 1810, Nelson occasionally visited his former employer, at first declaring himself quite satisfied with his position. In April 1811 JQA attended Nelson's baptism, "the first Roman Catholic Baptism that I had seen." By December

We cannot get into our Apartments for a week—And I am harrassed to death; for the place is so inconvenient[401] I have no suitable apartment for my Sister— Russian Houses have no Bed Chambers according to our ideas for *Lady* accomodation.[402]

4

Mons & Madame de Bray came to take leave—[403] He is a kind hearted pleasant and gentlemanly man not a dangerous one from either the shrewdness or brightness of his intellect: but one of those Routine Diplomats so often employed by the European Courts who practice every rule of ettiquette punctilliously keep a most hospitable and liberal House without any pretention of magnificence; which forms a centre of Réunion for the Corps where the superior minds can collect the best information of passing events and use it accordingly for the advantage of his Government— We are all very sorry to lose them they are a charming family and I am the only Lady left—a sad substitute even if our Salary permited the expence—

6

Thank God we now recieve Letters from our Children and friends in America— My Dear Sister Eliza was married to Mr John Pope of Kentucky a Senator of the U.S.[404] All well—

of that year, Nelson "looked and complained of being very unwell," and in August of the following year, he expressed the wish to be dismissed from service. The emperor evidently permitted him to spend a year in England to improve his health (D/JQA/28, 1, 10 Sept. 1810, 20 April, 4 Dec. 1811, 25 Aug. 1812, APM Reel 31; D/JQA/29, 21 Sept. 1813, APM Reel 32).

[401] The 2d version adds, "and ill contrived for a family."

[402] Just before midnight on 12 June 1810, the Adamses and Catherine Johnson moved from the Ville de Bordeaux hotel to a house owned by a Mr. Plinkey on New Street and the Moika Canal. Here JQA would have a study. The quarters were too small to accommodate Alexander Everett and Francis Gray, who lodged elsewhere (D/JQA/28, 12, 30 June, APM Reel 31).

[403] The 2d version adds, "They are going to spend the Summer with their Father at Narva in Levonia—"

[404] At this point in the 2d version LCA adds, "dates the 13 of April—" AA's letter to JQA of 31 Dec. 1809, endorsed as received on 1 June 1810, included reassuring words about GWA and JA2. In a letter to LCA of 12 Jan. 1810, AA approved of Eliza Johnson's decision to marry Sen. John Pope instead of Rev. Samuel Ripley, who would earn only $700 per year: "She has got absolution, without doing pennance" (both Adams Papers). JQA noted that a packet arrived on 6 June from Washington, D.C., with letters up to 23 Feb., under a department of state cover, for LCA and Catherine Johnson regarding Eliza's marriage to the senator on 11 Feb. (D/JQA/28, 6 June 1810, APM Reel 31). Letters from GWA and JA2 have not been found.

12TH

Moved into our Lodgings— My cares will now commence[405] and where is my authority for any thing?— God help me— The licencious manners of this place; and the familiar habits of my Countrymen are not easily controuled— All eyes are on a Foreign Minister more especially on such an one as my Husband—a marked man everywhere for great ability and statesmanship and already so distinguished by the Emperor and his Minister—

24

Dined at General Bettancourts ourselves my Sister and the Legation—[406] The House is Elegantly furnished— The Gen[l] a distinguished as Topographical Engineer and is at the head of the Polytechnic School— His Lady is an English Woman: uneducated and illiterate[407] but kind hearted warm in her attachments and hospitable—to her acquaintance—[408] They have three accomplished Daughters—the youngest a great beauty and all very amiable—[409] They danced the Spanish Bolero en Costume with Castanets very gracefully and we had a charming Evening and I always feel at home there—

25

Our lives have now assumed a more quiet aspect—[410] Parties are almost over for the Season— We attend the English Factory Chapel—Episcopalian—[411]

JULY 1ST.

All the fashionables are gone out of Town: we now remain much alone: and have the pleasure to see our own selected friends in a

[405] In the 2d version LCA replaced "commence" with "encrease."

[406] The 2d version adds, "and had a very pleasant time."

[407] The 2d version adds, "and very ambitious."

[408] The 2d version adds, "Her Husband is distinguished for great Military Science and also for strong mind and indefatigable industry and is a great favorite of the Emperor—"

[409] The 2d version notes that the daughters were educated in Spain.

[410] The 2d version adds, "out of doors.—"

[411] The merchants of the British Factory, as the Russia-based members of Britain's Russia Company were called, had established the English Factory Church, completed in 1754, on St. Petersburg's English Embankment. The chaplain at this time was Rev. London King Pitt (1773–1813) (Cross, *Banks of the Neva*, p. 4, 10, 90, 103–104, 113–114).

social manner—Mad Colombi M^rs. Fisher the Miss Bodes and the Americans[412]

4

Newspapers from Baltimore and no Letters—[413] What severe trials!!

6

Went to the Theatre: saw Mad Bourgoin an excellent Actress—The Piece was Molieres Tartuffe—Not equal to my expectations—

15

Taken very ill and confined to my bed—could not see any one. my husband also much indisposed—[414]

21

Resumed my seat in the Drawing Room and my usual occupations The Gentlemen of the Legation were here every Evening with other visitors and our time passed very pleasantly— M^r. Adams too often passed it alone studying Weights and measures *practically* that he might write a work on them: no article however minute escaped his observation and to this object he devoted all his time—[415]

[412] The 2d version lists her visitors as "Madame Colombi her two Sisters M^rs. Krehmer."

[413] The 2d version adds, "Poor loved John God Theee!" LCA had recently received a letter from JA2, but it has not been found (LCA to AA, 2 June 1810, Adams Papers). Evidently her grief for her son, who had died in 1834, was rekindled as she wrote the 2d version.

[414] The 2d version replaces the final sentence here with, "Mr Adams a bad Cough and cold—"

[415] At the end of June 1810 JQA had begun a comparative investigation of weights, measures, and coins in Russia and America. His interest in this subject would culminate in a report, prepared by JQA as secretary of state, in accord with a 3 March 1817 resolution of the Senate, and presented on 22 Feb. 1821, that considered "the proceedings in foreign countries, for establishing uniformity in weights and measures," "the regulations and standards for weights and measures in the several states of the Union," and "such propositions relative to the uniformity of weights and measures as may be proper to be adopted in the United States" (D/JQA/28, 27, 30 June 1810, APM Reel 31; *Report upon Weights and Measures*, Washington, D.C., 1821).

30

Accompanied my Sister to the Theatre: we had the use of the Duke de Mondragonis Lodge Box[416] Mr Fisher is a constant visitor[417] here He is established here as a Merchant and said to be doing well—[418] Catherine sick in her Chamber—

AUGST 5

Immediately after dinner Mr Adams took my Sister Charles and Martha in a row Boat and went up the River to Octa to see Mrs Krehmer at her Country House— Mrs. Krehmer was at Count Kochubeys but hastened home to recieve them with her Sister Mrs. Baily the English Consuls wife; and they passed a very pleasant Evening—[419] returned home in the boat and they went back to their party— There is no difference in Russia in the hours of Summer or Winter—

21

Went with my Husband my Sister & the two Smiths to see the Tauridan Palace It is singularly constructed having spacious apartments, and Saloons, and a natural Garden of considerable dimensions; with aviary, Trees of full growth all growing under one roof— It was built by Potemkin on the Bank of the Newa and presented by him to Catherine II.[420] It is ornamented with Statues and Pictures— The Empress Mother sometimes passes a few weeks there and is in a very delapidated condition—[421] Countess Litta is the Niece and Heiress of Potemkin—

[416] The 2d version adds, "We now had a Piano and could have some music— There are many Americans here and we see them almost every Eveng."

[417] The 2d version adds, "a Philadelphia."

[418] Miers Fisher Jr. (1786–1813) of Philadelphia, a merchant in St. Petersburg, would suffer a fatal fall down a flight of stairs in June 1813, the day after his marriage to a Russian woman. When JA was a delegate to the first Continental Congress in 1774, he had admired the "clever" library and sumptuous hospitality of the senior Miers Fisher, a lawyer and Quaker (JA, *D&A*, 2:126–127; Saul, *Distant Friends*, p. 63).

[419] The 2d version indicates her mother joined them and adds, "we sat half an hour."

[420] The 2d version replaces the previous sentence with the following: "It was built by Potempkin and was his favorite Palace— It belongs to the and is but little used at present— It has a Theatre in it like that of the Palace— It is beautifully situated on the banks of the Nèva—"

[421] In 1787 Catherine the Great had given Grigori Potemkin the title Prince of Tauris (the Crimea) to honor his military victories in that region. After Potemkin's death, the imperial family purchased the Tauride Palace and the best works of art it contained (Norman, *Hermitage*, p. 43, 56).

24

Letters from America now come more frequently God be thanked but the dreadful long Winter must come again—[422]

SEPT 1

Nelson left us to live with the Emperor—

Occasionally we frequent the Theatre and Kitty and Charles and myself take a drive— She often prefers to walk with the Gentlemen and frequently visits the Miss Bodes charming Girls with whom she is very intimate— We now begin to dine by Candlelight four o clock—

14

A large party of Americans to dine here.—

24

Went with Mr. Adams my Sister and Mr Smith to see the Palace at Peterhoff—[423] The Gardens are spacious and the Fountains very beautiful when in full play: but the Palace is in a State of decay and looks forlorn Mr J S Smith and Mr Jones[424] met us there and we all returned to dine— The Americans who are in St Petersburg spend most of their Evenings with us when we are at home and we have music and Cards.

29

At the Theatre returned at 11 The French Actors I like very well— The Ballets are fine Duport excellent—

[422] The 2d version adds, in a new paragraph, "Another Month gone."

[423] The Adams party traveled about nineteen miles from St. Petersburg to Peterhof, Peter the Great's summer residence on the southern coast of the Gulf of Finland. Work on the complex, with its palaces, gardens, fountains, and cascades, had begun in 1714, and it was officially opened in 1723. JQA's Diary provides a description of the curiosities and especially the "water works" that the visitors saw at Peterhof (Abram Raskin, ed., *Petrodvorets (Peterhof): Palaces and Pavilions, Gardens and Parks, Fountains and Cascades, Sculptures*, Leningrad, 1978, p. 9, 10, 12–13; D/JQA/28, 24 Sept. 1810, APM Reel 31).

[424] For Thomas Morton Jones, see Adventures, note 270, above. JQA facilitated Jones' presentation to the imperial family. He described Jones as a traveler of, as yet, "no particular profession" (D/JQA/28, 14 Sept., 26 Oct., APM Reel 31; Marjorie B. Cohn, *Francis Calley Gray and Art Collecting for America*, Cambridge, 1986, p. 35).

OCT 3

Again at the Theatre. the Duke de Mondragoni has lent me his Box whenever I choose to make use of it— One or other of the Gentlemen always went with us— It is here considered the duty of an Attachè—

8

Accompanied Mr Adams and Catherine to the German Theatre— I do not understand the language and cannot enjoy it— Paer's Music is very sweet but the Germans scream to the very utmost extent of their voices and although great Musicians I do not like their screeching and I found it all very stupid—[425]

10

Again at the German Theatre with Mr. Adams who is fond of it. We took Charles who begins to speak German and he was delighted— Mr. Gray came to our Box.

13

Made our visits of Ceremony to the Grandee's on the opening of the Winter— The Receptions are in the Even^g^ in full dress: but they are usually short.— Though you are frequently asked to pass Evening— If the Lady of the House is at her Card Table playing Ombre she seldom rises to recieve and you make your salutation and either remain half an hour or retire without taking leave a thing unknown there as it is considered the breaking of a party— A Russian Lady Sometimes follows you to the door of Apartment and there takes leave politely without disturbing her guests—

14

Invited to the Theatre at the Hermitage— The Emperor has given Orders as I am the only *Lady* of the Corps Diplomatique that my

[425] JQA reports that on 11 Oct. he "went with the ladies to the German Play" and saw a performance of the Italian composer Ferdinando Paer's opera *Achille*, which he admired (D/JQA/28, APM Reel 31; Grove *Dicy. of Music*).

Sister should be invited also[426] and this is considered one of the greatest honors ever confered upon a foreign young Lady; as well as the invitation to Minister of the second degree– This privilege is only assigned to Ambassadors[427] and we owed this distinction to my Sister's dance with His Imperial Majesty as also to the great partiality of the Emperor for my husband– It is very kind.

23

In the Evening I accompanied my Husband my Sister and my Boy who was dressed as a Bachus to a masked Ball– We went at about nine and were the first there always an awkward thing– The Empress Mother had a small party and the Duke was obliged to attend as a french play was to be performed: and the Actor who was engaged to manage his own Ball could not attend until released from his duties at the Palace and he did not arrive until eleven o clock–[428] As however a number of Children were there they were set to dancing and amused as well as they could until the whole party had arrived consisting of about 150 Persons and between thirty and forty Children–

The Children walked the Polonaise daned English Country dances; and the Russian Golobalst or Dove dance and some others–[429]

The Costumes were in great variety and admirable particularly Miss Pardoe who appeared as Madame de Pompadour and a young boy in the full costume of that age– She performed her part to admiration– Charles and Mad Vlodek opened the Ball they supped at eleven– the Supper was splendid and the animation of the bright and beautiful faces round the Table contrasted with the half anxious yet pleas countenances of the elegantly attired Mothers sparkling

[426] The 2d version adds, "that I may not be *alone*."

[427] During the first century of its history, the United States sent abroad only legations, of which the chief diplomat was a minister. In 1893 Congress began to elevate important missions to embassies, each headed by an ambassador, the highest-ranking diplomat (Julius W. Pratt, *A History of United States Foreign Policy*, 2d edn., Englewood Cliffs, N.J., 1965, p. 7–8).

[428] The 2d version adds, "Great part of the company did not come until that time." Armand de Caulaincourt hosted the children's masked ball (D/JQA/28, 25 Oct. 1810, APM Reel 31).

[429] An Englishman described the dove dance, or Golubetz, as "an imitation of the coaxing airs of turtle-doves or lovers." The dancing pair stands still, facing each other, and then "the man dances about with vehement motion, while the woman proceeds in gentle and delicate movements" (William Tooke, *View of the Russian Empire, during the Reign of Catharine the Second, and to the Close of the Eighteenth Century*, 3 vols., Dublin, 1801, 2:47).

with Diamonds who stood around them formed a scene of the most glowing beauty where the purest affections of the Soul seemed to beam from Maternal love alone—[430] The elegance of manners and the interest which he appeared to take in the general pleasure of the company consisting of the élite of St Petersburgh gave a high and finished grace to the Scene which exceeded all that I had ever met with— The Ombres Chinoise[431] and a Lottery were to conclude the party and Mr. Adams not choosing that Charles should accept any *gift* we returned home much pleased and gratified but very tired at two o clock I returned with my Sister and the Gentlemen being obliged to stay as Chaperone without waiting for Supper—

26

The Empress Mothers birthday— Mr Adams and the Gentlemen at Court in the Morning— In the Evening we went to the Palace at half past six; at Seven we were ushered into the Hermitage Theatre— The Emperor and the Imperial family came in at eight and took their Seats in a row of Chairs in Front—Immediately behind the Orchestra— The French Ambassador in the same line with[432] his Majesty took the Seat next the Grand Duke Michael— Behind them sat the Ambassadors St Julian and Stedinck and all the great Officers of the Crown and their Ladies for there are no Boxes— The Corps Diplomatique sat on the right hand second row; and the Hall was filled up by the Noblesse the Men on one side and the Women on the other.— The Piece was Cinderella[433]—The Music magnificent the Acting excellent and the Ballets beautiful— Some of the Songs were encore'd by the Emperor order and every thing was splendidly gorgeous as it is almost every where in St Petersburgh in the Imperial domain—[434] The distinction to Miss Johnson was a matter of wonder to all the world—

[430] The 2d version adds, "the serious loocks of the Nurses in attendance exceeds all description— The Ambassador him self giving the tone by his refined elegance and the pleasure he took in the delight of the Children—"

[431] Ombres Chinoises, literally, Chinese shadows, is a presentation in which the shadows of puppets or people are cast on a transparent screen as they act out a drama.

[432] The 2d version adds, "the last Person at the right hand of."

[433] Nicolas Isouard's opera *Cendrillon* (Don Michael Randel, ed., *The Harvard Concise Dictionary of Music and Musicians*, Cambridge, 1999; D/JQA/28, 26 Oct., APM Reel 31).

[434] The 2d version adds, "We after the Opera at 11 at night went through the Palace to see the Emperors Apartments."

NOV 7

Invited by Narishkin the Master of the Ceremonies to see the Anitchkoff Palace— It is very beautiful; fitted up with great taste by the Emperor for the Grand Dutchess Ann his youngest Sister[435] It contains every luxury that can be concieved with a refined delicacy under the immediate inspection of Alexander himself— We were invited to the Duke de Vicenza's but I was too unwell to go—as also to Madame Bettancourts.

8

Went to the F Ambassadors— The French Actors performed two little Opera's most delightfully and this was a real treat to me— Afterwards as usual a Ball and Supper until two in the morning. At this House and Madame de Brays I dance—

10

Went to the French Theatre; an amusement in which I delight— Mad^lle.^ George and Mad^e.^ Bourgoin are both excellent; and the dancing is very elegant— There is no noise; no trouble but great decorum and quiet— Recieved a second invitation to see the Annitchkoff Palace if I wished it— We accepted it: and discovered new beauties in every direction— The Bronzes and ornamental works are all made in Russia; and though not perfected with the elegance of the french; they are quite handsome and honorable to the genius of the Country, under their great Patron—

The China and Malaki Vases[436] are very beautiful—Every thing is couleur de Rose— As the Chapel was not consecrated we Ladies were permited to go into the Sanctuary—A place forbidden to Women we were told by the Priest in a very coarse mode of Speech— In

[435] The Anichkov Palace, built in the 1740s, was on Nevsky Prospect near the Fontanka Canal. JQA referred to it as "the Palace of St. Anne," which may have led LCA to believe that it was the residence of Grand Duchess Anna, but it was actually the official residence of Alexander I's favorite sister, Grand Duchess Catherine Pavlovna (1788–1819), recently married to Prince George of Holstein-Oldenburg (Norman, *Hermitage*, p. 70; D/JQA/28, 8, 10 Nov. 1810, APM Reel 31; Palmer, *Alexander I*, p. 76–77, 181, 418–419). See also Descriptive List of Illustrations, No. 10, above.

[436] Siberia was the source of the malachite from which the vases were fashioned (Johann Georg Kohl, *Russia*, London, 1844, p. 128).

10. "VIEW OF THE PALACE SQUARE FROM NEVSKY PROSPEKT," BY GABRIEL LUDWIG LORY THE ELDER, 1804

See page xiv

the Evening again at the Theatre— The use of the Dukes Box is a great privilege— On our return home found Letters announcing the Birth of another Son to M^rs. T. B. Adams[437]

14

Invited to stand Sponsors Mr Adams and myself and Mr Adams to the new born Child of our Butler requesting that the Christening might be performed in the Parlour and that the Gentlemen of the Legation would attend—[438]

15

We all met in the Drawing Room at two o clock— The Pastor of the Lutheran Church appeared accompanied by the Father Nurse and babe when it was found that a Man and Wife were not permited by the rules of that Church to stand together as Sponsors: and Catherine was substituted for me and as it was a boy M^r. Gray was selected by the Father of the Child as the second Godfather; and the Services were then performed— Mr Adams held the Child as he was a boy—

The Ceremony was short consisting of a prayer by the Pastor; Then repeating the Lords Prayer he holding his right hand on the Baby's head. Then the Apostles Creed of the Episcopalians then the Baptism with Water on the Childs head and forehead naming the Child John Charles Francis and terminating with a short Prayer— M^r. Adams gave fifty Rubles to the Father and five to the Nurse and all ended with a Collation and I imagine a handsome present from Mr Gray—

[437] The 2d version concludes, "Went to the Theatre when I got home heard that my Butlers Wife had a Son—", with the word "Butlers" written over "Brother."

As she wrote the sentence in the 1st version, LCA was probably working from the 2d version, with its confusion about the words "Butlers" and "Brother." She could not have received notice of the birth of a son to AHA and TBA, whom she always referred to as her brother. Their first son, named after his father, was born on 4 Aug. 1809, one day before JQA and LCA left Boston for Russia. JQA knew of the birth at that time and undoubtedly shared the information with LCA. Isaac Hull Adams, the second son of AHA and TBA, would be born on 26 May 1813 (D/JQA/28, 6 Aug. 1809, APM Reel 31).

[438] The butler Waldstein's wife, Marie, was LCA's chambermaid (D/JQA/28, 13 Nov. 1810, APM Reel 31).

19

Went to the Theatre after which went to a Supper and large party at Gen Bettancourts— The young Ladies played, Madame Colombit and Caroline Bettancourt on the Harp—Adeleline on the Trombone and Miss Lesseps on the Piano— Returned home at two as usual—

22

At the French Ambassadors— Saw two little Opera's performed Les Pages du Duc de Vendome and the Tableau Parlant. He has a small Theatre in the Palace and the French company frequently perform for him— In the first Piece the Pages were performed by Women—In the second the Female parts by men—A most disgusting travestie—[439] A very large and distinguished party got home at two— A charming School for young person's just entering into life. In fact for any who have a taste for dissipation

24

A Party at Home The Colombi's her Sisters The Bettancourts Baroness Strogonoff Mr. Harris Jones and the Family and Legation Fisher &ce Supped (Alas for Poor Harris the Cook forgot the Soup) we danced until one o'clock but his horreur at the oversight was not to be overcome— To Bed at two—

29

Walked out with my Sister and Mr Smith— Being quite fatigued I saw the Emperor behind us hastening on with great strides: and not intending to do any thing rude: and far from supposing that his Majesty would notice it I beckoned to my Servants to drive up and with my Sister got into the Carriage and drove on— On returning up the Street we met the Emperor but his Majesty turned his head away and looked at the River and took no notice of us at all I was very sorry but had no idea that *he* would be offended— The great distinction shown to my Sister, at the Invitation to the Hermitage

[439] *Les pages du Duc de Vendôme* and *Le tableau parlant* were works of the French composer André Ernest Modeste Grétry (1741–1813). The former opera was probably based on Adalbert Gyrowetz's *Die Pagen des Herzogs von Vendome* (Ivor Guest, *The Romantic Ballet in Paris*, Middletown, Conn., 1966, p. 37–38; Grove *Dicy. of Music*).

had occasioned so much talk I thought it was injudicious to encourage it—

DEC 5

My health became very precarious;[440] and the Winter being bither, to very mild I rode in a Sleigh with my Sister and Child or with Mr Adams As I could not bear the fatigue of the motion of a Carriage and four over the Stone pavements. We rode every day wraped in Furs and this exercise was smooth and delightful—

Mrs. Krehmer and her Daughters came and passed the Evening with us.— In the course of conversation she told me that the Emperor had seen all our Letters to our Family; and that one from Martha Godfrey the Nurse of my Boy very abusive of Himself and Constantine had excited a great desire to see her; and that he had in consequence sent for the Child— That he did think her at all handsome but that he was much please with the description and remarks which I had written of him to my Friends— I observed that it was very ungenerous of his Majesty after offering to send our dispatches by a Private and especial Courier to use the opportunity against *us*: for it was perfectly natural that with the idea of perfect safety attached to the conveyance of our Letters that we should describe our first impressions without disguise to our friends to whom they must certainly be very interesting— I knew that she would repeat this to the Emperor—[441]

13

Taken suddenly and severely ill—and continued so all Night

16

Convalescent; and resumed my rides— But as usual we met the Emperor but he turned his head away and did not look at us. I could not help laughing but was sorry when I found that he had

[440] LCA was expecting a child. She would give birth to Louisa Catherine on 12 Aug. 1811.

[441] In the 1828 presidential campaign, Isaac Hill, a Jacksonian, published an account of this incident in a *Brief Sketch of the Life, Character and Services of Major General Andrew Jackson*. Hill, however, twisted the story to give rise to accusations that JQA had served as a procurer of young women for Alexander I. The rumors circulated widely enough that some western Democrats came to refer to JQA as "The Pimp of the Coalition" (Robert V. Remini, *The Election of Andrew Jackson*, Phila., 1963, p. 117–118).

taken offence—for I knew that Mr. Adams would feel unpleasantly about it: as the subject would become very disagreeable if the Court as customary adopted the same tone—and the first fine day My Sister and I resumed our walks— We met the Emperor on the Fontalka and he immediately stoped us and looked and spoke a little coldly addressing my Sister; but at parting turned to me and said that it was essential to my health that I should take such exercise and desired that *we* should walk every fine day when he should hope to meet *us*.— The Gentlemen had all been as angry at the want of notice as they had been at his Majestys attentions— It was quite diverting to me who was acting in the capacity of a mere duenna— The Minister took no notice—

22

Charles was threatened with the Croup and I was in an agony of alarm— I took him into my own chamber and Mr Adams was obliged to occupy the Study— Dr Galloway staid and dined with us. I was quite sick myself— There came a notification from the Master of the Ceremonies Inviting Mr. Adams Miss Johnson and myself to a Ball on the Birth day of the Empress Mother—[442] Mr Adams informed him that my Child and myself were both sick and that Miss Johnson according to Ettiquette could not go alone—[443] He replied that he was ordered by the Imperial Family to say that Miss Johnson would be as already presented and be privileged to attend on all occasions when notified— Monsr. de Maisoneuve also observed that if Miss Johnson wished to be presented it would only be necessary for her to call on Countess Litta where the matter might be arranged when the Empresses came to Town—

24

This being the Emperors Birth day The Minister and Suite attended at the Circle— The Empress Mother told Mr Adams she hoped to see me at the Ball in the Evening— He said he feared that the State of my health must deprive me of the honor—when her Majesty kindly said she should much regret it—

[442] The ball was actually given to celebrate the emperor's birthday; see Adventures, 24 Dec. 1810, below.

[443] The 2d version adds, "and that we felt a great delicicy in taking her without the usual form of Presentation—"

25

Mr John S Smith left us early this morning for Berlin Vienna and Paris— He was very pleasant during his stay—

30

This day M^r. Jones left us— He called to take leave— He is going immediately—

31

We end this year in bad health and in worse spirits than ever— God help us these are honors dearly bought—

JAN 1ST. [*1811*]

This is a dull beginning for our New Year— Two of the Gentlemen have gone; and the others all dined out.— I thank my stars that my Sister is with me as things have turned out. What should I have done with all these young men?[444] A Young Lady, in the Family is quite an acquisition— She is a Companion to me and to them and their squabbles among themselves are quite amusing as I have nothing to do with them— They help to pass the time quite pleasantly—

5

My Sister and I passed the Evening with Baroness Strogonoff— quite a character— Her Husband is Ambassador at Naples but he

[444] The 2d version omits the remainder of the paragraph and concludes, "They would have been a perpetual plague—

"We rode out as usual and went to see the Frozen Market— This is quite a curiosity The Meats which supply the whole City being arrange in perfect order hard frozen to keep until the river opens."

The "Frozen Market," held in the open square near the Monastery of St. Alexander Nevsky during the week preceding Christmas, enabled the residents of St. Petersburg to provide themselves with meat for the winter (D/JQA/28, 2 Jan. 1811, APM Reel 31).

would not take her with him she is too eccentric and might have brought trouble on him—

9

A small party at home. Madame Strogonoff and her daughter; Madame Colombi and Sisters: Gen[l] Pardo and daughter Gen Watzderf and Count de Boze &c— Danced until one oclock Supper &ce and *Soup*— I was quite ill from fatigue

11

I was to unwell to go to Baroness Strogonoffs my Sister also we were obliged to decline—

12

Passed the Evening at Madame Colombi's We were to dance out the old Russian year and dance in the new one— It is the fashion to play many fortune telling tricks— I never drew any but *obstacles* a word written on a strip of paper and put under a Cup— The secret to surmount them was not taught— Returned late—

13

Went to the palace with M[r.] Adams and my Sister— The Emperor had sent an order that we should be admited by the Petites Entree's only used by the Imperial Family and the Ambassadors only and we were shown into the recieving Room of the Emperor— Count S[t] Julian alone was there when we went in and the French Ambassador came in soon after us— We were informed that this was a most extraordinary distinction ever granted to a foreign Minister at that Court and that it was the express order of the Emperor himself—

The Imperial Family soon came in and spoke very kindly to my Sister and myself— They were preceded into the Hall by a small guard of the Military and we followed by special order— On entering the Hall the Emperor called for the Grand Master of the Ceremonies order'd a Chair to be set and turning to *me*; told him that he Mons de Maisoneuve (my old friend) was to take me under his protection to sit or walk as most agreable; and not to suffer the Crowd to press on me for turning to me "un malheureux coude vous feroit un grand tort"—[445] That he was not to quit me during the Evening until he had seen me safe into my Carriage—[446] My astonishment and embarrassment was painful for I had no idea that my delicate situation had been observed by any one and it put me sadly to the blush—

The Emperor on and about an hour after still under the protection of my appointed Guardian we met the Emperor when he again accosted me and insisted that I should go and by the Empress who sat on an elevated Seat attended by her Ladies— I thankfully declined the honor—when he insisted and said dont you know that no one says Nay to the Emperor— I laughed and replied but *I* am a republican— He smiled and went on his way—

We soon went to Supper and then he came round and spoke to my Sister in English— He always spoke to me in French— I scarcely saw Mr Adams the whole evening or any of our party— Mr de Maisoneuve met me at the door of the Theatre again offered me his arm and we continued our Promenade until the Imperial Family had retired when I found our Carriage ready at the Emperors private entrance; and on taking leave of me the good old Gentleman said "that he hoped that he had faithfully performed the pleasant duty assigned to him by his Imperial and followed his orders punctually[”]— I thanked very sincerely as also all of the Imperial Family for such very great distinction for which I trusted they would be assured of my deep and lasting sense of gratitude— The old Gentleman had become acquainted with me on my arrival at Berlin many years before; who had been applied to by Mr. Adams for assistance in procuring *me* a Physician when I was siezed with a dangerous illness in consequence of the fatigues and anxieties which had suffered three

[445] A careless elbow could do you great harm.

[446] In the 2d version LCA added the following, in an entry dated 1 Jan. 1811: "He then Proceeded farther into the Hall and began the Pollonaise I was exceedingly embarrassed—but my good old Friend led me on gentliy every body making room and we walked until we met the Emperor again who stop'd me and said that I was wrong to walk in such a Crowd as I might be injured and desired me to go and take a Seat by the Empress who was sitting alone with the Grand Dutchess on a raised throne— The very idea startled me and I declined—when he said 'dont you know that no one says no to the Emperor' I answered Yes Sire! but I am a Republican! He smiled bowed and passed on— At Supper he again honored my Sister and myself with some conversation and we soon after returned to the Hall Mons de Maisonneuve again took my arm and we continued to move gently about until The Imperial Family retired when I found our Carriage ready and taking leave of me he said I trust I have fulfilled his Majestys orders punctually— I thanked him very sincerely as also the Imperial Family for this great distinc for which I was very grateful— The motive of all this I presume was political!!! Caulincourt was siezed with a swimming in his head and left the Hall immediately— After this Eveng the Empress desired that my Sister should be considered as *introduced*."

days after my arrival; only four months married and without a single female acquaintance— The Empress Mother desired, he said, that Miss Johnson should for the future consider herself as presented— The motive of all this I presume is political and owing to the flattering partiallity of the Emperor for my husband— Caulincourt was siezed with a swimming in the head and left the Hall immediately—

24

A Ball at Madame Lessceps I was too much exhausted to go—

Our Footman had a daughter born on New Years day and I was asked to stand God Mother with Miss Godfrey and Mr Gray as Proxies for the Duke of Oldenburgh and his Wife the Grand Dutchess Catherine The ceremonial was of the Greek Church— A Pope was introduced heading the party who accompanied the Parents the Babe and their friends; a Table was set covered with a handsome white damask Napkin with Candles and a Camels Pencil— I was prepared with a[447] Silver Cross; a Shirt; a Cap; and a piece of Showy Calico to wrap the Babe in—[448] The Tub was half filled with cold water: and the Child was presented to me to hold quite undressed by the Nurse and we were ranged by the Priest around the Tub he standing by the Table and the Sponsors close to him— The Pope took the Child from me made a prayer in a sort of Chant and dipped it three times into the Tub at each interval making the sign of the Cross on its forehead very much as in our ritual and blessing it— Then with a wet sponge he made the sign of the Cross on its breast and Shoulders & Feet having used a Camells hair pencil for the forehead and head and then the babe was put into my hands by the priest with a short prayer while the second God mother presented me with the Cross and Chain the Shirt, the Cap and at last the wrapper and the Gold Cross presented by Mr. Gray all of which Articles blessed during the dressing of the Child— After which being ranged in order around the Tub the Priest put a consecrated Taper in each of our hands and we marched three times in procession round the Bathing Tub The Pope or Priest as he is called when

[447] The 2d version adds, "String of beads with a."

[448] In the 2d version LCA added that she was informed that, as the baby's godmother, she must "promise to pay the Funeral expenses if it should die—"

aproaching the Table with all the company turning their backs to the Water and chanting the service in three times circling round the Tub are ordered to *spit* out the Devil and all his works and the Service is terminated by the Priest cutting of a piece of the Babes hair rolling it up and throwing it into the water in which the Babe was baptized— He then folded up the Napkin and Candles as his perquisite and they all retired to feast on a collation prepared for them in their own apartments— The name Echaterina—

26

I was taken very ill this day and Dr Galloway was sent for: the general routine of our lives was quiet— We rode out and walked accasionally— Frequently met the Emperor on the public walks who always stoped to speak to us very kindly and then passed on— My health was miserable and the family seemed to be broken up

In fact we all pined for home and I scarcely endure a longer separation from my loved Children— This was burthensome to all, surely a man loses more than he gains by exacting such a sacrifice— I had thought that one year would have been the extent of my stay— How could we be happy under such circumstances— To give birth to another Child in a strange land after all I had suffered was a cause of incessant fear and anxiety; and my Sister was deprived of the pleasures which were so attractive to young persons—

FEBY 1ST.

Invited to a Betrothal of the Daughter of Princess Belloselski— M^r. Adams had a Card and I was honored with a separate one— The young Lady is a Maid of Honor to the Empress; and she marries Col Prince Volkonski Aid to the Emper Alexander— A formal full dress visit is exacted in return— Madame de Bettancourt took Tea with us and my Sister accompanied her to Sup with Madame de Strogonoff—

5

Madame de Bettancourt and her daughters passed the Even^g with us— M^r. Adams quite sick in his Chamber

6

Rumours of War between Russia and France—A new anxiety—[449]

7

Went to a Childrens Ball at the French Ambassadors— It began very late and the Children were tired and sleepy— The Company out of sorts— The Children retired as usual and we remained until one o clock— The Ball was cold and heartless different altogether from any thing that we had seen before— Neither the Ambassador or the Gentlemen of the Legation appeared to interest themselves much in the entertainment of the company and the change was quite remarkable— Charles was dress in character as the Page in Beaumarche's Comedy of the marriage de Figarro—

8

Sick as usual after these fatigues which I cannot learn to support à la Russe— And now I am more delicate than ever—

9

Catherine at Baroness Strogonoffs— I still confined to my chamber— I must have been a strong woman or I could not have borne such climates and so much anxiety and suffering—

11

Went to a party at Madame Lessep's— Met several Strangers there— Madame Lesseps is a very sensible woman— Sensible women not always the most agreeable though the most valuable— The maxim of Men "that pretty is better than good." is almost universally adopted by them where money does not bias the taste—

[449] LCA is probably referring to a conversation that JQA recounted in his Diary in which Count Bussche Hunnefeldt, the minister from Westphalia, "talked about rumours of War between Russia, and France, to which he gives no credit." JQA further discounted the rumor the following month (D/JQA/28, 7 Feb., 28 March, APM Reel 31; *Repertorium*, 3:474).

20

At a Ball at Count Schencks— The Corps Diplomatiques with some of the élite of the Russian Court were the gusts— Everything in highest style of elegance and taste— Balls are almost all alike here; and it is rare that incidents occur worth describing—Suppers abundance of Champagne freely used by both Sexes: a Creps Table for the Elderly who play very high— The French a little down—

FEBY 26 [*21*]

Invited by the Empress Mother to witness the examination of the School of the Demoiselles Nobles under the especial patronage of her Majesty— Most of the Members of the Corps Diplomatic attended with their Legations and we were obliged to appear in full Court dresses— All the Ministers of State and the Imperial Family with the haute Noblesse of the Empire— The examination had began— The young Ladies went through every branch of their education and ended with dancing all sorts of dances: very fanciful and very gracefully performed— The number of Girls was eighty one— None of them are handsome— The performance of their Religious duties is strictly attended to and their long fasts reduce them so much that they look like Skeletons— Of course their complexions suffer—[450] We returned home at four in the Afternoon but wearied beyond measure— At ten o-clock went to a Ball at Count Romanzoffs— The Ball very dull: given on occasion of the marriage of the Princess Zéneides marriage with the Prince Volkonski— All the Corps Diplomatique and about 100 others— The invitation was to a Supper and I sat between Count Markoff and the Duke of Serra Capriola— The conversation turned upon America and Count Markoff mentioned many things that Talleyrand had told him of his Travels in the United States: particularly of the beauty of the Women and the easy morality of the husbands—Repeating in the coarsest man the atrocities of Chatelleux and other old writers who disgraced themselves by their utter want of truth— My situation was becoming so disagreeable that had not the Chancellor risen to re-

[450] On 21 Feb. JQA and LCA attended the second day of a two-day examination of the young women who had completed their studies at the Institute of the Order of St. Catherine. During the examination, the students demonstrated their proficiency in religion, geography, history, Russian literature, arithmetic, German language, French literature, experimental philosophy, singing, and dancing. In his Diary, JQA describes the proceedings, especially the experimental philosophy demonstration, in detail (D/JQA/28, APM Reel 31).

turn to the Ball Room I was so disgusted that I should certainly have made an esclandre to the horror of Mr. Adams and to the astonishment of Markoff an old Roué of eighty who was living only on the experience of younger men than himself to pass off his base and impure witicisms— I told him that it was very well known that Talleyrand never spoke truth—that therefore every one would estimate his assertions according to their worth.[451]

I was perfectly enragé which was very foolish— As Supper was not served until three did not reach home until after four—

What on earth is so disgusting as two old men chuckling over their past follies and vices!!!

24

Lent begins this day— Now for a little rest—

26

My Sister and Charles dined at Gen Bettancourts— In the evening Mrs. Bettancourt took my Sister and Mr Smith to the Masquearade for Foreigners— It is the last of the Season—

MARCH 1

The French Ambassador came to visit us; and said that he would come and dine with us tomorrow—a Short notice—

2

Company at dinner—Gen Caulincourt—Count Schenck: Baron Mullinem; Baron Blome: Chev. Krabbe Sec; Count de Buchi Kunnefeldt Westphalia Genl Watzderf Saxony: Genl Pardo Spain Gen Bettancourt Lady and daughters: Count Luxbourg Bavaria with Raynal Prevost and Rumigny of the french Embassy and very agree-

[451] For Talleyrand's visit to America, see *AFC*, 10:163. François Jean, Chevalier de Chastellux (1734–1788), who commanded French forces at Yorktown, wrote *Voyages de M. le marquis de Chastellux dans l'Amérique septentrionale dans les années 1780, 1781, & 1782*, Paris, 1786, published in English as *Travels in North America in the Years 1780, 1781, and 1782*, Dublin and London, 1787. Chastellux presented a generally positive view of the country, its institutions, and its people (Robert B. Downs, *Images of America: Travelers from Abroad in the New World*, Urbana and Chicago, 1987, p. 24–30, 222).

able men— Rayneval played and Sung after dinner and Clementine de Bode came in the Even. Mulinen goes away in three weeks—

16

My Sister and Charles again went and dined with Madame de Bettancourt— I was not able to go— A great change for my Sister—

19

The Gentlemen Mr. Gray and Mr Everett are very attentive to me and delicately polite in their presents of Fruit and delicacies which they think may be agreeable to me— I am truly grateful for their kindness which is highly appreciated by us all— Madame de Bettancourt and her daughters passed the Evening with us—

29

Went to visit Madame Colombi— She is so gay; so sensible; and so attractive it is impossible to know her without loving her— Her Fritz is also very agreeable: well educated and Lady like but not at all handsome though she has a fine person.— She is Maid of honor to the Princess Amalia Sister of the Reigning Empress. Clementine the youngest was very handsome but more serious— The Old Count was a grave and portly Spaniard with most of the characteristics of the Spanish and very jealous of his young and lively Wife the difference of age being at least twenty or twenty five years—[452]

APRIL 7

Dined at Baron Stedincks the Swedish Ambassadors— The company consisted of about fifteen or twenty persons— Madame Demidoff better known as the Duchesse de Grammont a French Lady one of the most fascinating creatures I ever saw and very much like the famous Pamela of Madame de Genlis who I knew as Mrs. Pitcairne; did the honors of the house— Count Demidoffs Brother who recalled to my mind the Mouton Blanc of Madame de Stael her

[452] Count Colombi had died of a "schirrous liver" and dropsy on the morning of the 28th. María Colombi's sisters were Fréderica and Clementine de Bodé y Kinnersley (D/JQA/28, 3 Nov. 1810, 28 March, 21 Sept. 1811, APM Reel 31; O'Brien, *Mrs. Adams*, p. 267).

husband–as handsome and as fade a Blond; Genl Watzdorf; Genl Briesen and M[r.] Lebenski with the Secreteries of the Count and ourselves. Madame de Grammont was the Grand daughter of the duc de Guiche– The Count is a most Charming old man and simple hospitality of his manners was quite paternal– Every body loved him– We returned home much pleased–[453]

MAY 13

We went to the Procession to Eaterinoff[454] but not to the Fr Ambassadors who is recalled to be made (it is said) Prime Minister to Napoleon– Inconstant expectation of Letters from my Children: all the time sick and unequal to any exertion–

14

The Duke de Vicence came in State to take leave of us in full Costume, and to introduce to us the Count de Lauriston who takes his place and is now Ambassador– The comparison was not advantageous to

The visit of introduction was especially to the Ladies– The Duke wore the diamonds presented to him by the Emperor as a mark of his personal regard and was altogether as M[r.] Harris would say in grande Tenu.[455] The Duke was a Militaire de la Cour refined and elegant.– Lauriston though handsome a rough and unpolished Guerrier–not comparable in any way to the Duke either in mind person or manners– Lauriston was a Son or Grandson of the famous Law of the S S Bubble–[456]

[453] The 2d version adds an entry for 30 April: "Sick all through the Month–"

[454] The Russian May Day procession of carriages from the Peterhof Gate to Catherinehof, about two miles outside of the city (D/JQA/28, 13 May 1810, APM Reel 31).

[455] In full dress.

[456] James Alexander Bernard Law, Comte de Lauriston (1768–1828), had replaced Armand de Caulaincourt as the French ambassador to St. Petersburg. He was the great-nephew of the economist John Law (1671–1729), whose father, a goldsmith and banker, had acquired Lauriston, an estate outside Edinburgh. Sentenced to death after killing a man in a duel, John Law escaped to the Continent. He eventually became a naturalized French citizen and finance official (*DNB*, entry on John Law; *Ann. Register*, 1829, p. 242). For Law's "System," which led to the Mississippi Bubble's collapse in July 1720, see *AFC*, 6:28, note 2.

Law's financial policies inspired John Blunt, a founder in 1711 of the South Sea Company. The ensuing South Sea Bubble burst in the fall of 1720 (*DNB*, entries on Sir John Blunt and Promoters of the South Sea Bubble).

23

My situation precludes me from entering into the dissipation of the day and I only visit among my intimate friends.—

Mr Adams and my Sister were reading Letters just recieved from America in his Study; when I went in to see him as usual in the morning to ask how he did: and I immediately saw by their distressed countenances that bad news had come to us— They could not conceal it from me and my heart collapsed with agony at the sudden shock in a dead fainting fit— My loved Sister Hellen had died in Childbirth and the Infant and the Cousin of Mr. Adams also Mrs. Norton—[457] The fright produced alarming consequences and a premature birth was threatened with dangerous symptoms for some hours. My Physician remained with me for many hours of intense suffering when a favorable change took place and perfect quiet was relied on for recovery—

Company was expected at dinner and apologies were sent to excuse us—

25

After appearing better for the whole day of yesterday I was again siezed with violent illness and hope was nearly crushed both for my life and that of my Child— Laudanum was freely resorted to by my Physician but it at first aggravated my illness but a second dose judiciously applied produced sleep and on awaking I was quite composed the crisis had passed and hope blessed hope was renewed—[458] It is at such moments that the heart is filled with fullness of joy: for in these moments the affections expand and all the best sympathies which lie dormant in the every day events of rush forth uncontroul'd and give assurance of their reality—

27

Slowly recovering God in his mercy has spared me— recieved Letters from our Children—[459] This was the best cordial in my weak State— They allayed my fears and assisted my recovery—

[457] Nancy Johnson Hellen died in childbirth, along with her infant, on 30 Dec. 1810, while Elizabeth Cranch Norton died of "Lung fever" on 25 Jan. 1811.

[458] The 2d version concluded the entry: "In the Evening the symptoms were more favorable and Mrs. Kienecke began to hope again."

[459] Not found.

31

Was able to sit in the Parlour the adjoining room to my Chamber and Mr. Harris kindly called to see me— He is very attentive—[460]

JUNE 26

Went to see a large three Decker Ship of War Launched— The rail gave way and we were saved with difficulty from precipitated into the Stream as She passed into the Water— The moment was fearful as the Crowd pressed down: but a gentleman caught me[461] and pulled me back just in time to save me— I had not time to be frightened, but we were glad enough to get home—[462]

JUNE 20 [28]

~~Went to the~~ Mr. Navarro brought Madame de Bezzara and introduced her to me— She is a remarkably sensible Woman: full of that worldly knowledge which adapts a Lady for a political Station— Shrewed observant and practiced without any excss of sensitive delicacy; feeling her consequence and her great superiority to her husband a small man every way she is full of anecdote knows every thing that passes and is ready to offer advice wherever it is needed. He was Minister from the Court of Portugal—[463]

JULY

Mr Plinky came to inform us that our House was Sold and that we must move out of it as soon as possible: that is in thirteen days as the Emperor had purchased it.— This was rather severe: To look

460 The 2d version adds, "Went to see the Launch—Stayed a very short time—"

461 At this point in the MS, LCA wrote "May 31" in the margin.

462 The boat launch, canceled on 1 June because the river level was too low, took place on 5 June. LCA's mishap occurred at a different vantage point from that of JQA, who stood with the diplomatic corps at the Admiralty as two naval vessels, the *Mironocatz* (the Peace Bearer) and the *Tchesma* were launched, along with a small galley for Grand Duchess Catherine (D/JQA/28, 1, 4, 5 June, APM Reel 31).

463 Portugal's chargé d'affaires in St. Petersburg, Chevalier Navarro de Andrade, had been recalled; his replacement, with the rank of minister, was Chevalier João Paulo Bezerra (*Repertorium,* 3:318, 319; *Correio Braziliense; ou, Armazém Literário*, 29 vols., London, 1808–1822, 9:179–180).

In the 2d version LCA added an entry for 30 June: "Went to The Theatre Saw Medlle. Geoge her Benefit—" JQA dates this event in his Diary to 29 June (D/JQA/28, APM Reel 31).

for a House: to find a suitable one and to move by the first of August which we thought to be absolutely necessary under the circumstances[464] both trying and distressing to me who had never entirely recovered from my illness and was not very well able to bear the fatigue and anxiety of a removal—

5

There was however no time to reason on the subject: and I accompanied Mr Adams in the search for Houses and we went to see one which was recommended to us opposite to the Palace at Kamini Ostroff— It is very pretty but too far out of Town being eith Miles from St Peterburg— Returned to town much fatigued to look farther—

7

Went to see the House which the Duke of Mondragoni left— It is very large; very expensive; and very Cold— We can procure nothing within our means the Rents are so high that we must submit to necessity and take the only house that offers although it must occasion another removal in October—

The House is taken and we have sent some of our Furniture out.[465]

8

Went out to Kaminoi Ostroff to make arrangements for the disposal of the Furniture of my Chamber got ready immediately— Every hour is of consequence to me. It is a trial both for body and mind: but God in his mercy gives me strength in my need— Madame de Bezzara and Mons Navarro were here in the Evening— Much exhausted—

[464] The 2d version explains that LCA was “expecting to be confined in a fortnight.”

[465] The new residence was on Apothecary Island, which, like Kamenny Ostrov, was one of the “garden islands” connected by bridges northeast of St. Petersburg. JQA engaged the house for the remainder of the summer. The location meant that he regularly walked nearly five miles to the city (J. G. Kohl, *Russia*, London, 1844, p. 176–177; D/JQA/28, 1 June, APM Reel 31).

9

Again went out into the Country to give Directions and make arrangements— Dreadfully fatiguing but there is no choice— My Sister helps—

10

Again at the house with Mr. Adams to arrange Books and Papers— Slow work for he reads a page in every book that passes through his hands—

11

Catherine Mr. Adams and Charles went out with his valua Papers and returned to dine: after which I accompanied them to Kaminoi Ostroff and we took possession of our new residence about half completed—

12

The situation is very pleasant—but from the windows of the Palace they can see into the house and Grounds all the time—

13

Several Gentlemen came out to dine with us— We have a good French Cook and they are always ready—

14

Not accustomed to the House yet— My Chamber very large and not half furnished—getting more comfortable however—but want rest—

16

Mr & Mrs. Bezzara came to Tea and passed the Evening with us— She seems much interested in my troubles and is very kind in her manners— She requests me to go and introduce her to Madame Litta— I cannot refuse but I am ashamed to go.

24

M[r] & Madame Bezzara Gen[l] Pardo; Mess Jouffrey Crabbe and Brancia Gen Waltzdorf Navarro Luxbourg and Harris—M[r.] Laval Baron Blome Count Bose and M[r.] Krehmer—came out to dine by invitation Baron Blome and M[r.] Laval came out after dinner having an engagement— It was ten o clock at night before they left us.

25

M[r] & M[rs.] Bezzara came according to appointment and I was obliged to accompany in full dress Mourning to introduce to Madame Litta at the Palace which was more than a Mile round from us as we had to cross the River— Countess Litta recieved us very kindly but begged that I would go home directly and not wait for Madame Bezzarras Presentation to the Empress.[466] As however She had no Carriage but mine I was obliged to remain nearly an hour before I could get home: and when the Countess came back from the Empress She took my hand and sent me off saying while she laughed that she had never taken leave of any body with so much pleasure in her life— We reached home in safety and they staid to pass the Evening with us mourning for the loss of their Service of Silver Plate which was all worn in holes on the land journey— This was a killing life—

29

M[r.] Labouchere came and passed the Evening with us— He is a most agreeable man and his conversation is very pleasant—

At last for a few days we have obtained a little quiet— I go down to the end of the Garden; have a Chair on the Bank of the River with Charles; and we catch Fish not worth eating— It is an indolent sort of an amusement that just suits me for I *do not think*— When I look forward I tremble: but I bow down with trust in him who has mercifully saved me through a life of trouble and granted to me so many blessings—

[466] The 2d version explains, "for she feared I should not reach my home in time for my Confinement—"

AUGST 11

This was a day of great suffering and dreadful anxiety to my Dear Husband— My Nurse arrived: and as we were eight miles from We were obliged to send to town for my requisite help Mrs Keinche came out and remained through the day— Mrs Bentzpon[467] here.

12

Continued quite ill— Mrs. Heinche left me to go and see a Lady in the City taking my Carriage Horses and Servants and did not return until six o clock in the Evening— This indiscretion nearly cost my life— My Child a Daughter the first that I was ever blessed with was born at half past seven o-clock an hour and a half after her return— My Sister went and announced her birth to her Father and he soon came in to bless and Kiss his Babe— God was very merciful to me for I had been in great danger ever since morning—

SEPT 9

This day my lovely little Babe was Christened— We dared not ask the Emperor to stand as Sponsor least it should not please in America— Mrs. Bezzara, Mrs. Krehmer, and Mr. Harris stod Sponsors and she was named after *me* by her Fathers special desire contrary to my wish— The Service was performed by the Rev London King Pitt Chaplain of the English Factory Chapel— The Witnesses present were the Chevalier Bezzara, Gen Waltzdorf, Count Bushe de Hunnefeldt, Chevalier Navarro, M^r^ & Mrs. Bentzon, daughter of J J Astor; M^r^ & Miss Krehmer Com Bainbridge Mess Blodget, Fisher, Gray J. Harris Junr Jones and some others with the Family made up the company— The Sponsors were strangely selected Madame de Bezzarra Roman Catholick Mrs. Krehmer Episcopalian, and Mr. Harris Quaker— The Company dined with us and I got through the fatigue pretty well—[468]

[467] Magdalen Astor Bentzon (1788–1832), the daughter of John Jacob Astor, and her Danish husband Adrian Bentzon, a former governor of St. Croix, sailed to St. Petersburg in the spring of 1811 to settle the terms of an agreement between Astor's American Fur Company and the Russian-American Company (Axel Madsen, *John Jacob Astor: America's First Multimillionaire*, N.Y., 2001, p. 31, 77–79, 88–89; Richard Henry Greene, *The Todd Genealogy; or, Register of the Descendants of Adam Todd*, N.Y., 1867, p. 43).

[468] The 2d version also notes that she "was Baptized according to the rites of the Church of England."

12

Mr. Jones and Mr. Gray took leave of us to visit Paris and London;[469] Mr. Gray presented a Small diamond Cross to my little daughter– during his residence with us he was always kind and as affectionate as a Son– Our Family was now diminished to the Secretary of Legation and we sensibly felt the loss of the Society of our young friends who cheered many an hour by their attentions and agreeable conversations–

30

Company at Dinner–Count Lauriston Mons Lonquerue his aid de Camp–Mons de Rayneval Sec of Legation; St Genet, Prevost, also Secretaries Madame de Rayneval Mr & Madame Lesseps Ct St. Julian; Messrs. Lebzeltern & Stummar Sec of Baron Blome & the Baron–Baron Schladon Prussian and Count Busche Hunnefeldt– They left us early–

10 [*OCTOBER*]

Moved into a House in the City selected by Mr. Adams, a miserable place but the only one that would suit our finances– The accommodations were altogether unfit for a family and it was in a very vulgar and unpopular part of the City–[470] Debt or meaness is the penalty imposed by the Salary of an American Minister

16

When Mr. Adams returned from his walk he informed us that he had met the Emperor who had stoped to converse with him– among the questions he had was whether I was confined yet. He answered that I had been confined in August! He then asked whether I had a Son or a daughter– My Husband answered a daughter the first he had ever had– What was she born in the Country? Yes Sire. He

[469] Alexander Everett had departed in July, intending to visit Stockholm before returning to America. Francis Gray and Thomas Morton Jones left on 17 Sept. (D/JQA/28, 10, 17 July, 17 Sept., APM Reel 31).

[470] JQA was reluctant to leave the Russian countryside, but his family had tired of it and winter was approaching. The city lodgings were on Voznesensky Prospect and Little Officer's Street, near the house they had rented from Mr. Plinkey (D/JQA/28, 3, 8 Oct., APM Reel 31; O'Brien, *Mrs. Adams*, p. 29).

shrugged his shouders and pretended he did not know it—[471] He felt I suppose what a serious inconvenience he had put me to— He enquired if my confinement had been fortunate? answer perfectly so he thanked his Majesty— How inquisitive!!! As he is informed of every thing concerning foreigners he knew all about it before he put these questions— I had not seen him since I left the City— Every thing is changed since the departure of Caulincourt—

NOV 19

We went to the Theatre where we saw Mad[lle.] George in Mérope—[472] She is a superb woman—very handsome and graceful—but there is something very stiff and cold in french tragedy— I do not think her equal to M[rs.] Siddons— While writing of Tragedy I do not know if we can form a correct Judgment as to the correctness of the performance. I often observe that the Children of a family after they have grown up: can never realize in idea of the manners and customs of the Age of the youth in which there Parents had been formed— And they generally disinclined to believe or to approve of the tales of the past which they look upon as fabulous or very much exaggerated—

This being the case although Authors write from historical facts they cannot impress themselves with the nice minutia of action and manner so perfectly as to convey to Actors the perfect truth of performance— And this is the reason why the characters in Tragedy are always stiff and stately or cold and uninteresting—or overstrained and vulgar— The domestic Tragedy is always touching because they are the Tragedies of every day life which speak to the heart and soul whether in tatters or in Royal Robes— My Babe was vaccinated this morning for the kinepock—[473] O she grows lovely—Such a pair of Eyes!! I fear I love her too well— Martha Godfrey refused to take care of her— She is learning french and German and is too busy conning french Verbs with her Master who Charles calls *ill parle*—

We all went to a great Ball at Count Besborodko's— We went at ten and returned at one— He is one of the richest Men in the Em-

[471] The 2d version adds, "And he does not say all he knows—because he cannot—"

[472] Marguerite Joséphine Georges (1787–1867) appeared in Voltaire's *Mérope* (*New Amer. Cyclo.*, 1883).

[473] Kinepox, or cowpox, is a mild disease affecting cows that, when communicated to humans, provides immunity to smallpox.

pire and this Ball was very magnificent– The Countess spoke nothing but Russian so that the Countess Kochubey a charming woman did the honors for her– These Balls are all very much alike: from the nature of pure russian society where an air posé is the height of elegance and good breeding, there is necessarily a want of that sparkling animation which makes french society so delightful– Such was the charm of Caulincourt City parties: and the Corps diplomatic mourned their meetings en petite Commitée with sincere regret– Lauriston did not come as a Courtier and took very little pains to please– He was a constant visitor at our house and on very social terms as he seemed extremely partial to Mr. Adams– Indeed he was styled the Father of Diplomacy among the Corps who all live with us upon terms of intimate friendship– Among the great characters of the day was Prince Adam Tchartorisky one of the most elegant Men I ever saw and highly respected at the Court– He was a Pole of a very distinguished Family and apparently adored by his Countrymen– His moral character was said to be irreproachable and it was whispered about that an attachment for an object every way above his reach rendered his heart cold to the charms of our Sex in consequence however alluring– Count Busche de Hunnefeldt was an amiable man a German Militaire with a good deal of the National bon hommie of the Nation without vulgarity and equally without polish–[474]

7 DEC–

Seized with a violent Fever– The Milk struck to my brain in consequence of a fright on finding that Charles had waked from his sleep and as I supposed ruptured a blood vessell: my fever ran so high and the delirium so violent that the Physician announced to Mr. Adams that if a change did not take place towards morning he must prepare for the worst– My Child was taken from me for the time–[475] The Children were both very ill and our complaint was said to be the Grippe

[474] The 2d version adds that the ball ended at 6 A.M.

[475] LCA did not attempt to wean her daughter until the summer of 1812. She had nearly completed the process in August of that year, but when her child developed severe dysentery and a fever, the doctors advised that nursing be resumed. The child rallied only briefly (D/JQA/28, 15, 16, 17, 20, 22, 23, 24 Aug., APM Reel 31).

10

Still considered in great danger but the head partially releaved— The Children severely ill

18

Myself out of danger and Charles better but my Babe very ill— All of us much reduced and very suffering.

JAN 28 [*1812*][476]

After a long protracted confinement by sickness and anxiety, I once again take my Station in the world for which I care so little— The aspect of Society is greatly changed— The Corps Diplomatique is no longer so brilliant and a Cloud has rizen to veil the future for a time— Mr Adams position is as high as ever with the Imperial Family and that is the *Sun-shine* of St Petersburgh—

29

A Letter full of wo announcing my Mothers death that of my brother in Law Mr. Buchanan; Mr Adams's Uncle and Aunt Cranch within twenty hours of each other: and the dangerous and hopeless illness of his only Sister— God help us!! Yet are we always praying for Letters:[477]

31

The severity of the weather exceeds all calculation— Raumures Thermometer thirty two and a quarter below Zero—[478] Full of mortal

[476] In the 2d version the entry for this date reads simply, "Rode out for the first time with Charles."

[477] In the 2d version LCA provides dates for the death of her mother, on 29 Sept. 1811, and, incorrectly, of JQA's uncle and aunt Cranch, on 15 and 16 Oct., respectively.

Two letters from AA, to JQA of 17 Nov. and to LCA of 26 Nov., brought news of the death of Catherine Nuth Johnson of "Billious fever of a very malignant kind"; of Andrew Buchanan in Baltimore on 5 Oct. of the same fever; and of Richard and Mary Smith Cranch on 16 and 17 Oct., respectively. Mary had been ill for months with a "pleurisy fever" and consumption, and, as she failed, Richard had been "beseiged with a lethargy which deprived him of his speech." AA2 had undergone a mastectomy in the hope of curing a cancer of the breast. Richard Forrest of the Department of State had written to JQA on 23 Nov. of the deaths of LCA's mother and brother-in-law (all Adams Papers).

[478] The temperature reading of –32.25° Réaumur, or –44.56° F, is improbable. In the "Mete-

affliction— My Poor Mother! After ten years of poverty dependence and severe suffering which at this great distance it was so utterly out of my power to mitigate or assuage— How different will home appear should we live to return.— Gods Will be done! He afflicts us in mercy for here we are placed amid many sore temptations—

FEB 11

My lovely beautiful Babe is very very ill—[479] Ah! the fountain of her precious existence is sapped by these constant shocks and I look at her with fear and trembling— Every one who sees her stops her in the Street and they all say "that She is born for Heaven." The Russians are very superstitious and I fear that with the impressions already made upon my weak mind during my four years residence in Berlin I am too ready to fall into this error— Toward Even^{g} my babe was better— I am not naturally melancholy but my trials are heavy.

16

Mr Adams & Charles dined out and my boy returned home highly delighted with a present which he had recieved of a Magic Lantern— We see the Americas frequently.[480]

3 [30] AUGUST

Went into the Country with my sick Child[481]

orological Observations" that JQA recorded in St. Petersburg from 1 Jan. 1811 to 24 April 1814, temperatures for the morning, noon, and evening of 31 Jan. 1812 are, respectively, –10.1, –6, and –6 F (D/JQA/49, APM Reel 51; John Henry Belville, *A Manual of the Thermometer; Containing Its History and Use as a Meteorological Instrument*, London, 1850, p. 11).

[479] The 2d version merely notes, "all consternation— Better towards Night."

[480] The longer version of Adventures ends here. The three entries that follow were added from the 2d version.

[481] At Dr. Galloway's urging, JQA had taken a month-long lease at Ochta, northeast of the city, in the hope that his daughter's ill health, attributed to teething, would improve in the country air (D/JQA/28, 26–31 Aug., APM Reel 31).

9 [*SEPTEMBER*]

Took my Babe back to the City in Convulsions Dr Simpson and Galloway both attend the Babe[482]

12 [15]

My Child gone to heaven[483]

[482] Most likely the British physician Robert Simpson (ca. 1749–1822), formerly in the service of the Russian Navy and now settled with his family in St. Petersburg (Cross, *Banks of the Neva*, p. 152).

For the infant Louisa's worsening ailments; LCA, JQA, and Catherine Johnson's exertions on her behalf; the treatments to which the doctors subjected her; and her death, see D/JQA/28, 7–15 Sept., APM Reel 31; JQA to AA, 21 Sept., Adams Papers; and O'Brien, *Mrs. Adams*, p. 248–252.

[483] On 17 Sept. William Steuben Smith, Levett Harris, Annette Krehmer, and Chevalier Bezerra joined JQA and CFA at the funeral service for the infant Louisa at the English Factory Church. Smith, Harris, and Krehmer went with JQA to the so-called Lutheran Cemetery on Vasilevsky Island, the resting place for those not of the Russian Orthodox faith, where the child was buried "on an elevated spot of ground, immediately behind the tomb of poor Blodget." The latter was an American merchant who had died of typhus on 8 Nov. 1811 (D/JQA/28, 8 Nov. 1811, 17 Sept. 1812, APM Reel 31; O'Brien, *Mrs. Adams*, p. 252).

Diary of Louisa Catherine Adams

OCTOBER 22 [*1812*][1]

I have procured this Book with a view to write my thoughts and if possible to avoid dwelling on the secret and bitter reproaches of my heart for my conduct as it regarded my lost adored Child whose death was surely occasion'd by procrastination Oh God I humbly bow myself in submission to thy allwise decree's and implore thy mercy to grant me strength to support the dreadful afflictions with which thou hast thought fit to try thy Servant—

[1] LCA's Diary for 22 Oct. 1812 – 15 Feb. 1814 is on p. 1–40 of M/LCA/1, APM Reel 264, a journal book, 7" x 8 1/2", bound in boards covered with marbled paper with a leather spine. The Diary pages are handmade, calendered paper, watermarked with the "Maid of Dort" motif, the date 1810, and the motto *Pro Patria*. Although this motif is typically Dutch, Russian paper mills also used it (Zoya Vasil'evna Uchastkina, *A History of Russian Hand Paper-Mills and Their Watermarks*, Hilversum, Holland, 1962, p. 212, plates 316, 317, 327). The journal book also contains LCA's Diary for 24 Jan. – 25 March 1819; verse by LCA, JQA, and others; a scene from Louis de Boissy's comedy *Le Français à Londres*, 1727, that LCA copied in English; two book lists; recipes; and notations on aids to health and beauty.

23

This day I have endeavourd to keep myself constantly employed but still my mind dwells on the past and nothing can fill the dreadful void in my heart my babes image pursues me where ever I go bitter reflection adds to my pangs and in religion alone do I find consolation—

humbly do I confess my sins great as is my punishment I have a full conviction of the justice and mercy of my God who will not reject the petition of a contrite spirit but will grant me strength to correct the evil propensities of my nature and teach me to subdue that pride of heart from which all my errors spring—

24

This day has passed without any thing to mark it and to relieve a little the sameness of my Sisters life I visited the Theatre while I was there I was amused, but on my return to my home how cold blank and dreadful! my first object used to be my Child but alas now I see only the spot on which she died and every thing recalls her last agonies—

25

This day Mr A. read prayers to me it has been my practice for some time to teach Charles his prayers and the commandments. Mr A expressed himself dissatisfied with my method and I suffer'd myself to be hurried away by my temper in a very unbecoming manner I am peculiarly unfortunate for what I undertake with the best intentions almost always turns out exactly contrary I read I work I endeavor to occupy myself usefully but it is all in vain my heart is almost broken and my temper which was never good suffers in proportion to my grief I strive against it and humbly implore heaven to fortify my soul and to teach me meekness and seregnation he complains of my being suspicious and jealous these were faults once foreign to my nature but they are insensibly acquired by a perpetual coldness and restraint operating on a naturally warm and affectionate disposition yet this is by no means sufficient as an excuse and it shall be my study to amend such distructive failings I was taught from my earliest youth never to feel ashamed to acknowledge a fault and it always appeared to me to be a great meaness to endeavour by falsehood or prevarication to conceal an error which I was not ashamed to commit— For those I love no sacrifice will ever be too great for me to make all I claim is a little indulgence and if I at any time desire what is unreasonable or improper affection and gentleness will always have full effect upon my mind it is surely enough to have the power of rejecting a request without making a rejection more painful by harshness or contempt I feel what a burthen I must be to all around me and it is this which has made me so solisitous to return home there is something in an American life more active and varied and the idea of seeing my children was an object on which my mind could rest with real pleasure in Mrs Adams I should have found a comforter a friend who would pity sufferings which *she* would have understood—[1]

[1] On 24 Feb. 1812 AA wrote that GWA and JA2 were doing well but warned of the consequences of a long absence, including the loss of parental influence. LCA responded on 13 June that ever since her arrival in St. Petersburg, when she realized that their stay would be lengthy, she had "solicited" to have the older boys sent to them (both Adams Papers).

NOVBR 6

My thoughts have been so very gloomy that I have refrian'd from writing some time and I dare not commit to paper all that passes in my mind in vain I strive to fly from them my babes image flits forever before my eyes and seems to reproach me with her death necesssity alone induced me to wean her and in doing it I lost her. Oh God thou didst know the agonies I felt e're I could bring my self to do it Thou didst think to fit to take her from me Oh Lord and I humbly bow myself in submission to thy will— I struggle in vain against the affliction that consumes me and I feel that all my wishes centre in the grave I am a useless being in this World and this last dreadful stroke has too fully convinced me what a burthen I am become— surely it is no crime to pray for death if it is wickedness I implore thy mercy Oh Lord to cleanse my heart and to teach me to bear my trials with fortitude— my heart is buried in my Louisa's grave and my greatest longing is to be laid beside her even the desire of seing my beloved Boys gives way to this cherished hope and I look forward with joy to "that Bourne from whence no traveller returns["][1]

[1] Shakespeare, *Hamlet*, Act III, scene i, lines 79–80.

11

I have had a dream which has made a strong impression on my mind I will write it down for want of other employment— Methought I was at the house in which I lived at Octa I was playing with my babe who appear'd in full health when I was suddenly called by my father who was setting in the next room with a party of Gentlemen to beg that I would go down into the Cellar to fetch him some wine feeling afraid to go alone I requested my Sister Hellen to accompany me she immediately complied we decended a flight of steps which appeared to lead to a deep Vault and at the bottom of the stairs I stumbled and fell over a body newly murder'd from which the blood still appear'd to stream I arose with difficulty and looked for my Sister who seem'd to stand as if immovable and as if just risen from the grave notwithstanding my terror methought I got three bottles and carried them to my father who upon examining them told me that they were bottles of Porter which was entirely spoilt with the usual inconsistency of dreams I got over all these painful impressions and was as at first playing with my Child who was all life and animation when the most tremendous storm of Thunder accompanied by most vivid flashes of Lightning suddenly arose the Sky was entirely obscured and I was left alone in undescribable terror I fell upon my knees and implored the mercy of Heaven when suddenly the Thunder ceased and I raised my eyes and beheld as it were a stream of Fire which extended completely across the Heavens in which was distinctly written "Be of good cheer thy petition is granted—[″] I fell flat upon my face in a swoon and awoke

27

It is long since I have written my spirits are still dreadful and nothing but constant occupation prevents me from dwelling with unremitted sorrow for my irreparable loss. I have just finished reading the Life of Diane de Poitiérs, the Mistress of Henry the Second, of France.[1] It has only served to convince me how little we can do of ourselves. after forty years of uninterrupted virtue, at an age when the passions are supposed to be dead, she suffer'd herself to be seduced, by a boy of eighteen. such things appear almost incomprehensible to the human mind and serve to shew how unstable man is. how often when we think we have attain'd to the highest state of perfection, of which human nature is capable, are we dashed from our elevation and degraded to the lowest stations of infamy. Such was the Dutchess de Valentinois, and however great her talents, and amiable her character, they contribute only to prove how ineffectual they are, to preserve us from error, and as an example to posterity, of the weakness and fragility of human virtue, unaided by an alwise and superintending providence— This subject naturally leads to the circumstances of the times, which I am hourly witnessing, and which are peculiarly impressive. we behold here, the Emperor of France, after sixteen years of the most unhear'd of successes, in the short space of one month, plunged into all the horrors. of extreme distress, flying for his life, pursued by Barbarians, a revolt in his Country, his Army totally overthrown, and surrounded by treachery, dashed instantaneously from the summit of Splendor, into such a scene of horror, and calamity—[2] what an awful lesson to mankind how infallable a proof that an Almighty power, rules and directs, all the events of the world, and for some wise purpose decrees such men to rise to such a height, to make their fall the more tremendous. The character of this man produces unceasing astonishment, and we cannot trace his rise, and see his fall, without shuddering at the length, to which a blind and inexhaustible Ambition, will lead mankind. and though conscious of the justice of his fall, we shrink with pity and horror from a fate so dreadful, so hopeless— Another dreadful crisis approaches and all Europe will probably again be plunged into a state of confusion we shall again behold a vast struggle for power and the lessons he has taught and the passions he has rouz'd may perhaps prove more fatal than the mischeifs which have been caused by his unlimitted power—

[1] Diane de Poitiers, *Diane de Poitiers, duchesse de Valentinois, manuscrit trouvé dans les ruines du Château d'Anet*, Paris, 1805.

[2] For Napoleon's disastrous retreat from Russia, see Diary, 5 Dec. 1812, and note 5, below.

27[1]

I passed the last evening at the Theatre and saw Maitré Gipps Les Voitures verrés & Je cherche un diner the second piece was amusing the Music very good—[2] I have just finished reading the life of the Dutchess de Mazarin who was the favorite niece of the famous Cardinal Mazarin and inherited a fortune of thirty millions notwithstanding which owing to an ill assorted Marriage and many imprudences she was reduced to live in a foreign Country upon a trifling pension granted her by Charles the second of England she appears to have been a Woman of wonderful Beauty great talents and wit but of a restless disposition and is a striking example of the inefficacy of Wealth to procure happiness Unable to endure the dreadful disposition of her tyranical and teazing husband she rashly deserted her family and by this means destroyed a reputation which she assures us was unspotted Madame was so fortunate as to possess the friendship of such a man as St Evremond which probably saved her from forfeiting that virtue which she boasts of having preserved.[3] Her's is a life from which we may derive peculiar advantages although her trials were such as few could support it is evident that the step she took led to evils of a much more serious nature and obliged her to relinquish those natural ties, and affections which can alone prove securities to virtue to me this is a striking lesson how often have I shrunk from the task imposed on me and thought myself the most wretched of human beings and how small have been my trials. Oh God two things yet weigh upon my heart and I offer my supplications to thee to

"If I am wrong thy grace impart
To find the better way.[\"][4]

[1] This is the second consecutive entry LCA labeled as "27."

[2] Emmanuel Dupaty, *Le séducteur en voyage, ou les Voitures versées*, Paris, 1807; Jean Toussaint Merle, *Je cherche un dîner*, Paris, 1810.

[3] Hortense Mancini, Duchesse de Mazarin, *La Duchesse de Mazarin: Mémoires*, Paris, 1808.

[4] "If I am right, thy grace impart, / Still in the right to stay; / If I am wrong, O teach my heart / To find that better way" (Alexander Pope, "The Universal Prayer," lines 29–32).

DECBR. 5

It is long since I have written my mind has been in such a state as to render it imprudent to set my thoughts on paper— Kitty has been very sick and the Doctor kindly told me that if we did not make haste and return home that the Climate would kill us both to me there is nothing frightful in this idea I am only desirous of mingling my ashes with those of my lovely Babe my only fear is that some one will take the place which I so ardently desire. as my senses are supposed to be affected I may be excused for expressing such a fear but I implore the friends I may leave should I die here to observe this my last request to lay me with my Infant and to let no one follow me to my grave at the moment of making this request I am in good health and spirits therefore I trust my petition will not be thought to proceed from caprice or a distemper'd imagination if I know myself I never was calmer or easier in mind and body than I am at this moment had I a Will to make it would be thought but prudent to make it in case of accidents therefore I indulge myself in the expression of this desire as my body is the only thing in the world over which I may pretend to have a right and that only conditionally even after death should I be ordained to be buried in this Country I again repeat as this will injure no one I hope it will meet with attention I cannot help smiling at my anxiety on this subject as I fear it will only tend to confirm the idea of my intelect being impaired—

I am reading a french work entitled—Dictionnaire des Hommes Illustres[1] it is extremely amusing and instructive it is full of anecdotes and Bon mots some of which I shall set down to impress them more strongly on my mind Gaspard Abeil was a french Poet but of a very inferior order—at the first performance of his tragedie of Coriolanus the scene begins with a dialogue between two Princesses "Vous souvient-il, ma Soeur, du feu Roi notre Pere,"[2] the actress who should have replied paused some time in consequence of which a wit from the Pit cried out "Ma foi, s'il m'en souvient, il ne m'en souvient guere,"[3] which produced such a general laugh that the piece was not permitted to go on Danchet wrote an epigram on this line

> Pour déchirer les Tyndarides,
> Abeille sillonant son front de mille rides,
> Lance sur eux ses traits divers:
> Ce Poéte n'est pas un homme du vulgaire
> Et vous, vous souvenes sans doute de ses vers;
> Ma foi, s'il m'en souvient, il ne m'en souvient guere.[4]

which he sent him in manuscript the Abbé return'd no answer to it and became one of the best friends of Danchet who expressed his sorrow for having written this piece and declared himself cured of his tase for Satire.

Alphonse King of Leon of Castile he form'd a Code of Laws known by the name of the Las Partidas his favorite study was Astronomy and the well known astronomical tables which bear his name are proofs of his science This Prince however became so foolishly vain of his Science that he one day said that "If God had consulted him when he made the World, he would have given him some good advice" how shocking to think that the human mind should become so perverted by the very advantages which ought to lead them to perfection— He was dethroned by his Son Alphonso King of Arragon surrnamed the magnanimus here we meet with an amiable and virtuous Prince— At the siege of Gayette when the provisions of the Town began to fail they sent all the old Men Women and Children of the City. Alphonso recieved them in his camp upon which some of his Officers reproached him "did you think said he I came here to make upon old Men Women and Children" There is another anecdote Seing a Transport laden with Soldiers and Sailors in great danger he gave orders to go immediately to their relief finding however that he was not obeyed he jumped into a boat to go to their assistance and to those who represented to him the danger of his attempt he answer'd "he had rather perish in attempting to save them than be a spectator of their death" there is something sublime in such an act which excites feelings of an undescribable nature which elevate a Man beyond mortality and produce a sense of wondering admiration to which there is no bounds—

He could not bear dancing and used to remark that the only difference between a man dancing and a madman was that the fit of the dancer was shorter

I find no similarity in the Characters of Annibal and Napoleon but a great deal between the latter and Alexander the great Napoleon is said to be in greater difficulties than ever but he has contrived to extricate himself from the most perilous situation at the head of 75 thousand men in the face of the whole Russian army combined it is however unquestionable that the greater part of his army is totally sacrificed owing entirely to his having delayed his retreat too long and his troops not being prepared for the severity of this Climate which this year as been greater than ever was known it is said that Napoleon has made his way into Prussia at the head of small band of chosen men that he stiles himself their Captain and marches on foot with all his Generals this if true is a trait which bespeaks the character of the man— The Emperor Alexander is gone to the army I suppose he intends to become as famous in pursuit as he is in retreat—[5]

[1] *Dictionnaire des portraits historiques, anecdotes et traits remarquables des hommes illustres*, 4 vols., Paris, 1768–1772.

[2] Do you recall, my Sister, the memory of the late king, our father?

[3] Faith! If I recall it, I recall it scarcely!

[4] Antoine Danchet, *Les Tyndarides*, Paris, 1708: "To tear apart the Tyndaridae, / The bee, furrowing his brow with a thousand wrinkles, / Flings at them his assorted arrows: / That poet is not of the vulgar crowd, / And you assuredly recall his verses: / Faith! If I recall it, I recall it scarcely!"

[5] Russia's uneasy alliance with France was strained by the commercial disruptions of the Continental System and by French incursions in east-central Europe. By the summer of 1811, Alexander I and Napoleon expected war, and through the winter they made plans for the military campaigns to come. JQA noted that in March 1812, when he encountered Alexander walking along the quay, the emperor confided to him, "I have done every thing, to prevent this struggle (cette lutte.) but thus it ends."

In April Alexander joined his troops on the western front. Napoleon's armies invaded Russian territory on 24 June. Two days later, Alexander left his army in the field and withdrew to Moscow. There he recruited troops and raised money before returning to St. Petersburg. In early September the French and Russian Armies met at the Battle of Borodino, seventy miles west of Moscow. Despite suffering extraordinary casualties, both sides claimed victory.

On 15 Sept. Napoleon entered Moscow, which was now evacuated and its buildings burned, mistakenly believing that Alexander would offer peace negotiations. With his lines of communication overextended and winter approaching, Napoleon withdrew from the city on 19 Oct., and by the following week the Grand Army was in retreat. News reached St. Petersburg in late October that the Russian armies had retaken Moscow.

During the calamitous retreat, Napoleon's men encountered severe winter weather and a newly emboldened Russian Army. Upon reaching the Prussian frontier, Napoleon abandoned what was left of his army and set out for Paris, accompanied by Armand de Caulaincourt. Alexander decided to pursue the French Army and left St. Petersburg on 19 December. He would not return to St.

Petersburg until Napoleon had been defeated and exiled to Elba (Palmer, *Alexander I*, p. 198–201, 204, 207–208, 213–216, 221–226, 231–237, 243–247, 250–257; D/JQA/28, 19 March, APM Reel 31).

DECBR. 23D

I have been reading the life of the Queen of Navarre it is very amusing and full of anecdotes of the court of Francis the 1st it is too romantic however to permit the possibility of forming a correct opinion of her character or of the circumstances attending her affection for the famous Duke De Bourbon she must however have been an extraordinary woman in every point of view—

I have just begun a work entitlled the Court of Louis the 14 and the Regent which is full of anecdotes of all the great persons of his day and shews the little as well as the great qualities of Louis it is written by Anquetil[1] The important events and principal anecdotes of the Court are related in such rapid succession that it is difficult for the mind to retain with any accuracy circumstances which are so mixed and many of them trifling. as the observations I may make in this book are not intended to be seen I shall indulge myself with writing my opinion on the different characters of this reign Louis the 14th appears to me notwithstanding all the éclat attached to his name to have been a man whose natural powers of mind were great but whose personal vanity was a counterpoise to this advantage self was the rule by which he measured every thing and every body and in the contemplation of his own perfections he shut his eyes I believe involuratarily to the real superiority of others himself was his standard of excellence and it never enter'd into his head to make a comparaison of any thing with himself and in this opinion a man in such a situation, surrounded by parasites must naturally be strengthen'd. The habit of viewing every one in an inferior light must naturally produce the consequence of blaming them for any ill which may ocur in the administration of Offices under their charge and Superiors seldom reflect sufficiently between planning and executing in this point Louis appears to me to have acted in several instances in the course of his reign in an unpardonable manner and to have caused many of the misfortune which befel him in the close of his career were I King if I was not immediately on the spot I would certainly leave the power of giving battle to my generals when the chance of war made it necessary and not oblige them to send from the frontier to my capital to know their orders one might as well if ones house was a fire send to beg the Kings permission to put it out before we attempted to stop the flames My Children guard against the silly failing of Vanity be assured there is no weakness so degrading to a great man and none of which such cruel advantages may be taken it is the almost natural failing of superior talents which universally produce such admiration as to lead us almost involuntarilly to view ourselves in too favorable a light and prevents us from weighing and comparing our actions with those of others of whom we are led to form unfavorable opinions merely from the habit of measuring their merits by our own standard we ought always to reflect that there are great varieties of excellence and that there are few characters from whom we may not derive some benefit and be assured that we are never further from perfection than when we flatter ourselves we have attain'd it of personal vanity I do not speak the course of nature is of itself a lesson from which we cannot fly however willing we may be to shut our eyes to the changes which take place in ourselves those which take place in the persons of those with whom we live and with whom we have grown must occasionally remind us that we are not exempted from the same infirmities it is from the mind therefore that we have the most to apprehend where the danger of vanity is the most to be dreaded as it is acquired insensibly and imperceptibly and is nursed by the adulation of the world untill it becomes insatiable of food and sinks a man to a blind adoration of himself destroys his taste for an intercourse with mankind in general and incapable of relishing the common occurrences and socialities of life which from indulging the idea of his own superiority become insipid and beneath his attention in short every thing that surrounds him must live for him and such an ascendancy does this passion acquire that no sacrifices however great and painful in those who are so unfortunate as to belong to him can satisfy for he is to much absorb'd in himself to imagine that people so inferior can feel otherwise than flatter'd and honour'd even at the expense of every thing which can render life desirable to persons whose qualifications do not fit them for so high a sphere remember my beloved Children that we are sent into this world to promote as much as possible the happiness of each other and that if heaven in its great mercy has granted us to attain any state of perfection we are still more call'd upon to act with humility and to support those who are not so equally gifted with us remember how few there are who become eminent and how many even who have reached to a splendid height have either been sunk to a state of imbecility or to the most dreadful of all deseases madness there are dreadful examples sent to warn us against this fatal passion by shewing us how *little* we are of ourselves and how easy it is for us to fall from the highest elevation to the lowest degradation of human misery. the misfortunes of Louis the 14 in the latter years of his reign where owing to this failing the infirmities which are brought on by age render'd him less able to contend against the troubles of his court and he suffer'd himself to be teazed and flatter'd into measures which produced the most serious misfortunes and at his death he bitterly bewail'd his error but alas it was too late too repair it—

[1] Louis Pierre Anquetil, *Louis XIV, sa cour, et le Régent*, Paris, 1789, published in English as *Memoirs of the Court of France, during the Reign of Lewis XIV*, Edinburgh, 1791.

29

Charles took his first lesson of Russian the 22 he is very unwell and I cannot help feeling very uneasy about him the loss of my darling baby which yet lies heavy at my Soul render'd me so timid that the most trifling thing alarms me I have no faith in my Physician in heaven alone I put my trust and my prayers will ascend to the throne of grace[1]

[1] The entry ends here, at the bottom of the page, with prominent ink stains on the page. The next several pages have been cut out and ink stains can be seen on the remnants of the missing pages and on the page that follows the gap. That page begins mid-sentence with the undated entry that follows.

[*ANTE* 27 *MARCH 1813*]

are almost too much for my constitution— They tell me that Mr Cabot is likely to die and I cannot describe the terror I feel lest they should usurp the little spot of earth which I have set my heart on that adjoins my Louisa's grave in vain I reason with myself the desire is uncontroulable and my mind is perpetually dwelling upon some means to procure this desired blessing

MARCH 27

With a grateful heart I return my thanks to Heaven for the restoration of my health and a new sense of the blessings which are still within my power and I trust in the mercy of my God to pardon the weakness of his creature— In reading the letters of Madame du

Noyer I have just met with the following lines which are very beautiful

Quand le Sauveur souffroit pour tout le genre humain
La mort, en l'abordant au fort de son supplice,
Parut toute et intérdite, et retera sa main,
N'osant pas sur son Maitre exercer son office.
Mais Jesus, en baissant la tête sur son sein,
Fit signe à l'implacable & sourde exécutrice,
De n'avoir point d'egard au droit de Souverain,
Et d'achever sans peur ce sanglant sacrifice
La barbare obéit, & ce coup sans pareil,
Fit trembler la nature, & pâlir le Soleil,
Comme si de sa fin le monde eût été proche:
Tout pâlis, tout se mút sur la terre & dans l'air,
Excepté le péché qui prit un coeur de roche,
Quand les rochers sembloient en avoir un de chair.
Par Le Comte de Modene.[1]

[1] While the Savior was suffering for the entire human race, / Death, upon approaching him in the throes of his torment, / Seemed dumbfounded, and withdrew her hand, / Not daring to exercise her office upon her Master. / But Jesus, lowering his head upon her breast, / Signaled to the implacable and unhearing execution'ress / Not to pay any heed to the Sovereign right, / And to fearlessly execute the bloody sacrifice. / The brute obeyed, and that nonpareil blow / Made the earth quake, and the Sun pale, / As if the end of the world were nigh: / Everything paled, everything moved upon the earth and in the air, / Except sin who assumed a heart of stone, / While stones seemed to have one of flesh. / By the Count of Modene (Anne Marguerite Du Noyer, *Lettres historiques et galantes*, 12 vols., Cologne, 1790, 4:208–209). Du Noyer describes the poem as being in the manner of the Count of Modene.

APRIL 4TH.

We have at length recieved letters from America—Which bring favorable accounts of the health of our friends and my dear Children to hear from them once in six or seven months is all that is left me as my prospect of ever seeing them more is now alas hopeless my health the Climate and this dreadful War have added to the improbability of our return this Summer for myself I scarcely can define my feelings much as I wish to see my Children my heart is torn at the idea of quitting for ever the spot where my darling lays and to which my whole soul is linked but my fears on Mr Adams's account render me desirous to leave a Climate in which he evidently suffers and which I fear will irreparably injure his constitution— Mr Harris joined me in the walk to day and made some observations on Mr A's looks which have contributed to render me more uneasy I will trust in the mercy of heaven to hear my prayers for his health and to save him from all danger he will listen to no advice therefore we must hope that the natural strength of his constitution and some striking event which may give an active occupation will remove the disease he is now threaten'd with— I have just closed a letter to Mrs Adams it is the first I have written for many months and it has rent my heart afresh—[1]

[1] On 4 April LCA wrote to AA of her concern about JQA's health, noting particularly that the cold climate affected his chest. JQA wrote in his Diary on 5 April that both he and CFA suffered from "Catarrhal Colds" (all Adams Papers; D/JQA/23, APM Reel 26).

AUGUST 14

What wonderful changes have taken place since I last took up this book even my health and spirits are so much amended that I scarcely know myself I offer up my prayers and thanks to the Almighty disposer of events for his great mercy in having raised me up and comforted me in my severe affliction and will ever put my trust in him for in heaven alone can I find consolation and I look forward with the hope of soon being reunited to my Angelic Babe—

Another great crises is speedily advancing and life will soon become even more burthensome than it has been for the last twelve Months in vain I ask myself what I apprehend a sort of vague indefinite something tells me that I have still some heavy trials to go through ere I shall be released from this world of sorrow—

They say I am ambitious if so why do not the vain projects of the world occupy my thoughts and fill my Soul when I compare myself with those to whom I am the most nearly connected when I see every thought devoted peace happiness family every thing neglected for this one object my heart decidedly assures me that for this great end I was not made and that were I of consequence enough to be any thing I should only prove a bar in the way of attaining it No! life has lost its principal charm and all I wish is to quit a World for which I have long been conscious I was not fitted to live happy in this world we must have something to soften the casualties to which the best of are liable and without one being who will open his ~~their living constantly together~~ heart to you though bound by the closest ties cast such a dreadful restraint over the most trifling things as to banish and destroy all confindence and by this means render the greatest blessings unavailing in promoting that portion of happiness which we are allowed to enjoy—

Astronomy

In the first place I wish to make myself acquainted with the Armillary Sphere, for instance, the names of the different Circles, the Horizen, the ~~Polar Circles,~~ the Ecliptic, the Equator, and the Tropics and the two Colures the Ecliptic is the Circle in which the Planets move round the Earth we must first begin our lesson of Astronomy by discovering the Polar Star. this star being situated near the Pole round which the other stars' move every day appears to continue always in the same spot at what hour or Season you look for it. it is the only one so situated all the other Stars' make circles round the Pole Star or more properly the Pole which forms the Centre of the motion or the Nave of the Wheel we shall observe in the course of our Lessons that these movements which are pure appearances proceed from the movement of the Earth but we must confine ourselves at Present like the ancient Astronomers to observing the Phenomenea without seeking their causes our course will in this way be more natural and easy— This Astronomy is I fear too difficult for me and requires a sort of attention of which I am incapable there is a great difficulty in discovering or grouping the Stars through Double Windows, and it requires a sort of exercise which my present state of health will not permit—[1]

[1] LCA's account may be derived from Joseph Jérôme le Français de Lalande, *Astronomie des dames* or *Abrégé d'astronomie*, 2d edn., both published in Paris, 1795. Lalande is one of the authors JQA used to guide his own astronomical observations. See, for example, D/JQA/29, 11, 16, 22, 27–29 Dec., APM Reel 32.

[*POST 25 JANUARY 1814*]

Although we saw but little of the Ministers when they resided here yet I miss them most unaccountably they left on the 25th: of January on their return home with every mark of disgust for the Climate the Manners and habits of the Russians they were no favorites here and their manner of living did not contribute to render them comfortable or to conciliate the good will or affection of their Country men[1] Public men in general do not pay sufficient attention to this point and are not sufficiently aware that in Foreign Countries (more especially here at St Petersburg) the Americans who reside have little eslse to do during a large part of the year but to weigh and measure every trifling error in the character of their ministers which in their own Country would pass totally unobserved and become here swelled into faults of magnitude there are most assuredly a certain stile of manners absolutely necessary to the station and if a man is incapable of conforming to them no matter from what cause he should immediately quit it The world in general judge only from what they see and seldom take the trouble to enquire whether what we term trifling omissions of etiquette or common rules of politeness are owing to a great superiority of intelect on our part or not but as long as we fill a station in high life such omissions become offences we must expect to be judged with as much severity and perhaps more than those who have half our pretentions I can never be surprized ~~at~~ this kind of censure as every person whose habits are so far fixed as to render it impossible to conform to the situations in which he may be placed is an improper person to fill a station in which a very small proportion of his time can be employed on public business and the essence of which depends on manners and deportment The melancholy accident which has lately occurred in the Spanish Ministers family seems to have revived all my painful feelings for my own irreparable loss how inscrutable are the ways of providence a Young Woman in the bloom of life with wealth, rank, beauty, and an adoring husband, surrounded by every enjoyment this world can afford cut of in the highest health a martyr to that most horrid of all suffering, *fire*. she languished 14 days ere her Soul was released, in excruciating torments, and then was removed to a better world; I trust to enjoy bliss everlasting.[2] the will of heaven be done the judgements of the Almighty are all wise and though beyond the conception of our limited understandings we must be convinced that so wise and benevolent a being in such examples must intend general good & thus warn us ever to be ready for that hour for which we can never be sufficiently prepared.—

[1] Albert Gallatin and James A. Bayard left St. Petersburg on 25 Jan. 1814 to travel to Ghent to begin peace negotiations with Britain (D/JQA/29, APM Reel 32; *DAB*).

[2] María Ramona Parada y Parada (1787–1814) had married the Spanish diplomat Eusebio de Bardají y Azara (1766–1844) in 1806. She died after her clothes caught fire at a stove (Didier Ozanam and Denise Ozanam, *Les diplomates espagnols du XVIIIe siècle*, Madrid, 1998, p. 174–175; D/JQA/29, 13, 25 Jan., APM Reel 32).

TUESDAY FEBR 1ST.

I have just returned from the melancholy office of attending poor Madame Bardasci funeral ceremony the Body is to be sent to Spain it is the first Catholic funeral I ever attended I dislike all that pomp and Shew which is displayed on such occasions but there is something delightful in the idea of the Soul being wafted to the presence of its maker accompanied by strains of almost heavenly harmony imploring mercy and peace—

I have just finished reading the Memoires of Madame de Lichtereau the Mistress of William Frederic 2 the endeavors to acquit herself of the heavy charges brought against her but without producing that conviction on the mind of her readers which she appears to expect it is very singular that she should have published the letters of the casual acquaintances she made many of which are filled with mere common place gallantries which I should suppose could afford no pleasure to the authors to have thus exhibited to the World.—[1]

The Memoires of Mlle Dumesnill are said to be an answer to Mlle Clairon they should rather be called a bitter sarcasm on the whole life and Memoires of this celebrated actress and written evidently with so much passion as to destroy in a great measure the effect the author is so desirous to produce when a Woman of 80 undertakes to write her memoires the world ought to be very charitable and make as much allowance as possible for the natural garulity of old age—which loves to dress former recollections in gawdy Colours and a Woman must possess a stronger mind than falls to the lot of poor humanity if her head is not a little turned by the unqualified admiration of *a world* during the space of thirty years[2]

[1] Wilhelmine Rietz, Countess of Lichtenau, *Mémoires de la comtesse de Lichtenau ecrits par elle-même en 1808*, Paris, 1809. The English version had been published in London in 1799.

[2] Marie Françoise Dumesnil, *Mémoires . . . en réponse aux mémoires d'Hippolyte Clairon*, Paris, 1798.

FEB 4

Doctor Beresford has just lent us Crabbs Tales which I think extremely pretty[1] there is something so easy, simple, and natural, in the verse, so forcible in the characters, that you can scarcly refrain from fancying yourself among the circle of your particular acquaintance and being assured that you have met the particular characters which he has so admirably drawn— As a Poet I should certainly never rank him with Walter Scott whose Verse to my ear the purest Melody but I infinely prefer him to Lord Byron who always appears to me to possess ideas too vast for expression and though in his Poetry you find many beauties the mind is left on the stretch to discover the precise ideas which he intended to convey— I have passed the enthusiastic age perhaps on this account I am less capable of appreciating their merit—

[1] Maria Joseph Crabb, *Tales for Children in a Familiar Style*, London, 1812.

7

Mr Adams gave me Dr Rush's work upon the deseases of the Mind to read[1] I have read it through although I confess it produced a very powerful effect upon my feelings and occasion'd sensations of a very painful kind since the loss of my darling babe I am sensible of a great change in my character and I often involuntarily question myself as to the perfect sanity of my mind in this state of spirits a person is apt to fancy himself afflicted with every particular symtom described the many melancholy circumstances which have occurred to me since my residence in this town have produced have cast a heavy gloom over me which I much fear nothing will ever correct in vain I struggle against it life has become a scene so barren that even the prospects which my beloved Children open to me appear too cold to yeild me a hope of future happiness

I am reading a Book entitled Lettres Elementaires sur la Chimie my mind must be differently organiz'd from those of other people nothing I read appears to be of service to me and even what I study most I find easiest obliterated from my memory— I have defer'd the study of this work untill I can purchase it requires time and particular attention—[2]

[1] Benjamin Rush, *Medical Inquiries and Observations, upon the Diseases of the Mind*, Phila., 1812, Shaw-Shoemaker, No. 26668.
[2] Octave Ségur, *Lettres élémentaires sur la chimie*, Paris, 1803.

15

I am now reading Manon L'Escaut a work of Prevost. it is said to be a very good thing the stile I like very well

Lines on a kiss
translated by Mr. Adams

You send me, Lady, by the Mail,
A Cheerless, joyless kiss!
How can a *paper* kiss avail

To touch my lip with bliss?
I to all favours, such as these
Stone cold shall ever be—
That fruit has naught, my taste to please;
Save, gathered from the tree.[1]

[1] The poem, attributed to "M. M," first appeared in a volume of the *Almanach des Muses*, an annual collection of poetry. It is reproduced, both in French and in another English translation, in *Letters from Paris, during the Summer of 1791*, London, 1792, p. 91.

Narrative of a Journey from Russia to France

It has often been a matter of regret to me that I kept no journal of my travels from St Petersburg, to Paris—and having little to occupy my mind or attention, I will even at this late period endeavour to sketch some of its incidents; merely by way of amusement, to fill up an hour which might be less profitably employed— It may perhaps at some future day serve to recal the memory of one, *who was*—and show that many undertakings which appear very difficult and arduous to my Sex, are by no means so trying as imagination forever depicts them— And that energy and discretion, follow the necessity of their exertion, to protect the fancied weakness of feminine imbecility—[1]

[1] This is LCA's account of her trip overland from St. Petersburg to Paris of 12 Feb. – 23 March 1815 to meet JQA, who had been negotiating the Treaty of Ghent. The 48-page narrative, dated 27 June 1836, is on p. 277–324 of M/LCA/5, APM Reel 268, a journal book, 7 3/4" x 9 1/2", bound in boards covered with marbled paper. The journal book also contains LCA's Diary for 6 Nov. 1835 – 28 May 1841, prose reflections, and verses by LCA and GWA. LCA wrote a second, undated version of the Narrative, in fifty unbound pages, 8" x 10", also in M/LCA/5. The editors have noted any additional or clarifying material from this version.

LCA's grandson Brooks Adams (BA) published an edited version of this work as "Mrs. John Quincy Adams's Narrative of a Journey from St. Petersburg to Paris in February, 1815," *Scribner's Magazine*, 34:449–463 (Oct. 1903).

Because LCA wrote this memoir 21 years after her journey, and without a Diary to guide her, her recollection of the route, the course of events, and some of the people she encountered is imperfect. LCA comments that "those who may read this memento mori, must endeavour to extract light from the chaos which lies before them." Readers can turn to Michael O'Brien, *Mrs. Adams in Winter: A Journey in the Last Days of Napoleon*, N.Y., 2010, for a reconstruction of the journey. That book provides a full map and period map details with information about the physical features of the lands through which LCA traveled, and it traces the towns along the route, with their post stations, hotels, cultural institutions, leading families, and local populations.

1815

On the 12th. day of Feby. at five o'clock in the evening of Sunday, I bade adieu to the splendid City of St. Petersburg, where I had resided upwards of five years;[2] in company with my Son Charles between 7 and 8 years of age; a french Nurse, who entered my service on that day, and two Men Servants, one of whom had lived with Mr. Smith; the other a released prisoner from the remnant of Napoleons Army,[3] who had been taken in that most disastrous Russian War, which terminated the career of that heretofore fortunate Soldier, in his transportation to the Island of St. Helena—

To avoid the disagreeable and painful feelings of parting with friends with whom I had formed a friendship of some standing; I chose the above hour while they were engaged at their dinner; and

[2] In Jan. 1814 President James Madison appointed JQA to head the commission to negotiate a treaty between the United States and Great Britain to end the War of 1812. JQA left St. Petersburg on 28 April, with LCA and CFA seeing him off at the Strelna post station. In a 27 Dec. letter to LCA, JQA described the signing and proclamation of the Treaty of Ghent and relayed his intention to go to Paris to await the president's orders. JQA wrote that whether or not he was appointed minister to Britain, as he had reason to expect, he had asked to be recalled from his post in Russia. Then he added, "I therefore now invite you, to break up altogether our establishment at St: Petersburg." JQA instructed his wife to dispose of any unwanted furniture, pack up the rest to be sent later, "and to come with Charles to me at Paris, where I shall be impatiently waiting for you." He supposed that she would leave in the middle of February, if the weather permitted, and he advised her to engage "a good man, and woman servant" and if possible to travel with another lady or acquaintance. He assured her that she would find "very tolerable" lodging at any of the post houses. Levett Harris, now elevated to chargé d'affaires, would assist her in financial matters and procure horses and a means of conveyance. JQA's fellow commissioners Albert Gallatin and James A. Bayard had recommended that she travel in "no other Carriage than a Kibitka," a Russian sleigh with a rounded hood to shelter the passengers. JQA wrote that he had informed his parents that if he was sent to England, he wanted GWA and JA2 to join them. In a subsequent letter, JQA allowed that LCA might wish to delay her journey until the end of February or early March, when the days would be longer and the snows "beaten down to a solid consistency," or still later, when she would have the option of traveling by water.

LCA replied to her husband's summons on 20 Jan. 1815, expressing her astonishment at the turn of events and her expectation that she would be "much imposed upon" as she attempted to sell their goods. She hoped to leave before 10 or 15 Feb., and, except for a short stop in Berlin to see old friends, she would travel quickly, "as my impatience to meet you is really and earnestly very great— We have both passed through disagreeable Scenes and shall only be able to forget them when we meet" (Bemis, *JQA*, 1:188–190; D/JQA/29, 28 April 1814, APM Reel 32; JQA to LCA, 27, 30 Dec. 1814, LCA to JQA, 20 Jan. 1815, all Adams Papers; O'Brien, *Mrs. Adams*, p. 58).

[3] LCA had hired Madame Babet, a French maid formerly employed by Madame Colombi; Baptiste, a prisoner of war who would provide service to earn his passage home to France; and another servant, probably John Fulling (LCA to JQA, 31 Jan. 1815, Adams Papers). For some uncertainties regarding the male servants' identities, see O'Brien, *Mrs. Adams*, p. 3, 306, note 2.

M^r. Wyer put me into the Carriage and gave the last directions to my Postillions—[4]

The weather was intensely cold; my Carriage on runners and the two Servants followed in a kibitka.[5] Every thing had been done by the Government, that the kindest politeness and interest could suggest, in the way of Passports[6] to make the journey easy; for which I felt truly grateful and to this attention I owed all the facilities which rendered my journey so easy— Night and day we proceeded until we arrived at Narva, where I stopped to rest at the best Inn in the place. We had been there but a few minutes, when a Gentleman was announced, who informed me that apartments had been prepared for me at the Governors, and that he would wait on me in person to escort me to his house, as Soon as convenient to myself— Intending to proceed very early in the morning, I declined the invitation; but received the visit of the Governor; and one from the Count de Bray the Bavarian Minister, who was at that time on a visit with his Wife and family at her Fathers— The Count brought me also a very polite invitation from the family to pass a few days

[4] Under the European post road system, administered by the individual states, a road was divided into posts for the purpose of determining charges. Post stations were located at regular intervals along the way, generally every six to twelve miles, which, under moderate conditions, might be traversed in one hour. At the post station, a traveler paid the charges for the units of distance traveled and for fresh horses and local postilions. One could also have a carriage serviced and find food and a place to sleep (O'Brien, *Mrs. Adams*, p. 53–56).

[5] On the advice of her friends in St. Petersburg, LCA traveled in a carriage that was mounted on runners for as far as was suitable for the road conditions. For 1,650 rubles (about $330), she purchased a berline, a large carriage, typically with four wheels, of which the rear two were larger; an enclosed passenger compartment with glass windows; a raised driver's seat in the front; and a serviceable suspension system. A carriage of this size required LCA to hire six horses and two postilions at each post station (LCA to JQA, 20 Jan., Adams Papers; M/JQA/13, Feb.–March 1815, Account Book 1809–1829, Minute of Expences of M^rs: Adams's Journey from S^t: Petersburg to Paris—from 12 Feb^y: to 23 March 1815, APM Reel 210; O'Brien, *Mrs. Adams*, p. 56–58).

[6] The 2d version adds, "and the Minister of the Interior had even offer to me the services of a *yager* to accompany me through the Imperial dominions."

LCA carried Russian and Prussian passports and a French passport issued in the name of the restored Bourbon king Louis XVIII by his ambassador in Russia, Comte Juste de Noailles. LCA evidently declined the offer of Osip Petrovich Kozodavlev, the Russian minister of the interior, of the services of a *yager* (or *jäger*), an attendant dressed in a huntsman's costume. Levett Harris noted that LCA also carried a *padarojna*—an order for post horses—to which was attached a "Circular Letter" from Kozodavlev to the postmasters on the road and "Letters of Credit and Recommendation" for Riga, Memel, Königsberg, and Berlin. Harris also noted that "Information has already been Given to the different persons addressed on this occasion who will hasten to Shew every attention to Mrs Adams" (LCA Russian passport, with a German translation, 28 Jan. 1815 [9 *Feb. N.S.*], MQA; LCA Prussian passport, 9 Feb., LCA French passport, 7 Feb., both Adams Papers; O'Brien, *Mrs. Adams*, p. 4; Levett Harris, Memorandum, 12 Feb. 1815, Adams Papers). For an additional passport LCA received later, see Descriptive List of Illustrations, No. 11, above.

with them, which I also rejected; being without my husband I wished to be as short a time on the road as possible

Very early in the morning I started *for* Riga, at which place we arrived in safety, and I found tolerable lodgings— Here we were overtaken by a thaw, and I was under the necessity of staying four or five days, to get my Carriage fixed and to dispose of my Kibitka—[7] Our provisions were all frozen ere we reached the City, and even the Madeira wine had become ice— Here for the first time I had some reason to doubt the honesty of my Servant A Silver Cup[8] belonging to my little boy was taken from the Carriage and there was little Doubt that he had made free with it— I was however under the necessity of overlooking the fact, in consequence of the terms of his engagement, and I could not prove it— We were barely settled in our Lodgings, when the Governor of Riga called to invite me to his house and to offer the use of his Carriage during my stay— I declined the invitation to take up my abode with him; but accepted an invitation to dine, and pass as much time at his house as I could during my sojourn in Riga This Gentleman was an Italian a great favorite of the Emperor Alexander, and one of the most friendly, Gentlemanly men I ever met with— The Marquis had married a German Lady who spoke very little french; but who appeared to possess all the amiable and domestic qualities of persons of that Nation—[9] During my stay I received every attention that politeness could offer— All the most distinguished persons in Town were invited to meet me, and I was forced to call up all the German I could muster, to answer to the kindness expressed for me by the Guests—

After a detention of four or five days we proceeded on our journey, and once or twice the Carriage sunk so deep into the Snow in Courland, that we had to ring up the inhabitants, who came out in numbers with shovels and pickaxes to dig us out— For this purpose the bell appeared to be commonly used, and the signal readily understood— Without accident or impediment of any other kind, we arrived in safety at Mittau, the Capital of Courland— Here I stopped to rest for some hours with a determination to proceed one stage more to sleep— The House was the best I had found: the people

[7] Because of the road conditions on the approach to Riga, the runners were removed and the carriage proceeded on wheels (LCA to JQA, 17 Feb. 1815, Adams Papers).

[8] In the 2d version LCA replaces "belonging" with "presented by the Baron de Bush Hunsfeldt the Westphalian Minister as a parting keepsake to my little boy."

[9] Marquis Filippo Paulucci and his wife, Wilhelmina (O'Brien, *Mrs. Adams*, p. 89–90).

very civil, and every thing comfortable—[10] In about an hour after my arrival Countess Mengs, a Lady with whom I was slightly acquainted at St. Petersberg called, and gave me a most kind and urgent invitation to her house; entreating me to remain with her some days she desiring to show all that was worth seeing in the Town to me, and to introduce me to some of her distinguished friends— As however my Letters were urgent for me to proceed on my journey as fast as I conveniently could; I thought it my duty to decline an invitation which would have been very pleasant and agreeable; the Countess being a Lady of great respectability, and superior attainments—[11] Immediately after my Dinner was removed, the Master of the House, after carefully shutting the doors and watchfully noting that no intruders were near; said he wished much to speak with me, upon a matter which he considered of vital importance to me; who as a friend for whom Countess Mengs had expressed herself much interested, he should feel very happy to serve. I expressed my thanks to him, and assured him I felt very grateful to the Countess, to whom I would certainly pay a visit if I had time— I requested him to be seated, and to inform me on what subject he had asked this interview— He again examined the doors with an appearance of great anxiety, and then sat down close to me, who felt not a little uncomfortable at all this *apparently terrible preparation*— I however assumed an air of great calmness and patiently awaited the *mighty tale*, which was to thrill my nerves with horror— He began by informing me that the last night a dreadful Murder had been commited on the very road which I was about to take, and to urge me to wait until the next morning, before I determined to proceed— I told him very coolly and decidedly that the plan of my journey was fixed, and as I only intended to travel four german miles farther that night and was to start so early with two well armed servants, I concieved I had nothing to apprehend; as the Postillions must be in the habit of passing the road constantly which was a very publick one, and that I should reach the place of my destination by nine or ten o clock that night— He looked very grave, and shook his head— He said that he had mentioned this subject incidentally, that he did not wish to alarm me—That he was an old man, and that he had daughters of

[10] The Hotel St. Petersburg, the proprietor of which was Jean Louis Morel, who had originally come to Mitau as a chef to the exiled Louis XVIII (same, p. 99–100).

[11] Possibly not Countess Mengs but rather Maria, Countess von Medem, the daughter of Count Peter von Pahlen, who owned estates in the region. Pahlen had taken a prominent role in the conspiracy against Paul I (same, p. 104, 323, notes 15, 16).

his own, and that he thought my situation such, as to entitle him to advise me, and to open my eyes to the danger of my position— He then informed me that the french Servant who I had with me, was well known in Mittau; that he was a Soldier in Napoleons Army; and had remained in that City two years—That he was known to be a desperate Vilain, of the very worst character; and that he did not consider my life safe with him, if I suffered him to proceed with me— At the same time he begged most earnestly that I would not dismiss him at *Mittau*, for fear he the Servant should suspect that I had received information there, and he might burn the House over his head— I told him that the man had behaved very well so far; that I had felt a mistrust of him, and did not like him; but that the Gentleman who had engaged him had entered into a bond, that he should be taken to his own Country; and that I was not to part with him unless he behaved improperly— That I had no pretence to make any charge against him, as he had been particularly active[12] and attentive; and that his conduct and manners were very respectful— He observed in answer that the case was difficult; and suggested to me, that I had better appear to place unlimited confidence in him; to seem to rely on him in any case of emergency; and to accept his advice if any difficulty occurred, and then act as opportunity offered when I was among my friends— He apologized for the liberty he had taken; begged me not to believe that his desire to have me stay, was a mere innkeepers wish to keep his company; but that his knowledge of the Man Servant had been the real motive of his conduct: and entreated that not a word of this conversation should be whispered, as it would equally endanger us both— I promised a perfect silence, and said, that I would willingly postpone my departure; but as the hour had arrived for that departure, and the Carriage would be at the door directly, I was fearful that a sudden change of purpose, would excite suspicion, and do more harm than good; and I assured him I thought his advice excellent, and should adopt it thro' the journey—[13] He rose to leave me, and I was immediately called to see the Countess, who had left a gay party at her house about a mile from the Town, and again urged me to change my mind, and to drive directly there, instead of pursuing my journey— All this I declined, I fear from a proud and foolhardy spirit; and that conviction

[12] The 2d version adds, "in the management of my arrangements; and that the other Man though good and honest was slow and timid—"

[13] From this point the 2d version continues in the hand of MCHA.

that however retarded, the difficulties of my path must be conquered, and it was as well to face them at once– Finding me determined; she took a very kind leave of me, and I got into the Carriage and began my ride under the most uneasy impressions After riding about four miles, the Postillion suddenly stopped, and informed us that he had missed the road–that the man who was accustomed to drive was sick, that he had never been that road before, and that he could not tell where he was– Until eleven o'clock at night, we were jolted over hills, through swamps, and holes, and into valleys, into which no Carriage had surely ever passed before; and my whole heart was filled with unspeakable terrors for the safety of my Child, for whom I offered the most ardent prayers to the ever protecting father of his Creatures– During this time my two servants were assiduous in their service, watchful and careful to prevent by every possible caution an overturn, or an accident to the Carriage– I consulted Baptiste frequently, and took his advice as to the best mode of proceeding, and at twelve o'clock at night the Horses being utterly worn out, and scarce a twinkling Star to teach of living light; we determined that Baptiste should ride one of the Horses, and endeavour to find a road through which we might be extricated from our perillous situation– He was absent about fifteen minutes, when we heard the trampling of a horse, and voices at a short distance– The palpitation of my heart encreased in its bounding motion until I thought it would have burst– My Child lay sweetly sleeping on his little bed in the front of the Carriage, unsusceptible of fear, and utterly unconscious of danger– Baptiste rode hastily up to the Carriage door, and informed me that he had found a house quite near– That he had awakend the family and that a Russian Officer had come to him, and after inquiring what he wanted, had offered his services to take us into the road, as it required great skill to keep the Carriage out of the gullies by which we were surrounded– He came up to me while Baptiste was speaking, and again I was obliged to tell my story in most execrable German, and as well as I could, express my thanks for the proposed service– lights were brought out; one of my men mounted *his* the (Officers) horse, and we proceeded at a foot pace, and reached the Inn in safety at about half past one; where I ordered refreshments for the gentleman, and Coffee for ourselves– He accepted a handsome present, made many polite speeches, and took leave; recommending the Inn-keeper to be attentive, and to see that horses should be ready at any hour that I might want them, he departed.– The House was very indifferent in its accommodations; I therefore expressed my satisfaction to my domestics for the prudence and discretion, which they had shown through this singular accident; and bade them be ready at an early hour with the Carriage and Horses; and after thanking most devoutly the Almighty for his protection through this hour of trial, I sought repose with renewed confidence in the persons attached to my service, and determined not to listen to any more bugbears to alarm my nerves, and weaken my understanding— I had contrived to conceal the bags of gold and silver which I carried in such a manner that neither of my Men Servants supposed that I possessed any; and as I carried Letters with me which I displayed, it was believed I took up only as much as I wanted at one town, until I reached another— I was likewise furnished with a Letter from the Government, recommending me to the protection of all whom I called on, and that any complaint should immediately be attended; to, as I was authorized to give information to the Minister of the Interior throughout the Russian territory, forming that portion of my journey—

What a pity that my romance should terminate in such a silly common place! but so it was; and as I was neither young, nor beautiful; no skill could colour it; or no varnish could heighten the tints, or add splendour to its effect— It is the simple unadorned truth; and nothing but the fanfaronade stories of the murder &c, which I had heard before the event, and immediately after, our relief from this fearful and harrassing anxiety; could have given an extraordinary interest, to so trifling an incident— Tis often thus in the realities of life, of themselves dull, straightforward, and simple; but made of painful importance by extraneous circumstances

> O'er which minds influence exerts; nor skill
> nor power to forsee.—[14]

We proceeded on our journey early in the morning, and no event of consequence occurred until we crossed the Vistula—[15]

It was four o'clock in the evening, and the ice was in so critical a state, I could with difficulty procure men and horses to go over— They informed me that I should have to make a very long and tedious détour, if I could not cross; that the passage over would be attended with great *risk*, if not danger; but if I had courage to attempt

[14] After "forsee," the 2d version adds, in LCA's hand, "unwilling yields to fate!"

[15] LCA's recollection of the location of these events may be incorrect. She would have reached the town of Shrunden in the Russian province of Courland, and the Windau, not the Vistula, River (O'Brien, *Mrs. Adams*, p. 112–113).

it, as there was no accommodation near, they would take long poles with Hooks, and attach the Horses to the extreme end of the Pole of the Carriage, and get over as well as they could— At five o'clock we started, the men going forward and sounding with their poles first, to find the firmest path; We got over and reached the other side of the River in safety, altho' the ice had given way on the border, and it required a violent effort in the horses, to prevent the coach from upsetting on the bank— I have forgotten the name of the Town, but we crossed from a small corner of Poland which lay on my route; and where I saw the most filthy and beggarly Village that I ever had beheld in any Country.— At this Town to which we had crossed, I remained a short time, and proceeded with the same horses to the next stage; and no other incident occurred worth notice until we reached the frontier of Prussia. Here I had to wait three hours for horses, and the people were so much inclined to be impudent, I was obliged to produce my Letter, and to inform the Master of the House, that I should write immediately to the Minister of the Interior, and complain of his Conduct— The entrance into Prussia was about 3 or 4 Miles farther on— The Man appeared to be much alarmed, made a great many apologies; and said the Horses should be ready immediately, and very *politely* obliged me to take a couple more than the usual compliment, as he thought the Carriage very heavy— This is an exaction to which travellers were constantly exposed, and to pay the tax was an absolute neccessity if you wished to avoid delay.— At the Prussian Gate, I was obliged to go through the formality of showing my Passports, and answering all the customery questions too tedious to enumerate—

We came suddenly upon a view of the Sea, and were apparently driving immediately into it, when Charles became dreadfully alarmed, and turning as white as a sheet, asked me if we were going into that *great water*— The Postillions did not seem pleased to cross the Hartz, and said there was a House that I could stop at until morning—[16] I enquired if there was any particular difficulty, but found that the principal objection was, that it would be *dark* before we should get across, and that it was a dreadful gloomy road— I asked at what time they expected to get in? they told me at about five o clock in the evening, and I immediately decided upon pursuing our route, as fast as we could— With much grumbling we again set forward, and as the Evening closed in, I began to repent my de-

[16] LCA is referring to the Baltic Sea and the Harz Mountains.

termination; for every thing around us looked blank and dreary, and the *terrible* without knowing why, or wherefore, seem'd to take its abiding place in our thoughts— Why is it that such thoughts appear to be annexed to peculiar situations? The ignorant, the learned, the romantic, the indifferent, alike fall into such moods, without any given cause; yet scorn the idea of superstition, or a thought of something hid beyond the ken of man— And yet how irrisistible is the pressure upon the strongest minds of this imperious spell; which

> Combats vain, 'gain'st reasons sov'reign sway
> And throws its mystic shadows 'thwart our way;
> Denying still her power to controul
> Subdues our Nature, and benumbs the Soul—
> O'erleaping learnings supercillious laws,
> The searching Spirit *seeks*! but where's the cause!

The Season of the year at which I travelled; when Earth was chained in her dazzling, brittle but solid fetters of Ice, did not admit of flourishing description, of verdant fields, or paths through flowery glebes; but the ways were rendered deeply interesting by the fearful remnants of mens fierry and vindictive passions; passively witnessing to tales of blood, and woes— Such are the graphic deleneations of Wars unhallowed march—that speak in thrilling language to the heart, where tongues of men are silent— Houses half burnt, a very thin population; women unprotected, and that dreary look of forlorn desertion, which sheds its gloom around on all the objects, announcing devastation and despair— These perpetual recurrences of lifes dire alarms; were the matters of inrest which forced themselves upon our attention— Onward we travelled until we arrived at Koenigsberg where we stopped a day. I delivered my Letter of credit and made arrangements to proceed; also some trifling purchaces of Amber, and should have gone to the theatre if I had not been unprotected by a Gentleman.— The next morning it rained so much I was detained until three o'clock in the afternoon; when we renewed our journey to-wards Berlin— Baptiste I believe that was his name (but no matter) began to assume a tone not by any means agreeable, and I began to be somewhat uneasy— I intimated to him that he might leave me as soon as he pleased, as I was in a Country where I was very well known, as I had lived four years in Berlin, and was acquainted with the King, and all the Royal Family— He said his great desire was to return to his own Country, and that he did not wish to leave me— That he understood I had *agreed* to take him the whole way— I told him that the performance of this *agreement* depended on his good behaviour, and that if he was diligent and attentive, I should have no wish to part with him— This conversation had a good effect, and he resumed his first tone, and was much more respectful; but there was something threatening in his look, that did not please me, but I was afraid to notice it— My other Servant was evidently much afraid of him, and avoided every thing that could put him out of humour— We had gone about seven miles, when the fore wheel of my Carriage fell to pieces, and we were more than a mile from any assistance— The Postillions said they could not return, neither could they proceed— the evening was setting in, and they advised that one of the two should go to a small place that we had passed on the road, and get some conveyance for me; as the road was in such a state it was impossible to walk— to this plan I assented, and after waiting a considerable time, the man return with a miserable common Cart, into which we got, and accompanied by Baptiste, turned our steps towards the place— It was little more than a hovel consisting of two rooms and a blacksmiths shop. One Woman made her appearance dirty, ugly, and ill natured; and there were two or three very surly ill looking men, whose manners were far from prepossessing or kindly— Baptiste explained our dilemma, and enquired if by any contrivance they could convey us back to the City— They answered doggedly that they could do no such thing, but that if we chose to stay there, they could make a wheel, so that we could go on in the morning— I consulted with the Servants and they both thought it a pity to return to the City— It would be midnight before I could procure a Carriage to take me there; they were armed, and one could keep watch at the door of my chamber; and the other would sleep in the Carriage, and this would prevent any accident— According to this plan I had my little boys bed brought in, and while he slept soundly my woman and I sat up, neither of us feeling very secure in the agreeable nest into which we had fallen— As I always had provisions in the Carriage we made out to eat something before we started, and at the next Stage we took our Coffee— Our wheel was very clumsy, and not painted, but it answered all the purpose to carry us through the famous road, which had been begun by Bonaparte from Kustrin, a fortress which we reached with much difficulty, and which bore the mutillating stamp of war, in all the pride of Bastion Stockade &ce that military skill atchieves, to give dignity to crime— On our way we met a travelling

Carriage labouring through the mud— The Servant stopped our drivers to ask concerning the desperate state of the road; and the Gentleman inside, enquired very politely of me, how many times I had been upset? informing me that he had seven times been exposed to this accident; I could not help laughing at his doleful account, and told him as I had not yet been so roughly dealt with, I hoped to escape the pleasure altogether— He informed me he was Count somebody I do not remember what, and that he was on his way to St. Petersburg— I wished him better luck and we parted— At Kustrin we found a tolerable house, but were not allowed to go within the fort— To my utter astonishment I heard nothing but the praises of the gallantry of Napoleon, and his Officers, and great regret at the damage done to this beautiful fortress; and learnt that from thence, I should travel over the most beautiful road in the world, which had been completed by his order, and that it would all have been finished in the same way, if the allies had not driven him away—

The desolation of this spot was unutterably dismal; and the guarded tone of the conversation, the suppressed sigh, the significant shrug, were all painful indications of the miseries of unholy Ambition, and the insatiate cravings of contaminating and soul corrupting War, with all its train of horrors— The Cossacks! the dire Cossacks! were the perpetual theme, and the cheecks of the Women blanched at the very name— We left Kustrin to pursue our journey, after the usual process of Passports &ce; and jogged on without any incident worth notice, excepting that one of the Postillions pointed out to us the small house, where that most lovely and interesting Queen Louisa of Prussia, had stayed with her sick Baby on their retreat from Berlin, after the French had taken possession of that City— My heart thrilled with emotion for the sufferings of one, whom I had so dearly loved, and I could not refrain from tears at the recital of her sufferings—[17] We arrived safely at Berlin and I drove to the Hotel de Russie, and established myself there for a

[17] On 14 Oct. 1806 Napoleon's armies decisively defeated Frederick William III's forces at the battles of Jena and Auerstädt. The route to Berlin was opened, and the French entered the capital on the 25th, with Napoleon arriving ceremonially on the 27th. As the French were advancing to Berlin, Queen Louise and her children fled eastward. On 20 Oct. the queen reached Küstrin, where she was reunited with her husband, who had fought at Auerstädt. The family retreated farther, eventually to Königsberg. Two of the royal children, Alexandrine (b. 1803) and Charles (b. 1801), had been alarmingly ill during their flight. The king and queen would not return to Berlin until Dec. 1809 (Palmer, *Alexander I*, p. 124–125; *Cambridge Modern Hist.*, 9:277, 280–281, 334; E. H. Hudson, *The Life and Times of Louisa, Queen of Prussia*, 2 vols., London, 1878, 2:220–221, 223, 225, 228, 230, 233; Constance Wright, *Beautiful Enemy: A Biography of Queen Louise of Prussia*, N.Y., 1969, p. xi, 137, 140).

week. the Carriage needed repairs, and our clumsy wheel to be painted, and Berlin was attractive to me—my poor and beloved George having been born there; independent of all these pleasant associations, which appear to re-connect us with the past; even when hope faints at the prospect of realizing the fearful changes produced by unrelenting Time— Memory; how ineffably beautiful is thy power! Years had elapsed; affliction had assailed the heart, with its keenest pangs of carking grief; disappointment had thrown its mingled hues of fear and care: and the loss of the loved and revered who had watchfully guarded youth *were* removed from us to greet our eyes no more, when we should return to the home to which we had looked with fond impatience; forgetting in the lapse of time and distance, that while we were participating in the luxuries, the pleasures, and the novelties of a Court, that desease and death might be crowning its work of destruction— Yet under all these impressions after an absence of forteen years, I entered Berlin with the pleasant recollections of the past; and youth seemed again to be deck'd with rosy smiles, and glad anticipations—and I wandered in the bright mazes of vivid recollections which every object called forth in fresher bloom, as if the scythe of time had left them glowing as of yore— I wrote a note immediately to one of my old friends, with a request to see her if disengaged, and waited with no little agitation to see one who had first known me as a young and blooming Bride, and who perhaps now might have lost all traces of the writer—

And now I must make a digression, and return to St Petersburg to relate a singular circumstance which occurred the night but one before I started on my journey— I went by invitation to the Countess Colombi's to take Tea with her and to bid her farewell— We had been very intimate— She was a charming woman and was apparently attached both to my Sister and myself— Much to her discomfort I found a Russian Lady there who had uninvited come to pass two or three days Countess Apraxin, was a fat coarse woman, very talkative, full of scandall, and full of the everlasting amusement so fashionable in Russian society, the bonne aventure—[18] After Tea she took the Cards, and insisted as I was going a journey,[19] that I should chuse a Queen, and let her read my destiny— I had never seen the woman before, and had never even heard her name until introduced

[18] Countess Ekaterina Vladimirovna, wife of Count Stepan Stepanovich Apraxin, whose palace in Moscow had been rebuilt after the conflagration of 1812 (O'Brien, *Mrs. Adams*, p. 194–195).

[19] From this point the 2d version is again in LCA's hand.

on my entrance that evening— I assented and she began— She said that I was perfectly delighted to quit Petersburg; that I should soon meet those from whom I had long been separated &ce &ce— That when I had atchieved about half of my journey, I should be much alarmed by a great change in the political world, in consequence of some extraordinary movement of a great man which would produce utter consternation, and set all Europe into a fresh commotion— That this circumstance which I should hear of on the *road*, would oblige me to change all my plans, and render my journey very difficult—but that after all I should find my husband well, and we should have a joyous meeting— I laughed and thanked her, and said I had no fear of such a circumstance, as I was so insignificant and the arrangements for my journey so simple, I was quite satisfied that I should accomplish it if I escaped from accidents, without meeting with any obstacles of the kind predicted; more especially as it was a time of Peace; and we were all very merry at the skill with which she had strung together so many improbabilities I took my leave, she expressing many kind wishes for my happiness, and said she hoped I should *remember*, to which I responded I was certain I could never forget her— I note this because it is an amusing and undoubted fact, and I was called on to remember it every moment during the latter part of my journey—

Countess Pauline de Neale flew to meet me with all the friendship which she had formerly shown me— We made arrangements to visit the Princesses Ferdinand, and Louisa Radzivil,[20] and also some of my old friends; and did not part until quite late with a mutual agreement, that she would pass as much time as possible with me while I staid— After a refreshing night I rose and prepared to make my visits, ordering a Carriage to be ready at the proper time, and gave all the necessary directions for the repairs of my *own*, to be dispatched as quick as possible, so as not to delay my journey— Every thing looked much as I had left it in the City, excepting the manners and the dress of the people— All the Nationality of Costume &ce had disappeared, and french was almost universally spoken— It was the same City that I had left in all its bearings The beautiful Linden Strasse! the fine Brandenburg Gate; the Bridges the Palaces, all spoke of former times; but yet it was cold, and flat, and there was a foreign air about it, which damped the pleasure I had expected, in revisitting the scenes of my youth— I missed many

[20] For Princess Ferdinand and her daughter Princess Radziwill, see Record, note 86, above.

objects which had formerly excited my admiration, and the perfect stillness seemed to cast a gloom over all the scenes, which had once been so gay, and brilliant, while gladdened by the smiles and affability of the young Queen, who won all hearts by her manners and her beauty—[21] According to appointment we waited on the Princesses who received me with all their wonted kindness[22] The Princess Louisa invited me to pass every Evening with her while I staid in Town; and laughingly said that though she could not entertain as she had *once* done, she would give me two dishes for my Supper, and a hearty welcome—No toilet was necessary, and she would show me her daughter—[23] Her husband and Son's she told me were at Vienna;[24] and that the great people of Berlin had suffered so much from the War, that there was no pretention of style among them, and they were glad to see their friends socially— I expressed my thanks for the flattering kindness shown me by her invitation, which I should do myself the honor to accept, and at the same time mentioned my regret, that the King, and the Prince were absent; as I had wished much to see them, and to have an opportu of offering thanks for much kindness formerly shown to me, of which I retained a most grateful sense— I made my Congé and departed to meet again in the evening—[25] The Princess was as little altered as possible, considering that time had not strewed roses in her path; but though the thorns had left some marks of their wounds, they had left traces of a softer shade of character on her face, than that which she possessed in the brilliancy of youth, and the entourage of splendid Royalty— My friends greeted me with the most unaffected warmth, and my reception was that of long separated and beloved Sisters: each vied with the other in marks of attachment making my stay a succession of delights— I saw all that was to be seen new, but

[21] The 2d version adds, "I was changed— She was gone 'to that bourne whence no traveller returns', but her image was associated in my mind with every surrounding object contrasting with vivid sadness the present and the past."

[22] In the 2d version, the sentence that follows begins with the additional words, "The Princess Ferdinand invited me to dine and."

[23] The 2d version adds, "a lovely little creature and an only one—" The child was probably Princess Louise's younger daughter, Wanda Radziwill (b. 1813) (Princess Louise, *Forty-five Years*, p. 24, 343).

[24] Prince Anton Radziwill was at Vienna with his sons Wilhelm (b. 1797) and Ferdinand (b. 1798). By the provisions of the Congress of Vienna, Prussia received two departments of the Grand Duchy of Warsaw, Posen and Bromberg, from which the Grand Duchy of Posen was constituted in May 1815. Prince Radziwill was appointed royal viceroy of the grand duchy (same, p. 24, 396–398; *Cambridge Modern Hist.*, 10:463).

[25] LCA had also attended to her *congé*, a formal permission to depart, before leaving St. Petersburg (LCA to JQA, 20 Jan. 1815, Adams Papers).

the object of most interest was the Mausoleum of the Queen at Charlottenburg in all its beauty;[26] decorated with a bower of evergreens; emblems of the undying love and respects of her subjects— How many interesting anecdotes I heard from the lips of the Princess concerning the War! more especially of the famed retreat of the suffering french— She rejoiced in their defeat; but she felt as a Christian, and she would permit no harsh and degrading language to be used in her presense; for the really great had fallen, and their punishment had overtaken them, in all the horrors that umitigated suffering could inflict; in addition to mortification and disgrace beyond the power of description— She told me that one day she received a Note on a dirty bit of paper, earnestly entreating her to see a person who was in great distress; that if she granted his petition she must see him alone, and with the greatest secrecy, as his life depended on not being known— At first she hesitated; but knowing from experience how much misery lurked about; she asked where the person was? and was told that a *Lady* who appeared in much trouble, was waiting for admittance— In a few minutes the person was introduced, veiled and dressed in a blue Satin Pelisse; who immediately after she had dismissed her attendants, fell at her feet, and implored her assistance as he was almost famished, had no clothes to his back but the dress he had on, which had been charitably given to him by a Lady as a disguise— It was the Count de Narbone; with whom she had been most intimate when Minister at Berlin some years before, who was flying from the Armies, in this utter and abject misery, who had thrown himself upon her mercy, to obtain the means of reaching Magdeburg— Prussia had not then become the avowed enemy of the French, and she gave him money, and clothes, and food— He reached the Fortress, but ~~was starved to death I~~ of Torgau and was killed by a fall from his horse I believe during the Siege He was one of the Master diplomats of the age,

[26] In the 2d version LCA replaced the remainder of this sentence with, "decorated with Green-house plants, embowering the Statue of the Queen which though beautiful did not at all convey the idea of the exquisite original— The lovely shrubs were tastefully arranged and the unfading emblems spoke of the undying love and respect of her subjects—"

In July 1810 Queen Louise became ill and died while visiting her family home in Mecklenburg. The much-admired sarcophagus of the queen by the sculptor Christian Daniel Rauch did not arrive in Berlin until 22 May 1815 and was not installed at the Charlottenburg mausoleum until the 30th, so in the 2d version LCA may be recalling a depiction of it or another sculpture of the queen (Palmer, *Alexander I*, p. 195; Ednah D. Cheney, *Life of Christian Daniel Rauch of Berlin, Germany*, Boston, 1893, p. 67–69).

and famed for the elegance of his manners—[27] One evening She had invited the Princess Wilhelm with a small party I was introduced This Lady was very handsome We sat round the Table with our work chatting; when the Princess Louisa asked me if I did not think the colour of her Gown was very gay— I acquiessed, and admired the richness of the Silk— She laughed, and observed, that she was rather *too old* for a bright couleur de rose; but she loved the dress, and must wear it, as it was a present from her Son, who had purchased it with the first money he had been allowed to Spend; and had immediately on his arrival in Paris gone to a Magazin and selected it himself, as a first offering to a mother he adored

Of my visit to Berlin I could write a Volume— The Brulhs; the de Néales; the Golofkins; the Zeinerts; the De Bergs; the Hardenbergs; the Hadzfeldt's; the Bishoffswerder, and many more, are names never to be forgotten by me, but always to be spoken of with affection— Count Caraman gave me a new Passport,[28] as I was not satisfied with the one which the French Ambassador had given me at St. Petersburg, and I again prepared to sally forth on my journey, having settled my Cash accounts with Mr Shieckler, and engaged the sympathy of the Néales in favour of a Capt Norman, an American, whom I had found dying of a fever in the upper story of the Hotel, for want of care and attention

Early in the morning I left the City of Berlin, for the last time with feelings both of gratitude and regret— There I had felt at *home*; all the sweet sympathies of humanity had been re-awakened; and the sterile heartlessness of a Russian residence of icy coldness, was thawed into life and animation—[29] In Petersburg for five long years I had lived a *Stranger* to all, but the kind regards of the Imperial family; and I quitted its gaudy loneliness without a sigh, except that

[27] Louis Marie Jacques Amalric, Comte de Narbonne-Lara (1755–1813), had served Napoleon as a soldier and a diplomat. He died at the fortress of Torgau in Saxony, where he was governor (O'Brien, *Mrs. Adams*, p. 161–162, 332, note 35; Princess Louise, *Forty-five Years*, p. 430).

[28] Victor Louis Charles de Riquet, Duc de Caraman (1761–1839), the Bourbon regime's minister plenipotentiary to Prussia, had been an émigré to Prussia. He was a particular friend of Princess Louise, and his son Adolphe was her protégé (*Repertorium*, 3:132; Princess Louise, *Forty-five Years*, p. 393, 409–410). For the passport he provided, see Descriptive List of Illustrations, No. 11, above.

[29] In the 2d version LCA replaces the previous sentence with, "There I had felt at home all the softer sympathies of humanity had been re-awakened in my heart into life and animation; and the sterile heartlessness of a Russian residence of icy coldness was thawed into joyous satisfaction and melted into affection by the kind testimonials of friends by whom I had believed myself long since forgotten—"

which was wafted to the tomb of my lovely Babe— To that spot my heart yet wanders with a chastened grief, that looks to hopes above—

The roads were sandy and our course lay through Pine barren woods— We proceeded quietly on our route occasionly meeting small straggling parties of disbanded Soldiers, loitering home; which meetings were by no means relished by any of us— In the Evening after dark I used to put on my Sons Military Cap and tall Feather, and lay his Sword across the window of the Carriage; as I had been told, that any thing that *looked* military escaped from insult— My two Servants rode on the box armed; and I was always careful to put away my *insignia* before I came to any house— My Friends in Berlin had advised me to avoid Liepsic, as I should have to cross the battle field so celebrated a year before,[30] and we went on a different route, to a fortified Town in Prussia, the name of which I cannot recollect— It had once been strong: but was now in a miserable condition though still guarded at the Gates by Soldiers— Being much fatigued; I passed the night there and was exceedingly astonished to learn from the Master of the House, that a rumour had arrived of the return of Napoleon to France; which he said created many jokes, as he was *Known* to be very safe at Elba!—but such a *rumour* was abroad, and in every body's mouth— I started with astonishment— True or false the coincidence was strange; and the bonne aventure of Countess Apraxin forced itself upon my mind in spite of my reason— I went to bed very tired, and for the first time left my purse with some gold in it upon the Table— My Childs Nurse who I had found perfectly honest; who had lived thirty years with Madame Colombi, who had given the strongest recommendations with her, slept in a bed with him, in the same room with me,[31] had carefully locked the doors on our going to bed—but when I rose in the morning, the lamp was gone out of the chamber, my purse was there, but the gold was gone!— I ordered the Carriage immediately, and again we pursued our route to Franckfort on the Maine, to which place the

[30] In the 2d version LCA writes, "and we took the route I think to Eisenach." LCA had, in fact, gone through Leipzig on 13 March on her way to Eisenach. She crossed the battlefields where the allied forces had routed Napoleon's armies at the Battle of Leipzig, also called the Battle of Nations, on 16–19 Oct. 1813. Eisenach had been ravaged by Napoleon's troops as they marched east to Jena in 1806 and as they advanced to and retreated from Leipzig in 1813 (O'Brien, *Mrs. Adams*, p. 165–166, 183–185, 191–193; Schom, *Napoleon Bonaparte*, p. 671, 675–680).

[31] The 2d version adds, about the nurse: "and had some property with which she wished to return to her relations in Paris and spend it among them—"

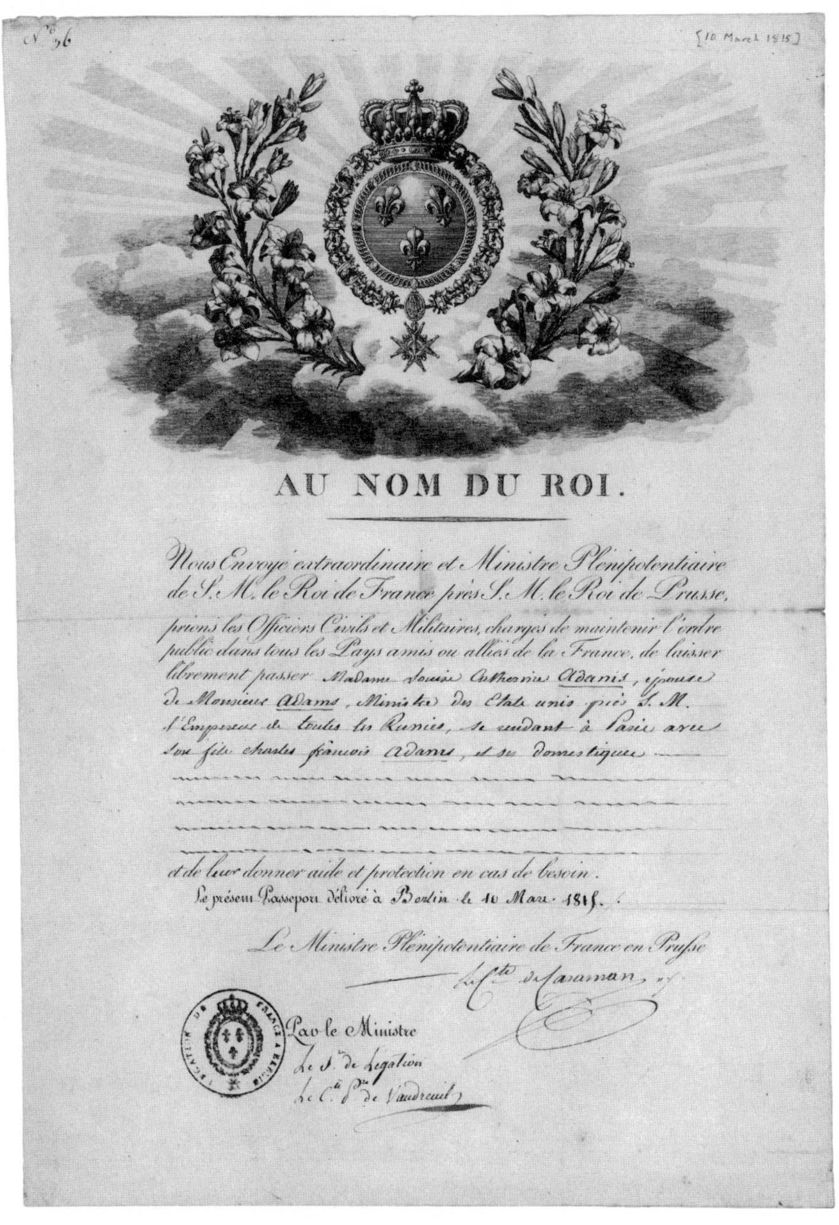

N° 36 [10 March 1815]

AU NOM DU ROI.

Nous Envoyé extraordinaire et Ministre Plénipotentiaire de S. M. le Roi de France près S. M. le Roi de Prusse, prions les Officiers Civils et Militaires, chargés de maintenir l'ordre public dans tous les Pays amis ou alliés de la France, de laisser librement passer Madame Louise Catherine Adams, épouse de Monsieur Adams, Ministre des Etats unis près S. M. l'Empereur de toutes les Russies, se rendant à Paris avec son fils Charles François Adams, et ses domestiques

et de leur donner aide et protection en cas de besoin.

Le présent Passeport délivré à Berlin le 10 Mars 1815.

Le Ministre Plénipotentiaire de France en Prusse

Le Cte de Caraman

Par le Ministre
Le S. de Légation
Le Cte P^re de Vaudreuil

II. LOUISA CATHERINE ADAMS' FRENCH PASSPORT, 10 MARCH 1815

See page xv

Banker at Berlin strongly advised me to go, and gave me Letters to two or three families there— Wherever we stopped to change Horses, we heard of the return of Napolen; and when we arrived at Hanau, we found that it was received with less doubt, and measures were already supposed to be adopted, for calling the disbanded Troops together— At about a mile before we entered the Town I had observed a number of mounds like Graves with Crosses at the feet, in the ditches on the sides of the roads— We enterred on a wide extended plain, over which was scattered remnants of Clothes; old Boots in pieces; and an immense quantity of bones, laying in this ploughed field— My heart throbbed; and I felt deadly sick ~~at my stomach~~ and faint; guessing where I was, when the Postillions pointed out a Board on which it was stated, that this was the Field of battle, where the Bavarians had intercepted the retreat of Napoleon, and that in this plain, ten thousand men had been slain— Conceive my horror at the sight of such a butchery![32] I could with difficulty keep from fainting, as fancy realized the torture, suffering, and anguish, thus brought before my eyes, with all the ghastly relics of the dead, exposed with savage barbarity to the view—[33] At Hanau a strongly fortified Town,[34] I was much questioned; and with some difficulty procured Horses, which however I was obliged to wait for, three or four hours. During this time, the people of the House were very civil and talkative; they spoke French fluently, and took great pains to point out to me the wonders that had been performed by Napoleon, and his Officers— three times they were beaten back[35] from the bridge, but at last took it against a strong force, and obtained possession of the Town— They showed me where their house had been struck by three bullets or rather cannon Balls, during the

[32] The 2d version adds, "my spirit sunk within me and I asked, Lord, what is man—that he should thus destroy?"

[33] It was at Hanau in 1813 that Napoleon and his troops, in retreat from the Battle of Leipzig, encountered and soundly defeated a much larger Austro-Bavarian Army (O'Brien, *Mrs. Adams*, p. 196–198).

[34] The 2d version adds, "the news of the return of Napoleon was confirmed." Napoleon had escaped from exile on Elba on 26 Feb. 1815 and landed in the south of France on 1 March with just over 1,000 men. Word of the landing reached Louis XVIII in Paris on 5 March. By the 7th, JQA had been informed, and the king had issued a proclamation declaring Napoleon a rebel and a traitor. As Napoleon advanced toward Paris, entering Grenoble on the 7th and Lyons on the 12th, his ranks swelled. By 16 March, when LCA reached Hanau, Napoleon was approaching Auxerre, about 300 miles away (same, p. 198–200).

[35] The 2d version substitutes, "while attempting to cross the River, but at last succeeded I believe by fording the River the bridge having been burnt," for "from the bridge, but at last took it against a strong force."

Action; and informed me that the French Officers had quartered there, a fact of which they seemed very proud— It was a very remarkable fact that in the course of my journey, I heard but little praise of the Allied Armies, and unceasing admiration of the exploits of the French;[36] yet suffering, and devastation, had followed their steps—but the renowned cruelties, and barbarities, of the Cossacks, seemed to have white washed all other crimes from their minds—[37] At this place I observed that my Servants began to grow uneasy, and frequently talked about conscripts, and a renewal of the Wars—for which neither appeared to have any taste—

Soldiers were mustering in every direction; and there was a life and animation, altogether different from the dull monotony, which had pervaded all the former part of my travels—[38] Feeling very uneasy; I pushed on with all the celerity that tolerable roads, and good Horses, six of which were always forced on me, would admit; and should have found many agreeable objects to attract my attention, if my mind had been more at ease— I arrived safely at Franckfort on the Maine, and sent my Letters to the Banker. A new dilemma of a very serious nature having occurred— My two Servants requested to speak to me, and informed me that circumstances having totally changed, since their engagement to attend me to France; in consequence of Napoleon's return, they must quit my service, and prefered to remain at Franckfort, to proceeding any farther; as there they would be likely to meet with opportunities of Service— *Here was a situation*— I could not compel them to stay; no bribe could induce them to go on in their state of Panic; and I was under the necessity of asking them to wait before they came to a final decision, until I had seen my Banker, with whom I would talk upon the subject— He came to see me almost immediately after the receipt of his Letter, and I informed him of my difficulty— He was very polite; and urged me very strongly to remain a few days in the City, and he would endeavour to make arrangements for me— He said the consternation was universal, and that it would be very difficult to find

[36] The 2d version adds, "There is in human nature a moral antipathy to treachery even against our worst enemies; and however we may be led into the support of it by artificial excitement; in moments of quiet and deliberation we are revolted by its atrocity—"

[37] The 2d version adds, "Friends and foes suffered alike from these ruthless miscreants and they were always mentioned with whispered exceations—"

[38] The 2d version adds, "The first a dreary picture of the past— The latter the glowing picture of ambitious hope— Power and oppression serving as lights and shadows in the dread realities of life—"

substitutes for the Servants, who were determined to leave me; and that my position was so unpleasant, he thought it required great prudence in my arrangements— I insisted that it would be better for me to get into France as soon as possible;[39] as I should probably[40] meet my husband on the frontier, and every moment would add to the difficulty, should I delay— At present the panic itself would prove advantageous; as it would require time to ascertain events, before the Governments could take decisive measures— He agreed with me in opinion; but said Troops would be assembled, and ordered to the Frontier directly, by way of precaution— As most of them had recently been disbanded, it would require time to collect them, but there was always danger from stragglers— He advised on the whole that it would be best to proceed, but thought I should change my intended route for one more circuitous but safer; and more likely to be quiet;[41] and he would try to find some person to go with me— I was to start at four o clock in the afternoon— He returned in a short time with a boy[42] of fourteen, the only creature he could find willing to go; and after arranging my money accounts, he put me into the Carriage and directed the Postillions as to the route to be taken— All went on very well— The boy was very smart, and active, and I thought it more prudent to take him withinside of the Carriage for fear of indiscretion— He had though so young been in the Russian Campaign with a prussian Officer; and told me a great many anecdotes concerning Napoleon during the retreat— Of his sitting among his Soldiers to warm himself! of his partaking of their Soup, when they had any! His kindness to them in the midst of their misery &ce &ce At the same time he expressed great hatred of the man, with all the petulance of boyish passion— It was singular to watch the workings of this young mind, swayed equally by admiration and detestation, uttered in the strong language of natural feeling— At ~~Manheim~~ Carlsrhue I stopped at a very good house intending to visit Princess Amalia, and Madlle. Bode— I sent to the Palace to enquire if I could see them— The Servant returned, and informed me that the Empress of Russia, and her Sister, had left ~~Carlsrhue~~ ~~Manheim~~ the day before for Munich—and the Grand

[39] The 2d version adds, "before the Armies could be prepared to move."

[40] In the 2d version LCA writes "possibly" rather than "probably."

[41] The banker, Simon Moritz von Bethmann (1768–1826), advised "that I must not think of going to Mayence but that I must go by Strasbourg" (LCA to JQA, 17 March, Adams Papers; *New Amer. Cyclo.*).

[42] The 2d version indicates that the boy was Prussian.

Dutchess of Baden was the only person at Court—[43] As I had no one to introduce me, I ordered my dinner, and concluded to prosecute my journey in the afternoon— I was much disappointed; as I intended to obtain some information, which I expected would have been profitable to me on the road— While I was at dinner The Master of the Inn came in, and informed me, that Napoleon had been taken, and that he had been tried immediately, and *Shot*— He said the news might be relied on, as it had just arrived at the Palace— I heard an exclamation of horror; and turning round, saw the boy who I had hired, as pale as a ghost, and ready to faint— he looked piteously at me saying "O that great Man! I did not expect that!"— Fortunately the Inn Keeper had left the room,[44] or he might have supposed me some violent Bonapartist, and the report would have been very unfavorable to my proceedings— At four o clock I was again on my way, and pursued my course through the Dutchy of Baden, without interruption or accident— Waggons of every discription full of Soldiers, were continually rushing towards the Frontier— roaring national Songs, and apparently in great glee at the idea of a renewal of hostilities— What a mere animal man may become! A machine worse than the brutes; for the instincts of the Brute creation lead only to fixed objects; while those of men termed rational; may be perverted by mere accidental causes, to the worst and basest purposes, even without an adequate motive for such excesses— When I retrace my movements through this long, and really arduous journey, I cannot humble myself too much in thankful adoration to the Providence which shielded me from all dangers, and inspired me with that unswerving faith which teaches, to seek for protection from above— Thus far not a word or look had been unpleasant; and could I have divested myself of that restless anxiety for the future, which pervades all mankind, I should have enjoyed the perpetual varieties, and changes constantly offered to my view; and the retrospection, would have furnished me stores of anecdotes, and information, at this time worthy to grace my subject, with the embellishments of wit, and the ornaments of picturesque taste— As

[43] The palace at Karlsruhe was the home of Karl Ludwig Friedrich, Grand Duke of Baden. He was the brother of Empress Elizabeth Alexeievna of Russia and of Princess Katharine Amalie Christiane Luise (called Princess Amalie or Amalia), whose maid of honor was Fréderica de Bodé y Kinnersley. The grand duchess was the former Stéphanie de Beauharnais, a relative of the Empress Josephine, whom Napoleon had adopted and made a *princesse de France* (O'Brien, *Mrs. Adams*, p. 266–267, 348, note 46).

[44] From this point the 2d version continues in the hand of MCHA.

it is I can only give a brief sketch of the road, and I fear very often with a defective Geography, making

"Confusion worse confounded"[45]

Research is not in my way— Indolence wars with exertion, and is too often victorious; and as I know nothing of style, or composition, those who may read this memento mori, must endeavour to extract light from the chaos which lies before them; and I wish them joy of the trouble—

We reached the Fortress of Kiel[46] opposite to Strazbourg on the Rhine, and here I was questioned, and troubled; and after some delay permitted to cross, which we accomplished with success, and landed in saftely— Here again I was stopped; my Passports demanded, my baggage taken off &ce— The Officer in command, recommended me to an excellent Hotel—and politely told me he would wait on me there— The House was excellent; and the Master of it came imediately to me, to receive my directions &ce &ce— I requested him to dismiss the Horses and Drivers, and that if he was at leisure I should be glad to consult him— He was a very respectable man of fifty years old or upwards, and in manners very gentlemanly— He told me the Officer would probably ask for Letters, and papers; and that as the moment was very *critical*, I had better cut the Seals before they took them, and in that state they would not read them, but suffer me to retain them— Here I found the Passport furnished me by Count Carnman of the greatest service, as his name was popular and well know—That of Mons. de Noaille being just the reverse—

The Officer came and informed me that my baggage would be allowed to pass, and that my Passports would be endorsed &ce and returned to me in the proper form— He said the Country was in a very unsettled state, and that it would require great prudence and caution, in the pursuit of my journey to Paris— Strazburg was very quiet, but it was impossible to foresee how long it would continue so— The Emperor had certainly returned; and was then on his way to the Capital—[47] I thanked him for his politeness; informed him it

[45] Milton, *Paradise Lost*, Book II, line 996.

[46] Kehl, in the Grand Duchy of Baden (O'Brien, *Mrs. Adams*, p. 263, 302).

[47] For Napoleon's progress toward Paris as LCA reached Strasbourg on 19 March; the collapse of the royalist order and Louis XVIII's flight; and Napoleon's arrival at the Tuileries on the night of 20 March, see same, p. 269–270, 277.

was my intention to remain at Strasbourg for a day at least, before I prosecuted my journey—

The Master of the Hotel then came to me and I represented to him the great difficulty I should find to travel without a Man Servant, and urged him to seek a respectable and confidential person to go with me as far as Paris— That I remunerate him handsomely, and pay his expences back; as the moment I met my husband, I should have no occasion for his services— That I must rely entirely upon the discretion of this person, in the management and arrangement of my route; and should depend on him for advice, and assistance— He said such a person would be very difficult to find; but that he had such a man in view, that he would see him directly, and prevail upon him to undertake the charge— After dinner I took a walk with my Son— The Town is very pretty, and I have sometimes thought that Wocester in Massachusetts looks a little like it— In the evening the Master of the House I have forgotten his name, introduced a most respectable looking person, the man he had recommended;[48] and we immediately enterred into engagements; I requested him to see that the Carriage was in order, and told him that on the next morning but one, I intended to depart for Paris, and to go on with as much rapidity as possible— He said he would be ready at the appointed time, and asked if the Boy was to proceed with me—and I had him up to know if he would not prefer to be discharged there, and to return home— He said no! his object was to find his old Master in Paris, and that he would rather go on— As he had rendered me good service, I could not refuse this; and a condition was made by Dupin, that he was not to talk at any of the Houses where we might stay, and that he was[49] either to be under my eye, or his, at all times—to which he readily agreed— The Woman who was with me, Madame Babet was a quiet and respectable person, older than myself, and very plain in her person, and manners, and very steady— On the former part of my journey she had been very useful; but as she spoke no german she could not be troublesome— The day at Strazburg was very tedious— My health was dreadful, and the excessive desire I had to terminate this long journey, absolutely made me sick— I had been a year absent from my husband, and five years and a half from my two Sons;[50] and the hope of soon again embracing

[48] Dupin.

[49] From this point the 2d version is again in LCA's hand.

[50] In the 2d version, after "my husband," LCA writes, "and five long long years and a half from my two eldest born Sons whom I had left in America with their Grand parents— War had

them, gave me strength to sustain the fatigue and excitement to which I was necessarily exposed— We pursued our route without impediment until one o'clock in the morning, when the Postillions insisted on my stopping at a very lonely house, to which proposition I acceded very unwillingly—[51] My Servant made me a sign, and said he thought it would be adviseable to wait there until daylight—and I could procure some refreshment for myself and my Son— We drove up to a miserable place in which we found a long room, with a pine Table, several very surly looking men, and nothing but common benches to sit on— Here I was obliged to sit, while they procured us a little milk, the only thing we could get— Charles seemed very much frightened as these men asked him several questions, and I was obliged to tell them the Child was too sleepy to talk— Dupin took the opportunity to ask if I could have some chamber where I could put the Child to sleep, and a door was opened into an adjoining chamber even more uncomfortable than the one we left— In this Chamber my Maid and I passed the night without going to bed; and heard the threatening conversation in the next room, and the boasts of what Napoleon was to do now that he had arrived, to drive out Louis dix huit and his beggarly Crew— Our Postillions were vociferous in their exclamations; and there were many bitter anathema's against the Allied Powers and the horrible Cossacks— I rejoiced when I found myself once more safely seated in the heavy Russian Carriage, and we renewed our journey with fresh spirits— I was much pleased with the conduct of Dupin, who appeared to me to be a very judicious and discreet person, possessing all the tact requisite to avoid threatened trouble, with a quiet smoothness of manner which enforced respect, and defied suspicion— At Nancy we stopped only to change Horses— The Square was full of Troops, who were mustering to express their delight at the return of the Emperor— Dupin told me that if we made good speed, we should keep in advance all the way; as it would require some hours for their preparation, and that we should reach Paris with ease before they could get

intervened and free communication in addition to the accustomed impediments from the Climate had conduced to add to my anxeties; and every Letter had brought me accounts of the loss of near and dear relatives whom I nevermore should see; had made me timid."

[51] LCA's account of her route from Strasbourg to Paris—according to which she passed through Nancy, Château-Thierry, Épernay, Châtillon-sur-Marne, Sens, Meaux, and Bondy—is improbable, as is her report that she traveled between 21 and 23 March. For O'Brien's more likely account of the approximately 300-mile route, in which LCA left Strasbourg on the morning of 20 March and made overnight stops in the vicinity of Velaine, Virtry-sur-Marne, and Port-à-Binson to reach Paris on the night of 23 March, see same, p. 272–274.

half way there— On we drove, and at night we stopped at Chateau Thierry— We got good beds, and comfortable refreshment; but poor Charles was much annoyed by a Gen d'armes, who told him he must be a good boy, and not speak a word on the road, for that little children of his age often did a great deal of mischief— He was very inquisitive; expressed great astonishment at my travelling towards Paris in such a state of things, and seemed by no means contented with my answers, which were very simple— The next morning we again set forward, every thing seemed propitious— The weather was fine; every thing quiet; the roads good, and all of us in renewed spirits; we thought we would stop to dine at Epernay— Here I was very comfortable; we had a capital dinner at one o'clock; and the Waiter said that I must have some Champagne as this was the fine Champagne Country and he doubted if I could find such in Paris. He was so urgent, I at last consented to have a bottle, which certainly was superior to any that I have ever tasted before, or since—[52] In less than an hour we were again on our way— He told me that the people of the Town did not expect the Troops to pass until the next day, and that I need not hurry— We had gone about a mile and a half, when we suddenly found ourselves in the midst of The Imperial Guards, who were on their way to meet the Emperor— The first notice I had of my danger, was hearing the most horrid curses, and dreadful Language from a number of women, who appeared to be following the troops Madame Babet was as pale as death, and trembled excessively; Presently I heard these wretches cry out, "tear them out of the Carriage; they are Russians take them out kill them." At this moment a party of the Soldiers siezed hold of the Horses, and turned their guns against the drivers— I sat in agony of apprehension, but had presense of mind enough to take out my Passports— A General Officer with his Staff, consisting of four or five, immediately rode up to the Carriage and addressed me— I presented my Passports, and he called out, that I was an American Lady, going to meet her husband in Paris— At which the Soldiers shouted "vive les Americains"—and desired that I should cry vive Napoleon! which I did waiving my handkerchief; they repeated their first cry adding "ils sont nos amis" A number of Soldiers were ordered to march before the Horses, and if we attempted to push on out of a walk, the order was to fire on us directly— The General and his suite rode on each side of the Carriage. He told me my situation

[52] From this point the 2d version continues in the hand of MCHA.

was a very precarious one; the army was totally undisciplined; that they would not obey a single order; that I must appear perfectly easy, and unconcerned; and whenever they shouted I must repeat the Viva's; that when we arrived at the Post House, he would use all his influence with the Lady of the House to admit me to pass the night, and advised that the next morning, I should delay my departure until the troops had all passed, and then take a circuitous route to Paris; as the whole Army would be in motion, to Greet the Emperor— I thanked him sincerely for his kind attention, and assured him I was ready to follow his advice. He complimented me on my manner of speaking french, and said that my perfect knowledge of the Language would contribute much to my safety, as no one would believe me to be a foreigner— My poor boy seemed to be absolutely petrified, and sat by my side like a marble statue— God in his great mercy seemed to give me strength in this trying emergency; for excepting a heightened and glowing colour in my Cheeks, there was no evidence of fear or trepidation: yet my heart might have been heard to beat, as its convulsive throbbings heaved against my side— In this way we journied; the Soldiers presenting their bayonets at my people with loud and brutal threats every half hour— The road lined on each side for miles with intoxicated men, ripe for every species of villainy, shouting and vociferating À bas Louis dix huit! vive Napoleon! till the whole welkin rang with the screech, worse than the midnight Owls most dire alarum to the startled ear—[53] At twelve o clock at night we reached the Post house— Genl Michell[54] spoke to the Lady, and she refused to take me: At length he awakened her sympathy, and she consented, *provided* I would consent to stay in a dark room; have my people concealed; and my Coach stowed away in some place where it could not be perceived— O how gladly I consented may readily be conceived— I was almost spent with the exertions I had made to master my feelings, and could not of borne up much longer— I was put into a comfortable room; a good fire was made; the shutters were close barred; and a very kind old gentleman came to me, and encouraged me with the hope, that we should get through the night without farther molestation— The

[53] From this point the 2d version is again in LCA's hand.

[54] The 2d version adds, "or Michaux." Gen. Claude Étienne Michel (1772–1815) had served Napoleon in St. Domingue against Toussaint L'Ouverture and in the later European campaigns. He accepted a commission from Louis XVIII but then resumed his former allegiance when Napoleon returned from Elba. On 18 June he died at Waterloo (O'Brien, *Mrs. Adams*, p. 284).

Gen[l] had gone on with the troops whose great object was to reach Toul, where Victor the Duc de Bellune then was; and that the cause of my detention, was the fear, that if he had information of their march, he would close the Gates against them, having refused to sustain the Emperor on his landing—[55] I was very ill all night; successive faintings, head ache, and sickness, made it impossible to sleep could I have divested myself of fear, which was out of the question; as the Soldiers were crowding into the house all night, drinking, and making the most uprorious noises— The Lady of the House came to my Chamber, followed by a woman with Coffee. She apologized to me for not being able to stay with me, but the moment was so *critical*, she had some Casks of wine opened, and brought out to amuse the gentlemen, and that she must be there, to "debiter des plaisanterie," or else she feared they might plunder her house— She was a showy pleasant faced woman, of about forty: of an assured and prompt spirit, and who seemed to possess that readiness, and playfulness of conversation, which is often so attractive in french women— Charles had fallen asleep—but Madame Babet really appeared to have lost her senses— She clasped her hands continually; while the tears rolled down her cheeks, crying out, that she was lost! for the Revolution was begun again, and this was only the beginning of its horrors— During my stay in my chamber, these ferocious creatures had attacked the poor boy, who was in my service with a bayonet, and forced him to burn his military Prussian Cap; and it was with great difficulty that his life was saved, by the dexterity of the Land-lady— Until five o clock in the morning it was utterly impossible to feel a moment of ease— After that time, the Doors were barred—and though stragglers frequently hola'd! and made a great knocking; no notice was taken, and we obtained refreshing repose— At nine o'clock I was up, and ordered preparations to be made for our departure. The Master of the House advised me to go to Chatillon sur marne; and when there, I could make suitable arrangements for the remainder of the journey— I endeavoured as well as I to express the high sense of obligation which they had conferred; to which they replied very handsomely; declaring that they felt a deep interest for me, and wished I would stay a day or two longer with them; they did not keep a house of publick entertain-

[55] Claude Victor-Perrin, Duc de Bellune (1764–1841), a former marshal to Napoleon who transferred his loyalty to the Bourbons (R. P. Dunn-Pattison, *Napoleon's Marshals*, 2d edn., Boston, 1909, p. 296–297, 300–304).

ment, but would be happy to see me as a visitor— With most heartfelt thanks I assured them of my gratitude for their very considerate kindness, and after taking an excellent breakfast, set out again on our journey, which according to the irish adage we found "the longest way round was the shortest way home—"

We took our route to Chatillon, where we arrived in the evening—Here some passengers in the Dilligence informed me that I had better not go on to Paris, as there were forty thousand men before the Gates; and a battle was expected to take place. This news startled me very much, but on cool reflection, I thought it best to persevere, as I was travelling at great expence,[56] and I was sure if any such danger existed Mr. Adams would have come to meet me, or by some means have conveyed intelligence to guide my course. Still as I had been under the necessity of changing my route, I could not be sure that he had heard from me at Strazburg,—[57] I consulted with Dupin; and he suggested the best plan; which was to push on to the environs of Paris, and if the difficulty accrued, I could remain within the means of communication, and find some opportunity of informing Mr. Adams— He told me that in consequence of my being almost the only traveller on the road going towards Paris; that a whisper was abroad, that I was one of Napoleons Sisters[58] going to meet him; and that this idea was so favorable to the promotion of my success, that *he* was *very mysterious* and only shrugged and smiled, at the suggestion— My six horses contributed somewhat to this notion, and proved very advantageous— It rained very heavily and the place was very gloomy— On we went again the day follow to Sens, and from thence to Meaux, where I arrived the 20th of March—[59]

[56] In the 2d version LCA adds, "a thing quite unsuitable to the paltry salary of an American Minister."

JQA calculated that LCA spent $48.61 for initial provisions and $1,606.38 for traveling expenses, which, with the $330 for her carriage, brought her total expenses to $1,984.99 (M/JQA/13, Feb.–March 1815, Account Book 1809–1829, Minute of Expences of Mrs: Adams's Journey from St: Petersburg to Paris—from 12 Feby: to 23 March 1815, APM Reel 210).

[57] Communication between LCA and JQA was difficult during her journey. LCA wrote to JQA from St. Petersburg on 12 Feb.; from Riga on 17 Feb. (a letter finished in Memel on the 20th); from Berlin on 5 March; and from Frankfurt on 17 March. JQA sent letters to LCA at Königsberg on 19 Feb.; at Berlin on 1 March; and, on 18 March, "in duplicates to Bondy and to Bourget the first stages from Paris, on the two roads by one of which my wife must arrive there." JQA eventually received all of LCA's letters, but JQA's letter of 19 Feb. is the only one found as a RC in the Adams Papers (all Adams Papers; D/JQA/29, 18, 22 March, APM Reel 32).

[58] In the 2d version LCA adds, "Princess Stephanie." Napoleon did not have a sister named Stephanie. LCA may have been referring to Stéphanie de Beauharnais, for whom see Narrative, note 43, above.

[59] In the 2d version LCA writes that she arrived on the 21st.

Here I dined– The Mistress of the House told me the most dismal tales of the atrocities of the Cossacs: The furniture of the house was almost in ruins; and she Showed me the Graves of six of the most beautiful young girls of the place, who had fallen victims to the murderous horrors of savage war, with all its detestable concomitants– They were laid side by side, and to judge from my landlady, their relics were embalmed by the sacred tears of undying affection, and the purest sympathies of unadulterated compassion– I was again on my way to Paris, pondering on the cruel evils to which the fiend like passions of men expose the world; when I observed a man on Horse back, who appeared to be making prodigious efforts to overtake us– With a mind already in some measure prepared for some catastrophy, and in the Foret de Bondy so long celebrated for Banditti exploits, it was natural that I should be ready for some disagreeable adventure–[60] My courage was fast oosing out, when by some accident the Postillions slackened their pace, and my imaginary highway man, came up very politely, and informed me, that for the last half hour he had been apprehensive that the wheel of my Carriage would come off, and that he had been fearful I should meet with a bad overset– We thanked him for his timely notice, and he rode off– Dupin examined the thing, and the only resourse was to fasten it as well as they could, and to turn back to the place where we had dined to get it repaired– The necessary repairs were atchieved; and notwithstanding it was late in the evening, we again penetrated the wilds of Bondy, once so famed, and arrived in perfect safety and without molestation at the gates of Paris; and descended at eleven o clock at the Hotel du Nord Rue de Richelieu–Mr. Adams not returned from the Theatre; but he soon came in, and[61] I was once more happy to find myself under the protection of a husband, who was perfectly astonished at my adventures; as every thing in Paris was quiet, and it had never occurred to him, that it could have been otherwise in any other part of the Country–[62] My Poor Maid

[60] Bondy was associated with murderous legends and with historical events, including the flight of Louis XVI and his family to Varennes; see O'Brien, *Mrs. Adams*, p. 291–293.

[61] In the 2d version LCA omits the previous thirteen words.

[62] JQA spent the evening of 23 March at the Théatre des Variétés, which, he noted in his Diary, consistently offered performances marked by "low and vulgar humour." When he returned home, "I expected to have found my wife's carriage in the yard, and was disappointed; but had scarcely got into my chamber when she arrived– It was eleven in the Evening–" He found his wife and child well and "was delighted after an absence of eleven Months to meet them again– They have been exactly forty days in coming from St. Petersburg" (D/JQA/29, APM Reel 32).

Servant went to her friends the next morning— The fright she had undergone was too much for her; and she was siezed with a brain fever, from which she had not recovered when I left Paris two Months after—[63] I was carried through my trials by the mercy of a protecting Providence; and by the conviction that weakness of either body, or mind, would only render my difficulties greater and make matters worse— My security and faith, was in my husband: who I was sure would have taken every precaution for our safety, had there been any danger. and thus I was lured on to accomplish an undertaking in itself simple, but by extraordinary circumstances rendered peculiarly interesting— A moral is contained in this Lesson— If my Sex act with persevering discretion, they may from their very *weakness* be secured from danger, and find friends and protectors: and that under all circumstances, we must never desert ourselves— I was fortunately neither young nor beautiful; a fact in itself calculated to prove my safegaurd; and I had others under my protection to whom the example of fortitude was essential; and above all the object which drew me on, was the re-union with my beloved husband, and alas, with my now departed Children— Years have rolled on: but memory recurs with delight to the past! that past, with all its associations pleasing and painful, which is left to glad the heavy march of time, and to rob it of its tedium— The rosy hours of youth have fled, and the Cypress and the Willow cast their deep and shadowy tinge oer the coming years, whose last remnant is at least blessed in the consciousness of innocence of guilt, however tainted by slander, and almost unremitting misfortune— Under this pressure may it please my Almighty Father to strengthen me in the faith—to teach me to subdue the erring passions of my nature; and while I abhor guilt, and wickedness; to be merciful to the Sinner, that I may be enabled to turn him from the evil of his ways, and lead him into the paths of Repentance; and when it is his will that I lay me down to sleep; that sleep, from which we wake no more, in this world; may I die in my Saviour Jesus Christ; in the full hope of those divine promises, which lead the purified Soul to heaven for evermore—

L C Adams
27th June 1836.

[63] In the 2d version LCA adds, "I am almost ashamed of the egotism of this detailed narative but a traveller cannot avoid speaking in the first person while relating his own history— and this must plead my apology—"